THE DEFINITIVE GUIDE TO SHOT GLASSES

By
Mark Pickvet

INTRODUCTION

To all shot glass collectors, I encourage you to join our club that was established in 1990. We publish a small 3-page news bulletin monthly that includes new information, new finds, information about collectors, where to obtain shot glasses, shot glasses for sale, and small free ads for our members. Dues are only for the cost of postage and printing. Please drop me a postcard or letter to:

> The Shot Glass Club of America
> P.O. Box 90404
> Flint, MI 48509

The newsletter encompasses all phases of collecting. From whiskey sample glass collectors, cut glass collectors, Depression Glass, advertising, souvenir or tourist glasses, sports, universities, pewter, foreign, patterns, and so on up to the present.

Our club goals include the sharing of information and the quest for identification of nearly every shot glass ever made. A nearly insurmountable task but with the help of our members, we are continuing to make headway. Our ultimate goal is to establish a museum and hopefully acquire a few significant collections for it. When one collects shot glasses quantity is one of the first things that comes to mind. Collectors like to count them in the hundreds and even thousands!

My first attempt at cataloging and sketching ended up with well over 1,000 glasses which can be found in: Shot Glasses: An American Tradition by Antique Publications 1989. I have tried to duplicate as little as possible in this edition at least in the way of sketches. The history has been expanded upon significantly though it was necessary to repeat a little of what was done in the first volume.

There were many errors and I have included a list of corrections here. New information is constantly surfacing from collectors, older and/or newer trade journals and catalogs, additional help from glass companies, and so forth. It can be frustrating (just ask most any collector!) when a trade journal lists a product from 1962-1963 and then finding it for sale in an earlier catalog dated 1958. Dating can be hazardous and frequently the collector must be relied on to tell us when and where a glass was acquired. We are always happy to receive new information - please forward whatever you might find or let us know of any discrepancies that you discover.

CORRECTIONS:

1) Since bar tumblers are so very common and manufactured from the mid 19th century to the present, the catalog classification "BTU" has been eliminated.

2) Pages 88, 89, and 90 have shot glasses with "IAG" numbers for "Iridescent Art Glass" which replaces PPP (Picture Patterns Pre-Depression). The Tiffany glass has been reclassified as #IAG020 and the early Lenox glass as #IAG010. Carnival Glass too was produced earlier than the Depression and also contains "IAG" numbers; the DMS (Depression Miscellaneous Shot) class has been altered to exclude Carnival Glass.

3) Page 96, the "IBS" (Identical in Beverage Set) has also been eliminated since only one glass had that classification. It was amended to "PPC" (Picture Patterns with Colorless or Clear designs).

4) Page 191, a picture correction for Hocking Glass Company's "Mayfair Open Rose" pattern. Page 229 also contains reproduction information.

5) Page 195, another picture correction for Fostoria's "Sunray" pattern.

6) Page 204, the pictured barrel-shaped shot glasses were all made by Bartlett-Collins in the 1950's rather than the 1940's.

7) Page 215, the set of Anchor Hocking fish patterns are a set of four rather than three. The "Old Cowhand" series has also been identified as a Bartlett-Collins introduction in 1959.

8) Page 216, the "Little Shot" design has also been identified as a Bartlett-Collins product produced in two separate sets of four. Some of the catalog numbers were amended to list the eight glasses concurrently.

9) Page 217, the "Sports" design is yet another Bartlett-Collins set of four. Once again the numbers were amended to list all in the set concurrently.

10) Page 219, the set of game birds was located in an earlier Federal Glass Company advertisement from 1956-1957. The catalog numbers were adjusted to place them with this earlier date; also, the rims were crafted with a more expensive platinum trim rather than silver.

11) Page 230, one final Bartlett-Collins set of four has been identified as a mid-1960's introduction.

DEDICATION

To my wife Robin for her typing, editing, and particularly her patience for all of the time I have invested in this subject.

ACKNOWLEDGEMENTS

I would like to continue to express my gratitude to my family members and friends who continue to pick up information and glasses for my collection in their travels. I would also like to pay particular attention to the members of The Shot Glass Club of America. Their valuable input especially those who allowed me to visit them in their homes to sketch and catalog their various collections. Helpful librarians, museum personnel, and glass company representatives were also excellent sources and their help was greatly appreciated. Finally, David Richardson and his fellow employees at Antique Publications also deserve a little thanks for the risk and effort put forth in publishing my work.

Robin Rainwater, Leota Pickvet, Louis Pickvet Jr., Louis Pickvet III, Fairy Pickvet, Juli Pickvet, Andrea Pickvet, Kate Pickvet, Michael Pickvet, Linda Eddy, Tom & Sandra Smith, David Smith, Bill & Kathy Willard, Rachel Moore, Robert & Sue Darnold, Joe & Sandy Dixon, Teri Sloop, Ella Kitson, Ward Lindsay, Robert Davidson, Kim & Kevin Mannor, Rick Patterson, Dr. Fred Svoboda, David Renner, Joe Renner, Linda Renner, Paul Traviglia & Jennifer Hood, Robert & Susan Lutton, Chris & Kelly Klebba, Rick & Karen Hoag, Teri Parsons, David Pilla & Cath Devost, Dr. Tom O'Connor, Matt & Linda Polzin, Richard & Linda Merchant, Jim & Carol Rainwater, Bill & Theresa Smola, Bobby & Mary Johnson and Larry Limonoff.

The University of Michigan libraries, Flint Public Library, Detroit Public Library, New York Public Library Annex, Historical Society of Pennsylvania, Widener Library at Harvard, Milwaukee Public Library, Toledo Museum of Art, Toledo-Lucas County Public Library, Corning Museum of Glass & Library, Nelson County Public Library of Bardstown, Kentucky, Jim Beam Distillery's American Outpost of Clermont, Kentucky, The Oscar Getz Museum of Whiskey History of Bardstown, Kentucky, The Library of Congress, and the Maker's Mark Distillery of Loretto, Kentucky.

The members of the Shot Glass Club of America: Mike Moyer, Walter H. McIntosh, Jere Lee, Fred Sweeney, Marvin C. Short, David H. Kuntz, Peter A. Loedding, Evelyn Radke, Kitty Culley, Hector M. Balderrama, Glen W. Duncan, Lois D. Irwin, Mark Edward Nelson, Ray Jaeger, Anna Mary Straub, Gerald J. Berghold, B.D. Kolwyck, Jeannine A. Wynn, Michael Galvin, Dan Siegrist, Edward Niderost, Virgil Stites, Al Cali, Ron Pytko, Merrily H. Finnegan, Michael Harbarth, John Sloate, J.W. Greenfield, Robert E. McCabe Sr., Ken Schwartz, Debbie Gillotti, Fred Simpson, Richard N. Sunderland, Bruce W. Hansen, Kenneth Koehler, James Sable, James L. Schwind, David L. Warren, Joe Miller, Kay Coleman, Bernard Lukco, Donald E. Poor, M.B. Bradley, Henry S. Anderson, Wilna Braun, Bill Gaylord, Florence S. Cook, Jim Kensil, Stan Sanders, George S. Lewis, Karl Fielding, Clement E. Zambon, David Smith, Robert Mraz, Erma Maine, Arthur Gould, George Koenig, Paul Van Vactor, Robert B. Hayden III, James E. Edwards, Barbara Edmonson, Tito Caldera, Beth Leffler, Ted Grekowicz, Diane Legner, Gary Fisher, David A. Wright, David Hazelmyer, Bill Butler, Patricia A. Copher, Leroy E. Pace, and all newer members who joined too recently to list.

TABLE OF CONTENTS

©Copyright 1992
Antique Publications
Box 553
Marietta, Ohio 45750
ALL RIGHTS RESERVED

PB ISBN# 0-915410-90-7

Chapter I
WHAT EXACTLY IS A SHOT GLASS?

A shot glass. What exactly is it? It seems like a rather simple question. "It's one of those rugged little things used for drinking 'shots' of whiskey. It's an advertising glass for distillers or distributors. It's a souvenir glass found in all of those tourist shops around the country. It's a tiny measuring glass." All are common answers and aid in the description of shot glasses. To the collector questions arise as to maximum and minimum height; maximum and minimum capacity; and style of glass. More questions arise. Are pharmaceutical glasses particularly those used throughout the 19th and early 20th centuries by the medical profession shot glasses? Are foots, stems, or handles all right? What about other tiny glass receptacles such as candleholders and toothpickholders? What about double shots, triple shots, sample glasses, dram glasses, and so on? Some questions are easy but others are not so simple.[1]

A survey conducted with The Shot Glass Club of America indicates that there is general agreement with the definition in <u>Shot Glasses: An American Tradition.</u> Shot glasses are whiskey tumblers which are small vessels made of glass designed for drinking distilled spirits in small amounts. Tumblers do <u>not</u> have foots, stems, or handles. The base of a tumbler is pointed or convex. Shot glasses are limited to two ounces in volume and strictly less than three inches in height. Minimum capacity is one ounce and the shortest height allowed is 1¾ inches. Thick bottoms and thick sides are common but not necessary.[2]

It might be just a bit easier or at least helpful to define what is not a shot glass. Glasses in this chapter without catalog numbers with the exception of double shots are not shot glasses. Pilsener glasses, wine glasses, champagne glasses, cocktail glasses, cordials, and brandy glasses all have foots and stems. Dram glasses are made of metal. Juice glasses and highballs are greater than two ounces. Fractional-shots are not true shot glasses since they contain less than one ounce of liquid. Toy mugs have handles. Bootglasses are not tumblers (base is not convex)

Champagne   Pilsener   Brandy   Highball

Wine   Sherry   Cocktail   Cordial

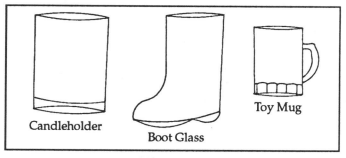

Candleholder   Boot Glass   Toy Mug

and typically contain about three ounces. Double shots are too tall. Triple-shots usually hold at least three ounces. Candleholders are designed to hold candles of 2" diameter and generally would contain more than two ounces if filled with liquid. All mentioned in this paragraph are not shot glasses.

The most difficult to distinguish by far is the toothpickholder. Many fit the definition of a shot glass and about the only major difference aside from the fact that they were designed to hold toothpicks; is that toothpickholders tend to taper inward as they proceed upward. In other words, the base diameter tends to be less than the

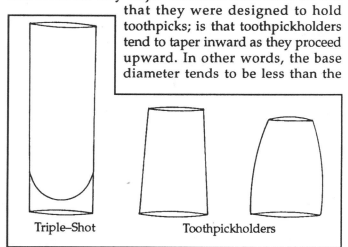

Triple–Shot   Toothpickholders

top diameter. Shot glasses ordinarily taper outward where the diameter is greater at the top. Of course there are always exceptions and that is where the confusion lies. Toothpickholders also tend to be cut, mold-patterned, or machine-patterned and are produced in a variety of colors. Cut crystal toothpickholders pose the

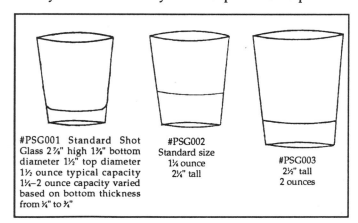

#PSG001 Standard Shot Glass 2⅞" high 1¾" bottom diameter 1½" top diameter 1½ ounce typical capacity 1¼–2 ounce capacity varied based on bottom thickness from ¼" to ¾"

#PSG002 Standard size 1¼ ounce 2¼" tall

#PSG003 2½" tall 2 ounces

most problems. Unless they are identified in some book, trade journal, or what have you, they will be difficult to distinguish from shot glasses.

Our definition of a shot glass is a broad one and encompasses a wide variety of small tumblers specifically designed for small measures of distilled spirits. The standard shot glass is quite common from its development over 100 years ago to the present. The standard is by far the most abundant of all shot glasses and is used for cut patterns, tourist motifs, advertising, patterns, pictures, and most anything else that has ever appeared upon on a shot glass.

Square shot glasses are 2½" tall glass tumblers with square bottoms and contain two ounces. Porcelain replicas are shot glasses completely covered inside and out with black enamel. Genuine porcelain has many of the same ingredients as glass and are considered shot glasses if the dimensions are correct. Plain shot glasses (PSG #'s) in a variety of shapes and sizes within the measurements listed in our definition are pictured here at the end of the chapter. Odd small tumblers within the required dimensions for the most part are impractical for drinking much else other than distilled spirits with the exception of miniatures that are usually children's toys such as tea sets. In fact much of the history of shot glasses begins with the development of toy whiskey tasters, the advent of ardent spirits, the places they were used, and the history of glassware and glassmaking.

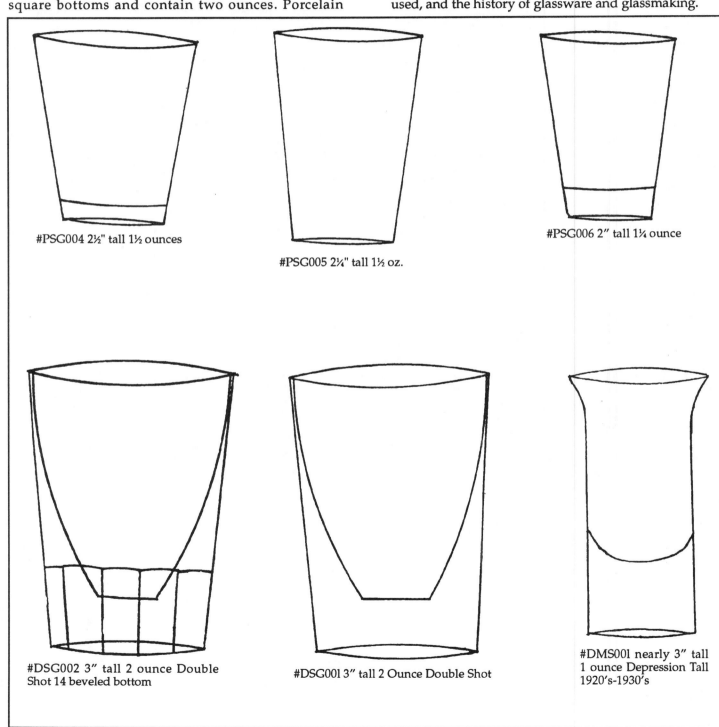

#PSG004 2½" tall 1½ ounces

#PSG005 2¼" tall 1½ oz.

#PSG006 2" tall 1¼ ounce

#DSG002 3" tall 2 ounce Double Shot 14 beveled bottom

#DSG001 3" tall 2 Ounce Double Shot

#DMS001 nearly 3" tall 1 ounce Depression Tall 1920's-1930's

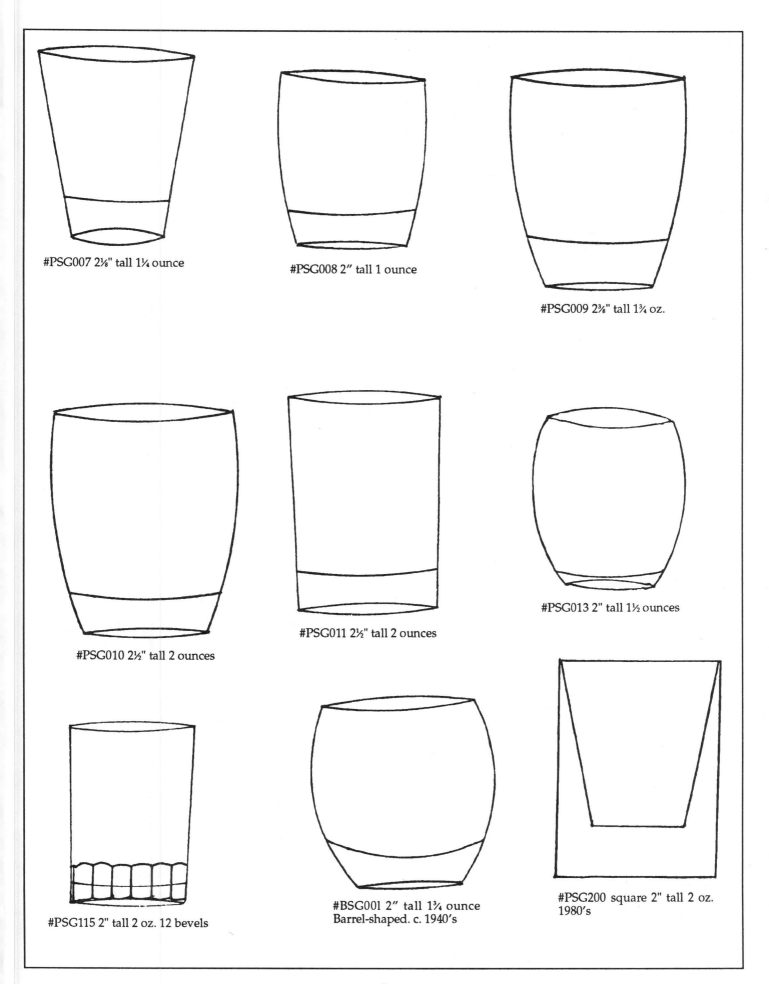

#PSG007 2⅛" tall 1¼ ounce

#PSG008 2" tall 1 ounce

#PSG009 2⅜" tall 1¾ oz.

#PSG010 2½" tall 2 ounces

#PSG011 2½" tall 2 ounces

#PSG013 2" tall 1½ ounces

#PSG115 2" tall 2 oz. 12 bevels

#BSG001 2" tall 1¾ ounce
Barrel-shaped. c. 1940's

#PSG200 square 2" tall 2 oz.
1980's

3

Chapter II:
THE HISTORY OF GLASSMAKING AND DRINKING VESSELS IN THE WORLD

A question that may never be answered is what brought on the development of the discovery of glass. Some believe that its invention was completely by accident. A desert nomad in ancient Egypt possibly lit a wood fire in a sand pit and the ashes may have fused with the sand into a glassy substance. Further experimentation was carried on from there. No matter how, the earliest archaeological records or surviving glass objects date with the ancient Egyptians roughly 3,500 years ago.

The prime ingredients of glass are silica, a form of sand, and ashes from plants or trees. Ash is an alkali that helps sand melt at a lower temperature. Stabilizing substances like carbonate of soda or lime are crushed into fine powders and added to the batch to aid in the fusion process as well as to protect against excessive moisture. Metals and other ingredients and additives were altered through the centuries but the basic formula has changed little.

The technique of core-forming with the Egyptians would not change until Roman times. Core-forming involves the construction of a core ordinarily a mixture of clay and dung. Hot glass was then spun around the core. The vessel then might be decorated with brightly colored glass threads that were weaved around it. The core-formed glass was quite dark or opaque.[3]

Ordinary citizens of ancient Egypt usually were not in possession of glassware. It was reserved for the wealthy such as high priests, nobles, the pharaoh's assistants, and even the pharaoh himself. Core-formed containers were made for ointments, oils, and perfumes. Such objects were present on thrones, buried with mummies in their cases, and even in the tombs of the pharaohs.

Core-forming continued for centuries but advances and new ideas followed and improved upon it. The Mesopotamians cast glass into mold-like containers. Simple clay molds may have lasted for only one good cast but molds did get their start here. Another innovative technique of the Mesopotamians was the finishing of the glass. After casting, the surface of the glass was polished by wheels fed with abrasives. These basic techniques of mold-casting and polishing would find their way into the 19th and 20th centuries of America.

The second significant step in the history of glassmaking other than its actual discovery was the art of glassblowing. Around 50 B.C. or just over 2,000 years ago, the Romans developed the process of blowing short puffs of air through a hollow metal tube into a gather or molten blob of glass. Glassmakers could heat up a batch of glass, inflate a bubble quickly at the end of the rod, and then work it while it was still warm into many shapes and sizes. Glass did not have to be cast or core-formed any longer.

With the advent of blowing, glass was no longer a luxury product used exclusively by the rich. The Romans produced a great variety of glass and fortunately a good deal of it survived or was recreated from archaeological digs. The most popular were

Core-formed ancient Egyptian drinking vessels ¼ to ½ scale

Roman Gladiator Beaker about 3¾" tall
c. 1st century A.D. hand-blown

drinking vessels. Drinking cups were primarily used for drinking fermented beverages. Gladiator beakers and souvenir beakers depicting gruesome gladiator scenes, battles, heroes, chariots, and so forth were designed for drinking wine. Glass was also blown into molds and bottles were made with the same scenes. Other popular shapes were figureheads, gods, and particularly grapes and grapeclusters to celebrate wine and the vines it was derived from. The same grapeclusters and fortunately different tourist scenes can be found on 20th century shot glasses in America.

The Romans experimented with many styles of decorating their glass that would also work its way into the American glass industry. The Greeks had borrowed cutting techniques from the Mesopotamians but learned to cut shallow grooves and hollows more precisely similar to that of gemstones. The Romans advanced further with cutting, engraving, and abrading on stone wheels. A glass object was held against the wheel and fed with an abrasive paste. Light, deep, and fancy cuts were made based for the most part on the cutter's skill.

Enamelling developed long before glassware. The painting of cave walls, rocks, clay, pottery, and so forth have been a part of every culture since the advent of civilizations. The Romans enamelled their glassware much like we do today only without the complex machinery. With the Romans, colored glass was pulverized into a powder, mixed with oils like a paint, and then applied to the glass. The glass was then reheated to permanently fuse the enamel. Romans for the most part manipulated cold glass and did cold painting as well.[4]

Up until the 5th century the Romans ruled the western world and the advances by the West were

found somewhere within their vast empire. In the East, China delved into glassmaking in the form of beads and jade-like carved glass figurines about the same time as the Romans. Much of it was exported or traded away since it was not highly regarded. The Chinese would spend more time creating the best porcelain in the world for the coming centuries. Later, but not until the 18th and 19th centuries would glass become somewhat popular in China. Cut glass snuff bottles for inhaling opium and porcelain replicas of vases were made of glass. It would be the Middle East or the Islamic world and then on to Europe for the new advances in the history of glassmaking.

Islamic glass dates as far back to the 8th century. The Romans had experimented with some cameo or relief cutting but the Islamic cutters took it a step further. Relief cutting is a difficult and expensive process. It involves outlining a design on a glass surface and then carefully cutting away the background but not completely in order to leave the original design raised or in relief. Relief-cut glass was once again for the rich only. Plants, geometric patterns, fish, Koran quotations, and a

Islamic Drinking Vessel. Long handles, necks, & spouts were typical along with decorations covering the entire glass. c. 10th-11th century ¼ scale

wide variety of other designs were highlighted in relief upon vases, perfume sprinklers, beakers, bottles, etc.

Common items for ordinary people might include bowls, bottles, and glasses primarily for wine consumption. Enamelling was also done on lamps which housed oil for full and floating wicks. The period of Islamic glass ended early in the 15th century in 1401 when the Mongol conqueror Tamerlane destroyed Damascus and captured the glass artisans. He brought them and their skills to Samarkand.[5]

Europe cast in the middle ages did very little with glass for decades. A few primitive vessels such as bowls and glasses but hardly anything of note for years and years. The 12th century coupled with the rise in power of the Catholic Church finally was responsible for a new chapter in glass history.

Gothic architecture and the creation of the stained-glass window began that chapter. Stained materials from oils, plants, and vegetable matter were added to glass mixtures. The development of coloring glass with some experimental metals was cast as thin flat cakes, cut into small pieces, and then formed into mosaics. Brilliantly colored glass was included in some of the finest European architecture. Huge cathedral windows sparkled in shades of all colors.[6]

In the new millennium, it is not hard to understand that the first glassmakers guild and the hub of glassmaking world would fall into the city of Venice. Venice by the early 13th century became the major trade center of the western world. Venetian glassmakers formed a guild to guard their trade secrets and commercial production of glass flourished once again.

With the hazards associated with the great furnace fires, the glass industry was ordered in 1291 to move all of their operations to the nearby island of Murano. The rulers feared that Venice might burn if an accident occurred in one of the glasshouses. The glass trade was such an integral part of the commerce of Venice, that Venetian glassmakers were forbidden by law to leave Murano. The penalty for escape was death though many did manage to do so.

All was not bad for the glass craftsmen on Murano. Their skills and reputation were highly regarded and their daughters were allowed to marry noblemen. For the most part the city of Venice had a monopoly on glassmaking. Their craftsmen held the secrets for furnace construction, glass formulas including the proportion of ingredients, the use of tools, and toolmaking. Knowledge was passed down to their sons or only those admitted to the guild. The secrets were well guarded until 1612 when Antonio Neri made them available in his book titled: L'arte Vetraria which translates into The Art of Glass. Neri was a master glass craftsmen and understood the complete process involved in its production. It is easy to see that Neri enjoyed his trade for he is famous for saying: "Glass is more gentle, graceful, and noble than any metal and its use is more delightful, polite, and sightly than any other material at this day known to the world."

The biggest impact Venetians had on the evolution of glassmaking was the development of cristallo in the 16th century. Next to the discovery of glass itself with the Egyptians and the invention of glassblowing with the Romans, the creation of a nearly colorless glass formula was a very significant innovation. The glass was adapted to the world's finest mirrors far superior to those made of bronze, steel, or polished silver. Venetians produced glass beads for jewelry and rosaries that rivaled that of gemstones. Glass jewelry

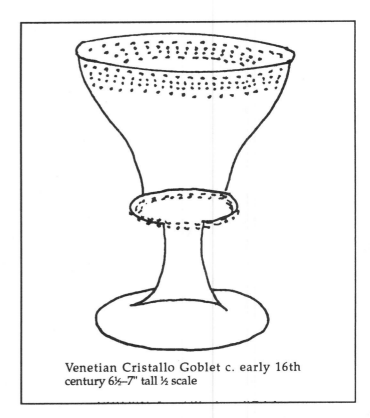

Venetian Cristallo Goblet c. early 16th century 6½–7" tall ½ scale

was used for barter in the African slave trade.

Venetian glass was produced in colors that would resurface in Art Glass in the 19th century and Depression Glass in America in the early 20th. Emerald green, dark blue, amethyst, reddish-brown, and later in the 17th century a milky-white glass flowed from the factories on Murano. The monopoly and production of fine Venetian glass dominated the world market through most of the 17th century.

Glass aided science and technological advances. Clear optical lenses for microscopes, telescopes, improved eyeglasses, test tubes, beakers, flasks, tubing, and a host of other laboratory apparatus were vital for scientific experimentation. The Venetian cristallo did not interfere with chemicals and one could see the reactions through the clear glass. Much of the Venetian styles were created for the wealthy. Anyone of importance in the western world graced their tables with glass wine goblets, fancy bowls, and vessels from Venice. The Venetian glasscutters were the first to use diamond point engraving. Up to the 17th century, India was the sole source of diamonds and the majority of trade between east and west passed through Venice. With diamonds readily available, they adapted them to their cutting wheels.

The one serious complaint with Venetian glass that surfaced was its frailty. There was no question that the glass was exquisite and the best made in the world to that point; but it was thin, fragile, and not easily transported. It broke easily in shipment and the quest for a more durable and stronger formula would be invented with the English.[7]

Meanwhile a few other glasshouses sprang up around northern Europe. Europe was still in the midst of the feudal system and a few glasshouses existed near the manor of a nobleman. More iron in the soil produced glass of a pale green color. Wood ashes or potash was readily available and served to aid in the melting of the sand mixture. These so-called "Forest Glasshouses" made windows and drinking vessels.

Huge drinking vessels were particularly popular in Germany where beer could be drunk in large quantities. Some held several quarts and amazingly enough, some drinkers tried to drain them in a single gulp. Some lost

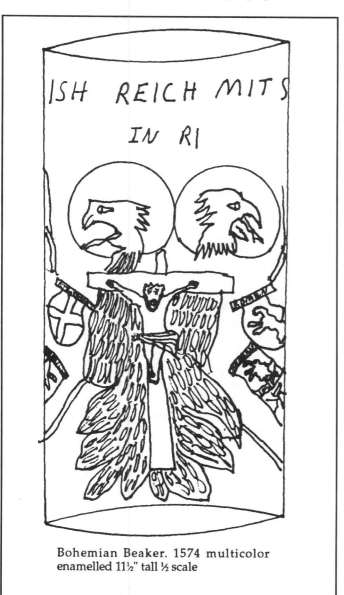

Bohemian Beaker. 1574 multicolor enamelled 11½" tall ½ scale

their bets while others succeeded but the practice was frowned upon by some like Martin Luther who referred to these vessels as "Fool's Glasses."

In the late 16th and 17th centuries, Germans and Bohemians began cutting and decorating their glass. Their drinking glasses contained patriotic designs, coats of arms, biblical figures and references, mythological figures, and scenes of daily life. They experimented with the formulas of making glass and actually developed a form of crystal that was easier to cut than the thin Venetian cristallo. In Bohemia and Brandenburg particularly, this new glass could be cut on rapidly rotating stone and copper wheels. The Germans were responsible for the perfection of wheel engraving and engraved much the same designs as were enamelled. As the center of the West's trade shifted away from Venice, so did the advances in glassmaking. The English would adopt the Venetian style and then begin their own unique technological advances beyond the experts at Murano.[8]

One might be asking at this point what this brief world history of glassmaking has to do with the lowly shot glass. If one looks closely enough, the shot glass has adapted many of the characteristics associated with this early glassware. Aside from the porcelain or ceramic shot glasses that we have included in our definition, a shot glass is a 'glass' drinking vessel. The same basic formula of sand and ash are used to create them. Through the ages one of the principle uses of glass was for drinking vessels to hold waters, wines, and beers. A shot glass is a drinking vessel also used for fermented beverages, only of a stronger nature.

Depression shot glasses contain the colors that were perfected in Venetian glassware. Souvenir scenes began with the Romans and thousands of shot glasses portray our own tourist attractions. The scenes of daily life on early glassware is certainly shared by us today: games, sports, nautical themes, animals, cars, planes, universities, products, holidays, soft drinks, flowers, hotels, political campaigns, clubs, and so on are all pictured on modern shot glasses. The coat of arms popular with early German glassware are still found on their souvenirs today and especially on fraternity and sorority shot glasses in America. The enamelling, cutting, and particularly the copper wheel engraving of the Germans would be borrowed by the early American glass industry and applied to small drinking vessels. Much of the background of our designing and decorating can be traced to their early history of glassware.

Chapter III
EUROPEAN AND ENGLISH INFLUENCE ON GLASSMAKING AND DRINKING PATTERNS

England did little in the way of original glassmaking until the 17th century. In the 13th century some window glass and a few crude drinking glasses were produced. In 1571, Giacomo Verzelini and 9 other Italian glassmakers escaped to London from Antwerp. Three years later Verzelini received a patent from Queen Elizabeth to make glass like the Venetians from whose secrets he had known. For about 100 years, England produced glass in the Venetian style.

In 1615, English glassmakers were forced to switch to coal as fuel for their furnaces. Wood was outlawed as fuel because of a severe shortage and what was available was reserved for shipbuilding. Coal posed a problem for it was dirtier and the fumes produced could easily ruin molten glass during the process of blowing.

The first significant item that England produced for export was the "black bottle" in the mid-17th century. It was actually a very dark green due primarily to the iron

English Black Bottle with Owner's Initials (Dark Green in Color) 1686 ⅓ scale

English Black Bottle (Dark Green in Color) 1657 ⅓ scale

and elements present in the sand that was used. It was nearly black and that served to protect its contents from light. The bottle was made of thick glass that was very durable. Unlike the fragile thin Venetian glassware, the black bottle rarely broke in shipping. For over 100 years, England was the biggest supplier of bottles to the western world.[9]

The goal of England was to find a cross between Venetian glass and the black bottle. They wanted the crystal clear elegance of cristallo but with the durability of the black bottle. The solution came in 1676 with George Ravenscroft. Ravenscroft had lived several years in Venice but he was an englishman and glassmaker. He perfected a formula for heavy lead glass which is still regarded as a good formula today.

The new batch held great advantages and was a factor in the ending of Venetian dominance. When heated, it remained in a workable condition longer which allowed the glass artisan to make fancier and more time-consuming designs. It was superior in clarity, weight, and light-capturing ability. The workability of the first true lead crystal was responsible for a host of new stem formations particularly in goblets. Airtwists, teardrops, knops, balusters, and others refracted light as never before.

The English further experimented with refraction in their cutting techniques. Prior to the early 18th century, England borrowed cutting techniques from the Germans and Bohemians. The new style involved covering the surface of glass with an orderly geometric pattern of facets. This patterning combined with the new glass maximized refraction which in turn caused it to sparkle brightly. The new patterning was applied to chandeliers, candlesticks, centerpieces, and drinking glasses. Rooms in English houses were dark and candles were heavily taxed and therefore expensive. Glass served to lighten and replaced more and more candles until it too was eventually taxed.

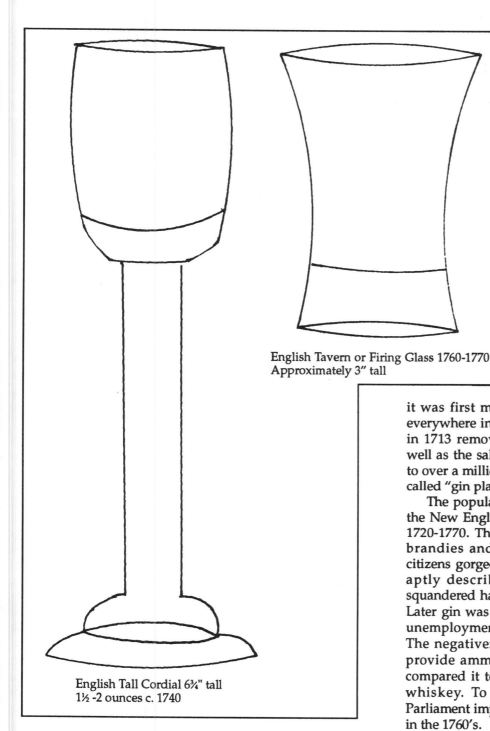

English Tavern or Firing Glass 1760-1770
Approximately 3" tall

English Dram Glass Metal
(silver or iron) 2½" tall
2½ oz. c. 1720's

English Tall Cordial 6¾" tall
1½ -2 ounces c. 1740

The new lead glass was thicker and easier cut than the Venetian glass. As early as 1689, political messages were engraved upon stemware. One such glass was engraved to celebrate the end of Roman Catholic rule when William III of Orange assumed the throne. Those who supported the Catholic King James and his sons were known as Jacobites and also engraved glasses in their support. Some Jacobites were actually charged and convicted of treason for possessing such glasses.[10]

In 1690, the same administration under William of Orange passed: "An Act for the Encouraging of the Distillation of Brandy and Spirits." New drinking styles and the lifting of taxes on distilled spirits encouraged their growth and influenced glassware as well. The introduction of gin named for Ginievre or Geneva where it was first made overtook England. Stills sprang up everywhere in the early 1700's. Furthermore Parliament in 1713 removed all restrictions on the distillation as well as the sale of spirits. Annual production soon rose to over a million gallons of gin which brought on the so-called "gin plague."

The popularity of gin paralleled the development of the New England rum industry in America from about 1720-1770. The wealthy English aristocrats drank fine brandies and expensive wines while the common citizens gorged on gin and beers. The poor of England aptly described in the books of Charles Dickens squandered hard fought pennies on the new cheap gin. Later gin was blamed for crime, idleness, begging, and unemployment of the middle-classes and poor alike. The negativeness would carry over to America and provide ammunition for temperance reformers who compared it to the problems associated with rum and whiskey. To combat the gin plague in England, Parliament imposed a 20 shilling per gallon tax upon gin in the 1760's.

The use of stronger, more powerful distilled spirits produced dramatic changes in the development of glassware and other drinking vessels. The bowls of wine glasses were reduced to as low as one ounce. It was impossible to drain pints or half-pints consistently of strong liquors. Dram glasses made of metal or tiny glass bowls on long stems and bases only held an ounce or two. Dram glasses cheaply-made were frail and broke easily, but were quite popular and used in the practice of dramming. Dramming was where several small toasts of of rum, brandy, whiskey, or gin were drunk in succession in lodges, taverns, and dram shops. Dramming carried over to America but ended in England by about 1840. Parliament earlier in the 19th century placed additional high taxes on the sale and distillation of spirits. They did this to further encourage the general population to switch from hard liquors like gin and whiskey to beer.

The development of the much sturdier firing glass followed dram glasses in the late 18th century. As they were slammed upon the table the resulting noise was like a "musket firing." Unlike dram glasses, firing glasses withstood significant abuse and banging. Firing glasses were heavy and were the first glass vessels to consistently contain a thick base. The base might be as much as an inch thick with the average about half that amount. Firing glasses might also contain separate bases similar to wine glasses but without the separate stem and separate bowl.[11]

The glass industry prospered in England and they exported glass in large quantities. A bit of glass was shipped to the far east in the 17th century but much more in the 18th. The English East India Company exported significant amounts of glass to India; second only to what they shipped to America. In 1780, Parliament lifted a 35 year ban on exportation of Irish glass. Irish glass was tax free and many of England's skilled glassworkers moved to Ireland. English and Irish glass was virtually identical in style and impossible to distinguish one from the other. Glassworkers in Ireland turned out huge quantities for American markets across the Atlantic. Glassmaking cities such as Dublin, Belfast, Cork, and probably the most famous city for fine glass, Waterford; survived well into the 19th century. America's founding fathers and people that had access to glassware on America's east coast, used British and Irish-made glass well into the 1820's until the invention of the mechanical pressing machine. Glassware imported by America included water glasses, decanters, firing glasses, wine glasses and other stemware, rummers, drams, fluted glasses, finger basins, bottles, punch jugs, liquors or cordial glasses, salts, mustards, butter keelers, globes, and about anything the English and Irish factories turned out.[12]

While American glass companies were gearing up in the 19th century, England and Ireland lost a significant share of their largest market; however, they still exported a good deal of glass to America. More glass found its way into domestic life and more decorations were applied to it. Glasses with landscapes, architecture, city views, nature, and portraiture were engraved, stained, or enameled upon English glassware. Beakers contained entire maps of famous battles and other scenes of daily life.

In 1845, Parliament finally removed the excise tax on English glass. By the 1850's, England still had the reputation of producing some of the finest glassware in the world. In 1851, The World's Fair in London dubbed The Great Exposition of the Works of Industry of All Nations contained a huge display of glass. The Crystal Palace Exhibition featured a giant building containing 400 tons of sheet glass or about 300,000 hand blown panes. The displays and products at this exhibit could not but help stimulate the glass industry. Complete matching table sets of glassware that would later be produced in great quantity in America during the Great Depression had its roots in England. Table service items included stemmed drinking glasses in many different shapes and sizes, water beakers, beer tankards, decanters, bowls, sugar bowls and creamers, salt shakers, butter dishes, honey jars, flower vases, candlestick holders, and bonbon dishes.

A variety of other glass items other than tableware were made in England too. Jugs, water basins, powder boxes, jewelry dishes and boxes, toothbrush holders, soap dishes, and other glass objects. The hand pressing method invented in America found its way back to England. The new imitation cut glass was pressed into boots, shoes, baskets, birds, fruits, and some of the first boot-shaped drinking glasses. Paperweights were popular in England in the mid-19th century. England and other European countries were the first to spark a revival of cameo-cut glass not done since the Islamic glasscutters. John Northwood was credited for the new revival of relief cutting in cameo colors. A blue or plum color cased in white with classic Greek and Roman themes was raised on vases, flasks, glasses, plaques, etc.

England, Ireland, and other European countries were definitely important influences on the evolution of the shot glass. Much of our American traditions, the ideas carried down with us, and the immigrants with glassmaking skills all had their origins in Europe and particularly England. The advent of ardent spirits and dramming carried over the Atlantic Ocean to the New World. Thick-bottomed glasses originated with the English-made firing glass. Technological and practical advances in glassmaking such as the use of coal as fuel, new lead crystal formulas, and smaller drinking vessels were all inherited from Great Britain. On top of that virtually all of our glassware was imported well into the 19th century was British or Irish-made. The new geometric pattern cutting and decoration techniques were borrowed from England. The black bottle was certainly a common item in eastern America and the first uses of glass by Americans would be for bottles and windows.

Much in the way of tableware and unique uses of glass was just another of the long list of items borrowed from Europe. Political glassware was duplicated in later 19th century America in the way of campaign tumblers. These tumblers typically displayed portraits of presidential candidates and American symbols such as the flag and the bald eagle. Along with the new techniques, America's first glassworkers and generations that followed would be skilled craftsmen from Europe. Though English law prohibited emigration of its glassworkers, a few along with some Germans and French would be responsible for getting the American glass industry off the ground.

Chapter IV:
THE HISTORY OF DRINKING SPIRITS IN AMERICA AND THE FIRST TEMPERANCE MOVEMENT

"A man hath no better thing under the sun than to eat and to drink and to be merry."

ECCLES. 8:15.

Many of the glass creations throughout time in the Old World as well as the New World were geared to the consumption of beverages. Beverages can influence the type of glassware used for them. Champagne glasses, wine glasses, cordials and so on all contain distinct differences and are used for specific liquids. Beer mugs, water tumblers, bar tumblers, firing glasses, and further on down to the shot glass are no exception. So it does seem reasonable to study the history of alcohol since it is very closely related to the creation of tiny glass vessels. After all, shot glasses were created to drink spirits in tiny amounts.

Alcohol is formed by the spontaneous fermentation of fruits and grains. It has been around for thousands of years, long before glassware. Immortal beings were invented by people to celebrate drinking and to give reverence to the protectors of the vine. Gestin was a Sumerian goddess present in the minds of her people over 6,000 years ago. Osiris was the ancient Egyptian god of wine as was Gestin. Dionysus was the Greek god of wine about 2,500 years ago. Socrates, one of the great early Greek philosophers commented on drink: "So far as drinking is concerned, you have my hearty approval, for wine does moisten the soul and lull our griefs to sleep."

Intoxicating festivals in honor of the gods and great drinking holidays might last several days. The name of Dionysus was renamed Bacchus by the Romans but the only thing that changed was the size of the festivals. Romans held even larger celebrations for a variety of occasions in honor of Bacchus. Of course heavy drinking of wine accompanied the harvest, death, and rebirth of the vine. Frequent passages can be found in the Bible espousing the benefits of alcohol. "Give wine unto those that be of heavy hearts." PROV. 31:6. "Let us eat and drink; for tomorrow we shall die." ISA. 22:13.

The drinking of wines and other alcoholic beverages was present throughout the known world for centuries. Religions integrated its use into their services. The Western world brewed beers to accompany wine-making. Mead became a popular fermented beverage in the Middle Ages around 500 A.D. Mead consisted of water, honey, malt, and yeast. The Viking God Thor was admired for being able to outdrink any mortal or immortal being. Thor fit in with the stereotypical Viking warrior – a large muscular thick-skinned warrior sailing the Northern world with little but his courage and large stocks of mead and beer. Other European explorers and

sailors refused to drink water stored on their ships until the wines and beers were consumed.

Whiskey and other stronger distilled spirits originated in the later Middle Ages but beer was by far the most common drink. Large breweries existed on most European feudal estates. It was served at breakfast, lunch, and dinner. Some estimates for beer consumption reached as high as two gallons a day per capita. A monastic grading system using X's evaluated the brew. One 'X' was weak; 'XX' was a bit stronger; and then 'XXX' was the strongest and the best.[13]

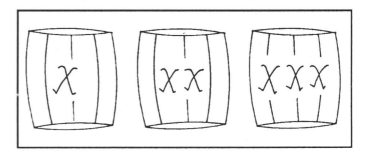

"This is what I now propose:
In a tavern I shall die
With a glass up to my nose
And God's angels standing by
That they may indeed declare
As I take my final tot
May God receive with loving care
Such a decent drunken sot."

(14th century Latin toast, author unknown).

Beer was drunk by the pilgrims on the Mayflower and other forms of of alcohol were present in early colonial America. The Puritans believed that alcohol was

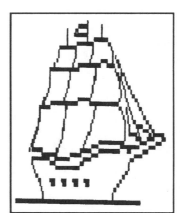

a gift from God and it was used as a restorative or cureall. It was often prescribed for common sicknesses such as colds, the flu, fevers; and other not so ordinary like nervous breakdowns, diseases, and childbirth. Alcohol was a nutritional and a dietary staple. In the beginning, the ingredients necessary had to be imported from England including grapes, berries, apples, and hops. Hops grew wild in New England but the seeds and strains used in the brewing process were shipped in from the mother country.

Apples surprisingly were not native to the New World. Once the seeds were transplanted from England, apple trees grew quite nicely in America. So well in fact, that fermented cider became the most popular beverage in the American colonies. It was produced very easily; simply by crushing apples with stones and allowing the resulting juice to sit in barrels over the winter. By spring, most of it aged into hard cider. Some was stored for lengthier periods of time. When available, honey and sugar were added to increase the potency a bit and this apple champagne was a rare treat. Cider was so common that it was drank by adults and children alike at all meals and between meals.

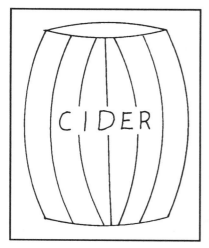

Beer was not that uncommon but did not enjoy any where near the popularity of cider. With the aid of a malster, farmers brewed their own beers from the malted grains of corn, barley, and others. A small commercial brewery was set up in 1634 in Massachusetts Bay Colony but did not survive for long. The beer was not that good for several reasons. One was the poor quality water; but the most significant reason for failure was the English method of brewing. It did not work in America. Yeast that floated on top of a batch or vat of barley malt reacted with the air and produced poor tasting, bitter beer. Along with the water, the early beer to the mid-19th century was cloudy and down right rank at times.

The word "whiskey" originated in Scotland around 1494; a name given to their distilled grains. Some argue that George Thorpe of Virginia distilled America's first corn whiskey along the James River in 1620. It is a fact that the early colonists experimented much with fermentation but had very little success at distilling hard liquors. The Scots drank a small dose or morning dram of their whiskey to get the body going after a night's rest and supposedly to prevent chills, fever, and malaria. The colonists borrowed the practice but it was more commonly a dose of cider in the morning. Corn whiskey would not be produced in any quantity until the 1790's.

The early colonial farmers in the 17th and early 18th centuries attempted wine-making as well. Many experimented with most any fruits, vegetables, or plant matter. The mixture was mashed, boiled, sweetened primarily with honey or possibly sugar when available, and then fermented. Whatever was available was used in the mixture. Fruits seemed to work best and might include strawberries, raspberries, huckleberries, blackberries, cranberries, blueberries, elderberries, gooseberries, currents, and other wild berries. Many of the berries were rather sour and the wine that was produced was barely drinkable. The vegetables were even worse. Corn silk or stalks, celery, beets, turnips, carrots, squashes, pumpkins, onions, tomatoes, spinach, and whatever else was given a whirl. Herbs, flowers, tree leaves, birch bark, pine twigs, persimmons, hickory nuts, goldenrod, dandelion, roots, and a wide variety of plants were experimented with. Surprisingly some like dandelion wine was drinkable but since we see little today in the way of beet or squash wine; it is obvious that the majority of winemaking was a failure.

"Oh, we can make liquor to sweeten our lips
of pumpkins, of parsnips, of walnut tree chips."
(Early colonists' song; unknown author).

Alcohol was a normal and beneficial product as considered by the Puritans. In 1673, Increase Mather stated: "Drink is in itself a creature of God, and to be received with thankfulness."[14] Drunkenness though was looked upon in extreme disfavor. One of the earliest recorded punishments in America for drunkenness was applied to John Holmes in 1633. He was fined 40 shillings in Plymouth County and made to sit in the stocks. Increase Mather also said: "The wine is from God, but the drunkard is from the devil."[15] Other than stocks and fines, Puritans punished habitual drunkards with whippings, hard labor, and were sometimes made to wear a mark of shame. The rigid life of the Puritan and the discipline associated with daily living resulted in infrequent drunkenness in the 17th century.

The problems associated with drunkenness would not arise until the introduction of rum. The first rum was imported to America in the 1650's from the West Indies on English ships. Rum was a potent spirit distilled from molasses and sugar cane. Cotton Mather, the son of Increase, was worried that rum would ruin the social class of America. No doubt he was worried about his position in the social hierarchy and that intoxication would crumble the current structure. Cotton Mather stated that: "The flood of excessive drinking. . . . would soon drown Christianity."[16]

It was not until the early 1700's when the first rum distilleries were built in America. In 1722, the price of rum was about 3 shillings 6 pence per gallon. By 1738 with the rum trade in full swing and the increased production of American distilleries, the price dropped to two shillings. It was so cheap that common laborers could afford to get drunk daily. With the drop in price, rum threatened to overtake cider as the national drink. In addition to what they purchased on their own, common laborers, farmers, sailors, and the like were given daily rations of rum by their employers. A family who had little else but cider might go through a hundred barrels a year taking into consideration a husband, wife, numerous children, various guests, and numerous occasions. Rum reduced that amount.

Rum was very potent compared to what had been previously available. Beer contained little more than 5% alcohol, wine about 18%, cider only about 10%; while rum like the gin of England contained 40-50% alcohol. Rum was often mixed in punches or flip which was a combination of rum, beer, sugar, and then warmed by plunging a hot poker from a fireplace directly into a mug. By the mid-18th century, every important town on the east coast including Boston, Charleston, New York, Philadelphia, and so on all contained at least one rum distillery.

Rum was so common and popular that it actually became a unit of trade or standard of currency. It could be traded for flour, tobacco, and other goods. Rum was exchanged for slaves in the 18th century up to the American Revolution when the British naval blockade cut off molasses and sugar cane from the West Indies. Like cider, rum was used by physicians as a common remedy for sickness, pain, and to restore health and energy. Following ancient traditions, rum was also used in times of celebration or important events. Funerals, weddings, births, barn or house raisings, public meetings, church service, and church events such as the ordination of a minister was all celebrated with rum.

Records prior to 1768 on alcohol production and consumption are sketchy at best. More formal record-keeping was not completed until 1768 on rum and molasses imports. The first set of books only lasted until about 1772 when the early beginnings of the Revolutionary War was cause for disruption. Good recordkeeping resumed after the war. The rum and molasses trade accounted for ⅓ of all American imports before and after the Revolution. Rum was shipped easily, withstood all climates, and actually increased in value as it aged. All of American's eastern states were heavily involved in the rum trade. Not only was it traded for African slaves, but also for such things as rice in South Carolina, tar and tobacco in North Carolina, and salted fish in Massachusetts. After the Revolutionary War, America traded for the most part with the non-British West Indies or those of the French, Spanish, and Danish West Indies.

One problem that arose during the Revolution was the cutting off of the rum and molasses supplies by the British that Americans relied heavily upon. This was the first turning of America to distilled grain spirits. Whiskey had been distilled for quite some time but could not meet the demand with the absence of rum. Evan Williams was the first to distill corn whiskey in Kentucky in 1783, but Elijah Craig got most of the credit. There were other Europeans in America before Columbus, but like the Spanish captain, Craig brought the secrets and speculation out in the open. Craig was a Baptist minister and is often noted as the first distiller of Kentucky bourbon whiskey. Corn grew better than the less hardy wheat and rye so it was natural that much of the early whiskey would be produced from corn. Whiskey production increased dramatically as rum was scarce but there were no commercial distilleries for grainbased whiskey as there were for the production of rum. After the war, rum regained its position but it would be doomed for several reasons at the turn of the century.

In the late 1780's, molasses was harder to obtain. France joined Britain in the West Indies and distilled their own rum. Erratic supplies and higher prices were the result. In 1789, import duties were imposed on rum and molasses driving the prices further up. Meanwhile as American grain production rose, whiskey became cheaper. By 1790, Americans still consumed twice the amount of rum as grain spirits and fruit brandies. That statistic would soon change. Another important factor in the decline of rum was the rising American nationalism. Imported goods were looked upon in disfavor since we were not truly independent with our reliance upon them. More taxes doubled the price of rum and since excellent import records were kept, taxes were not as easily evaded like those of whiskey distillers. American-made spirits soon became our third most important industrial product after cloth and tanned hides. Some argue that it was the first abundant and inexpensive product of American technology. With all of these pressures, the rum industry nearly died out by 1802.

Consumption of hard spirits fell during the Revolutionary War but increased dramatically afterward. By 1790, the average adult drank 6 gallons per capita of pure alcohol annually or over 2 ounces a day. By 1800 it was up to 7 gallons and that figure remained steady through 1830. About 65% of the alcoholic intake was from distilled spirits. The remaining 35% consisted of cider for the most part and some wine and beer.[17] John Kobler estimates that omitting non-drinkers and those without access to spirits and averaging illicit stills, the average per capita intake of those drinking may easily have exceeded 12 gallons.[18]

Cider never wavered and by the 1830's, 15 gallons of it was consumed annually per person. Cider sold on the average for about $3. to $4. per barrel but might drop to as low as 50¢ with a bumper apple crop. The rural north was a popular place for cider production and consumption since apple trees grew well in that region of the country. Cider presses were quite common for commercial production and the labor required was low-skilled. Cider was often fortified with distilled spirits to raise the alcoholic content. To increase the potency further, applejack was the term used for the 20% alcohol that was poured off cider after it had been left outside on a cold night to freeze. Normal cider was ordinarily 10–12% alcohol. Other drinks using cider were also created such as cider royal which was hard cider mixed with apple brandy.

"Cider is the Devil's Kindling–wood."
(Henry A. Reynolds M.D.)

Other alcoholic beverages that figured into the American diet were wine, beer, and brandies; but to a much lesser extent. Good beer would not be available until the 1850's or just before the Civil War. Wine was generally imported and by 1770 the average American only drank a little less than a pint of wine annually. From 1770-1870, wine consumption only rose to about ⅓ of a gallon per year which was equal to the amount of cider consumed in a week. Brandy was made from strawberries, raspberries, pears, apples, and most frequently peaches. Distilled pears were named "perry"; distilled peaches likewise were called "peachy." Various punches and mixtures like sangaree which was a wine concoction sweetened with sugar and brandies were also drunk. Manathan was a mixture of beer, rum, and sugar; its name was changed to hotchpotch when warmed. Sillabub (wine, sugar, and milk) and meridian (brandy and tea) were two other names but not as common as those where rum was the prime ingredient.

Prior to the mid-19th century, there was no good way to store fruits like apples and peaches. They were of course eaten fresh, sometimes dried, but most likely converted to alcoholic beverages. It was simply the best way of preserving them. Drinks such as cider and whiskey enabled people to wash down heavily oiled foods, dried breads like cornbread, spoiled foods, moldy bread, stale cheese, and salty meats. Early on, Americans had no ovens and fried everything in lard or butter.

Men as one might expect did the majority of the drinking; however, women and children were not exactly abstainers in the least. According to the American Temperance Society (ATS), by the late 1820's; 9 million women and children drank 12 million gallons of distilled spirits annually and 3 million men drank 60 million gallons. The ATS also provided statistics on daily consumption rates for men. According to their estimates, half the men drank 2 ounces per day; ¼ drank 6 ounces (habitual drinkers); ⅛ drank 12 ounces (topers and occasional drunks); and the remaining ⅛ of the men drank 24 ounces a day (drunkards). They also claimed that there were about 100,000 female drunkards in the late 1820's.

The tavern was by far the most popular place next to the everyday home for a man to drink. Men socialized in groups at taverns and discussed crops, concerns, political events, and the latest news. Though the tavern or pub was a popular establishment in England, Britain was alarmed with them since revolutionary talk most likely originated in American taverns. To illustrate the concerns of the British, members of the Boston Group met at Chase's Distillery in 1769 to celebrate the anniversary of Boston's protest to the Stamp Act. It was noted that no less than 45 toasts were drunk. The first naturally was to the king and queen symbolizing that Americans still advocated ties with England. The last toast supporting the new Whig position was a threat to those who further wished to exploit the colonists: "strong halters, firm blocks, and sharp axes to all such as deserve either!"[19] Organized meetings by Americans

were even more popular after the war in these taverns. A tavern was a significant step in reaching manhood. Fathers were rather proud of their sons when they were able to match them glass for glass. Tavern logs show that between 1810-1835, a typical customer purchased liquor in half-pint amounts.

Landlord, fill the flowing bowl,
until it doth run over,
for tonight we'll merry be,
tomorrow we'll be sober.
(18th century tavern song; unknown author)

Some popular terms associated with taverns was dramming, tippling, tipplers, and the grog shop. Dramming was more difficult in America because of the unavailability of small drinking vessels. Some were imported from England but for the most part Americans toasted with mugs and crude tankards. The practice might still be called dramming but actual dram glasses were a rarity. Tippling was the art of drinking in a tavern. A tippler was much like a social drinker and was not as harsh a word as "drunkard". A few illegal tippling houses sprang up here and there to serve those where drinking was prohibited. They might serve Indians, slaves, apprentices, debtors, problem drunkards, and so forth; but most establishments prior to the Civil War era were respectable. A grog shop was simply another name for a tavern or a place to obtain grog.

From Green's Anti-Intemperance Almanac:

The Grog Shop
O come let us all to the grog-shop:
The tempest is gathering fast–
There surely is naught like the grog-shop
To shield from the turbulent blast.

For there wille be wrangling Willy
Disputing about a lame ox;
And there will be bullying Billy
Challenging negroes to box:

Toby Fillpot with carbuncle nose
Mixing politics up with his liquor;
Tim Tuneful that sings even prose,
And hiccups and coughs in his beaker.

Dick Drowsy with emerald eyes,
Kit Crusty with hair like a comet,
Sam Smootly that whilom grew wise
But returned like a dog to his vomit

And there will be tippling and talk
And fuddling and fun to the life,
And swaggering, swearing, and smoke,
And shuffling and scuffling and strife.

And there will be swapping of horses,
And betting, and beating, and blows,

And laughter, and lewdness, and losses,
And winning, and wounding and woes.

O then let us off to the grog-shop;
Come, father, come, Jonathan, come;
Far drearier far than a Sunday
Is a storm in the dullness of home.

(originally written 1831)

Tavern owners were respected and usually prominent members of the community. Ordinarily it required a license to operate a tavern. The leaders or the society's elite issued licenses only to voters (white male property owners) and church members. Some laws required taverns to keep sufficient supplies on tap or risk losing their license. Prior to the Civil War, Virginia only allowed one tavern per county. It was ordinarily built next to the county courthouse so that all associated with the case could gather for a drink. Sometimes disputes were settled there out of court. Other times the trial might take place in the tavern since it was often the only building large enough to contain many spectators. Many other public buildings including churches were built around taverns. It became a tradition for good luck to seal a bottle of rum or whiskey in the cornerstone of a church, tavern, or public building. Even with ordinances like Virginia's, permits and licensing of new taverns grew dramatically in the later 18th and throughout the first half of the 19th century. John Adams expressed some concern but was ridiculed. Benjamin Franklin wrote in his <u>Pennsylvania Gazette</u> in the March 29, 1764 edition that taverns were becoming "a. . . . pest of society." [20] Complaints in the beginning were not taken very seriously.

Data is tougher to obtain on women. The social order of the time period did not allow them many opportunities to drink in public. What they lacked in the way of public drinking; they certainly made up for in private. Women for the most part stayed away from potent spirits. Rather, they enjoyed highly sugared cordials. Stomach elixirs or alcoholic medicines were consumed by women regularly and sickness was often faked by them as an excuse to drink. Pregnant women were often prescribed rum and milk. Women were allowed to drink at some social functions like society dinners, evening parties, and public baths where mint juleps were popular.

Children and even babies, white males particularly; were given alcohol. Babies with the hearty approval of doctors were given rum and whiskey when teething. Children were often expected to finish off the sugary residue at the bottom of his or her parents' nearly empty glass. The argument of the parents was that children would become accustomed to liquor and it would later protect them from becoming drunks. A father naturally had to get his son ready for the tavern.

Southern slaves were given watered down spirits as an extra work incentive at planting and harvesting time. Holidays like Christmas were also times that slaves were provided with spirits. Laws were instituted prohibiting blacks from drinking but they were rarely enforced. Slaves that were allowed to have tiny garden patches and animal pens often traded vegetables and hams for distilled spirits. Many taverns admitted blacks as long as they had money or foodstuffs to pay for their drink.

The force of whiskey had the most adverse effects on Indians. Indians were often cheated with whiskey that was watered down 10 or 15 to one and then fortified with pepper and tobacco. Liquor was traded with the Indians for furs and pelts. Often times when Indians did get the real thing, they were quite unaccustomed to it. Habitual drinking disrupted Indian culture, encouraged wars, and led to tribal disintegration.

Indian tribes placed high value on trances and hallucinations. Strong drink was a way to bring them on. During a drunken revelry, they often beat their wives, each other, and self torture could be part of a ceremony. The Quakers would later help them in the 1800's to forsake spirits. Two important chiefs who renounced rum were Pontiac and Tecumseh. Both led major uprisings but sadly both were killed and most of their followers met the same fate. Ironically Pontiac met his death when a Kalkaskian Indian was bribed by an Englishman with rum. The defeat of Tecumseh by Governor William Henry Harrison at the battle of Tippecanoe just before the War of 1812 led to a popular saying. "Tippecanoe and Tyler Too" was one of the first great political slogans that aided Harrison in winning the presidential election of 1840. Harrison doled out hundreds of barrels of cider during political rallies and speeches.

John Tyler was Harrison's vice president and assumed the presidency when Harrison died of pneumonia after only a month from his inauguration. Numerous toasts would follow and catchy phrases or sayings would find their way later on many advertising items such as glassware. "Fifty-four forty or fight" was a boundary dispute with Britain over the Oregon Territory. It was settled at the 49th parallel rather than the 54th without fighting. "Remember the Alamo", "Pike's Peak or Bust", "The Union Forever", were just a few others.

It seems as though nearly everyone in the country was drinking for a variety of reasons and occasions. The nation's laborers were given drinking breaks in the morning (typically 11:00 a.m.) and afternoon (4:00 p.m.). Frequently, town bells tolled at these hours to announce the drinking break. Drinking in factories was done for new arrivals of employees, old ones retiring, marriage proposals, new babies, etc. Outside the job, most any special occasion was celebrated with a great deal of drinking such as dances, barbecues, pig roasts, balls, after harvests, land clearings, barn-raisings, elections, and when women gathered to sew a quilt. Bottles were passed at trials between judges, lawyers, clients, defendants, plaintiffs, and spectators. Western newlyweds were commonly presented with a good bottle of whiskey to be drunk before the honeymoon night. The clergy up to the 1820's were heavy drinkers. The military or army was made up of serious drinkers. The election or promotion of officers was another excuse

for drinking. It was believed that the army would revolt without their twice daily 2-4 ounce rations of rum or whiskey.

Drinking accompanied gaming, cards, horseracing, and duelling. Some college boards tried to ban drink from their campuses but met with little success. Hangings and the most important holiday of all, the 4th of July; was accompanied by heavy drinking binges. Those in monotonous jobs or with no roots or social ties drank the most. Examples would be the army, lumberjacks, factory workers, stagecoach drivers, river boatmen, canal builders, and new immigrants. ⅕ of a man's consumption was in a tavern. The rest for the most part was consumed at home. The common man drank whiskey at mealtime. The upper classes would have a varied stock of cordials, brandies, and whiskey. The rich stored them in bottles while ordinary men used jugs. Small drams and later shots would be consumed at their leisure (i.e. morning, breaks, bedtime, etc.)

Whiskey might be bought at a local distillery if one was nearby, but for the most part it was purchased at the general store. Whiskey was the most important product sold at the general store and accounted for ¼ of the total sales. The economic growth of a general store depended upon the availability of spirits and it was more important to stock them than flour and sugar. Whiskey was used as currency as rum had been previously. Distilled spirits were also available at Inns and when travelling and upon steamships. Riverboats were highly profitable from alcohol sales and many were little more than gambling boats and floating taverns. Southern Comfort used a steamboat as their trademark for their whiskey.

As time went on new drinks were created. Hot drinks were made for cool weather. A hot toddy consisted of whiskey or rum, sugar, and hot water. A hot sling was similar only gin was substituted for whiskey. Lemon juice, cherry brandy or bitters might be added to the mixture. The mint julep, a favorite drink of women was made up of peach brandy or whiskey, sugar, ice, and crushed mint. The fireplace of a home or tavern was a comfortable place to sit, relax, and drink.

Alcohol was so entrenched in our society. Like the Puritans it was prescribed for all illnesses. Supposedly, it cured fevers, colds, snake-bites, frosted toes, and even broken bones. Mental disorders, relaxants for tension, cures for depression, and so on were all curable by alcohol; so the early doctors believed. There were some though who had a different opinion. Americans became so seasoned and accustomed to alcohol that as time went on, ever increasing amounts were needed to reach the stage of intoxication. Greater quantities led to terrible physical troubles such as nausea, vomiting, and the dreaded delirium tremens (D.T.'s). A case of the delirium tremens began with irritation and anxiety; then muscle spasms and a period of paranoia or hallucina-tions. Images associated with D.T.'s included crawling snakes and spiders upon one's body, falling into bottomless pits, and monsters like the demon rum. The disorder was caused by an addiction to alcohol and then the sudden withdrawal of it. The adverse effects of alcohol and then abuse were recognized and many began speaking out against them.

#DSG200 double shot Black Design. 1980's 87.7 proof, distilled from peaches & oranges.

"After supper pap took the jug, and said he had enough whiskey there for two drunks and one delirium tremens."

Mark Twain (Huckleberry Finn)

By the mid-18th century, abuses of alcohol became more and more recognized and found their way into print. The first scientific arguments that alcohol could be poisonous began around the 1720's-1730's. In 1732 the new colony of Georgia banned spirits. Illegal tippling houses and the argument that South Carolina traders dealing in rum were soaking up great profits in Georgia particularly with the Indians led them to lift the ban. In the 1740's, an illness named the West Indies Dry Gripes was blamed on rum. The painful stomach disorder was caused by lead-poisoning from distilling rum in lead stills but it was associated with rum. In an attempt to reduce the consumption of rum somewhat, the General Court of Massachusetts outlawed rum and wine at funerals, but it did little in the way of reducing intake.

The Quakers were some of the first early opponents of both liquors and slavery. Although they usually passed a bottle around during their gatherings, they progressively lowered their intake throughout the 18th century. Anthony Benezet was a wealthy Quaker from Philadelphia and wrote his first pamphlet in 1774: The Mighty Destroyer Displayed in Some Account of the Dreadful Havock made by the Mistaken Use as well as Abuse of Distilled Spirituous Liquors. The title is nearly an essay itself and attacks excessive use of alcohol. He attacked both rum and slavery in his next pamphlet: The Potent Enemies of America Laid Open also published in 1774 in Philadelphia. He followed up with another one in 1775: The Nature and Bad Effects of Spirituous

Liquors.[21] Benezet believed that the American Revolution could not be a success without abolishing slavery and liquor alike. The "Friends" as Quakers referred to themselves slowly followed Benezet's teachings. In 1777, the Quaker followers were ordered not to sell or distill grain because of war-time bread shortages. In 1784, the Friends were not allowed to import or sell any distilled spirits. The restrictions continued and in 1788, Quakers were advised by their leaders not to use spirits as medicine without caution. In 1789, the Friends were outlawed from using spirits at births, marriages, and funerals. The reduction of liquor from all phases of everyday living was quite radical thinking especially when one considers that spirits were a common part of most religious ceremonies, activities, and celebrations.

The Methodists were the only other religious institution to condemn the use of alcohol in the 18th century. In the very late 1700's (1780's–1790's), Methodism was religion based on rejecting old traditions and they saw alcohol as another obstacle in the way of church reform. It didn't always work in practice though for ministers including Methodists were expected to receive a drink at each stop or house visited on their pastoral rounds. Methodist preachers in out of the way rural areas easily drank even though the church frowned upon it and eventually forbade it.

The first to provide scientific evidence on the negative effects of alcohol in the United States was Dr. Benjamin Rush. He first studied at the Edinburgh College of Medicine in the 1760's and then returned to America. He was the army surgeon general during the Revolutionary War cut was also considered America's foremost physician during this time. Rush knew and admired Benezet and used his pamphlets in his research. Rush labeled alcoholism as a disease noting dependence and the pain of withdrawal. He backed his arguments with firsthand knowledge of treating people's diseases. Rush's complaints focused on distilled spirits and believed that fermented drinks like wine were healthful. He pointed out that distilled spirits caused chills when cold, stomach problems, vomiting, shaking or tremors, liver disorders, colic, rashes, gout, apoplexy, jaundice, diabetes, epilepsy, and insanity.

Rush published numerous articles supporting anti-drinking sentiment. He voiced that our soldiers were in poorer condition because of drink. He urged alternatives to rum and whiskey including water, beer, vinegar, wine, cider, milk or buttermilk, molasses, brown sugar, and various mixtures or combinations of them. His most famous essay was written in 1784 which outlined the problems and sicknesses that spirits were responsible for: An Inquiry into the Effects of Spirituous Liquors (sometimes named: An Inquiry into the Effects of Ardent Spirits Upon the Human Mind and Body or simply Inquiry). 170,000 copies of this essay were distributed by 1850.[22]

From Rush's Inquiry, he described distilled beverages and their effects as follows: "In folly, it causes him to resemble a calf, – in stupidity, an ass, – in roaring, a mad bull, – in quarreling and fighting, a dog, – in cruelty, a tiger, – in fetor, a skunk, – in filthiness, a hog, – and in obscenity, a he-goat."

In 1789, Rush's work continued on and he published a meter or chart outlining the effects of all forms of liquids from water on down to hard liquors. It was named: "A Moral and Physical Thermometer" where he argued that water, milk, and beer gave one health, wealth, long life, happiness, etc.; wine, cider, and the like brought cheerfulness and strength; but then more potent mixed drinks caused sickness and disease; and finally at the very bottom, hard distilled liquors brought on crime, suicide, and death.

Throughout Rush's life until his death in 1813, drinking rates did not decline in the least but rather increased somewhat. He was discouraged but he did bring awareness to the growing problem. Rush founded and taught at the Philadelphia College of Medicine and his students spread his views throughout the country by the end of the 18th century. Reformers were still much in the minority; use of spirits was simply too prevalent in our society. He did come to the conclusion that the only way to reduce consumption was by the intervention of the clergy and the religious orders present in America. The Quakers and the Methodists were already on their way and later temperance groups would adopt this plan. Rush's other ideas included petitioning to limit the number of taverns, heavy taxes, and harsh punishment for public drunkenness. So many of his ideas and works were borrowed by temperance organizations that Dr. Benjamin Rush earned the reputation as being: "The

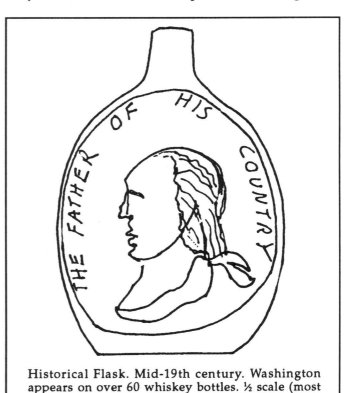

Historical Flask. Mid-19th century. Washington appears on over 60 whiskey bottles. ½ scale (most presidents & other historical figures in the 19th century are also pictured upon flasks).

Father of the American Temperance Movement" in the next century. However, our founding fathers and other leaders were alarmed and well aware of intoxication and drunkenness, they did little in the support of Rush.

Though Benjamin Franklin as mentioned earlier referred to taverns as pests, he was also fond of saying: "If God had intended man to drink water, he would not have made him with an elbow capable of raising a wine glass."[23] Prior to the war, George Washington had his own still and an apple orchard at Mt. Vernon in which to distill spirits and make cider. Washington grew his own wheat, corn, and collected over 2,000 local grape vines in an attempt to make wine. He experimented with fermentation but the duties as Colonel and later as

Commander-in-Chief took him away and ended his attempts at wine-making. As Colonel Washington prior to the Revolutionary War, he was popular with his troops and drank with them but rarely to excess. Washington drank beer, wine, and some distilled spirits but not heavily. Before and well after the war, America's leaders were still using glass drinking vessels imported from England or Ireland.

Thomas Jefferson was a good friend of Benjamin Rush and since Rush primarily argued against hard liquor and believed that wine was healthful if taken in moderation, Jefferson received little flack for his wine-making hobby. Jefferson toured Bourdeaux several times as America's minister to France after the war, and he

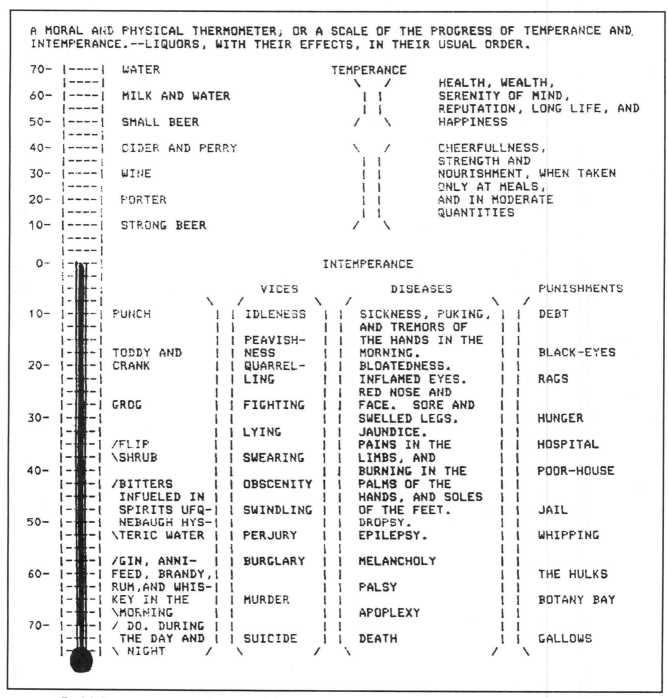

Rush's Thermometer – reproduced in various forms from the late 1700's through all of the 19th century.

then ordered hundreds of bottles of wines. Jefferson along with several of his friends like Henry Clay and John Calhoun planted their own vineyards and were America's foremost wine connosieurs. John Marshall and Andrew Jackson shared their taste for wine. Aaron Burr reportedly had the best wine cellar in the country. It was still somewhat unpatriotic to drink foreign wine so Jefferson did his best to encourage others to start their own vineyards.

John Adams expressed great concern about the amount of drinking going on in the country. Of course Adams enjoyed a large tankard of cider at breakfast time. Cider was his favorite and at times, Adams drank little else.

The first to do something about the growing problem was Alexander Hamilton though his intentions were for raising revenue rather than curbing consumption. The new nation needed money desperately to pay the war debts and excise taxes on the manufacture, sale, or consumption of commodities were one of the few taxes other than customs' duties permitted by the federal government under the Constitution. Hamilton won with the use of two powerful arguments: the tax would raise money and reduce drunkenness all in one easy swipe of the pen. In actuality, it accomplished nothing; it brought in little in the way of revenue and consumption of alcohol continued to rise. The excise tax in 1791 passed on whiskey, snuff, loaf sugar, and carriages. All were

America's 2nd president, John Adams, drank huge amounts of cider in tankards.

accepted except by the frontiersmen concerning whiskey. At first Congress only allowed import duties but it raised hardly any money, so they extended it to all distillers. The New England states supported it, the middle states split, and the rural South and West opposed it. Rush was naturally an avid supporter and fought for it. 11¢ a gallon was placed on spirits distilled from imported ingredients (i.e. molasses for rum) and 9¢ a gallon on domestic spirits distilled from grains.

The large commercial distillers surprisingly were in support of the tax but only in the hope that it would put the small distillers and hence their competition out of business. It was those in the rural areas like the South and the West that fought the taxes. The West at the time of the tax was namely Kentucky, Tennessee, and western Pennsylvania. The general population did not particularly care much for it either and in an attempt to appease them, Congress exempted personal stills from taxation.

The frontiersmen barely operated at a subsistence level. They owned their own stills, consumed their own whiskey, and couldn't pass much tax on to the purchaser. Not much money circulated in the West and the tax had to be paid in currency. Jugs of whiskey were frequently used as currency or payment and that was unacceptable to the federal tax collectors. American grain was still too bulky and transportation over land and water was too difficult prior to trains, ships, canals, and further improvements. Grain was best distilled and transported that way. The frontiersmen resented the agents snooping around their property. Jefferson, an agrarian himself had not agreed with Hamilton and had mentioned that the tax clashed with Revolutionary principles.

The hatred of the tax by the common people grew especially when arrests were made for moonshining and not paying the tax. Federal agents went as far as to wreck stills or shoot them up. Stills were an important investment and holding of rural people. It was ordinarily several days journey to the nearest courthouse which angered and inconvenienced the settlers even more. Finally violence broke out in resistance to the tax. Government representatives were tarred and feathered, seared with hot irons, mailbags were taken at gunpoint, and some had their homes burned in resistance. One tax collector called in an army platoon but the platoon was outnumbered and surrendered. There was even one brief rumor that the rebellers were going to establish a Trans-Alleghenian nation separate from the United States.

In 1792, the tax was modified to provide more exemptions but they still didn't work. Rumors that 500 armed men in rebellion reached Congress. As many as 7,000 protesters appeared at the trial of several moonshiners at Parkinson's Ferry in western Pennsylvania. Washington panicked and gathered 12,950 troops and took Hamilton along with him to put down the rebellion. When it came down to it, the rebellers were simply scared, poorly organized, and poor men who owned little and would not think of opposing Washington in any sort of combat. The great Whiskey Rebellion of 1794 was ended with no bloodshed or opposition. Two ringleaders were captured and sentenced to death, but were later pardoned by Washington. Everything associated with the tax from its inception to the Whiskey Rebellion had been very unpopular and a failure. Some argue that the Whiskey Rebellion was the most indiscreet act of Washington's presidential career.[24]

In the 1790's, Washington increased the amount of

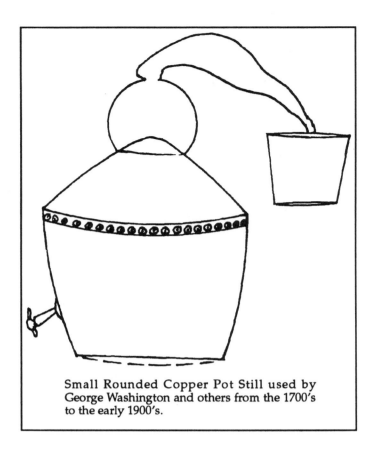

Small Rounded Copper Pot Still used by George Washington and others from the 1700's to the early 1900's.

distilling at Mt. Vernon. He hired a new estate manager named James Anderson. Anderson was an old Scotsman who instituted large scale distilling at Washington's home. Soon they were processing the grains of Washington's neighbors and the distilling operation was somewhat profitable. Unfortunately for Anderson, he put all of his efforts forth into distilling and did little else in the way of improvements around Mt. Vernon. Washington fired him for that reason but the distilling continued. Though our leaders spoke out against the abuse of strong liquors, they did hardly anything of note in the way of change.

On President Jefferson's recommendation in 1802, the excise tax on whiskey was finally removed. Wine was always an important item in Jefferson's budget. When he became president one of his first goals was to stock the wine cellar of the White House. Jefferson's annual salary was $25,000, but in his first presidential administration he entertained frequently. He invented the Presidential Cocktail Party and in his first year as president, he spent $6,500 on food and $2,400 on wines. Of course he ordered the majority of his wines from France and personally attended to his wine cellar. He figured out actual consumption figures and purchased wine accordingly.[25] Winemaking and drinking was still reserved for the elite. The common man drank whiskey and cider.

The repeal by Jefferson of the whiskey tax was the final blow to the rum industry. The ingredients needed to make whiskey were cheap and plentiful. Water, grain, and wood to fuel the stoves or still bowls were all abundant in America. The constant increase in European immigration and stillmaking skills flowed into America. The most expensive and complicated part in distilling

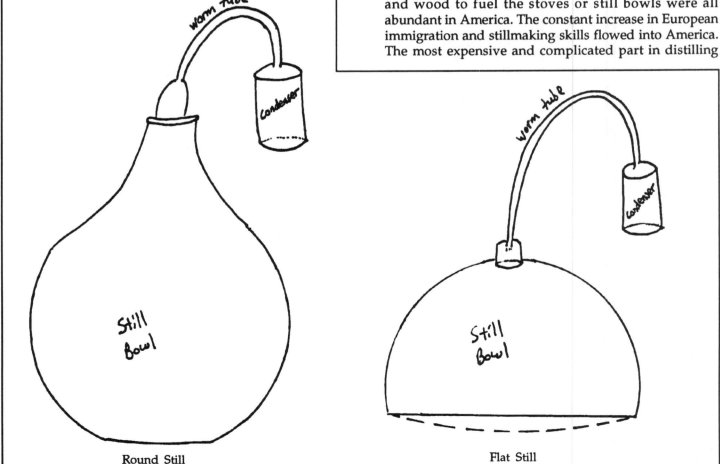

Round Still

Flat Still

whiskey from the beginning was the still. The early 1800's was a time of invention, Yankee ingenuity, and advances in stillmaking.

A still is a device that converts grain into whiskey. Fermented matter or the mash is placed in a closed container known as the still bowl. The mash is heated until an alcoholic steam is produced. The steam then escapes at an opening at the top of the still bowl and flows through a pipe named the "worm" which is cooled by air or by passing through tubs of cold water. Finally the steam is then recaptured as a liquid in a second closed container referred to as a condenser. Each time a distiller adds mash to the still bowl a batch is made. A run is a series of batches. The middle of a run usually produces the best whiskey. Great heat is not needed since the fermented matter or mash already contains alcohol which boils at a lower temperature than water. At the end of a batch, a watery waste free of alcohol remains in the bowl.

The most common material for the worm tube and the still itself is copper. America borrowed stillmaking skills from who else but England. In 1800, taxes were imposed by Parliament based on the capacity of English stills. To pay less taxes, flat shallow stills were created by the English. As a result they heated more rapidly and saved on fuel but the resulting smaller batches required more labor to operate. In the 18th century American stills were larger and rounder since fuel was abundant, there was little taxation, and labor was in short supply. In the early 1800's, America switched to these flatter stills to cut expenses and to reduce the amount of a new excise tax imposed by Hamilton on still capacity just like the English. One advantage of the flat stills was that they produced better quality whiskey. Rum distillers could not use flat stills since the rapid heating scorched and ruined molasses.[26]

Rum manufacturers were basically commercialized in the first place. They used large efficient stills that made bigger batches and required less labor. Whiskey distillers were small-time operators lacking capital, huge grain supplies, and large markets in the early 19th century. Rum manufacturers held the advantage until the invention and perfection of an advanced still known as the perpetual still. With the end of the tax on whiskey in 1802 and the decline of rum, over 100 patents were issued by the federal government from 1802–1815 for new stills.

A perpetual still contained a heat exchanger that saved on both fuel and cooling water. A third chamber called a condensing tub was built around the main condenser which was fashioned into the shape of a sphere or globe. Mash was added through a tube at the top of the structure which fed into the bowl. The bowl was then heated as with any still and the alcoholic steam rose in the globe. The advantage of the perpetual still was that the heat given off by the globe as steam cooled the warmed mash in the surrounding tub before it reached the bowl. In turn, the mash in the tub absorbed the heat from the globe and aided in cooling the

alcoholic vapors in the globe. In earlier still models, the heat given off by the condenser was wasted. A perpetual still eliminated coiled worms and water tubs for cooling. Since it captured the heat of the condenser, less fuel was needed to operate a perpetual still. Furthermore, it could be fed continuously which eliminated batches and hence the name "perpetual." The small stills of whiskey distillers were almost as efficient as those used by the large rum manufacturers which allowed the small producer to be more competitive.[27]

The typical farmer in the early 19th century rarely owned a large commercial still. The copper material for worms, bowls, boilers, and so on were expensive and a large still required construction by highly skilled craftsmen. Round and flat stills were quite common with a smaller rural farmer. Stills allowed them to easily transport their perishable fruits and grains. Whiskey was not perishable and was worth much more. A bushel of corn in the early 1800's might fetch 25¢ to 50¢. That same bushel when converted to whiskey produced 2½ gallons worth $1.25. The leftover water waste from the still bowl or sometimes referred to as slop was fed to the hogs. When the price of whiskey fell in the 1820's to as low as 25¢ a gallon, grain was still too difficult to move in any other form.

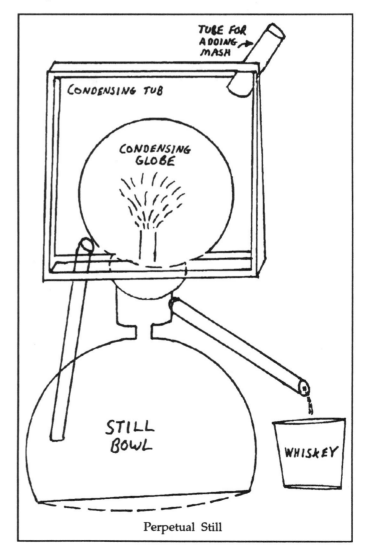

Perpetual Still

21

A horse over land could barely carry enough grain to feed itself over lengthy distances. On the other hand, that same horse could carry up to six times the amount of corn in distilled form. Water transport was getting under way but frequent delays in early shipping caused grain to rot. The conversion of grain into whiskey never slackened. It increased particularly in the West which remained the Ohio Valley, Kentucky, Tennessee, and Indiana. Those three states continue to lead the nation today in whiskey production. The western region did suffer as an abundance of whiskey drove the prices down. The cheap whiskey further undercut the dying rum market.

From the late teens up to about 1840, major changes were launched in the whiskey marketplace. Steamboats were built in droves and travelled the new waterways. New canals opened up new markets. New Orleans was one of the premier trading metropolis' of the United States but the new canal and river network north opened up the East for western grain. Cheap water transportation not only opened new markets for cattle such as hogs and cows and whiskey; but for the raw grain used to manufacture grain-based spirits. The capital more prevalent in the East was used to build huge distilleries like those previously constructed for rum. By 1840, the region of Ohio, upstate New York, and southern Pennsylvania distilled half of the nation's grain spirits. These large commercial operations effectively put the smaller ones in the West out of business.

Whiskey helped to bind the East and West together. Looming ever in the distance were temperance reformers. Good old American-made corn whiskey was patriotic and had that reputation for wholesomeness as most alcoholic beverages. Large commercial distilleries actually aided temperance reformers in the beginning somewhat. By removing the small distillers from local society, ordinary people relied on them less for distilling their grain. Distilling became associated with the upper class. The amount of drinking of whiskey was appalling and peaked about 1830. According to the Journal of Studies on Alcohol, total annual consumption per adult (those aged 15 and over) in 1830 reached 7.1 gallons in absolute or pure alcohol. Well over half of that was grain whiskey. 7.1 gallons is about 909 ounces which figures to about 2½ ounces per day per person of pure alcohol. That means the average person was drinking the equivalent of 5 ounces of 100 proof whiskey per day! Hard cider and perhaps a little wine were also included in the 7.1 gallon figure. The problems of alcohol abuse, drunkenness, and intoxication were hardly unnoticeable. The first major temperance movement sparked by Benezet and Rush was well organized in the early 19th century.

In the early 1800's, the first temperance society named: The Union Temperate Society of Moreau & Northumberland was established in Moreau, New York, by Bill J. Clark. He and his followers applied Rush's theories and agreed to abstain from all spirits except for wine at public dinners and for medication only

ALCOHOLIC BEVERAGE CONSUMPTION IN ABSOLUTE ALCOHOL PER CAPITA FOR THOSE 15 YEARS OF AGE AND UP. FROM THE JOURNAL OF STUDIES ON ALCOHOL.					
YEAR	SPIRITS	WINE	CIDER	BEER	TOTAL
1710	1.7	<.05	3.4	-	5.1
1770	3.2	<.05	3.4	-	6.6
1785	2.6	.1	3.4	-	6.1
1790	2.3	.1	3.4	-	5.8
1795	2.7	.1	3.4	-	6.2
1800	3.3	.1	3.2	-	6.6
1805	3.7	.1	3.0	-	6.8
1810	3.9	.1	3.0	.1	7.1
1815	3.7	.1	3.0	-	6.8
1820	3.9	.1	2.8	-	6.8
1825	4.1	.1	2.8	-	7.0
1830	4.3	.1	2.7	-	7.1
1835	3.4	.1	1.5	-	5.0
1840	2.5	.1	.4	.1	3.1
1845	1.6	.1	-	.1	1.8
1850	1.6	.1	-	.1	1.8
1855	1.7	.1	-	.2	2.0
1860	1.7	.1	-	.3	2.1
1865	1.6	.1	-	.3	2.0
1870	1.4	.1	-	.4	1.9
1875	1.2	.1	-	.5	1.8
1880	1.1	.2	-	.6	1.9
1885	1.0	.1	-	.9	2.0
1890	1.0	.1	-	1.0	2.1
1895	.8	.1	-	1.2	2.1
1900	.8	.1	-	1.2	2.1
1905	.9	.1	-	1.3	2.3
1910	.9	.2	-	1.5	2.6
1915	.8	.1	-	1.5	2.4
1920	.9	-	-	-	.9
1925	.9	-	-	-	.9
1930	.9	-	-	-	.9
1935	.7	.1	-	.7	1.5
1940	.6	.2	-	.8	1.6
1945	.7	.2	-	1.1	2.0
1950	.7	.2	-	1.1	2.0
1955	.7	.2	-	1.0	1.9
1960	.8	.2	-	1.0	2.0
1965	1.0	.2	-	1.0	2.2
1970	1.1	.3	-	1.2	2.5
1975	1.1	.3	-	1.3	2.7

prescribed by a doctor. As incentive to enforce these restrictions, they imposed 25¢ penalties for members drinking and 50¢ for drunkenness. The time limit imposed was one year and the initial test was a success.

As Dr. Benjamin Rush had advocated, the movement to reduce drinking of potent spirits would not be a success until the clergy of the various religious sects became active. A new antiliquor campaign began around 1810 with a group of Evangelical Calvinist ministers. Justin Edwards, Moses Stuart, Leonard Woods, and Ebenezer Porter all published articles against spirits in the Panopolist, a religious periodical created and edited by Edwards. After the War of 1812, the movement picked up speed and new organizations were formed.

Just after this war, the Massachusetts Society for the Suppression of Intemperance was founded. It was formed by a combination of clergymen, politicians, and business leaders to curb drinking, gaming, and profane language. They argued that drinking was morally wrong and appealed to merchants, sea-captains, manufacturers, businessowners, and community leaders to eliminate alcohol as a fringe benefit to their respective workers. Using Rush's studies, they claimed that alcohol was a depressant and caused their workers to be less productive.

One of the first temperance pamphlets that ministers would add to their sermons was printed in 1814 by Andover's New England Tract Society. Temperance gained momentum and more and more of their unions sprung up all along the Atlantic coast from Maine to the Carolinas. Reformers drafted constitutions, signed pledges, and attempted to turn popular drinking celebrations like the 4th of July into dry affairs. Literature appeared in droves and establishments selling liquor were prime targets. Alcohol was blamed as it had been in England during the Gin Plague for poverty, unemployment, crime, begging, and so forth. Written in several temperance publications, The Green & Delaware Moral Society in 1815 stated: "The thing has arrived to such a height, that we are actually threatened with, becoming a nation of drunkards." Temperance references could be found in literature both in support and against.

"There is some sneaking Temperance Society movement about this business. . ." said one crewman to another when ginger and water was offered to an exhausted sailor rather than some hard liquor.

     Herman Melville (Moby Dick 1851 chap. LXXI)

Though many of the claims made by these societies were grossly exaggerated, some were certainly truthful. Municipalities began significant recordkeeping and more people in major cities were arrested and convicted for drunkenness than any other crime. The adverse effects of intoxication were readily visible. Wife beatings, child abuse, assaults, fighting, public support for the mentally deranged, and the squandering of money on whiskey when it was needed for more essential items were all pointed out. The health problems recorded by Rush were not ignored either.

The temperance movement slackened somewhat in the early 1820's but reduction or outright abstinence would become part of the Protestant revival or the Great Awakening in 1815. Reverend Lyman Beecher, a Presbyterian minister was one of the first to urge outright prohibition of distilled spirits. Beecher used powerful religious arguments in his: "Six Sermons on the Nature, Occasions, Signs, Evils and Remedy of Temperance."[28] He was a popular outspoken preacher who drilled into his followers that the use of spirits was Unchristian. His pamphlets and tracts from these famous sermons circulated as much as Rush's Inquiry. Earlier in 1812, the Presbyterians had ordered their ministers to preach against intoxication. By 1827, Presbyterians supported temperance and eight years later, they adopted Beecher's teachings and fought for total abstinence. The Methodists supported temperance by 1828 and in 1832, they also advocated outright prohibition.

Previously the great rural religious revivals most popular in the South and on the frontiers were times of great occasion and drunken revelry; however, the new reform movement condemned alcohol. Presbyterians and particularly the Methodists gained converts. Other religions took note and jumped on the bandwagon. The Congregationalists and Southern Baptists supported the antidrinking movement; however, most Baptists were against it. The Reverend Justin Edwards followed Beecher's speeches and founded a new chapter named: "American Society for the Promotion of Temperance" in 1826. The Presbyterians encouraged membership and it grew dramatically and the name was shortened to "American Temperance Society" two years later. Temperance reformers were hostile, pushy, and arrogant in imposing their views upon others. Like Beecher, they mixed abstinence in with religion and made it a requirement for salvation. Women surprisingly were a majority of the participants in the movement prior to the Civil War; men would be in the next movement afterward.

One important victory of temperance was to encourage the use of alternate beverages but the fight would not be an easy one. America was plagued with poor quality water. Water from rivers like the Ohio and Mississippi were left to stand in cups until the sediment settled to the bottom. Some rivers were too dirty and the settling water never cleared. Rain water was collected in cisterns on the roofs but drought or lack of rain often left them empty. Water had to be thawed in winter and it was still muddy. The best and clearest water was in low-lying springs but the average pioneer built their homes above the water line, generally up upon a hill. It was a great inconvenience and unwanted task to haul water over and up long distances. Some private well drilling took place but impurities like sand, salt, lime, iron, and the like made the water taste awful.

Many considered water unfit for human consumption and associated it with the lower creatures like horses, cows, and pigs. Water was also associated with the poor who had nothing better to drink. It was mixed with molasses, vinegar, sassafras, ginger, and other spices or flavors if no liquor could be had. Impure water caused sickness like dysentery and diarrhea. Milk was ordinarily reserved for children when it was available but it caused troubles as well. At 12¢ a quart, milk was double the price of whiskey. Supplies of milk were erratic since storage and transportation were nearly impossible. Cows that grazed on wild jimson plants produced poison milk and isolated outbreaks of milk poison raised fears against it. Tea was not very popular. It was considered unpatriotic since it was imported from England. Americans still had tea parties but served alcohol instead! Tea was expensive but cost less than coffee. Tea though not common outsold coffee until the late 1820's when coffee prices fell to15¢ a pound.

Temperance societies attempted to get Americans to drink tea, coffee, water, beer, and some wine. With their support, Congress removed taxes on coffee and the price dropped to 10¢ a pound. A cup of coffee after the tax cut cost the same as a glass of whiskey punch. Wine was generally too expensive but remained stocked in the cellars of the wealthy. Madeira wine from Spain was a favorite and above average in potency for wines in general at about 20% alcohol. Society's elite also drank expensive but milder Rhine and Bourdeaux wines which varied from 7–14%. Wine was supported by temperance until they realized that distilled spirits were being added to wine to raise the alcoholic content to as much as 30%. When people were getting drunk on wine, temperance added it to their list of banned spirits.

Reformers at times went too far and outright lied to convince people to give up their favorite drinks. For instance, Dr. Armstrong of the Moreau Temperance Society said that Madeira wine got its nutty flavor from cockroaches dissolved in it. Rum was cursed more than any other with the ever reoccurring demon. The demon was portrayed in a variety of forms as a winged devil or as an evil being escaping out of a bottle like a Genie. Furthermore, the demon destroyed or killed people and temperance advocates encouraged parents to frighten their children with this hideous demon.

Beer was advocated as another substitute for spirits but problems arose with it as well. Successful brewing of beer did not take place in America until the 1840's with the influx of German immigrants and brewmasters. A new yeast was introduced that sank to the bottom and didn't react with the air like the old American bitter brews. Germans called their new beer lager and aged it in a cool storeroom for weeks. A cold house which couldn't operate in the summer heat was part of the large capital outlay required for a brewery. Another factor that discouraged brewing was the skilled labor required. It took years of apprenticeship to become a master brewer. One more strike against beer was that it didn't transport or store as well as whiskey. Beer would often turn sour or go flat before kegs or barrels were emptied. The German immigrants overcame these obstacles in the mid-19th century. The first German brewer to successfully produce fine lager in America was a man named Wagner operating in Philadelphia in 1842. Soon after, Anheiser-Busch, Schlitz, Pabst, Schaefer, and Muller

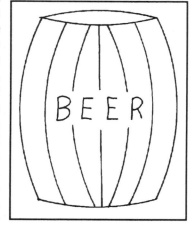

(Miller) all ran successful breweries. Beer drinking would challenge that of whiskey just prior to the Civil War.

Beer on average was only about 5% alcohol and never more than 10%. However teetotalers or those who fought for total abstinence from all alcoholic beverages attacked it as well. Beer before the good German brews was considered filthy by teetotalers and drugged with unmentionable things. That left only water, milk, tea, coffee, and a few fruit drinks as acceptable liquids for human intake. Fortunately for reformers, new methods of purifying water helped remove some of the impurities. Literature followed on the healthful and

wholesome benefits of cold clear water. Water was toasted at temperance meetings as if it had been wine. Temperance was growing.

By 1829, membership in the American Temperance Society and its numerous affiliates reached 100,000. In 1830, they claimed that 400 Boston ships sailed with no spirits aboard and 168 of 186 registered whalers of New Bedford, Massachusetts were free of them as well. By 1831, membership was up to 170,000 and boasted 2,200 local affiliates. In 1834, 7,000 groups numbered about 1,250,000. 1835 membership figures reached 1½ million and a claim that 4,000 distilleries were put out of business.[29] Great strides were made in the 1830's which is supported by consumption figures in the Journal of Studies on Alcohol. The figure on average adult consumption was cut by 56% from 1830 to 1840. Universities and the medical profession formed temperance organizations. The movement spread to northern Europe and groups were established in England, Norway, Sweden, Finland, and Ireland.

The New York State Temperance Society (NYSTS) founded by Edward Delevan in 1829 convinced former presidents Madison, John Quincy Adams, and Andrew Jackson to sign pledges abstaining from distilled spirits. Later he convinced future presidents all the way through Andrew Johnson (12 in all) to make the pledge. From 1829-1834, the NYSTS distributed 4½ million temperance pamphlets and in 1839, they claimed that 85% of all ministers and a majority of physicians in New York were strong temperance supporters. Later in the 1830's, Dr. Thomas Seawall, professor of anatomy and physiology at Colombian College, Washington D.C., lectured with drawings of mutilated and damaged human organs in various stages. Supposedly the deterioration was a direct and devastating effect of alcohol. His drawings were reproduced in many temperance tracts. Edward Delevan for the most part at his own expense circulated 150,000 of Seawall's stomach diagrams.

Massachusetts went as far as to pass the nation's first prohibition law in 1838 outlawing the retail sale of distilled spirits. It was unpopular and they had over estimated the temperance movement. The law was quickly repealed. The pledge to abstain in the very least meant no whiskey, no rum, no tavern, and no drinking at celebrations; many were not ready to make that sacrifice. The Oregon Territory adopted a prohibition law in 1844 but it was so remote and sparsely populated that it was ignored and unenforced.

"Temperate drinking is the downhill road to intemperance."

(motto of The National Philanthropists – 1826)

Temperance did have an effect on those associated with whiskey and consumption. The late 1830's on up was a tough time for those associated with the liquor trade. Many distillers, manufacturers, and tavern owners lost customers and went out of business. Arrests

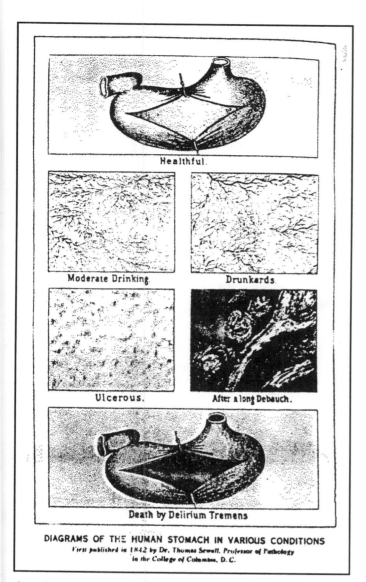

DIAGRAMS OF THE HUMAN STOMACH IN VARIOUS CONDITIONS
First published in 1842 by Dr. Thomas Sewall, Professor of Pathology
in the College of Columbus, D. C.

for drunkenness and disorderly conduct declined. Liquor was no longer given to laborers or used at as many celebrations. The armed forces cut back and the Navy went as far as to pay their enlisted men and officers alike 6¢ a day for not drinking their daily ration. Secretary of War John Eaton during the Jackson Administration in 1830 was the leader behind this idea of compensation. The new Secretary of War Lewis Cass in 1832 substituted coffee and sugar but a so-called "fatigue ration" of whiskey was still allowed to alleviate strains of combat. Cass was a lifelong abstainer and blamed the majority of army desertions on liquor and banned it from forts, camps, and garrisons.

Temperance pressures on farmers persuaded them to chop down their apple trees so no more cider could be made. Cider presses by the 1840's were outlawed for temperance members. In the 1830's some temperance hotels were formed that did not offer liquor. Dry boatlines were created to discourage drinking while travelling. Businessmen were encouraged to ban spirits in all phases of their activities. Insurance companies were persuaded to offer 5% discounts on ships run by sailors who abstained from drinking. Political candidates with similar views were funded by temperance organizations.

Lincoln as a young lawyer joined the Washington Temperance Society and spoke out against intemperance. Lincoln also had a business partner named William Berry and together they owned a country store in New Salem, Illinois that sold liquor. Although Lincoln did not drink and advocated temperance, he never fought for abstinence nor did he align himself with any political party over liquor legislation.

Tons and tons of literature flowed from the presses of the American temperance organizations. Publications circulated throughout the country including articles, mass mailings, newspapers, journals, sermons, pamphlets, public speeches and meetings, and on and on. Statistics were part of the good recordkeeping practices of many temperance groups such as the annual reports completed by the American Temperance Society. These reports were published every year from 1828-1854 and the only change was in their name. In 1837 the American Temperance Society became the American Temperance Union. Other important publications was the Andover Journal of Humanity (1829-1833) and Delevan's Albany Temperance Recorder (1832-1843). The three listed here were probably the most important because they were read by professionals, business leaders, and the clergy. By 1851, the American Tract Society reported that it had distributed 5 million pamphlets on temperance. The Order of Good Samaritans established in New York in 1857 broke new ground the next year by being the first society to admit both women and blacks. Consumption by 1845 fell to less than 2 gallons of absolute alcohol, nearly ¾ less than it had been 15 years earlier.

The entertainment industry prospered during temperance. There was money to be made as lecturers, theatrical producers, the fruit juice industry, and those making white ribbons. Temperance plays in the 1840's and shows in lecture halls, concert rooms, museum auditoriums, and theaters sprang up. The Drunkard was one of the most popular. It was adapted to the stage by William H. Smith and present at P.T. Barnum's great shows. The shrieks of one struck by the awful delirium tremens left a powerful impression on the viewers. Later in her career, Carry Nation actually had a vaudeville act. Entertainment was one medium that helped spread the word about reform.

One of America's most prolific writers wrote numerous book-length fiction supporting temperance thoughts. Timothy Shay Arthur (T.S. Arthur) wrote over 20 temperance novels and his most famous work in 1854 was titled: Ten Nights in a Barroom which was also adapted to the stage. The book was about a local miller who sells his mill to buy a tavern where all sorts of awful things happen. A little girl comes to beg her father to come home but she is hit in the head with a heavy bar tumbler. The story continues with more tragic events that indulging in alcohol is responsible for. Arthur wrote novels before, after, and during the Civil War.

There was some dissension in the first early temperance movement. Moderate supporters allowed beers, wines, and cider while teetotalers wanted complete abstinence. In the 1840's, state legislatures were reluctant to ban alcohol state-wide but rather left the decision to cities, towns, and counties. "Local Option Laws" were passed by popular vote at town meetings. Some voted for partial restrictions; others for total abstinence. In the elections held the following years, decisions were often reversed. Banning was not effective if liquor could be easily purchased in the next town. Illegal traffickers could easily be found in a dry town for those who wished to drink.

More changes occurred in the 1850's. Slavery and temperance were intertwined since both were considered immoral and economically wasteful. Prior to the abolitionist movement, slavery was considered less a problem than alcohol. A slave only lost control of his body while a drunkard lost control of his soul.

With the driving force of Neal Dow, Maine enacted a statewide prohibition law in 1851 outlawing the manufacture and sale of intoxicating liquors. Dow was born to a Quaker family and earned his wealth in the timber business. He obtained the title of colonel with his money through political favor rather than serving any form of military duty. When not involved in his business enterprises, Dow spent the majority of his life on a crusade against intemperance. He collected petitions for outright state-wide prohibition and submitted them to the legislatures. He backed candidates with his great financial resources and personally authored the prohibition bill that was unaltered when it became Maine law. He was mayor of Portland in 1851 and 1855 and reinforced the police with his own spies and agents to pursue illegal establishments, distributors, and bootleggers. Unauthorized sellers were fined $10. for the first offense; $20. for the second; and $20. as well as 6 months in jail for the third. He personally authorized illegal searches and found contraband liquor in trunks; barrels marked apples, flour, or sugar; and even coffins. Dow became a national hero and popular with temperance societies who named him: "The Napolean of Temperance". From his unearned rank of colonel, he was promoted to the rank of brigadier general during the Civil War. He was captured by the South in 1863 and spent 8 months in Libbey Prison at Richmond, Virginia. After the war he became a temperance publicist and lecturer.

Despite Dow's great efforts in Maine, illegal liquor was easily obtainable there. The first bootleggers and speakeasies arose. A bootlegger was literally a man who carried a bottle of liquor in his boot offering illegal drinks in alleyways or other secret out of the way places. Speakeasies were private clubs or illegal establishments that served drinks to members. Liquor was smuggled in to Portland in a wide variety of forms that Dow occasionally found. Doctors prescribed it freely since liquor was legal for medicinal purposes. Many doctors capitalized on it by opening their own drugstores to dispense these medicines. In short, the law failed.

Twelve other states followed Maine's lead in 1855 (Connecticut, Delaware, Indiana, Iowa, Massachusetts, Michigan, Minnesota, Nebraska, New Hampshire, New York, Rhode Island, and Vermont). Governor Horatio Seymour vetoed New York's prohibition law but he was overridden. It did not effect his political career much for he was the democratic presidential candidate in 1868 but lost to Lincoln's vice-president Andrew Johnson.

Women took on some of the law enforcing of the new prohibition laws. Margaret Freeland of Syracuse, N.Y., was the first to smash in a door and use a club to break bottles and glasses of an establishment. She had previously begged a rumseller not to sell her husband anymore who had violent tendencies when drunk. The rumseller pressed charges but dropped them when he in turn was threatened with prosecution for illegal rum selling. Violence spread most particularly in the midwest where groups of women in Indiana and Ohio axed barrels, bars, and broke bottles, mirrors, and glasses. They were rarely prosecuted because for the most part they targeted illegal establishments. Abraham Lincoln as a lawyer defended one such group and got them off with a simple reprimand. Women shamed and embarassed lawmakers by claiming that it was up to them to carry out the rough work of enforcement. Moreover, the women were prominent members of a community and the mothers, daughters, wives, aunts, cousins, or sisters of them. The courts often ruled in their favor and husbands and lawmakers backed them up out of humiliation.

Most of the early prohibition laws contained exemptions for personal use of alcohol. Beer and wines were allowed in some states. Beer consumption more than doubled from 1850 to 1860 as the new German breweries produced large quantities of quality beer. The laws did not last long. Liquor either legal or illegal was obtained with little trouble. Prohibition was waning by the late 1850's and only five states still had prohibition laws by 1863. As the laws were lifted illegal dispensers numbered fewer and fewer; women then had less to justify any destruction. The coming of the Civil War, the issue of slavery, and the clash of the rival powers effectively ended the first prohibition movement. The war and the issues associated with it took the focus away from alcohol.

Lincoln did manage to excise a tax upon alcohol during the Civil War: Internal Revenue Act in 1862 which taxed many things including liquor. Money was needed for the war and the taxes included a $20. license fee for liquor retailers, a $1.00 per barrel of malt, and 20¢ per barrel of distilled liquor. The one thing the tax did other than raising government revenue was that it supported a persuasive argument against prohibition. Prohibition would result in the immense loss of government money that the taxes provided.

We will end our discussion on early drinking patterns here at the conclusion of the first prohibition movement and its consequent failure. Many of these social events would have a direct relationship to the shot glass. The process of dramming would be replaced by the "shot" but was basically the same practice. The political sayings would find their way on to shot glasses as well as some of the first political advertising. Finally pharmaceutical shot glasses would be used more frequently by the class of doctors prescribing and dispensing measures from them.

About this time directly before the Civil War, the first shot glasses made by American glass companies were being manufactured in the East. Now that we have the background of drinking patterns in our early society, we can follow the innovations in the glass industry that would in turn directly influence drinking styles. Without whiskey and its history of consumption, shot glasses may never have been produced.

Chapter V

THE EARLY HISTORY OF GLASSMAKING IN THE UNITED STATES

The American glass industry had a rocky beginning. In 1607, the Jamestown Colony settlers brought glassblowers along with them. America had an abundance of all the necessary ingredients: a good source for ashes, plenty of sand, and massive forests for fuel. A small glasshouse was built the very next year but closed without producing any worthwhile glass. The Germans with some success but not much would be the next immigrants to attempt glassmaking in the New World.

In 1739, a German immigrant by the name of Caspar Wistar built a factory in New Jersey. He hired skilled German glassworkers and became the first commercially successful glass manufacturer in the United States. As it had been in the forest glasshouses of Europe, the basic necessities or practical uses of glass was for bottles and windows. Wistar also produced some crude tableware and a few scientific glass vessels for Benjamin Franklin. It was surprising that any glass was made at all since England banned the manufacturing of glass in the colonies. The Wistar house did not survive for long.

From 1763-1774, another German by the name of Henry W. Stiegel operated a glasshouse in Manheim, Pennsylvania. Stiegel acquired some of the former workers from Wistar's business and employed a few other foreign workers from both Germany and England. He went bankrupt in 1774 but did manage to create some window and bottle glass. The American Revolution officially closed this glasshouse permanently.

One year after the Revolution, once again another German opened a glass factory. In 1784, John Frederick Amelung produced a fair amount of hand-cut tableware; much of it engraved. Amelung's factory actually made Benjamin Franklin a pair of bifocals. To continue the trend of failure, Amelung shut down in 1795.

There were many reasons for these failures even though there was a great demand for glass in the colonies. Foreign competition and the pressure of the English Government was one reason for the failure. Glasshouses or manufacturing plants were well established in England and Ireland to produce large quantities of cheaper glass. Early Americans lacked the capital and many of the skills necessary to make glass. Transportation problems made shipping too difficult and costly across the Alleghenies. People out west used bowls and teacups to consume spirits or more often the bottle itself.

The Alleghenies were a disadvantage to the East but a boom to those living in eastern Ohio, northern West Virginia, and western Pennsylvania. The mountains served as a barrier to foreign and eastern glass long before the great canals were built. In 1797, the first frontier glasshouse about 60 miles south of Pittsburgh was constructed by Albert Gallatin, an immigrant from Switzerland. Later in the same year, a bottle factory was built in Pittsburgh by James O'Hara and Isaac Craig. This factory was named the Pittsburgh Glass Works and a year later they merged with Gallatin's New Geneva Glass Works. They did manage to hand blow windows, bottles, and a bit of tableware. They never were very successful and sold out to Edward Ensell.

The Pittsburgh and surrounding area was an ideal place to manufacture glassware. Wood for fuel was readily available and later great coal deposits were also present in the area. Sand and sandstone deposits lie along the numerous riverbeds. Red lead for fine crystal was available in the Illinois Territory. The commercial markets were wide open in every direction but east. North to Canada, west to the Pacific, and south to the major trading center of New Orleans and the Gulf of Mexico. Rivers abounded for easy transportation of glass. With all of this going for them, early attempts still ended in failure.[29]

America's first true successes in glassmaking can be traced to many but one figure stands out in particular. Deming Jarves not only founded many companies, but obtained foreign workers, the proper ingredients and formulas, and wrote an important volume in 1854: Reminiscences of Glassmaking.

In the 1790's, the Boston Crown Glass Company was chartered to produce window glass and managed to do so, but very little. Their only significance in history is that they were the first to introduce lead glass in America. Many of the workers left and went on to form the Boston Porcelain and Glass Company in 1814. They built a factory in 1815 and made a bit of lead crystal before failing in 1817. Deming Jarves with three associates (Amos Binney, Daniel Hastings, and Edmund Monroe) purchased the holdings of the Boston Porcelain and Glass Company and incorporated it into a new company in 1818. In East Cambridge, Massachusetts, it was dubbed The New England Glass Company.

From the very beginning, they operated profitably and continually reinvested in new equipment and recruited skilled workers from Europe. Jarves assumed a leading role as first agent and manager. He was a prosperous businessman and held a monopoly on red lead production early on in America. Red lead is vital for making fine lead crystal. Jarves left New England Glass in 1826 and went on to form the Boston and Sandwich Glass Company, another successful operation.[30]

What Jarves was accomplishing in the East, the team of Bakewell, Ensell, and Pears, was working on the

West. In 1807, Edward Ensell founded a small glass company in Pittsburgh but it was purchased by Benjamin Bakewell and associates in 1808. Benjamin sent his son Thomas Bakewell and a trusted clerk named Thomas Pears on numerous trips to Europe to hire experienced glassworkers. Thomas Pears split in 1818 to start a bottle factory but it failed and rejoined the Bakewells. He quit again in 1825 and moved to Indiana but came back once again in 1826. He died soon after but his son John Palmer Pears became manager of the glasshouse and the name changed to Bakewell, Pears, and Company.

These early successes were somewhat of a rarity. The first period or the Early American Period of American glass lasted from 1771 to 1830. Several glass companies were founded east and west of the Alleghenies, but nearly all failed. Cheap European glass and the lack of protective tarriffs hurt eastern glassmakers. In the West, skilled workers were difficult to obtain and the capital necessary was not often available to sustain long term growth and operation. A few depressions such as the one after the War of 1812 was also another factor in those shutdowns. For the most part except for a few enterprising men, the first period was marked distinctly with unprofitability and failure.

The Middle Period was the second period in American glass history and dates from 1830 the 1880. The Baldwin Bill in 1830 placed import duties and high tariffs on foreign imports which severely limited them. The new tariffs worked and the glass industry in the United States was well under way. Along with the taxes, the American invention of a mechanical pressing machine in the late 1820's led to the mass production of glassware. The invention of this hand-press was America's greatest contribution to glassmaking. It was as important as the discovery of lead crystal, glassblowing, and the invention of glass itself. Handpressing revolutionized the industry. Machine pressing was very fast and could be run with less-skilled workers.

Pressed glass was made by forcing melted glass into shape under pressure. Early on a plunger was used to force or press molten glass into iron molds. A mold was made up of two or more parts and imparts lines or seams where the mold comes apart. With each piece the mold was reassembled and filled once again. Some of the marks left by the mold were hand-finished to remove them. Molds might contain patterns within them. Molds were usually hinged and could be full-size piece molds or separate for more complicated objects. Candlesticks, vases, table glass, and especially matched sets of tableware were easily manufactured by hand-pressing.

Pressed glass was certainly not the only technique utilized by America's glassworkers. Huge amounts of fine cut glass, engraving, coloring, casing, flashing, blowing, flute-cutting, and so on appeared from the glass factories in the United States. Pressed glass was slowly overtaking fine expensive hand-cut blown glass in America's Middle Period but would not do so until the early 20th century.

America's Middle Period is important to shot glass history for that is the time the first barware and shot glasses were produced. A series of tumbler-like vessels called French Lacy Glass were developed in the middle

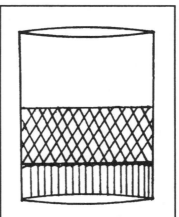

1st Toy Whiskey Taster c. early 1830's #WTT003 3-piece mold-blown. Pontil Mark on bottom. Color: clear. 1¾ " tall, 1 ounce capacity. Produced in New England. (from The Corning Glass Museum of Glass).

period but all had separate bases and were larger than two ounces in terms of capacity. The first whiskey tasters appear to have been hand-blown into a three-piece mold prior to extensive use of the hand press. It was a tiny tumbler only 1¾" in height and contained a volume of 1 ounce. It dates to the 1830's in the New England area.

The need was always there for windows and bottles. Bottles were not used much for water, coffee, tea, milk, juices, etc.; rather their primary function was for rum, whiskey, and wines. In the West particulary, drinking vessels were needed for hotels, taverns, and eventually the saloon. Fancy tableware was more prevalent in the East while the West tended to be more practical; however, it was Deming Jarves who emphasized cheaper mold-blown glass for lesser items like bowls, tumblers, and simpler dishes.

During the Middle Period from the later 1840's through the 1870's, American glass companies sporadically produced milk glass or a derivative coined "fiery opal." It was the American term for opaque white glass that glows when held to the light. It might show a pale blue where the glass is thin. It was rarely popular and did not sell well. Some tableware including a small whiskey tumbler or taster were created in this opal glass.

"Fiery Opal" #WTT010 2" tall 1½ oz. c. 1850's-1860's. Toy Whiskey Taster.

The Brilliant Period of American glass-making was the following era from 1880 to 1915. It was characterized by deep cutting, exceptional brilliance or sparkle, heavy lead, and very elaborate or ornate tableware. This era would be the peak of America's best cut glassware. Cut glass is completed by steel or iron wheels revolving in a trough while a stream of water mixed with abrasives drips down on the wheel from above. This is known as roughing and is responsible for the initial cut. Heavier wheels were used to make deeper and sharper cuts. The glass then goes to a hard stone wheel with water still dripping upon it and here the rough cut is smoothed out. A polisher would then polish it on a wooden wheel. The final stage would involve a buffer to apply the finishing touches upon a buffing wheel. Buffing was replaced with acid polishing in the 1890's but true craftsmen argued that acid polishing was inferior since it wasn't permanent and gradually wore away. Acid polishing also left a dull finish obstructing the brilliance of the piece slightly. [32]

The aim of a cutter was to remove imperfections and impart facets to capture light (the prismatic effect). American inventions improved on cutting. Flat-edged wheels made square-ended cuts and convex-edged wheels made hollowed cuts. Americans added mitre-edged wheels which made curved or V-shaped cuts. Invented around the 1870's, mitre-edged wheels freed cutters from the dependence on straight-line cuts. Wheels were not only made of stone and steel, but also copper and carborundum. Electricity when available was used to power the wheels as well as to provide the craftsmen with better lighting in which to see by. More and more steps were added to the cutting process as finer wheels and less abrasives made cutting more precise.

Copper wheel cutting or engraving was the end of the evolutionary scale for the finest cut glass. Up to 150 wheels of various diameters from the very large down to the size of a pin were utilized. A copper wheel engraver kept the pattern in his mind without outlining it upon the glass. Glass was held to the wheel which instantly cut through or roughened the surface so to speak. It was then rubbed off with oils using one's fingers. The process of cutting and rubbing was repeated and altered back and forth. Before electricity, the lathe was operated by a foot-powered treadle. A power operated lathe made possible large stone wheels including diamond-point cutting wheels. It might take weeks, months, and even years to finish a piece on copper wheels. Cameo engraving was done with copper wheels. Stone wheels were primarily used for depth while copper was best for the fine detailed work. It is rather easy to see that the best and finest cut glass was completed on copper wheels. Copper wheel engravers were compensated more than cutters and were some of the most skilled in the trade of glassmaking.

Along with blowers, copper wheel engravers commanded some of the highest wages. In the 1880's, they might make as much as $6. a day. Common cutters about $3.50 to $4.00 a day. Ordinary workmen maybe $14. to $20. a week based on a 6-day work week. The higher wages were certainly incentive for foreign workers. English and Irish glassmakers only made $7. to $9. a week; Germans and Austrians much less at $3. per week. American wages were typically 3 to 4 times greater than their European counterparts. One disadvantage was that

European glassmakers produced cheaper glass even after a 45% tariff was placed on imported glass in 1888. America's own advantages was the abundance of cheap fuel and advanced mechanization.

To make fine cut glass, a quality hand-blown blank was necessary. Many decorating companies purchased blanks of high quality lead glass from major glass companies for their cutters to work. Traditionally blowers had to be very skilled and years of training and hard work were only two of the prerequisites desired. The ability to work effectively under pressure and in poor conditions were two more. One had to work near a blinding furnace with roasting heat and eye-watering smoke. Hands were scorched and dirtied with coal dust. It was surprising indeed that such exquisite objects could be blown from these stoke-hole like conditions. Under such pressures, the glassblower had the utmost skill, control, patience, steady nerves, and judgement; all mixed with creativity and occasional bouts of spontaneity. In short, glassblowing was an art.

There were many other positions one could partake in the glassmaking trade. A gatherer was one who gathered a blob of molten glass at the end of a blowpipe, pontil, or gathering iron for the blower. Cutters usually apprenticed for three years at a small salary ordinarily after completing 8 grades of formal education. The best might work up to copper wheel engravers. At the turn of the 20th century, women held some jobs though glassmaking was primarily a man's business. Women dusted glass in showrooms and salesrooms, distributed glass to cutters, updated catalogs, made drawings of blanks, waxed the glass before an acid dip, and washed or dried glass before packaging it. A rare enameller or cutter might have been female.

The production of glass itself was not an easy, inexpensive, or safe practice. The basic ingredients of sand, potash, lead for the best crystal, lime or soda for cheaper glass, and a few other additions were mixed in a huge clay pot and heated to extreme temperatures. A batch was termed "metal" by chemists and the best metal batch always contained the highest lead content of a particular company's glass products. Molten glass had to be gathered by a worker to press into a mold or for the blower. Several tools were available to them. A pontil was used to remove expanded glass objects from the blowing iron but it did leave a mark. It was later replaced with a special rod called a gadget. A gadget had a spring clip on the end of it to grip the foot of a glass piece and hold it while another worker trimmed the rim and applied what finishing touches as were needed.

Ovens were important especially those with a glory hole. A glory hole was a small-sized opening in the side of the oven where objects could be reheated and reworked without destroying the original shape. A lehr was an annealing oven that toughened glass through gradual cooling. A muffle kiln was a low temperature oven for firing on enamels.

A variety of other terms and tools were associated with glassmaking that are not heard everyday. Moil was waste glass left on the blowpipe or pontil. Pucellas were like tongs and were used to grasp glass objects. Arrissing was the process of removing sharp edges from glass. Cracking-off was for removing a piece of glass from the pontil by cooling, gently tapping, and then dropping it into a soft sand tray. Fire polishing was the art of reheating objects at the glory hole to remove tool marks. Glass did not always turn out perfectly and sickness resulted. Sick glass was not properly tempered or annealed and showed random cracks, flaking, and possibly disintegration. Seeds were tiny air bubbles in glass indicating an underheated furnace or impurities caused by flecks of dirt.

A variety of other techniques were present in American glass including some original ideas. Cutting was primarily done in geometric patterns. Pictorial, cameo, or sometimes referred to as "intaglio" designs were all cut. Acid etching was the process of covering glass with an acid-resistant layer, scratching on a design, and then permanently etching that design with acids. Acid polishing gave cut glass a polished surface by dipping the entire object into a mild solution of sulfuric or hydrofluoric acid. Hand painting and firing on enamels were two additional techniques. Embossing required a mold into which glass was blown or pressed. Sandblasting was a distinct American process where a design is coated with a protective layer and then the exposed surfaces were sand-blasted with a pressurized gun. Trimming with enamels like silver, gold, and platinum were in use in the 1900's prior to World War I. Staining, gilding, mongram imprinting, rubber stamping, and silk screening were other cheaper methods of decorating glass prior to the first world war. In 1913, a gang-cut wheel was invented in America to make several parallel incisions at once. It made rapid and inexpensive cutting possible such as cross-hatching and blunt-edged flower petals. One of the most important to the early shot glasses was fluting. Fluting or bevels were vertically cut decorations in long narrow

sections by wheels and somtimes molding. Barware was often cut this way.

There were primarily two types of shot glasses produced in the mid-19th century prior to the sample glass era; fancy hand-cut or molded and bar tumblers. A variety of hand-cut or molded patterns were produced that no one company bothered to obtain patents for. Common patterns including shot glasses and other forms of tableware were the Ashburton, Bull's Eye, Cable, Thumbprints, Hamilton, Comet, Grapes, Pineapples, Ribs, Sunbursts, Aztec, Pillars, and so forth.[33]

Whiskey and bar tumblers in a variety of shapes and sizes were far more practical for bars, taverns, and hotels especially in the West. Common flute-cut designs included arched, pillared, pointed, rounded, and even heavy molded flutes. Those companies that typically marketed bar tumblers held no patents and one advertisement for the average bar items in terms of glassware appears little different from any other. Flutes tend to be in even numbers around the bar tumbler (i.e. 6, 8, 10, 12, 14, or more) but an occasional odd number can be found. Furthermore, color experimentation in glass is present on some of the bar tumblers produced in the later 19th century. Blues especially those derived from cobalt and vaseline-colored shot glass-sized tumblers are some of the most common of this time period. Vaseline glass is made with a small amount of uranium that imparts a light greenish-yellow color which gives a greasy appearance like vaseline. Bar tumblers are so ordinary and of limited variation that they are not catalogged here.

A semi-automatic blowing machine was invented in the United States in the 1890's that allowed tumblers to be processed with greater speed and less skill. A rotating table equipped with several molds surmounted by a plunger operated by compressed air. Thin-blown or sham tumblers were the cheapest and sold for as little as 35¢ a dozen. Heavier glasses with flute-cut bottoms or

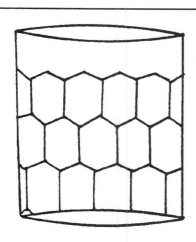

#NCP100 Ashburton pattern. c. 1840's-1870's. Whiskey Tumbler. Color: clear. 2" tall, 2 oz.

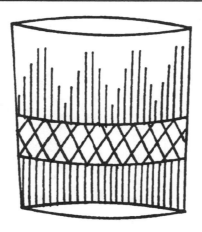

#NCP104 Hamilton pattern. c. 1840's-1870's. Whiskey Tumbler. Color: clear. 2" tall, 2 oz.

#NCP111 Ribbed Ivy pattern. c. 1840's-1870's. Whiskey Tumbler. Color: clear. 2" tall, 2 oz.

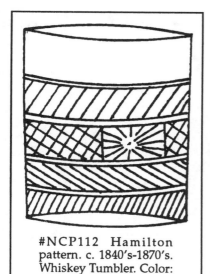

#NCP112 Hamilton pattern. c. 1840's-1870's. Whiskey Tumbler. Color: clear. 2" tall, 2 oz.

sides sold for 50¢ to $1.00 per dozen. Finer crystal with possible engraving might sell for up to $7.00 a dozen.

The end of the chapter lists companies who produced shot glasses or bar tumblers during the first three periods of American glassmaking. The final brilliant period ended when the market for fine glass decreased, cheaper glass formulas were invented, labor strikes, another increase in imports, more machine-made glass, and simply the expense of brilliant finely-cut lead crystal was beyond the means of the ordinary citizen. Cut glass was a luxury and sales fell with the economy. A novelty shot glass in the 1880's or 1890's contains one of the earliest known sayings ever to appear upon a shot glass: "Just a Thimblefull." The words were embossed in a 3-piece mold. The unique feature about this glass that when turned upside down, it is a replica of a giant thimble.

The mid-19th century particularly in the later two periods of glassmaking, factories sprung up everywhere. The Industrial Revolution sparked with increased mechanization and transportation was a boom to the glass industry. Improved river and rail transportation made retail distribution possible on a large scale across the country. 200,000 miles of railroad tracks were laid by 1900 and canals connected all major waterways for shipping glass. The telegraph and telephone improved communication and freight prices cheapened as more competition and

routes were established. Packaging improved with tissue paper and other soft coverings to cushion glass shipped in barrels and crates.

With the Industrial Revolution came the labor revolution as well. In the second half of the 19th century, Pittsburgh arose as the leading area for glass production in the United States but production, profits, and prices declined in the depression of the mid-to-late 1870's. In 1874, the Western Flint and Lime Glass Protective Association was established. In 1875, the union advised its workers to shut down all glass operations in Pittsburgh for two months to reduce stock and to hopefully raise prices of glassware. Management naturally did not look favorably on unions trying to dictate production output. It was one of the first of several bitter disputes that would last until 1891; and then only temporarily.

Union grievances consisted of poor working conditions in the glass factories, the hiring of foriegn workers who accepted lower wages, firing of members for supporting unions, shorter hours and better pay, and child labor. Workers might work up to 14 hours a day 6 days a week. Children were utilized to hand-operate the blower's mold—a foot device invented by Michael Owens for opening and closing. Higher-paid engravers might work 16 hours a day during backlogs and actually supported their elbows on cushions because of the long free-hand work. Another common argument that originated with workers were complaints that too many of them were being replaced by machines! A common complaint today with the increase in robotics.

Companies were having a rough time surviving the depression of the 1870's and were incensed by the numerous work slow-downs, lockouts, and outright strikes. In 1877, a big strike where 10 or 19 Pittsburgh glass factories closed as well as some shutdowns in the East. In 1878, the Glass Pressers Union struck and shut down 11 of 13 pressed glass companies in Pittsburgh. Bakewell and Pears were one of the two

Low cut arched or molded flutes.

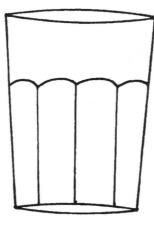

High cut arched or molded flutes.

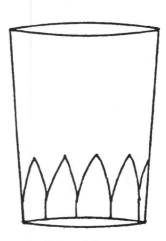

Pointed flutes.

BAR TUMBLER EXAMPLES

Wide Flutes

Narrow Flutes

#WTT005 Vaseline. c. 1840-1860 Whiskey taster. 1¾ " tall, 1 oz. New England made. (from the Corning Museum of Glass). (also clear in color).

that did not close because they did their best to deal with their workers and had previously negotiated a special agreement.

Striking was even more frequent in the 1880's. The strikes were badly managed and too many separate unions representing many interests were striking at different times. Foreign competition and cheaper glass products continued to invade and hurt the American glass industry. Pittsburgh could still claim half the American market for glass. The disputes were temporarily resolved when 18 large glass manufacturers in Pittsburgh and the surrounding area merged to form the United States Glass Company in 1891. The company did its best to control the workers' output which only led to more strikes and work stoppages. The disputes continued on into the early 1900's and strikebreakers were hired at times and

violence broke out between them and the strikers. The company did manage to survive and produce some quantity of glassware.[34]

Pittsburgh glassmakers tended to make more practical glass like bar tumblers, bottles, and windows. By 1880, ¼ of all glass made in the United States was for liquor flasks, patent medicine bottles, and home preserving jars. John Landis Mason in 1858 made the first "Mason Jars" for home canning. All were produced by blowing molten glass into molds and then hand-finishing the necks and lips. Pittsburgh glass companies did make some fine cut crystal and experimental glass of the new art style.

In the midst of the Brilliant Period, this new "Art Nouveau" or "Art Glass" was created in the 1880's and lasted well into the 1890's. Artists, designers, and other creative people who had not previously worked in glass turned their talents into some of the most unique and spectacular glass objects. Some have a legitimate argument that the Brilliant Period and the introduction of art glass began with the Philadelphia Centennial Exhibition in 1876. Glassmakers displayed some of their finest pieces to date at this exhibition including cut crystal chandeliers and a 17' glass fountain. The fountain was ornamental with cut crystal prisms lit by 120 gas jets and surmounted by a glass figure of liberty.

These expositions were not exclusive to America for the first designer-artists in this new art glass were French. In 1878, Rousseau and Galle displayed their fancy glass at the Paris Exposition Universelle. From the time Admiral Perry opened trade with Japan to the West, Rousseau was deeply influenced by oriental art. This renewed interest in Orientalism in the form of rugs, porcelain, prints, and so on was popular in America throughout the art nouveau period. Rousseau and Galle did not limit themselves to oriental influence but rather combined it with traditional German and Italian

#WTT004 Light cobalt blue. c. 1840-1860 Whiskey taster. 1¾ tall, 1 oz. New England made. (from the Corning Museum of Glass).

#NCP210 Molded 3-piece clear design. 2⅛" tall 1½ oz. c. 1880's-1890's.

33

Renaissance shapes. Galle more than Rousseau was the inspiration for this period. The new art form not only appeared in glass but in architecture, paintings, posters, book illustrations, furniture, wallpaper, fabric, embroidery, jewelry, and numerous others. Unlike many of the cut glass manufacturers where identification is at times impossible, Galle signed his works which sparked others to continue this tradition.

Art glass was richly ornamental with little in the way of rules. It was full of originality displaying crackle effects, metal particles, asymmetrical designs, long sinuous lines, weaving tendrils, flowing rhythms, and wild color effects. Colors and opaqueness were experimented with as well and impractical items made of glass had no constructive use except for display as a work of art. Whimsies abounded and such things as insects, animals, fruits, paperweights, and other recurring themes in nature were all recreated in glass. Rather than pretty flowers; thistle pines, pine cones, and simple plants like the grains of wheat were present upon this new glass. Two of the most famous American art glass sculpters were Louis Comfort Tiffany and Frederick Carder.

Tiffany was an American painter who visited Paris in 1889 and observed Galle's works in person at the Exposition Universelle. He was also the son of the jewelry magnate who had founded Tiffany & Co., the world famous jewelry store. Louis Comfort Tiffany began his work in glass by producing stained glass windows without using stains or paints. The color, detail, and illusion were created within the glass itself by plating one layer of glass over another. He broadened his work to include lamps and was one of the first to experiment with "iridescent" glass and named it "favrile" or "Tiffany Favrile." He derived it from the English word fabrile which means: "Belonging to a craftsmen or his craft."

Iridescence was produced by firing on combinations of metallic salts for a wide variety of coloring effects. Luminous colors and metallic luster produced a silky smooth or delicate patina upon Tiffany's glass. According to Tiffany, his main inspiration was the decayed objects from Roman glass discovered in archaeological excavations.

With great success at presenting his works at the World's Exposition in Chicago in 1893, orders poured in and he further expanded his work to other art forms. Tableware, vases, flowers, unique shapes, and a few shot glasses were blown from Tiffany's skilled hands. Unwittingly, his designs were never decorated or painted; they were made by combinations of different colored glass during the blowing operation. His goods were displayed in Europe such as the 1900 Paris Exposition which inspired rising young European artists. Shot glasses made by Tiffany are the most valuable.[35]

Frederick Carder was an apprentice of the famous English glass artisan John Northwood. He emigrated from Stourbridge, England and founded the Steuben Glass Works in Corning, New York. Carder created several varieties of lustrous lead art glass such as aurene, an ornamental iridescent form. He sold Steuben to the Corning Glass Works in 1918 but continued to produce some of the finest crystal forms in the world through 1936 for Corning. Carder's glass was also exhibited at numerous national and international expositions, galleries, and museums.

#IAG020 Tiffany Favrile-gold luster with silver highlights. 2 oz., 2½" tall, 6-sided. Initialed on bottom "LCT." 1890's-early 1900's.

The problem with art glass was the same as that of the fine, brilliantly cut crystal. It was too expensive for the ordinary average citizen. A pressed substitute did arrive for expensive Tiffany, Steuben, and the English Victorian glass; and that was carnival glass. Most all of the carnival glass made in the United States was in the years 1905-1925. At its beginning, carnival glass borrowed its name from Tiffany Favrile, Aurene, and added others like New Venetian Art, Parisian Art, Aurora, and Art Iridescent.

The techniques of making this glass were borrowed from Tiffany and other art glass artisans. Color is natural in glass based on various oxides that are present in the sand. Ordinarily iron and common metals produce light green to brown glass. By adding metallic oxides as well as variations in heat, length of time in the furnace, and minor formula changes can all affect color. Carnival glass has a base color which is the color of the glass before any iridescence is fired upon it. The base color is usually present on the bottom underside of an iridized glass object.

There were two major groups of colored carnival glass. The bright carnival colors consisted of red, blue, green, purple, amethyst, amber, and marigold. The pastel colors were a bit rarer and were made up of clear, white, clambroth, lavender, aqua, and smoky. Red was the rarest and one of the most expensive since gold was required to produce it. Marigold was the most popular carnival color and is the one most envisioned when one thinks of carnival glass. Marigold was an orange-colored flashing applied to clear glass and then sprayed iridescence. Pastels usually had clear bases with a very light coating of iridescence. Lavender naturally had a purple tint; aqua a bluish-green tint; smoky a light gray; and clambroth a pale yellow. Other opaque or opalescent forms were present too.

The glass itself was first manufactured into vases

and bowls. As its popularity increased, water sets, table sets, punch bowls, berry and ice cream sets, dresser sets with matching cologne bottles, other bottles (wines, whiskey, and soda), powder jars, trays, hatpin holders, lamps, paperweights, mugs, beads, advertising items, souvenir pieces; and yes even shot glasses all followed. Unlike the fancy art glass, it was sold in china shops, general stores, mail order, and used as containers for food products like pickles and mustard. It was the first to be used as prizes or promotional items for tea companies, candy companies, and furniture stores as would be Depression Glass later. It was exported to England and other parts of Europe but the fad would be a short-lived one.

By the late teens, the demand lessened; and by the early 1920's, the fad was over. The new modern decor of the 1920's had no place for this odd glassware. Manufacturers sold their remaining stock to fairs, bazaars, and carnivals (hence the name "Carnival Glass") at below wholesale prices to rid themselves of it. Collectors packed it away until the 1950's. There were four major companies that produced the majority of carnival glass: The Fenton Art Glass Company of Williamstown, West Virginia; The Imperial Glass Company of Bellaire, Ohio; The Millersburg Glass Company of Millersburg, Ohio; and The Northwood Glass Company of Wheeling, West Virginia.[36]

#IAG030 Marigold Carnival Glass. 2⅛" tall, 1½ oz. c. 1910-1920.

The Fenton Art Glass Company was founded in 1905 by two brothers, John and Frank L. Fenton in Martin's Ferry, Ohio. Frank had previously been a designer for others and created new designs for Fenton. In 1907, they moved to Williamstown, West Virginia where carnival glass became the company's best-seller. Jacob Rosenthal joined them and was instrumental in developing many of Fenton's secret formulas and experimental glass. As with common iridized glass, they sprayed metallic compounds on various colors of glass and then refired the pieces. Fenton was most famous for cobalt blue carnival glass. From 1910-1920 they made little else but discontinued all carnival production on 1921 as sales plunged.

In Bellaire, Ohio, in 1902, Edward Muhleman founded The Imperial Glass Company. Imperial began with pressed jars, lampshades, and tumblers. They made great quantities of carnival glass from 1910-1924 mostly in two patterns; Lustre Rose and Imperial's Grape. They named their most famous color "Helios" for the Greek Sun God. Helios' pieces consisted of a green base color coated with gold or silver iridescence. Imperial survived the downfall of carnival and the Depression and are still in operation today. To the confusion of modern collectors, Imperial began reproducing carnival in the early 1960's using some of the original molds.

John Fenton left The Fenton Art Glass Co. in 1910. With the aid of yet another Fenton brother Robert; they founded The Millersburg Glass Company in Millersburg, Ohio. They named their carnival glass "Rhodium Ware" and it is quite rare. A few limited shapes and colors were produced mostly in the form of punch bowl sets and table sets. Most identification was completed from an archaeological dig from the site of the old Millersburg factory. Broken glass shards, chips, and pieces were uncovered and reconstructed. The company

#IAG031 Blue Carnival Glass. Fenton Art Glass Co. 2" tall, 1 oz. 6 flutes. c. 1910-1921.

suffered the same fate as carnival glass. When it died out so did they. Millersburg went bankrupt and the molds were sold for scrap metal.

Harry Northwood was the son of the famous English glass artisan John Northwood. Harry came over to America in 1884 and joined several glass firms as designer and manager. In 1902, he went into business for himself as The Northwood Glass Company of Wheeling, West Virginia. The art influence was present in his early tableware and colored glass. Northwood decorated glass with gold and opalescent edges. From 1910-1918, they made carnival glass in some quantity for it sold well without much advertising. The famous Northwood trademark of an 'N' with a line under it enclosed within a circle appeared on much of their glassware. The company did not fair well as the demand for carnival glass weakened. The Northwood Glass Company disbanded in 1923.

A few other companies that produced limited carnival glass were The Cambridge Glass Co., The Jenkins Glass Co., The Heisey Glass Co., The Indiana Glass Co., and The Federal Glass Co. The remaining part of this chapter also contains brief histories of glass companies in the 19th and early 20th century who produced barware or shot glasses in some form or capacity.

New England Glass Company (Libbey)

It seems appropriate to begin with the New England Glass Company. Though there were trials and near bankruptcies along the way, New England Glass who's name changed to Libbey in 1892 was simply the most successful glass company in both the 19th and 20th centuries. From the beginning in 1818, they made high quality blown and pressed glassware. They utilized all known techniques available including cutting, engraving, gilding, etching, embossing, etc. Much of the company's early success belongs to Thomas Leighton, an English immigrant. Though English law forbade emigration of its skilled glassworkers, Leighton managed to escape in 1826. He was a skilled blower and seved as superintendant for 20 years. Furthermore he had six sons who became glassworkers; two of which would inherit his position. He also convinced two glassblowing cousins to emigrate from Scotland in 1829.

New England Glass managed to import a steady supply of highly-skilled glass masters from Europe. Two early notables were Francois Pierre, a fancy glassblower; and Joseph Burdakin, an expert cutter. The company's most skilled engraver was Louis F. Vaupel who was a master with copper wheels by the time he emigrated to the United States from Germany at age 26. Vaupel came from a family of excellent German engravers and started work at New England in 1851. For 34 years he was head of designing and engraving.

Trouble began in the mid-19th century when they had difficulty competing with the many factories in and around Pittsburgh. Though they were the first to use coal, it had to be imported from long distances. The introduction of a cheaper lime glass ironically by one of Thomas Leighton's sons at another company undercut the more expensive lead crystal market. Management refused to switch to lime and this, added with other expenses and problems forced the company to move to the Midwest. A series of strikes were launched over wages and grievances by Local 64 of the American Flint Glass Workers' Union in 1886.

The 1870's were a most trying time for New England. In 1872, William L. Libbey became the company's last agent and a year later they barely survived the country-wide depression. In 1878, the holdings were leased to Libbey and his son Edward entered the business as clerk. In 1880, Edward became a partner and the name W. L. Libbey and Son was attached to New England Glass Works. Edward's father died in 1883 and to avoid bankruptcy, Edward sold several patent lines to Tiffany's in New York including Amberina, Wild Rose or Peachblow, Pomona, Agata, and Maize.

With costly fuel, worker discontent, financial troubles, and incentives from Toledo, Libbey loaded 50 train cars full of machinery and headed west for Ohio in 1888. Toledo offered Edward Libbey a 4-acre factory site and 50 lots for workers to build homes. Large reserves of the less dirty natural gas for fuel was present in abundant supplies. 1888 was also an important year for a major acquisition; not in the form of additional land or factories, but of Michael J. Owens.

Owens was hired as a glassblower from Wheeling, West Virginia and had been working in glass factories since age 10. His Irish immigrant parents were poor and his education limited but he was an excellent speaker and union leader. He had the experience of the glass worker and was sympathetic to them. In a bold move Libbey placed him in charge of production at age 29 at the new Toledo plant. From 1888-1889 the plant lost money but from 1890-1892, a major turnaround came about. Edison General Electric offered a huge contract to Libbey to produce light bulbs after a major strike shut down the Corning Glass Works in New York. Some of the strikers in Corning were hired by Libbey and a separate plant in Findlay, Ohio was leased to meet production. The name of the company also changed officially in 1892 to: "Libbey Glass Company."

In 1893, Edward Libbey gambled again. At a huge financial risk, he obtained exclusive rights to build and operate a complete glass factory at the massive World's Colombian Exposition in Chicago. He did it at his own expense but it propelled Libbey into the largest cut glass manufacturer in the world. The glasshouse at the fair was managed by Owens and featured handblowing and cutting. A 10¢ admission was charged, but it was so successful that the price was increased to 25¢ and the crowds still increased. Furthermore, patrons could apply the admission price to purchase glass souvenirs. Over 2 million people visited Libbey's outstanding display and the name "Libbey" from that point on became well-known and famous. They were presented with a gold medal at the exposition for excellence in cut glass and led the way into America's Brilliant Period.

With Libbey's backing, Owens formed the Toledo Glass Company to produce machine-made lamp chimneys and tumblers. Edward Libbey remained the largest stockholder in Libbey Glass but turned control over to his associates in order to spend more time with Toledo Glass and the Owens Bottle Company. In 1903, Michael Owens invented an automatic blowing machine that revolutionized the industry. It was the first machine to produce flat glass automatically and it led to the formation of Owens-Illinois Inc.

#PPC005 standard. Libbey Colonna pattern (No. 304). 1905. (originally sold for $8.00 per ½ dozen (see ad below).

#PPC006 2½" tall, 2 oz. whiskey tumbler c. 1920 clear w. etched pattern representing grain leaves piece of a beverage set Libbey Glass Co.

Further mechanization led to automatic blown bottles, jars, tumblers, and shot glasses; all at a much lower cost. This technology spawned yet another company: "Libbey-Owens Sheet Glass" which is presently Libbey-Owens-Ford Inc. Libbey Glass would eventually fall under the parent company of Owens-Illinois Co.

Meanwhile in 1901, Edward Libbey founded The Toledo Museum of Art to house the best collections of Libbey glassware. Second only to Corning, Toledo houses one of the largest collections of American-made glass. Libbey entered another exhibition, namely the St. Louis World's Fair in 1904. They created a large collection of cut and engraved glass specifically for the fair including a 25" cut glass punch bowl. The punch bowl was pictured on the cover of the April 30, 1904 edition of Scientific American and was dubbed: "The Largest Piece of Cut Glass in the World." Libbey went home with another gold medal for excellence and with reputation intact. Prior to World War I, Libbey also carried a line of tough heat-resistant chemical glass for use in laboratories like beakers, flasks, test-tubes, etc.

Libbey along with the rest of the glass industry suffered during the years just before World War I, the decline of cut glass, and the end of the Brilliant Period. Cheaper products and further automation were substituted for cut glass. The public's taste in home decorative accessories changed. Hand-cutting was nearly eliminated as cheaper imitations were pressed from machines. Furthermore, certain required chemicals particularly metals were unavailable or hard to come by because of the war. Libbey continued to produce expensive cut glass but it did not sell well. In 1915, Libbey introduced a cheap, thin glass that required less cutting time and referred to it as "Lightware." It did not go over well and sales were very disappointing. In 1917, Libbey revived Amberina, a popular pattern in the 1880's, but it too flopped. They did survive this new crisis and the Depression as well.[37]

The Boston and Sandwich Glass Company

As mentioned earlier, Deming Jarves left New England Glass and went on to establish Boston and Sandwich in 1826. The firm produced large quantities of mold blown and pressed glassware. To gain recognition and increased reputation like so many other glassmakers, they displayed their goods and won several awards at fairs and exhibitions.

In relation to shot glass history, Boston and Sandwich made one of the first identifiable toy whiskey tasters around 1840. They were small enough to be considered shot glasses and fit the definition in terms of dimensions and capacity. Other tiny capacity tumblers had their life's beginnings as toys such as "Pillar," "Barney," and "Tasters." As more and more orders poured forth for them, their production increased and the word 'toy' was soon dropped.

Boston and Sandwich did not patent their designs nor did many others in the later 19th century. Boston and Sandwich produced table sets including shot

Tumbler Ad reproduced directly from a 1905 Libbey Sales Catalog.

No. 643. Mixing Tumbler. $5.00 each.

No. 575. High Ball Tumbler. $15.00 the half dozen.

No. 502. Table Tumbler, $12.00 the half dozen.

No. 290. Champagne Tumbler, $10.00 the half dozen.

No. 251. Whiskey Tumbler. $9.00 the half dozen.

No. 304. Whiskey Tumbler. $8.00 the half dozen.

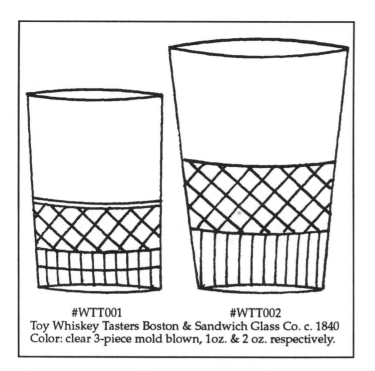

#WTT001   #WTT002
Toy Whiskey Tasters Boston & Sandwich Glass Co. c. 1840
Color: clear 3-piece mold blown, 1oz. & 2 oz. respectively.

glasses in many of the unpatented NCP (Nineteenth Century Patterns) designs. Major strikes that encouraged Libbey to leave the East fell hard upon Boston and Sandwich. Along with the disruption of labor, they also suffered from the fuel problem, cheap lime glass, and intense competition from Pittsburgh, eastern Ohio, and West Virginia. They were unable to remain afloat and closed in 1888.

Bakewell, Pears, and Company

Through several name changes beginning as early as 1807; Bakewell, Pears, and Company emerged as a successful glass operation, the oldest in Pittsburgh to survive more than a few years. Before 1840, their specialty was glass furniture knobs and handles. Though the Pittsburgh area was an ideal place for industrial glass production, a unique set of problems responsible for shutting down over 50 glasshouses in and around the surrounding area by 1850. A depression after the War of 1812, foreign and eastern competition as transportation improved, the Panic of 1837, and an over abundance of glass factories all within the same geographical region pressured many over the brink of failure.

Bakewell & Pears shut down in 1840 for these reasons but resurfaced in 1845 with a new factory. The wholesale and retail market particularly America's West always belonged to Pittsburgh early on. Bakewell & Pears expanded into tableware and barware especially for taverns, hotels, general stores, and saloons. From the late 1840's through the 1870's, they shipped significant quantities of heavy fluted barware and the like to the big western markets. They occasionally made a few novelty items like a dish shaped in the form of the liberty bell for America's centennial and handled beer mugs shaped as barrels. They also had the distinction of being the first American glassworks to supply the Whitehouse with a tableset for President Monroe.

They did manage to patent some of their designs except for the common NCP glasses and simpler barware. They applied and received a patent for a mechanical hand-press and claimed to be the first glass factory to press glassware entirely by machine. Companies emphasizing finer hand-cut crystal would probably not dare make that claim. Sales fell off in the 1870's primarily due to the countrywide depression and Bakewell, Pears, and Company shut down in 1882.[38]

McKee Brothers

The brothers Samuel and James McKee first made glass in 1834. They began in Pittsburgh creating windows, bottles, and flasks. Business flourished and in the 1840's, operations were expanded to include a wide variety of table and barware. Surprisingly they did not

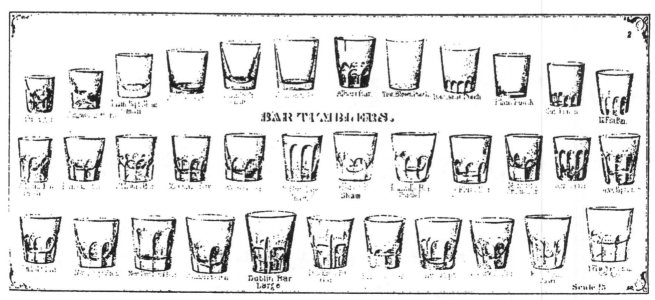

One of Bakewell, Pears, & Company's first Bar Tumbler advertisements reproduced directly from an old trade catalog. c. 1850's.

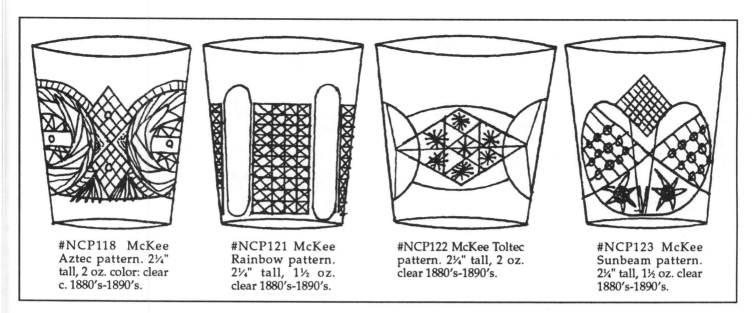

#NCP118 McKee
Aztec pattern. 2¼"
tall, 2 oz. color: clear
c. 1880's-1890's.

#NCP121 McKee
Rainbow pattern.
2¼" tall, 1½ oz.
clear 1880's-1890's.

#NCP122 McKee Toltec
pattern. 2¼" tall, 2 oz.
clear 1880's-1890's.

#NCP123 McKee
Sunbeam pattern.
2¼" tall, 1½ oz. clear
1880's-1890's.

establish their own factory until 1850 when they teamed up with James Bryce. The union was short-lived and 4 years later, they went their separate ways.

The McKee's continued to operate under McKee and Brother until 1864 when yet another brother entered the business. Stewart McKee joined and the name officially changed to: "McKee Brothers." They filed a few limited patents but failed to do so for the popular "Aztec" pattern in which shot glasses were produced. This particular pattern was copied extensively by others and was renamed "Whirling Star" or "New Mexico." McKee probably had more cut pattern shot glass-size vessels than any other 19th century glassmaker counting patented, unpatented, and tiny bar or whiskey tumblers.

The McKee's were a fairly big success in glass compared to the average Pittsburgh glass companies. In 1899, they merged with the National Glass Company for four years and then switched to the Thatcher Glass Manufacturing Company. Thatcher operates today in Jeannette, Pennsylvania.[39]

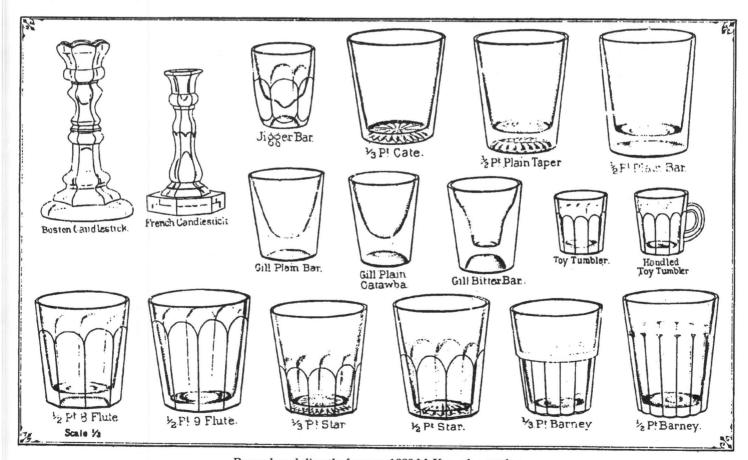

Reproduced directly from an 1880 McKee sales catalog.

Bryce Brothers

As noted, James Bryce first entered the glass business with Samuel and James McKee in 1850. For four years the company name was Bryce, McKee, and Co. With the McKees; bottles, lamps, tableware, and barware were all manufactured. After the separation in 1854; Bryce, Richards, and Company were formed. In 1865 it was named Bryce, Walker, and Company. 1886 was when it officially became Bryce Brothers. Under the leadership of James Bryce in Mt. Pleasant, Pennsylvania, they primarily specialized in handblown stemware and some barware for hotels, homes, and restaurants. Bryce Brothers became part of the United States Glass Company in the great merger of 1891. Much of their glass through the Depression was still marketed under the "Bryce Brothers" name. Eventually their division was purchased by Lenox in 1965.

Hobbs, Brocunier & Company

Hobbs, Brocunier & Company was founded in Wheeling, West Virginia in 1820. Through the years they produced some bottles, tableware, and tumblers. They produced a variety of the unpatented patterns but did in fact establish their own. They experimented with color later on and even delved into porcelain or porcelain-like glassware. A light peach-colored coating was applied to some of their glass during the 1870's and 1880's including a shot glass. They referred to it as "Morgan Porcelain Replica." Porcelain replicas would not surface again for about 100 years for shot glasses. They were fairly successful and were commissioned by various political factions to make campaign tumblers.

The biggest contribution that Hobbs, Brocunier & Co. made to glass-making had rippling and even devastating effects on the entire American glass industry. That was the introduction of a less expensive lime glass formula as a substitute for lead. William L. Leighton Sr. (son of Thomas Leighton from New England Glass Co.) joined Hobbs & Brocunier in 1864

#NCP200 Hobbs, Brocunier & Co. c. 1870's to 1880's 1½ oz. whiskey tumbler or standard size shot glass color: clear "101" pattern.

TUMBLERS.

Reproduced directly from an old trade catalog of Hobbs, Brocunier & Company. c. 1870's-1890's.

and was the inventor of the new lime formula. Previously, very cheap glass could be made with silica, lime, and potash or soda but it was far removed from lead in terms of quality. Leighton substituted bicarbonate of soda for soda ash and the new resulting lime-soda glass was nearly as clear as lead. Most companies switched to remain competitive. Few survived such as Boston and Sandwich who did not make the change. Hobbs, Brocunier and Co. operated quite successfully with the new formula and eventually became part of the United States Glass Company in 1891.[40]

Rochester Tumbler Company

Established in 1872 in Rochester, Pennsylvania; the Rochester Tumbler Co. led by its first president Henry C. Fry and 13 others; specialized in the mass production of tumblers and related tableware including barware. Within 5 years they marketed over 300 different patterns. Most were flutes, pillars, and simple variations of them. Others included many of the unpatented ribs, thumbprints, and so on. They made them in all sizes from shot glasses to punch bowls.

One advertisement boasted capacity of 200,000

Rochester Tumbler advertisement from the Crockery and Glass Journal, September 9, 1875.

tumblers in a week. They exported tumblers primarily to the western United States but occasional shipments were ordered from Japan, Canada, South America, the West Indies, and Europe. Rochester was yet another company that joined United States Glass in 1891.[41]

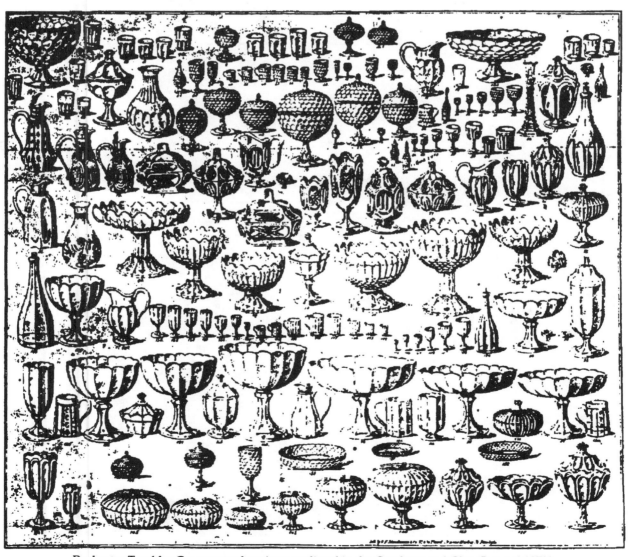

Rochester Tumbler Company advertisement listed in the Crockery and Glass Journal 1870's.

King, Son, & Company

The Cascade Glass Works was established in 1859 in the Pittsburgh region. Early on it barely survived and was reorganized in 1864 as Johnson, King, and Company. One final change in 1869 led to King, Son, & Company. For a while they prospered and became a major manufacturer of pressed, blown, and cut glassware in Pittsburgh. Numerous advertisements for barware were marketed under Cascade. Later, identical advertisements were changed to King, Son, & Company. They did patent a few designs but borrowed much from older companies like Bakewell & Pears. They also experimented somewhat beginning in the 1870's but the majority of their work was typically in clear lead crystal or lime glass. King, Son, & Co. were another in the ever-growing list that were swept into the United States Glass Company in 1891.[42]

Duncan Miller Glass Company

George Duncan first owned a glass factory in the 1860's which later became George Duncan & Sons in 1874 in Washington, Pennsylvania. His son-in-law happened to be Augustus Heisey. George Duncan Sr. died a short time after in 1876 but his sons James

Duncan and George Duncan Jr. continued the business. In 1886 it became Duncan & Heisey as Heisey managed the plant even after it became part of the United States Glass Company in the infamous merger of 1891.

Up to the merger, the company produced for the most part lime glass tableware and some bar tumblers in the traditional unpatented patterns including pillars, flutes, and the like.

#NCP119 King, Son, & Co. Pillar pattern color: cobalt blue. Molded flutes. c. 1870's. (also clear in color).

George Jr. and James sold out to U.S. Glass but joined up with Earnest Miller. The new Duncan Miller Glass Company was established soon after and expanded into beer and ale glasses, pitchers, jugs, cruets, and some novelty items including frosted glass of the Depression

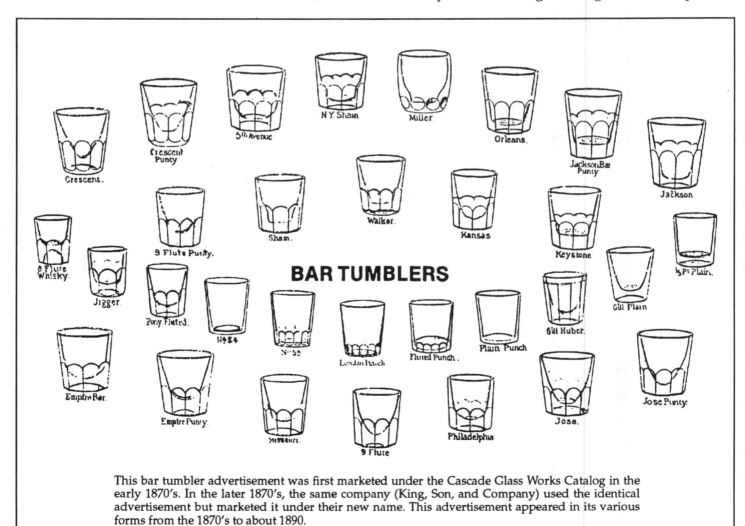

BAR TUMBLERS

This bar tumbler advertisement was first marketed under the Cascade Glass Works Catalog in the early 1870's. In the later 1870's, the same company (King, Son, and Company) used the identical advertisement but marketed it under their new name. This advertisement appeared in its various forms from the 1870's to about 1890.

Reproduced directly from an old trade catalog of King, Son, & Company c. 1870's-1880's.

era. They would patent some of their designs right before and during the Great Depression. (see Chapter VIII for Depression examples).[43]

A. H. Heisey Company

Augustus Henry Heisey began his life in Hanover, Germany; born 1842. As a young boy his family migrated to Merittown, Pennsylvania. After graduating from Merittown Academy, young Augustus began his first job in the printing business but changed his career to enter the glass business. His first job was with King, Son, & Co. It did not last long for in 1861, he enlisted in the Civil War as a private. In four short years to the end of the war, Augustus Heisey was continuously promoted to the rank of major. When the war was over, he rejoined King & Son for a short time but accepted a new position with Ripley Glass Company; also located in Pittsburgh.

In 1870, Heisey married Susan Duncan, the daughter of George Duncan Sr. Soon after he joined his brother-in-law James E. Duncan in the reorganization of George

Duncan & Sons. The corporation operated successfully and Heisey stayed on as manager of the factory even after it became a branch of the U.S. Glass Co. Augustus Heisey was not an artisan or glassmaker, but rather an administrator, supervisor, and an outstanding travelling salesman promoting glassware.

In the early 1890's, he gave up his managerial position with U.S. Glass and went to work for a few mining companies in New Mexico and Arizona. His love for glass brought him back to eastern Ohio in 1895. He bought a farm in Newark, Ohio and converted it to a glass factory with his own name: "A. H. Heisey & Company." In the beginning, his factory pressed fine tableware exclusively; but later they expanded into blowing, etching, and cutting. Heisey's factory produced tableware including barware and little else. A few odd pieces from smaller contracts such as glass baskets, auto headlamps, and a few other miscellaneous items were also made.

To the great appreciation of collectors and historians, Heisey patented all of his glass which makes

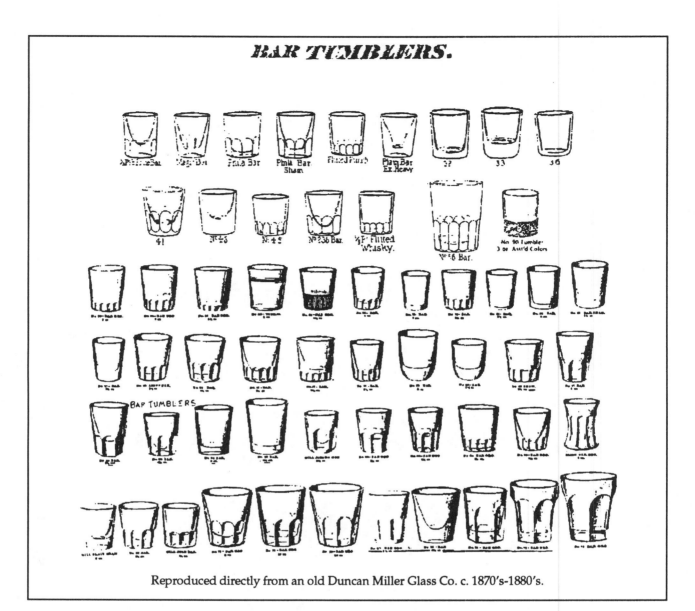

BAR TUMBLERS.

Reproduced directly from an old Duncan Miller Glass Co. c. 1870's-1880's.

identification of the majority of his products possible. Heisey's two sons joined the glass operations in the early 1900's and carried the company through the Depression. The earliest known national Heisey advertisement appeared in Harper's Bazaar in 1912. The famous Heisey trademark on much of their larger ornate

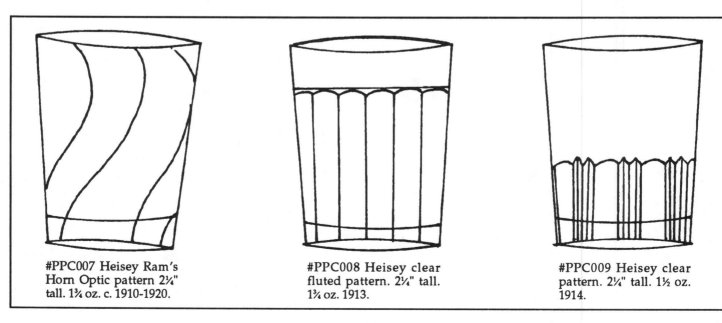

#PPC007 Heisey Ram's Horn Optic pattern 2¼" tall. 1¾ oz. c. 1910-1920.

#PPC008 Heisey clear fluted pattern. 2¼" tall. 1¾ oz. 1913.

#PPC009 Heisey clear pattern. 2¼" tall. 1½ oz. 1914.

pieces is the "Diamond H." It is simply the capital letter "H" within a 4-sided diamond (see Heisey ads for example). The Diamond H was pressed on some pieces or simply was a sticker. A more elaborate "Plunger Cut Glass" trademark surrounding the Diamond H in 3 concentric semicircles was another mark of Heisey.[44]

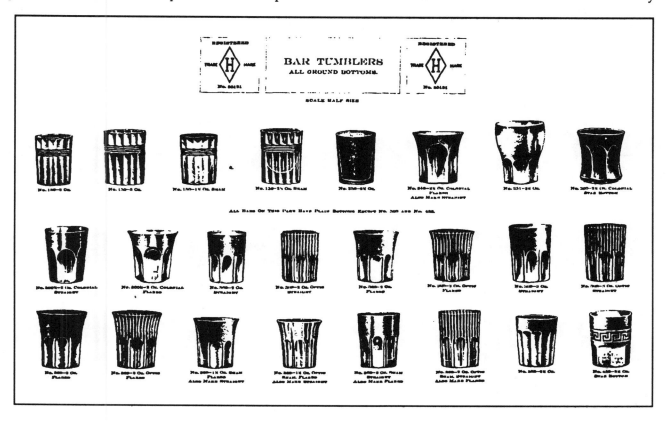

Heisey Bar Tumbler Advertisements from the late 1890's to the early 1900's. Reproduced directly from old trade catalogs of A.H. Heisey Company.

C. Dorflinger & Sons

Christian Dorflinger was born in France in 1828 and learned the glass trade from his uncle at St. Louis Glass Works of St. Louis, France. At a young age he learned the art of etching, cutting, enameling, and blowing. His family moved to America in 1846 and Christian promptly obtained a job as a skilled glassblower. Soon after with some financial backing, he established the Long Island Flint Glass Works in Brooklyn, New York; 1852. After a few years of successful operation, Dorflinger was able to buy out his financers.

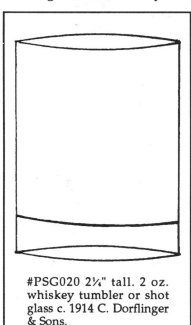

#PSG020 2¼" tall. 2 oz. whiskey tumbler or shot glass c. 1914 C. Dorflinger & Sons.

In 1858, he built a new factory named the Greenpoint Glassworks. Trouble arose not with the business but with his health. Illness forced him to retire in the 1860's. The Long Island plant was sold and control of Greenpoint was handed over to two trusted employees. Dorflinger soon became bored and though he could not take a full-time role in the glass operation itself, he built another factory further west in White Mills, Pennsylvania, in 1865.

He hired many of the skilled European immigrants who had been employed at the Brooklyn plant. A cutting shop was added in 1867.

Christian Dorflinger passed his excellent skills in glass to his three sons: William, Louis, and Charles. The name of the company became C. Dorflinger & Sons officially in 1881. Two grandsons (Dwight and Charles) also entered the business in 1900 to carry on the family tradition. As a manufacturing firm, Dorflinger & Sons produced crystal and colored blanks to other decorators in great quantity. They made their own fine-cut crystal in America's Brilliant Period that rivalled that made anywhere. Dorflinger was also one to experiment with coloring occasionally.

The teen years in the early 20th century was a most difficult time for C. Dorflinger & Sons. They did not sacrifice their fine quality for cheaper lime glass. The elder Christian Dorflinger died in 1915 and though on a limited basis because of his health, he had always been an integral force and great source of information, experience, and knowledge. During World War I, potash necessary for fine crystal was nearly impossible to buy. The coming of Prohibition was tough on stemware and barware sales. In 1921, the factory closed.[45]

Pairpoint Glass Works

In 1837, Deming Jarves built another factory in south Boston under Jarves and Comerais. It was named the Mt. Washington Glass Works. William L. Libbey worked there as bookkeeper in 1851. It closed in 1861 but the interest was purchased by W. L. Libbey and Timothy Howe. Howe died soon after in 1866 and Libbey was able to buy out his interest. Meanwhile the New Bedford Glass Company formed in 1866 only operated until 1870. Libbey bought it as well and moved all operations to Massachusetts and carried on the name of Mt. Washington Glass Works. Libbey left in 1872 for New England Glass and turned the management of Mt. Washington over to Captain Henry Libbey.

Mt. Washington operated with some success but did not survive the depression of 1873 and the factory closed a year later. The company was able to reorganize in 1876 and expanded well under the new ownership of Frederick Shirley, Robert G. Toby, Robert King, and A. H. Seabury. Their specialty consisted of opal globes, shades for electric or gas lamps and lights, and other handblown and cut glass. They were the only factory in America capable of manufacturing a complete cut-crystal chandelier. Hundreds of patient hours of cutting were required for each chandelier and at the Philadelphia Centennial in 1876, Mt. Washington won an award for excellence for their fine glassware. Mt. Washington also produced brilliant-cut lamps, lampshades, vases, and art glass. Molds were used to some extent but they were lined with beeswax and all pieces were finished by hand to remove all mold marks. It is nearly impossible to distinguish between some hand-cut and mold-pressed glass by Mt. Washington.

Always a company dedicated to fine glassmaking and experimentation, Mt. Washington invented one of their most noteworthy forms in 1881. Burmese glass had a coral color around the edges that was made with gold and uranium oxide. Queen Victoria of England ordered a tea set and four vases of Burmese glass from Mt. Washington. Burmese glass consisted of a blending of color tones from flesh pink at the top of an object to a yellow at the bottom. It was finished with satin or gloss. Only one other factory in the world was able to produce Burmese glass and that was Thomas Webb & Sons in England. Webb was licensed under Mt. Washington's patent. Burmese was discontinued in 1900 because of the expense involved.

Mt. Washington Glass Works also invented other forms of glass working with gold. Peachblow was a combination of cobalt and gold that turned glass into a dusty-rose color. Rose-amber was a combination of gold and amber. Other art forms included iridescence with gold and silver, satin glass, and cameo engraving. In fact, Mt. Washington was one of the first companies in America to perform cameo or relief-cutting upon their glassware.

Production expanded to toothpickholders, paperweights, fancy barware, typcial unpatented pattern-ware, table-ware, and so on. They were always best known for chandeliers and lampshades even after the Pairpoint Manufacturing Company purchased them in 1894. Their overall quality was some of the best in the United States and unsurpassed in their specialty areas. T. J. Pairpoint, the superintendent of Pairpoint Manufacturing worked primarily in metals such as silver, tin, zinc, and copper. Silver tea sets, knives, forks, spoons, cake baskets,

#NCP120 Mt. Washington Glass Co. (Pairpoint) Strawberry Diamond & Fan pattern. 2¼" tall. 2 oz. c. 1880's-1890's

metal tableware, casters, candlesticks, cigarette and cigar cases, jewel cases, and so on were all manufactured in metals by Pairpoint. When the Mt. Washington Glass Works was purchased, some glass and metal items were united. Fine glass goblets with metal mounts or stems for example.

The name of the glass operation in 1894 was changed to Pairpoint Glass Works. They prospered well into the Depression era with more elegant hand-cut glass. However, the cheaply-made mass produced Depression-ware took its toll on Pairpoint. Pairpoint's glass division shut down in November of 1937. The next year it was sold to J. B. Kenner Inc. who in turn resold it to Thomas Tripp, Isaac Babbitt, and Chester West in 1939. These three hired Robert Gunderson to head the glass division and went as far as to name it the Gunderson Glass Works Inc. From 1939-1952, the glass was still considered Pairpoint. In 1952, Gunderson died but the name went through another change to Gunderson-Pairpoint. A final change to Bryden's Pairpoint from 1957-1958 did not last for long. Bryden moved to Spain in 1958 and remained overseas until 1970. The plant shutdown in the meantime and burned in 1965. When Bryden returned, a new factory was opened in Sagamore, Massachusetts where fine hand-made glass is still made today.[46]

Corning Glass Works

In 1827, John Hoare founded the Brooklyn Flint Glass Works in New York. Through shaky times, the company finally went bankrupt in 1864 and Hoare left. Amory Houghton Sr. and his son Amory Houghton Jr. purchased Brooklyn in 1866. They survived a fire in 1867 and their first patented product was a glass window blind available in various colors: amber, green, blue, and purple. With much labor unrest in Brooklyn, they moved further west to Corning, New York. Corning was

a transportation hub with the Chemung Feeder Canal that connected with the Erie Canal. Railroads also ran north from Pennsylvania for the transportation of coal as a cheap fuel source. Thomas Hawkes, a gifted artisan ran a cutting shop within the factory.

Major troubles occurred in 1869. The canal dam went out which suspended shipping. Railroads were sporadic and frequently off schedule. The coal they received was full of slate and did not work as well as expected. Competition from Christian Dorflinger's factory especially in White Mills, Pennsylvania did not help matters. Fine-cut American glassware was in a slight decline. In 1870, the Corning Flint Glass Works went bankrupt. A year later a businessman from Boston bought them out but Amory Houghton Jr. continued to manage the plant.

In 1872, a rebound began and profitability returned particularly with the window blinds. New talented Bohemian engravers were hired from Europe. The mid-1870's were a bit rough when a Corning bank failed and a fire caused $35,000. worth of damage. A boost was given to the glass industry as a whole with the Philadelphia Centennial Exposition in 1876. Corning was not represented with any products but one of their craftsmen did work there. 1880 was another boost to the glass industry when the republican James Garfield won the presidential election. The republicans supported protective tariffs against lower wages paid by Europeans which was crucial for the Eastern cut-glass companies competing with Europe for the huge New York market. Corning expanded in 1880 and blew their first light bulb blanks and associated closely with Thomas Hawkes and his company (Hawkes & Co.). The 1880's were a time when Corning produced some barware and the common unpatented patterns including whiskey tumblers. Later in 1889, Hawkes won a grand prize at the Exposition Universelle in the midst of the Brilliant Period. Corning earned the reputation as "The Crystal City."

During the union troubles and greta mergers in the 1890's, many cutting companies combined with Corning as well. An influx of foreigners including Italians, English, Irish, and Bohemian engravers moved in to Corning. A small depression and over production in the 1890's was one factor leading to mergers and the scaling down of many companies. Corning survived and by the early 1900's, more companies moved to the city of Corning; most notably Steuben in 1903. Cut glass reached its peak in 1905 in Corning where nearly 500 cutters were employed. As the Brilliant Period was coming to a close and the market decreasing for fine cut glass, Corning began a trend of cost-cutting. Lower quality was produced for the middle-class which increased sales somewhat but reduced the need for some skilled labor.

Many small companies closed after 1905 and up to World War I. Europe was able to provide some blanks and raw materials such as potash but most was cut off during the war. In 1918, Corning purchased the Steuben Glassworks which survived the post-war depression in

1920. Corning continued to produce stemware of every kind even through Prohibition. Those who could afford to drink still did in fancy stemware but barware did suffer drastic cuts. In the Wellsboro, Pennsylvania plant in 1926, Corning Glass Works installed a ribbon machine which was an automatic blowing device used to manufacture light bulbs. After 1939, it was also used for Christmas tree ornaments. The new automation allowed for the blowing of 2,000 bulbs a minute or 3 million in a day. Corning is well known today for the largest museum and library on glassware as well as the Steuben Glass Factory.[47]

Fostoria Glass Company

The Fostoria Glass Company was established in Fostoria, Ohio in 1887. L. B. Martin was the first president and W. S. Brady, the first secretary. Together they founded Fostoria. Ohio was chosen for clean natural gas supplies at low rates, but only four years later, the gas ran out. The factory's furnace was rebuilt in 1891 and moved to Moundsville, West Virginia.

Fostoria was and is today a hand-house that survived the onslaught of mass production and machine-made glassware. Very few can make that claim. Fostoria manufactured fine hand-cut crystal tableware. They were able to introduce colored glassware early on in the Depression years in 1924. That coupled with a highly successful advertising campaign insured their survival. A huge expansion in 1925 which included employment of 650 workers made Fostoria one of the largest hand-made glass factories in the country. W. A. B. Dalzell assumed the presidency in 1902 and served until 1928. Dalzell was responsible for much of Fostoria's success during the early 20th century. Later Dalzell's son William F. Dalzell and grandson David Dalzell were also instrumental in the future and present survival of Fostoria.[48]

United States Glass Company

There were several key reasons why so many companies united on July 1, 1891. Much of it had to do with labor. The companies wished to monitor production, share losses, as well as to compete with the smaller cheaper lime glass companies that sprang up throughout the 1870's and 1880's. Excessive competition drove prices down which was another priority in the long list of changes desired. The major concern was to provide a united front against labor.

#NCP300 United States Glass Co. "Pennsylvania" pattern 1890's to early 1900's 1½ ounce whiskey tumbler or standard shot glass 2¼" tall. color: clear

18 companies in all were part of the deal: Adams & Company, Bryce Brothers, Challinor Taylor, & Company, George Duncan & Sons, Richards & Hartley, Ripley & Company, Gillider & Sons, Hobbs Glass Company, Colombia Glass, King, Son, & Company, O'Hara Glass Company, Bellaire Goblet Company, Nickel Plate Glass Company, Central Glass Company, Doyle & Company, A. J. Beatty & Sons (2 Beatty plants–1 in Tiffin, Ohio and another in Steubenville, Ohio), and the Novelty Glass Company. All factories would still be operated by the current owners and would continue to make what they had in the past. Only

#PPC001 Fostoria 1641 pattern 1909-1913 2¼" tall. 2 oz.

#PPC002 Fostoria 'Prince Gold' pattern 1909-1913 2¼" tall. 2 oz.

#PPC003 Fostorian 'Sylvan Line' pattern 1909-1913 2¼" tall. 2 oz.

now the output would be controlled. To the bain of identification, all catalogs from the 18 companies were combined under the United States Glass Company.

The unions and particularly the skilled glass workers were in uproar and organized the Great Strike of 1893-1896. Violence was typical through this period between strikers and strikebreakers. U.S. Glass was able to manufacture glass during the strike but at a reduced capacity. Many of the older companies shut down and all but two were sold during the Depression. In 1938, the main offices moved from Pittsburgh to Tiffin, Ohio and only one factory remained in operation in each of these two cities. In 1951, the Pittsburgh plant closed and the Tiffin plant was purchased by Continental Can in 1966. Continental Can sold it to the Interpace Corporation in 1969 which still operates it as a subsidiary producing stemware under the 'Tiffin' name.

Conclusion

The 19th and into the very early 20th century was a time when the first true shot glasses came about in America. They were frequently referred to as toys of whiskey tasters but were in fact small whiskey tumblers with the correct dimensions. One pattern developing in this era is the versatility of the designs applied to shot glasses. Very few glass objects can claim the variety of decorating techniques used upon them including flute-cuts, mold-blown, piece molds, hand-pressed, finely-cut, fancy art designs, opalescence, carnival or iridescence, enamelling, coloring, etching, and most every if not all techniques known. In the following chapters, new innovations with advertising, coloring, transfers, and every new design technique conceived are applied to shot glasses.

#NCP211 Molded 3-piece clear or gold coated design. 1½" tall, 1 oz. c. 1880's-1890's.

Chapter VI:

THE LATE 19TH AND EARLY 20TH CENTURY PRE-PROHIBITION YEARS

The 1860's up to 1919 was an explosion era for one particular type of shot glass; the whiskey tumbler known as the sample glass. Whiskey distillers proliferated and the rise of the urban and western saloons also marked this period of time. On the opposite end, a new wave of temperance reform coupled with women's movements effectively destroyed the saloons and the sample glasses; but not the drinking and the social aspects associated with them.

The Civil War disrupted production and particularly commerce of both glassware and whiskey. Transportation was more difficult and at times heavier drinkers were recruited as soldiers. Drink was more readily available to Union soldiers especially as the war wore on. Part of Lincoln's liquor tax in 1862 was to raise much needed revenue but it was also aimed as a curb to the public intoxication of Union soldiers. The United States Navy also abolished spirits-rations for enlisted men in 1862. In the late years of the war particularly 1863-1864, the South's economy collapsed and the inflationary price of whiskey cost as much as $65.00 per gallon. Grain sources were needed by the South for food and a good bushel of corn rose to $50.00. General Grant's drinking binges on the Union side were legendary but most scholars agree that Grant only drank during slow periods of inactivity.[49]

After the war, an explosion of distilleries opened across the country but primarily east of the Mississippi River and along the California coast. So many in fact that by the end of the 19th century, numerous mergers, overproduction, bankruptcies, and of course

temperance; all served to reduce this overabundance. The Post-Civil War era was also a time of significant advertising. Bottles, signs on streets and shops, newspapers, magazines, mail, trade cards, pictures, tins, crocks, jugs, and especially bottles and glasses all contained advertising for whiskey products.

The earliest sample glasses date back to the later 1880's while most were present in the early 1900's prior to America's entry into World War I. A sample glass is simply a glass tumbler decorated with some form of advertising. The advertising was somehow alcohol related for proprietors, distillers, store-owners selling whiskey, pharmacists, doctors dispensing liquor, saloons, clubs, and so on. The word 'sample' originated from the sales gimic of salesmen, peddlers, agents, and so on who offered free samples of the product that they were promoting.

Most sample glasses were in tumbler form and some were small enough for single measures or "shots" of whiskey. Thus, many of them qualify as shot glasses. Barware and bar tumblers including cheaper sham glasses were all utilized for sample use. Sample glasses might or might not have flutes and could be of heavy construction on the bottom and along the sides. Cheaply-made thin shams were more fragile but were much less expensive. Shams were nicknamed "shells" or "shot-shells" because of their eggshell thinness. They may even be somewhat rarer since they were so easily breakable and lost during natural disasters like earthquakes, floods, fires, etc.

Thousands of sample glasses were made by most

#WSB025 2¼" tall, 2 oz. Sample Glass. Etched white design.

#SD009 2⅜" tall, 2 oz. Sample Glass. Etched white design.

#WAL015 2⅛" tall, 1½ oz. Sample Glass. Etched white design.

any company involved in tumbler production. A variety of decorating techniques were applied by glass companies as well as individual decorating establishments. The lettering could be pressed into a mold, enameled, flashed, stained, or monogrammed. The vast majority contained a lightly-colored white acid etching or a rubber stamping of white pigment. Both do not wear all that well but the pigment specifically tends to fade or eventually rub off. White was not used exclusively, other colors like orange or red beading were applied in the form of a continuous row of small relief beads or chips of glass.

The more elaborate the design applied to a sample glass, the more valuable it is today. Some simply contained the name of the distiller. Others had logos, grain, wheat, or corn stalks and husks; fancy lettering; silver dollars or coins; bottles; barrels; shields; and many others. Cheaper designs might only list a name in one or two words. Rarity also plays a part in determining the value of such glasses. Some one-of-a-kind are worth more than one hundred dollars while typical or common items are valued less than ten dollars. Other price-determining factors include condition, region, and age.[50]

Many sample glasses were given away as promotional items, sold in general stores, and readily available around distilleries. An illegal drink might be served in one since they were readily concealed. Distillers sent them along with whiskey shipments for advertising and to spread the company name around. From 1898-1918, the Hayner Distilling Company in Dayton, Ohio, claimed to be the largest mail-order house in the nation for whiskey distribution. Hayner of course advertised on sample glasses. Beer brewers did the same but for the most part used larger sample tumblers and mugs. Many examples of sample glasses that are shot glass-size are displayed here and at the end of the chapter.

A saloon was a typical place or destination of a sample glass. Heavier and more durable glassware was the mainstay in terms of vessels for commercial use. Bar tumblers in shot glass size were made in significant quantities in the later 19th century particularly when whiskey was sold and drank in single ounces. Real men did not sip their whiskey but downed it straight in one gulp. The saloon was the western counterpart of the grog shop.

The beginning of the mass movement West can be traced to the California Gold Rush in 1848-1849. It was followed by a host of other settlers and occupations: trappers, silver miners, mountainmen, sailors, lumberjacks, ranchers, cattle-drivers, cowboys, etc. The first western saloons were cheaply built in a tent or shack and a row of beer or whiskey barrels served as the bar. No licenses were required and the only investment needed was for a stock of liquor and a place of most any sort to put it. Immigrants such as German and Irish opened many such saloons.

Like the New England tavern, the saloon could serve in many functions as a county court house, post office, way station for stagecoaches, theater, assayer's office, political campaign headquarters, eatery, etc. Judge Roy Bean ran a combination courthouse/saloon named "The Jersey Lily" at Langtry, Texas. While not serving in a judicial capacity, Bean tended bar. The saloon was a social place for meetings, card games, news, and other games.

The typical western saloon was much more rowdy and downright dangerous compared to the old American taverns. Poker games particularly if someone was caught cheating might end up in a shooting or knifing. The Colt .45 and other weapons were more prevalent and present upon one's body than the old days out East. Single men had little to do in the way of entertainment west except for the saloon. Not only could a good game of cards be drawn up but billiards, checkers, dances, lotteries, and an occasional prizefight with loads of wagering were additional forms of

#WSD012 2¼" tall, 1½ oz. Sample Glass. White writing.

#WSD015 2⅜" tall, 2 oz. Sample Glass. Beaded white writing. 10 Flutes.

#WSE018 2¼" tall, 2 oz. Sample Glass. Etched white design.

#WSC080 2¼" tall, 2 oz. Sample Glass. "7-11" is orange; remaining is etched white lettering.

#WSF018 2¼" tall, 1¾ oz. Sample Glass. Etched white writing.

#WSI006 2⅛" tall, 2 oz. Sample Glass. Etched white design.

entertainment. As more and more drinking went on, the chance of violence in terms of brawling, fighting, assaults, and the unleashing of handguns intensified.

After the Civil War, whiskey was cheap, distilled in huge quantities, and transported easily on rail, ship, or by ox, horse, and mule. Hundreds and maybe even thousands of brand names some colorful in nature were all applied to bottles, sample glasses, and a variety of other advertising means. A "Cowboy's Cocktail" was nothing short of straight whiskey. "Red-Eye," "Gut-Warmer," "Tarantula Juice," "Dakota Dynamite," "Old Joe Gideon," "Firewater," "Tonsil Tickler," "Tornado Juice," "Nose Paint," and "Grizzly Bear's Milk" were a few others. "Bravemaker" made one wild like an Indian on the warpath. "Bumblebee Whiskey" was the whiskey with a sting. "Old Forty Rod" brought a man down at that distance. "Taos Lightning" was guaranteed to strike you dead on the spot. "Skull-Bender" supposedly had an extremely high alcoholic content and sold for as much as 25¢ (2-bits) a glass. "Mormon Juice" induced polygamic hallucinations by making a man see his wife in triplicate. "Snakehead Whiskey" was by far the deadliest since each barrel was rumored to contain two diamondback rattlesnake heads, a plug of tobacco, and a tablespoon of gunpowder. One can only wonder if the guns alone were killing men in saloons.[51]

Legendary towns with their saloons pictured on modern tourist shot glasses today abounded in America's West. The Bucket of Blood in Lettavre, Montana; The Pioneer Club in Leadville, Colorado; Aspen's Red Onion; The Nugget and The Silver Dollar in San Antonio, Texas; and other cities like Tombstone, Arizona; Dodge City, Kansas; and Cripple Creek, Colorado just to name a few. The oldest drinking establishment surviving today is the Red Barn in Georgetown, Colorado. The bullet-ridden bar was hauled by oxcart from Kansas. Large diamond-dust French mirrors also survived the overland trek to the Red Barn. A dispute with the sign painter who altered the name to read: "We Sell the VERY WORST Whiskey" was left the way it was was very popular with the miners in Georgetown.

Deadwood in the Black Hills of South Dakota had one of the highest concentrations of saloons and distilleries anywhere. There were 75 whiskey mills in the town's first year of existence and more were added later. Saloons in Deadwood outnumbered all other buildings at a 5 to 1 ratio. Calamity Jane (Martha Jane Canary) frequented the Green Front (a saloon in Deadwood). By far the most famous liquor establishment in Deadwood was Nuttal and Mann's Number Ten; Wild Bill Hickok's hangout. Hickok was going to take over the marshalling of Deadwood but with his reputation as an able gunman, the citizens had little desire to have their town cleaned up. The townspeople hired the gambler Jake McCall to kill Hickok. In a rare instance, Hickok was sitting with his back to the door playing poker in the Number Ten. McCall shot him in the head leaving Hickok holding what is now known as the "Dead Man's Hand:" both black aces, both black eights, and the jack of diamonds. Hickok was buried in Deadwood's Boothill Cemetery.[52]

Thirst Comes First.
Drink till you burst!
Everything else can wait!

(Old Saloon Sign)

The origin of the word saloon is a French term for a specialized room such as a drawing room. Dining saloons, billiard saloons, and beer saloons soon followed. America adapted it as a drinking place. A carving or mirror especially that of a nude woman was quite common hung on the wall behind the bar. Early on, many of America's urban saloons were respected establishments serving a variety of social functions. It was a place to talk, read newspapers, unwind, and play a game of pool or cards. Bowling alleys were popular in saloons as well or a back room known as the sample room.

Travelling salesmen, peddlers, local distributors, as well as others were allowed to display their goods in this sample room. Undoubtably, sample glasses were used and free samples were presented to the proprietor in these special rooms. The sample room was often reserved for the wealthier men of importance and for general get-togethers, business meetings, or maybe even a prearranged highstakes poker game. Imported beer, Cuban cigars, and hard liquor, whether imported or domestic were common items housed in the sample room for the distinguished clientele. One can only guess at the quantity and variety of sample glasses or whiskey tumblers that passed through these sample rooms throughout the country during this period of our history.[53]

Larger backrooms in saloons were used for union meetings, clubs, weddings, christenings, dances, and a host of other festivities. Fine city saloons provided clean restrooms, first aid for fights and accidents, and might occasionally run a soup kitchen giving handouts to the poor and beggars. A rare few along the eastcoast, San Francisco, New Orleans, and others scattered in the West were deluxe upper-class establishments. Fancy paintings, marble floors and fireplaces, cherry or walnut curved wooden bars, fancy cut glass mirrors and windows, hand-cut blown stemware, and pianos were a few examples of the expensive decor. Fancy meats, cheeses, fruits, sausages, smoked fish, salmon, pies, pastries, and so on accompanied the best in liquor. Waitresses might wear fancy outfits such as cocktail aprons sporting pink elephants which were popular beginning in the later 1800's. Many of these designs and styles would wind up later as pictured on shot glasses.

Most saloons were dirty, smelly places particularly as the Industrial Revolution brought on a new class of urban saloons. From 1880-1900, the number of saloons doubled in the United States. The ideal location was on a street corner near a large factory. A corner provided two separate entrances and proprietors gladly cashed workers' checks. Windows were covered with posters, plants, bottles, and what have you to hide or block out what was going on inside. Today, strict laws prohibit visibility of the inside of most bars and places where alcohol is consumed.

Urban saloons sheltered crooks, gamblers, and prostitution. Illegal gambling with cards, dice, lotteries, and so forth were ready forms available in a saloon. With the crap and roulette tables followed con artists and criminals. Saloons worsened at the turn of the century and became the focal point for slum life. Habitual drunkards spent their last dollar on a cheap bottle of whiskey. Saloon owners cheated customers by filling expensive bottles of whiskey with cheaper brands or added tobacco and hot peppers to watered-down whiskey to simulate that extra bite of stronger spirits. The food served was dry, salty, and greasy which encouraged patrons to drink. Salty peanuts and pretzels, smoked fish, extra dry sausages, and saurkraut; all drove one to thirst. Naturally, heavy drinking was common practice as well as a run of drinks; when one person bought a round everyone else was expected to reciprocate.[54]

In the late 1880's through Prohibition, large investors and brewers became the majority of saloon owners. They possessed the capital necessary to set up saloons along railroad routes and in the larger cities. Small retailers had difficulty competing and either went out of business or became the agents of brewers, wholesalers, and investors. Over 75% of the saloons were owned by

#WSH005 2¼" tall, 2 oz. Sample Glass. Molded Writing (bottom underside reads: "FOR PRIVATE USE").

#WSP120 2½" tall, 2 oz. Sample Glass. Etched white writing.

#WSS130 2⅛" tall, 1⅞ oz. Sample Glass. Beaded orange design.

liquor wholesalers and breweries by 1890. Beer was beginning to replace whiskey as the drink of choice across the country. German brewmasters set up huge breweries in Milwaukee and St. Louis sending thousands of barrels West. In 1880, lager production in America reached 13½ million barrels. It doubled by 1890 to 27 million. Huge 5¢ foaming mugs of beer only added to the abundance of whiskey. As the state of saloons turned for the worse, a new wave of temperance was on the horizon.

New forceful arguments against drinking, new data, and specifically some of the political power brewers and distillers were wielding ignited reform. The United States Brewers Association was established in 1862 and was able to get Lincoln's tax reduced to 60¢ a barrel through effective lobbying. They backed candidates who did not support temperance including Grant in the 1871 presidential election. A bit later in the 1880's, the National Protection Association was organized by the liquor industry and they pooled their resources to bribe newspapers and back politicians. The organization of beer and liquor industries and the victories won alarmed reformers.

Foreign immigrants and prejudice were blamed for much of the drinking problems in the country but it would soon expand to all connected to alcohol in any shape or form. Both men and women of English, Irish, or Scottish descent led the way in convictions for drunkenness and disorderly conduct. Ethnic celebrations and customs were particularly focused specifically on those involving drink. Blacks who were rarely served in white establishments were said to have violent tendencies when drunk by Southern reformers.

Prohibitionists could not get either the republicans or the democrats to support temperance; therefore, their only solution was to establish their own political party. James Black organized the National Temperance Society and Publication. With the cooperation of other serious reformers such as Neal Dow, Black was able to form the National Prohibition Party in 1869. It was shortened to the Prohibition Party (PP) later and allied with other social causes of the day such as the new woman's movement.

The PP ran Black for president in 1872 but did not muster much of any support. General Green Clay Smith ran in 1876 and only received 9,000 votes; Neal Dow did little better in 1880. 1884 was the year that the PP had an effect on the presidential election. John P. St. John had been a top republican candidate but switched to the PP when the republican party would not take the dry effort seriously. St. John received 150,000 votes that would most likely have gone to the republicans had he not run for a separate party. The republican Blain ended up losing to Grover Cleveland the democrat who won by a slim 1,000 votes.[55]

New arguments surfaced for temperance reform after the Civil War but many were exaggerations or old wives' tales. Some unproven scientific theories worked their way around the country and into speeches. The fermentation process was considered poison of unnatural origin since it involved dead vegetable matter going through a further process of decay. In short, it was a function of death. The hereditary argument first sprang up with Franklin Pierce in the 1850's. Pierce's mother was an alcoholic and he was criticized for his heavy drinking, but many believed it was in his family genes.

"... speed the day ... when no young man ... who pollutes his lips with the drunkard's cup shall presume to seek the favors of our precious daughters."
Susan B. Anthony

The female leaders of the day not only pushed for suffrage but prohibition as well. Lucy Stone, Elizabeth Cady Stanton, Amelia Bloomer, and Susan B. Anthony

#WSO040 2⅛" tall, 2 oz. Sample Glass. Etched white design.

#WSS024 2⅜" tall, 2 oz. Sample Glass. Etched white writing.

#WSW090 2¼" tall, 2 oz. Sample Glass. Beaded orange design.

#WSH003 2⅛" tall,
2 oz. Sample Glass.
Etched white writing.

WSO014 2⅛" tall, 2 oz.
Sample Glass. Etched
white writing.

#WSP012 2¼" tall,
2 oz. Sample Glass.
Etched white design.
13 Flutes.

were just some of the female rights' activists also advocating temperance. A bow of white ribbon was the membership badge for women promoting prohibition. The most influential by far was Frances Willard.

Willard began her training at the Milwaukee Female College in 1857 and then entered Northwestern Female College the following year. She graduated in 1860 and taught in 10 different schools and colleges during the next 16 years. She became president of Northwestern Female College in 1871 but resigned when it merged with the previous all male Northwestern University. Part of it was that she had once been engaged to Charles Henry Fowler, the men's president but Willard's homosexual tendencies might also have been a factor. In the early 1870's, Willard placed her energies into the temperance cause.

In 1874, the National Woman's Christian Temperance Union (WCTU) was formed effectively united several small sects. Willard declined the position of presidency but accepted a lesser position as recording secretary. She believed that she did not have quite enough experience yet in temperance to assume the leading role; instead, it went to Annie Wittenmyer. Willard became the president of the WCTU in 1879 and was in all actuality the driving force behind it.

"Woe unto them that are mighty to drink wine,
and men of strength to mingle strong drink."
Isaiah 5:22.

Willard personally wrote thousands of letters, articles, and gave numerous speeches on temperance. The WCTU fought for the end of gambling and racetracks; urged preachers to substitute grape juice for wine in sacramental offerings, argued for prison reform, 8-hour workdays, peace, educational reform, and most every social cause imaginable. They supported anything to do with temperance including "Lemonade Lucy"

Webb Hayes, the wife of President Rutherford B. Hayes. Lucy barred alcohol from all Whitehouse functions. Rutherford B. Hayes was not for total abstinence and Lucy's ways were somewhat unpopular. Hayes was not reelected in 1881. The ultimate goal of the WCTU was Constitutional Prohibition.

In 1880, the WCTU created a Department of Scientific Temperance Instruction in Schools and Colleges. They petitioned and fought local and state legislatures to include teaching of temperance as compulsory in schools. They also organized a campaign at teachers and publishers for educational reform. It worked and every state but Arizona passed such laws by 1900. They were also the first to recognize birth defects as the result of women who drank heavily while pregnant.

Willard and the WCTU's impact was felt most on temperance and suffrage. Liquor was associated with unequalness in women's social condition. In all 45 separate departments were established at the WCTU protesting everything including attacks on athletics, tobacco, hygiene, morals, etc. The WCTU became the largest, best-organized, and most powerful temperance organization until the formation of the Anti-Saloon League. In 1882, the WCTU allied with the PP and claimed some responsibility for the support given to St. John in the 1884 election. In 1883, Willard founded the World's WCTU which was present in 51 countries. Willard was easily the most celebrated woman of her day. Willard had no children nor had she ever married.[56]

The WCTU worked well with unions such as the Knights of Labor, and tried to bring together suffragists, populists, and other groups but failed. From that point things slid down hill and the WCTU's "Do Everything" policy was weakening. There was only one Frances Elizabeth Willard and when she died in 1898, there was no one to assume her all-encompassing role. In fact, the only other significant woman known nationally next to

Willard in the WCTU and the temperance movement was Carry Nation. The saloon-bashing Nation painted a picture quite different from that of Willard, Anthony, and the other uppercrust Protestants of the WCTU.

In the late 1860's, the smashing up of saloons resumed. Dr. Dioclesian Lewis (DIO) was not a true doctor but advertised himself that way when teaching and lecturing. Dio was a well-known figure and supporter of woman's rights, ran girl's schools, and encouraged women to destroy saloons through violent means. He aided in the development of the WCTU. Women held a particular advantage in that it was strictly taboo to shove, touch, or kick a lady. Many saloonkeepers stood by or left as their bars were destroyed; but others did not. Occasionally, women were beaten, drenched with water or liquor, egged, pelted with stones and bottles, and threatened with guns, knives, and even dogs. Women usually attacked in large groups and when arrested, overcrowded local jails and were freed soon after with simple reprimands or small fines. Peaceful, nonviolent protests such as long prayer meetings in front of liquor establishments were completed as well. Carry Nation scoffed at such peacefulness and was the epitomy of the violent female saloon-smasher.

"I Will Carry A Nation for Temperance."
(Carry Amelia Nation's motto–middle initial "A.").

Born 1846, Carry Nation was corny, vulgar, psychotic, and had a complete family history of mental disorders. Her mother died in an insane asylum. Her brother, sister, and nephew were also unbalanced. At age 19, she married a physician Charles Gloyd who drank and smoked heavily. Gloyd's health deteriorated quickly and Carry was quite repulsed by him. She believed that he was transmitting horrible diseases to her. Gloyd died leaving her 6 months pregnant and with a strong dislike for drink and tobacco. To make matters worse, her daughter had physical problems and ended up in an asylum for the mentally deranged. Her hatred intensified to include the places alcohol and tobacco were used or served. Carry remarried and moved to Texas to plant cotton with her new husband David Nation but it failed to work out as planned and they returned to Kansas.

Kansas went dry in 1882 and Carry joined a local WCTU branch to fight the illegal liquor establishments still in existence. In 1888, she became president of the county WCTU chapter in Medicine Lodge, Kansas; and was able to get those illegal places shut down. Her violence would begin in the neighboring town of Wichita. With a Bible in one hand and a hatchet in the other, she screamed obscenities and broken quotes from the Book during her rampages.

"You besotted, lawbreaking, booze-sodden, soul-killing, filth-smeared spawn of the devil . . . "
Carry A. Nation speaking to a saloonkeeper.

Carry was specifically enraged with nudity and sex of any sort; especially the common nude hung behind the bar only increased her rage. Carry Nation was a large, obese, meanlooking, and middle-aged woman when she began her wrecking tours. She spread throughout Kansas including Kiowa and Topeka on her initial trek while her husband constantly begged and pleaded for her to return home. Her first arrest was in Wichita when she trashed the bar of the best hotel in town. Drys turned her loose on bail and reluctantly the WCTU who by the way did not advocate violence; at least provided Carry with defense counsel.

Carry used her fists, rocks, iron bars, sledgehammers, canes, billard balls and cuesticks, or whatever was available to break backbar mirrors, crush bottles, tear up tables and chairs, and destroy those poor sample glasses prized by collectors today! When arrested she posed for cameramen behind bars often on her knees upon a cement floor reading the Bible. She gained converts and armed other women to accompany her. Carry's personal mascot of course was a bright-edged hatchet hidden under her cloak. She encouraged other women to take up hatchets. From the Midwest to the Eastcoast including such cities as Des Moines, Chicago, St. Louis, Cincinnati, Atlantic City, New York, and Philadelphia; Carry inspired hatchet crews and led the destruction.

Carry Nation was a fanatic and arrested repeatedly; but the publicity she created often forced local officials and police to shut down illegal establishments. She attracted big crowds and earned additional money as lecturer, autographing pictures, and selling souvenir hatchets. Furthermore, she published a newspaper named: "The Smasher's Mail." Near the end of her career, she carried along 3 hatchets with the following names: "Faith," "Hope," and "Charity." Carry died in 1911 and an annual festival in Holly, Michigan is held every year where she had once destroyed a saloon.[57]

There is room for debate as to whether or not Carry Nation did more harm than good. The WCTU reluctantly offered some support but censured her dramatically. Eventually they disowned her and her violent ways of protesting.

The Saloons Must Go!
Motto of the Anti-Saloon League.

With more power than the WCTU, the formation of the Anti-Saloon League was a major blow to intemperance. Reverend Howard Hyde Russell, a Protestant minister, created the Ohio Anti-Saloon League in 1893 and served as its first superintendent. Other leagues formed quickly in Washington D.C., Massachusetts, Pennsylvania, and onward. All formed together into a national organization at a convention in 1895. Russell presided over it as well.

The goal of the League was to abolish the use of alcohol completely with special attention to the most popular place in which it was served; the saloon. Russell

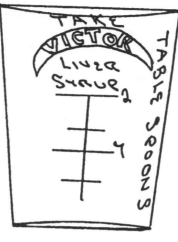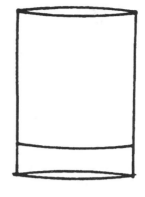

#WSV003 2¼" tall, 2 oz. Sample Glass. Etched white writing. Front represents a German Baptist Conference of 1899 signifying that all religious sects obviously did not support temperance.

#WAA001 1¾" tall, 1 oz. Late 19th century pharmaceutical glass—pale green tint. Bottom underside reads in molded writing: "BREVETE 2 S.G.D.C."

illicited the use of nearly 60,000 churches, spread great amounts of propaganda unlike ever before, ran highly successful fundraising operations, recruited thousands of volunteer speakers, encouraged well-educated young ambitious ministers to join his staff, obtained thousands of signatures on petitions and pledges, and attacked the political arena. By the early 1900's, the Anti-Saloon League was represented well in every state and territory in America. The rural Methodists, Presbyterians, Congregationalists, and Bible-Belt Baptists all joined the effort. Catholics, Jewish, and some Baptists did not but still advocated temperance and moderation.

One of Russell's most notable acquisitions was the talents of Wayne Bidwell Wheeler. Wheeler was a lawyer for the Ohio League in 1898 and became general counsel later for the national league. Wheeler was very influential in the Ohio legislature ousting those in favor of alcohol and backing those for abstinence. Wheeler's initial victories and methods in Ohio were applied to the national league.

Voting lists based on a candidate's record were set up and significant lobbying efforts were utilized. Candidates were backed as did the brewers and distillers. The League engineered the extension of local option laws for townships and then to counties. When significant parts of a state were dry, they would then shoot for state-wide prohibition. The Anti-Saloon League gave support to democrats and republicans with "Dry" views but paid little attention to the Prohibition Party. The PP blamed the League for stunting its growth and were adverse to the League's methods; however, the League became so powerful that the PP had little option but to join with them. Former prohibitionists, feminist leaders including the WCTU, reformers, and political activists also united with the League. All worked together for national prohibition; the supreme goal.

So much propaganda in the form of newspapers, magazines, leaflets, pamphlets, charts, new posters in color, and pledges were published in huge quantities. At its peak the Anti-Saloon League Year Book numbered more than 15 million annual copies. As keeping with tradition, nearly every conceivable social and health problem was blamed upon drink. Alcohol increased crime, divorce, sickness, and insanity. It increased the risk of social diseases like syphillus, gonorrhea, and tuberculosis. Furthermore, it still encouraged black men to rape white women. There was some truth in the complaints; some were untrue such as the racial claims but all were definitely exaggerated. Overall, the League was the power and force behind the drive for national prohibition.[58]

The liquor industry fought back but not quite with the intensity or whole-hearted commitment as the League professed. The United States Brewers Association and The National Liquor Dealer's Association black-listed businesses that advocated temperance, bought pledges from candidates, and organized major meetings in saloons. The League used

PLEDGE of the
Woman's Christian Temperance Union

PLEDGE

I hereby solemnly promise, GOD HELPING ME, to abstain from all distilled, fermented and malt liquors, including wine, beer and cider; and to employ all proper means to discourage the use of, and traffic in the same.

Name

Date

After signing this Pledge, retain it, but send name to Mrs. Geo. F. Pashley, 429 McDonough St., Brooklyn, N. Y., State Supt. work among Soldiers and Sailors.

IF YOU ARE AN ALCOHOLIC
. . . signing this will do you little good. For alcoholism is either a disease in itself or the symptom of a psychic disorder which will power cannot cure.

WCTU Pledge reproduced directly from a late 19th century WCTU pamphlet.

churches for their own meetings which was to the League's advantage. One serious problem with the liquor industry was that they were opposed to women's groups and suffrage for women. Furthermore, the Brewer's and Liquor Dealer's Associations assumed that prohibition would fail and were not as well organized nationally as the forces receptive to it.

Further pressures by the temperance movement in the Post-Civil War era forced doctors, pharmacists, and those patenting medicines to label them differently and use other words as substitutes for whiskey or alcohol. The names were as imaginative as those used by the whiskey distillers for their products. Bitters such as "Prickly Ash Bitters," "Stomach Bitters," and "Hostetters Bitters" still contained anywhere from 20 to 50% pure alcohol. Hostetters was often labelled at 44%. Many of these names can be found on pharmaceutical glasses, proprietor advertising, and other glasses used for doling out liquor as medicine in small shot-size doses. A few of the more colorful names include: "Balsam of Life;" "Panacea;" "Painkiller;" extracts like "Medical Extract" and "Physical Extract;" "Vegetable Compound;" "Liver Syrup" (see German Baptist glass) or "Remedy for Liver Trouble;" tonics such as "Wigwam Tonic," "Arabian Tonic," and "Beef Tonic;" "Herbs" or "Native Herbs;" "Doctor Bunkus's Discovery;" "Swamp Root;" and elixirs like "Stomach Elixir." All were promoted as cure-alls for the same pains and problems complained about a century earlier coupled with the new discoveries in disease and suffering.

As the Anti-Saloon League continued with local option and county-wide prohibition; they worked their way up to the state level fighting for Constitutional Amendments. Some required popular votes to amend a state's Constitution such as Kansas, Maine, Rhode Island, and the Dakotas. Kansas went dry in 1882 except for medical and scientific purposes; Maine in 1884; and North Dakota in 1889. President Cleveland imposed Prohibition on the Territory of Alaska. Rhode Island briefly enacted prohibition from 1886-1889 but repealed and never attempted it again. Prohibition was a dismal failure in South Dakota because of the numerous rowdy towns like Deadwood. Local authorities could not take on drinking mobs and saloons lasted long after statewide prohibition laws.

Speakeasies especially arose after the so-called "High License" fees were invented. These fees could be as high as $1,000. annually and were basically used for obtaining permits to sell or dispense alcohol. The respectable wealthier hotel and bar owners readily paid them and still conducted a profitable business for their rich clientele. Common men frequented the illegal establishments for cheaper and lower quality spirits. Enforcement did increase and a common weakspot with saloons was that nearly always they lost out on some legal technicality in violation of some local or state ordinance. It might be selling liquor after midnight, serving minors, allowing gambling, holding an expired license, and a host of other violations.

Temperance martyrs also played a role in the fight against inebriety and intemperance. Sioux City, Iowa was another dangerous place with roughly 100 illegal saloons present in 1886. Channing Haddock was a Methodist preacher who denounced these lawbreakers. Haddock was shot and killed by a brewer, John Arensdorf. Arensdorf was acquitted which further inflamed reformers. Likewise, a son of a Baptist preacher in Mississippi a year later was shot and killed by an antiprohibitionist. By the early 1900's, only Kansas, Maine, and North Dakota still possessed Constitutional laws on Prohibition. A new wave of amendments and prohibition would soon rise again.

On March 3, 1903; a law was enacted by Congress stating: "That no intoxicating liquors of any character will be sold within the limits of the Capitol Building of the United States."[59] A significant step in the enforcement of a ban on liquor sales to Indians in the Oklahoma Territory, was the appointment of William "Pussyfoot" Johnson by President Theodore Roosevelt in 1906. Previously, Johnson had been an agent and spy for prohibitionists across the country exposing voting frauds by antiprohibitionists, drinking in colleges and

WAB005 2¼" tall, 1¾ oz.
Molded clear writing with measuring lines on rev.

#WAA004 2" tall, 1¼ oz.
Molded clear writing.

#WAK009 2¼" tall, 1½ oz.
Molded clear writing with measuring lines on rev.

camps where it was outlawed, bootlegging in the South, and those serving liquor without licenses in the Senate and House restaurants in Washington D.C.

Roosevelt commissioned Johnson as a special officer and Congress supported the measure with a $25,000. grant to suppress liquor sales. With the appropriation, Johnson hired additional gunslingers, deputized gunmen, and with his own gun went to work. As did the women crusaders like Carry Nation, Johnson broke up illegal establishments smashing bottles, our poor whiskey sample glasses, other barware, barrels, pool tables, and then typically torched the place as a finishing touch. Those who resisted were arrested and even shot. Johnson was a big, burly, rough man and earned the nickname "Pussyfoot" for carefully stalking his prey often at night. Brewers tried to ship whiskey under near-beer labels as Non Tox, Uno, Ino, Longhorn, and Tin Top; but Johnson discovered them all. Johnson fit in well with Roosevelt's adventurous and cavalier style of doing things and he was further promoted to "Chief Special Officer" for all Indian Reservations in Minnesota, Idaho, Montana, New Mexico, and the Dakotas.

In Johnson's 5 years of Indian service, he and his deputies killed at least 25 men and arrested nearly 5½ thousand criminals with about an 80% conviction rate. Millions of dollars worth of saloons, liquor, and bar accessories were destroyed on Johnson's rampages. 8 of Johnson's deputies lost their lives too in the line of duty.[60]

Howard Taft appointed a new Commissioner of Indian Affairs who did not like Johnson's methods. Furthermore, one of Johnson's hand-picked men was charged with murder for killing a man during a raid. He was cleared but Johnson had had enough with the new administration and resigned in 1909. Johnson went on to work as director of the World League Against Alcoholism and edited the Anti-Saloon League's American Issue. As publicity agent for the League, he lost an eye from a stone thrown at him by a mob of antiprohibitionists during a speech given in London. Speaking out could be dangerous and many other temperance leaders were shot, beaten by mobs, had their homes blown up with dynamite, slashed with knives, and had bottles and rocks thrown at them.

Additional statewide Prohibition Amendments popped up again as the Anti-Saloon League pressed on with unrelenting attention. Georgia and Alabama enacted laws in 1908; Tennessee in 1910; Washington in 1915; and Puerto Rico, the Territory of Alaska, and Washington D.C. in 1917. The 1913 Webb-Kenyon Interstate Liquor Act forbade the shipment of liquor into dry states. Also in 1913, the Anti-Saloon League finally emphasized Constitutional Prohibition Laws for the entire nation. In 1916, as general council of the League, Wayne Wheeler 'wheeled' much power pressuring senators, representatives, and presidents to support nationwide prohibition. Numerous marches on Washington D.C. were completed by the League and the WCTU.

As with the Civil War, prohibitionists did not make the same mistake with World War I. They combined their views with the war effort. Distilling they argued, used up valuable sources of grain, sugar, and other ingredients needed for war rationing. The League supported the food control bill and it was linked to unpatriotic behavior. Beer was pro-German with the brand names and backing. Both Kaiser Wilhelm and booze must go according to the doctrine of "Wheelerism." Of course drinking toasts like "To Hell With Kaiser" were also not unpopular. Only beer and wine production was allowed under this bill though distilled spirits were not strictly outlawed. Some distilleries did offer their services including the use of their facilities to the government during the war. For example, N.E. Squibb, president of Indiana Distillers Associated notified President Woodrow Wilson that they had placed their properties for the manufacture of alcohol for munitions at the disposal of the federal government.

It certainly did not stop any laws for in 1917, alcohol was outlawed for the military. On March 3, 1917, the Reed "Bone-Dry" Amendment forbade U.S. Mail to carry . . . "no letter, postcard, circular, newspaper, pamphlet, or publication of any kind containing any advertisement of spiritous liquors. . ."[61] It was later amended on October 3, 1917 to exclude alcohol use for governmental, scientific, medicinal, mechanical, manufacturing, industrial, and sacramental purposes of churches. Hawaii Territory also went dry in 1918.

The actual drafting of the Prohibition Amendment or the 18th Amendment was completed in 1914 by Wayne Wheeler, the Reverend Purley Baker, and James Cann. It was known as the Hobson-Sheppard Bill since Representative Hobson introduced it in the House and Senator Sheppard in the Senate. Marchers for the League and WCTU personally handed legislatures copies of the proposed amendment during one of the marches. A majority in the House actually supported it in a vote of 197-190 but a ⅔ vote majority was necessary.

The 1917 Food Control Bill was enacted by Congress as a wartime measure that excluded foodstuffs for war from the manufacture of alcohol. As mentioned beer and wine were saved, but only temporarily. The push for National Prohibition was intensified with World War I. The Brewers Association and The National Wholesale Liquor Dealers Association naturally fought it but it was too little too late. Popular public support was leaning to anti-intemperance. Women could vote in 12 states by 1920 and 10 of those 12 adopted laws prohibiting drink by popular vote. Women too were actively engaged in the WCTU and the League. Wheeler also had the support of Secretary of Navy Josephus Daniels and former Secretary of State William Jennings Bryan; both abstainers and popular speakers. To give the liquor industry a year to adapt, Wheeler altered the proposed national amendment slightly at the request of Congress. In 1917, the Senate voted in favor of it 65-20 and the House 282-128.

GLASS SOUVENIRS

The only high grade popular priced line on the market. **Fired colors and gold, will not fade or wash off.**

Will be lettered with "Souvenir of (name of your town)" or "Compliments of (your name)." Be sure to state plainly the lettering desired. We can furnish without lettering at same prices if desired. As decorating is done after receipt of order, shipment cannot be made in less than two or three weeks.

Special Note:—Customers must order at least **one gross** either of one number or asst'd We cannot make smaller shipment.

1C950, Oval Pin Tray—6 in. ruby, embossed gold edge......Doz. 82c

1C951, Sherbet — Full size, ruby, gold edge.................Doz. 82c

1C952, Wine—Ruby bowl, crystal stem and foot, gold edge.Doz. 82c

1C973—As 1C952, emerald green.
Doz. 82c

1C968, Toothpick Holder—2¼x2¼, emerald green, gold decorated jewel base, gold edge.
Doz. 82c

1C955, Gypsy Kettle—2½x2, ruby, 3 gold feet, gold edge, metal ball handle...Doz. 82c

1C971—As 1C955, emerald green...Doz. 82c

1C953, Mug—3x2⅝, block diamond crystal base, balance ruby, gold edge......Doz. 84c

1C969—Shape as 1C953, 2¾x2¾, emerald green, gold decorated crystal jewel base.
Doz. 82c

1C956, Hatchet—6¼ in., ruby, gold edges.
Doz. 85c

1C970—As 1C956, emerald green.   " 82c

1C959, Coal Hod—4 in.. crystal base, ruby sides, gold edge, metal ball handle..Doz. 85c

1C974—As 1C959, emerald green, gold decorated base and edge.
Doz. 85c

1C977, Covered Oval Jewel Box—4½ in. emerald green, solid gold feet, gold edges.
Doz. 87c

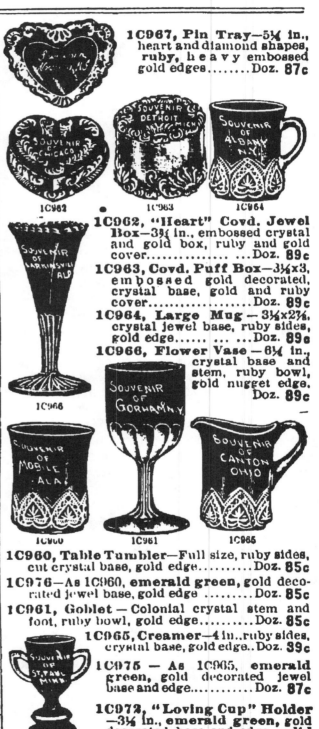

1C967, Pin Tray—5¼ in., heart and diamond shapes, ruby, heavy embossed gold edges.......Doz. 87c

1C962, "Heart" Covd. Jewel Box—3¾ in., embossed crystal and gold box, ruby and gold cover.............. ...Doz. 89c

1C963, Covd. Puff Box—3½x3, embossed gold decorated, crystal base, gold and ruby cover..................Doz. 89c

1C964, Large Mug — 3½x2⅞, crystal jewel base, ruby sides, gold edge...... ...Doz. 89c

1C966, Flower Vase — 6¼ in., crystal base and stem, ruby bowl, gold nugget edge.
Doz. 89c

1C960, Table Tumbler—Full size, ruby sides, cut crystal base, gold edge..........Doz. 85c

1C976—As 1C960, emerald green, gold decorated jewel base, gold edge ....Doz. 85c

1C961, Goblet — Colonial crystal stem and foot, ruby bowl, gold edge..........Doz. 85c

1C965, Creamer—4 in..ruby sides, crystal base, gold edge..Doz. 89c

1C975 — As 1C965, emerald green, gold decorated jewel base and edge...........Doz. 87c

1C972, "Loving Cup" Holder —3½ in., emerald green, gold decorated base and edge, solid gold handles........ .Doz. 85c

It was introduced officially to the House by Andrew Volstead for which the act was named ("The Volstead Act"). Ironically, Volstead never joined a temperance society when it was fashionable to do so and rarely spoke out against intemperance. He did believe that it was lawful and moral and should be enforced. Volstead altered the 18th Amendment slightly and verified its constitutionality. It became law on January 16, 1919. The last blow to the liquor industry was when they lost their one year grace period; the Agricultural Appropriation Bill did not remove its dry clause. Wilson vetoed the Prohibition Amendment but was overridden.

"After one year from the ratification of this article the manufacture, sale or transportation of intoxicating liquors within, the importation thereof into, or the exportation thereof from the United States and all territory subject to the jurisdiction thereof for beverage purposes is hereby prohibited."

Secton I; 18th Amendment to the Constitution (Prohibition or the Volstead Act).

Section II of the 18th Amendment granted states very little power, only to prohibit liquor. States could no longer enact their own liquor laws. "The Congress and the several states shall have concurrent power to enforce this article."[62] All states eventually ratified it except Rhode Island and Connecticut.

The Amendment was altered and amended several times. Exceptions by government permit were allowed for sacramental wine, medicine (1 pint per patient per 10 day period), and beer had to be reduced to 5% alcohol or less. The law officially took effect on January 17, 1920. Wheeler and the Anti-Saloon League had finally achieved their goal of nationwide prohibition, at least from a legislative standpoint.

170,000 saloons were either destroyed or closed. Many distilleries had already shut down by September 17, 1917 under the wartime food conservation regulation. The production of sample glasses slowly trailed off; and very few were made beyond 1915. All production ended by 1919. Prohibition effectively killed lawful drinking and many of the vessels including barware and sample glasses that accompanied it.

Those that survived the destruction of the saloons were sold, packed up, stored away, given away, kept as momentoes and souvenirs, and tossed out. Sample glasses probably wouldn't sell well today since they are rather plain-looking and cheaply-made. Some collectors go as far to say that they all look the same while others boast of the sheer quantity they possess in their collection and the excitement of finding unique additions. One thing is sure though; the passage of the 18th Amendment was also the end of a shot glass era. Sample glasses along with saloons are now part of America's past history.

The remaining pages of this chapter illustrate other sample glasses and old pharmaceutical shot glasses from the 1880's up to Prohibition.

One last innovation just before World War I, was the introduction of ruby red and emerald green personalized glass souvenirs. In most all cases, one had to order a minimum of 12 dozen or 1 gross but for state fairs, major cities, and other attractions; 144 sold easily. Today, many companies require over a thousand of a particular design as a minimum order. Ruby red tourist items including shot glasses were also available through much of the Depression era.

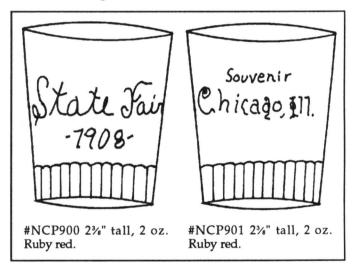

#NCP900 2⅜" tall, 2 oz. Ruby red.

#NCP901 2⅜" tall, 2 oz. Ruby red.

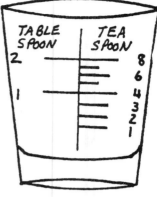

#WAB009 Obverse.

#WAB010 Obverse.

Reverse for both.

Each are 2¼" tall and 2 oz. Color: clear or light purple tinge. Molded writing.

#WSA120 2¼" tall, 2 oz. Sample Glass. Etched white writing.

#WSB035 2¼" tall, 1¾ oz. Sample Glass. Etched white writing.

#WSC092 2¼" tall, 2 oz. Sample Glass. Etched white design.

#WSC190 2" tall, 1¾ oz. Sample Glass. Etched white design.

#WSG020 2⅛" tall, 2 oz. Sample Glass. Etched white design.

#WAD005 2¼" tall, 1¾ oz. Sample Glass. Etched white design.

#WSD003 2" tall, 1¾ oz. Sample Glass. Etched white writing.

#WSF010 2⅛" tall, 2 oz. Sample Glass. Etched white design.

#WSF030 2⅛" tall, 2 oz. Sample Glass. Black & White label applied to the bottom (inside glass).

#WSH035 2" tall, 1½ oz. Sample Glass. Etched white design.

#WSY020 2" tall, 1½ oz. Sample Glass. Etched white writing. Note: "Markley" spelled in reverse is "Yelkram."

#WSK040 2¼" tall, 2 oz. Sample Glass. Etched white writing.

#WSH050 2⅛" tall, 2 oz. Sample Glass. Etched white design.

#WSS005 2" tall, 1½ oz. Sample Glass. Etched white writing.

#WSM020 2⅛" tall, 2 oz. Sample Glass. Etched white design.

#WSO005 2⅛" tall, 1¾ oz. Sample Glass, 13 flutes. Etched white design.

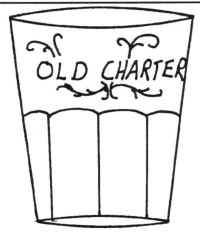

#WSO009 2¼" tall, 2 oz. Sample Glass, 9 flutes. Etched white design.

#WSO080 2⅜" tall, 1¾ oz. Sample Glass. Etched white writing.

#WSR060 2¼" tall, 2 oz. Sample Glass. Etched white writing.

#WSR090 2¼" tall, 2 oz. Sample Glass. Etched white writing.

#WSR104 2⅛" tall, 1¾ oz. Sample Glass. Etched white writing.

#WSS023 2⅛" tall, 1¾ oz. Sample Glass. Etched white writing.

#WSS040 2¼" tall, 2 oz. Sample Glass. Etched white writing.

#WSW082 2⅛" tall, 1¾ oz. Sample Glass. Etched white design.

#WAA002 2¼" tall,
1½ oz. Molded clear
writing.

#WAB007 2" tall, 1 oz.
Molded clear writing.

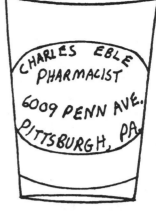

#WAE008 2¼" tall, 1½ oz.
Molded clear writing.

#WSB003 2½" tall, 2 oz.
Sample Glass. Etched
white writing.

#WSB006 2¼" tall, 2 oz.
Sample Glass. Etched
white writing.

#WSB008 2¼" tall, 2 oz.
Sample Glass. Enamelled
white writing.

#WSC058 2¼" tall, 2 oz.
Sample Glass. Etched
white design.

#WSC064 2¹⁄₁₆" tall,
1½ oz. Sample Glass.
Etched white design.

#WSD008 2⅜" tall, 1¾ oz.
Sample Glass. Etched
white writing.

#WSG120 2⅛" tall, 1½ oz. Sample Glass. Etched white writing.

#WSH120 2¼" tall, 2 oz. Sample Glass. Etched white design.

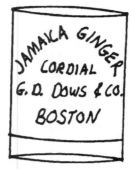

#WSJ010 1⅝" tall, 1 oz. Sample Glass. Clear molded writing.

#WSL030 2¼" tall, 2 oz. Sample Glass. Etched white design.

#WSN030 2⅜" tall, 2 oz. Sample Glass. Etched white design.

#WSO022 2¼" tall, 1½ oz. Sample Glass. Etched white design. 12 flutes.

#WSO028 2⅛" tall, 1½ oz. Sample Glass. Beaded white writing.

#WSO030 2" tall, 1½ oz. Sample Glass. Etched white design.

#WSO035 2⅛" tall, 1½ oz. Sample Glass. Etched white writing.

#WSO060 2¼" tall, 1½ oz. Sample Glass. Etched white design.

#WSS002 2¼" tall, 1½ oz. Sample Glass. Etched white design.

#WSS140 2¼" tall, 1½ oz. Sample Glass. Etched white design with inner panels.

#WST020 2³⁄₁₆" tall, 1¾ oz. Sample Glass. Etched white writing with inner panels.

#WST040 2½" tall, 2 oz. Sample Glass. Etched white design.

#WSW018 2⅛" tall, 1½ oz. Sample Glass. Etched white writing.

#WSW032 2⅛" tall, 1½ oz. Sample Glass. Etched white writing.

#WSF024 2¼" tall, 1½ oz. Sample Glass. Beaded white writing.

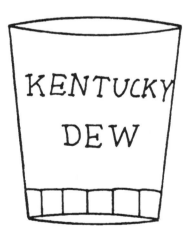

#WSK028 2⅛" tall, 1½ oz. Sample Glass. Etched white writing. 12 flutes.

Chapter VII:

THE PROHIBITION YEARS 1919-1933

Upon passage of the 18th Amendment, the country was immediately divided into 10 separate departments. Each was led by an assistant commissioner. Each and every state was assigned a federal prohibition director, assistant, and legal advisor. Initially 1,500 gun-toting revenue agents were employed by the federal government; this number would double as time went on. The appointment of as many as 3,000 total agents was still woefully inadequate even with the help of the Coast Guard; Customs; Immigration; and state, county, and local police.[63]

Liquor poured in from the outside and illegal distilling from deep inside America's borders was gearing up to set records in that form of unlawful production. Most that entered from the outside was smuggled in from Canada and Mexico by car, truck, train, boats, and airplanes. Liquor was concealed under seats, car hoods, and even wired to the chassis. Upon one's person, illegal liquor was carried in rubber tubing around one's waist, in hollow canes, in hip flasks, stashed in inner pockets, hidden in boots, and even concealed in baby carriages! Illegal spirits were also carried in by pack animals, floating barrels, and packaged in products such as jars, barrels, cans, and even in the poles of Christmas trees. European smugglers met 'rum-runners' out at sea while the long established rum trade from the West Indies was on the rise again. Legal Canadian imported liquor doubled during Prohibition while the illegal trade increased many times over that.

Home brewing and distilling became one of America's favorite hobbies. Section 29 of the Volstead Act allowed manufacture and possession of fruit juices for home consumption. Winemaking at home flourished and grape production grew steadily throughout Prohibition. Grape juice was often labeled: "Caution: Will Ferment and turn into Wine." Labelling also warned that if concentrated grape juice was dissolved in water and stored for 20 days that it would turn into wine. With the amount of grape juice sold, it was estimated by the government that 678 million gallons of wine were drunk in the five years 1925-1929; 3 times as much compared to the 5 years leading up to Prohibition. Related wine-making products sold very well: grape crushers, presses, fermenting tubes, gelatins (used to settle sediments), crocks, kegs, bottles, and corks. All perfectly legal and it added up to 220 million in sales in the five years 1925-1929.

Wine production and consumption was hardly anything compared to beer. Billions of gallons of home-brewed beer were made during the so-called "Dry" years. Brewing materials like malt syrups, malts, hops, yeast, bottles, caps, capping machines, rubber hosing, alcohol gauges, vats, and so on all sold extremely well. National production figures of malt syrup in 1926 and 1927 peaked at nearly 888 million pounds and only 10% had any commercial use. Malt syrup advertisements and labels pictured on cans illustrated drunken animals such as mules, camels, and donkeys; common themes on shot glasses in the 1940's and 1950's.

Furthermore, Americans distilled alcohol in their homes too. It was obviously illegal but steam cookers, coffee percolators, wash boilers, and simple tea kettles were all used to distill alcohol. A one-gallon portable copper still complete with coils could be purchased for $5. to $6. at a local department or general store; or by mail from a Sears or Wards catalog. With the use of a United States Farmer's Bulletin from before Prohibition (readily available at most any local library), one could easily observe and learn the process of distilling alcohol from grains, vegetables, fruits, and most things the pilgrims had experimented with 300 years earlier. Every other home based on annual sales of these copper boilers owned one. Bathtub Gin was the all-around favorite home-distilled beverage during the great dry-wet spell. Bathtub Gin was a concoction of boiling mash made up of fruits, grains, and possibly vegetables; glycerine and juniper oil were the other additives. All ingredients were thoroughly mixed together in a bathtub. Nearly all juniper oil consumed in America was imported from Italy and Austria and served little purpose except for flavoring gin. From 1920-1925, juniper oil imports increased by just over 22%. The taste of gin was easily disguised in cocktails.

> Mother's in the kitchen
> Washing out the jugs;
> Sister's in the pantry
> Bottling the Suds;
> Father's in the cellar
> Mixing up the hops;
> Johnny's on the front porch
> Watching for the cops.
>
> (Popular Prohibition tune; unknown author)

Aside from the small time operations experimented with in one's home; major illegal stills were further perfected, constructed, and put into operation. From the years 1876 up through 1919, Internal Revenue agents seized 66,794 illegal stills. That seems to be a significant number until it is compared to the seizures in the 1920's. In the late 1870's seizures numbered about 1,000 per year; less than 500 through most of the 1880's per year as temperance was growing; about 2,000 at the turn of the century; and a peak of about 4,000 in 1915. The first three years of Prohibition seizures surpassed the 54,000 mark combined. The all time high for a one year period was a little over 29,000 in 1925![64]

It might cost about $50,000. to set up a large distilling operation of 10-20 stills each capable of

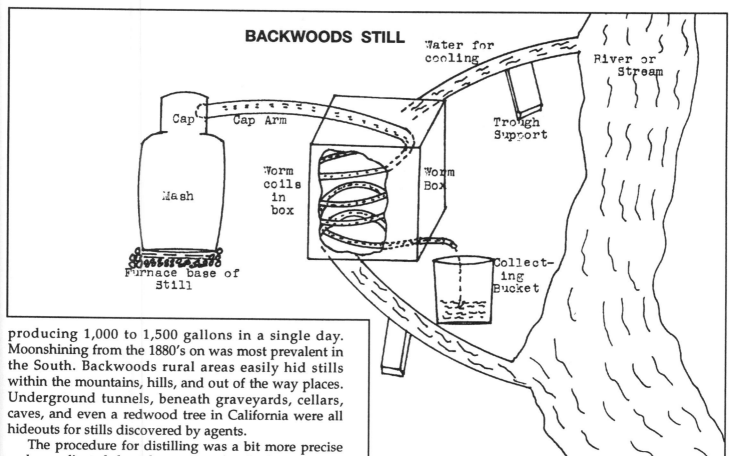

BACKWOODS STILL

Water for cooling

River or Stream

Cap

Cap Arm

Trough Support

Mash

Worm coils in box

Worm Box

Collecting Bucket

Furnace base of Still

producing 1,000 to 1,500 gallons in a single day. Moonshining from the 1880's on was most prevalent in the South. Backwoods rural areas easily hid stills within the mountains, hills, and out of the way places. Underground tunnels, beneath graveyards, cellars, caves, and even a redwood tree in California were all hideouts for stills discovered by agents.

The procedure for distilling was a bit more precise and complicated than the perpetual still of old but the basic process changed little. Alcohol boils at 172 degrees. The ground corn mash is poured into boiling water and heated to this temperature. The starchy mixture gelatinizes and it is allowed to cool for about an hour. On the top of the mush within the still, one gallon of ground rye and 3/4 gallon of malt is added. After another hour of waiting, the rye and malt is stirred into the mush about a half a foot and a gallon of warm water is then added. This slow gradual mixing prevents overcooking of the malt which would destroy the batch or at the very least reduce its quality. One additional hour of soaking ending with a thorough stirring and then the final steps are ready. Dissolved yeast along with a little more malt is the last addition. The final heating and capping is all that is remaining. The cap is placed only when vaporization begins. The alcoholic steam moves through the copper worm-tubing which is usually surrounded in a worm box of water for cooling. The cooling transforms the vapor to liquid immediately which is collected in a bucket or pail.[65]

Some of the devices utilized for stillmaking were rather unique. Zinc garbage cans made excellent stills and sewer grates forged of heavy iron were great for standing stills over a fire. Large steam boilers also worked well as stills. Car radiators readily available at junk yards and auto parts stores were adapted as condensers. Natural gas burners eliminated much of the smoke of wood fires which in turn reduced the risk of detection. With this new technology and perfection of distilling methods, alcohol purity during the best runs

varied from 140 up to as high as 190 proof.

The 18th Amendment did allow for some legal uses of alcohol but all were abused. Alcohol could be manufactured for insecticides, explosives, varnishes, and other products. Prohibition regulations required that alcohol be denatured; or in other words, totally unfit to drink. Furthermore it had to be marked by a skull and crossbones and labelled as "Poison." Labels naturally were falsified as denatured and sold to bootleggers. Commercial production was also allowed for medicinal and religious uses. A huge increase in medicinal prescriptions were written by accommodating physicians; thousands more than before the dry years. Sacramental wines found their way into illegal liquor shops.

The denatured regulations caused serious health problems especially for those who attempted to extract the alcohol from industrial products for human consumption. Highly toxic industrial alcohols were not diluted or mixed properly. Thousands of deaths occurred from alcohol poisoning particularly from wood products containing alcohol. "Jake Foot" was a neurological disorder caused by a mixture of gingerroot, alcohol, and a denaturing chemical tricresyl phosphate. Jake Foot often led to paralysis. About the only health benefit of Prohibition was that in its first few years, the death rate for cirrhosis of the liver was cut in half.

Bootlegging, smuggling, and speakeasies had long been in affect to combat previous state and local option

69

#PDP014 standard gold & black designs (enamelled-1960's). Prohibition regulations required denatured alcohol to be labelled with this symbol.

laws. In the 1920's it was so much more profitable. Prior to national prohibition, straight whiskey or drinks mixed with a shot (1 ounce) cost 10-15¢ or two for 25¢. In the early 1920's, the price went as high as 50¢ or more for a single shot; but as illegal supplies increased, prices nearly went back to what they were before Prohibition. The pricing did make it somewhat more difficult for the poor to obtain; however, some spent what little cash in their possession on alcohol.

Alcohol could be obtained wherever organized crime had an outlet. Outlets varied from place to place much like today's crack houses since the odds of discovery increased the longer one remained rooted in one place. An outlet could be a candy store, tea room, clubs, laundries, and drugstores were especially ideal since legal dispensation in the form of prescriptions was allowed. Other places consisted of cigar stores, soda fountains, delicatessans, confectionaries, backrooms of barber shops, general stores, malt shops, hardware stores, five and dimes, behind partitions in shoe stores, garages, motorcycle delivery agencies, paint shops, fruit stands, grill rooms, restaurants, groceries, vegetable markets, athletic clubs, dance studios, boarding houses, and nearly every type of business conceivable.

Alcohol was most easily consumed in cities. The speakeasy was sort of like an urban saloon but unlike the saloons of old, it tended to serve the affluent who organized them into private clubs. They could easily afford the expensive prices for imported or the best domestic liquors at 3 to 6 times the prior prices. Fancy speakeasies were decorated with neon lighting, water fountains, jazz musicians, and other forms of entertainment were present. Nightclubs where the entrants were carefully screened were established and local police were easily bribed to leave them alone.

In New York alone, there were a minimum of 5,000 speakeasies by 1922. In 1927, the police commissioner of New York, Grover A. Whelan estimated that there were 32,000 speakeasies within the city. Congressman William P. Sirovich placed the figure closer to 100,000. Speakeasies were usually prepared for raids with hidden wine cellars and emergency plans for disposing of alcohol. One such place called the Club 21 had an electrical device that dumped shelves of liquor behind the bar; the bottles dropped down a shoot and shattered on sharp angle irons projecting out from the sides; and finally landed in a pile of rocks and sand in which the liquor seeped through, leaving no evidence.[66]

At the extreme opposite of the elegant speakeasies were the rough bars usually located in the worst part of town; rougher than the past saloons. Raw liquor and industrial products like wood alcohol were served. Sometimes drinks were drugged to knock customers out and then they were robbed. Killers and organized crime figures could be found in these places. It might serve as headquarters where strategy and hits were planned. Multiple murders and car to car shootouts between rival gangs or with federal agents were not uncommon in the big cities. The Tommy Gun was effective for cutting one down from a fast moving street car. Sam "Golf Bag" Hunt, a bootlegger got his nickname from carrying a Tommy Gun in a golf bag. A larger violin case could easily hide the weapon of choice of Prohibition gangsters. Women wouldn't dare get involved or attempt to break up one of these operations for they too might be riddled with bullets or sent down a river or lake with nothing but cement shoes.

Organized crime flourished during Prohibition since the prices of alcohol skyrocketed initially. Great profits could be made from smuggling, bootlegging, moonshining, and robberies. Railcars were robbed frequently of medicinal and sacramental liquors. Government warehouses stocking great quantities of alcohol were prime targets. Prohibition soon became the height of lawlessness in America. Prohibition agents were easily bribed and were a common sight in speakeasies.

The Anti-Saloon League gave up what came to be a serious concession to Congress. To obtain the support of Congress, Prohibition agents were not subject to civil service rules which allowed whatever political party in favor to appoint agents and commissioners. Poorly qualified people were appointed strictly on the basis of political favor rather than minimum qualifications. A large amount were fired, replaced, and convicted of a long list of offenses, usually collaboration and bribery. There were some hard core agents who did not succumb to the pressures who followed in the tradition of Pussyfoot Johnson; Eliot Ness and his band of "Untouchables" for example. The team of Izzy and Moe were quite successful at tracking down bootleggers. The gossip reporter Walter Winchell was yet another colorful character. History tends to favor the more ruthless organized crime figures such as Al Capone, Big Bill Dwyer, George Remus, Jack Diamonds, Dutch Schultz, and so on. Liquor history would be incomplete without exploring some of these interesting figures more closely.

The business Al Capone assumed was long in operation before he was working his way up the ranks of organized crime. Big Jim Colosimo followed by his nephew Johnny Torrio worked with prostitution, racketeering, bribery, and gambling in the old saloons around Chicago prior to Prohibition. Illegal liquor was an added bonus to the existing business. Capone with his growing reputation and special skills became the chief lieutenant and enforcer for Torrio. Capone narrowly escaped a hit upon him from George "Bugs" Moran and his rival gang. Capone's chauffeur was killed while Capone himself narrowly escaped.

Torrio eventually pleaded guilty to bootlegging charges in 1925 but was given 5 days to arrange his affairs before confinement. In that time he was shot 4 times by Bugs Moran's gang. Torrio did survive and had had enough of the business. He turned operations over completely to Al Capone. By the end of 1926, Capone ruled Chicago. He held control of numerous businesses including nightclubs, speakeasies, and other private clubs. The illegal trade was his main money maker and with approximately 1,000 gunmen working under him, there was little in the way of liquor business in and around Chicago that he did not control. Estimates at his annual income were placed at 100 million dollars but Capone himself admitted that 30 million of that was used for bribes and payoffs each year.

Capone was actually held in favor by the public but much of his popularity was lost after the infamous Valentine's Day Massacre. On February 14, 1929; 7 members of Moran's gang were lined up along a wall by 5 men which seemed like a routine raid. Two of the five were uniformed policemen and the remaining three were plainsclothesmen. The 7 men were frisked, relieved of their weapons, and then were systematically executed by 100 bullets and a few shot gun blasts. A later investigation revealed that only 8 bullets had missed their target. It was one of the severest sanctions against his competition and went down in history as the worst gangland killing during Prohibition.[67]

Capone was spending the majority of his time in his Miami mansion but enforcers were more and more determined to get him especially after the brutal Valentine's Day killing. Capone was picked up later in 1929 on a concealed weapon's charge and served 10 months of a 1 year sentence. His notorious career was finally shattered when he was put away for good on charges of federal tax evasion in October of 1931. In prison his venereal disease intensified and was partially responsible for his insanity and eventual death.

Jack "Legs" Diamond picked up his name from being fast on his feet as a young thief. Many consider him one of the most barbarous of all gang leaders during the Prohibition era. He had a long history of crime involvement and illegal liquor was simply another outlet for more illegal profit. Aside from bootlegging, Diamond was into hijacking, kidnapping, extortion, gambling, and other rackets as well.

Diamond often tortured those he held for ransom by burning the bare soles of their feet with matches and cigarettes. He himself killed many of his rivals and ordered hits upon them too. He was not well liked but lived long enough to earn a new nickname: "The Clay Pigeon." He obtained this new name from the underworld because he amazingly was shot so many times and still survived. His luck ran out in 1929 when he was finally shot to death in the city of New York.

George Remus was a successful lawyer in Cincinnati and bought into the liquor business in 1920. Remus had government permits for distilling medicinal liquor. On top of that he purchased warehouses that were properly bonded to store liquor and a drug company to dispense it. Of course temptation overcame him and he sold millions of gallons to associate bootleggers. He bought the Jack Daniels distillery in St. Louis, Missouri that had been relocated there when Tennessee went dry.

Remus naturally had his own gang of killers and gunmen as well as issuing bribes to various officials, inspectors, and the like. His main illegal dispensing operation was located in a place called Death Valley Farm in southern Ohio. This location suffered a serious raid and Remus was convicted, sentenced to three years in prison, and fined $30,000. He was able to bribe the warden for special treatment but later the warden himself was convicted for conspiracy and accepting bribes.

While in prison, Remus' wife spent over two million dollars of his money and began seeing and eventually sleeping with Franklin Dodge. Dodge happened to be the Prohibition agent who had had much to do with Remus' arrest. Remus was not at all happy with these circumstances and shot his wife soon after his release from behind bars. He was found not guilty by reason of insanity and was forced to spend 6 months in an asylum. He lost his position, wealth, and his past associates had to find other suppliers. As a result, Remus was left without money, his businesses, or contacts. He moved to Kentucky and spent a quiet life with a second wife until he died in 1952.

"A boy has never wept nor dashed a thousand kim."
Last words of Dutch Schultz dying from multiple gunshot wounds.

Arthur Flegenheimer alias Dutch Schultz and sometimes known as the "Bronx Beer Baron" was also from New York City. Like so many others, he was long involved with organized crime before passage of the Volstead Act. Schultz was an associate of Big Bill Dwyer and served as Dwyer's most important customer. Schultz was yet another brutal crime leader. He murdered or had those murdered who refused or failed to give him his cut or piece of the action within his territory. The police of Manhattan attributed at least 138 killings to Schultz but there were probably dozens more. Schultz like Jack Diamond, was gunned down before Repeal.

The most powerful man in the rum-running industry was William Vincent "Big Bill" Dwyer of New York. Many cities boasted with pride when they claimed to be the wettest in the nation; New York was tops, even over Chicago. Dwyer was yet another shrewd businessman and invested enormous capital from illegal liquor sales into hotels, nightclubs, a brewery, gambling casinos, professional hockey and football teams, and racetracks. Along with that he ran illegal lotteries, number games, and sports' betting operations.

Big Bill's speedboats were outfitted with airplane engines that propelled his boats at speeds in excess of 60 mph; fast enough to outrun any Coastguard vessels. Dwyer allied with all the major New York mafioso families and bribed agents, policemen, and the Coastguard. In fact, Dwyer had four Coastguard ships on the take which added to his importing success. Eventually an undercover agent in Dwyer's gang obtained evidence on the Coastguard but promised them immunity if they would testify against Dwyer. They did and Big Bill was sentenced to two years in prison. Meanwhile he conducted his business while in prison through intermediaries and contacts. When his term was up, his business unlike George Remus' was still well intact with little in the way of change.[68]

Walter Winchell was born in 1897 in New York City and grew up working around theaters and vaudeville. He joined the Navy briefly in 1917. His vaudeville career was not going well but his experience did make contacts. He was able to find new employment as a drama critic and then as popular gossip columnist working his way up to bigger and better newspapers. He also occasionally worked part-time as a radio gossip commentator.

Winchell was not prone to violence but out of fear carried a gun with a legal permit. During Prohibition, he knew personally many gangsters including the violence and wars between them. The FBI was highly suspicious of Winchell since at times he found out more than they. Winchell's car was also equipped by New York Police Department permission with a short-wave radio receiver, red lights, and siren. Winchell often beat the police to the crime scenes. Winchell for safety's sake was careful to stay on the good side of gangsters and portrayed them favorably in his articles. He was also around to report on major busts and seizures of illegal liquor. Winchell was simply New York City's most popular reporter during the Prohibition years.

"There's sad news here. You're under arrest."
Fond saying of Isidor (Izzy) Einstein.

Isador "Izzy" Einstein was a 40 year old postal clerk who weighed 250 pounds but only stood 5'5" tall. His good friend Moe Smith was a former boxer and now managed a boxing club and owned a cigar store. The two became prohibition agents in New York City. The team of Izzy and Moe were most famous for their clever disguises. They dressed as fruit and vegetable vendors, derelicts, actors, football players, fishermen, coal shovellers, meter inspectors, conductors, sailors, firemen, and a hundred others. They exposed illegal caches, dispensers, and host of others associated with illegal liquor. Izzy loved the limelight of acting and the team's popularity but Moe tended to shun the publicity.

From 1920-1925, Izzy Einstein and Moe Smith arrested nearly 5,000 lawbreakers, raided 3,000 speakeasies, and confiscated over 5 million bottles of illegal liquor worth about $3.00 per bottle. Up to 1926, ⅕ of all prosecutions involving 18th Amendment violations in New York City were arrests made by Izzy and Moe. That was an incredible figure considering that there were a total of 178 prohibition agents operating in New York. Izzy and Moe were too good at what they did. They embarassed their superiors with their numerous successful arrests and widespread popularity. Both were dismissed for political reasons and became insurance salesmen. Wayne Wheeler stuck up for them but it did little good.[69]

Eliot Ness was born in Chicago in 1903 and graduated from the University of Chicago. He was hired in 1929 by the United States Justice Department to lead Chicago's Prohibition Bureau. He was only 26 but his duties were clearly marked out to investigate and harass Al Capone. Ness led a 9-man team of young men in their 20's like himself. All were highly dedicated and unbribable which earned them the name: "The Untouchables."

They obtained notoriety from serious raids on illegal breweries, speakeasies and so on (especially those thought to be part of Capone's empire) which attracted public attention. Ness actually invited reporters to raids for first-hand pictures and stories. Ness and his band of loyal followers were able to obtain supporting evidence to prove that Capone was evading taxes. It is doubtful that Capone would have been convicted or even tried without the work of The Untouchables. After Prohibition, Ness went on to head the Alcohol Tax subdivision of the Treasury Department and held other government positions through the 1940's. From there, he went into private business.

Overall the Prohibition Bureau with agents like Ness did manage some success. Many lost their lives as enforcers of Prohibition. 55 prohibition agents, 15 Customs and Immigration officials, and 5 Coastguard's men; all were killed in the line of duty. During the years 1920-1933, 150 bootleggers and associated criminals were shot and killed and many more wounded; 600,000 arrests were made; 10 million gallons of distilled liquor was confiscated; over 1 billion gallons of malt liquor seized; and 1¾ million distilleries from small time household to large commercial-size stills were closed. The illegal trade was so firmly rooted by the early 1930's that both production and consumption was up to about where it was prior to World War I.

Key American figures such as labor leader Samuel Gompers, Mayor LaGuardia of New York, and millionaire Pierre Dupont were ardent antiprohibitionists. President Harding loved whiskey and served it to his friends during weekly poker games at the White House. A new movement against Prohibition and the mobilization of their forces was growing through the 1920's. The Crusaders, The National Association Opposed to Prohibition, The Moderation League, The American Legion, and The American Federation of Labor to name a few. The most powerful formed by Dupont and over 50 other millionaires was the Association Against the Prohibition Amendment (AAPA).

The Anti-Saloon League remained strong until the death of Wayne Wheeler in 1927. Bishop James Cannon became president of the League in 1928 but the League's image was tarnished when Cannon was accused of adultery and misappropriation of campaign funds in 1930. Another blow to temperance was the popularity of illegal drinking and a new attitude by America's women.

In the 1920's, drinking was no longer associated with saloons and drunkards. Instead it became glamorous and the illegal aspect made it appealing by adding a degree of intrigue and danger. The success of Hollywood and early moving-picture making exhibited drinking as the 'in thing.' Drinking was fashionable, sophisticated, and followed the new trends of color, radio, and the phonograph. A man impressed his friends and added to his reputation by being able to obtain the best imported or the highest quality American liquors.

The 19th Amendment granted women suffrage and many including the Anti-Saloon League believed that Prohibition would never be overturned with women eligible to cast votes. What they did not count on was the changing attitudes of women and the leadership of Pauline Sabin, the wife of Charles Sabin who happened to be the Treasurer of the AAPA. Pauline Sabin was the first woman to serve on the Republican National Committee and was a chief organizer of the Women's Organization for National Prohibition Reform. It obviously angered the WCTU but that organization was steadily losing membership and support; and was in a serious state of decline. The new modern woman was influenced by the entertainment industry, aspirations of the wealthy, and a socially acceptable drinking attitude. The old WCTU was a generation apart, out of fashion, and out of touch with the modern woman.[70]

Liquor was a key issue in the 1928 presidential election. Herbert Hoover advocated top priority in enforcing and defending the 18th Amendment rather than making any radical changes. Al Smith wanted to change the definition of "intoxicating liquors" within the Amendment to exclude beer and wine. Hoover won and was able to endorse a new law that was enacted: The Jones "Five and Ten Law." This law increased penalties for bootlegging to 5 years in jail and/or $10,000 fine. It also threatened purchasers with felony convictions if they failed to reveal their sources. It was supported by the Anti-Saloon League but not by the common people. Ratting on, narking, or informing was generally unacceptable and considered cowardly. Simply put, Prohibition was on the downswing.

While Prohibition and its supporters were failing, the AAPA was growing. They argued that repeal of the 18th Amendment would reduce tax burdens and help recovery of the stock market crash by putting people back to work. Brewers and distillers supported the AAPA wholeheartedly and added money to the cause. Antiprohibitionists pointed out the corruption of public officials, distrust in government, rampant widespread drinking, criminal empires, the interference of an individual's rights, and that Prohibition threatened a new wave of communism similar to the Bolshevick Revolution in Russia. Not only was Prohibition responsible for increases in crime but the most compelling argument of all was that studies showed that about 11 billion dollars was lost in tax revenue. Enough money that would have balanced the budget in 1933. It was a strong case for when America was drowning in its worst depression.

By 1932, membership in the AAPA numbered over half a million and they heavily supported Franklin Deleanor Roosevelt in the presidential election. Both Hoover and Roosevelt supported Repeal but the nation's depression was more of an issue than liquor. Hoover did lose much of his former dry supporters but Roosevelt fought harder in his campaign for Repeal. Hoover, his administration, and his republican supporters were blamed for the Great Depression and without effective policies to end it. Democrats, especially those in support of Repeal won great victories along with Roosevelt and replaced a republican majority in Congress.

Roosevelt legalized beer sales within a week of his inauguration. On December 5, 1933, the 21st Amendment (Repeal) was short and sweet with only two sections: "The eighteenth article of amendment to the Constitution of the United States is hereby repealed."[71] The first section automatically allowed the importation, manufacture, and sale of alcohol. "The transportation or importation into any State, Territory, or Possession of the United States for delivery or use therein of intoxicating liquors, in violation of the laws thereof, is hereby prohibited."[72] The second section delegated to states all authority for regulation of alcohol. Enough states ratified this reversal of the 18th Amendment to satisfy the ¾ necessary. Repeal had won convincingly. Knocked down temporarily but never out, John Barleycorn immortalized in the writings of Jack London was given new life.

Prohibition certainly had devastating effects on the shot glass and barware industry. The need for them tumbled in the late teens and early 1920's. One could simply no longer advertise liquor products upon anything since it was obviously illegal to do so. This as mentioned in the prior chapter completely ended whiskey sample glass production and advertising. Barware sales dropped drastically but stemware held its own. Rich, affluent, upperclass citizens continued to serve drinks such as wine in elegant hand-cut stemware. The fancy speakeasies needed a steady supply of quality crystalware.

The time period after Prohibition more than made up for the lack of shot glasses during. The beginning of Depressionware and decorated tumblers was soon on the rise. Along with them, the ending of Prohibition was responsible for a large quantity of Post-Repeal, antiprohibition, and humorous propoganda that poked fun at the forces against intemperance and celebrated Repeal. The decorations applied to shot glasses were popular targets for such sentiments. One need only turn the pages to the next two chapters for examples.

Chapter VIII:
DEPRESSION GLASS 1920-1940

"Brother, can you spare a dime?"
         (beggar's common Depression phrase)

A generation had lived without experiencing a depressed national economy. There had been no serious economic downswings since the 1890's in the United States. Several factors were responsible for the Great Crash of the stock market in October of 1929 and the consequent Great Depression that followed in the 1930's.

The Agricultural Marketing Act of 1929 set up a Federal Farm Board along with an appropriation of $500. million. The board could then make loans to cooperatives and supposedly help farmers market their crops more effectively. Instead, this newly established board had no control over production or of sustaining prices which in turn left no protection from overproduction or poor economic conditions. The support farmers were fighting for left them quite unhappy. Furthermore, the Hawley-Smoot Tariff enacted in 1930 increased rates on many farm goods as well as manufactured products. President Herbert Hoover signed the bill despite widespread opposition by most leading economists. The resulting tariff raised the cost of living, encouraged inefficient production, and hampered exports of agricultural surpluses. This only served to provoke foreign bitterness and retaliation in return.

Through the first ¾ of 1929, the stock market soared but the strong upward movement was due primarily to widespread speculation and manipulation of securities. The banks as did the savings and loans of the 1980's; gambled on loans for strictly speculative purposes and very risky investments. A variety of other warning factors included overstocking of business inventories, a 4-fold drop in consumer spending, declines in commodity prices, and increases in interest rates. Meanwhile the stock market illogically boomed despite many of these poor economic indicators.

On October 23, 1929; security prices fell drastically from frenzied, panic selling. The panic was temporarily halted when a group of New York bankers united under the leadership of J.P. Morgan & Co. They pooled their resources to hold the market together.

"The fundamental business of the country…is on a sound and prosperous basis."
  President Herbert Hoover (4 days before the Great Crash).

On Black Thursday, 12,894,650 shares were dumped on the New York Stock Exchange breaking the previous record.[73] Five days later on October 29, 1929; the volume soared to 16.4 million shares. The Great Crash was here. Between September 3, 1929 to November 13, 1929; The Dow Jones Industrial Average dropped from 381 to 199. The Average would eventually bottom out at 36 in 1932. The Gross National Product at $103. billion in 1929 was cut nearly in half in 1933.[74]

4,305 banks closed between 1929 and 1932 robbing depositors of 2¾ billion dollars. The savings of millions who had little else in the way of resources were lost. The Great Crash was a shock to many especially business leaders who believed that the continued prosperity of

#DMS604 standard. Black design. 1930's, celebrating Repeal. Also in Depression Tall versions (#DTP302, black design or red & blue design, page 31, Shot Glasses: An Amercian Tradition).

#DMS500 2½" tall, 2 oz.

Reverse of #DMS500, 501, and 502.

Set of 3 humorous shot glasses depicting Carry Nation wielding an ax and anti-saloon and anti-drinking sentiments. Black & white labelled design around each glass. Early 1930's (page 37, Shot Glasses: An American Tradition).

America was insured. From 1929-1932, 100,000 businesses failed including many in the glass trade. Corporate profits fell from $8.4 billion in 1929 to $3.4 billion in 1932.

4 million Americans were unemployed by October of 1930, 1 year after the crash; but things only worsened. 7 million were out of work a year later and then a peak of 11 million by the fall of 1932. Fully ¼ of the labor force was unemployed by 1933. With savings lost or exhausted, middle class and working class people in great numbers not only lost their jobs but their homes and eventually adequate food and nutrition for their families.

Foreclosures, droughts, dust storms, and other poor weather conditions for farming forced America from what had once been a surplus agricultural producing nation to one of inadequacy. Prices too fell so low that farmers could not make enough profit to pay their mortgages and debts. Wheat sold for $2.00 a bushel right after World War I and the price still remained over $1.00 in 1929. In the midst of depression, the price fell to 38¢ per bushel. Cotton, corn, and other grains fell drastically as well.

Hoover displayed public optimism and tried to convince the nation that the Depression would not last long. To combat it; taxes were reduced, government projects and public works were created to employ more, businesses were persuaded to keep both prices and wages up, and the Federal Reserve Board and the Farm Board were called upon to fund price stabilizing efforts.[75] Nothing seemed to work and the Democrats jumped on Hoover and the failures of recovery efforts. "Hoovervilles" were small communities of poverty built of cardboard, packing crates, and whatever materials could be found. A "Hoover Blanket" was yesterday's newspaper and a "Hoover Flag" was an empty pocket turned inside out.

Bread lines were long and soup kitchens existed in nearly every major city. Both ran out of food frequently. Private charity and unemployment were incapable of meeting even a small percentage of America's needy. Large percentages of the population were cut off from all sources of relief simply because of the lack of resources. Children often picked through garbage and

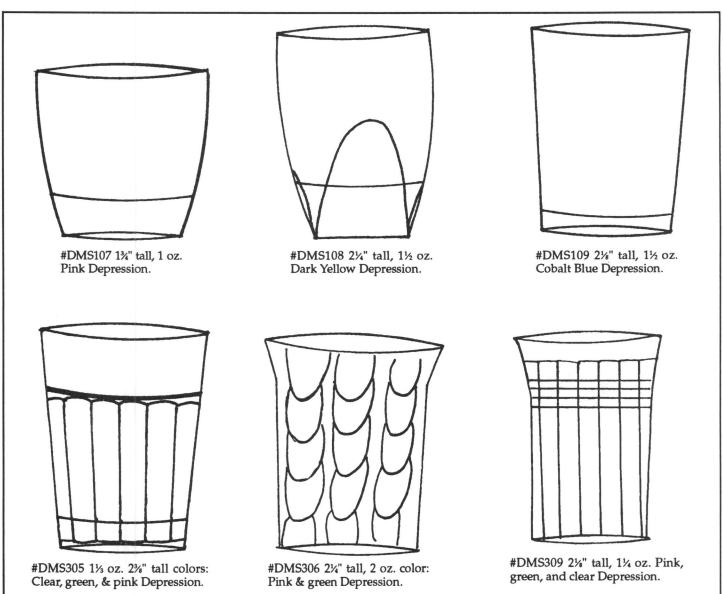

#DMS107 1¾" tall, 1 oz. Pink Depression.

#DMS108 2¼" tall, 1½ oz. Dark Yellow Depression.

#DMS109 2⅛" tall, 1½ oz. Cobalt Blue Depression.

#DMS305 1⅓ oz. 2⅜" tall colors: Clear, green, & pink Depression.

#DMS306 2¼" tall, 2 oz. color: Pink & green Depression.

#DMS309 2¼" tall, 1¼ oz. Pink, green, and clear Depression.

dumpsters for rotting food. Families lost their dignity first in bread lines and then resorted to begging.

The Great Depression not only gripped America but spread to Europe which forced them to dump American securities in their own desperate need for money. Many allies were unable to make payments to America on old WWI debts owed. England and every major power except Italy, France, and the United States were forced off the gold standard due to runs on the most powerful international banks. The Depression wore on with no light visible at the end of the tunnel.

"We are at the end of our rope. There is nothing more we can do."

President Herbert Hoover (on the last day of his presidential administration).

Hoover was finally voted out of office in the election of 1932. Franklin Deleanor Roosevelt was full of energy, vitality, and charm. Many thought that when he was stricken with polio and lost the use of his legs in 1921, his career would be ended. That was certainly not the case.

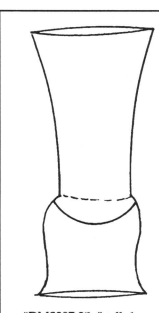

#DMS207 2¹⁵⁄₁₆" tall, 1 oz. Green, blue, & pink colored Depression glass.

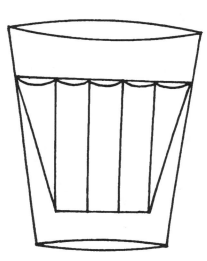

#DMS310 2¼" tall, 1½ oz. Thick green-colored Depression glass.

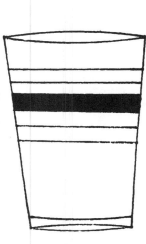

#DWE041 2¼" tall, 1¼ oz. 5 etched lines on a light ruby red-colored Depression glass.

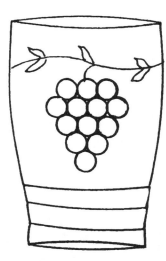

#DWE012 2⅜" tall, 1½ oz. Etched grape pattern on clear Depression glass.

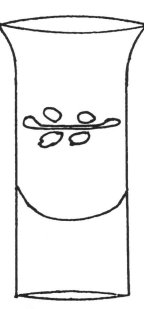

#DWE014 Depression Tall, clear etched pattern.

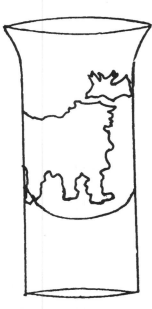

#DWE015 Depression Tall, clear etched pattern.

"The only thing we have to fear is fear itself."
FDR; March 4, 1933 (inauguration address).

Roosevelt acted fast. Within a week bills were passed incredibly fast through both houses of Congress on emergency banking regulations, a reduction in veteran's expenses, and of course the legalizing light wines and beers. Celebrations of Repeal and a new optimism despite the middle of the Depression breathed through America. "Happy Days are Here Again" celebrating Repeal and FDR's victory assailed signs, headlines, and advertising media like shot glasses. Humorous items as well were present.

From the beginning, FDR roused America into a new sense of nationalism and confidence in government. Roosevelt turned his efforts to agriculture and manufacturing in an attempt to turn them around. He was able to institute mortgage relief, price controlling, government buying of excess crops to maintain prices, and cutting down on farm production and soil banking to stabilize and even raise prices. Droughts were even more prevalent in the mid-1930's and actually aided the strategy of decreased production and increased prices. Likewise industry was favored by successful bills by Congress giving private trade associations authority to fix prices, divide markets, and stabilize production. Fair

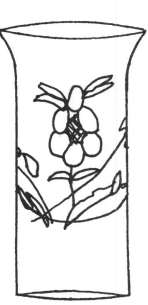

#DWE016 Depression Tall, etched design on ruby red glass.

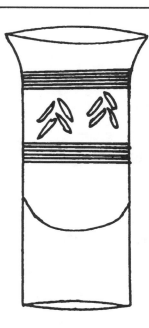

#DWE017 Depression Tall, clear etched pattern.

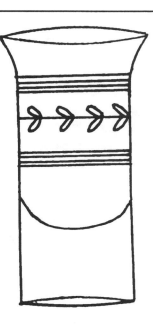

#DWE018 Depression Tall, clear etched pattern.

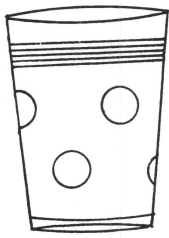

#DWE019 2¼" tall, 2 oz. Etched pattern on a clear Depression glass.

#DPG049 2¼" tall, 2 oz. Inside panels on a clear Depression glass.

#DMS603 standard. Black enamel design on a frosted Depression glass.

competition was temporarily exempt from anti-trust laws. To win the support of labor, federal guarantees were given to the rights of trade unions to organize and institute collective bargaining.

Under the early days of Roosevelt's New Deal, $3.3 billion was appropriated to the Public Works Administration which employed thousands. Other public and conservation groups were created such as the Civilian Conservation Corps. One of the most famous and ambitious projects under these new organizations was the Tennessee Valley Authority. Powerhouses, electricity, dams, trees, and other improvements were all built or planted as both a conservation and industrial effort.

The New Deal rekindled confidence above all else that the depressed nation surely needed. Its combination of capitalist order managed by the government along without hindering the personal freedoms of its people was able to stimulate economic growth. By the end of the 1930's and the early beginning of the next decade, America was able to dig itself out of its worst Depression in history.[76]

To focus on the glass industry in particular, the Depression era was certainly an interesting period. More than most industries, an intense battle between hand-made glasshouses and machine-made glassware began. Mass produced machineware won simply on price alone. It was cheaply-made and usually flawed, but the

#DMS007 Depression Tall, 3 yellow bands in the middle & 4 green bands.

#DMS313 2¼" tall, 1¾ oz. Yellow, red, orange, black and molded clear lines on a Depression glass.

#DTP103 Depression Tall, red & white dots around glass.

#DTP306, 307, and 308. All are Depression Tall with enamelled white designs. U.S. Glass Co. 1930-1935. (DTP310 was also produced by U.S. Glass 1930-1935).

#DTP310 Depression Tall, red & black enamelled design.

price was 2, 3, 4, and even more times less than expensive quality hand-made crystal. Most glass companies that did not convert to automation could not compete with such prices as two for a nickel tumblers. A series of mergers, buyouts, and outright failures were no exception to the glass industry as well as other manufacturing firms.

Initially, there was a big boost to the glass industry as a whole during the post WWI period but then the Depression hit. The inexpensive machine-made glassware still sold surprisingly well but price cutting and competition to the point of selling glass products less than the cost to produce did not help matters. The profit margin was much less on low-priced glass and companies needed to sell more to maintain those profits; a difficult goal to achieve in a depressed economy. One last obstacle to the survival of American glass companies was that imports nearly tripled for hand-cut glass. The new automation was able to compete to some extent with these cheap foreign products.

Despite these troubles, more patterns, shapes, and colors were produced during the Depression than in any other time period in American glass history. Depression Glass encompasses American-made glassware in two decades, the 1920's and 1930's. Though many glass historians end at three, a fourth period named: "The Modern American Period" has been added by others. Colorful Depression Glass was geared to common people and since it sold so cheaply, typical middle class and working class Americans could easily afford it. In fact, complete table sets numbering well over 50 matched pieces were available and purchased from stores, mailorder, factory outlets, and wherever else they were sold.

Modern Americans particularly women who had a direct say on what or what would not be present in their homes, shunned the gaudy art and carnival glass for the new simple colors of the new Depression Glass. Color was also added to cars, a distinct improvement from the dreary black colors of old. Appliances were no exception either to color enhancement and the modern kitchen was thrust into a new fad. As with carnival glass, the new colorful glass was given away at carnivals and fairs. Entire sets were given away with major purchases such as furniture and appliances. Smaller pieces were packed away as prizes or bonuses in cereal boxes, oatmeal cans, laundry soap boxes, and other containers.

Depression era glass was not only a time of technological advances in machinery, but also a period of color mastery and the beginnings of widespread commercial enamelling. The chemistry of coloring from both metallic and nonmetallic agents was perfected and added to large batches of glass. Ordinarily, separate smaller pots were used for each color. Nonmetallic coloring agents such as sulphur, selenium, tellurium, and phosphorous were generally used in combination with metals to heighten or intensify certain colors.

Manganese imparts a purple color and is the oldest known dating back to Egyptian times around 1400 B.C. Copper was also used by the ancient Egyptians and produces a lighter blue. The rich dark blues are associated with cobalt, the most powerful deep blue coloring. Cobalt blue glass was found in King Tutankhamen's (King Tut) tomb; in stained church windows of the 12th century; and used as a pottery glaze for both the Tang and Ming Dynasties of China. Lead of course produces the finest of clear crystal. Silver also produces crystal but not as fine as lead. Chromium imparts a dark green color. Iron, long an undesirable impurity tends to make glass a dull brown or murky

Set of 3 Depression Tall (DTP001, 002, & 003) with stickers attached to the exterior. Reverse of sticker shows a nude side (multicolored stickers).

#DTP301 1 oz. Depression Tall Black writing, black horse, & yellow rider or Blue writing, red horse, & red outline of rider.

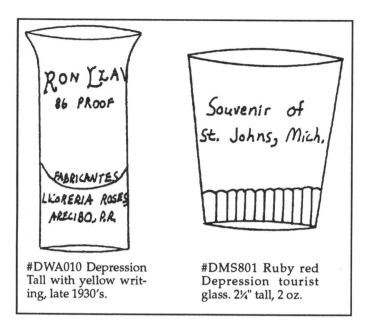

#DWA010 Depression Tall with yellow writing, late 1930's.

#DMS801 Ruby red Depression tourist glass. 2¼" tall, 2 oz.

green; but iron can be mixed with chromium for dark green bottle glass or with sulphur and carbon to make amber. Rarer colors such as nickel for smoky-colored glass and uranium for a prominent yellow were used a little. Brilliant ruby-red glass was created from gold and this discovery was credited to Andreas Cassius in 1685.

It seems as though every coloring agent or technique for non-opaque glass was utilized by Depression Glass companies. Pink was the most common and since it is not as scarce as other colors, it is usually valued less than green or amber. Green was a close second in terms of quantity and the majority of popular Depression patterns were manufactured in both pink and green. In terms of beauty as well as value, many would argue that cobalt blue and ruby red are overwhelming favorites. Obviously, anything requiring gold is certainly worth more but the deep rich coloring of both ruby and cobalt possess their own merits.

Other innovations and decorating techniques added to the mass-produced colored glassware. Some copper wheel engraving survived as well as acid-etching, but machines were developed to do some etching. Needle etching by machine was fairly cheap in that fine lines were cut through a wax coating and subsequent etching with acid. Crackling was another technique and was completed by plunging a hot glass into cold water to induce numerous cracks over the entire surface of the glass. The cracked glass was then reheated and reformed in the mold. Frosting consists of an all-over acid etch to impart a murky light gray somewhat opaque in coloring. Both crackling and frosting were advertised as giving glassware "a Cool" or frosty appearance to combat hot summer days. In all actuality, neither did anything in the way of temperature reduction.

New techniques of enamelling were invented or refined; especially those involving machines. Finely ground enamels suspended in liquid mediums like thick paint were applied to glassware in exactly the right position by machines. Each color was applied separately and when finished, the glass was slowly heated to about

550 degrees to fuse the enamel. Slow cooling was the final step. Crests, monograms, and similar designs were also applied through apertures cut within a silk screen. A few rare stickers depicting nude women but only on the inside were also applied to later Depression Glass in the 1930's. The side showing is of a fully-clothed woman while the inner side of the sticker contains the nude side.

Shot glasses or small whiskey tumblers were frequently present in large sets of identical patterned glassware. Companies patented their patterns but unpatterned glass was once again made by all especially common flute-cut glasses. More shapes and varieties of shot glasses were made during the Depression era than any other. A special Depression shot glass was made in great quantities. Most held exactly an ounce and were about ⅛" shorter than 3" in height (listed as "Depression Tall" beneath pictures). Depression Tall shot glasses were etched, enamelled, frosted, or produced in one simple color such as pink, green, ruby red, cobalt blue, etc. This new tall glass lasted well into the 1940's but disappeared before a resurgence in the 1980's. Since Prohibition lasted through much of the Depression, liquor advertising would not return until the time period after Repeal namely the mid-1930's. A few specially made tourist or personal advertising shot glasses particularly in ruby red were also available to buyers in the modern American period of glass. The remaining chapter pictures miscellaneous shot glasses produced during the 1920's and 1930's including company histories of those making shot glasses during this time period.

Libbey

After World War I; Westlake Machine Company, a subsidiary of Libbey refined a light bulb machine that in turn was similar to Owens' bottle machine. What was unique about it was that it mass produced tumblers without seams by blowing them into a paste mold. It was basically an inexpensive process to make tumblers in great numbers especially for hotels, institutions, restaurants, etc. It is for the most part the way they make them today only with more modern, better, and longer-lasting machinery. Shot glasses naturally are made this way.

When Edward Libbey's associates assumed control of the company in 1920; the name officially changed to Libbey Glass Manufacturing Company. J.D. Robinson Sr. followed by his sons Joseph and J.D. Jr. were responsible for the company through much of the Depression years, particularly when Edward Libbey died in 1925. Meanwhile in 1924, Libbey patented a tumbler advertised as "Safeedge" or "Safeguard." The moil or excess glass was burned off of these new safeedge tumblers and the heat-strengthened rim was guaranteed with a replacement if the rim ever chipped. Two grades of glass were used for safeedge tumblers, an expensive lead and a cheaper limeware. Shot glasses were also made under this new patent for tumblers.

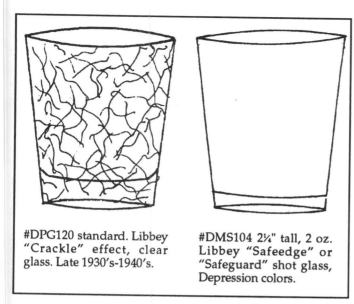

#DPG120 standard. Libbey "Crackle" effect, clear glass. Late 1930's-1940's.

#DMS104 2¼" tall, 2 oz. Libbey "Safeedge" or "Safeguard" shot glass, Depression colors.

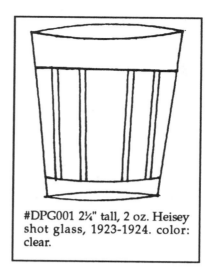

#DPG001 2¼" tall, 2 oz. Heisey shot glass, 1923-1924. color: clear.

As with most glass companies, Libbey had a rough time in the early 1930's. In 1931, the Robinson's hired A. Douglas Nash, former sales executive of the Tiffany factory in Corona, New York that went out of business. In 1933 a line of glass introduced known as the Libbey-Nash series was a very expensive hand-cut crystal that sold from $15. to $2,500. per dozen. The Victoria cameo engraved chalice which required 80 hours of hand engraving on a copper wheel was the most expensive piece. It was excellent finely-made brilliant glass but needless to say, the timing of its introduction was way off. Sales were terrible during the Depression and Libbey lost so much money that it nearly destroyed them. Nash left and joined the Pittsburgh Plate Glass Co.

In 1935, Owens-Illinois originally formed by Edward Libbey, Michael Owens, and associates bought out Libbey Glass for 5 million and continued to operate the company as a subsidiary. In 1937, Libbey won a contract with Walt Disney to produce and decorate tumblers with Snow White and the 7 Dwarfs. The movie was immensely popular and 8 separate tumblers with a picture of each title character enamelled upon the surface were filled with cottage cheese and shipped to thousands of dairies across the country. The immense popularity of the decorated tumbler many believe had its beginning here. Libbey survived the Depression with its successful mass production of tumblers.[77]

A.H. Heisey Company

During the Depression, Heisey followed the trends and produced colored glassware, milk glass, a bit of iridescent, and some silver trimming and rimming. In 1936, they patented their own acid-etching method. A glass article was soaked in an 80% solution of hydrofluoric acid up to an hour which etched surfaces at different elevations. They were quite successful at etching which pulled them through hard times and into the next decade.

The most notable Heisey etched patterns were Heisey Rose, Ivy, Minuet, Orchid, Plantation Ivy, and Rosalie. Heisey did market some barware including shot glasses for hotels, clubs, and restaurants. In 1956, the Heisey factory closed for good and the existing molds were sold to Imperial Glass of Belaire, Ohio. Imperial used many of them to continue producing Heisey's patterned glass.[78]

Steuben Glass Company

During World War I, the Steuben Glass Works was classified by the government as a nonessential industry producing luxury items. Like so many others, they were denied rights to purchase raw materials needed for the war effort. Rather than closing, Frederick Carder sold the company he had founded to the Corning Glass Works in 1918. Carder remained on as managing director but loss of control of the plant as well as the loss of his son in World War I action who he had planned on succeeding him, were two very serious blows. With further resolve and a long vacation, Carder continued on and was given a free-hand at the factory. Carder's temper and gruffness were legendary.

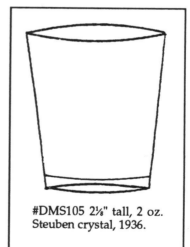

#DMS105 2⅛" tall, 2 oz. Steuben crystal, 1936.

"Can't you see that damn' flat spot on the goblet's bowl? They'll make it rotten enough in the blowing room without your help! You're nothing but a damn' Yankee kid, and more trouble to me than a row of 'ouses!"

Frederick Carder speaking to a young apprentice named Paul Gardner.[79]

Surprisingly, Steuben joined the color fad of the 1920's. From 1920-1927, Steuben produced glass in all of the ordinary Depression colors. In 1933, Arthur A. Houghton assumed the presidency of Corning and all production in color ended.

"Our company's mission...is to produce the most perfect crystal the world has ever known."

Arthur A. Houghton Jr.

Corning scientists developed a new optical glass for lenses. This new grade of crystal was of unusual purity and brilliance. Not only was it the finest of crystal but it also possessed an inherit workability. Houghton decided to use it exclusively for all glassware made by Steuben. The new glass had such a degree of clarity that it was virtually free of flaws and nearly as pure as natural spring water. One need only set a piece of Steuben glass next to any other fine crystal object to see the difference. One would be hard-pressed to find crystal made anywhere in the world to rival that of the new Steuben. Occasionally a few Steuben shot glasses have been produced.[80]

Monongah Glass Company

Monongah had its beginning in Fairmont, West Virginia in 1903. They operated quite successfully especially after the downturn of World War I. By the late 1920's, they were probably in the top 5 manufacturers of pressed and blown tumblers in the country. A good deal of their glassware was trimmed in gold or platinum by hand which was a very expensive process. Sales fell

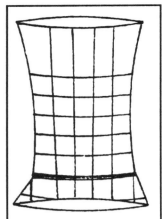

#DPG070 1¾ oz., 2½" tall "Key Block" pattern Monongah Glass Co. colors: green & rose-pink late 1920's-early 1930's

sharply at the end of the decade and by the early 1930's, they were threatened with bankruptcy. The company's interest was purchased then by Hocking Glass Company.

The Federal Glass Company

First organized in Columbus, Ohio in 1900, Federal Glass began as a hand-made glass operation but soon changed completely to automation. They were one of the first to do so and as a consequence, they were never in danger of

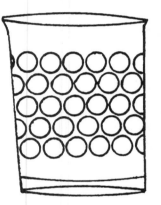

#DPG081 1⅞" tall, 1 oz. Federal "Raindrops Optic Design" pattern. Clear or green in color, 1929-1933.

#DPG031 standard. Federal "Platinum Band" or "Gold Band" patterns. 1936-1938. Reproduced in 1961 by Anchor-Hocking as "Gold Edge" or "Hairline" patterns in 1961.

Federal advertisements first appeared in various publications in 1944. Note, glasses with the 'F' inscribed within a shield are Post-Depression.

collapsing during the Depression. As early as the mid-1920's, Federal was one of the biggest if not the biggest manufacturer of machine-made tumblers and jugs in America.

Coloring was no stranger to Federal. In 1926, they mass-produced machine-made green tumblers. They soon added all of the other popular Depression colors of pink, blue, amber, red, and so on. In shot glasses, these colors are present in Depression Tall glasses which Federal also mass-produced. Federal also experimented with platinum and gold banding or rings mostly in the later 1930's as colors were phased out. These rings or bands appear on many tumblers including those of shot glass size into the later 1940's.

In 1944, Federal added a trademark (see ad) which consisted of an 'F' inscribed within a shield. According to Federal, this new "Hi-Bright Tumbler" was remarkably stong and able to resist rough handling. The firm also expanded into the food service industry and supplied restaurants, bars, fountains, institutions, and hospitals. In 1958, they became a subsidiary of the Federal Paper Board Company and continue to produce glass products today.

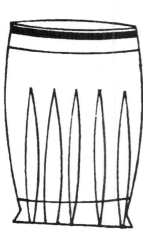

#DPG076 2¼" tall, 1¼ oz. Federal, 1930's-1949. Clear with 2 gold bands & square bottom.

#DPG077 standard. Federal "Rose" pattern. Depression colors, 1936-1938.

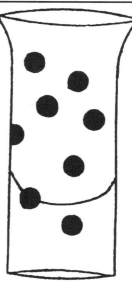

#DPG071 Depression Tall, Federal "Polka Dot" pattern 1936-1938. (white, black, red, green, blue, yellow, or orange)

#DPG072 Depression Tall, Federal "Palm Beach" pattern. 10 bands in fiesta colors: Chinese red, ivory, yellow, Yale blue, & Jade green.

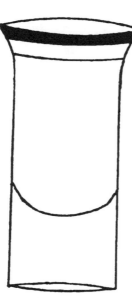

#DPG073 Depression Tall, Federal "Platinum Band 2" or "Gold Band 2" patterns.

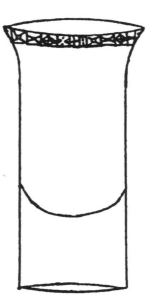

#DPG074 Depression Tall, Federal "Excrustation" pattern. Gold or Platinum designs.

a#DPG075 Depression Tall, Federal "Wally" pattern, 12 bands of gold or Platinum.

Hazel-Atlas Glass Company

Two separate side by side factories in Washington, Pennsylvania merged in 1902. The Hazel Glass Company and The Atlas Glass and Metal Company combined to form Hazel-Atlas and offices were set up in Wheeling, West Virginia. Both factories continued to produce glass but other locations were added and geared to automation. Like Federal, Hazel-Atlas was also fully automated by the mid-to-late 1920's and suffered little during the Depression.

Hazel-Atlas was selling so many tumblers and tableware that additional factories were added in Ohio, Pennsylvania, and West Virginia in the 1930's. Hazel-Atlas did not produce any colored glassware until a bit of green in 1929. It sold well and other colors were added the following year. One of the famous Hazel-Atlas shot glass patterns was the "White Ship," "Angel Fish," and "Windmill." All three were a light cobalt blue or amethyst with a fired on white enamel and came in a variety of tumbler sizes, pitchers, plates, and other tableware. From the time the company was established much of their glass contains the easily defined tradmark "  ." Hazel-Atlas sold out to Continental Can in 1956 who in turn sold the operation to Brockway Glass Company in 1964.

#DPG010 1½ oz., 2¼" tall "Lydia Ray" pattern Hazel Atlas Glass Co. Depression colors late 1920's-early 1930's

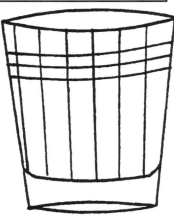

#DPG011 1½ oz., 2¼" tall "Modern Tone Wedding Band" pattern Hazel Atlas Glass Co. Depression colors 1934-1942

#DTP200 "Sailboat," #DTP201 "Angelfish" (pictured), and #DTP202 "Windmill" patterns. Hazel-Atlas Depression Tall shot glasses. Cobalt blue & Amethyst. See <u>Shot Glasses: An American Tradition</u>, page 39.

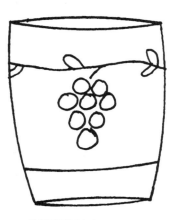

#DWE011 1¼ oz. beverage sham 2" tall Bartlett Collins Sapulpa Glass Co. mid-1930's colors: rose & green

original advertising by Bartlett Collins:

English version: Beverage Sham capacity 1¼ oz. 12 doz. in carton wt. 20 lbs.

Spanish version: Para Licores capacidad 1¼ oz. 12 dnas. cartor Pesos 20 lbs.

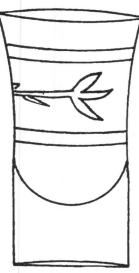

DWE050 1½ oz. whiskey tumbler or shot glass clear w. etching Bartlett Collins Sapulpa Glass Co. 2⅞" tall mid-1930's.

Bartlett-Collins Company

The first glass factory west of the Mississippi River was formed by the unlikely team of Bartlett and Collins. Collins was experienced in the glass industry and was from America's Eastcoast while Bartlett had made his money in Oklahoma from oil. The firm established a glasshouse in Sapulpa, Oklahoma and by 1931 were still the only factory operating out West.

Since the company's location was physically closer to the Mexican border than any other; Bartlett-Collins had a virtual monopoly on the Mexican market. Most every advertisement listed by them was also cross-referenced in Spanish. Bartlett-Collins' only Depression glass colors were pink and green but they had experimented with rose and amber lustres and a bit of iridescence prior to the Depression. Early on they were famous for lamps which they produced in colors, iridescence, enamelled,

and engraved. In the 1940's and on, they became a major decorator of tumblers especially with western themes including many shot glass designs.

Imperial Glass Corporation

When carnival glass faded, Imperial produced fairly large amounts of mold-pressed imitation-cut glass in crystal and Depression colors. Further decorations with cuttings, etchings, and gold trims were also applied to their products. Slow to automate, Imperial shut down production and closed its doors in 1931. The company was able to reorganize from the Imperial Glass Company to the Imperial Glass Corporation.

New lines of pressed colored glass were added. The two most notable that survived well after the

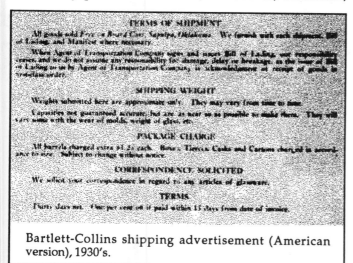

Bartlett-Collins shipping advertisement (American version), 1930's.

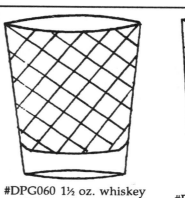 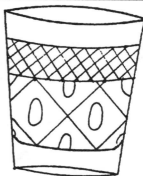

#DPG060 1½ oz. whiskey tumbler or shot glass 2¼" tall Imperial Glass Co. "Diamond Quilted" or "Flat Diamond" pattern 1920's-1931 colors: green & pink.

#DPG061 1½ oz. whiskey tumbler or shot glass 2¼" tall "Cape Cod" pattern Imperial Glass Co. colors: clear and carnival 1920's-1931.

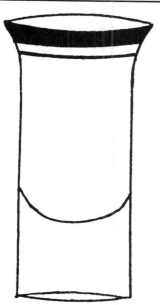 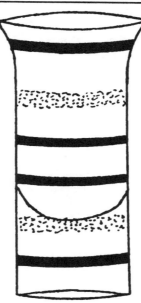 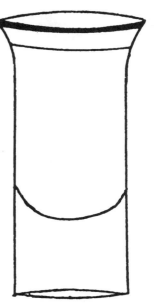

#DPG100 Depression Tall, Bartlett-Collins "Gold Band" pattern. Yellowish-gold bands. Late 1930's-1948.

#DPG1010 Depression Tall, Bartlett-Collins "Band Ice" pattern. 4 yellowish gold bands & 2 frosted bands. Late 1930's-1948.

#DPG102 Depression Tall, Bartlett-Collins "Gold Hairline" pattern. Gold bands. Late 1930's-1950.

Depression were "Cape Cod" and "Imperial Candlewick" developed in the mid-1930's.

Imperial in 1958 purchased the molds of Cambridge and Heisey. The molds were not destroyed but were utilized to produce reissues of both company's former patterned glassware. In the 1960's, a resurgence of "New Carnival" glass enabled Imperial to issue new iridescent glass in the original molds that had long rested in cold storage. Much of the new carnival glass was marked to avoid confusion with the old. In 1973, Imperial became a subsidiary of Lenox who for a while continued to make many of Imperial's old lines of glassware.[81]

Jeannette Glass Company

In 1901, the Jeannette Glass Company was named for the city in which it was established; Jeannette, Pennsylvania. Production began as bottles exclusively but the manufacture of bottles nearly ended by World War I. Jeannette switched to tableware and after the war, they progressively became more and more automated. By 1927, all hand operations ended in favor of complete automation at Jeannette. A few older Jeannette articles have a trademark which consists of a "J" inscribed within a triangle (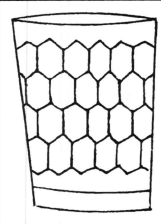).

The move to automation was a fortunate one particularly when one considers that the majority of hand glasshouses either changed or went out of business during the Depression years. Jeannette was the first to produce large amounts of machine-made colored Depressionware. Jeannette experimented a little with iridescence before adding green lines in 1925. Pink followed in 1927. Up to 1932, Jeannette made large quantities of pink, green, and clear machine-made Depression glassware. Many colors were added throughout the remaining 1930's including

#DPG030 2" tall, 1 oz. Jeannette "Hex Optic" or "Honeycomb" pattern. 1928-1932 Pink, green, or clear in color.

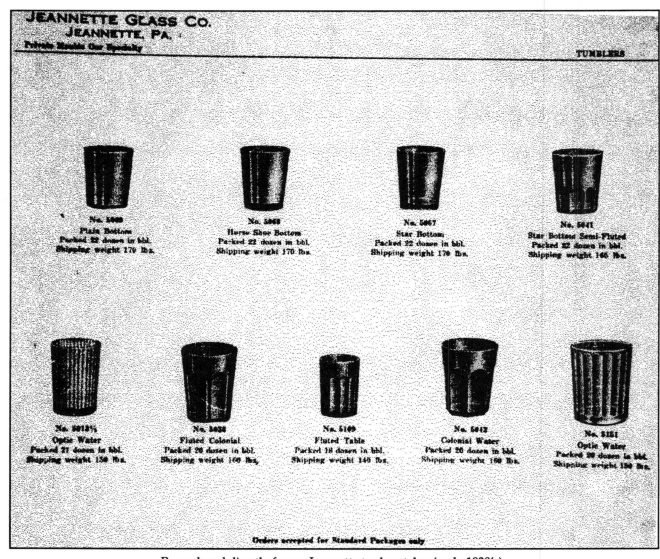

Reproduced directly from a Jeannette trade catalog (early 1920's).

an opaque green, an opaque blue, ultramarine, amber, and others. Some pink items were revived and reissued in the 1940's and 1950's. In 1961, the company purchased the former McKee factory also in Jeannette, Pennsylvania and continues to make glass today at this location.

Westmoreland Glass Company

The Westmoreland Specialty Company was established in Grapeville, Pennsylvania in 1890. They developed a new pressing method dubbed "Cut and Shut." An object was pressed upside down into a mold and the plunger travels through the knockout piece inside the top. Next it is snapped up on the bottom and the top is warmed in and finished. The final stage consisted of warming the vessel to close in or "Cut and Shut" the bottom of the object with a snap tool.[82]

For a while Westmoreland produced some foods for their glass containers but they dumped the foods to concentrate exclusively on glass production. Westmoreland joined the transparent color bandwagon of the 1920's with amber, green, blue, rose pink, and a few experimental combinations such as crystal and black or black and topaz. An opaque white had been one of the

#DPG090 1½ oz. whiskey tumbler or shot glass 2¼" tall. "English Hobnail" pattern. Westmoreland Specialty Co. 1930's. colors: pink, green, blue, & amber; reissued in crystal in the 1960's.

company's favorites from nearly its beginning but they did issue some pieces in an opalescent blue in the early 1930's. By the mid-1930's, as the popularity of colored glass decreased, Westmoreland returned to primarily colorless or crystal glass production. Westmoreland was one of the few rare hand-made glass operations to survive the Depression. The company lasted until 1985 and have always been famous for their "English Hobnail" patterns. Many earlier designs have been reproduced throughout the company's history.

Hocking Glass Company

Hocking opened their first glass factory in Lancaster, Ohio in 1905. They naturally began as a small hand operation but for the most part converted to automation in the mid-to-late 1920's. Aside from common tableware and tumblers, Hocking produced glass globes for lanterns, lamp chimneys, and novelty glass items. They were one of the first to advertise "Two for a Nickel" tumblers for machine-made mass produced tumblers.

Early on, Hocking went full force into machine-patterned glassware. Throughout the 1920's, Hocking produced glass in green, pink, amber, blue, canary, topaz, etc. An opaque white was added in 1932. In terms of different types of shot glass designs produced during the Depression, Hocking is the outright winner. Numerous patterns such as the "Roulette," "Colonial Knife and Fork," and "Mayfair Open Rose" were produced in colors; but for shot glasses and other tumblers, there are more banded ring patterns than any other. In fact, most Depression enamelled ring patterns are most likely a Hocking product or invention though a few others such as Federal and Bartlett-Collins also made some ringed glassware.

Hocking in the later 1930's branched into the container business with beer bottles and glass baby food

#DPG042 2¼" tall, 1½ oz. Hocking "Mayfair Open Rose" pattern. 1931-1936. Pink only–reproduced 1970's-1980's (see Chapter X). Also pictured is a correction from Shot Glasses: An American Tradition, page 32. (other colors besides pink are reproductions).

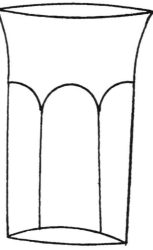

#DPG043 1½ oz. whiskey tumbler or shot glass. 2½" tall. "Knife and Fork" pattern. Hocking Glass Co. colors: green, pink, & crystal. 1934-

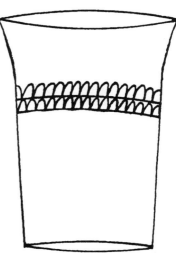

#DPG044 1½ oz. whiskey tumbler or shot glass. 2½" tall, Hocking Glass Co. colors: green & pink. 1936-1938. "Roulette" pattern.

#DPG024 standard. Hocking "Stripe Decoration 64" pattern. Red, yellow, & black stripes from top to bottom.

#DPG025 standard. Hocking "Stripe" pattern. 1932-1933. Red, yellow, black and green stripes from top to bottom.

#DPG026 standard. Hocking "All Over Stripes" pattern. 1933. Alternating bands of red & white or blue & white stripes.

#DPG027 standard. Hocking "Multi-colored Stripe" pattern. 1933. Red, yellow, & green stripes.

#DPG028 standard. Hocking "Striped Decoration 42" 1933. Bands of yellow at top, black at bottom, red & clear in the middle.

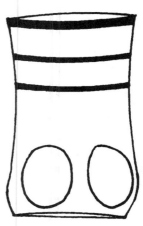

#DPG029 standard. Hocking "Crystal Punch Line" pattern with or without stripes; red, yellow, & black with stripes. 2¼" tall, 1½ oz.

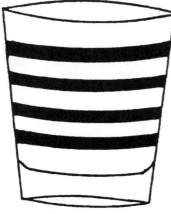

#DPG034 standard. Hocking "4-color Banded Decoration" pattern 1934-1938. Tangerine, yellow, green, & blue stripes from top to bottom.

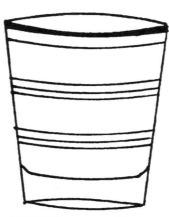

#DPG035 standard Hocking "Gold Band" & "Gold Hairline" pattern. 1933. Gold line near top & gold rim; rest of bands are clear.

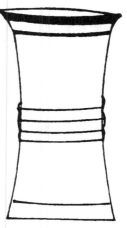

#DPG036 standard. Hocking "Gold Band & Hairline" pattern. 1933. 2¼" tall, 1½ oz. 2 gold lines near top; rest are clear.

jars. Hocking was also able to take over a few companies that went bankrupt during the Depression including the Lancaster Glass Company, the Monongah Glass Company, and the Standard Glass Company. In 1937, Hocking merged with the Anchor Cap and Closure Corporation of Long Island City, New York; another huge manufacturer of containers. With the merger, the new Anchor-Hocking Glass Corporation easily became the nation's leading container manufacturer.

Beginning in the 1940's, Anchor Hocking began using a trademark found upon the bottom of most of their glassware. It consists of an "H" and an anchor " 𝖩 ." Later in the 1980's, a new trademark with an anchor inscribed within a square is also present on the underside of glass objects " 🔲 ." Today Anchor-Hocking Corporation has over 20 manufacturing plants and is the world's largest manufacturer of glass tableware. In terms of shot glass production, they are only second to Libbey in producing the "standard" size.

The remaining part of the chapter illustrates other shot glasses produced during the Depression era or America's Modern Period of glassware.

#DPG040 Depression Tall. Hocking "Stripe" pattern. Late 1920's-1930's. Applied color bands of red & white.

#DPG047 standard. Hocking "Diamond & Lattice" pattern. 1933. Red and white enamelled design.

#DPG037 standard. Hocking "Striped Decoration 88" pattern. 1933. White, yellow, red, green, & red stripes from top to bottom.

#DPG038 2¼" tall, 1½ oz. Hocking "Striped Decoration 88" pattern. 1933. White, yellow, red, green, & red stripes from top to bottom.

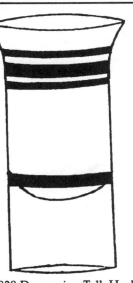

#DPG039 Depression Tall. Hocking "Stripe Decoration 97" pattern. 1933. Widest band near the top is white, the other three are red.

#DPG041 standard. Hocking "Ring" pattern. 1920's-1933. Several color patterns.

#DPG045 standard. Hocking "Crossed Spirals" pattern. Black & white spiral bands. 1933.

#DPG046 standard. Hocking "Balloon" pattern. 1933. Green & orange circles around glass.

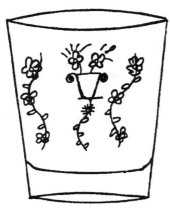

#DWE020 2" tall, 2 oz. Duncan & Miller "First Love" pattern. Etched. 1930's-early 1940's.

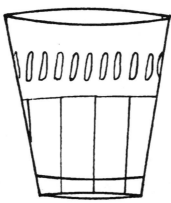

#DPG021 2¼" tall, 2 oz. Duncan & Miller "Waterford" pattern. 1930's. Clear.

#DPG022 2¼" tall, 2 oz. Duncan & Miller "Astaire" pattern. 1930's. Clear.

#DPG032 & 033 standard. Federal "Glacier 21" or "22" patterns. 1936-1938. Platinum Bands (032) or Gold Bands (033).

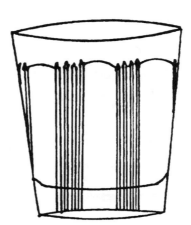

#DPG050 2¼" tall, 2 oz. Fostoria "Sunray" pattern. 1935-1944 clear. Picture is a correction from Shot Glasses: An American Tradition, page 33.

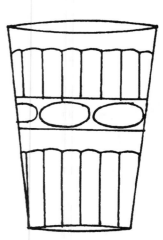

#DPG051 2½" tall, 2 oz. Fostoria "Hermitage" pattern. 1935-1945. Depression colors.

#DPG065 2¼" tall, 1¼ oz. New Jersey Glass Company. 1930's. Light Copper Blue.

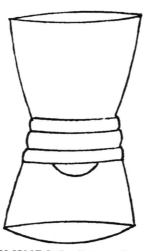

#DMS307 2½" tall, 1 oz. Bryce Brothers Co. 1930's. Clear.

#DWA006 Depression Tall with orange writing. Late 1930's.

Chapter IX:
CONSERVATISM AND THE BEAT GENERATION:
THE 1940'S & 1950'S

At the turn of the 20th century, America was on a wave of growth funnelled by invention, technology, industrialization, and the rise of powerful large corporations. The glass industry was no exception as many smaller companies were overtaken by larger, more machine-production oriented corporations. Big business would argue that the standard of living was raised for all including the common or skilled laborer such as a glass blower or machinist as the nation progressed.

Naturally, a new set of problems arose. Irresponsible wealth and the abuse of power was blamed on big business. The exploitation of the worker, urban poverty, prejudice, and lack of equality for women were more critical examples. The exploitation and depletion of natural resources, pollution, and international disputes followed the new America.

The United States sought to solve some of these problems by government regulation of business, conservation or replacement of resources, establishing national parks and preserves, alleviating poverty, and isolating itself from world problems. All did not work particularly when America entered World War I and the Depression. The war was won but the victory was hollow, unconvincing, and bitterness remained. The Depression only increased poverty to its highest level in American history. FDR's New Deal fought hard against poverty and the new wave of experimentation brought confidence back. The domestic victories were pushed aside as foreign threats to national security were extremely serious especially with the bombing of Pearl Harbor by the Japanese on December 7, 1941.

America under FDR had done its best staying out of the war hoping that Hitler and the Axis would be defeated without American intervention. Four days after the Pearl Harbor bombing, Germany and Italy declared war on America and Congress returned the favor with the same declaration. The nation's factories geared for war and in the first 6 months of 1942, over $100 billion was placed by the federal government for war contracts. Fully ⅓ of America's economical output was for war-related goods. The gross national product because of the new war effort more than doubled from 1940 to 1945. National debts soared too but unemployment was nearly eliminated. Tires, gas, meat, and other essentials had to be rationed through coupon allotments.

Minorities such as blacks and hispanics were able to find more work but wages were lower and the most menial tasks were reserved for them. Over 6½ million women were hired in factories with the shortage of men fighting the war overseas. At the time, protest about disparity in women's lower wages compared to men's was unheard of. Most women considered their jobs patriotic and temporary until the end of the war. The huge increase in double-income families had much of its beginning here and the lack of day care centers for the care of children was certainly not an issue.

> "The defeat of Germany...will leave Japan exposed to overwhelming force, whereas the defeat of Japan would not by any means bring the war to an end."
> Winston Churchill (On a visit to Washington D.C., December 1941).

On the war front, America had to choose between Germany and Japan on who they would concentrate the most military action. FDR agreed with Churchill that Germany provided both more of a technological threat and naval threat to the United States over Japan. The Japanese for the most part were only a threat to Southeast Asia while Germany controlled most of Europe's Westcoast and threatened to move across the Atlantic. An invasion on Germany's position in North Africa in 1942 led by General Eisenhower met with some success particularly over the great Field Marshal Rommel, Germany's "Desert Fox." Germany under Hitler also had difficulty maintaining two separate fronts between Eastern Europe and Russia.

From the South the Allies invaded Italy forcing Mussolini, the powerful ally of Hitler and dictator of Italy, out of power. General George Patton led another front from the North invading German occupied Normandy, France. Ultimately, Germany was squeezed from the South by Eisenhower, the Northwest from Patton, and the East by Russia. The Japanese were not ignored in the Pacific. Much of Japan's naval power was eliminated with the battle of Midway when Japanese losses totalled four aircraft carriers and numerous other ships and planes. Admiral Nimitz, the commander of the Pacific fleet and General Douglas MacArthur led the ground forces on the Japanese offensives.

> "I realize the tragic significance of the atomic bomb...We have used it in order to shorten the agony of war, in order to save the lives of thousands and thousands of young Americans. We shall continue to use it until we completely destroy Japan's power to make war. Only a Japanese surrender will stop us."
> President Harry S. Truman's radio address; August, 1945.

With the death of Roosevelt from a massive cerebral hemorrage on April 12, 1945, Harry S. Truman assumed the presidency. The war was well in hand and only 18 days after FDR's death, Hitler committed suicide within his personal bunker. On May 7, 1945 Germany

#PPD204 standard. gold & black design. "ONE FOR THE ROAD COFFEE THAT IS." 1950's.

#PPD279 standard. Red, yellow, & black design. 1950's.

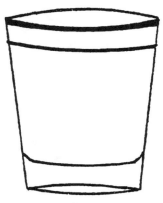

#PML001 1½ oz. standard shot glass w. 1 oz. measuring line gold rim. 1940's. color: clear.

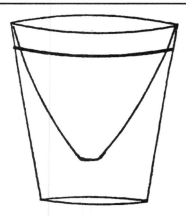

#PML007 1 oz., 2¼" tall w. ⅓ oz. 1940's. measuring line (white) color: clear.

surrendered unconditionally but the Japanese forces refused to follow suit and became more fanatical with suicide missions. Political thinkers and intelligence reports estimated that it would cost a million American lives to defeat Japan and force their surrender. The only other option to prevent such a loss was the decision to use the new atomic bomb. The bomb was the latest technological creation by a group of some of the world's finest physicists led by J. Robert Oppenheimer. Japan indeed surrendered after such a weapon leveled two Japanese cities and directly or indirectly killed hundreds of thousands of Japan's people.

The end of the war left America as a world superpower but the fears of Nazism were transferred to communism. The Cold War was on and the anti-communist prophets of Senator Joe McCarthy and Secretary of State John Foster Dulles briefly carried a wave of censorship, persecution, and fear. The Truman Doctrine was a form of containment legislation to protect certain countries from communism and to pledge U.S. support to all governments fighting against it. The Korean War was a result of such legislation and the fears of communism were not abated until its end.

The post World War II era was also a time of excitement and the first births of the baby-boom generation. The new "Beat Generation" of the 1950's challenged the morality standards of old. 2.5 million new immigrants entered the United States in the 1950's. The nation's population grew by 28 million in the same decade compared to only 19 million in the 40's and a scant 9 million in the Depression-wracked 30's. By the end of the 1950's, America's suburban population increased by 50%.

The introduction of television, rock 'n roll, hamburger joints, new movie stars, custom cars, the drive-in, consumerism including the sale of 9.3 million

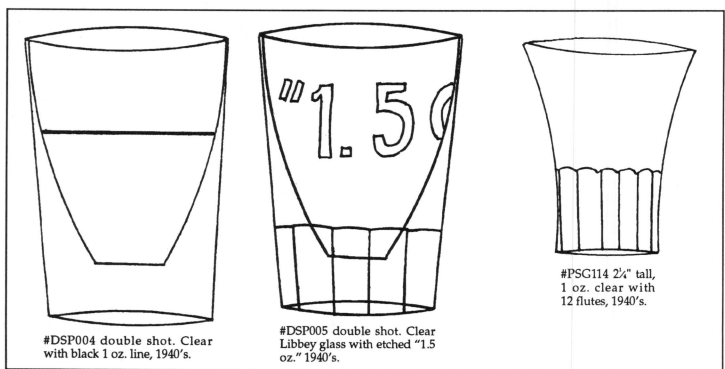

#DSP004 double shot. Clear with black 1 oz. line, 1940's.

#DSP005 double shot. Clear Libbey glass with etched "1.5 oz." 1940's.

#PSG114 2¼" tall, 1 oz. clear with 12 flutes, 1940's.

motor vehicles in 1955 alone, and a new suburban America; seemed to shape the 1950's almost into a state of reserved conformity. An uncommitted generation suggested by some with acceptance of middle-class; lack of protest; secure in the way things were; and contentment with a new car, suburban home, a steady job, and a company retirement plan. The only dissent against the supposed American dream was from the "Beatniks" who were often simply dismissed as "Rebels without a Cause." Conformity was the only thing to protest and followers of James Dean and Marlon Brando could only shun responsibility and "be cool." The use of alcohol stabilized in the 1940's and rose slightly near the end of the 1950's (see chart page 58) but a rise in drunken fatalities particularly with automobiles also accompanied the beatniks and hipsters. Faster cars and drag-racing on back streets did not mesh well with alcohol.

A new wave of civil rights protest and equal rights for women also had its roots in the 1950's. The Supreme Court decision of Brown vs. Board of Education in 1954 ordered the integration of public schools and that the former "separate but equal" doctrine was unconstitutional. Rosa Parks a year later refused to give up her seat to a white man on a bus in Montgomery, Alabama which led to more segregation legislation. The first Civil Rights Bill was approved in 1957 by Congress since Reconstruction. It was enacted to protect the voting rights of blacks. Women's protest was growing too, but as with minorities; the movement was still small-time and not as organized or powerful as it would be in the following decade. The wage disparity affecting minorities and women had still changed little if at all. Native American Indians and blacks pictured here on shot glasses were quite common in the late 1940's and early 1950's but phased out soon after.

Drinking, alcohol, and any issues associated with them were virtually unheard of. With the nation's Depression, the coming of World War II, and the after war period; the old prohibition forces seem to have been pushed aside. The Federal Alcohol Administration Act of 1935 which later became the responsibility of the Bureau of Alcohol, Tobacco, and Firearms under the Treasury Department; held the authority to issue permits to importers, manufacturers, wholesalers, and warehouses of alcohol products to conduct business. They were also responsible for the regulation of labelling, advertising, interdiction, and tax collection.

Distilled beverages were taxed higher than beer or wine. Many manufacturers and distributors who were able to get back on their feet labelled their products as "High Strength," "High Test," "High Proof," "Extra Strength," "Extra Strong," and so on. Some of it was exaggerated and as a regulation measure, the federal government prohibited beer and wine below 14% alcohol or 28 proof to advertise or list alcholic content unless it was required by state law.

Thirty states went wet at the onset of Repeal but that still left 18 who continued Prohibition. The last state to

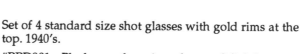

Set of 4 standard size shot glasses with gold rims at the top. 1940's.

#PPD001	Black man throwing a boot at 2 fighting cats from a window. Two different color patterns: orange & black or yellow & black
#PPD002	Brown, green, and yellow pictures of 2 large monkeys, 2 small monkeys, a palm tree, and grass. Brown writing: "Here's Looking at You"
#PPD003	Brown and yellow pictures of four monkeys. Brown writing: "Bottoms Up"
#PPD004	Black, white, and red pictures of black cannibals roasting a white person. "Down the Hatch"

#PPA005 standard. Black & red design, 1940's

#PPA006 standard. Red & white design, 1940's.

#PPA007 standard. Red & black design, 1940's.

#PPA008 standard. Green & white design with gold rim, 1940's.

#PPA051 standard. Federal. Red design, 1954.

#PPA052 standard. Federal. Blue design, 1954.

#PPD111 standard. Red & black design, 1940's.

#PPD113 standard. Anchor-Hocking. Black & white design, 1950's.

#PPD175 standard. Black design (rev: anchor). 1950's. Reproduced 1980's.

overturn Prohibition was not completed until 1966. A few dry counties and localities still exist today. Unlike WWI where drinking was labelled as unpatriotic and a waste of vital food resources, the second world war brought on no such thoughts. Supply and demand were reduced somewhat and at times there was difficulty for manufacturers to obtain the necessary raw materials; however, alcoholic products were readily available. A significant part of the drinking-age population was overseas but beer was very popular in military camps. The officers' quarters might be stocked with finer more potent liquors. Overall

World War II was the last straw for the hope of any renewed popular temperance movements.

The popularity of drinking establishments, the new bars, and related operations surfaced during and after the war. Toasts that had once been to "The Stars and the Bars," "Remember the Maine," and "To Hell with the Kaiser" were replaced during World War II with: "Remember Pearl Harbor," "Keep 'em Flying," and "Get America Moving Again;" all celebrated the war and a new wave of progressivism. Shot glasses for practical usage were basically flute cut, plain, standard, simple double shots, plain with measuring lines; and nothing

8 barrel-shaped shot glasses. Catalog numbers BSG010, 011, 012, 013, 014, 015, 016, and 017. All are 2" tall, 1¾ oz., and have red & black designs (monkeys have lightly-colored yellow faces). All were originally made in 1956 by Bartlett-Collins. (Correction from Shot Glasses: An American Tradition which listed their date in the 1940's).

#ANF007 standard.
White writing. 1940's.
Note: all "Calvert"
glasses were made
after Repeal.

#ANF008 2½" tall, 2 oz.
Red designs, 1940's.
Atlas-Mason glass.

#ANF015 standard.
Orange writing, 1940's.
Thick-sided glass.

#ANF017 standard.
White writing, 1940's;
rev: red writing:
"Kentucky Gentlemen."

#ANF050 standard.
Orange writing, 1940's.
Federal glass with 12
inside flute panels.

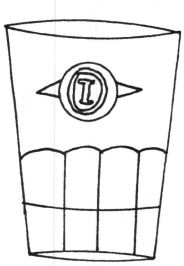

#ANF051 2½" tall, 2 oz.
White design, 9 flutes,
1940's. Rev: ½, 1, & 1½
oz. measuring lines.

#AFT005 standard. White
& red design, 1950's.

#AFT006 2½" tall, 2 oz.
White design, 1950's. Rev:
gold "H & H."

#AFT051 2⅛" tall, 1½ oz. White
writing: "Gota de Iva," 1950's.
Inside panels, 12 flutes.

#AFT101 standard. Red design, Federal glass, thick sides, 1950's. Rev: ⅞ & 1⅛ oz. measuring lines.

#AFT200 standard. White designs, 1950's.

#ANF016 standard. Red designs, 1940's.

#AFT003 standard. White designs, 1950's. Rev: ½, 1, & 1½ oz. measuring lines.

fancy which seemed to fit in with America's conformist, conservative, "don't rock the boat" state of being.

Dating from Repeal and more prevalent by the 1940's and 1950's, simple toasts found enamelled upon hundreds of shot glasses included: "Here's Looking at You," "Bottom's Up," "Here's How," "Down the Hatch," "Here's To It," "One For the Road," "Just a Swallow," and "Here's Mud in Your Eye" just to name a few. The decorated enamelled tumbler soon became the most popular medium for shot glass production. A return to advertising by Post-Repeal liquor manufacturers and distributors also found their way upon shot glasses only the designs were fancier than the old white-pigmented or lightly etched sample glasses.

It was not easy for many who were in legitimate liquor businesses to get back on their feet after the great wet-dry spell of Prohibition. Many had reorganized into grocery, supply, or beverage stores. Milton S. Kronheim worked in his father's saloon at age 11; by the time he was 14 in 1902, he opened his own liquor store. When D.C. went dry in 1917, Kronheim turned to a clothing store and bail bonding business. When Prohibition was lifted, Kronheim returned to liquor wholesaling supplying the White House during the Roosevelt and Truman years.

Another notable character was Paul Jones who began as a salesman for the R.M. Rose & Co. of Tennessee and

Georgia. After the Civil War, he established Paul Jones & Company in Louisville, Kentucky and purchased the Four Roses brand from R.M. Rose. Paul Jones marketed other brands such as Four Star Whiskey and Red Star Gin. As a wholesaler in the late 19th century up to Prohibition, Jones travelled the country buying and selling barrels of whiskey in large quantities. At the onset of Prohibition, the Paul Jones Company was able to bottle much of it for medicinal use under "Paul Jones," "Four Roses," and "Antique;" all common names advertised upon shot glasses from the 1940's and on. The Paul Jones Company spent millions of dollars on advertising and eventually sold out in the early 1950's.

Probably the most famous character in whiskey history was Jack Daniel. Dan Call, a farmer and preacher, took young Jack on at age 11 as an apprentice to his distilling operation. Three years later in 1860, Call gave up distilling but Jack continued with the help of a friend's father. They pedalled what they made as far away as Huntsville, Alabama. After the Civil War, Jack acquired a piece of property near Lynchburg, Tennessee known as the Cave Spring Property. Here in the 1880's, the Jack Daniel Distillery was officially registered and processed true sour mash whiskey. The famous No. 7 Brand had its origins here but no one is sure as to how the name originated. One legend has it that 7 barrels were apparently lost in a shipment and when they were indeed found, a clerk marked "No. 7" on the invoices that travelled with them. Orders soon poured in for the "No. 7" brand.

Jack hired his nephew Lem Motlow and the Jack Daniel's No. 5 Brand can be traced to Motlow. A Jack Daniel's product named: "The Belle of Lincoln" was thought to be disrespectful to women by Lem since there was a picture of a woman on the bottle; so Lem renamed it "No. 5." When Tennessee went dry in 1910, the Lynchburg distillery closed but a new operation was relocated in St. Louis, Missouri. As mentioned earlier, the gangster George

#AFT001 standard. Green & white or green & gold designs, 1950's.

Remus bought them out but lost control of it during his prison and asylum confinement. With some difficulty, Motlow was able to reopen the Jack Daniel's distillery in Lynchburg after Repeal but even to this day, the distillery operates in a dry county. As far as shot glasses are concerned, more examples of Jack Daniel's Old No. 7 have been found advertised on shot glasses from the sample era to the present than any other brand of whiskey. In 1956, Jack Daniels sold out to the Brown-Forman Corporation.[83]

Aside from a resurgence of advertising, the 1940's and 1950's still contained a variety of other decorating techniques applied to shot glasses. Barrel-shapes, enamelled inner-eyes to produce a 3-dimensional effect, a few nudes on standard size shot glasses, racial designs, numerous animals including drunken examples found on the old malt syrup cans of Prohibition, enamelled matched sets of four, and numerous other examples pictured here and at the end of the chapter.

Colored glass of the Depression was nearly eliminated for two major reasons. One is that many of the metals needed for coloring were needed for weapons; and the other was that color simply went out of style. One final look at Libbey, America's largest shot glass maker; and Cambridge, a significant shot glass producer in the 1940's and 1950's, are also listed here.

In 1939, Libbey was able to manufacture stemware by machine. They also introduced one last line of hand-cut crystal named: "Modern American." After a few years of poor sales and the onset of WWII, Libbey ended their own era of hand-made glass. Like all other major glass manufacturers, Libbey did qualify as an industrial essential. Tumblers were heat-treated for extra strength which was perfected and required by the armed services. Other glass products made for the war by Libbey and others were radar, x-ray, and electronic tubes.

In the Post-WWII era, Libbey emerged as a modern manufacturing firm with increased efficiency, high-speed machinery, and huge-volume capacity. In 1947, Libbey purchased Cataract-Sharpe of Buffalo, New York; a highly advanced automated company. In 1959, automatically blown stemware possessed "Safeedge" rims while bowls were cut with automatic mitred-patterns. Libbey not only introduced machine-cut patterned shot glasses but also numerous machine-enamelled patterns. Libbey also had an exclusive contract with Coca-Cola through the 1950's to produce all Coca-Cola glass products. One shot glass featuring Coca-Cola was produced by Libbey in the 1950's ("Coke Adds Life to Parties" catalog #AFT100).

In 1962, Libbey built a massive tableware factory

#PPD005 standard. Multicolored nude picture on inner side of glass (2 separate designs–not a sticker). 1940's.

#PPD006 standard. Multicolored nude sticker (nude on reverse side of sticker– not the inner side of glass). 1940's.

#PPA032 standard. West Virginia Glass Company "Strutting Rooster" design. Multicolored with gold rim, 1950.

#PPA033 standard. West Virginia Glass Company "Pink Elephants" design. Multicolored with gold rim, 1950.

near Los Angeles to serve the large growth West Coast markets. Libbey's modern products dating from the late Depression era particularly machine-made tumblers including shot glasses have a blown in "L." The L might be inscribed in a circle with an etched star, in the circle itself, or without the circle at all. Two tiny numerals may also be present on the underside of Libbey's products.

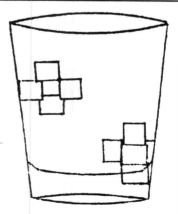

#PPE021 standard. Pink & black design with inside eyes, 1940's.

#PPE022 standard. Pink & black design with inside eyes, 1940's.

#PPA422 standard. Libbey; red, white, & black design of 2 horses and a dog, 1950's.

#EPG111 standard. Libbey etched pattern around glass, 1950's.

Set of four standard size shot glasses with enamelled white interiors and black inside eyes. Catalog numbers (left to right) PPE005, 006, 007, and 008. Black and orange enamelled exterior design. 1940's.

Set of four Bartlett-Collins standard size shot glasses. "Animal" designs, 1959-1961. Catalog numbers (left to right) PPA204, 205, 206, and 207. All are black & red enamelled exterior design.

#PPD203 2¼" tall, 1¾ oz. Libbey "Horseless Carriage" design. Red, black, & green design, 1950's.

#EPG150 standard. Cambridge etched "Laurel Wreath" pattern. 1949-1953.

#EPG154 standard. Cambridge etched "Star" pattern. 1949-1953.

The one on the left indicates the year and the one on the right the quarter of that year in which the item was manufactured. Today, there is a better than average chance that a standard U.S. made shot glass was produced by Libbey even though the design may have been applied by another decorator.[84]

One final company worth mentioning in shot glass history is Cambridge. Under the direction of Arthur J. Bennett, Cambridge built a factory in Ohio in 1902. Bennett acquired the controlling interest in 1909 and remained as Cambridge's leader for 30 years until 1939. At that time he sold his interest to Wilbur L. Orme, his son-in-law.

During World War II and particularly the period afterward, a final decline of expensive hand-made, etched, and hand-cut glassware was the final blow to those who had squeaked through the Depression. A new wave of cheap foreign glass and the huge volume of automation forced Cambridge into a very uncompetitive situation. As a result the factory closed in 1954. It reopened briefly in 1955 under new ownership and once again in 1956; however, they were unable to turn a profit and the final closing was in 1958. In 1960, Imperial Glass Company of Bellaire, Ohio purchased all rights to the Cambridge name and assets of the former company including all surviving and existing molds. Some of the molds were utilized by Imperial for glass production.

As far as shot glasses go, it is possible that Cambridge introduced more etched and cut patterns than any other company from the 1940's through the early 1950's. Some of the patterns were quite common such as the "Laurel Wreath" which were produced by others. Cambridge was also one of the first to offer mold-patterned glass with the design cut or patterned within the interior of the object rather than the exterior as tradition would dictate.[85]

The remaining pages of the chapter picture other shot glasses produced during the 1940's and 1950's.

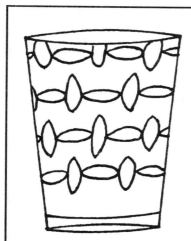

#PPC039 2⅛" tall, Cambridge inside cut pattern, 1½ oz. 1944-1948.

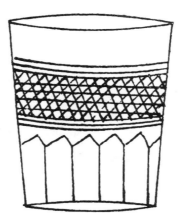

#PPC042 standard. Cambridge clear pattern. 1949-1953.

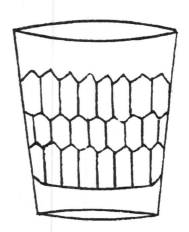

#PPC043 standard. Cambridge clear "Bijou" pattern. 1949-1953.

#EPG101 standard. Etched pattern around glass with gold rim, 1940's.

#EPG102 2" tall, 1½ oz. Etched pattern. 1940's.

#EPG103 2" tall, 1½ oz. Etched pattern around glass. 1940's.

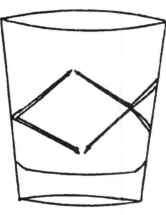

#EPG104 standard. Etched diamond pattern around glass, 1940's.

#EPG105 standard. Etched leaves around glass, 1940's.

#EPG120 2¼" tall, 1 oz. Federal etched flower and vine pattern around glass, 1940's, 14 flutes.

#EPG160 standard. Etched star (rev: identical). 1940's. Reproduction of McKee "Star" pattern.

#EPG161 2¼" tall, 1 oz. Etched pattern (rev: identical). 1940's.

#PPD090 standard with thick sides, 1 oz. Red design, 1940's.

#PPC011 standard. Federal clear diamond pattern. 1940's. 12 flutes.

#PPC015 2¼" tall, 2 oz. Gunderson Glassworks (Pairpoint) "Hex" design (hand-cut), 1940's.

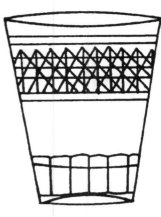

#PPC021 2⅛" tall, 1⅛ oz. 1940's. 14 flutes.

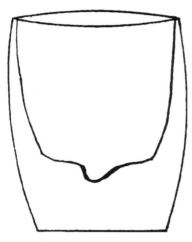

#PSG109 2⅜" tall, 1½ oz. Steuben whiskey jigger or shot glass. 1947, crystal.

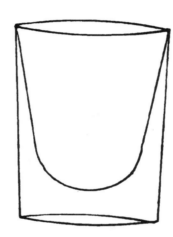

#PSG116 2¼" tall, 1¼ oz. Heisey "Country Club" barware pattern. 1940's, crystal.

#PPD050 standard. White design, 1940's. Rev: "WHEN THINGS ARE LOW HIGHEST ONE HERE AT CEDAR GARDENS MT. CLEMENS."

#PPD112 standard. Red & black design, 1940's.

#PPD155 standard. 4 black & red "barbershop quartet" design, 1950's.

#PPD220 2" tall, 1 oz. Anchor Hocking. Black design, 1950's.

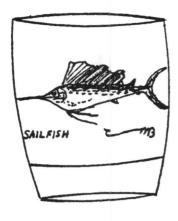 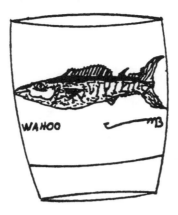 

SAILFISH WAHOO TARPON

DOLPHIN

Set of 4. Each are 2" tall, 1 oz. 1950's. Catalog numbers (left to right) #PPA120 "Sailfish," #PPA121 "Wahoo," #PPA122 "Tarpon," and #PPA123 "Dolphin." Correction from Shot Glasses: An American Tradition – page 58 lists as a set of three.

Set of 4 standard size with tints applied to the underside (pink, blue, red, purple, green, and other tints). Black enamelled designs, originally 1959 by Bartlett-Collins. Reproduced numerous times since 1959. "Old Cowhand" design.

#PPD265

#PPD266

#PPD267

#PPD268

Two separate sets of four standard size shot glasses. All have red & black enamelled designs. Both sets originally 1956 by Bartlett Collins. "Little Shot" design.

Correction from Shot Glasses: An American Tradition (pages 58 and 61). The catalog numbers are amended here to list them concurrently.

#PPD269

#PPD270

#PPD271

#PPD272

#PPD160

#PPD161

Set of four standard size shot glasses with tints applied to the underside (green, red, pink, yellow, blue, and other tints). Black enamelled designs, originally 1959 by Bartlett-Collins. Reproduced numerous times since 1959.

Correction from <u>Shot Glasses: An American Tradition</u> (pages 52, 59, and 62). Two of the catalog numbers are amended here to list them concurrently. Also, #PPD162 was listed incorrectly as 1940's.

"Sports" design.

#PPD162

#PPD163

#PPA111 standard. Red design, 1950's.

#PPA112 standard. Blue design, 1950's.

#PPA113 standard. Pink design, 1950's.

#PPA114 standard. Pink, green, & black design, 1950's.

#PPA304 2" tall, 1 oz. Black design, 1950's.

#AFT012 2¼" tall, 1½ oz. Black design with platinum bands or gold with gold bands. 1950's.

#AFT120 standard. Blue writing, 1950's.

#PPA009 standard. Red & black design. 1940's.

#PPA010 standard. Red & black design. 1940's.

#PPD218 2" tall, 1 oz. Anchor Hocking. Black design, 1950's.

#PPD219 2" tall, 1 oz. Anchor Hocking. Black design, 1950's.

#PPC060 standard. Fostoria "Whirlpool" pattern. One continuous curved etched line around glass. 1940's.

Set of four standard size shot glasses. All have black pictures and writing on reverse. PPA053 "Ring Necked Pheasant," PPA054 "Canvas-back," #PPA055 "Canada Goose," and #PPA056 "Grouse." All also have platinum bands at the very top (rim).

Correction from Shot Glasses: An American Tradition pages 77-78. The catalog numbers were changed from PPA500-504 to reflect the older age of the glasses.

An earlier advertisement from 1956-1957 by Federal Glass Co. list them as the "Sportsman's Rumpus" set. They were later reproduced.

Chapter X:

RADICALISM & BABY-BOOMERS OF THE 1960'S AND THE SILENT '70'S

"World peace, like community peace, does not require that each man love his neighbor – it requires only that they live together in mutual tolerance, submitting their disputes to a just and peaceful settlement."

John F. Kennedy, speech given at American university, Washington, D.C. June 10, 1963.

Peace, love, flower children, a new Left, LSD, marijuana, antidiscrimination, assassinations, economic booms, even faster cars, classic rock 'n roll, civil rights, widespread protest, an immoral war, transcendentalism, free-wheeling sex, draft-dodging, reform, and radicalism are just a few terms that often describe the 1960's. The drinking of alcohol was associated with a new type of binging – the party. These new drinking patterns especially with the upcoming or growing up of the baby-boom generation established here in the '60's have changed little today except for the realization, caution, and problems of mixing driving with alcohol. Consequently, the 1970's was a period of disillusionment, lack of participation, conservatism, and a sluggish economy.

The longest sustained economic boom in American history took place in the 1960's. The Gross National Product doubled in the United States. Much of it was caused by budget deficits created for the Vietnam War. The General Agreement on Tariffs and Trade in 1967 also stimulated European and other foreign prosperity. Japan was well on its way to become the world's top economic power with $20. billion in exports by 1970. Brazil too became very industrialized.

The election of a young vibrant president in John Fitzgerald Kennedy and promises of new attacks on racial injustice and poverty with positive government action seemed to be a renewed continuation of progressivism. New political and social reform movements especially with blacks and women pressured the government to make lawful changes. Kennedy sought people with ideals, intellectuals, and new blood to enter the government in hopes of changing America into a better sense of morality, duty, and responsibility.

Meanwhile, relations with Russia were uneasy and the Cold War was in a state of perpetuation. Direct confrontations between the two superpowers were avoided; however, Third World countries became the battleground for democracy versus communism. Khrushchev's policies were simply to fuel national liberation wars in order to exploit insurgencies while Kennedy counterattacked with the Peace Corps and the development of counter-insurgency doctrines and schools. Kennedy too attempted to use force at the embarassing Bay of Pigs to overthrow Castro in Cuba. It failed but progress was being made in Central and South America. The hottest spot though shifted to Southest Asia.

The Kennedy Administration had inherited the crisis in Laos. To protect an infiltration effort, North Vietnam sent men and supplies to the Viet Cong in South Vietnam along the Ho Chi Minh trails. Kennedy backed the South Vietnamese with a small force of Green Beret instructors in the spring of 1961. This violated an earlier agreement set in Geneva in 1955; however, the Kennedy Administration believed that the far superior numbers of the South Vietnamese resistance would easily overthrow the North Vietnamese. Things did not progress as planned. Civil War broke out in Vietnam and both China and Russia were supporting the Viet Cong.

#ASX050 and #ASX051. Set of two 1964 standard size campaign shot glasses. Red designs (reverse of #ASX051 has a picture of a boot).

#ASX060 standard. Black or red writing, 1960's.

Thousands more American military advisors were sent.

Another crisis in Europe involving Germany and the surge of refugees from East to West, nearly 30,000 a month, brought Kennedy and Khrushchev in conflict again. The solution in August, 1961 was the erection of the Berlin Wall to eliminate the mass migration West. Yet another crisis in the following year involving missiles in Cuba placed by the Soviet Union nearly led to a nuclear war. Russia backed off as America threatened to remove the missiles if Russia did not. After the cuban Missile Crisis, a test ban treaty on nuclear weapons was agreed upon; outlawing all such tests in air, water, or outer space.

One positive result of the competition by the superpowers was the advances in science and space. In 1961, the Russian cosmonaut Yuri Gagarin was the first man placed in orbit around the Earth. A month later, Kennedy was able to achieve his newly declared goal of placing a man on the moon before the decade would end. Other scientific examples were the development of lasers, integrated circuits, the first successful heart transplant in 1967, and scientific solutions to agricultural troubles.

"This Administration has outstripped all previous ones in the breadth of its civil rights activity. Yet the movement, instead of breaking out into the open plains of progress, remains constricted and confined."

Martin Luther King Jr., 1962.

On the domestic front, black discontent and Southern resistance grew against discrimination in restaurants, shops, services, and other public places. Mass protest against discrimination was led by Dr. Martin Luther King Jr. including a quarter of a million people in front of the Lincoln Memorial in Washington, D.C. in 1963. Some success was achieved by blacks against segregation and poverty as the Civil Rights Act was passed in 1964.

Still, as John Kennedy and Martin Luther King Jr. seemed to portray a new appeal to American idealism, their respective assassinations plunged many to believe that America was overly corrupt and that moral reform was hopeless. Urban ghettoes erupted into riots but the

#PDP002 standard. 4 yellow & brown flower blooms around glass, 1960's.

#PDP012 standard. Jeannette "Hellenic" design. Gold, white, & green, 1960.

#PDP021 standard. Dark brown design around top of glass, 1960's.

#PDP022 standard. 3 gold & black coins around glass, 1960's.

#PDP023 standard. Orange, black, & gold design around glass, 1960's.

#PDP024 standard. 4 gold & white leaves around glass, 1960's.

#PDP025 standard. Libbey "Golden Foliage" design. Gold & white. Golden Foliage was introduced in 1956 though shot glasses did not appear until the early 1960's.

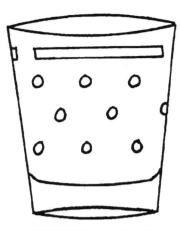

#PDP026 standard. Yellow designs around glass, 1960's.

#PDP027 standard. Red & black hearts, diamonds, clubs, & spades around glass, 1960's.

#PDP028 standard. Bartlett-Collins "Rocket Burst" design. Red & green around glass, 1960-1961.

#PDP029 standard. Federal "Inca" design. Turquoise & gold around glass, 1960.

#PDP030 standard. Federal "Topsy Turvey" Turquoise & gold around glass, 1962.

(Note: It is believed that the Federal Glass Co. is responsible for most if not all turquoise & gold tourist shot glass designs of the 1960's).

new president, Lyndon Baines Johnson sought to continue his predecessor's policies. Johnson referred to his domestic programs as the "Great Society."

"...a place where the city of man serves not only the needs of the body and the demands of commerce but the desire for beauty and the hunger for community."
President Lyndon B. Johnson on his "Great Society."

Johnson campaigned heavily in the 1964 presidential election for his Great Society and won a convincing victory over Barry Goldwater. Along with the Civil Right's legislation, other bills were enacted increasing federal aid to Medicare, Medicaid, education, low-income housing, the arts, a job corps, head start programs, and welfare services. By the end of the 1960's, those below the poverty level in 1959 was cut in half; however, much can be attributed to the strength of the economic boom.

But then there was Vietnam. Johnson plunged America into its biggest failure ever in what a majority according to opinion polls believed to be an immoral war. Over half a million American troops caused an incredible amount of destruction and death against a small country while suffering heavy losses on their own. Despite intense bombing and fighting, America failed to end the war. The unjust war was yet another reason for American protest. Antiwar declarations spread across college campuses, were led by prominent literary figures, were present in music, and aided in the reviving of feminism.

"Hell no, we won't go."
(popular Vietnam draft-dodger's saying).

Not only did protest for the war escalate into massive political movements, but a variety of other cultural and environmental concerns were now present.

#ASX006 standard. Red & white design. 1960's.

#ASX007 2½" tall, 2 oz. Gold & white design. 1960's.

#ANS009 standard. Gold writing. 1970's.

#ANS010 standard. Black writing. Optional Rev: blue picture of Halley's Comet. 1970's.

#ANS011 standard. Clear lettering on frosted glass, 1970's.

#ANS022 2½" tall, 2 oz. Yellow designs. 1970's.

#PHS090 standard. Green design. Rev: "Season's Greetings . . . 1969." (Coca-Cola commemorative edition, 1969).

#TTN033 standard. Yellow & white design, 1970's.

#TTX012 standard. Red design (rev: outline of state with flag), 1970's.

Cleaning up America, a new Leftist movement, the creation of the National Organization for Women in 1966, and even a movement for homosexual rights emerged in the later 1960's. Membership in extreme radical groups surged such as Students for a Democratic Society and the Black Panthers. New counter-culture non-political bands developed rejecting traditionalism such as group communes and personal habits as with beards, long hair, miniskirts, and the use of hallucinogens. Simple patterns picturing flowers, hearts, steps, leaves, and so on could be found upon everyday items like clothing, wallpaper, and even shot glasses.

In 1968, Johnson withdrew from the presidential contest as a new Kennedy; Robert F. and Eugene McCarthy were assured of victories in the democratic primaries. Another assassination of Robert F. Kennedy once again, seemed to enforce that America and morality were not intertwinable. Hubert Humphrey won the democratic nominaton since his only serious opposition had been Kennedy. The Republican Richard M. Nixon campaigned heavily with a secret plan to end the war quickly. Nixon surprisingly won and was counted on to enforce middle-class values and stabilization. Nixon ended up further intensifying the American people's distrust in government.

Nixon once a famous red-hunter with Joe McCarthy showed great initiative in improving relations with Russia and China; the highlight of his presidential career. However, the war in Vietnam spread to neighboring neutral countries like Laos and Cambodia.

Note: The easiest way to tell the difference between the Mayfair original and reproduction is in the stem of the flower. The original has the stem of the flower forking at the end like an 'A' shape while the reproduction follows a single line to the end of the stem.

#PHS100 standard. Red design. 1977. Coca-Cola's first annual holiday shot glass.

#DPG042 (see p. 191) (original-pink only)

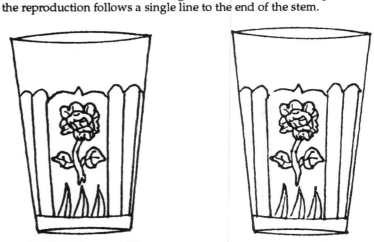

#PPC080 2¼" tall, 1½ oz. Reproduction Depression–pink, green, or cobalt blue. 1977-present.

#DSA306 Double Shot. Red & clear design. 1970's.

#DSA308 Double Shot. Red or black design. 14 flutes, 1970-present.

#TUS050 standard. Red, white, & blue, 1970's.

The North Vietnamese used Cambodia to strike against South Vietnam which prompted Nixon to exercise bombing raids over Cambodia. The most intense widespread college protest ever in American history involving 1½ million students was a direct result of the invasion of Cambodia. Four students were killed and 10 more wounded for violently protesting the invasion by National Guardsmen at Kent State University in Ohio on May 4, 1970.

"When dissent turns to violence, it invites tragedy."
President Richard M. Nixon commenting on Kent State after describing student agitators a few days earlier as "Bums."

The 1960's certainly carried on into the very early 1970's as Nixon sought solutions to ending the war. At a high point of 543,400 American ground troops in Vietnam in April of 1969; the number was reduced to only 60,000 by September, 1972. Nixon relied mostly on increased air and naval power. Cease-fires were agreed upon in late 1972 and early 1973 as America eventually pulled out. On the home-front with his personal insecurity and strong suspicions of those around him, Nixon set off a fanatical and unlawful drive to destroy those he considered his enemies. The end result was the shocking scandal of Watergate. Nixon was forced to resign to escape further humiliation and impeachment.

The return of caution in America and a neo-conservatism of the mid-1970's was partially fueled by a sluggish economy, energy and resource shortages such as the natural gas crunch of 1979, environmental troubles like the Three Mile Island Nuclear Reactor in 1979, and a suspicion of science and technology as many federal projects were killed or delayed. The mistrust of government brought on by Watergate weakened support for government reform plans by liberals. In the Bakke decision of 1978, school busing and racial quotas were opposed. Civil rights for homosexuals were also opposed in the Dade County referendum of 1977. The Equal Rights Amendment for women was also rejected. Compared to the movements and vocalization expressed in the 1960's and very early '70's, the rest of the 1970's became a silent decade.

The economy was on the downturn as a severe recession hit both the United States and Europe in 1974-1975. Oil price hikes, monetary instability as the United States cut ties to the gold standard, the decline of the dollar, and protectionist moves by industrial companies were all poor economic indicators. Furthermore, research spending and business investment declined. As a result, the end of the 1970's brought on severe inflation in America, up to 18% in 1979.

The gains achieved since WWII from the economy to women and minorities were beaten back in the '70's as the distribution of income changed little. The new industrial technology aided destruction and further contamination of the environment. The low-cost of energy was now a thing of the past. The depletion of nonrenewable forms of natural energy led to a greater dependence on foreign resources. As a result, inflation skyrocketed and reduced the average person's spending power per dollar.

The 1960's and 1970's also contained a radical shift in advertising and material items. New car models, clothing, suburban life, widespread television advertising, and a host of other styling changes present with each new successive generation. In the world of shot glasses, the radical 1960's produced many simple enamelled pictured patterns; new campaign shot glasses not seen for decades; a special Coca-Cola 1969 commemorative edition to celebrate peace, Woodstock, and the end of the 1960's; and the beginnings of tourist memorabilia as the baby-boomers traveled everywhere. The great cross-country car trips with the improvement of America's vast highway network funneled the rise of tourist shops certainly had its beginning in the 1960's. Shot glasses were a cheap but durable souvenir for both adults or children and literally millions of tourist shot glasses have been available from this time period onward.

Advertising especially whiskey distillers of brand names were only interrupted by Prohibition but continued onward into the 1960's and 1970's. Gone were many of the old sayings like "Down the Hatch" or "Just a Swallow" upon shot glasses; however, expansion into other everyday walks of life were present. Games, cards, colleges, souvenir, the 1976 Bicentennial celebration, and even the first reproductions of old popular patterns found their way upon shot glasses.

The remaining pages list shot glasses made during the 1960's and 1970's.

Set of 4 standard-size shot glasses. Bartlett-Collins "Buzz" assortment. Black & red designs. 1965-1967. #'s PPA430, 431, 432, and 433.

Correction from Shot Glasses: An American Tradition, page 52 lists PPA430 as 1940's. Also the number was amended to reflect the more recent date of the glass.

Set of 4 2½" tall, 2 oz. shot glasses. Catalog numbers PPA505, PPA506, PPA507, and PPA508. All have black designs with gold rims, 1970's.

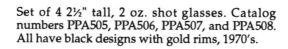

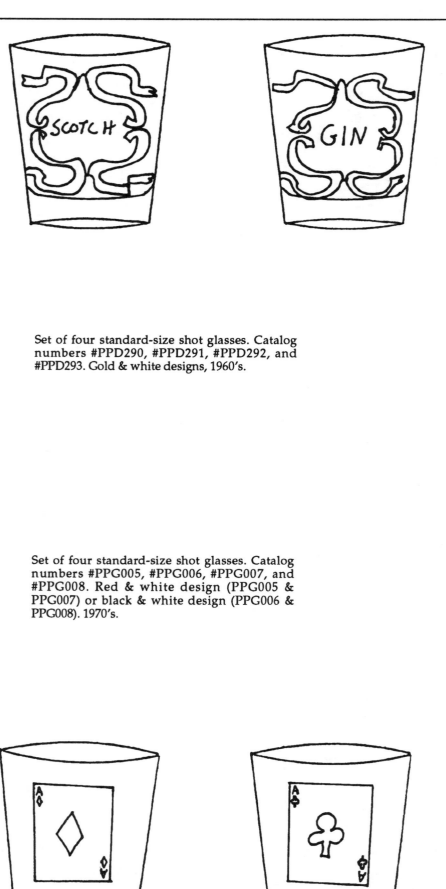

Set of four standard-size shot glasses. Catalog numbers #PPD290, #PPD291, #PPD292, and #PPD293. Gold & white designs, 1960's.

Set of four standard-size shot glasses. Catalog numbers #PPG005, #PPG006, #PPG007, and #PPG008. Red & white design (PPG005 & PPG007) or black & white design (PPG006 & PPG008). 1970's.

Set or two standard-size shot glasses. #PPG020 and #PPG021. Red & white designs. 1970's (identical on reverse).

#ANS102 standard. Red writing, 1970's.

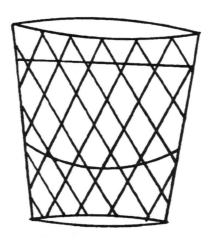

#ANS140 standard. Gold writing, 1975.

#PPC071 2⅛" tall, 1⅝ oz. Black-tinted patterned glass. 1970's.

#PDP031 standard. Anchor Hocking "Golden Lace" design. Gold & white design around glass, 1961.

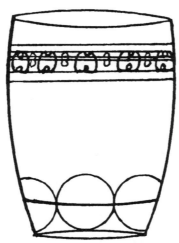
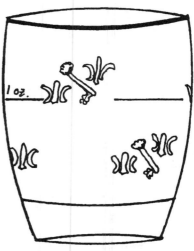

#PDP032 standard. Gold, white, & purple design around glass, 1960's.

#PDP104 2⅜" tall, 1¾ oz. White design around glass with 7 circular bevels, 1970's.

#PDP105 2½" tall, 2 oz. Gold design around glass with gold rim, 1970's.

#PDP120 2⅛" tall, 1⅓ oz. Brown porcelain, 1970's.

#UMI011 standard. Green design, 1970's.

#UWI010 standard. Gold design, 1970's.

#TAK011 standard. Red, yellow, black, & white design, 1970's.

#TAK012 standard. Blue & gold design with bear, totem poles, flag, & mouse; 1970's.

#TAR050 standard. Red design, 1970's.

#TCA001 standard. Turquoise & gold design (rev: bus & camera crew), 1960's.

#TCA030 standard. Gold & black design, 1970's.

#TCA031 standard. Gold & black design, 1970's.

#TCA032 standard. Gold &
black design, 1970's.

#TCA040 standard. Gold &
black design, 1970's.

#TCA050 standard. Gold &
black design (identical on
reverse), 1970's.

#TCA051 standard. Gold &
black design, 1970's.

#TCA060 standard. Black
design on white background
(Taiwan-made), 1970's.

#TCA070 standard. Gold &
black design, 1970's.

#TCO002 standard. Turquoise
& blue design. 1960's.

#TCO022 standard. Gold &
black design, 1970's.

#TCO030 standard. Red
design on white background
(rev: "Summit House"), 1970's.

#TFL051 standard. Green design, 1970's.

#TGA011 standard. Blue design, 1970's.

#TGA012 standard. Black design, 1970's.

#THI020 standard. Blue & gold design, 1970's.

#THI021 standard. Red design, 1970's.

#THI022 standard. Black & gold design, 1970's.

#TIA010 standard. Red & black design, 1970's.

#TLA010 standard. Black design, 1970's.

#TMI021 standard. Red design, 1970's.

#TMI029 standard. Green, red, & brown design, 1970's.

#TMI035 standard. Black writing with gold rim, 1970's.

#TNC020 standard. Blue design, 1970's.

#TNE010 standard. Red & black design (rev: "Crystal Palace Saloon"), 1970's.

#TNV001 standard. Turquoise & gold design, 1960's.

#TNY002 standard. Turquoise & gold design, 1970's.

#TOH003 standard. Turquoise & gold design, 1960's.

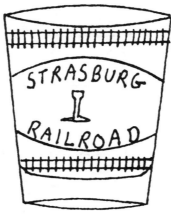

#TPA001 standard. Turquoise & gold design, 1960's.

#TPA030 standard. Violet-blue design, 1970's.

Chapter XI:

THE END OF THE 20TH CENTURY: THE 1980'S AND 1990'S

At the beginning of 1980, the population of the United States was just under 222 million. It had doubled since 1920 but the post-war baby boom slackened after 1957. Women began marrying later, seeking careers, putting off children; and with new inflation, children were becoming more and more expensive to care for. Women also no longer wished to be pregnant for a significant part of their life and tied down with many children. New birth control methods such as the pill, sterilization procedures, and legalized abortions also aided in reducing the size of families. As a result the birth rate steadily declined and fell below the 2-children per family mark. The population of the country was only increasing because of immigration; without it the United States would be in a state of decline.

The baby boom population (roughly 1945-1957) continue as a disproportionate number in the current population curve. From the unrest of the sixties, middle-age changed many from radicals to conservative traditionalists. Like the immediate post-WWII era, many have settled into a quiet complacent 'don't rock the boat' way of life. The social impact of the baby boomers may have yet one more stage of transition in 2010 when the largest percentage ever of America's population will attain senior citizen status.

By 1980, women outnumbered men by 5½ million and the goal of equality has returned with new vigor. "Equal pay for equal work," the ending of sexual discrimination in employment, day care centers, and equal access to all professions and education; were all the battle cries of American women. Black American statistics produce somewhat of a mixed picture of progress. By 1980, black families earning over $25,000 increased by 50% and the number of black college students quadrupled from the mid-1960's to 1980. However, the majority of black jobs are at the bottom end and the unemployment rate is usually at least double that of whites.

More voices from the minority world were heard particularly from Hispanic and Native American Indians. The fastest growing American minority since the late 1960's have been people of Hispanic decent. High birth rates and both illegal and legal immigration have greatly increased the Hispanic population in the United States. Projections predict that Hispanics will overtake blacks early in the next century. For a long time, Mexicans entered the United States to satisfy the country's need for inexpensive manual agricultural labor. New pride in their identity and conquests for better working conditions and wages led by Caesar Chavez have also aided in the advance of Hispanics; however, as with blacks, Hispanic people still lag far behind whites in terms of economic equality.

Once termed the "Vanishing Americans," American Indians at least voiced the terrible conditions of their peoples. Over half live on extremely poor reservations and are at the very end of unemployment, health conditions, income, educational level, and so forth. A few books such as Vine Deloria Jr.'s Custer Died For Your Sins in 1969 and Bury My Heart at Wounded Knee by Dee Brown in 1971 illustrated the plight of the Indian in America. Films from Little Big Man in 1970 to Kevin Costner's Dances With Wolves in 1990 also portrayed the Indians as a proud humane culture and victims rather than the senseless bad guys in the westerns of old. Indians today have a long way to go to achieve egalitarianism but recent victories in court battles over restoration of lost land, water, mineral, and fishing rights have them making steady gains.

As many of those who had rebelled in the sixties quietly backed into the mainstream of the seventies; but shadows of counterculture still survive. Language, dress, sexual freedom, and especially new and more powerful drugs are present in today's society. While LSD and heroin fell out of fashion, crack cocaine has rivaled the number one drug (marijuana) in terms of popularity. New personal fulfillment, the greed of the Reagan years and the self-centered "Me Decade" emerged in the 1980's.

The Bush years have been filled with promises of a "Kindler and Gentler" nation by President George Bush; however, the reduction of the middle-class during his predecessor's two terms left a larger underclass. The United States was able to overcome the failure of Korea and Vietnam with the victory of Saddam Hussein and the liberation of Kuwait in the Persian Gulf War of 1991, but poverty, lack of education, lack of health care for all, the drug problem, and a variety of other troubles are waiting attention on the home-front. Alcohol too as many now classify as an additional drug still holds a prominent place in society.

There is little voice for absolute prohibition and little question of the morality of drinking moderately. People naturally drink with meals, at celebrations like weddings or parties, to relax, etc. Negative reasons for consumption include an escape from problems, cures for fears, to block out unsatisfactory feelings, and to forget one's troubles as with any other drug. Modern intoxication is often described in 5 stages: (1) Happy—one is talkative, sociable, and somewhat uninhibited. (2) Excited—one is emotional, erratic, and exercises poor judgement. (3) Confused—one is disoriented, moody, and slurs speech. (4) Stupor—one is unable to walk, barely conscious, and frequently vomits. (5) Coma—the stage of unconsciousness, no reflexes, and death may result.[86]

Though alcohol is accepted, its abuse, medical problems, and social troubles are readily known. Chemically ethyl alcohol is C_2H_5OH and is a colorless liquid with a sharp burning taste. Alcohol is a depressant that slows the activity of the brain by knocking out or numbing nerve control centers. Modern beer is 4-7% alcohol; ordinary wine 9-14%, stronger fortified wines like port or sherry are 18-21%, and hard liquors like whiskey, bourbon, gin, vodka, and rum are 40-50%. 12 ounces of beer or 5 ounces of wine or 1½ ounces (shot) of whiskey each contain about .6 oz. of pure alcohol. A typical 1½ ounce shot of whiskey contains 150 calories with little nutritional value (i.e. no minerals, protein, or vitamins).

"The use of alcohol in medicine as a tonic, a stimulant or for food has no scientific value and should be discouraged."
From the regulations adopted 1917 by the House of Delegates of the American Medical Association.

Modern medicine would not quite go as far as the 1917 agreement. Alcohol is an ingredient in many medicines and is used at times as a mild sedative. Alcohol rapidly enters the bloodstream, all parts within just a few minutes. It is slowed by food in the stomach. It takes the average adult body about an hour or so to break down one drink. The liver is responsible for 90% of that process while the lungs and kidneys account for the remaining 10%. Black coffee, cold showers, and fresh air all have no effect on blood alcohol content. The more that is drunk, the harder the liver must work to clear the bloodstream. Modern medical problems of alcohol overindulgence can lead to brain damage; cancer of the mouth, throat, esophagus, and stomach; heart disease; cirrhosis of the liver; ulcers, gastritis; damage to adrenal and pituitary glands; and severe birth defects.

Men currently account for 75% of all alcohol consumed in America. 60% of adult women drink regularly while 90% of college age women drink. Overall, 20-39 year olds in America consume 56.1% of the total alcohol drunk in America.[87] Alcohol affects women differently from men. Women can become more intoxicated than men since on average a woman has a much higher fat content than a man. Alcohol does not diffuse rapidly into fat which leaves a higher concentration in a woman's bloodstream. The most notable negative affect concerning women is drinking while pregnant.

The birth defect best known as Fetal Alcohol Syndrome affects 1% or 35,000 of all babies born in the United States each year. Symptoms include mental retardation, physical deformities, decreased birthweight, and miscarriages. The Surgeon General recommends that women do not drink at all while pregnant since even moderate drinking can cause serious damage to a fetus.[88]

Aside from medical problems, there are also social troubles associated with drunkenness particularly when drinking is mixed with driving. Drunken driving accidents are declining but they still account for about ½ of all highway deaths annually which number about 25,000. At 4,000, alcohol related crashes are the leading cause of deaths for teens annually. The worst drunk driving accident in history occurred on May 14, 1988. Larry Mahoney was driving the wrong way on I-71 in Carrollton, Kentucky and ran into a school bus killing 3 adults and 24 teenagers. Mahoney was sentenced for 16 years on multiple counts of wanton endangerment and second degree manslaughter. In 1982, 30% of drivers were drunk in fatal crashes; in 1989, it has dropped to 24.2%. Drunk driving arrests are also down about 40% from 1973 to 1990 based on blood alcohol levels of 10% or greater as registered on breathalyzer tests.

"You Should Have Called For a Lift Earlier."
MADD poster illustrating a coffin with pall-bearers.

Candy Lightner founded Mother's Against Drunk Driving (MADD) after losing her daughter to a drunk driver in 1980. MADD with intense lobbying and campaigning has succeeded in getting tougher drunken driving laws in many states. Higher drinking ages, stricter laws, and harsher penalties have been partly responsible for reducing drunk driving accidents. There is still a ways to go. According to the Insurance Institute for Highway Safety, teenage drunk driving accidents alone cause $6 billion dollars of losses in property damage, hospital costs, and lost work. A recent University of Michigan Medical School and School of Public Health surveyed 5,600 5th and 6th grade students in southeastern Michigan. The report revealed that 15% of 5th graders and 19% of 6th graders drank alcohol in unsupervised situations.[89] Another report from the Insurance Institute reveals that as many as 97% of young men aged 19 and 20 in Washington, DC were able to buy alcohol without question though the legal age is 21 in all states. In some states like Albany, New York where enforcement is taken more seriously, 44% of underage buyers were still successful in purchasing alcohol. These figures do not take into consideration alcohol purchased for underage drinkers by older friends and relatives.[90] As a spinoff from MADD, some high schools across the country have established SADD chapters or Students Against Drunk Driving.

Penalties are also getting stiffer and innovative for convicted drunk drivers. A test device introduced in California in 1987 has been made mandatory for some of those convicted. This breathalyzer gadget detects alcohol on ones breath and is attached to the ignition of the driver's car. If the driver has had as little as one strong drink or two ordinary alcohol-containing drinks, the device will lock the ignition and not allow the driver to start the car for a fifteen minute interval; then the driver must try and pass the test again.

Aside from driving while intoxicated, other social problems include family abuse, other accidents, and decreased employment. 50% of all spouse abuse is attributed to alcohol and 38% of child abuse shares the same cause. Drunken arrests, lost employment, lower productivity, and accidents operating machinery and other devices besides cars while intoxicated add up to a total loss of $120 billion dollars annually.[91] Airplane pilots too have lost their jobs due to inebriety. A good portion of violent crimes and homicides are also attributed to alcohol abuse.

These troubles at least are well-known and recognized by a wide variety of organizations. Along with MADD and SADD, is RADD or Rockers Against Drunk Driving. RADD was founded in 1987 by radio programmer Ken Anthony in San Jose, California. RADD has been supported by such notable rock bands as The Rolling Stones; Crosby, Stills, & Nash; Jackson Browne; and a host of others. Many older anti-liquor and prohibition groups still survive today. The Prohibition Party is headquartered presently in Denver, Colorado. The Anti-Saloon League today is the American Council on Alcohol Problems and is located in Washington, DC. The WCTU boasts ¼ million members and occasional articles appear in their publication: "The Union Signal." The Children of Alcoholics Foundation Inc. is yet another group fighting the abuse of alcholics. Of course, AA or Alcoholics Anonymous has chapters established in every major city across the country.

Consumption figures for per capita alcohol have been on the downswing the past 10 years (see charts below). Beer consumption has dropped 7% from 1980-1987; wine decreased 14% in the same period; and distilled spirits are down a whopping 23%. According to The National Restaurant Association, alcohol consumption is down 17% from 1980-1987. Though there is still the belief that alcohol enhances social life, increased awareness and treatment of its problems seem to be making headway. Warning labels applied to tobacco products in the 1960's have recently been required for all beer, wine, and liquor sold in the United States:

1. According to the Surgeon General, women should not drink alcoholic beverages during pregnancy because of the risk of birth defects.

2. Consumption of alcoholic beverages impairs your ability to drive a car or operate machinery, and may cause health problems.

Naturally, alcohol and the vessels used to drink it have played an important role in the country's history not to mention the various distilleries and liquor industry. A few rare companies or distilleries have managed to last several generations without merging or selling out. At least one example bares closer scrutiny, The James B. Beam Distillery Company of Clermont, Kentucky.

In 1788, Jacob Beam packed all of his belongings including a copper still, his wife, and two sons upon a second-hand wagon and headed for Kentucky through the Cumberland Gap. Jacob made a successful living raising corn, hogs, and fruit. With a bit of rye and barley

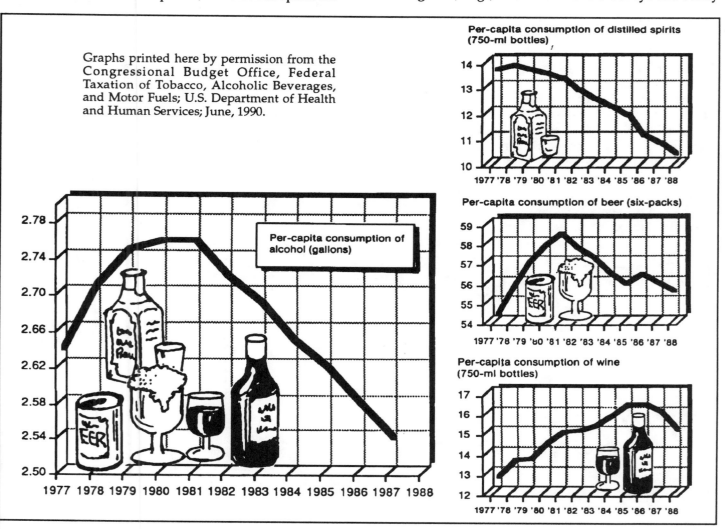

Graphs printed here by permission from the Congressional Budget Office, Federal Taxation of Tobacco, Alcoholic Beverages, and Motor Fuels; U.S. Department of Health and Human Services; June, 1990.

Per-capita consumption of distilled spirits (750-ml bottles)

Per-capita consumption of beer (six-packs)

Per-capita consumption of alcohol (gallons)

Per-capita consumption of wine (750-ml bottles)

mixed with his corn and iron-free water rushing down Kentucky's hills, Jacob was able to distill a fine bourbon who's formula has changed little today. The first Beam Distillery was a water mill for grinding grain. Jacob Beam was the mill operator and took as his fee a percentage of the grain that was ground which he in turn used to mash and distill his own bourbon whiskey.

By 1795, Jacob Beam became a full-time commercial distiller as reputation of his good whiskey developed. Jacob's son David Beam and grandson David M. Beam expanded and moved the business to Nelson County. The

#ANE020 standard.
Black writing, 1980's.

reason for the move was to place the operation closer to the railroad for easy shipment. By 1880, a fourth generation by the name of James Beauregard Beam entered the family-run business at age 16. The whiskey was named for James Beauregard and with tradition, Jim's son T. Jeremiah Beam also joined the business in 1913.

The distillery closed temporarily during Prohibition but Jim was able to reopen it in Clermont, Kentucky directly after Repeal. At this time the official name of "Jim Beam" was applied to a square bottle upon a white label. The design of the bottle and label have not changed since. Today, the grandson of Jim Beam, Booker Noe is the 6th generation of the oldest family-run operation in Kentucky.[92] Jim Beam is famous for the hundreds of unique novelty and collector decanters produced since Prohibition. A few shot glasses have been produced including a porcelain collection of one each from the years 1979-1982.

Other fine bourbons such as Maker's Mark, Old Grand

Dad, and others can also be found upon shot glasses. In 1964, the United States Congress actually declared bourbon as "America's Native Spirit." There are literally federal regulations to determine what qualifies as a bourbon. At least 51% of the grain used must be corn and to protect its flavor, bourbon cannot be distilled at more than 160 proof. Bourbon must also be stored for a minimum of two years in new, charred, white oak barrels.

The glass industry has never wavered though the majority of companies today are very large. Glass continues to have a vital place in cars, homes, medical equipment, lenses, eye-glasses, airplanes, televisions, space shuttles, telescopes, satellites, art, and of course tableware and souvenirs. The rise of the decorating companies over the last 20 years has been phenomenal. Most simply order the glasses in huge quantities from such perennial powers as Libbey and Anchor-Hocking; and then apply decorations to them with enamels, transfers, decals, gold, pewter, and so on.

In the 1980's and 1990's, shot glasses can be found coated with black enamel as in porcelain replicas, genuine porcelain articles are new for the very late 1980's and early 1990's; the return of the Depression Tall style shot glass is here; frosted shot glasses exist in great quantities; silver coated shot glass souvenirs are new for the very late eighties and nineties; tourist glasses are now available in every state; square shot glasses are decorated with the same variety as standard glasses; advertising is abundant as ever; and souvenir glasses are reaching into the millions in annual production. The 1980's and 1990's have also seen the introduction of huge sets of glasses. Shot glasses are available for all professional hockey, basketball, football, and baseball teams. Several 50 piece state sets include the 50 flags, 50 framed state capitols and tourist sites, and the 50 state shields. A railroad set that numbers over 100 is by far the largest.

It might be easier to say what has not been applied to a shot glass compared to what has. Two major decorating companies are still Fort and Culver. Both provide high quality shot glasses compared to ordinary decorated items. The price certainly reflects it but the

#ANS030 2¾" tall, 1⅓ oz. Brown porcelain.

#ANE004 2¾" tall, 1⅓ oz. Blue porcelain.

#ANE005 2¾" tall, 1⅓ oz. Yellow porcelain.

#ANE006 2¾" tall, 1⅓ oz. Green porcelain.

craftsmanship is definitely superior. Culver decorates holiday and souvenir glasses in 22 kt. gold. The famous framed gold Culver tourist glasses are available across the country. Fort is the leading pewter souvenir producing company in the country. Their products in the past were excellent but new for the 1990's is the introduction of 2-tone bronze and pewter objects applied primarily to the exterior of square shot glasses. I believe that Culver and Fort are producing the top collectibles of the future for shot glass collectors today.

The shot glass from the bar tumbler days of old retains its use today. Bars use them for quick measuring and dispensing shots of hard liquor. Shots are given at holidays, weddings, and other toasts. A nice heavy U.S. made shot glass can take a beating and has even more durable features than the firing glasses of old. Relying on century's old tradition, occasionally a toast of some sort can be heard today with a shot glass high in hand filled with good old American bourbon.

> If all be true that I do think,
> There are five reasons we should drink;
> Good wine–a friend–or being dry–
> Or lest we should be by and by–
> Or any other reason why.
>
> 16th Century Latin Epigram.

Drinking began with America's first permanent settlers in the early 17th century. Surviving was difficult in the new country and alcohol played an important role as a food staple and medicine. The next century brought on Rush and others concerned with temperate drinking but the drinking of rum, cider, and dramming only increased. American whiskey also became one of the country's most important native products.

The 19th century was the true rise of the shot glass. Not only were bar tumblers and sample glasses made in significant quantities but fine cut glass and art glass were also tuned to some shot glass production. The 20th century was the time of successful national Prohibition movement that ended sample glass production and legal drinking; however, the Depression era more than made up for the lack of sample glasses.

The 20th century was marked with so many innovations in shot glass decorating that it seems like nearly everything possible has been applied. Only the future and the next century will tell what is yet to be developed. The remaining part of the chapter illustrates the numerous examples of shot glasses produced in the 1980's and 1990's.

> Fifteen men on the Dead Man's Chest–
> Yo-Ho-Ho and a bottle of rum!
> Drink and the devil had done for the rest–
> Yo-Ho-Ho and a bottle of rum!
>
> Robert Louis Stevenson, Treasure Island.

#ANE011   #ANE012   #ANE013

#ANE014   #ANE015

#ANE016 standard.
Red design, 1980's.

Set of 5 standard-size shot glasses–#ANE011, #ANE012, #ANE013, #ANE014, and #ANE015. All have gold & black designs, late-1980's.

#ANE007 square. Etched
white writing, 1980's.

#ANE009 standard. Red
design, 1980's.

#ANE017 standard. Black
design, 1980's.

#ANE018 2½" tall, 2 oz. Gold
design, 1980's.

#ANE019 standard. Black
writing, 1980's.

#ANN010 standard. Green
or red design, 1980's.

#ANE021 standard. Green
design, 1980's.

#ANE022 standard. Blue
design, 1980's.

#ANE025 standard. Red &
black design, 1980's.

#ANE026 standard. Blue & white design, 1980's.

#ANE027 standard. Red, white, & blue design, 1980's.

#ANE028 standard. Red, white, & black design, 1980's.

#ANE029 standard. Red design, 1980's.

#ANE030 standard. Green & red design, 1980's.

#ANE031 standard. Black & white design, 1980's.

#ANE035 standard. Green, red, & yellow design, 1980's.

#ANN050 standard. Gold, red, & yellow design, 1990's.

#DSA307 Double Shot, Green design, 1980's.

#ANE062 standard. Red writing, 1980's.

#ANE063 standard. Black design, 1980's.

#ANE070 standard. Pewter circle att. to exterior, 1980's.

#ANE090 standard. Green design, 1980's.

#ANE100 standard. Multi-colored design, 1980's.

#ANE101 standard. Gold, red, & blue design on a frosted glass, 1980's.

#ANE110 standard. Brown design, 1980's.

#ANE120 standard. Red, white, & blue design, 1980's.

#ANE121 standard. White, red, & yellow, 1980's.

#ANE122 square. Pewter circle att. to exterior, 1980's.

#ANE140 standard. Multi-colored design, 1980's.

#ANE141 square. Multi-colored design, 1980's.

#ANE180 square. Pewter symbol att. to exterior, 1980's.

#ANE045 standard. Red design, 1980's.

#ANE046 standard. Red & white design, 1980's.

#ANE047 standard. Black design on white background, 1980's.

#ANE048 standard. Red writing on yellow background, 1980's.

#ANE049 standard. Red & black design with clear lettering, 1980's.

#ANE050 standard. Orange & white design, 1980's.

#ANE051 standard. Black & white design, 1980's.

#PHS112 standard. Red design on white background, 1980's.

#ANE055 standard. Red & black design, 1980's.

#PHS140 standard. Red design, 1980's.

#PHS141 standard. Red design, 1980's.

#PHS142 standard. Red design, 1980's.

#PHS143 standard. Red & black design, 1980's.

#ANE057 standard. Black & orange or dark green & orange design, 1980's.

#ANE059 standard. Red & blue design, 1980's.

#PHS160 standard. Blue design, 1980's.

#PHS160 standard. Blue writing, 1980's.

#PHS164 standard. Blue design, 1980's.

#PHS012 standard. Culver 22 kt. gold, white, & frosted design, 1980's.

#PHS013 standard. Culver 22 kt. gold, white, & frosted design, 1980's.

#PHS014 standard. Culver 22 kt. gold, green, & red design, 1980's.

#PHS015 standard. Culver 22 kt. gold, green, & red design, 1980's.

#PHS016 standard. Culver 22 kt. gold, red, white, & green design, 1980's.

#PHS200 standard. Culver 22 kt. gold, red, & green "Yule Horn" design, 1990's.

#PHS201 standard. Culver 22 kt. gold, red, & green "Poinsettia" design, 1990's.

#PHS202 standard. Culver 22 kt. gold, red, & frosted design, 1990's.

#PHS203 standard. Culver 22 kt. gold & frosted "Golden Stag" design, 1990's.

#PHS204 standard. Culver 22 kt. gold, white, black, & frosted design, 1990's.

#PPA623 standard. Blue & white design, 1980's.

#PPA628 standard. Pink & bluish-green design, 1980's.

#PPA637 square. Fort pewter design, 1980's.

#PPA660 standard. Black & brown design, 1980's.

#PPA638

#PPA639

#PPA640

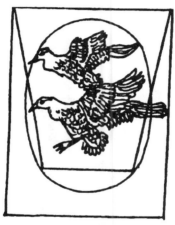

#PPA641

Set of 4 square shot glasses #PPA638, #PPA639, #PPA640, and #PPA641. Fort 2-tone "Ducks" with pewter designs upon bronze shields. 1980's.

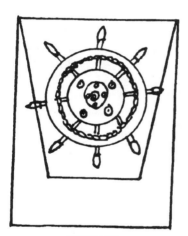

Set of 4 square shot glasses #PPD465, #PPD466, #PPD467, and #PPD468. Fort "Nautical Shots" with pewter designs attached to the exterior. 1980's.

#PPD468

#PPD465

#PPD466

#PPD467

#PSG201 standard. Black porcelain replica (coated with black enamel inside and out), 1980's.

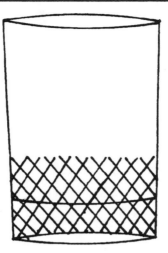

#PPC204 2½" tall, 2 oz. Clear crystal pattern, 1980's.

#PPC205 2" tall, 1 oz. Molded flower pattern upon a frosted glass, 1980's.

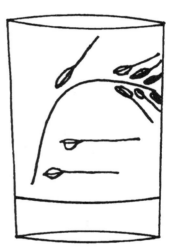

#EPG600 2½" tall, 2 oz. Etched pattern around glass, 1980's.

#EPG601 standard. Etched pattern around glass, 1980's.

#PDP200 2" tall, 1 oz. Gray and white onyx design. Early 1980's.

#PDP202 standard. Brown design, 1980's.

#PDP203 standard. Gold & blue design, 1980's.

#PDP404 standard. White writing, 1980's.

#PPD405

#PPD406

#PPD407

#PPD408

Set of 4 standard shot glasses #PPD405, #PPD406, #PPD407, and #PPD408. Black designs, 1980's.

#PPD430 standard. Orange, black, & blue design, 1980's.

#PPD438 Depression Tall with multicolored design, 1980's.

#PPD439 2½" tall, 2 oz. Multicolored ship with gold lines and rim; id. on rev., 1980's.

#PPC300 standard. Culver 22 kt. gold, red, & black "Tortoise" pattern, 1990's.

#PPD500 standard. Culver 22 kt. gold "Shell Gold" pattern, 1990's.

THE AMERICAN ART CHINA COMPANY RAILROAD COLLECTION:

All are standard size shot glasses with railroad advertising, 1980's.

#ANE300 "The Alaska Railroad" Black, blue, & yellow design.
#ANE301 "Amtrak" Red, blue, & black design.
#ANE302 "Atlantic Coast Line" Red, white, & blue design.
#ANE303 "B & O" Blue & yellow design.
#ANE304 "Bangor and Aroostock" Blue & white design.
#ANE305 "BM" (Boston and Maine) Blue, black, & clear design.
#ANE306 "Burlington Northern" Green & white design.
#ANE307 "Burlington Route" Red, yellow, and black design.
#ANE308 "C and O for Progress" Yellow & blue design.
#ANE309 "CSX Corporation" Dark blue, light blue, and white design.
#ANE310 "CSX Transportation" Blue and white design.
#ANE311 "California Western Railroad" Red, yellow, black, and white design.
#ANE312 "California Zephyr" Multicolored design.
#ANE313 "Canadian National Railway" Red, white, and black design.
#ANE314 "Canadian Pacific" Red, white, brown, and tan design.
#ANE315 "Central Railroad Company of New Jersey" Red and white design.
#ANE316 "Chessie System" Blue and orange design.
#ANE317 "Chicago Burlington and Quincy" Multicolored design.
#ANE318 "Chicago & Eastern Illinois" Multicolored design.
#ANE319 "Chicago & Illinois Midland" Red, yellow, & black design.
#ANE320 "Chicago Missouri and Western Railway" Red, yellow, and black design.
#ANE321 "Chicago and North Western System" Red, white, and black design.
#ANE322 "Clinchfield Railroad" Black and white design.
#ANE323 "CS" (Colorado Southern) Red and black design.
#ANE324 "Conrail" Blue and white design.
#ANE325 "Cotton Belt Route" Blue and white design.
#ANE326 "The D & H" Blue and yellow design.
#ANE327 "D & RGW RR Royal Gorge Route Scenic Line" Red and white design.
#ANE328 "Delaware and Ulster RR" Multicolored design.
#ANE329 "E" (Erie) 2 varieties–Light blue and white or dark blue and white designs.
#ANE330 "Erie" Yellow and black design.
#ANE331 "E Erie Lackawanna" Brown and white design.
#ANE332 "French Lick West Baden Southern Ry." Green and yellow design.
#ANE333 "Frisco" Red and white design.
#ANE334 "Frisco Lines" Red and white design.
#ANE335 "G M & O" Red and yellow design.
#ANE336 "Georgia R.R. Old Reliable 1834" Red and white design.
#ANE337 "Grand Trunk Railway System" Multicolored design.
#ANE338 "Great Northern Railway" Red, white, and blue design.
#ANE339 "Green Mountain Rutland" Multicolored design.
#ANE340 "Illinois Central" Green, white, and black design.
#ANE341 "Illinois Terminal Railroad Company" Multicolored design.
#ANE342 "Jersey Central Lines" Multicolored design.
#ANE343 "Kansas City Southern Lines" Red and white design.
#ANE344 "Katy" Red and white design.
#ANE345 "L & A Railway The Better Way" Red, white, and black design.
#ANE346 "L & N" 2 varieties – Red and clear or red and white designs.
#ANE347 "Lehigh Valley Railroad" Black, red, and yellow design.
#ANE348 "M-K-T Katy Lines" Red and white design.
#ANE349 "Manufacturers Railroad" Multicolored design.
#ANE350 "Maryland and Pennsylvania Railroad" Black and yellow design.
#ANE351 "The Milwaukee Road" Red, white, and black design.
#ANE352 "Missouri Pacific Lines" Red and white design.

#ANE353 "Missouri Pacific Lines" and "Texas Pacific Lines" Red and white design.
#ANE354 "Mo-pac" Red, white, blue, and black design.
#ANE355 "Monon The Hoosier Line" Red and white design.
#ANE356 "Monon" Red and yellow design.
#ANE357 "New York Central System" Red, black, and white design.
#ANE358 "New York Central System" Black and gray design (large oval).
#ANE359 "The New York New Haven and Hartford Railroad" Black and white design.
#ANE360 "Nickel Plate Road" Blue and white design.
#ANE361 "N S Norfolk Southern" Gray and black design.
#ANE362 "N W Norfolk and Western" Black and white design.
#ANE363 "Northern Pacific Railway" Red, white, and black design.
#ANE364 "Oregon Pacific & Eastern Railroad" Blue and white design.
#ANE365 "Pacific Electric Comfort Speed Safety" Red, yellow, and gray design.
#ANE366 "Penn Central" Green and white design.
#ANE367 "Pennsylvania RR" Red & white design.
#ANE368 "Providence & Worcester Railroad" Brown, orange, and white design.
#ANE369 "Pullman" Multicolored design.
#ANE370 "R F & P" Blue and white design.
#ANE371 "Reading Lines" Black and white design.
#ANE372 "Richmond Fredericksburg" Red, white, and blue design.
#ANE373 "Richmond Washington Line" Orange and blue design.
#ANE374 "Rio Grande Main Line Thru the Rockies" Multicolored design.
#ANE375 "Rio Grande The Action Railroad" Orange and black design.
#ANE376 "Rock Island" 2 varieties–Black and white or red and white designs.
#ANE377 "R P R" Red and white design.
#ANE378 "S P S F" Red and yellow design.
#ANE379 "Sacramento Northern" Green, white, yellow, and gray design.
#ANE380 "Santa Fe" 3 varieties–Blue and white or blue, white, and black or red, yellow, and black designs.
#ANE381 "Santa Fe" and "Southern Pacific Lines" Blue, yellow, white, and black design.
#ANE382 "Seaboard Air Line Railroad" Black, white, and red design.
#ANE383 "Seaboard Coast Line Railroad S C L" Red, white, and blue design.
#ANE384 "Seaboard System Railroad" Red, yellow, white, and black design.
#ANE385 "Sierra Railroad Company Rail Transportation" Black and white design.
#ANE386 "Soo Line" Red and white design.
#ANE387 "Soo The Milwaukee Road" Red and white design.
#ANE388 "S R The Southern Serves the South" Green and yellow design.
#ANE389 "S P Southern Pacific" Red, white, black, and gray design.
#ANE390 "Southern Pacific" Brown, white, and yellow design.
#ANE391 "Southern Pacific Lines" Blue, yellow, and white design.
#ANE392 "Spokane Portland and Seattle RY." Red and white design.
#ANE393 "Strasburg" Multicolored design.
#ANE394 "T and P The Texas Pacific Railway" Red, black, and white design.
#ANE395 "Union Pacific" 2 varieties–All white or red, white, and blue designs.

#ANE396 "Union Pacific Overland" Red, white, and blue design.
#ANE397 "Union Pacific" and "Mo-pac" and "Western Pacific" Multicolored design.
#ANE398 "Virginia Truckee" Red, white, and yellow design.
#ANE399 "Wabash Follow the Flag" Red, white, and blue design.
#ANE400 "Western Maryland Fast Freight Line" Black, yellow, and red design.
#ANE401 "Western Pacific" Red, white, and black design.
#ANE402 "Durango & Silverton Narrow Gauge R.R. The Silverton" Black and white design.

#ANE403 "The Durango & Silverton Narrow Gauge Railroad" Black, yellow, and white design.
#ANE404 "Burlington Northern" and "Great Northern Railway" and "Spokane Portland Seattle Route" and "Burlington Route" and "Frisco Lines" and "Northern Pacific Railway" Multicolored miniature designs.

Those listed below and on the next page are railroad shot glass examples.

#ANE300   #ANE301   #ANE302

#ANE311   #ANE313   #ANE317

#ANE332   #ANE336   #ANE338

#ANE348

#ANE353

#ANE374

#ANE381

#ANE386

#ANE396

#ANE401

#ANE402

#ANE404

The 26-team baseball shot glass set. All are standard-size, late-1980's.

#SGA001 Atlanta Braves.
#SMD001 Baltimore Orioles.
#SMA001 Boston Red Sox.
#SCA002 California Angels.
#SIL001 Chicago Cubs.
#SIL002 Chicago White Sox.
#SOH002 Cincinnati Reds.
#SOH001 Cleveland Indians.
#SMI003 Detroit Tigers.
#STX002 Houston Astros.
#SMO001 Kansas City Royals.
#SCA003 Los Angeles Dodgers.
#SWI001 Milwaukee Brewers.

#SMN001 Minnesota Twins.
#CNS001 Montreal Expos.
#SNY010 New York Mets.
#SNY001 New York Yankees.
#SCA004 Oakland Athletics.
#SPA010 Philadelphia Phillies.
#SPA011 Pittsburgh Pirates.
#SMO002 St. Louis Cardinals.
#SCA005 San Diego Padres.
#SCA006 San Francisco Giants.
#SWA001 Seattle Mariners.
#STX001 Texas Rangers.
#CNS002 Toronto Blue Jays.

#SCA003 standard, Red, white, & blue design. (1 version has reverse writing: "1988 World Series").

#SCA005 standard. Brown and orange design.

#SIL001 standard. Blue and red design.

#SMA001 standard. Orange, blue, & white design.

#SOH002 standard. Red and white design.

#SWI001 standard. Blue, yellow, and white design.

The 28-team football shot glass set. All are standard-size, late-1980's.

#SGA100 Atlanta Falcons.
#SNY100 Buffalo Bills.
#SIL100 Chicago Bears.
#SOH101 Cincinnati Bengals.
#SOH100 Cleveland Browns.
#STX100 Dallas Cowboys.
#SMI100 Detroit Lions.
#SCO100 Denver Broncos.
#SWI100 Green Bay Packers.
#STX101 Houston Oilers.
#SIN100 Indianapolis Colts.
#SMO100 Kansas City Chiefs.
#SCA100 Los Angeles Raiders.
#SCA103 Los Angeles Rams.

#SFL101 Miami Dolphins.
#SMN100 Minnesota Vikings.
#SMA100 New England Patriots.
#SLA100 New Orleans Saints.
#SNY101 New York Giants.
#SNY102 New York Jets.
#SPA100 Philadelphia Eagles.
#SAZ100 Phoenix Cardinals.
#SPA101 Pittsburgh Steelers.
#SCA101 San Diego Chargers.
#SCA102 San Francisco 49ers.
#SWA100 Seattle Seahawks.
#SFL100 Tampa Bay Buccaneers.
#SDC100 Washington Redskins.

#SCA102 standard. Multicolored – 3 versions: 1) No reverse. 2) Rev: "Superbowl XXIII." 3) Rev: "SB XXIII CHAMPIONS."

#SCO100 standard. Multicolored design.

#SDC100 standard. Multicolored design.

#SFL100 standard. Orange, white, red, and black design.

#SLA100 standard. Black, white, and tan design.

#SMA100 standard. Multicolored design.

#SOH100 standard.
Multicolored design.

#SOH101 standard. Multicolored
design. (1 version has reverse
writing: "Superbowl XXIII").

#STX100 standard.
Blue, gray, black, and
white design.

The 26-team basketball shot glass set. All are standard-size, late-1980's.

#SGA110 Atlanta Hawks.
#SMA110 Boston Celtics.
#SNC110 Charlotte Hornets.
#SIL110 Chicago Bulls.
#SOH110 Cleveland Cavaliers.
#STX110 Dallas Mavericks.
#SCO110 Denver Nuggets.
#SMI110 Detroit Pistons.
#SCA110 Golden State Warriors.
#STX111 Houston Rockets.
#SIN110 Indiana Pacers.
#SCA111 Los Angeles Clippers.
#SCA112 Los Angeles Lakers.

#SFL110 Miami Heat.
#SWI110 Milwaukee Bucks.
#SMN110 Minnesota Timberwolves.
#SNJ110 New Jersey Nets.
#SNY110 New York Knicks.
#SFL111 Orlando Magic.
#SPA110 Philadelphia 76ers.
#SAZ110 Phoenix Suns.
#SOR110 Portland Trailblazers.
#STX112 San Antonio Spurs.
#SWA110 Seattle Supersonics.
#SUT110 Utah Jazz.
#SDC110 Washington Bullets.

#SFL110 standard. Orange,
red, and black design.

#SMA110 standard. Green,
white, and black design.

#SMI110 standard. Red,
white, and blue design.

#SNC110 standard.
Multicolored design.

#SCT001 standard. Green,
white, and blue design.

The 21-team hockey shot glass set. All are standard size, late-1980's.

#SMA120 Boston Bruins.
#SNY122 Buffalo Sabres.
#CNS010 Calgary Flames.
#SIL120 Chicago Blackhawks.
#SMI120 Detroit Redwings.
#CNS011 Edmonton Oilers.
#SCT001 Hartford Whalers.
#SCA120 Los Angeles Kings.
#SMN120 Minnesota North Stars.
#CNS012 Montreal Canadians.
#SNJ120 New Jersey Devils.

#SNY121 New York Islanders.
#SNY120 New York Rangers.
#SPA120 Philadelphia Flyers.
#SPA121 Pittsburgh Penguins.
#CNS013 Quebec Nordiques.
#SMO110 St. Louis Blues.
#CNS014 Toronto Maple Leafs.
#CNS015 Vancouver Canucks.
#SDC120 Washington Capitals.
#CNS016 Winnipeg Jets.

#SMI120 standard. Red,
white, and black design.

#SNJ120 standard. Red, green,
and white design.

#SNY120 standard. Blue,
red, and white design.

#SFL120 standard. Red and green design, 1980's.

#SOH130 standard. Green design, 1980's.

#SWI010 standard. Green design (early 1980's version).

#SUS008

#SUS009

#SUS010

Set of four square shot glasses. Fort "Sports" set. All have pewter designs attached to the exterior, 1980's. #SUS008, 009, 010, and 011.

#SUS011

#UAL012 standard. Red, white, and gray design, 1980's.

#UAZ010 standard. Multi-colored design, 1980's.

#UCA010 standard. Red, white, and tan design, 1980's.

#UFL010 standard. Orange, green, and white design, 1980's.

#UIA010 standard. Yellow and black design, 1980's.

#UKY013 standard. Black and white design, 1980's.

#UKY014 standard. Blue and white design, 1980's.

#UKY015 standard. Black design, 1980's.

#ULA010 standard. Red, white, and black design, 1980's.

#UMA010 standard. Red and white design, 1980's.

#UMI059 standard. Blue & yellow design on pewter att. to exterior, 1980's.

#UMI061 standard. Blue and yellow design, 1980's.

#UMI062 square. Blue design, 1980's.

#UMI063 square. Blue and yellow design, 1980's.

#UMI085 standard. Green and white design, 1980's.

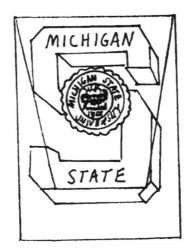

#UMI086 square. Green and white design, 1980's.

#UMI102 standard. Red design, 1980's.

#UMI103 standard. Gold, blue, and black design, 1980's.

#UMI105 standard. Green and white design, 1980's.

#UNC022 standard. Blue and white design, 1980's.

#DSU110 Double Shot. Green design, 1980's. 14 flutes.

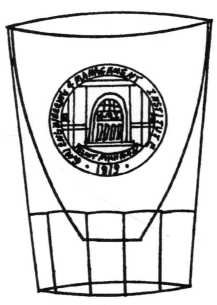

#DSU111 Double Shot. Yellow and blue design, 1980's. 14 flutes.

#DSU112 Double Shot. Blue design, 1980's. 14 flutes.

#UNC030 standard. Red, white, and black design, 1980's.

#UNV010 standard. Red and black design, 1980's.

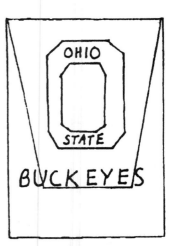

#UOH011 square. Red and gray design, 1980's.

#UOH012 standard. Red and black design, 1980's.

#UOH030 standard. Brown and orange design, 1980's.

#UOH035 standard. Dark pink design, 1980's.

#UOH040 square. Brown design, 1980's.

#UOH045 square. Blue writing, 1980's.

#UPA010 standard. Blue design, 1980's.

#UTN020 standard. Purple design, 1980's.

#UUS017 standard. Multi-colored design, 1980's.

#UUS018 standard. Multi-colored design, 1980's.

#UUS019 standard. Multi-colored design, 1980's.

#UUS020 standard. Multi-colored design, 1980's.

#UUS021 standard. Multi-colored design, 1980's.

#UUS022 standard. Multi-colored design, 1980's.

#UUS023 standard. Etched white writing, 1980's.

#UUS024 standard. Red writing, 1980's.

The 50 State Shield shot glass collection. All are multicolored (greater than 4 colors) designed, standard-size, and produced in the early 1980's.

#TAL103 Alabama.	#TLA101 Louisiana.	#TOH106 Ohio.
#TAK103 Alaska.	#TME104 Maine.	#TOK104 Oklahoma.
#TAZ102 Arizona.	#TMD100 Maryland.	#TOR101 Oregon.
#TAR102 Arkansas.	#TMA101 Massachusetts.	#TPA103 Pennsylvania.
#TCA145 California.	#TMI124 Michigan.	#TRI103 Rhode Island.
#TCO102 Colorado.	#TMN106 Minnesota.	#TSC100 South Carolina.
#TCT103 Connecticut.	#TMS102 Mississippi.	#TSD101 South Dakota.
#TDE105 Delaware.	#TMO101 Missouri.	#TTN111 Tennessee.
#TFL113 Florida.	#TMT101 Montana.	#TTX106 Texas.
#TGA103 Georgia.	#TNE102 Nebraska.	#TUT102 Utah.
#THI115 Hawaii.	#TNV102 Nevada.	#TVT102 Vermont.
#TID102 Idaho.	#TNH101 New Hampshire.	#TVA102 Virginia.
#TIL104 Illinois.	#TNJ103 New Jersey.	#TWA102 Washington.
#TIN103 Indiana.	#TNM104 New Mexico.	#TWV101 West Virginia.
#TIA102 Iowa.	#TNY107 New York.	#TWI103 Wisconsin.
#TKS101 Kansas.	#TNC100 North Carolina.	#TWY101 Wyoming.
#TKY114 Kentucky.	#TND101 North Dakota.	

The following 2 pages illustrate examples of state shield shot glasses:

#TAL103

#TCO102

#TCT103

#TDE105

#TIA102

#TID102

#TKS101

#TME104

#TMO101

#TMS102

#TMT101

#TNE102

#TNH101

#TRI103

#TSD101

#TUT102

#TVT102

#TWA102

The 50 State framed tourist shot glass collection. Each illustrates 5 framed tourist sites from each respective state. All are standard-size, available in red & black or blue & white color designs, and were produced in the mid-1980's. Note other framed glasses with this style are also in existence including cities, Canada, and older state shot glasses.

#TAL102 Alabama.	#TLA100 Louisiana.	#TOH103 Ohio.
#TAK101 Alaska.	#TME102 Maine.	#TOK103 Oklahoma.
#TAZ101 Arizona.	#TMD104 Maryland.	#TOR100 Oregon.
#TAR101 Arkansas.	#TMA100 Massachusetts.	#TPA102 Pennsylvania.
#TCA113 California.	#TMI103 Michigan.	#TRI102 Rhode Island.
#TCO101 Colorado.	#TMN104 Minnesota.	#TSC102 South Carolina.
#TCT102 Connecticut.	#TMS101 Mississippi.	#TSD100 South Dakota.
#TDE104 Delaware.	#TMO100 Missouri.	#TTN109 Tennessee
#TFL107 Florida.	#TMT100 Montana.	#TTX104 Texas.
#TGA102 Georgia.	#TNE101 Nebraska.	#TUT100 Utah.
#THI112 Hawaii.	#TNV101 Nevada.	#TVT101 Vermont.
#TID100 Idaho.	#TNH100 New Hampshire.	#TVA101 Virginia.
#TIL101 Illinois.	#TNJ102 New Jersey.	#TWA101 Washington.
#TIN101 Indiana.	#TNM101 New Mexico.	#TWV100 West Virginia.
#TIA101 Iowa.	#TNY106 New York.	#TWI101 Wisconsin.
#TKS100 Kansas.	#TNC103 North Carolina.	#TWY100 Wyoming.
#TKY113 Kentucky.	#TND100 North Dakota.	

Illustrated below and on the following 2 pages are examples of the framed state tourist shot glasses:

#TAK101

#TAL102

#TAR101

#TDE104

#THI112

#TIA101

#TKS100

#TME102

#TMS101

#TKY113

#TMT100

#TND100

#TNM101

#TOK103

#TOR100

#TRI102

#TSC102

#TSD100

#TVA101

#TVT101

#TWA101

#TWI101

#TWV100

#TWY100

The 50 State Flag tourist shot glass collection. All are standard-size, multicolored, illustrate each state's respective flag, and were first produced in 1990. Flags for Canada, Mexico, Puerto Rico, and the United States are also available (see foreign chapter for Canada and Mexico).

#TAL400 Alabama.
#TAK400 Alaska.
#TAZ400 Arizona.
#TAR400 Arkansas.
#TCA400 California.
#TCO400 Colorado.
#TCT400 Connecticut.
#TDE400 Delaware.
#TFL400 Florida.
#TGA400 Georgia.
#THI400 Hawaii.
#TID400 Idaho.
#TIL400 Illinois.
#TIN400 Indiana.
#TIA400 Iowa.
#TKS400 Kansas.
#TKY400 Kentucky.

#TLA400 Louisiana.
#TME400 Maine.
#TMD400 Maryland.
#TMA400 Massachusetts.
#TMI400 Michigan.
#TMN400 Minnesota.
#TMS400 Mississippi.
#TMO400 Missouri.
#TMT400 Montana.
#TNE400 Nebraska.
#TNV400 Nevada.
#TNH400 New Hampshire.
#TNJ400 New Jersey.
#TNM400 New Mexico.
#TNY400 New York.
#TNC400 North Carolina.
#TND400 North Dakota.

#TOH400 Ohio.
#TOK400 Oklahoma.
#TOR400 Oregon.
#TPA400 Pennsylvania.
#TRI400 Rhode Island.
#TSC400 South Carolina.
#TSD400 South Dakota.
#TTN400 Tennessee.
#TTX104 Texas.
#TUT400 Utah.
#TVT400 Vermont.
#TVA400 Virginia.
#TWA400 Washington.
#TWV400 West Virginia.
#TWI400 Wisconsin.
#TWY400 Wyoming.

Illustrated below and on the following 2 pages are examples of the framed state flag shot glasses (Puerto Rico #TPR400 and the United States #TUS400 are also shown here).

#TAK400

#TAL400

#TAZ400

#TCO400

#TFL400

#TGA400

HAWAII
"ALOHA STATE"

#THI400

KANSAS
"SUNFLOWER STATE"

#TKS400

MARYLAND
"OLD LINE STATE"

#TMD400

MAINE
"PINE TREE STATE"

#TME400

MISSOURI
"SHOW ME STATE"

#TMO400

MISSISSIPPI
"MAGNOLIA STATE"

#TMS400

MONTANA
"TREASURE STATE"

#TMT400

NORTH DAKOTA
"FLICKERTAIL STATE"

#TND400

NEW HAMPSHIRE
"GRANITE STATE"

#TNH400

NEW MEXICO
"LAND OF ENCHANTMENT"

#TNM400

OHIO
"BUCKEYE STATE"

#TOH400

SOUTH DAKOTA
"THE SUNSHINE STATE"

#TSD400

TEXAS
"LONE STAR STATE"

#TTX400

VIRGINIA
"OLD DOMINION"

#TVA400

WASHINGTON
"EVERGREEN STATE"

#TWA400

WYOMING
"EQUALITY STATE"

#TWY400

PUERTO RICO

#TPR400

#TUS400

#TAK102 standard. Gold, black, and blue-gray design, 1980's.

#TAL121 standard. Black design, 1980's.

#TAZ100 standard. Multi-colored design, 1980's.

#TAZ120 standard. Black design, 1980's.

#TAZ130 standard. Red design on black porcelain rep., 1980's.

#TAZ140 standard. Gold & black design, 1980's.

#TAZ150 standard. Multi-colored design on black porcelain rep., 1980's.

#TCA101 standard. Blue and white design, 1980's.

#TCA102 standard. Black, blue, and white design, 1980's.

#TCA103 standard. Multi-colored design, 1980's.

#TCA104 standard. Pink, black, and blue design on frosted glass, 1980's.

#TCA105 standard. Culver 22 kt. gold and frosted design, 1980's.

#TCA106 standard. Black and white design, 1980's.

#TCA107 standard. Yellow, white, and blue design on frosted glass, 1980's.

#TCA108 standard. Yellow and blue design, 1980's.

#TCA109 standard. Green and blue design around glass, 1980's.

#TCA110 standard. Multi-colored design, 1980's.

#TCA111 standard. Pewter circle att. to exterior, 1980's.

#TCA112 standard. White
and green design on pewter
att. to exterior, 1980's.

#TCA114 standard. Blue
and white design, 1980's.

#TCA115 standard. Blue
and green design on frosted
glass, 1980's.

#TCA116 standard. Gold and
black design on a clear or
frosted glass, 1980's.

#TCA117 standard. Gold
designs on black porcelain
rep., 1980's.

#TCA118 standard. Multi-
colored design, 1980's.

#TCA119 standard. Blue
and black design, 1980's.

#TCA122 standard. Orange
and black design, 1980's.

#TCA123 standard. Blue and
white design, 1980's.

#TCA124 standard. Blue, red, and yellow design, 1980's.

#TCA125 standard. Blue and black design, 1980's.

#TCA126 standard. Blue, orange, and red design, 1980's.

#TCA127 standard. Blue and white design, 1980's.

#TCA128 standard. Gold and white design on black porcelain rep., 1980's.

#TCA129 standard. Orange, blue, and design, 1980's.

#TCA132 standard. Multi-colored design, 1980's.

#TCA133 standard. Red design, 1980's.

#TCA134 standard. Blue, red, and black design, 1980's.

#TCA135 standard. Red, blue, and black design, 1980's.

#TCA136 standard. Multi-colored design, 1980's.

#TCA137 standard. Black design on a blue, orange, or yellow background, 1980's.

#TCA138 standard. Etched design, 1980's.

#TCA139 standard. Brown design, 1980's.

#TCA140 standard. Multi-colored design, 1980's.

#TCA141 standard. Multi-colored design, 1980's.

#TCA142 standard. Gold and black design on a black, orange, or white background, 1980's.

#TCA143 Depression Tall. Orange and light blue design, 1980's.

#TCA144 standard. Multi-colored design on black porcelain rep., 1980's.

#TCA160 standard. Multi-colored design, 1980's.

#TCA170 standard. Black design on blue, orange, or yellow background, 1980's.

#TCO130 standard. Culver 22 kt. gold and frosted design, 1980's.

#TCO140 standard. Black and white design, 1980's.

#TDC121 standard. White design, 1980's.

#TDC122 standard. Green design, 1980's.

#TDE106 standard. Black and orange design, 1980's.

#TFL106 standard. Orange design on a white background, 1980's.

#TFL108 standard. Orange and white design, 1980's.

#TFL109 standard. Multi-colored design, 1980's.

#TFL110 standard. Multi-colored design, 1980's.

#TFL111 standard. Blue and white design, 1980's.

#TFL112 standard. Culver 22 kt. gold and frosted design, 1980's.

#TFL125 standard. Red and gold design, 1980's.

#TFL147 standard. Green design, 1980's.

#TFL160 2¼" tall, 1½ oz. Etched design (Disney World Castle), 1980's.

#TGA101 standard. Red and white design, 1980's.

#TGA131 standard. Black and orange design on frosted glass, 1980's.

#THI113 standard. Gold and black design, 1980's.

#THI114 standard. Black and white design, 1980's.

#THI120 standard. Gold design, 1980's.

#THI125 standard. Gold and black design on frosted glass, 1980's.

#THI130 standard. Green and brown design, 1980's.

#TID101 standard. Gold and black design, 1980's.

#TID103 standard. Blue and black design, 1980's.

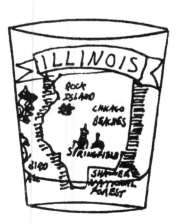

#TIL100 standard. Red and black design, 1980's.

#TIL102 standard. Multi-colored design, 1980's.

#TIL103 standard. Multi-colored design on porcelain glass, 1980's.

#TIL122 standard. Blue writing, 1980's.

#TIL123 standard. Silver metallic design, 1980's.

#TIL140 standard. Red design, 1980's.

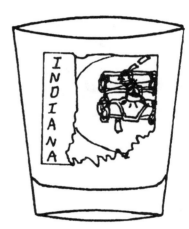

#TIN102 standard. Multi-colored design, 1980's.

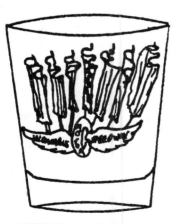

#TIN120 standard. Multi-colored design, 1980's.

#TIN121 standard. Gold and black, 1980's.

#TIN122 standard. Multi-colored design, 1980's.

#TIN123 standard. Multi-colored design, 1980's.

#TKY112 standard. Light blue and gold design, 1980's.

#TLA122 standard. Black and gold design, 1980's.

#TLA123 standard. Black design, 1980's.

#TLA124 standard. Culver 22 kt. gold and frosted design, 1980's.

#TMA131 standard. Pewter design att. to exterior, 1980's.

#TMA132 standard. Red lettering, 1980's.

#TMA133 standard. Black and red design, 1980's.

#TMA134 standard. Blue design, 1980's.

#TMA135 standard. Multi-colored design, 1980's.

#TMA150 standard. Black design, 1980's.

#TMD105 standard. Red and black design, 1980's.

#TMD131 standard. Black and yellow design, 1980's.

#TMD134 standard. Black, red, and green design, 1980's.

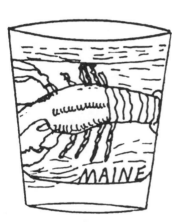

#TME103 standard. Red designs, 1980's.

#TMI109 standard. Multi-colored design on black porcelain rep., 1980's.

#TMI110 standard. Blue and black design on frosted glass, 1980's.

#TMI111 standard. Black design, 1980's.

#TMI112 standard. Red and black design, 1980's.

#TMI113 standard. Blue design on frosted glass, 1980's.

#TMI114 standard. Red, white, and blue design on pewter att. to exterior, 1980's.

#TMI115 standard. Blue design on pewter att. to exterior, 1980's.

#TMI116 standard. Multi-colored design, 1980's.

#TMI117 standard. Orange and black design, 1980's.

#TMI118 standard. Black design, 1980's.

#TMI119 standard. Black design, 1980's.

#TMI121 standard. Dark yellow and black design on frosted glass, 1980's.

#TMI122 standard. Blue-green and pink design on frosted glass, 1980's.

#TMI123 standard. Yellow, red, and black design, 1980's.

#TMI129 2" tall, 1 oz. Multi-colored design, 1980's.

#TMI139 standard. Gold design on black porcelain rep., 1980's.

#TMI141 standard. Red or black design, 1980's.

#TMI142 standard. Multi-colored design, 1980's.

#TMI143 standard. Dark pink design, 1980's.

#TMI147 standard. Blue design, 1980's.

#TMI152 standard. Pewter design att. to exterior, 1980's.

#TMI153 standard. Blue design on frosted glass, 1980's.

#TMI163 standard. Blue, white, and black design, 1980's.

#TMI164 Depression Tall. Blue and white design, 1980's.

#TMI165 Depression Tall. Blue and white design, 1980's.

#TMI166 Square. Black design, 1980's.

#TMI167 standard. Multi-colored design on frosted glass, 1980's.

#TMI168 standard. Blue, white, and pink design on frosted glass, 1980's.

#TMI175 standard. Black and blue.

#TMI176 standard. Blue and black design on frosted glass, 1980's.

#TMI177 standard. Culver 22 kt. gold and frosted design, 1980's.

#TMI178 standard. Multicolored design on porcelain, 1980's.

#TMI179 Square. Pewter design att. to exterior, 1980's.

#TMI189 Square. Multicolored design on pewter att. to exterior, 1980's.

#TMI198 standard. Blue and white design on black porcelain rep., 1980's.

#TMI199 standard. Multicolored design on porcelain, 1980's.

#TMI200 standard. Etched white design, 1980's.

#TMI201 standard. Black design on frosted glass, 1980's.

#TMI202 standard. Multicolored design on porcelain, 1980's.

#TMI203 standard. Orange, blue, and black design, 1980's.

#TMI204 standard. Red & black or blue & white design, 1980's.

#TMI209 standard. Multicolored design on aluminum att. to exterior, 1980's.

#TMI210 standard. Blue and white design on a black porcelain rep., 1980's.

#TMI211 standard. Blue and black design on porcelain glass, 1980's.

#TMI212 standard. Culver 22 kt. gold and frosted design, 1980's.

#TMI213 standard. Multicolored design on porcelain glass, 1980's.

#TMI215 standard. Red design, 1980's.

#TMI216 standard. Multicolored design, 1980's.

#TMI217 standard. Multi-colored design, 1980's.

#TMI218 standard. Pewter design att. to exterior, 1980's.

#TMI270 standard. Gold and black design, 1980's.

#TMI271 standard. Blue and white design on a black porcelain rep., 1980's.

#TMI272 standard. Multi-colored design on pewter attached to exterior, 1980's.

#TMI280 standard. Black design on red background, 1980's.

#TMI480 standard. Silver metallic design, 1990's.

#TMN105 standard. Black and red design, 1980's.

#TMN131 standard. Culver 22 kt. gold and frosted design, 1980's.

#TMN132 standard. Red, white, and black design, 1980's.

#TMN150 standard. Black design, 1980's.

#TMT102 standard. Gold and black on frosted glass, 1980's.

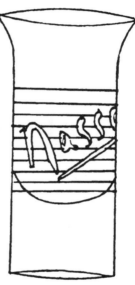

#TNA100 Depression Tall. Orange and yellow design, 1980's.

#TNC102 standard. Blue and white design, 1980's.

#TNJ129 standard. Gold and black design, 1980's.

#TNM103 standard. Multicolored design on porcelain glass, 1980's.

#TNM103 standard. Multicolored design, 1980's.

#TNV100 standard. Multicolored design, 1980's.

#TNV112 standard. Black
design, 1980's.

#TNV113 standard. Gold
and black design, 1980's.

#TNV114 standard. Culver
22 kt. gold and frosted
design, 1980's.

#TNV115 standard. Red and
blue design, 1980's.

#TNV151 standard. Red
and gold design, 1980's.

#TNV160 standard. Brown,
white, and black design, 1980's.

#TNV170 standard. Yellow,
black, and blue design, 1980's.

#TNV171 standard. Gold and
black design, 1980's.

#TNY130 standard. Gold
and black design, 1980's.

#TNY140 standard. Culver 22 kt. gold and frosted design, 1980's.

#TOH102 standard. Red and black design, 1980's.

#TOH104 standard. Multi-colored design, 1980's.

#TOH105 standard. Multi-colored design on porcelain glass, 1980's.

#TOH111 standard. Gold and white design, 1980's.

#TOH126 standard. Red, blue, and yellow design, 1980's.

#TOH128 Depression Tall. Orange and light blue design, 1980's.

#TOH129 standard. Culver 22 kt. gold and frosted design, 1980's.

#TOH130 standard. Gold and black design, 1980's.

#TOH150 standard. Black
design, 1980's.

#DST550 Double Shot. Black
design, 1980's.

#TOH160 standard. Blue
and white design, 1980's.

#TOH480 standard. Silver
metallic design, 1990's.

#TOK120 standard. Black
design, 1980's.

#TPA155 standard. Yellow
design, 1980's.

#TPA155 standard. Red,
white, and blue design on
pewter att. to exterior, 1990's.

#TPA156 standard. Pewter
design att. to exterior, 1980's.

#TPA160 standard. Red and
black design, 1980's.

#TPR100 standard. Red, white, and blue design, 1980's.

#TPR101 standard. Pewter design att. to exterior, 1980's.

#TRI100 standard. Multi-colored design, 1980's.

#TRI101 standard. Multi-colored design, 1980's.

#TRI120 standard. Black design on white, blue, yellow, or orange background, 1980's.

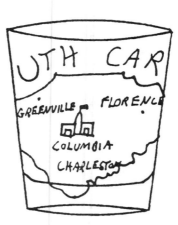

#TSC101 standard. Red and black design, 1980's.

#TSC103 standard. White design on dark yellow glass, 1980's.

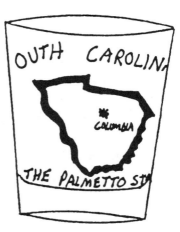

#TSC104 standard. Red design, 1980's.

#TSC131 standard. White design on frosted glass, 1980's.

#TSC132 standard. Orange, black, and green design, 1980's.

#TSC133 standard. Multi-colored design, 1980's.

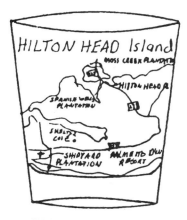

#TSC160 standard. Black and orange design, 1980's.

#TSD120 standard. Black design, 1980's.

#TTN110 standard. Black design on blue or yellow background, 1980's.

#TTN112 standard. Orange and black design on frosted glass, 1980's.

#TTN113 standard. Multi-colored design on porcelain glass, 1980's.

#TTN121 standard. Orange design, 1980's.

#TTN122 standard. Black design, 1980's.

#TTN137 standard. Red and blue design, 1980's.

#TTN138 standard. Blue and black design on frosted glass, 1980's.

#TTN139 square. Pewter design att. to exterior, 1980's.

#TTN142 standard. Blue and green design on white background, 1980's.

#TTN143 standard. Multicolored design, 1980's.

#TTN151 standard. Black and gold design on frosted glass, 1980's.

#TTN167 standard. Red and gold design, 1980's.

#TTN168 standard. Gold and black design, 1980's.

#TTN169 standard. Blue, yellow, and black design, 1980's.

#TTN171 standard. Yellow and black design, 1980's.

#TTN180 standard. Yellow and black design, 1980's.

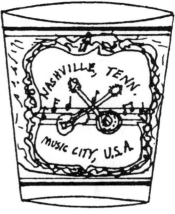

#TTN421 standard. Culver 22 kt. gold and tortoise design, 1990's.

#TTX101 standard. Black design on blue, yellow, or orange background, 1980's.

#TTX102 standard. Black design on blue, yellow, or orange background, 1980's.

#TTX103 standard. Red design, 1980's.

#TTX105 standard. Orange and black design, 1980's.

#TTX121 standard. Gold and black design, 1980's.

#TTX141 standard. Red, black, white, and blue design, 1980's.

#TTX142 standard. Multi-colored design, 1980's.

#TTX150 standard. Multi-colored design, 1980's.

#TTX401 standard. Culver 22 kt. gold and tortoise design, 1990's.

#TUT101 standard. Black design on yellow, orange, or blue background, 1980's.

#TUT103 standard. Red, white, and blue design on pewter att. to exterior, 1980's.

#TUT120 standard. Black and gold design, 1980's.

#TVA100 standard. Red and black design, 1980's.

#TVA120 standard. Grayish-blue and white design, 1980's.

#TVA121 standard. Black design, 1980's.

#TVT420 standard. Black design, 1990's.

#TVT421 standard. Blue or red design, 1990's.

#TVT422 Square. Black design, 1990's.

#TWA100 standard. Green and black design, 1980's.

#TWA120 standard. Orange, green, and blue design, 1980's.

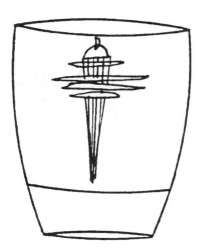

#TWA121 2⅜" tall, 1¾ oz. Etched design, 1980's.

#TWI100 standard. Black design, 1980's.

#TWI102 standard. Multi-colored, 1980's.

#TWI122 Depression Tall, Yellow, orange, and black design, 1980's.

#TWI123 standard. Red design, 1980's.

#TWI124 standard. Blue, white, black, and orange design, 1980's.

#TWI125 standard. Red and black design, 1980's.

#TWI126 standard. Blue, black, and green design, 1980's.

#TWI127 standard. Red and white design, 1980's.

#TWI128 standard. Culver 22 kt. gold and frosted design, 1980's.

#TWI140 standard. Blue and black design, 1980's.

#TWI141 standard. Green design, 1980's.

#TWV102 standard. Multi-colored design on porcelain glass, 1980's.

#TWV103 standard. Multi-colored design, 1980's.

#TWY130 standard. Blue design, 1980's.

#TWY131 standard. Green, brown, and gold design of frosted glass, 1980's.

#TWY132 standard. Culver 22 kt. gold and frosted design, 1980's.

#TWY133 standard. Gold and black design, 1980's.

#TUS101 standard. Red, white, and blue design on frosted glass, 1980's.

#TUS102 standard. Multi-colored design, 1980's.

Chapter XII:
FOREIGN SHOT GLASSES

In 1970, America issued a record 2.2 million passports. Heavy overseas travel increased steadily in the 1960's and beyond. Tourism as in the United States is big business in Europe. Shot glasses sold as souvenirs serve much the same function as in America. They are a very inexpensive souvenir and appeal to collectors.

Taiwan manufactures a cheaper, lighter glass product. The name "TAIWAN" or "MADE IN TAIWAN" ordinarily appears on the bottom underside. Other times the symbol " </> " also represents a Taiwan-made glass. Most shot glasses decorated in Taiwan will have an American design applied to them and are sold in the states.

The capital "D" upon the bottom underside of a Canadian 2-ounce glass is a government mark. These glasses along with standard U.S.-made and Taiwan shot glasses are easily decorated with Canadian themes. A few more countries particularly in Europe have been offering shot glasses for sale in some quantity since the 1960's. Germany, France, and England are still the leaders but others like Austria, Switzerland, and Sweden are now offering tourist glasses for sale in ever-increasing amounts. Korea is making most if not all of the genuine porcelain shot glasses sold in America. The discovery of the first Australian shot glass was purchased by a collector on a recent trip to Sydney. Many of the islands like the Bahamas now have a wide variety of souvenir shot glasses available. As time goes on, I believe that we will see even more souvenir glasses from around the world.

#FHT101 standard. Green and blue design, 1980's.

#FHT102 standard. Blue and red design, 1980's.

#FHT103 standard. Green design, 1980's.

#FHT104 standard. Pink and blue design, 1980's.

#FHT105 standard. Black design, 1980's.

#FHT106 standard. Multicolored design on frosted glass, 1980's.

#FHT107 standard. Blue, yellow, and black design on frosted glass, 1980's.

#FHT108 standard. Multi-colored design on frosted glass, 1980's.

#FHT109 standard. Black design on a blue background, 1980's.

#CNS001 standard. Red and blue design, 1980's.

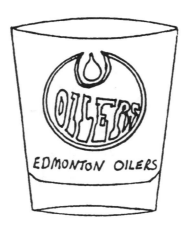

#CNS011 standard. Blue, white, and orange design, 1980's.

#CNT060 standard. Black design on a yellow background, 1980's.

#CNT106 standard. Red and blue or blue and white design, 1980's.

#CNT107 standard. Red writing on black porcelain rep., 1980's.

#CNT108 standard. Red and black design, 1980's.

#CNT109 2½" tall, 2 oz.
Multicolored design, 1980's.

#CNT111 2½" tall, 2 oz.
Multicolored design, 1980's.

#CNT185 standard.
Yellow design, 1980's.

#CNT217 standard. White
and gray design, 1980's.

#CNT218 standard.
Red design on yellow
background, 1980's.

#CNT219 2½" tall, 2 oz.
Multicolored design
with gold rim, 1980's.

#CNT271 standard. Black
or blue design, 1980's.

#CNT400 standard.
Red, white, and black
design, 1980's.

#FEA103 2½" tall, 1½ oz. Black,
white, and brown design with
gold rim, 1970's.

#FEA104

#FEA105

#FEA106

Set of 4 2" tall 1 oz. shot glasses. All have black, white, and gold designs, 1980's.

#FEA107

#FET104 2¼" tall, 2 oz. Metallic silver design on yellow glass, 1970's.

#FET212 2¼" tall, 1½ oz. Multicolored design, 1980's.

Set of two 2" tall, 1 oz. shot glasses.
#FFP052 (Red and white design) and
#FFP053 (Black and white design), 1970's.

#FFP054 2" tall, 1 oz. Blue design, 1970's

#FET206

#FET207

#FET208

#FET209

#FET210

#FET211

Set of six 2¼" tall, 1½ oz. shot glasses. All have multicolored designs with gold rims, 1980's.

#FFP055 2" tall, 1 oz. Red, white, and black design, 1970's.

#FFT101 2" tall, Multicolored design with gold rim, 1980's.

#FGA010 2" tall, 1 oz. Etched white design, 1980's.

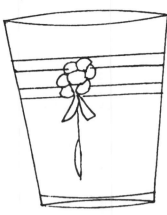

#FGE050 2" tall, Etched design, 1970's.

#FGP115 2⅝" tall, 1½ oz. Multicolored fake gems and gold design with gold rim, 1980's. 8 arched flutes.

#FGP200 2" tall, 1 oz. Multicolored design with gold rim, 1990's.

#FGT110 2" tall, 1 oz. Multicolored design with gold rim, 1980's.

#FGT111 2" tall, 1 oz. Multicolored design with gold rim, 1980's.

#FGT112 2" tall, 1 oz. Multicolored design with gold rim, 1980's.

#FGT113 2" tall, 1 oz. Multicolored design with gold rim, 1980's.

#FGT200 2" tall, 1 oz. Multicolored design with gold rim, 1990's.

#FGT201 2¾" tall, 1⅛ oz. Multicolored design with gold rim, 1990's.

#FRP100 2⅛" tall, 1½ oz. Green clover leaves around glass with gold rim, 1990's.

#FXT400 standard. Multi-colored design, 1990's.

#FWT100 2" tall, 1 oz. Blue and yellow design, 1980's.

#FST200 2" tall, 1 oz. Multicolored design, 1980's.

#FST201 2¼" tall, 1 oz. Multicolored design with gold rim, 1980's.

#FST202 2¾" tall, 1¼ oz. Multicolored design with gold rim, 1980's.

#FUA110 2½" tall, 2 oz. Blue design, 1980's.

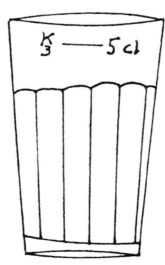

#FAM100 2⅝" tall, Clear molded 5 centiliter line, 1980's.

#FAT400 2¾" tall, Multicolored design with gold rim, 1990's.

Chapter XIII:
CATALOGING

The method of catalogging has not changed from <u>Shot Glasses: An American Tradition</u>. Two new codes have been added: "ANN" for Advertising 1990's, and "DWA" for Depression With Advertising. Furthermore an additional new code "IAG" (Iridescent Art Glass) has replaced the old class "PPP" (Picture Patterns Pre-Depression). One final change in codes is the elimination of the "IBS" classification. Only one glass had ever been classified as "IBS" (see page 96). A few additional letters were added under the foreign section since new discoveries from countries who had previously not had shot glasses available are now present.

AFT Advertising 1950's.

ANE Advertising 1980's.

ANF Advertising 1940's.

ANN Advertising 1990's.

ANS Advertising 1970's.

ASX Advertising 1960's.

BSG Barrel-shaped glasses.

DMS Depression miscellaneous shot glasses.

DPG Depression pattern glass (known patterns).

DTP Depression Tall shot glass with picture.

DWA Depression shot glass with advertising.

DWE Depression with etching.

EPG Etched pattern glass.

JSG Jumbo shot glasses (replicas of the standard).

LNF Libbey's 1950's less tapered glass.

MSG Measuring shot glass.

NCP 19th century patterns.

PDP Pattern designed picture.

PHS Picture with holiday design.

PML Plain with measuring lines.

PPA Picture patterns with animals or wildlife.

PPC Picture patterns with clear designs.

PPD Pictures with pictured designs.

PPE Picture patterns with inside eyes.

PPG Picture patterns with games.

PSG Plain shot glass.

SGF Shot glass – fractional (less than one ounce).

WTT Whiskey taster – toy.

Foreign shot glasses, except for those from Canada, are catalogued with three letters beginning with the letter "F". The second letter represents a country or commonwealth. "CN" is used for the first two letters of Canadian shot glasses. The third letter represents a simplified category. Double shots are also classified similar to Canadian glasses – "DS" is used for the first two letters while the third letter represents the same simplified category listed below:

<u>Second Letter</u>		<u>Third Letter</u>	
A	Austria.	A	Advertising.
C	Cayman Islands.	C	Color.
D	Denmark.	E	Etched.
E	England.	M	Measuring.
F	France.	P	Picture or Pattern.
G	Germany.	S	Sports.
H	Bahamas.	T	Tourist or Souvenir.
I	Israel.	U	University.
J	Jamaica.		
K	Korea.		
M	Middle East.		
R	Ireland.		
S	Switzerland.		
T	Italy.		
U	Australia.		
V	Virgin Islands.		
W	Sweden.		
X	Mexico.		

Examples: FEA would be an advertising glass from England. CNE would be an etched glass from Canada. DSU would be a double shot glass with a college or university design.

The letters S, T, and U are also used in front of state abbreviations to represent sports, tourist, and university shot glasses respectfully. Examples: SAL would be a sport shot glass from Alabama; TID would be a tourist glass from Idaho; and USD would be a university shot glass from South Dakota.

AL	Alabama.
AK	Alaska.
AZ	Arizona.
AR	Arkansas.
CA	California.
CO	Colorado.
CT	Connecticut.
DE	Delaware.
DC	District of Columbia.
FL	Florida.
GA	Georgia.
HI	Hawaii.
ID	Idaho.
IL	Illinois.
IN	Indiana.
IA	Iowa.
KS	Kansas.
KY	Kentucky.

LA Louisiana.
ME Maine.
MD Maryland.
MA Massachusetts.
MI Michigan.
MN Minnesota.
MS Mississippi.
MO Missouri.
MT Montana.
NA Nassau.
NE Nebraska.
NV Nevada.
NH New Hampshire.
NJ New Jersey.
NM New Mexico.
NY New York.
NC North Carolina.
ND North Dakota.
OH Ohio.
OK Oklahoma.
OR Oregon.
PA Pennsylvania.
PR Puerto Rico.
RI Rhode Island.

SC South Carolina.
SD South Dakota.
TN Tennessee.
TX Texas.
UT Utah.
VT Vermont.
VA Virginia.
WA Washington.
WV West Virginia.
WI Wisconsin.
WY Wyoming.
US United States.

The letters WA respresent a whiskey sample shot glass with local advertising such as from saloons, pharmacists, doctors, liquor distributors, etc. The third letter is the first letter of the dealer, distributor, proprietor, etc. Example: #WAA002 Adlerika or #WAB007 William Black, druggist.

The letters WS represent whiskey sample shot glasses and a third letter is added for the brand of the whiskey as applied upon the glass. Examples: #WSB006 Beaver Falls whiskey and #WSK028 Kentucky Dew.

APPENDIX I:
NOTES, FOOTNOTES, AND SOURCES

[1]Harold Newman, <u>An Illustrated Dictionary of Glass</u>, London: Thames and Hudson Ltd. 1977; provides 2 definitions of a shot glass. The early definition and origin of the word "shot" is: "A glass vessel to be filled with lead shot. It was used to support as well as clean quill pens." The second and more recent revised definition states: "A small drinking glass similar to a whiskey glass, so called mainly in the U.S. where they are used for serving a single measure (shot) of whiskey. My definition takes into consideration small capacity (single shot) and from surveys through "The Shot Glass Club of America."

[2]Mark Pickvet, <u>Shot Glasses: An American Tradition</u>, Marietta, Ohio: Antique Publications Inc. 1989, page 5. Definition of a shot glass.

[3]Chloe Zenwick, <u>A Short History of Glass</u>, New York, 1990. Pictorial history of world glassware from the Corning Museum of Glass.

[4]David Whitehouse, <u>Glass of the Roman Empire</u>, New York, 1988. History of Roman glassware and glassmaking techniques.

[5]Robert J. Charleston, <u>Masterpieces of Glass</u>, New York, 1980. Examples and history of Islamic glass.

[6]Phoebe Phillips, <u>The Encyclopedia of Glass</u>, New York, 1981, pages 48-57. Brief history & development of mosaics and stained glass in the Middle Ages.

[7]G. Mariacher, <u>Three Centuries of Venetian Glass</u>, Corning, 1957. European expert on Venetian glass - works were translated to English 1940's-1950's.

[8]Karel Hettes, <u>Venetian Trends in Bohemian Glassmaking in the 16th and 17th Centuries</u> from "Journal of Glass Studies" Volume V, 1963.

[9]Derek C. Davis, <u>English Bottles and Decanters 1650-1900</u>, New York, 1972. Various examples of the English "Black Bottle" and others.

[10]Rex Ebbott, <u>British Glass of the 17th and 18th Centuries</u>, London, 1971.

[11]G. Bernhard Hughes, <u>English Glass for the Collector 1660-1860</u>, New York, 1968. English liquor glass illustrations and parliamentary laws affecting spirits.

[12]E. M. Elville, <u>English and Irish Cut Glass 1750-1950</u>, New York, 1951. History of Irish glassmaking cities.

[13]<u>Falstaffs Complete Beer Book</u>, New York, 1973. Various authors – Frederic Birmingham on monastic beer grading.

[14]Increase Mather, <u>Diary</u>, Cambridge: Samuel Green, editor; 1900.

[15]Increase Mather, <u>Diary</u>.

[16]Cotton Mather, <u>Social Considerations</u> (puritan writing), Boston, 1708.

[17]Statistics from: <u>Journal of Studies on Alcohol</u>, 1976, pages 360-361.

[18]John Kobler, <u>Ardent Spirits: The Rise and Fall of Prohibition</u>, New York, 1973, page 31. John Kobler is a well-known authority on Prohibition.

[19]William Iverson, "<u>A Short History of Toasts and Toasting</u>" Playboy Magazine article, 1963. Reprinted in <u>The Booze Book</u> edited by Ralph Schoen, Chicago, 1974, page 106.

[20]Benjamin Franklin, <u>Pennsylvania Gazette</u>, Philadelphia: article first published March 29, 1764.

[21]Anthony Benezet, <u>Remarks on the Nature and Bad Effects of Spiritous Liquors</u>, Philadelphia: article written in various publications and numerous pamphlets throughout the late 18th and 19th centuries; originally 1784.

[22]Dr. Benjamin Rush, <u>An Inquiry into the Effects of Spiritous Liquors</u>, Philadelphia: essay written in various publications and numerous temperance pamphlets throughout the 18th and 19th centuries, originally 1784; from <u>The Autobiography of Benjamin Rush</u>, editor George W. Corner, Princeton University Press, 1948.

[23]Benjamin Franklin, <u>Pennsylvania Gazette</u>. Quoted from <u>The Late Demon Rum</u> by J. C. Furnas; New York, 1965, page 43.

[24]James Thomas Flexner, <u>Washington The Indispensable Man</u> (biography), New York, 1969, pages 315-323.

[25]Merril D. Peterson, <u>Thomas Jefferson & The New Nation</u> (biography), New York, 1970, page 729.

[26]Jess Carr, <u>The Second Oldest Profession, An Informal History of Moonshining in America</u>, Englewood Cliffs, New Jersey; 1972. Stills and Stillmaking techniques.

[27]W. J. Rorabaugh, <u>The Alcoholic Republic, An American Tradition</u>, New York, 1979. Perpetual Stills pages 70-73.

[28]Reverend Lyman Beecher, Six Sermons on the Nature, Occasions, Signs, Evils and Remedy of Temperance, New York, first published in pamphlet form in 1825; from the autobiography edited by Barbara Cross, Harvard edition, 1961.

[29]Lowell Innes, Pittsburgh Glass 1797-1891, Boston, 1976. Background and beginnings of glass in & around Pittsburgh; pages 3-11.

[30]Deming Jarves, Reminiscences of Glass-making, Boston, 1854. Popular and widespread pamphlet on early American glassmaking.

[31]George and Helen McKearin, American Glass, New York: 1968, page 26.

[32]Deming Jarves, Reminiscences of Glassmaking; (glassmaking techniques practiced in early to mid-19th century America).

[33]Collector Note: These items pose significant identification troubles. Rarely can they be traced to any one company and later reproductions add to the confusion.

[34]Lowell Innes, Pittsburgh Glass 1797-1891, pages 460-463.

[35]Henry Winter, The Dynasty of Louis Comfort Tiffany, Boston, 1971.

[36]Bill Edwards, The Standard Encyclopedia of Carnival Glass, Paducah, KY: 1982, pages 5-8; and Sherman Hand, The Collector's Encyclopedia of Carnival Glass, Paducah, KY: 1978, pages 3-7.

[37]A Century of Glass Manufacture 1818-1918 by Libbey Glass Co. – only 100 original copies issued by the company (from Toledo-Lucas County Public Library).

[38]Thomas C. Pears III, Bakewell, Pears, & Co. Glass Catalogue, Pittsburgh: 1977, pages 1-6.

[39]Sandra McPhee Stout, The Complete Book of McKee, North Kansas City, 1972.

[40]American Pottery & Glassware Reporter, 1879-1889: numerous small articles on the development of Hobbs, Brocunier & Co.

[41]Rochester Tumbler Advertisement – The Crockery and Glass Journal, September, 1875 edition.

[42]Pennsylvania Glassware 1870-1904, editors of the Pyne Press, Princeton: 1972, page 4.

[43]Neila Bredehoft, George Fogg, and Francis Maloney; Early Duncan Glassware, Boston: 1987, pages 1-2.

[44]Viola N. Cudd, Heisey Glassware, Brenham, 1969.

[45]C. F. Dorflinger & Sons, Cut Glass Catalog Collection 1881-1921.

[46]Leonard E. Padgett, Pairpoint Glass, Des Moine, 1979.

[47]Estelle Farrar and Jane Spillman, The Complete Cut & Engraved Glass of Corning, New York, 1979.

[48]Hazel Marie Weatherman, Fostoria Its First Fifty Years, Springfield, IL: 1972, introduction section.

[49]W. E. Woodward, Meet General Grant (biography), New York, 1928.

[50]Barbara Edmonson, Old Advertising Spirits Glasses; Chico, CA: 1988. Pages 16-19 illustrates one pricing formula for old advertising glasses including whiskey sample glasses.

[51]Oscar Getz, Whiskey: An American Pictorial History, New York, 1978. (Also items of note include material on display at the Oscar Getz Museum of Whiskey History in Bardstown, Kentucky).

[52]Watson Parker, Deadwood: The Golden Years; Lincoln, NB: 1981, pages 196-197.

[53]Robin Rainwater, assistant editor; "A SHOT of News," monthly newsletter; April, 1991 edition, page 1.

[54]John Kobler, Ardent Spirits: The Rise and Fall of Prohibition, New York; 1973, pages 172-180.

[55]Roger C. Storms, Partisan Prophets: A History of the Prohibition Party, Denver, 1972.

[56]Frances Willard, Woman and Temperance or The Work and Workers of the WCTU, New York, 1972.

[57]Robert Lewis Taylor, Vessel of Wrath, New York, 1966.

[58]K. Austin Kerr, Organized for Prohibition: A History of the Anti-Saloon League, New Haven, 1985.

[59]Liquor Laws compiled by Gilman G. Udell, Washington, DC; 1978, page 1 (Public Law No. 162, 57th Congress, 2nd session).

[60]Frederick Arthur McKenzie, "Pussyfoot" Johnson (biography), New York, 1920.

[61]Liquor Laws compiled by Gilman G. Udell; pages 14-15 (Public Law No. 380 64th Congress).

[62]18th Amendment of the Constitution of the United States (National Prohibition); Section II.

[63]John Kobler, Ardent Spirits The Rise and Fall of Prohibition, New York, 1973.

[64]Alcohol & Tobacco Tax Division, document #5574, <u>Distilled Spirits: History of Taxation and Law Enforcement</u>, 1966.

[65]Jess Carr, <u>The Second Oldest Profession: An Informal History of Moonshining in America</u>: New Jersey; 1972, page 75.

[66]John Kobler, <u>Ardent Spirits: The Rise and Fall of Prohibition</u>, pages 234-236 (a narrative from Charlie Berns).

[67]Thomas Coffey, <u>The Long Thirst: Prohibition in America 1920-1933</u>, New York; 1975, pages 256-257.

[68]John Kobler, <u>Ardent Spirits: The Rise and Fall of Prohibition</u>, pages 260-266.

[69]Thomas Coffey, <u>The Long Thirst: Prohibition in America 1920-1933</u>, pages 176-177.

[70]Norman H. Clark, <u>Deliver Us from Evil: An Interpretation of American Prohibition</u>, New York; 1976, pages 201-202.

[71]21st Amendment of the Constitution of the United States (Repeal), Section 1.

[72]21st Amendment of the Constitution of the United States (Repeal), Section 2.

[73]"The New York Times;" October 25, 1929 edition (headline).

[74]"The New York Times;" September 23, 1979 edition (summary and statistics of the Great Crash of the Depression).

[75]Eugene Lyons, <u>Herbert Hoover: A Biography</u>, New York; 1964 (Hoover's policies to combat the Depression).

[76]Kenneth S. Davis, <u>FDR: The New Deal Years 1933-1937</u>, New York; 1986 (First 100 days of Roosevelt's New Deal), pages 42-103.

[77]Carl U. Fauster, <u>Libbey Glass Since 1818: Pictorial History & Collector's Guide</u>, Toledo, 1979.

[78]Viola N. Cudd, <u>Heisey Glassware</u>, Brenham, Texas; 1969.

[79]Paul V. Gardner, <u>The Glass of Frederick Carder</u>, New York; 1971, page 45.

[80]Mary Jean Madigan, <u>Steuben Glass: An American Tradition in Crystal</u>, New York, 1982.

[81]Virginia Scott, <u>The Collector's Guide to Imperial Candlewick</u>, Athens, GA; 1980, page 4.

[82]Lowell Innes, <u>Pittsburgh Glass 1797-1891</u>, page 67 (process of "Cut and Shut" as described by Westmoreland Glass Company).

[83]Ben A. Green, <u>Jack Daniel's Legacy</u>, Nashville, 1967.

[84]Carl U. Fauster, <u>Libbey Glass Since 1818: Pictorial History & Collector's Guide</u>, Toledo, 1979.

[85]Mark Nye, <u>Cambridge Stemware</u>, Miami; 1985. Introduction section.

[86]Michigan Substance Abuse & Traffic Safety Information Center: <u>What Everyone Should Know About Alcohol</u>, 1989 publication.

[87]U.S. Department of Health and Human Services, <u>Spectrum: Alcohol Problem Prevention for Women by Women</u>, Rockville, MD: 1988.

[88]<u>Annual Report</u> from the Surgeon General of the U.S. Public Health Service, 1990.

[89]UMARC – The University of Michigan Alcohol Research Center, Ann Arbor, MI: 1988 pamphlet.

[90]Insurance Institute for Highway Safety, <u>Status Report</u>, March 16, 1991 edition.

[91]Additional statistics from UMARC, 1988 pamphlet.

[92]<u>The History of Jim Beam Bourbon</u>, pamphlet produced in 1990 by The James B. Beam Distillery Company of Clermont, Kentucky.

Appendix II:
GLOSSARY

Absorption – A process of taking in or absorbing alcohol in great quantity to the point of unconsciousness.

Acid Etching – The process of covering glass with an acid-resistant protective layer, scratching on a design, and then applying hydrofluoric acid to etch the pattern into the glass.

Acid Polishing – The technique of giving cut glass a polished surface by dipping it into a hydrofluoric acid bath.

Advertising Glass – A glass vessel displaying information about a manufacturer, distiller, shop, company, doctor, pharmacist, brand of whiskey, bar, restaurant, and so on.

Alcohol – The intoxicating agent in distilled, brewed, or fermented beverages. Any beverage that contains it is often referred to as alcohol such as beer, wine, and whiskey.

Ale Glass – An early 17th century English glass with capacity of 3-5 ounces, short-stemmed, and used for drinking ale or beer.

Alky – High proof ethyl alcohol. A term used by bootleggers and moonshiners during Prohibition.

Annealing – A process that toughens glass and eliminates stress by heating and gradually cooling in an annealing oven or lehr.

Apple Champagne – Hard cider fermented with honey and sugar (sometimes carbonated).

Apple Jack – The highly alcoholic content (about 20%) that was poured off cider after it had been set outside on a cold night to freeze.

Ardent Spirits – Strong distilled liquor such as whiskey with a minimum of 40% alcoholic content (80 proof).

Arrissing – The process of removing sharp edges from glass.

Art or Art Nouveau Glass – Expensive hand-blown glass with unusual effects of color, shape, and design. Art Glass is primarily ornamental and was most popular from the 1880's up to 1920.

Bar Tumbler – A glass tumbler with or without flutes produced in the United States in various shapes and sizes beginning in the mid-19th century primarily for hotels and saloons.

Barrel-shaped Shot Glass – A 2" tall, 1¾ ounce whiskey tumbler in the shape of a barrel produced by Bartlett-Collins in the mid-1950's.

Base Color – The color of glass before any coating is applied – usually the color of carnival glass before it is iridized.

Batch – In distilling, each time a distiller adds mash into the still bowl. In glassmaking, the mixture of raw materials fused together before heating.

Bathtub Gin – A home distillation brew using a boiling mash made up of fruits, grains, or vegetables and then adding glycerine and juniper oil (frequently mixed within one's bathtub during Prohibition).

Beading – The process where chips or small relief beads are fused to a glass object in the form of a continuous row.

Beaker – A large drinking vessel that usually contains a wide mouth.

Beer – A mild alcoholic beverage made from malted grain such as barley, flavored with hops, and then brewed by slow fermentation.

Best Metal – The highest quality batch of glass made by a company using the purest ingredients and highest lead content.

Bevel – Slanted or angle cuts usually beginning at the bottom or sides of a glass object (flutes).

Binge – Drinking to the point of intoxication.

Bitters – A name for strong liquor or medicinal alcohol popular in the late 19th and early 20th centuries.

Bitters Bottle – Small bottles used for containing bitters or tonics made in the United States in the mid-19th and later 19th century.

Black Bottle – A dark green English invention in the mid-17th century used for transporting and storing various beverages such as water, beer, wine, rum, etc.

Blank – An uncut piece of glass ordinarily a bowl or vase that has been specifically made of heavy, high-quality glass.

Blowing – The process of blowing air through a metal tube or blowpipe in order to shape the molten glass blob attached to the end.

Blowpipe – A hollow metal tube used to gather molten glass from the pot and then to blow air through in order to shape the glass.

Boot Glass – A small glass vessel shaped like a boot. Boot glasses ordinarily contain about 3 ounces when filled.

Bootleg Liquor – Liquor obtained illegally during Prohibition.

Bootlegger – One involved in the manufacturing, smuggling, or transporting of illegal alcoholic liquor.

Booze – Intoxicating liquor usually related to excess drinking.

Booze Bottle – a flask made in America in the 1860's in the form of a 2-story house by the Whitney Glass Works for Edmund G. Booze. (note the word "Booze" derives from "Bouse," a 17th century word meaning to "Carouse.").

Booze-Buster – A law enforcement officer employed to combat the illegal liquor trade or a temperance reformer also involved in the fight against liquor.

Bourbon – A whiskey distilled from a fermented mash consisting of a least 51% corn grain and stored in brand new charred oak containers for a least 2 years.

Brandy – An alcoholic beverage distilled from fruit juices such as peach, apple, cherry, etc.

Brandy Glass – A short rounded glass with a foot and very tiny stem; shorter but wider as compared to a rounded wine glass.

Bumper – Another term for a firing glass.

Cameo Engraving – Engraving process where the background is carved away to leave the design in relief. (see relief cutting).

Candleholder – A small glass tumbler-like vessel designed to hold candles of 2" in diameter (candleholders are typically greater than 2 ounces when filled with liquid).

Carnival Glass – Pressed glassware with a fired-on iridescent finish made in the United States 1905-1925 (reproductions were produced later beginning in the 1960's).

Cast Glass – Glass made in simple molds and then surface-ground with polishing wheels fed by abrasives.

Champagne Glass – A tall glass with foot and stem with a large round but shallow bowl.

Cheaters – Small whiskey tumblers with thick glass bottoms and walls that were made to look like they held more than in actuality.

Cider or Hard Cider – A popular alcoholic beverage in Colonial America made by crushing apples in a press, fortified with distilled spirits until it reached approximately 10% in alcoholic content.

Cider Royal – A Colonial American mixture of hard cider and apple brandy.

Cobalt Blue – Metallic color agent producing the most powerful deep dark blue color within glass.

Cocktail Glass – A tall glass with foot, stem, and an angled or straight-edged bowl.

Condenser – The second closed container of a still that collects the alcoholic steam in the distilling process.

Condensing Globe – The condenser in a perpetual still that is spherical in shape.

Copper Wheel Engraving – Process of hand-engraving by holding a glass to a revolving copper wheel which instantly cuts through the surface. Some of the best glass ever produced was done by highly-skilled copper wheel engravers who kept the cutting pattern in their mind while altering the cutting with rubbing oil continuously.

Cordial Glass – a miniature wine-glass with foot, stem, and tiny bowl of small capacity (note that a cordial though of similar capacity, is not a shot glass because of the foot and stem).

Core Forming – A process of glassmaking by spinning glass around a core.

Cracking Off – The process of removing an object from the pontil. Cooled by scoring, then the pipe is gently tapped, and the object falls into a sand tray or v-shaped holder held by an assistant.

Crackling – A decorating technique applied to glassware by plunging a hot object into cold water to induce cracks; and then reforming the piece within a mold.

Cristallo – A nearly colorless highly esteemed soda glass invented by Venetian glassmakers in the 16th century.

Crystal – Colorless glass containing a high lead content.

Cut Glass – Heavy flint glass cut with geometric patterns into the glass with grinding wheels and abrasives. The design is then further smoothed and polished. Cutting originated in Germany and then was introduced in the United States in the late 18th century.

Delirium Tremens (DT's) – A disorder caused by the sudden withdrawal of alcohol from those addicted to it. Symptoms include irritation, spasms, shaking, and paranoia.

Demon Rum – A term given to rum by early 19th century temperance reformers who wished to purge it from American society.

Depression Glass – Mass-produced, inexpensive, and primarily machine-made glass dinner sets and giftware in clear and many colors produced in America between 1920 and 1940.

Depression Tall Shot Glass – A rugged shot glass originating from the Depression era of glass that is just under 3" in height, typically contains exactly 1 ounce in capacity, and has a very thick bottom.

Diamond-Point Engraving – Hand cutting or machine cutting of glass with a diamond point tool (note hardened metal by heat treating to a sharp point has since replaced the more expensive diamonds for machine cutting).

Dionysus – The Greek God of Wine so named approximately 2,500 years ago. Harvest, death, rebirth, and other celebrations given in his honor were accompanied by heavy drinking of wine.

Distilled Spirits – The process by which alcohol is created by heating a mash in a closed container and capturing the steam in another container (condenser); the steam is very high in alcoholic content.

Double Shot Glass – A 3" tall whiskey tumbler with a capacity of 2 ounces; the bottom may or may not be fluted.

Dram Glass – Small English or Irish-made glasses of metal used for drinking a single measure of strong liquor. Most were made between 1750 and 1850 and imported to the United States.

Dramming – A popular drinking style that originated in England in the 18th century consisting of drinking several small toasts in succession.

Dram Shops – Shops that once served liquor or drams in small amounts.

Drunk Tank – A prison cell and early form of punishment for drunkenness.

Drunkenness – The state of intoxication from habitual use of liquor.

Elixir – An alcoholic mixture sweetened with sugar commonly used by 19th and early 20th century doctors and others as a cure-all.

Embossing – Mold blown or pressed glassware. The design is applied directly upon the object from the mold.

Enamelling – A liquid medium similar to paint applied to glassware and then permanently fused on by heating.

Encased Overlay – A single or double overlay design further encased in clear glass.

Engraving – The decoration of glass by holding the piece against the edge of revolving wheels made of stone, copper, or other materials.

Etching – See Acid Etching.

Fermented Beverages – Usually weaker beverages such as beer and wine (less alcoholic content than distilled liquor) created by an active enzyme in yeast that transforms organic compounds such as fruits and grains spontaneously.

Fire Polishing – Reheating a finished piece of glass at the glory hole in order to remove tool marks (more commonly replaced with acid polishing).

Fired-on Iridescence – A finish applied to glass by adding metallic salts after which the glass is refired.

Firing Glass – A small glass vessel with thick base, waisted sides, and possibly a stem or base that could withstand considerable abuse. The resulting noise of several being slammed at once was compared to that of a musket "firing." Some were made of metal and most were made in the 18th and early 19th centuries in both Europe and America.

Flashed-on Iridescence – A finish applied to glass by dipping hot glass into a solution of metallic salts.

Flashing – A very thin coating (thinner than a casing or overlay) of a different color from that of the base color.

Flint Glass – The American term for fine glassware made in the 19th century. A name for lead glass though original experimenters used powdered flints as a substitute for lead oxides.

Flip – A popular Colonial American drink consisting of a punch concocted of rum, beer, nutmeg (if available), sugar, and then warmed by plunging a hot poker from a fireplace directly into a drinker's mug.

Fluting – Vertically cut decoration in long narrow sections such as bevels (usually wheel-cut but sometimes molded).

Flux – A substance such as soda, wood ash, potash, and lead oxide added to the basic ingredients in order to stabilize and lower the melting point of a batch of glass.

Folded Foot – The turned-over edge of the foot of a wine glass or similar glass object to give added strength to the vessel.

Foot – The part of a glass other than the base on which it rests.

Footmaker – An assistant to a glassmaker who forms the foot of the glass in the glassblowing process.

Fractional Shot – A small glass tumbler with capacity of less than 1 ounce.

Frosted Glass – A light opalescence or cloudy coloring of a batch of glass using tin, zinc, or an all-over acid etching as in Depression glass. A frosted coating can also be applied on the surface of clear or crystal glass by spraying on white acid (a solution of ammonium bifluoride).

Full Lead Crystal – Colorless glass containing a minimum of 30% lead.

Gadget – A special rod developed to replace the pontil to avoid leaving a mark on the foot. A spring clip on the end of the gadget grips the foot of a just-finished piece of glass while the worker trims the rim and applies the finishing touches on the glass.

Gadrooning – A decorative band derived from a silver form made of molded, applied, or deep cut sections of reeding.

Gaffer – A term of respect for an experienced head glassmaker dating back to the 16th century.

Gall – A layer of scum at the surface of a batch of glass during the heating process of a batch of glass that must be skimmed off.

Gather – A blob of molten glass attached to the end of a blowpipe, pontil, or gathering iron.

Gestin – A Summerian Goddess and protector of the vine; created approximately 6,000 years ago.

Gin – A colorless alcoholic beverage distilled from grain and flavored with juniper berries.

Gin Glass – A drinking glass used for drinking gin similar in shape to a wine glass but smaller in size.

Glass – A hard, brittle, artificial substance made by fusing silicates (sand) with an alkali (soda or potash) and sometimes with metallic oxides (lead oxide or lime).

Glasshouse – The building that contains the glass-melting furnaces and in which the actual handling and shaping of molten glass takes place.

Glory Hole – A small-sized opening in the side of the furnace used for inserting cool glass objects in order to reheat them without melting or destroying the shape (sometimes named the reheating furnace).

Goblet – A drinking vessel with a large bowl of various sizes and shapes that rests on a stemmed foot.

Grog – A term used in the 19th century and earlier for alcoholic drinks (most commonly rum).

Grog Shop – A tavern, place, or barroom where liquor or grog was served.

Half Lead Crystal – Colorless glass containing a minimum of 24% lead content (lower quality than full-lead crystal).

Hand-Blown Glass – Glass formed and shaped with a blowpipe and other hand-manipulated tools without the use of molds.

Hand-Pressed Glass – Glass that is made in hand-operated mechanical presses.

Hard Liquor – Strong distilled spirits such as grain whiskey that is a minimum of 40% alcohol or 80 proof.

Highball Glass – A tall narrow tumbler of at least 4-ounce capacity used for mixed drinks.

Hops – A vine or plant from the mulberry family that is ripened, dried, and then added to malt liquors like beer to impart a bitter taste.

Hotch Potch – A Colonial American drink consisting of a warmed mixture of beer, rum, and sugar.

Hot Sling – A cool weather drink developed in the early 19th century consisting of gin, sugar, and hot water.

Hot Toddy – A cool weather drink developed in the early 19th century consisting of whiskey or rum, sugar, and hot water.

Hydrofluoric Acid – An acid similar to hydrochloric acid but weaker that attacks silica and is used to finish and etch glass.

Intemperance – Habitual or excessive use of alcoholic beverages.

Intoxication – The state of drunkenness affected by the overuse or excessive drinking of alcoholic beverages.

Iridescence – A sparkling rainbow-colored finish to glass produced by adding metallic salts.

Iridized – Glass that has been coated with iridescence.

Jigger – A measure used in mixing drinks that

ordinarily holds 1–1½ ounces. Jiggers that are glass tumblers are shot glasses.

Jumbo-Shot Glass – A replica of a standard shot glass but over 2 ounces.

Kiln – An oven used for firing or refiring glass objects.

Lager – A term given by Germans to quality beer that they produced in America beginning in the mid-19th century using a new yeast product.

Lead Crystal – Crystal or colorless glass made with a high lead content, usually 30% or more.

Lehr – An annealing oven with a moving base that travels slowly through a controlled loss of heat until the objects can be taken out at the opposite end. The rate of speed is adjustable as needed.

Lime Glass – A glass formula developed by William Leighton as a substitute for lead glass. Calcined limestone was substituted for lead which made glass cheaper to produce. Lime glass also cooled faster than lead glassware but was lighter and less resonant.

Liquor – Distilled alcohol or strong spirits as opposed to weaker fermented beverages.

MADD – Mother's Against Drunk Driving – A feminist movement organized to combat and eliminate drunk-driving.

Malster – One who converts grains into malt in the distilling or brewing process by softening the grain in steeping water and then allowing it to germinate.

Malt Liquor – Fermented beverages such as beer produced with malt.

Manathan – A Colonial American drink mixture consisting of rum, beer, and sugar.

Mash – Fermented matter consisting of grains, fruits, or vegetables that is heated in the still bowl and produces an alcoholic steam.

Mead – An ancient fermented beverage popular in the Middle Ages made of water, honey, malt, and yeast.

Measuring Shot Glass – A shot glass with measuring lines that is designed for measuring liquids in small amounts (usually in teaspoons, tablespoons, milliliters, and centiliters).

Meridian – A Colonial American drink consisting of brandy and tea.

Metal – A term used by chemists for a batch of glass (see Best Metal).

Milk Glass – A semi-opaque opalescent glass colored by a compound of arsenic or calcined bones.

Mitre Cut Engraving – Glass cut with a sharp groove on a V-edged wheel.

Moil – Waste glass left on the blowpipe or pontil.

Mold – A wooden or iron form used to shape glass. Pattern or half-molds are used before glass is finished expanding. Full or 3-part molds are used to give identical or same-size shapes to glassware.

Molded Glass – Blown glass given its final shape by the use of molds.

Moonshining – Manufacturing, smuggling, or transporting of illegally distilled corn whiskey.

Mountain Dew – A term used for illegal distillers or moonshiners for whiskey.

Muffle Kiln – A low temperature oven used for refiring glass to fix enamelling.

Near-Beer – Beer considered nonalcoholic that was brewed with less than 5% alcohol. Developed during Prohibition since it was legal.

Near-Cut – Pressed glass patterns similar to designs of hand-decorated cut glass.

Needle Etching – A process of etching glass by machine. Fine lines are cut by a machine through a wax coating upon glass and then hydrofluoric acid is applied to etch the pattern into the glass.

New Carnival – Reproduction iridescent glass made since 1962, sometimes with the original carnival glass molds.

Onyx Glass – A dark-colored glass with streaking of white or other colors made by mixing molten glass with various color mediums.

Opalescence – A milky or cloudy coloring of glass using tin or zinc.

Opaque Glass – Glass that is so dark in color that it does not transmit light (milk glass for example).

Osiris – The Egyptian God of Wine and lord of the dead worshipped and praised approximately 5,000 years ago.

Pattern Glass – Glass produced by mechanically pressing it into molds.

Perpetual Still – An early 19th century still invention that added a 3rd chamber called a condensing tub that was built around the condensing globe. It eliminated coiled worms and water tubs for cooling and reduced the amount of fuel needed.

Pillar Cutting – A decorative pattern of cut glass in the form of parallel vertical ribs in symmetrical pillar shapes (similar to flute cutting).

Pilsener Glass – A tall narrow glass vessel with foot primarily used for beer drinking.

Plain Shot Glass – A shot glass with no markings, designs, lines, or pattern (may contain flutes or bevels only).

Pontil – A solid shorter iron used to remove expanded objects from the blowing iron which allows the top to be finished. Prior to the 19th century, it left a mark but since then has been grounded flat (also called pontie, ponty, or puntee).

Porcelain Replica Shot Glass – A shot glass enamelled upon the entire exterior surface made to resemble genuine porcelain; usually a black coating.

Porcelain Shot Glass – A shot glass made from ceramic or a non-metal substance such as clay and then fired at a high temperature.

Pot – A vessel made of fired clay in which a batch of glass ingredients is heated before being transferred to the furnace. Many varieties include open, closed, smaller for colored glass, and so on but most only last 3-6 weeks before breaking up. Modern pots hold 1,100 to 1,650 pounds of glass.

Pot Arch – A furnace in which a pot is fired before being transferred to the main furnace for melting.

Pressed Glass – Hot molten glass mechanically forced into molds under pressure (important American invention in the 1820's).

Pressing – The process begins with molten glass poured into a mold which forms the outer surface of an object. A plunger lowered into the mass leaves a smooth center with a patterned exterior. Flat plates and dishes are formed in a base mold and an upper section folds down to mold the top (like a waffle iron).

Prohibition – A law forbidding manufacture, transportation, and sale of alcoholic liquors except for medicinal or sacramental purposes. 18th Amendment passed January 16th, 1919 and repealed December 5, 1933.

Proof – A unit of alcohol strength equal to half the actual pure percentage of alcoholic content (i.e. 100 proof is 50% alcohol, 50% water).

Pub – The British name for a tavern or bar where alcoholic beverages are sold and consumed.

Pucellas – A glassmaker's tool shaped like tongs used for gripping or holding glass objects while being worked.

Punch – A popular Colonial American beverage made with rum and fruit drinks.

Relief Cutting – A difficult and expensive method of cutting glass by designing an outline on the surface and then cutting away the background. The design was then raised in relief similar to that of cameo engraving.

Repeal – The 21st Amendment to the United States Constitution enacted December 5, 1933 that overturned the 18th Amendment (Prohibition).

Rib Mold – A pattern mold for bowls, bottles, tumblers, etc. which is marked with heavy vertical ribbing.

Rotgut – A slang term for whiskey; also the poor quality whiskey of the last run of a moonshiner from repeated distillations of the same mash.

Ruby Red – A gold metallic coloring agent that produces the most powerful red color within glass.

Rum – An alcoholic beverage distilled from molasses.

Rummer – An etched or engraved drinking glass with a large bowl, foot, and stem.

Rummy – A drunkard or one intoxicated from excessive drinking of rum.

Run – A series of batches using the same mash in the distilling process.

Rye Whiskey – A grain whiskey distilled from rye.

Saloon – An establishment prior to Prohibition for the sale and consumption of alcoholic beverages.

Sample Room – A backroom most typically found in a saloon where business was conducted and liquor samples provided.

Sand – The most common form of silica used in making glass. The best sands are found along inland beds near streams of low iron content and low amounts of impurities.

Sandblasting – An American-developed process where the design on a piece of glass is coated with a protective layer and then the exposed surfaces that remain are sandblasted with a pressurized gun to create the design.

Sangaree – A punch consisting of wine sweetened with sugar or brandy.

Schnapps – A liquor of high alcoholic content usually sweetened or flavored with a variety of ingredients (i.e. peach, peppermint, etc.).

Seeds – Tiny air bubbles in glass indicating an underheated furnace or impurities caused by flecks of dust or dirt.

Sham – Thin, fragile glass tumblers.

Sherry Glass – A tall glass with foot and stem with a shallow angled or straight-edged bowl.

Shot – A single measure of liquor most typically one ounce.

Shot Glass – A small whiskey tumbler with a capacity of at least 1 ounce but no more than 2 ounces; and a height of at least 1¾" but strictly less than 3".

Shot-Shells – Thin-shelled shot glasses easily breakable so named for their fragile 'egg-shell' thinness (many whiskey sample glasses were made this way).

Sickness – Glass not properly tempered or annealed that ordinarily shows random cracks, flaking, and eventually disintegrates.

Sillabub – A Colonial American drink consisting of wine, sugar, and warm milk.

Skittle – A small fire-clay pot used for melting a specialized small batch of colored glass or enamel.

Sour Mash – Whiskey made by scalding down a new batch of mash with spent mash, yeast, and water rather than just water. Spent mash gives the next batch more of a sour flavoring.

Souvenir Shot Glass – A shot glass produced primarily after the 1950's (a few specialized glasses were produced in the late 1890's and early 1900's in ruby red and green) depicting cities, states, countries, tourist attractions, etc. Designs are typically enamelled, transferred, and etched.

Speakeasy – Private clubs invented after the Civil War but most popular during Prohibition where illegal alcoholic beverages were sold and consumed.

Spirits – A general term for distilled liquor.

Sprayed-on Iridescence – Adding iridescence to glass by spraying it with particles of metallic salts.

Spun Glass – Glass threading that was originally spun by hand upon a revolving wheel. Glass fibers are automatically spun by machines today.

Square Shot Glass – A square glass tumbler (top and bottom are square in shape) that is 2½" tall and has a

capacity of 2 ounces; first made in the United States in the 1980's.

Standard Shot Glass – The most abundant type of shot glass: 2¼" tall, 1⅜" bottom diameter, 1⅞" top diameter, and 1¼ - 2 ounce capacity based on varying bottom thickness.

Still – A device used to distill liquor by vaporization.

Still Bowl – A closed container in which fermented matter is heated in the distilling process.

Tavern – A popular Colonial American establishment where alcoholic beverages were sold and drunk.

Tazza – An unusually wide dessert cup or serving plate with or without handles mounted on a stemmed foot (sometimes adapted for drinking alcoholic beverages).

Teetotaler – Temperance reformers who advocated total abstinence of alcoholic beverages.

Temperance – The movement or argument for moderation or abstinence of alcoholic beverages.

Thumping – The process of banging whiskey tumblers, firing glasses, or other drinking vessels upon a table or similar article.

Tippler – One who continuously drinks liquor in small amounts such as shots.

Tonic – A carbonated beverage such as water that is added to alcohol.

Toothpickholder – A small glass or ceramic receptacle of small capacity designed to hold toothpicks; usually cut or patterned and tend to taper inward rather than outward as compared to shot glasses.

Tourist Shot Glass – A shot glass depicting tourist attractions (see Souvenir Shot Glass).

Toy Mug – A miniature glass vessel in the shape of a mug with a handle and a capacity of 1– 1½ ounces.

Toy Whiskey Taster – A small glass tumbler first made in America around 1840 for the tasting or consuming of whiskey in tiny amounts.

Trailing – The process of pulling out a thread of glass and applying it to the surface of a glass object in spiral or other designs.

Transfers – A complete design printed on a paper backing that are removed from the article, applied to glassware, and fired on in a special enamelling lehr.

Tumbler – A drinking vessel without foot, stem, or handle; and contains a pointed or convex base.

Vaseline Glass – Glass made with a small amount of uranium which imparts a light greenish-yellow color (a greasy appearance like vaseline).

Venetian Glass – The finest glassware produced in Europe in Venice, Italy from the 13th through 17th centuries.

Victorian Glass – English-made glass from about the 1820's through the 1940's characterized by colors, opaqueness, opalescence, art glass, and unusual designs and shapes. Named for Queen Victoria (1837-1901).

Vodka – A colorless grain spirit distilled from mash made up of wheat or rye.

Volstead Act – The Prohibition Amendment named after Andrew Volstead, a United States Representative who introduced the 18th Amendment to Congress and verified its Constitutionality.

Wear Marks – Tiny barely visible scratches on the base, foot, or rim which indicate normal wear and tear through years of usage.

Wheels – Cutting wheels developed from lapidary equipment. Large stone wheels are used for deep cuts and smaller various-sized copper wheels are used for finer engraving.

Whimsey – A small unique decorative glass object made to display a particular glassmaker's skill (sometimes called a frigger).

Whiskey – Hard or strong liquor distilled from fermented mash. The most common grains used in the mash are corn, rye, and barley.

Whiskey Rebellion – A brief rebellion primarily in Western Pennsylvania in the late 18th century to protest the excise tax passed by Congress in 1791 on distilled spirits. The rebellion was defeated when George Washington assembled an army of 12,950 men but no bloodshed took place. The tax was removed in 1802 on Thomas Jefferson's recommendation.

Whiskey Sample Glass – Small whiskey tumblers or cordials with a capacity of up to 4 ounces used for sampling whiskey or other distilled spirits. Sample glasses were produced in the late 19th century on up to Prohibition (1919). Most contained advertising of a distiller or brand of whiskey. (also referred to as Pre-Prohibition Advertising Glasses).

Whiskey Tumbler – A small shot-glass sized drinking vessel without foot, stem, or handle with a pointed or convex base used for drinking distilled spirits in small amounts.

Wine – The fermented juice of grapes or other fruits containing a maximum alcoholic content of 25% (milder than distilled spirits).

Wine Glass – A tall glass with foot and stem with a large round deep bowl. As a unit of measurement or serving size, 4 ounces is the most prevalent.

Worm – The twisting, turning pipe of a still where the alcoholic steam passes from the still bowl to the condenser.

Appendix III:
PRICE GUIDE

Listed below is a basic price guide of shot glasses based on shape, design, decoration, etc. The following specific price list includes updates in values for all glasses listed or pictured in: *Shot Glasses: An American Tradition.*

Advertising-general	$1.00 - $2.00
Advertising-beer, whiskey, national, etc.	$2.00 - $3.00
Aluminum-attached to the exterior	$1.00 - $2.00
Bar Tumblers	$.50 - $10.00
Barrel-Shaped	$4.00 - $5.00
Crystal	$5.00 - $25.00
Culver 22 kt. Gold	$4.00 - $6.00
Cut Glass	$10.00 - $50.00
Depression Colors	$4.00 - $10.00
Depression Tall	$3.00 - $4.00
Depression Tall – Modern Tourist	$2.00 - $3.00
Etched	$5.00 - $7.00
European-Small Rounded	$2.00 - $3.00
Fort Square with Pewter	$10.00 - $12.00
Fort Square with Bronze and Pewter	$12.00 - $15.00
Frosted	$2.00 - $3.00
Frosted with Gold Designs	$3.00 - $5.00
General	$1.00 - $3.00
General with Gold Designs	$3.00 - $5.00
Inside or Inner Eyes	$3.00 - $4.00
Pewter – Large Circle	$7.00 - $10.00
Pewter – Small Circle	$6.00 - $8.00
Pewter – Shield Design	$6.00 - $8.00
Porcelain	$5.00 - $10.00
Porcelain Replicas	$2.00 - $3.00
Porcelain Tourist	$3.00 - $4.00
Sample Glasses	$8.00 - up
Silver-Coated	$5.00 - $7.00
Soda or Pop	$7.00 - $10.00
Sports	$3.00 - $4.00
Square	$5.00 - $7.00
Square – Etched	$7.00 - $10.00
Square – Pewter	$10.00 - $15.00
Taiwan	$1.50 - $3.00
Taiwan – Tourist	$1.50 - $3.00
Turquoise & Gold Tourist	$3.00 - $4.00

PRICE LIST

Cat. No.	Good	Mint	Cat. No.	Good	Mint	Cat. No.	Good	Mint
AFT001	2.00	3.00	ANE060	2.00	3.00	ANE339	2.00	3.00
AFT002	2.00	3.00	ANE061	1.50	2.00	ANE340	2.00	3.00
AFT003	2.00	3.00	ANE062	1.50	2.00	ANE341	2.00	3.00
AFT004	2.00	3.00	ANE063	1.50	2.00	ANE342	2.00	3.00
AFT005	2.00	3.00	ANE070	4.00	6.00	ANE343	2.00	3.00
AFT006	2.00	3.00	ANE080	2.00	3.00	ANE344	2.00	3.00
AFT010	2.00	3.00	ANE090	1.50	2.00	ANE345	2.00	3.00
AFT011	2.00	3.00	ANE100	2.00	3.00	ANE346	2.00	3.00
AFT012	5.00	7.50	ANE101	3.00	4.50	ANE347	2.00	3.00
AFT050	2.00	3.00	ANE110	2.00	3.00	ANE348	2.00	3.00
AFT051	2.00	3.00	ANE120	3.00	4.00	ANE349	2.00	3.00
AFT100	10.00	12.50	ANE121	3.00	4.00	ANE350	2.00	3.00
AFT101	7.50	10.00	ANE122	10.00	12.50	ANE351	2.00	3.00
AFT110	2.00	3.00	ANE140	2.00	3.00	ANE352	2.00	3.00
AFT120	2.00	3.00	ANE141	4.00	6.00	ANE353	2.00	3.00
AFT200	1.50	2.00	ANE180	10.00	12.50	ANE354	2.00	3.00
ANE001	7.50	10.00	ANE300	2.00	3.00	ANE355	2.00	3.00
ANE002	5.00	7.50	ANE301	2.00	3.00	ANE356	2.00	3.00
ANE003	2.00	3.00	ANE302	2.00	3.00	ANE357	2.00	3.00
ANE004	5.00	7.50	ANE303	2.00	3.00	ANE358	2.00	3.00
ANE005	5.00	7.50	ANE304	2.00	3.00	ANE359	2.00	3.00
ANE006	5.00	7.50	ANE305	2.00	3.00	ANE360	2.00	3.00
ANE007	5.00	7.50	ANE306	2.00	3.00	ANE361	2.00	3.00
ANE009	2.00	3.00	ANE307	2.00	3.00	ANE362	2.00	3.00
ANE010	2.00	3.00	ANE308	2.00	3.00	ANE363	2.00	3.00
ANE011	3.00	4.50	ANE309	2.00	3.00	ANE364	2.00	3.00
ANE012	3.00	4.50	ANE310	2.00	3.00	ANE365	2.00	3.00
ANE013	3.00	4.50	ANE311	2.00	3.00	ANE366	2.00	3.00
ANE014	3.00	4.50	ANE312	2.00	3.00	ANE367	2.00	3.00
ANE015	3.00	4.50	ANE313	2.00	3.00	ANE368	2.00	3.00
ANE016	2.00	3.00	ANE314	2.00	3.00	ANE369	2.00	3.00
ANE017	2.00	3.00	ANE315	2.00	3.00	ANE370	2.00	3.00
ANE018	2.00	3.00	ANE316	2.00	3.00	ANE371	2.00	3.00
ANE019	2.00	3.00	ANE317	2.00	3.00	ANE372	2.00	3.00
ANE020	2.00	3.00	ANE318	2.00	3.00	ANE373	2.00	3.00
ANE021	2.00	3.00	ANE319	2.00	3.00	ANE374	2.00	3.00
ANE022	2.00	3.00	ANE320	2.00	3.00	ANE375	2.00	3.00
ANE025	3.00	4.00	ANE321	2.00	3.00	ANE376	2.00	3.00
ANE026	3.00	4.00	ANE322	2.00	3.00	ANE377	2.00	3.00
ANE027	3.00	4.00	ANE323	2.00	3.00	ANE378	2.00	3.00
ANE028	3.00	4.00	ANE324	2.00	3.00	ANE379	2.00	3.00
ANE029	3.00	4.00	ANE325	2.00	3.00	ANE380	2.00	3.00
ANE030	3.00	4.00	ANE326	2.00	3.00	ANE381	2.00	3.00
ANE031	3.00	4.00	ANE327	2.00	3.00	ANE382	2.00	3.00
ANE035	3.00	4.00	ANE328	2.00	3.00	ANE383	2.00	3.00
ANE045	7.50	10.00	ANE329	2.00	3.00	ANE384	2.00	3.00
ANE046	7.50	10.00	ANE330	2.00	3.00	ANE385	2.00	3.00
ANE047	7.50	10.00	ANE331	2.00	3.00	ANE386	2.00	3.00
ANE048	7.50	10.00	ANE332	2.00	3.00	ANE387	2.00	3.00
ANE049	7.50	10.00	ANE333	2.00	3.00	ANE388	2.00	3.00
ANE050	7.50	10.00	ANE334	2.00	3.00	ANE389	2.00	3.00
ANE051	7.50	10.00	ANE335	2.00	3.00	ANE390	2.00	3.00
ANE055	7.50	10.00	ANE336	2.00	3.00	ANE391	2.00	3.00
ANE057	7.50	10.00	ANE337	2.00	3.00	ANE392	2.00	3.00
ANE059	7.50	10.00	ANE338	2.00	3.00	ANE393	2.00	3.00

Cat. No.	Good	Mint	Cat. No.	Good	Mint	Cat. No.	Good	Mint
ANE394	2.00	3.00	ANS140	2.00	3.00	CNT170	2.00	3.00
ANE395	2.00	3.00	ASX001	2.00	3.00	CNT180	2.00	3.00
ANE396	2.00	3.00	ASX002	3.00	4.50	CNT181	2.00	3.00
ANE397	2.00	3.00	ASX003	2.00	3.00	CNT182	2.00	3.00
ANE398	2.00	3.00	ASX004	2.00	3.00	CNT183	2.00	3.00
ANE399	2.00	3.00	ASX005	2.00	3.00	CNT184	2.00	3.00
ANE400	2.00	3.00	ASX006	2.00	3.00	CNT185	2.00	3.00
ANE401	2.00	3.00	ASX007	2.00	3.00	CNT200	2.00	3.00
ANE402	2.00	3.00	ASX050	2.00	3.00	CNT201	2.00	3.00
ANE403	2.00	3.00	ASX051	2.00	3.00	CNT202	2.00	3.00
ANE404	2.00	3.00	ASX060	2.00	3.00	CNE203	2.00	3.00
ANE900	1.50	2.00	BSG001	2.00	3.00	CNT204	2.00	3.00
ANF001	2.00	3.00	BSG010	4.00	6.00	CNT205	2.00	3.00
ANF002	2.00	3.00	BSG011	4.00	6.00	CNT206	2.00	3.00
ANF003	2.00	3.00	BSG012	4.00	6.00	CNT207	2.00	3.00
ANF004	2.00	3.00	BSG013	4.00	6.00	CNT208	2.00	3.00
ANF005	2.00	3.00	BSG014	4.00	6.00	CNT209	2.00	3.00
ANF006	2.00	3.00	BSG015	4.00	6.00	CNT210	2.00	3.00
ANF007	2.00	3.00	BSG016	4.00	6.00	CNT211	2.00	3.00
ANF008	2.00	3.00	BSG017	4.00	6.00	CNT212	3.00	4.50
ANF015	2.00	3.00	CNE100	5.00	7.50	CNT213	3.00	4.00
ANF016	2.00	3.00	CNM100	1.50	2.00	CNT214	2.00	3.00
ANF017	2.00.	3.00	CNS00L	3.00	4.00	CNT215	2.00	3.00
ANF050	2.00	3.00	CNS002	3.00	4.00	CNT216	5.00	7.50
ANF051	2.00	3.00	CNS010	3.00	4.00	CNT217	2.00	3.00
ANN010	2.00	3.00	CNS011	3.00	4.00	CNT218	2.00	3.00
ANN050	2.00	3.00	CNS012	3.00	4.00	CNT219	2.00	3.00
ANS001	3.00	4.50	CNS013	3.00	4.00	CNT230	2.00	3.00
ANS002	3.00	4.50	CNS014	3.00	4.00	CNT240	2.00	3.00
ANS003	3.00	4.50	CNS015	3.00	4.00	CNT250	2.00	3.00
ANS004	3.00	4.50	CNS016	3.00	4.00	CNT260	2.00	3.00
ANS005	2.00	3.00	CNS110	5.00	7.50	CNT270	2.00	3.00
ANS006	2.00	3.00	CNS120	5.00	7.50	CNT271	2.00	3.00
ANS007	3.00	4.50	CNT010	2.00	3.00	CNT400	2.00	3.00
ANS008	2.00	3.00	CNT011	2.00	3.00	DMS001	1.50	2.00
ANS009	3.00	4.50	CNT012	2.00	3.00	DMS001	5.00	7.50
ANS010	3.00	4.50	CNT050	2.00	3.00	DMS001	25.00	30.00
ANS011	3.00	4.50	CNT060	2.00	3.00	DMS002	1.50	2.00
ANS020	2.00	3.00	CNT070	2.00	3.00	DMS003	4.00	6.00
ANS021	2.00	3.00	CNT100	2.00	3.00	DMS004	1.50	2.00
ANS022	2.00	3.00	CNT101	2.00	3.00	DMS005	10.00	12.50
ANS025	2.00	3.00	CNT102	2.00	3.00	DMS006	2.00	3.00
ANS030	5.00	7.50	CNT103	2.00	3.00	DMS007	4.00	6.00
ANS040	1.00	1.50	CNT104	2.00	3.00	DMS100	3.00	4.50
ANS050	1.50	2.00	CNT105	2.00	3.00	DMS102	3.00	4.50
ANS051	1.50	2.00	CNT106	2.00	3.00	DMS103	3.00	4.50
ANS052	1.50	2.00	CNT107	2.00	3.00	DMS104	3.00	4.50
ANS053	1.50	2.00	CNT108	2.00	3.00	DMS105	10.00	12.50
ANS054	1.50	2.00	CNT109	2.00	3.00	DMS106	3.00	4.50
ANS055	1.50	2.00	CNT110	2.00	3.00	DMS107	3.00	4.50
ANS056	1.50	2.00	CNT111	2.00	3.00	DMS108	3.00	4.50
ANS070	2.00	3.00	CNT120	2.00	3.00	DMS109	10.00	15.00
ANS071	2.00	3.00	CNT121	2.00	3.00	DMS200	1.00	1.50
ANS080	1.50	2.00	CNT130	2.00	3.00	DMS201	1.00	1.50
ANS100	1.50	2.00	CNT140	2.00	3.00	DMS202	2.00	3.00
ANS101	1.50	2.00	CNT150	2.00	3.00	DMS203	4.00	6.00
ANS102	2.00	3.00	CNT151	2.00	3.00	DMS204	1.50	2.00
ANS120	1.50	2.00	CNT160	.50	.75	DMS205	4.00	6.00

Cat. No.	Good	Mint	Cat. No.	Good	Mint	Cat. No.	Good	Mint
DMS206	2.00	3.00	DPG050	4.00	6.00	DPT308	3.00	4.00
DMS207	4.00	5.00	DPG060	4.00	6.00	DTP310	3.00	4.00
DMS208	3.00	4.50	DPG061	4.00	6.00	DWA006	3.00	4.50
DMS300	.75	1.00	DPG061	15.00	20.00	DWA010	3.00	4.50
DMS301	1.00	1.50	DPG065	10.00	15.00	DWE010	5.00	7.50
DMS302	2.00	3.00	DPG070	4.00	6.00	DWE011	5.00	7.50
DMS303	2.00	3.00	DPG071	3.00	4.50	DWE012	4.00	6.00
DMS304	2.00	3.00	DPG072	3.00	4.50	DWE013	4.00	6.00
DMS305	3.00	4.50	DPG073	5.00	7.50	DWE014	3.00	4.00
DMS306	4.00	6.00	DPG074	6.00	8.00	DWE015	5.00	7.50
DMS307	2.00	3.00	DPG075	10.00	13.00	DWE016	10.00	12.50
DMS308	1.00	1.50	DPG076	5.00	7.50	DWE017	5.00	7.50
DMS309	4.00	6.00	DPG077	3.00	4.50	DWE018	5.00	7.50
DMS310	4.00	6.00	DPG080	4.00	6.00	DWE019	4.00	6.00
DMS311	15.00	20.00	DPG081	4.00	6.00	DWE020	5.00	7.50
DMS312	15.00	20.00	DPG090	20.00	25.00	DWE040	3.00	4.50
DMS313	2.00	3.00	DPG100	3.00	4.50	DWE041	4.00	6.00
DMS500	2.00	3.00	DPG101	5.00	7.50	DWE050	4.00	6.00
DMS501	2.00	3.00	DPG102	3.00	4.50	DWE060	4.00	6.00
DMS502	2.00	3.00	DPG120	4.00	6.00	EPG100	5.00	7.50
DMS601	2.00	3.00	DSA300	1.00	1.50	EPG101	5.00	7.50
DMS602	4.00	6.00	DSA301	1.00	1.50	EPG102	4.00	6.00
DMS603	4.00	6.00	DSA302	1.00	1.50	EPG103	4.00	6.00
DMS604	2.00	3.00	DSA303	1.00	1.50	EPG104	4.00	6.00
DMS800	20.00	25.00	DSA304	1.00	1.50	EPG105	4.00	6.00
DMS801	20.00	25.00	DSA305	2.00	3.00	EPG110	5.00	7.50
DMS900	15.00	20.00	DSA306	1.00	1.50	EPG111	5.00	7.50
DPG010	4.00	6.00	DAS307	1.00	1.50	EPG120	5.00	7.50
DPG011	4.00	6.00	DSA308	2.00	3.00	EPG130	5.00	7.50
DPG020	4.00	6.00	DSA500	2.00	3.00	EPG150	5.00	7.50
DPG021	4.00	6.00	DSP001	.75	1.00	EPG151	5.00	7.50
DPG022	4.00	6.00	DSP002	.75	1.00	EPG152	5.00	7.50
DPG023	4.00	6.00	DSP003	1.00	1.50	EPG153	5.00	7.50
DPG024	3.00	4.50	DSP004	1.00	1.50	EPG154	5.00	7.50
DPG025	3.00	4.50	DSP005	1.00	1.50	EPG160	5.00	7.50
DPG026	3.00	4.50	DST550	2.00	3.00	EPG161	4.00	6.00
DPG027	3.00	4.50	DSU110	2.00	3.00	EPG200	5.00	7.50
DPG028	3.00	4.50	DSU111	2.00	3.00	EPG210	4.00	6.00
DPG029	3.00	4.50	DSU112	2.00	3.00	EPG220	4.00	6.00
DPG030	4.00	6.00	DTP001	5.00	7.50	EPG230	10.00	15.00
DPG031	5.00	7.50	DTP002	5.00	7.50	EPG500	2.00	3.00
DPG032	10.00	13.00	DTP003	5.00	7.50	EPG501	2.00	3.00
DPG033	7.50	10.00	DTP010	3.00	4.00	EPG502	2.00	3.00
DPG034	3.00	4.50	DTP100	3.00	4.00	EPG503	2.00	3.00
DPG035	3.00	4.50	DTP101	3.00	4.00	EPG504	2.00	3.00
DPG036	3.00	4.50	DTP102	10.00	12.50	EPG600	2.00	3.00
DPG037	3.00	4.50	DTP103	3.00	4.00	EPG601	2.00	3.00
DPG038	3.00	4.50	DTP200	10.00	12.50	FAE100	12.00	16.00
DPG039	3.00	4.50	DTP201	10.00	12.50	FAM100	1.00	1.50
DPG040	3.00	4.50	DTP202	10.00	12.50	FAT400	3.00	4.00
DPG041	3.00	4.50	DTP300	3.00	4.00	FBT100	2.00	3.00
DPG042	50.00	60.00	DTP301	3.00	4.00	FCT100	2.00	3.00
DPG043	4.00	6.00	DTP302	3.00	4.00	FDT100	2.00	3.00
DPG044	4.00	6.00	DTP303	3.00	4.00	FEA100	2.00	3.00
DPG045	3.00	4.50	DTP304	3.00	4.00	FEA101	2.00	3.00
DPG046	3.00	4.50	DTP305	3.00	4.00	FEA102	2.00	3.00
DPG047	3.00	4.50	DPT306	3.00	4.00	FEA103	2.00	3.00
DPG049	4.00	6.00	DTP307	3.00	4.00	FEA104	3.00	4.00

Cat. No.	Good	Mint	Cat. No.	Good	Mint	Cat. No.	Good	Mint
FEA105	3.00	4.00	FGP105	2.00	3.00	LNF010	4.00	6.00
FEA106	3.00	4.00	FGP106	3.00	4.50	MSG001	2.00	3.00
FEA107	3.00	4.00	FGP107	3.00	4.50	MSG002	2.00	3.00
FET100	2.00	3.00	FGP108	3.00	4.50	NCP100	50.00	75.00
FET101	2.00	3.00	FGP109	3.00	4.50	NCP101	50.00	75.00
FET102	2.00	3.00	FGP110	2.00	3.00	NCP102	50.00	75.00
FET103	2.00	3.00	FGP111	3.00	4.50	NCP103	50.00	75.00
FET104	2.00	3.00	FGP112	2.00	3.00	NCP104	50.00	75.00
FET200	2.00	3.00	FGP113	2.00	3.00	NCP105	50.00	75.00
FET201	2.00	3.00	FGP114	3.00	3.00	NCP106	50.00	75.00
FET202	2.00	3.00	FGP115	3.00	4.50	NCP107	50.00	75.00
FET203	2.00	3.00	FGP200	2.00	3.00	NCP108	50.00	75.00
FET204	2.00	3.00	FGT100	2.00	3.00	NCP109	50.00	75.00
FET205	2.00	3.00	FGT101	2.00	3.00	NCP110	50.00	75.00
FET206	2.00	3.00	FGT102	2.00	3.00	NCP111	50.00	75.00
FET207	2.00	3.00	FGT103	2.00	3.00	NCP112	50.00	75.00
FET208	2.00	3.00	FGT104	2.00	3.00	NCP113	50.00	75.00
FET209	2.00	3.00	FGT105	2.00	3.00	NCP114	50.00	75.00
FET210	2.00	3.00	FGT106	2.00	3.00	NCP115	50.00	75.00
FET211	2.00	3.00	FGT107	2.00	3.00	NCP116	50.00	75.00
FET212	2.00	3.00	FGT108	2.00	3.00	NCP117	50.00	75.00
FFC001	1.00	1.50	FGT109	2.00	3.00	NCP118	50.00	75.00
FFP010	1.00	1.50	FGT110	2.00	3.00	NCP119	50.00	75.00
FFP011	.75	1.00	FGT111	2.00	3.00	NCP120	50.00	75.00
FFP012	1.00	1.50	FGT112	2.00	3.00	NCP121	50.00	75.00
FFP050	1.00	1.50	FGT200	2.00	3.00	NCP122	50.00	75.00
FFP051	2.00	3.00	FGT201	2.00	3.00	NCP123	50.00	75.00
FFP052	2.00	3.00	FHT100	2.00	3.00	NCP200	50.00	75.00
FFP053	2.00	3.00	FHT101	2.00	3.00	NCP201	50.00	75.00
FFP054	2.00	3.00	FHT102	2.00	3.00	NCP210	10.00	15.00
FFP055	2.00	3.00	FHT103	2.00	3.00	NCP211	10.00	15.00
FFP100	1.00	1.50	FHT104	2.00	3.00	NCP300	25.00	50.00
FFP200	2.00	3.00	FHT105	2.00	3.00	NCP900	20.00	25.00
FFP201	2.00	3.00	FHT106	2.00	3.00	NCP901	20.00	25.00
FFP202	2.00	3.00	FHT107	2.00	3.00	PDP001	2.00	3.00
FFP300	2.00	3.00	FHT108	2.00	3.00	PDP002	2.00	3.00
FFP310	2.00	3.00	FHT109	2.00	3.00	PDP003	2.00	3.00
FFP400	2.00	3.00	FIP100	2.00	3.00	PDP004	2.00	3.00
FFP500	2.00	3.00	FJT100	2.00	3.00	PDP005	2.00	3.00
FFT100	2.00	3.00	FKE100	4.00	6.00	PDP006	2.00	3.00
FFT101	2.00	3.00	FMP100	2.00	3.00	PDP007	2.00	3.00
FGA010	2.00	3.00	FRP100	2.00	3.00	PDP008	2.00	3.00
FGE050	2.00	3.00	FST200	3.00	4.00	PDP009	2.00	3.00
FGE100	6.00	8.00	FST201	3.00	4.00	PDP010	2.00	3.00
FGE101	6.00	8.00	FST202	3.00	4.00	PDP011	2.00	3.00
FGE102	6.00	8.00	FTP010	2.00	3.00	PDP012	2.00	3.00
FGE103	6.00	8.00	FUA110	4.00	6.00	PDP013	2.00	3.00
FGE104	6.00	8.00	FVT100	2.00	3.00	PDP014	2.00	3.00
FGE105	6.00	8.00	FWT100	2.00	3.00	PDP015	2.00	3.00
FGE106	6.00	8.00	FXT400	2.00	3.00	PDP016	2.00	3.00
FGE107	6.00	8.00	IAG010	300.00	400.00	PDP017	2.00	3.00
FGE108	6.00	8.00	IAG020	400.00	500.00	PDP018	2.00	3.00
FGE109	6.00	8.00	IAG030	20.00	25.00	PDP019	2.00	3.00
FGP100	2.00	3.00	IAG031	20.00	25.00	PDP020	2.00	3.00
FGP101	2.00	3.00	JSG001	2.00	3.00	PDP021	1.00	1.50
FGP102	2.00	3.00	JSG002	2.00	3.00	PDP022	2.00	3.00
FGP103	2.00	3.00	LNF001	1.00	1.50	DPD023	2.00	3.00
FGP104	2.00	3.00	LNF002	3.00	4.50	DPD024	2.00	3.00

Cat. No.	Good	Mint	Cat. No.	Good	Mint	Cat. No.	Good	Mint
PDP025	2.00	3.00	PHS201	5.00	7.50	PPA321	2.00	3.00
PDP026	2.00	3.00	PHS202	5.00	7.50	PPA400	2.00	3.00
PDP027	2.00	3.00	PHS203	5.00	7.50	PPA401	2.00	3.00
PDP028	2.00	3.00	PHS204	5.00	7.50	PPA411	2.00	3.00
PDP029	3.00	4.00	PML001	1.00	1.50	PPA412	2.00	3.00
PDP030	3.00	4.00	PML002	1.00	1.50	PPA420	2.00	3.00
PDP031	3.00	4.00	PML003	1.00	1.50	PPA421	2.00	3.00
PDP032	2.00	3.00	PML004	1.00	1.50	PPA422	2.00	3.00
PDP100	2.00	3.00	PML005	1.00	1.50	PPA430	2.00	3.00
PDP101	2.00	3.00	PML006	1.00	1.50	PPA431	2.00	3.00
PDP102	1.00	1.50	PML007	1.00	1.50	PPA432	2.00	3.00
PDP103	2.00	3.00	PML100	1.00	1.50	PPA433	2.00	3.00
PDP104	2.00	3.00	PML101	1.00	1.50	PPA504	2.00	3.00
PDP105	2.00	3.00	PML200	1.00	1.50	PPA505	2.00	3.00
PDP120	4.00	3.00	PPA001	2.00	3.00	PPA506	2.00	3.00
PDP200	10.00	12.50	PPA003	2.00	3.00	PPA507	2.00	3.00
PDP201	2.00	3.00	PPA004	2.00	3.00	PPA508	2.00	3.00
PDP202	2.00	3.00	PPA005	2.00	3.00	PPA600	5.00	7.50
PDP203	2.00	3.00	PPA006	2.00	3.00	PPA601	5.00	7.50
PDP210	2.00	3.00	PPA007	2.00	3.00	PPA602	5.00	7.50
PHS001	5.00	7.50	PPA008	2.00	3.00	PPA603	5.00	7.50
PHS002	5.00	7.50	PPA009	2.00	3.00	PPA620	1.00	1.50
PHS003	5.00	7.50	PPA010	2.00	3.00	PPA623	2.00	3.00
PHS004	5.00	7.50	PPA030	2.00	3.00	PPA624	2.00	3.00
PHS005	5.00	7.50	PPA031	2.00	3.00	PPA625	2.00	3.00
PHS006	5.00	7.50	PPA032	2.00	3.00	PPA626	2.00	3.00
PHS007	5.00	7.50	PPA033	2.00	3.00	PPA627	2.00	3.00
PHS008	5.00	7.50	PPA039	2.00	3.00	PPA628	2.00	3.00
PHS009	5.00	7.50	PPA040	2.00	3.00	PPA630	10.00	12.50
PHS010	5.00	7.50	PPA050	2.00	3.00	PPA631	10.00	12.50
PHS011	5.00	7.50	PPA051	2.00	3.00	PPA632	10.00	12.50
PHS012	5.00	7.50	PPA053	4.00	6.00	PPA633	10.00	12.50
PHS013	5.00	7.50	PPA054	4.00	6.00	PPA634	10.00	12.50
PHS014	5.00	7.50	PPA055	4.00	6.00	PPA635	10.00	12.50
PHS015	5.00	7.50	PPA056	4.00	6.00	PPA636	10.00	12.50
PHS016	5.00	7.50	PPA110	2.00	3.00	PPA637	10.00	12.50
PHS090	7.50	10.00	PPA111	2.00	3.00	PPA638	12.00	15.00
PHS100	7.50	10.00	PPA112	2.00	3.00	PPA639	12.00	15.00
PHS101	7.50	10.00	PPA113	2.00	3.00	PPA640	12.00	15.00
PHS102	7.50	10.00	PPA114	2.00	3.00	PPA641	12.00	15.00
PHS103	7.50	10.00	PPA120	2.00	3.00	PPC001	35.00	50.00
PHS104	7.50	10.00	PPA121	2.00	3.00	PPC002	35.00	50.00
PHS105	7.50	10.00	PPA122	2.00	3.00	PPC003	35.00	50.00
PHS106	7.50	10.00	PPA123	2.00	3.00	PPC005	35.00	50.00
PHS107	7.50	10.00	PPA200	2.00	3.00	PPC006	35.00	50.00
PHS108	7.50	10.00	PPA201	2.00	3.00	PPC007	5.00	7.50
PHS109	7.50	10.00	PPA202	2.00	3.00	PPC008	5.00	7.50
PHS110	7.50	10.00	PPA203	2.00	3.00	PPC009	5.00	7.50
PHS111	7.50	10.00	PPA204	2.00	3.00	PPC010	1.00	1.50
PHS112	7.50	10.00	PPA205	2.00	3.00	PPC011	1.00	1.50
PHS140	7.50	10.00	PPA206	2.00	3.00	PPC015	20.00	30.00
PHS141	7.50	10.00	PPA207	2.00	3.00	PPC020	1.00	1.50
PHS142	7.50	10.00	PPA300	2.00	3.00	PPC021	1.00	1.50
PHS143	7.50	10.00	PPA301	2.00	3.00	PPC030	1.00	1.50
PHS160	7.50	10.00	PPA302	2.00	3.00	PPC031	1.00	1.50
PHS161	7.50	10.00	PPA303	2.00	3.00	PPC039	2.00	3.00
PHS164	7.50	10.00	PPA304	2.00	3.00	PPC040	2.00	3.00
PHS200	5.00	7.50	PPA320	2.00	3.00	PPC041	2.00	3.00

Cat. No.	Good	Mint	Cat. No.	Good	Mint	Cat. No.	Good	Mint
PPC042	2.00	3.00	PPD203	2.00	3.00	PPD408	2.00	3.00
PPC043	2.00	3.00	PPD204	2.00	3.00	PPD420	2.00	3.00
PPC044	2.00	3.00	PPD210	2.00	3.00	PPD430	2.00	3.00
PPC045	2.00	3.00	PPD211	2.00	3.00	PPD438	3.00	4.00
PPC050	2.00	3.00	PPD218	2.00	3.00	PPD439	2.00	3.00
PPC051	1.00	1.50	PPD219	2.00	3.00	PPD440	5.00	7.50
PPC060	6.00	8.00	PPD220	2.00	3.00	PPD441	5.00	7.50
PPC070	.50	.75	PPD250	1.50	2.00	PPD442	5.00	7.50
PPC071	2.00	3.00	PPD251	1.50	2.00	PPD443	5.00	7.50
PPC080	3.00	4.50	PPD252	1.50	2.00	PPD450	2.00	3.00
PPC200	1.00	1.50	PPD253	1.50	2.00	PPD460	10.00	12.50
PPC201	25.00	35.00	PPD265	2.00	3.00	PPD461	10.00	12.50
PPC202	2.00	3.00	PPD266	2.00	3.00	PPD462	10.00	12.50
PPC203	25.00	35.00	PPD267	2.00	3.00	PPD463	10.00	12.50
PPC204	6.00	8.00	PPD268	2.00	3.00	PPD464	11.00	13.50
PPC205	2.00	3.00	PPD269	2.00	3.00	PPD465	10.00	12.50
PPC230	5.00	7.50	PPD270	2.00	3.00	PPD466	10.00	12.50
PPC231	5.00	7.50	PPD271	2.00	3.00	PPD467	10.00	12.50
PPC300	5.00	7.50	PPD272	2.00	3.00	PPD468	10.00	12.50
PPD001	2.00	3.00	PPD279	2.00	3.00	PPD500	5.00	7.50
PPD002	2.00	3.00	PPD280	1.00	1.50	PPE001	3.00	4.00
PPD003	2.00	3.00	PPD290	3.00	4.00	PPE002	3.00	4.00
PPD004	2.00	3.00	PPD291	3.00	4.00	PPE003	3.00	4.00
PPD005	3.00	4.00	PPD292	3.00	4.00	PPE004	3.00	4.00
PPD006	3.00	4.00	PPD293	3.00	4.00	PPE005	3.00	4.00
PPD020	2.00	3.00	PPD300	1.50	2.00	PPE006	3.00	4.00
PPD021	2.00	3.00	PPD301	1.50	2.00	PPE007	3.00	4.00
PPD022	2.00	3.00	PPD302	1.50	2.00	PPE008	3.00	4.00
PPD023	2.00	3.00	PPD303	1.50	2.00	PPE010	3.00	4.00
PPD040	1.50	2.00	PPD304	1.50	2.00	PPE011	3.00	4.00
PPD041	1.50	2.00	PPD305	1.50	2.00	PPE012	3.00	4.00
PPD042	1.50	2.00	PPD306	2.00	3.00	PPE020	3.00	4.00
PPD050	2.00	3.00	PPD307	2.00	3.00	PPE021	3.00	4.00
PPD090	2.00	3.00	PPD308	2.00	2.00	PPE022	3.00	4.00
PPD100	2.00	3.00	PPD309	2.00	3.00	PPE100	3.00	4.00
PPD101	2.00	3.00	PPD310	1.50	2.00	PPE101	3.00	4.00
PPD110	2.00	3.00	PPD311	1.50	2.00	PPE102	3.00	4.00
PPD111	2.00	3.00	PPD312	1.50	2.00	PPE103	3.00	4.00
PPD112	2.00	3.00	PPD313	1.50	2.00	PPG001	2.00	3.00
PPD113	2.00	3.00	PPD314	2.00	3.00	PPG002	2.00	3.00
PPD150	2.00	3.00	PPD315	2.00	3.00	PPG003	2.00	3.00
PPD151	2.00	3.00	PPD318	1.50	2.00	PPG004	2.00	3.00
PPD152	2.00	3.00	PPD319	1.50	2.00	PPG005	2.00	3.00
PPD153	2.00	3.00	PPD320	1.50	2.00	PPG006	2.00	3.00
PPD154	2.00	3.00	PPD321	1.50	2.00	PPG007	2.00	3.00
PPD155	2.00	3.00	PPD330	1.50	2.00	PPG008	2.00	3.00
PPD160	2.00	3.00	PPD337	2.00	3.00	PPG010	2.00	3.00
PPD161	2.00	3.00	PPD338	2.00	3.00	PPG020	3.00	4.00
PPD162	2.00	3.00	PPD339	2.00	3.00	PPG021	3.00	4.00
PPD163	2.00	3.00	PPD340	2.00	3.00	PPG100	5.00	7.50
PPD170	1.50	2.00	PPD400	5.00	7.50	PPG111	5.00	7.50
PPD171	1.50	2.00	PPD401	2.00	3.00	PSG001	.35	.50
PPD172	1.50	2.00	PPD402	2.00	3.00	PSG002	.35	.50
PPD173	1.50	2.00	PPD403	1.50	2.00	PSG003	.35	.50
PPD175	1.50	2.00	PPD404	1.50	2.00	PGS004	.35	.50
PPD200	2.00	3.00	PPD405	2.00	3.00	PGS005	.35	.50
PPD201	2.00	3.00	PPD406	2.00	3.00	PGS006	.35	.50
PPD202	2.00	3.00	PPD407	2.00	3.00	PGS007	.35	.50

Cat. No.	Good	Mint	Cat. No.	Good	Mint	Cat. No.	Good	Mint
PSG008	.35	.50	SGF100	1.50	2.00	STX001	3.00	4.00
PSG009	.35	.50	SGF101	2.00	3.00	STX002	3.00	4.00
PSG010	.35	.50	SGF102	1.50	2.00	STX100	3.00	4.00
PSG011	.35	.50	SGF103	3.00	4.00	STX101	3.00	4.00
PSG012	.35	.50	SIL001	3.00	4.00	STX110	3.00	4.00
PSG013	.35	.50	SIL002	3.00	4.00	STX111	3.00	4.00
PSG020	5.00	7.50	SIL100	3.00	4.00	STX112	3.00	4.00
PSG040	.50	.75	SIL110	3.00	4.00	SUS001	3.00	4.00
PSG100	.35	.50	SIL120	3.00	4.00	SUS002	10.00	12.50
PSG101	.35	.50	SIN100	3.00	4.00	SUS003	10.00	12.50
PSG102	5.00	7.50	SIN120	3.00	4.00	SUS004	10.00	12.50
SPG103	.35	.50	SLA100	3.00	4.00	SUS005	10.00	12.50
PSG104	.35	.50	SMA001	3.00	4.00	SUS006	10.00	12.50
PSG105	.35	.50	SMA100	3.00	4.00	SUS007	10.00	12.50
PSG106	.75	1.00	SMA110	3.00	4.00	SUS008	10.00	12.50
PSG107	.75	1.00	SMA120	3.00	4.00	SUS009	10.00	12.50
PSG108	.75	1.00	SMD001	3.00	4.00	SUS010	10.00	12.50
PSG109	10.00	12.50	SMI001	3.00	4.00	SUS011	10.00	12.50
PSG110	.35	.50	SMI002	3.00	4.00	SUT110	3.00	4.00
PSG111	.35	.50	SMI003	3.00	4.00	SWA001	3.00	4.00
PSG112	.75	1.00	SMI100	3.00	4.00	SWA100	3.00	4.00
PSG113	.35	.50	SMI110	3.00	4.00	SWA110	3.00	4.00
PSG114	.50	.75	SMI120	3.00	4.00	SWI001	3.00	4.00
PSG115	.50	.75	SMN001	3.00	4.00	SWI010	3.00	4.00
PSG116	5.00	7.50	SMN100	3.00	4.00	SWI100	3.00	4.00
PSG200	1.50	2.00	SMN110	3.00	4.00	TAK010	2.00	3.00
PSG201	1.50	2.00	SMN120	3.00	4.00	TAK012	2.00	3.00
SAZ100	3.00	4.00	SMO001	3.00	4.00	TAK011	2.00	3.00
SAZ110	3.00	4.00	SMO002	3.00	4.00	TAK100	2.00	3.00
SCA001	3.00	4.00	SMO100	3.00	4.00	TAK101	2.00	3.00
SCA002	3.00	4.00	SMO110	3.00	4.00	TAK102	2.00	3.00
SCA003	3.00	4.00	SNC110	3.00	4.00	TAK103	2.00	3.00
SCA004	3.00	4.00	SNJ110	3.00	4.00	TAK400	2.00	3.00
SCA005	3.00	4.00	SNJ120	3.00	4.00	TAL100	2.00	3.00
SCA006	3.00	4.00	SNY001	3.00	4.00	TAL101	2.00	3.00
SCA100	3.00	4.00	SNY010	3.00	4.00	TAL102	2.00	3.00
SCA101	3.00	4.00	SNY100	3.00	4.00	TAL103	2.00	3.00
SCA102	3.00	4.00	SNY101	3.00	4.00	TAL120	2.00	3.00
SCA103	3.00	4.00	SNY102	3.00	4.00	TAL121	2.00	3.00
SCA110	3.00	4.00	SNY110	3.00	4.00	TAL400	2.00	3.00
SCA111	3.00	4.00	SNY120	3.00	4.00	TAR050	2.00	3.00
SCA112	3.00	4.00	SNY121	3.00	4.00	TAR100	2.00	3.00
SCA120	3.00	4.00	SNY122	3.00	4.00	TAR101	2.00	3.00
SCO100	3.00	4.00	SOH001	3.00	4.00	TAR102	2.00	3.00
SCO110	3.00	4.00	SOH002	3.00	4.00	TAR400	2.00	3.00
SCT001	3.00	4.00	SOH100	3.00	4.00	TAZ001	2.00	3.00
SDC100	3.00	4.00	SOH110	3.00	4.00	TAZ020	2.00	3.00
SDC110	3.00	4.00	SOH130	2.00	3.00	TAZ021	2.00	3.00
SDC120	3.00	4.00	SOR110	3.00	4.00	TAZ025	2.00	3.00
SFL100	3.00	4.00	SPA001	3.00	4.00	TAZ040	2.00	3.00
SFL101	3.00	4.00	SPA002	3.00	4.00	TAZ100	2.00	3.00
SFL110	3.00	4.00	SPA010	3.00	4.00	TAZ101	2.00	3.00
SFL111	3.00	4.00	SPA011	3.00	4.00	TAZ102	2.00	3.00
SFL120	2.00	3.00	SPA100	3.00	4.00	TAZ120	2.00	3.00
SGA001	3.00	4.00	SPA101	3.00	4.00	TAZ130	3.00	4.00
SGA100	3.00	4.00	SPA110	3.00	4.00	TAZ140	3.00	4.00
SGA110	3.00	4.00	SPA120	3.00	4.00	TAZ150	2.00	3.00
SGF010	15.00	20.00	SPA121	3.00	4.00	TAZ400	2.00	3.00

Cat. No.	Good	Mint	Cat. No.	Good	Mint	Cat. No.	Good	Mint
TCA001	3.00	4.00	TCO001	2.00	3.00	TFL110	2.00	3.00
TCA030	2.00	3.00	TCO002	2.00	3.00	TFL111	2.00	3.00
TCA031	2.00	3.00	TCO020	2.00	3.00	TFL112	5.00	7.50
TCA032	3.00	4.00	TCO021	2.00	3.00	TFL113	2.00	3.00
TCA040	2.00	3.00	TCO022	2.00	3.00	TFL120	2.00	3.00
TCA050	2.00	3.00	TCO030	2.00	3.00	TFL121	2.00	3.00
TCA051	3.00	4.00	TCO100	2.00	3.00	TFL122	6.00	8.00
TCA060	2.00	3.00	TCO101	2.00	3.00	TFL123	6.00	8.00
TCA070	3.00	4.50	TCO102	2.00	3.00	TFL124	2.00	3.00
TCA100	2.00	3.00	TCO120	2.00	3.00	TFL125	5.00	7.50
TCA101	2.00	3.00	TCO125	2.00	3.00	TFL140	2.00	3.00
TCA102	2.00	3.00	TCO126	5.00	7.50	TFL141	2.00	3.00
TCA103	2.00	3.00	TCO130	5.00	7.50	TFL142	2.00	3.00
TCA104	2.00	3.00	TCO140	2.00	3.00	TFL143	2.00	3.00
TCA105	5.00	7.50	TCO400	2.00	3.00	TFL144	2.00	3.00
TCA106	2.00	3.00	TCT100	2.00	3.00	TFL145	2.00	3.00
TCA107	2.00	3.00	TCT101	2.00	3.00	TFL146	2.00	3.00
TCA108	2.00	3.00	TCT102	2.00	3.00	TFL147	2.00	3.00
TCA109	2.00	3.00	TCT103	2.00	3.00	TFL150	2.00	3.00
TCA110	2.00	3.00	TCT120	6.00	8.00	TFL160	5.00	7.50
TCA111	7.50	10.00	TCT121	6.00	8.00	TFL400	2.00	3.00
TCA112	6.00	8.00	TCT400	2.00	3.00	TGA010	2.00	3.00
TCA113	2.00	3.00	TDC010	2.00	3.00	TGA011	2.00	3.00
TCA114	2.00	3.00	TDC011	2.00	3.00	TGA012	2.00	3.00
TCA115	2.00	3.00	TDC100	2.00	3.00	TGA100	2.00	3.00
TCA116	3.00	4.00	TDC101	2.00	3.00	TGA101	2.00	3.00
TCA117	3.00	4.00	TDC102	2.00	3.00	TGA102	2.00	3.00
TCA118	2.00	3.00	TDC120	2.00	3.00	TGA103	2.00	3.00
TCA119	2.00	3.00	TDC121	2.00	3.00	TGA120	2.00	3.00
TCA120	2.00	3.00	TDC122	2.00	3.00	TGA130	2.00	3.00
TCA121	2.00	3.00	TDE100	10.00	12.50	TGA131	2.00	3.00
TCA122	2.00	3.00	TDE101	2.00	3.00	TGA400	2.00	3.00
TCA123	2.00	3.00	TDE102	2.00	3.00	THI020	3.00	4.00
TCA124	2.00	3.00	TDE103	2.00	3.00	THI021	2.00	3.00
TCA125	2.00	3.00	TDE104	2.00	3.00	THI100	2.00	3.00
TCA126	2.00	3.00	TDE105	2.00	3.00	THI101	2.00	3.00
TCA127	2.00	3.00	TDE106	2.00	3.00	THI102	2.00	3.00
TCA128	3.00	4.00	TDE400	2.00	3.00	THI103	2.00	3.00
TCA129	2.00	3.00	TFL001	3.00	4.00	THI104	5.00	7.50
TCA130	2.00	3.00	TFL002	3.00	4.00	THI105	2.00	3.00
TCA131	2.00	3.00	TFL020	2.00	3.00	THI106	2.00	3.00
TCA132	2.00	3.00	TFL021	2.00	3.00	THI107	2.00	3.00
TCA133	2.00	3.00	TFL025	2.00	3.00	THI108	2.00	3.00
TCA134	2.00	3.00	TFL026	2.00	3.00	THI109	2.00	3.00
TCA135	2.00	3.00	TFL030	2.00	3.00	THI110	2.00	3.00
TCA136	2.00	3.00	TFL031	2.00	3.00	THI111	2.00	3.00
TCA137	2.00	3.00	TFL050	2.00	3.00	THI112	2.00	3.00
TCA138	4.00	6.00	TFL051	2.00	3.00	THI113	5.00	7.50
TCA139	2.00	3.00	TFL100	2.00	3.00	THI114	2.00	3.00
TCA140	2.00	3.00	TFL101	2.00	3.00	THI115	2.00	3.00
TCA141	2.00	3.00	TFL102	2.00	3.00	THI120	3.00	4.50
TCA142	2.00	3.00	TFL103	2.00	3.00	THI125	3.00	4.50
TCA143	3.00	4.00	TFL104	2.00	3.00	THI130	2.00	3.00
TCA144	3.00	4.00	TFL105	2.00	3.00	THI400	2.00	3.00
TCA145	2.00	3.00	TFL106	2.00	3.00	TIA010	2.00	3.00
TCA160	2.00	3.00	TFL107	2.00	3.00	TIA100	2.00	3.00
TCA170	2.00	3.00	TFL108	2.00	3.00	TIA101	2.00	3.00
TCA400	2.00	3.00	TFL109	2.00	3.00	TIA102	2.00	3.00

Cat. No.	Good	Mint	Cat. No.	Good	Mint	Cat. No.	Good	Mint
TIA400	2.00	3.00	TLA120	2.00	3.00	TMI104	2.00	3.00
TID100	2.00	3.00	TLA121	2.00	3.00	TMI105	2.00	3.00
TID101	2.00	3.00	TLA122	2.00	3.00	TMI106	7.50	10.00
TID102	2.00	3.00	TLA123	2.00	3.00	TMI107	2.00	3.00
TID103	2.00	3.00	TLA124	5.00	7.50	TMI108	2.00	3.00
TID400	2.00	3.00	TLA400	2.00	3.00	TMI109	3.00	4.00
TIL010	2.00	3.00	TMA100	2.00	3.00	TMI110	2.00	3.00
TIL011	2.00	3.00	TMA101	2.00	3.00	TMI111	2.00	3.00
TIL012	2.00	3.00	TMA120	2.00	3.00	TMI112	2.00	3.00
TIL100	2.00	3.00	TMA121	2.00	3.00	TMI113	2.00	3.00
TIL101	2.00	3.00	TMA122	7.50	10.00	TMI114	6.00	8.00
TIL102	2.00	3.00	TMA130	2.00	3.00	TMI115	6.00	8.00
TIL103	3.00	4.00	TMA131	7.50	10.00	TMI116	2.00	3.00
TIL104	2.00	3.00	TMA132	2.00	3.00	TMI117	2.00	3.00
TIL120	2.00	3.00	TMA133	2.00	3.00	TMI118	2.00	3.00
TIL121	2.00	3.00	TMA134	2.00	3.00	TMI119	2.00	3.00
TIL122	2.00	3.00	TMA135	2.00	3.00	TMI120	2.00	3.00
TIL123	5.00	7.50	TMA150	2.00	3.00	TMI121	2.00	3.00
TIL140	2.00	3.00	TMA400	2.00	3.00	TMI122	2.00	3.00
TIL400	2.00	3.00	TMD100	2.00	3.00	TIM123	2.00	3.00
TIN011	2.00	3.00	TMD101	2.00	3.00	TMI124	2.00	3.00
TIN100	2.00	3.00	TMD102	2.00	3.00	TMI125	2.00	3.00
TIN101	2.00	3.00	TMD103	2.00	3.00	TMI126	2.00	3.00
TIN102	2.00	3.00	TMD104	2.00	3.00	TMI127	2.00	3.00
TIN103	2.00	3.00	TMD105	2.00	3.00	TMI128	2.00	3.00
TIN120	2.00	3.00	TND120	2.00	3.00	TMI129	2.00	3.00
TIN121	2.00	3.00	TMD121	2.00	3.00	TMI130	2.00	3.00
TIN122	2.00	3.00	TMD122	2.00	3.00	TMI131	3.00	4.00
TIN400	2.00	3.00	TMD130	2.00	3.00	TMI132	2.00	3.00
TKS001	2.00	3.00	TMD131	2.00	3.00	TMI133	2.00	3.00
TKS020	2.00	3.00	TMD132	2.00	3.00	TMI134	2.00	3.00
TKS100	2.00	3.00	TMD133	2.00	3.00	TIM135	2.00	3.00
TKS101	2.00	3.00	TMD134	2.00	3.00	TIM136	2.00	3.00
TKS400	2.00	3.00	TMD400	2.00	3.00	TMI137	2.00	3.00
TKY001	2.00	3.00	TME100	2.00	3.00	TMI138	6.00	8.00
TKY100	2.00	3.00	TME101	6.00	8.00	TMI139	3.00	4.00
TKY101	2.00	3.00	TME102	2.00	3.00	TMI140	2.00	3.00
TKY102	2.00	3.00	TME103	2.00	3.00	TMI141	2.00	3.00
TKY103	3.00	4.00	TME104	2.00	3.00	TMI142	2.00	3.00
TKY104	2.00	3.00	TME400	2.00	3.00	TMI143	2.00	3.00
TKY105	2.00	3.00	TMI001	2.00	3.00	TMI145	2.00	3.00
TKY106	2.00	3.00	TMI002	3.00	4.50	TMI146	2.00	3.00
TKY107	2.00	3.00	TMI020	2.00	3.00	TMI147	2.00	3.00
TKY108	2.00	3.00	TMI021	2.00	3.00	TMI150	6.00	8.00
TKY109	2.00	3.00	TMI025	2.00	3.00	TMI151	6.00	8.00
TKY110	2.00	3.00	TMI029	2.00	3.00	TMI152	7.50	10.00
TKY111	2.00	3.00	TMI030	2.00	3.00	TMI153	2.00	3.00
TKY112	2.00	3.00	TMI035	2.00	3.00	TMI160	2.00	3.00
TKY113	2.00	3.00	TMI039	2.00	3.00	TMI161	2.00	3.00
TKY114	2.00	3.00	TMI040	2.00	3.00	TMI162	2.00	3.00
TKY120	2.00	3.00	TMI041	2.00	3.00	TMI163	2.00	3.00
TKY130	2.00	3.00	TMI042	2.00	3.00	TMI164	3.00	4.00
TKY140	2.00	3.00	TMI050	2.00	3.00	TMI165	3.00	4.00
TKY141	2.00	3.00	TMI060	2.00	3.00	TIM166	5.00	7.50
TKY400	2.00	3.00	TMI100	2.00	3.00	TMI167	2.00	3.00
TLA010	2.00	3.00	TMI101	2.00	3.00	TMI168	3.00	4.00
TLA100	2.00	3.00	TMI102	2.00	3.00	TMI170	2.00	3.00
TLA101	2.00	3.00	TMI103	2.00	3.00	TMI171	2.00	3.00

Cat. No.	Good	Mint	Cat. No.	Good	Mint	Cat. No.	Good	Mint
TMI172	2.00	3.00	TMI280	2.00	3.00	TNJ121	2.00	3.00
TMI173	2.00	3.00	TMI400	2.00	3.00	TNJ122	2.00	3.00
TMI174	2.00	3.00	TMI480	5.00	7.50	TNJ123	2.00	3.00
TMI175	2.00	3.00	TMN100	2.00	3.00	TNJ124	2.00	3.00
TMI176	2.00	3.00	TMN101	2.00	3.00	TNJ125	2.00	3.00
TMI177	5.00	7.50	TMN102	2.00	3.00	TNJ126	2.00	3.00
TMI178	3.00	4.00	TMN103	2.00	3.00	TNJ127	2.00	3.00
TMI179	10.00	12.50	TMN104	2.00	3.00	TNJ128	2.00	3.00
TMI180	2.00	3.00	TMN105	2.00	3.00	TNJ129	5.00	7.50
TMI181	2.00	3.00	TMN106	2.00	3.00	TNJ150	2.00	3.00
TMI182	6.00	8.00	TMN120	2.00	3.00	TNJ400	2.00	3.00
TMI189	10.00	12.50	TMN130	2.00	3.00	TNM010	2.00	3.00
TMI190	2.00	3.00	TMN131	5.00	7.50	TNM100	2.00	3.00
TMI191	2.00	3.00	TMN132	2.00	3.00	TNM101	2.00	3.00
TMI192	2.00	3.00	TMN140	2.00	3.00	TNM102	3.00	4.00
TMI193	2.00	3.00	TMN150	2.00	3.00	TNM103	2.00	3.00
TMI194	2.00	3.00	TMN400	2.00	3.00	TNM104	2.00	3.00
TMI195	2.00	3.00	TMO010	2.00	3.00	TNM400	2.00	3.00
TMI196	3.00	4.00	TMO011	2.00	3.00	TNV001	3.00	4.00
TMI197	2.00	3.00	TMO012	2.00	3.00	TNV010	2.00	3.00
TMI198	3.00	4.00	TMO100	2.00	3.00	TNV011	3.00	4.00
TMI199	3.00	4.00	TMO101	2.00	3.00	TNV100	2.00	3.00
TMI200	5.00	7.50	TMO110	2.00	3.00	TNV101	2.00	3.00
TMI201	2.00	3.00	TMO120	2.00	3.00	TNV102	2.00	3.00
TMI202	3.00	4.00	TMO400	2.00	3.00	TNV110	2.00	3.00
TMI203	2.00	3.00	TMS100	2.00	3.00	TNV111	2.00	3.00
TMI204	2.00	3.00	TMS101	2.00	3.00	TNV112	2.00	3.00
TMI205	2.00	3.00	TMS102	2.00	3.00	TNV113	5.00	7.50
TMI206	2.00	3.00	TMS400	2.00	3.00	TNV114	5.00	7.50
TMI207	2.00	3.00	TMT100	2.00	3.00	TNV115	2.00	3.00
TMI208	3.00	4.00	TMT101	2.00	3.00	TNV150	3.00	4.00
TMI209	2.00	3.00	TMT102	3.00	4.00	TNV151	3.00	4.00
TMI210	3.00	4.00	TMT400	2.00	3.00	TNV160	2.00	3.00
TMI211	2.00	3.00	TNC010	3.00	4.00	TNV170	2.00	3.00
TMI212	5.00	7.50	TNC020	2.00	3.00	TNV171	3.00	4.00
TMI213	3.00	4.00	TNC100	2.00	3.00	TNV400	2.00	3.00
TMI215	2.00	3.00	TNC101	2.00	3.00	TNY001	3.00	4.00
TMI216	2.00	3.00	TNC102	2.00	3.00	TNY002	3.00	4.00
TMI217	2.00	3.00	TNC103	2.00	3.00	TNY010	2.00	3.00
TMI218	7.50	10.00	TNC120	2.00	3.00	TNY020	2.00	3.00
TMI220	2.00	3.00	TNC400	2.00	3.00	TNY100	2.00	3.00
TMI221	2.00	3.00	TND100	2.00	3.00	TNY101	10.00	12.50
TMI222	2.00	3.00	TND101	2.00	3.00	TNY102	5.00	7.50
TMI223	2.00	3.00	TND400	2.00	3.00	TNY103	2.00	3.00
TMI224	2.00	3.00	TNE010	2.00	3.00	TNY104	6.00	8.00
TMI225	2.00	3.00	TNE100	2.00	3.00	TNY105	2.00	3.00
TMI226	2.00	3.00	TNE101	2.00	3.00	TNY106	2.00	3.00
TMI227	2.00	3.00	TNE102	2.00	3.00	TNY107	2.00	3.00
TMI228	2.00	3.00	TNE400	2.00	3.00	TNY120	2.00	3.00
TMI229	2.00	3.00	TNH100	2.00	3.00	TNY121	2.00	3.00
TMI240	2.00	3.00	TNH101	2.00	3.00	TNY122	2.00	3.00
TMI241	2.00	3.00	TNH400	2.00	3.00	TNY130	2.00	3.00
TMI250	2.00	3.00	TNJ100	10.00	12.50	TNY140	5.00	7.50
TMI251	2.00	3.00	TNJ101	2.00	3.00	TNY400	2.00	3.00
TMI260	2.00	3.00	TNJ102	2.00	3.00	TOH001	3.00	4.00
TMI270	2.00	3.00	TNJ103	2.00	3.00	TOH002	3.00	4.00
TMI271	3.00	4.00	TNJ110	2.00	3.00	TOH003	3.00	4.00
TMI272	5.00	7.50	TNJ120	2.00	3.00	TOH020	2.00	3.00

Cat. No.	Good	Mint	Cat. No.	Good	Mint	Cat. No.	Good	Mint
TOH021	2.00	3.00	TPR100	2.00	3.00	TTN129	2.00	3.00
TOH100	5.00	7.50	TPR101	2.00	3.00	TTN130	2.00	3.00
TOH101	2.00	3.00	TPR400	2.00	3.00	TTN131	2.00	3.00
TOH102	2.00	3.00	TRI100	2.00	3.00	TTN132	2.00	3.00
TOH103	2.00	3.00	TRI101	2.00	3.00	TTN133	6.00	8.00
TOH104	2.00	3.00	TRI102	2.00	3.00	TTN134	2.00	3.00
TOH105	3.00	4.00	TRI103	2.00	3.00	TTN135	2.00	3.00
TOH106	2.00	3.00	TRI120	2.00	3.00	TTN136	2.00	3.00
TOH110	2.00	3.00	TRI400	2.00	3.00	TTN137	2.00	3.00
TOH111	5.00	7.50	TSC100	2.00	3.00	TTN138	2.00	3.00
TOH120	2.00	3.00	TSC101	2.00	3.00	TTN139	10.00	12.50
TOH121	3.00	4.00	TSC102	2.00	3.00	TTN140	2.00	3.00
TOH122	3.00	4.00	TSC103	2.00	3.00	TTN141	6.00	8.00
TOH123	2.00	3.00	TSC104	2.00	3.00	TTN142	2.00	3.00
TOH124	2.00	3.00	TSC120	2.00	3.00	TTN143	3.00	4.00
TOH125	2.00	3.00	TSC130	2.00	3.00	TTN150	2.00	3.00
TOH126	2.00	3.00	TSC131	2.00	3.00	TTN151	3.00	4.00
TOH127	2.00	3.00	TSC132	2.00	3.00	TTN155	10.00	12.50
TOH128	3.00	4.00	TSC133	2.00	3.00	TTN156	2.00	3.00
TOH129	5.00	7.50	TSC160	2.00	3.00	TTN157	2.00	3.00
TOH130	2.00	3.00	TSC400	2.00	3.00	TTN158	2.00	3.00
TOH150	2.00	3.00	TSD001	3.00	4.00	TTN159	2.00	3.00
TOH160	2.00	3.00	TSD020	2.00	3.00	TTN160	5.00	7.50
TOH400	2.00	3.00	TSD100	2.00	3.00	TTN161	7.50	10.00
TOH480	5.00	7.50	TSD101	2.00	3.00	TTN162	2.00	3.00
TOK010	2.00	3.00	TSD120	2.00	3.00	TTN163	2.00	3.00
TOK100	2.00	3.00	TSD400	2.00	3.00	TTN164	2.00	3.00
TOK101	3.00	4.00	TTN010	2.00	3.00	TTN165	2.00	3.00
TOK102	2.00	3.00	TTN011	2.00	3.00	TTN166	3.00	4.00
TOK103	2.00	3.00	TTN012	2.00	3.00	TTN167	3.00	4.00
TOK104	2.00	3.00	TTN030	2.00	3.00	TTN168	3.00	4.00
TOK120	2.00	3.00	TTN031	2.00	3.00	TTN169	2.00	3.00
TOK400	2.00	3.00	TTN032	2.00	3.00	TTN170	2.00	3.00
TOR100	2.00	3.00	TTN033	2.00	3.00	TTN171	2.00	3.00
TOR101	2.00	3.00	TTN050	2.00	3.00	TTN180	2.00	3.00
TOR400	2.00	3.00	TTN100	2.00	3.00	TTN400	2.00	3.00
TPA001	3.00	4.00	TTN101	2.00	3.00	TTN421	5.00	7.50
TPA020	2.00	3.00	TTN102	2.00	3.00	TTX010	2.00	3.00
TPA030	2.00	3.00	TTN103	2.00	3.00	TTX011	2.00	3.00
TPA100	2.00	3.00	TTN104	2.00	3.00	TTX012	2.00	3.00
TPA101	3.00	4.00	TTN105	2.00	3.00	TTX020	2.00	3.00
TPA102	2.00	3.00	TTN106	5.00	7.50	TTX100	2.00	3.00
TPA103	2.00	3.00	TTN107	2.00	3.00	TTX101	2.00	3.00
TPA120	2.00	3.00	TTN108	2.00	3.00	TTX102	2.00	3.00
TPA130	2.00	3.00	TTN109	2.00	3.00	TTX103	2.00	3.00
TPA140	2.00	3.00	TTN110	2.00	3.00	TTX104	2.00	3.00
TPA141	2.00	3.00	TTN111	2.00	3.00	TTX105	2.00	3.00
TPA142	2.00	3.00	TTN112	2.00	3.00	TTX106	2.00	3.00
TPA150	2.00	3.00	TTN113	3.00	4.00	TTX120	5.00	7.50
TPA151	2.00	3.00	TTN120	2.00	3.00	TTX121	3.00	4.00
TPA152	2.00	3.00	TTN121	2.00	3.00	TTX130	2.00	3.00
TPA153	2.00	3.00	TTN122	2.00	3.00	TTX140	2.00	3.00
TPA154	2.00	3.00	TTN123	2.00	3.00	TTX141	2.00	3.00
TPA155	6.00	8.00	TTN124	2.00	3.00	TTX142	3.00	4.00
TPA156	7.50	10.00	TTN125	2.00	3.00	TTX150	2.00	3.00
TPA160	2.00	3.00	TTN126	2.00	3.00	TTX400	2.00	3.00
TPA400	3.00	4.00	TTN127	2.00	3.00	TUS050	2.00	3.00
TPR010	2.00	3.00	TTN128	6.00	8.00	TUS100	2.00	3.00

Cat. No.	Good	Mint	Cat. No.	Good	Mint	Cat. No.	Good	Mint
TUS101	2.00	3.00	TWY133	3.00	4.00	UOH011	5.00	7.50
TUS102	2.00	3.00	TWY400	2.00	3.00	UOH012	2.00	3.00
TUS104	2.00	3.00	UAL010	2.00	3.00	UOH030	2.00	3.00
TUT100	2.00	3.00	UAL011	2.00	3.00	UOH035	2.00	3.00
TUT101	2.00	3.00	UAL012	2.00	3.00	UOH040	4.00	6.00
TUT102	2.00	3.00	UAR001	2.00	3.00	UOH045	4.00	6.00
TUT103	6.00	8.00	UAR010	2.00	3.00	UOK010	5.00	7.50
TUT120	3.00	4.00	UAZ010	2.00	3.00	UPA010	2.00	3.00
TUT400	2.00	3.00	UCA010	2.00	3.00	UTN010	2.00	3.00
TVA100	2.00	3.00	UFL010	2.00	3.00	UTN020	2.00	3.00
TVA101	2.00	3.00	UIA010	2.00	3.00	UWI010	2.00	3.00
TVA102	2.00	3.00	UIN001	3.00	4.00	UUS001	2.00	3.00
TVA120	2.00	3.00	UIN010	2.00	3.00	UUS002	2.00	3.00
TVA121	2.00	3.00	UIN021	2.00	3.00	UUS003	2.00	3.00
TVA130	2.00	3.00	UKY010	2.00	3.00	UUS004	2.00	3.00
TVA400	2.00	3.00	UKY011	2.00	3.00	UUS005	2.00	3.00
TVT100	2.00	3.00	UKY012	2.00	3.00	UUS006	2.00	3.00
TVT101	2.00	3.00	UKY013	2.00	3.00	UUS007	2.00	3.00
TVT102	2.00	3.00	UKY014	2.00	3.00	UUS008	2.00	3.00
TVT400	2.00	3.00	UKY015	2.00	3.00	UUS009	2.00	3.00
TVT420	2.00	3.00	ULA010	2.00	3.00	UUS010	2.00	3.00
TVT421	2.00	3.00	UMA010	2.00	3.00	UUS011	2.00	3.00
TVT422	5.00	7.50	UMI001	2.00	3.00	UUS012	2.00	3.00
TWA100	2.00	3.00	UMI010	2.00	3.00	UUS013	2.00	3.00
TWA101	2.00	3.00	UMI011	2.00	3.00	UUS014	2.00	3.00
TWA102	2.00	3.00	UMI050	4.00	6.00	UUS015	2.00	3.00
TWA120	2.00	3.00	UMI051	2.00	3.00	UUS016	2.00	3.00
TWA121	5.00	7.50	UMI052	2.00	3.00	UUS017	2.00	3.00
TWA400	2.00	3.00	UMI053	2.00	3.00	UUS018	2.00	3.00
TWI010	2.00	3.00	UMI054	3.00	4.00	UUS019	2.00	3.00
TWI100	2.00	3.00	UMI055	2.00	3.00	UUS020	2.00	3.00
TWI101	2.00	3.00	UMI056	2.00	3.00	UUS021	2.00	3.00
TWI102	2.00	3.00	UMI057	2.00	3.00	UUS022	2.00	3.00
TWI103	2.00	3.00	UMI058	10.00	12.50	UUS023	2.00	3.00
TWI120	5.00	7.50	UMI059	6.00	8.00	UUS024	2.00	3.00
TWI121	5.00	7.50	UMI060	2.00	3.00	WAA000	6.00	8.00
TWI122	3.00	4.00	UMI061	2.00	3.00	WAA001	6.00	8.00
TWI123	2.00	3.00	UMI062	5.00	7.50	WAA002	8.00	12.00
TWI124	2.00	3.00	UMI063	5.00	7.50	WAA004	8.00	12.00
TWI125	2.00	3.00	UMI080	2.00	3.00	WAB005	8.00	12.00
TWI126	2.00	3.00	UMI081	2.00	3.00	WAB007	8.00	12.00
TWI127	2.00	3.00	UMI082	2.00	3.00	WAB009	8.00	12.00
TWI128	5.00	7.50	UMI083	10.00	12.50	WAB010	8.00	12.00
TWI140	2.00	3.00	UMI084	10.00	12.50	WAC010	8.00	12.00
TWI141	2.00	3.00	UMI085	2.00	3.00	WAD005	8.00	12.00
TWI400	2.00	3.00	UMI086	5.00	7.50	WAE008	8.00	12.00
TWV100	2.00	3.00	UMI087	2.00	3.00	WAK009	8.00	12.00
TWV101	2.00	3.00	UMI100	2.00	3.00	WAK018	8.00	12.00
TWV102	3.00	4.00	UMI102	2.00	3.00	WAL015	8.00	12.00
TWV103	2.00	3.00	UMI103	2.00	3.00	WAP001	8.00	12.00
TWV400	2.00	3.00	UMI105	2.00	3.00	WAP004	8.00	12.00
TWY001	3.00	4.00	UNC010	2.00	3.00	WAP005	8.00	12.00
TWY100	2.00	3.00	UNC020	2.00	3.00	WAT009	8.00	12.00
TWY101	2.00	3.00	UNC021	2.00	3.00	WAT038	8.00	12.00
TWY120	2.00	3.00	UNC022	2.00	3.00	WSA002	10.00	15.00
TWY130	2.00	3.00	UNC030	2.00	3.00	WSA120	10.00	15.00
TWY131	3.00	4.00	UNV010	2.00	3.00	WSB003	8.00	12.00
TWY132	5.00	7.50	UOH010	2.00	3.00	WSB006	10.00	15.00

Cat. No.	Good	Mint	Cat. No.	Good	Mint	Cat. No.	Good	Mint
WSB008	8.00	12.00	WSH005	10.00	15.00	WSR090	10.00	15.00
WSB013	10.00	15.00	WSH006	10.00	15.00	WSR104	10.00	15.00
WSB025	15.00	20.00	WSH035	15.00	20.00	WSS002	10.00	15.00
WSB035	10.00	15.00	WSH050	50.00	75.00	WSS005	8.00	12.00
WSC058	8.00	12.00	WSH120	20.00	25.00	WSS023	10.00	15.00
WSC064	10.00	15.00	WSI006	15.00	20.00	WSS024	8.00	12.00
WSC080	15.00	20.00	WSJ010	10.00	15.00	WSS040	10.00	15.00
WSC092	35.00	50.00	WSK028	10.00	15.00	WSS130	20.00	25.00
WSC190	35.00	50.00	WSK040	10.00	15.00	WSS140	20.00	25.00
WSD003	10.00	15.00	WSL030	20.00	25.00	WST020	15.00	20.00
WSD004	8.00	12.00	WSM020	15.00	20.00	WST040	15.00	20.00
WSD008	8.00	12.00	WSN030	15.00	20.00	WSV003	20.00	25.00
WSD009	20.00	25.00	WSO005	15.00	20.00	WSV004	10.00	15.00
WSD012	10.00	15.00	WSO009	15.00	20.00	WSW018	8.00	12.00
WSD014	8.00	12.00	WSO014	10.00	15.00	WSW032	8.00	12.00
WSD015	8.00	12.00	WSO022	10.00	15.00	WSW082	20.00	25.00
WSE018	8.00	12.00	WSO028	8.00	12.00	WSW090	20.00	25.00
WSF001	10.00	15.00	WSO030	8.00	12.00	WSY020	8.00	12.00
WSF010	15.00	20.00	WSO035	10.00	15.00	WTT001	100.00	125.00
WSF018	8.00	12.00	WSO040	10.00	15.00	WTT002	100.00	125.00
WSF024	10.00	15.00	WSO060	20.00	25.00	WTT003	100.00	125.00
WSF030	10.00	15.00	WSO080	8.00	12.00	WTT004	100.00	125.00
WSG020	35.00	50.00	WSP012	10.00	15.00	WTT005	100.00	125.00
WSG120	8.00	12.00	WSP120	8.00	12.00	WTT010	100.00	125.00
WSH003	10.00	15.00	WSR060	10.00	15.00			

BIBLIOGRAPHY

The Alcohol Beverage Industry. *Social Attitudes and Economic Development.* Washington DC: Distilled Spirits Council of the United States, Inc. 1982.

Alcohol & Tobacco Tax Division. *Distilled Spirits: History of Taxation and Law Enforcement.* Internal Revenue Service documents (Document #5574, 1966).

Amelung, John. *Remarks on Manufactures, Principally on the Established Glass-House near Frederick-Town in the State of Maryland.* New Bremen, MA: Published by author, 1787.

American Council on Science and Health. *The Responsible Use of Alcohol: Defining the Parameters of Moderation.* New York: ACSH Publication; January, 1991.

American Pottery and Glassware Reporter, numerous articles and editions, 1870's-1880's.

America's Future: Opposing Viewpoints, from *The Opposing Viewpoints Series.* San Diego: Greenhaven Press Inc. 1990. (series editors David L. Bender and Bruno Leone).

Anderson, Sonja & Will. *Beers, Breweries, & Breweriana.* New York: Sonja & Will/Anderson; publishers, 1969.

Angus-Butterworth. *British Table and Ornamental Glass.* New York: Arco Publishing Co., Inc. 1956.

Annual Report of the Commissioner of Internal Revenue, 1875-1990.

Annual Reports from the Commissioner of Prohibition.

Archer, Margaret and Douglas. *Imperial Glass.* Paducah, KY: Collector Books, 1978.

Arthur, Timothy Shay. *Ten Nights in a Barroom, and What I Saw There.* Boston: Phillips, Sampson Co. 1854.

Association Against the Prohibition Amendment. "Scandals of Prohibition Enforcement." March 1, 1929 edition.

Avila, George C. *The Pairpoint Glass Story.* New Bedford: Reynolds-Dewart Printing, Inc. 1968.

Barber, Edwin A. *American Glassware.* Philadelphia: Press of Patterson & White Co. 1900.

Barbour, Harriot Buxton. *Sandwich: The Town That Glass Built.* Boston: Houghton Mifflin Co. 1948.

Barret, Richard Carter. *Popular American Ruby-Stained Pattern Glass.* Manchester, VT: Published by Richard Carter Barret and Frank L. Forward, 1968.

Batty, Bob H. *A Complete Guide to Pressed Glass.* Gretna, LA: Pelican Publishing Co., Inc. 1978.

Beam, James B. Distillery Co. *The History of Jim Beam Bourbon.* Historical Pamphlet produced by the company; Clermont, KY: 1990.

Beecher, Reverend Lyman. *Six Sermons on the Nature, Occasions, Signs, Evils and Remedy of Temperance.* East Cambridge, MA: Harvard Belknap Press. Autobiography edited by Barbara Cross, 1961.

Benezet, Anthony. *Remarks on the Nature and Bad Effects of Spiritous Liquors.* Article, Philadelphia 1775.

Bennett, Harold and Judy. *The Cambridge Glass Book.* Iowa: Wallace-Homestead Book Co. 1970.

Bishop, Barbara & Martha Hassell. *Your Obdt. Servt., Deming Jarves.* Sandwich, MA: The Sandwich Historical Society, 1984.

Blum, John M. etal. *The National Experience: A History of the United States.* New York: Harcourt Brace Jovanovich, Inc. 1981.

Boston & Sandwich Glass Co. Boston: Lee Publications. 1968.

Bredehoft, Neila. *The Collector's Encyclopedia of Heisey Glass 1925-1938.* Paducah, KY: Collector Books, 1986.

Bredehoft, Neila; Goff, George; & Francis Maloney. *Early Duncan Glassware: Geo. Duncan & Sons 1874-1892.* Boston: Published by authors, 1987.

Brodie, Fawn M. *Richard Nixon: The Shaping of His Character.* New York: W. W. Norton & Co. 1981.

Butler Brothers: Fall, 1910 Catalog. (At the turn of the century, Butler Brothers was one of the largest distributors of glassware and general merchandise of the day).

The Cambridge Glass Co. Ohio: National Cambridge Collection Inc. 1978.

Carr, Jess. *The Second Oldest Profession, An Informal History of Moonshining in America.* New Jersey: Prentice-Hall Inc. 1972.

Charleston, R. J. *English Glass.* London: George Allen and Unwin. 1984.

Charleston, Robert J. *Masterpieces of Glass: A World History from the Corning Museum of Glass.* New York: Harry N. Abrams, 1980.

Chase, Mark E. and Michael J. Kelly. *Contemporary Fast-Food and Drinking Glass Collectibles*. Radnor, PA: Wallace-Homestead Book Co. 1988.

Clark, Norman H. *Deliver Us from Evil: An Interpretation of American Prohibition*. New York: W. W. Norton & Co., Inc. 1976.

Coffey, Thomas M. *The Long Thirst: Prohibition in America 1920-1933*. New York: W. W. Norton & Co., Inc. 1975.

Coleman, Emmet G. editor. *The Temperance Song Book*. New York: American Heritage Press. 1907.

The Complete Book of McKee. Kansas City, MO: The Tuga Press. 1974.

Concerning the Prescribing of Medicinal Liquors. U.S. Treasury Department, Bureau of Industrial Alcohol. Regulations 11, May, 1933.

Cook, Fred J. *The Dutch Schultz Story*. "True Detective" (periodical). April, 1960.

Cosentino, Geraldine and Regina Stewart. *Carnival Glass*. New York: Western Publishing Co., Inc. 1976.

Cudd, Viola N. *Heisey Glassware*. Brenham, TX: Herrmann Print Shop. 1969.

Davis, Derek C. *English Bottles and Decanters 1650-1900*. New York; World Publications Inc. 1972.

Davis, Kenneth S. *FDR: The New Deal Years 1933-1937*. New York: Random House. 1986.

Department of the Treasury, Bureau of Alcohol, Tobacco, and Firearms. *Information for Specially Denatured Spirits Applicants and Tax-Free Alcohol Applicants*. September, 1985 Publication.

Diamond, Freda. *The Story of Glass*. New York: Harcourt, Brace, and World Inc. 1953.

Dibartolomeo, Robert E. editor. *American Glass Volume II: Pressed and Cut*. New York: Weathervane Books. 1978.

Dorflinger C. & Sons. *Cut Glass Catalog 1881-1921*. Hanover, PA: Everybody's Press Inc. 1970.

Ebbott, Rex. *British Glass of the 17th and 18th Centuries*. London: Oxford University Press. 1972.

Editors of the Pyne Press. *Pennsylvania Glassware 1870-1904*. Princeton: Pyne Press. 1972.

Edmonson, Barbara. *Old Advertising Spirits*. Oregon: Maverick Publications. 1988.

Edwards, Bill. *The Standard Encyclopedia of Carnival Glass*. Paducah, KY: Collector Books. 1982.

Elville, E. M. *English and Irish Cut Glass 1750-1950*. New York: Charles Scribener's Sons. 1951.

Falstaff's Complete Beer Book. Edited by Frederic Birmingham. New York: Universal Award House Inc. 1973.

Farrar, Estelle Sinclaire and Jane Shadel Spillman. *The Complete Cut & Engraved Glass of Corning*. New York: Crown Publishers Inc. 1978.

Fauster, Carl U. *Libbey Glass Since 1818*. Toledo, OH: Len Beach Press. 1979.

Flexner, James Thomas. *Washington The Indispensable Man* (biography). New York: Penguin Inc. 1969.

Florence, Gene. *The Collector's Encyclopedia of Depression Glass*. New York: Collector Books. 1990.

Franklin, Benjamin. *The Autobiography and Other Writings*. Philadelphia: completed in 1788. New York: L. Jesse Lemisch, editor; Signet. 1961.

Franklin, Benjamin. *Pennsylvania Gazette* (article). Philadelphia: March 29, 1764.

Furnas, J. C. *The Late Demon Rum*. New York: G. P. Putnam's Sons. 1965.

Gardner, Paul V. *The Glass of Frederick Carder*. New York: Crown Publishers, Inc. 1971.

Getz, Oscar. *Whiskey: An American Pictorial History*. New York: David McKay Co., Inc. 1978.

Green, Ben A. *Jack Daniel's Legacy*. Nashville: Rich Printing Co. 1967.

Hand, Sherman. *The Collectors Encyclopedia of Carnival Glass*. Paducah, KY: Collector Books. 1978.

Harrington, J. C. *Glassmaking at Jamestown: America's First Industry*. Richmond, VA: The Dietz Press Inc. 1952.

Heacock, William and Fred Bickenheuser. *The Encyclopedia of Victorian Colored Pattern Glass*. Marietta, OH: Antique Publications Inc. 1978.

Heisey's Collector's Guide to Glassware For Your Table. Edited by Lyle Conder. Gas City, IN: L-W Book Sales. 1984.

Hettes, Karel. "Venetian Trends in Bohemian Glassmaking in the 16th and 17th Centuries" from *Journal of Glass Studies*. Volume V. 1963.

Horan, James D. *The Desperate Years: A Pictorial History of the Thirties* (photograph collection only).

Huether, Anne. *Glass and Man*. New York: J. B. Lippincott Co. 1965.

Hughes, G. Bernard. *English Glass for the Collector 1660-1860*. New York: Macmillan Co. 1968.

Imperial Glass Corporation: *The Story of Handmade Glass*. Pamphlet published by Imperial (24 pages), 1941.

Innes, Lowell. *Pittsburgh Glass 1797-1891: A History and Guide for Collectors*. Boston: Houghton Mifflin Co. 1976.

Insurance Institute for Highway Safety. *Status Report*. March 16, 1991 edition; Volume 26, No. 3.

Iverson, William. *A Short History of Toasts and Toasting*. Article, Chicago: 1963 Playboy Magazine, Playboy Press.

Jarves, Deming. *Reminiscences of Glassmaking*. Boston: Eastburn's Press. 1854.

Journal of Studies on Alcohol. Chart and statistics from pages 360-361, 1976 edition.

Kearns, Doris. *Lyndon Johnson & The American Dream*. New York: Harper & Row, Publishers. 1976.

Kerr, K. Austin. *Organized for Prohibition: A New History of the Anti-Saloon League*. New Haven, CT: Yale University Press. 1985.

Ketchum, William C. Jr. *A Treasury of American Bottles*. New York: The Ridge Press Inc. 1975.

Klamkin, Marian. *The Collectors Guide to Depression Glass*. New York: Hawthorn Books, Inc. 1973.

Kobler, John. *Ardent Spirits: The Rise and Fall of Prohibition*. New York: G. P. Putnam's Sons. 1974.

Kovel, Ralph and Terry. *The Kovel's Antique and Collectibles Price List*. (18th edition). New York: Crown Publishers Inc. 1985.

Krause, Gail. *Duncan Glass*. New York: Exposition Press. 1976.

Krout, John Allen. *The Origins of Prohibition*. New York: Russell & Russell. 1953.

Lee, Ruth Webb. *Early American Pressed Glass*. New York: Ferris Printing Co. 1946.

Lee, Ruth Webb. *Sandwich Glass*. New York: Ferris Printing Co. 1947.

Lyons, Eugene. *Herbert Hoover: A Biography*. New York: Doubleday & Company, Inc. 1964.

Madigan, Mary Jean. *Steuben Glass: An American Tradition on Crystal*. New York: Harry N. Abrams, Inc. 1982.

Manley, Cyril. *Decorative Victorian Glass*. New York: Von Nostrand Reinhold Co. 1981.

Mariacher, G. *Three Centuries of Venetian Glass*. Corning, NY: Corning Museum of Glass (translation). 1957.

Marshall, Mac. *Beliefs, Behaviors, & Alcoholic Beverages*. Ann Arbor, MI: University of Michigan Press. 1979.

Martin, Ralph G. *A Hero For Our Time: An Intimate Story of the Kennedy Years*. New York: Macmillan Publishing Co. 1983.

"Master Detective" (periodical). *The Nine Lives of Legs Diamond*. May, 1969 edition.

Mather, Cotton. *Social Considerations* (article). Boston: 1708.

Mather, Increase. *Diary*. Cambridge: Oxford University Press. 1900. (Samuel Green, editor).

McKean, Hugh F. *The "Lost" Treasures of Louis Comfort Tiffany*. New York: Doubleday & Co. Inc. 1980.

McKearin, George and Helen. *American Glass*. New York: Crown Publishers Inc. 1968.

McKenzie, Frederick Arthur. *"Pussyfoot" Johnson* (biography). New York: Fleming H. Revell Co. 1920.

Mendelson, Jack H. and Nancy K. Mello. *Alcohol Use and Abuse in America*. Boston: Little, Brown, & Co. 1985.

Michigan Substance Abuse & Traffic Safety Information Center. *What Everyone Should Know About Alcohol*. Lansing, MI: 1989 publication.

Miller, Robert; editor. *Wallace-Homestead Price Guide to Antiques and Pattern Glass* (8th edition). Iowa: Wallace-Homestead Book Co. 1982.

Mish, C. Frederick; editor in chief. *Websters Ninth New Collegiate Dictionary*. Springfield, MA: Merriam Webster Inc., Publishers. 1983.

Morgan, Edmund S. *American Slavery, American Freedom*. New York: W.W. Norton and Co. 1975.

Morgan, Edmund S. *The Puritan Dilemna*. Boston: Little, Brown, & Co. 1958.

Morgan, Ted. *FDR: A Biography*. New York: Simon and Schuster. 1985.

Mothers Against Drunk Driving. *National Newsletter.* Hurst, TX: MADD publication, various monthly editions 1980-1991.

Naisbitt, John and Patricia Aburdene. *Megatrends 2000: Ten New Directions for the 1990's.* New York: William Morrow and Co., Inc. 1990.

Nation, Carry A. *The Use and Need of the Life of Carry A. Nation* (autobiography). Topeka, KS: F.M. Steves & Sons. 1909.

National Highway Traffic Safety Administration, U.S. Department of Transportation. Annual Reports 1965-1990.

Newman, Harold. *An Illustrated Dictionary of Glass.* London: Thames and Hudson Ltd. 1977.

The New York Times. October 25, 1929 and September 23, 1979 editions.

Nye, Mark. *Cambridge Stemware.* Miami: Mark A. Nye. 1985.

Padgett, Leonard E. *Pairpoint Glass.* Des Moines: Wallace-Homestead Co. 1979.

Papert, Emma. *The Illustrated Guide to American Glass.* New York: Hawthorn Books, Inc. 1972.

Parker, Watson. *Deadwood: The Golden Years.* Lincoln: University of Nebraska Press. 1981.

Pears, Thomas C. III. *Bakewell, Pears & Co. Glass Catalogue.* Pittsburgh: Davis & Warde, Inc. 1977.

Peterson, Merrill D. *Thomas Jefferson & The New Nation* (biography). New York: Oxford University Press. 1970.

Phillips, Phoebe; editor. *The Encyclopedia of Glass.* New York: Crown Publishers Inc. 1981.

Pickvet, Mark. *Shot Glasses: An American Tradition.* Marietta, OH: Antique Publications Inc. 1989.

Relating to Permits As Provided in Title II National Prohibition Act for the Manufacture of and Traffic in Intoxicating Liquors for Nonbeverage Purposes. U.S. Treasury Department, Bureau of Industrial Alcohol. Regulations 2, April 1, 1931.

Revi, Albert Christian. *American Pressed Glass and Figure Bottles.* New York: Thomas Nelson and Sons. 1968.

Ring, Carlyn. *For Bitters Only.* Boston: The Nimrod Press Inc. 1980.

Rinker, Harry. *Warman's Americana and Collectibles.* Elkins Park, PA: Warman Publishing Co. 1986.

Rorabaugh, W.J. *The Alcoholic Republic: An American Tradition.* New York: Oxford University Press. 1979.

Rush, Dr. Benjamin. *An Inquiry into the Effects of Spiritous Liquors* (essay). Originally written 1784.

Rush, Dr. Benjamin. *Autobiography* (edited by George W. Colner). Philadelphia: Princeton University Press. 1948.

Schoenstein, Ralph. *The Booze Book.* Chicago: Playboy Press. 1974.

Schwartz, Marvin D.; editor. *American Glass Volume I: Brown and Molded.* New York: Weathervane Books. 1978.

Scott, Virginia R. *The Collectors Guide to Imperial Candlewick.* Athens, GA: Published by author, 1980.

Sichel, Franz. *Glass Drinking Vessels.* San Francisco: Lawton & Alfred Kennedy Printing. 1969.

Spectrum: Alcohol Problem Prevention for Women by Women. Rockville, MD: U.S. Department of Health and Human Services; Public Health Service; Alcohol Drug Abuse, and Mental Health Administration. 1981.

Spillman, Jane Shadel. *American and European Pressed Glass in the Corning Museum of Glass.* Corning, NY: The Corning Museum of Glass. 1981.

Storms, Roger C. *Partisan Prophets: A History of the Prohibition Party.* Denver: National Prohibition Foundation. 1972.

Stout, Sandra McPhee. *The Complete Book of McKee.* North Kansas City: Trojan Press. 1972.

Taylor, Robert Lewis. *Vessel of Wrath: The Life and Times of Carry Nation* (biography). New York: The New American Library. 1966.

The Toledo Museum of Art. *Libbey Glass: A Tradition of 150 Years.* Toledo: The Toledo Museum of Art. 1968.

Udell, Gilman G.; Superintendant – Document Room of the House of Representatives. *Liquor Laws.* Washington, DC: U.S. Government Printing Office. 1978.

The University of Michigan Alcohol Research Center (UMARC). Ann Arbor, MI: Pamphlet. 1988.

U.S. Department of Health and Human Services, Alcohol and Health, January 1990; Congressional Budget Office, Federal Taxation of Tobacco, Alcoholic Beverages, and Motor Fuels, June 1990. Editorial Research Reports.

U.S. Department of Health and Human Services. *Annual Report from the Surgeon General of the United States.* Public Health Service. 1990.

U.S. Department of Health and Human Services. Various Washington, DC publications including: "Helping Your Pre-Teen say 'No," 1986; "Alcohol Health & Research World," 1989; "Facts About Teenage Drunk Driving," 1990; "Alcohol Some Questions and Answers," 1981; "Teaching About Drinking," 1981; "Alcohol Research: Meeting the Challenge," 1985; and "Epidemiology of Alcohol-Related Problems in the United States," 1988.

Wakefield, Hugh. *19th Century British Glass.* New York: Thomas Yoseloff Publishing. 1961.

Watkins, Lura Woodside. *Cambridge Glass.* Boston: Marshall Jones Co. 1930.

Weatherman, Hazel Marie. *Colored Glassware of the Depression Era.* Missouri: Weatherman Glass Books. 1974.

Weatherman, Hazel Marie. *Colored Glassware of the Depression Era II.* Missouri: Weatherman Glass Books. 1974.

Weatherman, Hazel Marie. *Fostoria: Its First Fifty Years.* Springfield, IL: The Weatherman's, Publishers. 1979.

Weatherman, Hazel Marie and Sue Weatherman. *The Decorated Tumbler.* Missouri: Glassbooks Inc. 1978.

Whitehouse, David. *Glass of the Roman Empire.* Corning, NY: The Corning Museum of Glass. 1988.

Willard, Frances E. *Woman and Temperance or the Work and Workers of the Woman's Christian Temperance Union.* New York: Arno Press. 1972.

Wilson, Kenneth M. *New England Glass and Glassmaking.* New York: Thomas Crowell Co. 1972.

Winter, Henry. *The Dynasty of Louis Comfort Tiffany.* Boston: Henry Winter. 1971.

Witcover, Jules. *85 Days: The Last Campaign of Robert Kennedy.* New York: G.P. Putnam's Sons. 1969.

Woodward, W.E. *Meet General Grant* (biography). New York: Horace-Liveright Inc. 1928.

Wright, Lawrence. *In the New World: Growing Up With America From the Sixties to the Eighties.* New York: Vintage Books. 1987.

Young, David R. (director), etal. *America in Perspective.* Boston: Houghton Mifflin Co. 1986. (Oxford Analytica subtitled: *Major Trends in the United States Through the 1990's).*

Zerwick, Chloe. *A Short History of Glass.* New York: Harry N. Abrams, Inc. Publishers. 1990.

INDEX

ABOUT THE AUTHOR

ALEX HAAS has more than ten years' hands-on experience in all aspects of the restaurant industry. He was a chef at the MGM Grand in Las Vegas and ran his own kitchen in Lincoln, Nebraska, where he developed a new menu and recipes for the restaurant. He received his undergraduate degree from the University of Alabama, Huntsville, and his master's degree from the University of Nebraska.

Haas is a nationally recognized expert on the various types of low carb eating regimens and has participated in many radio, newspaper, and television interviews across the country concerning low carb dieting. He has also been the low carb resource for WAFF-TV in Huntsville, Alabama. Haas lives in New Market, Alabama.

ALEX HAAS

EVERYDAY
LOW CARB
COOKING

240 Great-Tasting

Low Carbohydrate

Recipes the Whole

Family Will Enjoy

MARLOWE & COMPANY
NEW YORK

*Everyday Low Carb Cooking: 240 Great-Tasting Low
Carbohydrate Recipes the Whole Family Will Enjoy*

Copyright © 1996, 2002 by Alex Haas

Published by
Marlowe & Company
An Imprint of Avalon Publishing Group Incorporated
161 William Street, 16th Floor
New York, NY 10038

An earlier edition of this book was originally
published as *Everyday Low Carb Cookery* in 1996.

Library of Congress Cataloging-in-Publication Data
Haas, Alex.
   Everyday low carb cooking : 240 great-tasting low
   carbohydrate recipes the whole family will enjoy /
   by Alex Haas.
      p. cm.
Previous ed. has title: Everyday low carb cookery.
Includes index.
ISBN 1-56924-520-7 (trade paper)
    1. Low-carbohydrate diet—Recipes. I. Haas,
  Alex. Everyday low carb cookery. II. Title.
RM237.73 .H33 2002
641.5'635—dc21
2002075110

9 8 7 6

Designed by Pauline Neuwirth, Neuwirth & Associates

Printed in the United States of America
Distributed by Publishers Group West

This book is dedicated to my parents, Lois and Alex Sr.,
both of whom might have been with us a little longer
had they eaten this type of food.

CONTENTS

ONE of the secrets to the success of any eating regimen is variation. It's wonderful to be able to tell folks that they can eat roast beef and salad with blue cheese dressing and they can lose weight, they won't be hungry, their cholesterol and triglycerides will normalize, their hair will grow back, and people of the opposite sex will fall to their knees and worship them. And all of this is true (well, mostly). However, after they've had roast beef and salad with blue cheese dressing three times in two weeks, they start looking for the pita bread and sprouts. It doesn't matter how good the eating regimen is for your health; you won't tolerate being bored.

This book is designed to provide virtually an infinite amount of variation in your low carbohydrate diet regimen. I have compiled more than 240 recipes, including over a dozen barbecue recipes, over three dozen recipes associated with beef, over two dozen recipes that include cheese, about four dozen recipes with chicken, a dozen of which are chicken wing recipes (I believe chicken wings are the world's most perfect diet food), about two dozen dessert recipes, about a dozen and a half recipes where the main ingredient is eggs, about three dozen recipes for some kind of pork, about four dozen recipes for salads and salad dressings, a dozen slaws and several vinaigrettes, about two dozen recipes involving sauces, almost two dozen recipes associated with seafood, and about two dozen soup recipes. There are also a dozen or so suggestions for how you can embellish your grilled hamburgers. These recipes are culled from Cajun, Southern U.S., Southwestern U.S., Northeastern U.S., Mexican, German, Russian, Korean, Thai, French, Hungarian, Italian, Cuban, Polish, Portuguese, Czech, Vietnamese, and Irish cuisines.

Much of the praise I've received on the previous edition of *Everyday Low Carb Cooking* (*Everyday Low Carb Cookery,* 1996) mentions how I use everyday foods in my recipes. I use garlic powder, onion powder, various dried herbs, and bottled lemon and lime juice. I do this because I want to reduce the amount of time it takes to prepare meals. If you want to take the extra few minutes to dice fresh garlic or squeeze fresh limes, then do it. I do use some special ingredients, such as Fish Sauce, in certain recipes. They are discussed in detail below.

Part of the reason that I've done this is because folks want to spend a minimum amount of time during the week cooking. Unfortunately, when you are low carbing it, you can't just go to the corner grocery store, grab a bunch of low carb foods, bring them home, and eat your meal. You are going to have to spend some time cooking. How much time is considered acceptable? The chefs on TV aim for less than one hour and I agree with that, so any cooking time under sixty minutes is considered very good. This is enough time for you to grill your steak or cook your main dish, fix your salad, and heat up a bowl of soup that you prepared over the weekend. Most of the main courses in this book can be ready in 30–45 minutes. Keep in mind that time is the essence of good food; it can't be hurried. There have been times in the past when it took me 2–3 days to make a slaw, and I consider it time well spent.

I recently had a discussion with another chef about whether these recipes can actually be said to emulate the originals if we leave out certain high carbohydrate items. He was looking at one of the chowder recipes and commented that he wouldn't know what chowder would taste like without potatoes. My experience with chowders is that most of them have potatoes in them and I have some sympathy for the purists. Can we have pies and cheesecakes without crusts? Personally, I think we can and the recipes reflect this. We as low carbers can't have potatoes or graham cracker crust. It's for this reason that I use the word "style" in the name of many recipes. These are not the real thing, but they're close. And quite frankly, it doesn't matter as long as the dish tastes good.

LOW CARB COOKING TIPS ▶

I suggest that you make some Salad Onions (see page 84) and Ketchup (see page 234) immediately as these are used in many other recipes. If you are fond of Thousand Island Dressing (see page 44), then you will need to make Chili Sauce (see page 235) and Sweet Relish (see page 85) which takes a couple of days to "pickle."

THE BEST TIME TO COOK

You will find that you do most of your cooking on the weekends, when you have more free time. This is the best time to prepare and freeze your soups, make your salad dressings and sauces, and cook some of the more "gourmet" dishes included in this book. Because you have decided to eat low carb, you are going to become both the food manufacturer and the food packager. Remember that you can't just go to the grocery and pick up low carb basic foods the way you can with low-fat foods. You have to make them yourself. Some of these recipes, such as barbecue ribs, take a couple of hours of cooking time. However, this is similar to making bread or pickling foods in that although the dishes take a lot of time to make, the amount of time you actually spend cooking is minimal.

COOKING PROTEIN

Protein should be cooked slowly over lower temperatures. Slow cooking will cause proteins to be tender when they're done. This is what Crock-Pot cookery is all about—long, slow cooking. This is true for baking and frying, as well as the barbecue and smoking.

It might appear that there is a preponderance of "boiled meat" in these recipes. This is done to tenderize the meat and to ensure that there is a significant amount of stock left to make the flavorful sauces. These stocks contain the meat flavors that, when combined with vegetable flavors, are the foundation of good cooking. If you don't have stock available, use water with a bouillon cube (although there is about 1 gram of carbs in a bouillon cube), or use commercially prepared canned stock, some of which contain no carbohydrates.

COOKING POULTRY

A long time ago, my father taught me that different parts of the chicken or turkey cook at different rates. Without getting into the reasons why, please note that white meat cooks in about ¾ of the amount of time that it takes to cook an equal amount of dark meat. I mention this because in several of the chicken recipes that are made with breast meat, I specify a time for cooking based on the use of white meat. You are encouraged to use dark meat in these recipes but if you do, you need to cook it longer. You can increase the cooking time by ¼ to ½.

VEGETABLES

When you are cutting vegetables, make sure that you always use a stainless steel knife. The reason for this is that there is less oxidation produced with a stainless steel knife than with a non-stainless knife. There are several recipes in this book in which most of the water is cooked out of the vegetables. This process is not unknown to those of you who make spaghetti sauce from scratch or who grew up in the South, which has traditionally suffered the image of "overcooking" vegetables. Water dilutes the flavor.

HOT PEPPERS

Many of the recipes in this book call for some form of hot peppers, to your taste, of course. Keep in mind that if you don't have the specified kind of peppers, you can use whatever kind of peppers you have available. Won't the substitution of red cayenne sauce for pickled jalapeños affect the flavor of the dish? It sure will, but this is just another minor variation that you can enjoy. Also remember that various kinds of hot sauces and peppers have different strengths, in terms of heat, so you should add any hot sauces slowly in order to keep yourself from burning out on the recipe.

STOCKS

Stocks are the building blocks for good cooking. They are the combinations of meat flavors and vegetable flavors, but because this cookbook is dedicated to everyday cooking, I do not give instructions on making stocks. Fortunately, this is one of the foods you can buy off the shelf so you can spend your cooking time preparing other low carb basics. In recipes for soups, I try to list all of the ingredients for making the stocks so that the proper flavors are included. In other recipes two substitutes are readily available and will provide this combination of flavors: canned stock and bouillon cubes. These are not as good at the real thing, but they are quicker and easier. Try to find canned stocks and bouillon cubes that don't have any carbs. I consider stocks and bouillon cubes to be freebies and don't include them in the carb counts.

SOUPS

Most soups take a long time to make, whether you make a large quantity or a smaller quantity. You can make a quart of soup in fifty minutes or a gallon of soup in one hour. Therefore, I encourage you to make a larger quantity of soup, upward of three quarts, if possible, and freeze what you don't use so that you can have it later.

POZOLE

There are several types of *pozole* in this book. *Pozole* is a Mexican-style soup that is traditionally served with raw vegetables, cheese, and other accompaniments. The method of serving it deserves a special mention. Place some combination of the accompaniments in the bottom of your bowl, pour the hot soup over it, and sprinkle cheese on it. The raw vegetables include some small amount of any of the following: sliced lettuce, avocado slices, sliced radishes, diced onions, sliced green onions, and diced tomatoes. The other accompaniments include lime or lemon wedges, dried or fresh oregano, cumin, hot pepper flakes, diced fresh cilantro, fresh or pickled jalapeños, and crushed pork rinds. Don't forget to count the carbs if you add any of these.

SALADS

Keep in mind that your average salad should be about two cups total of any vegetables and will require about four tablespoons of salad dressing.

GARLIC

Jeff Smith, the Frugal Gourmet, once said something to the effect of, "If you have a mate who doesn't like garlic, get a new mate." Though I agree with his sentiment entirely, I realize that there are some folks who are not so enamored with garlic, so I decided that moderation should prevail.

SNACKS

One thing that you can do for snacks is to make a double recipe of whatever you're cooking and then refrigerate or freeze it. These can be microwaved as needed. The best thing about this is that you know what the carbohydrate count is because you made it. You don't have to worry about the labels being accurate.

PICKLING

Several of the recipes I provided formally involve pickling, and others, such as salad recipes, informally involve the pickling process. Two that come immediately to mind are the Salad Onions (see page 84) and Sweet Relish (see page 85), both of which are used extensively in other recipes. Pickling is the use of acid and/or salt (and to some extent refrigeration) over time to preserve whatever it is that we are pickling. The length of time needed to pickle a food is a function of the surface area. Diced onions and cucumbers pickle in about a day. The recipes in this book include pickled items that many of us normally do not eat, such as the Salad Onions, and this may give your diet more variety. Keep in mind that vinegar-pickled items, as a rule, do not freeze well, but they shouldn't need to be frozen because they are already preserved.

EXTRA THINGS YOU WILL NEED

Xanthum gum is a soluble fiber, similar to pectin. It is used as a thickener and doesn't have any carbs. Typically, it takes an hour or more to dissolve and it can't be hurried. Xanthum gum is available through most health food stores.

Orange and *lemon flavoring* are used in many of the Cuban recipes that originally called for sour orange juice.

ITEM AVAILABILITY

Generally, everything in these recipes is readily available in most grocery stores. There are a few items that you might be unfamiliar with or you might have trouble finding. For instance:

Unsweetened coconut—available through health food stores. You can also get coconut powder in stores that sell Indian food, but it may not be unsweetened.

Fish Sauce—available in most Asian food stores. Either Philippine or Thai is satisfactory.

Chili Paste—available in most Asian food stores. I was able to find it in the specialty section in my regular grocery.

DEGLAZING

In several instances, I have asked you to deglaze the pan in a recipe. For those of you who are unfamiliar with the term, it means you should add the specified liquid to the hot pan. While it is boiling off, it will lift some of the brown, cooked-on stuff from the bottom of the pan.

NOMENCLATURE

The following are the designations used throughout this book:

1 t.	=	1 teaspoon		
1 T.	=	1 tablespoon	=	3 t. by volume
1 c.	=	1 cup	=	16 T. by volume
2 c	=	1 pint		
2 pints	=	1 quart		

MEASUREMENTS AND QUANTITIES

You should note that the quantities in the recipes are only suggestions and should, for the most part, be considered as "more or less." If you think a recipe needs more garlic (you are blessed), then write it in the margin for the next time you make it. The same goes for salt, vinegar, or any other ingredient in a recipe, with a couple of exceptions. In any of the pickling recipes, the salt and vinegar should be considered to be minimum amounts. If you want to add more, that's fine, but do not add less. Do not forget to account for the added or subtracted carbs.

FOOD SAFETY

With **marinades**, after you have marinated the meat, you can't use the marinade again unless it is cooked. I strongly recommend that if you don't cook the marinade with the meat, toss the leftovers. When cooking **poultry**, it must be cooked well done because of *salmonella* contamination. As concerns the **level of doneness**, there have been recent reports in the media about the effects of eating undercooked (non-fowl) meats and how folks have gotten sick from it. I recommend that all non-fowl meats be cooked to at least medium level. As concerns the *E. coli* that was making people sick, this is a surface organism. The problem occurs because ground meat is virtually all surface, so any meat that is ground, such as hamburger or sausages, must also be cooked well done. As concerns **fish**, there are no recipes for raw fish in this book. All the diseases that were endemic in Japan from eating uncooked fish became endemic in California with the rise of sushi bars there. All fish must be cooked well done.

COOKING UTENSILS

A quick word about cooking utensils: I use the word "nonreactive" in describing pans that will be used to hold or cook an acid. This means that you should not use an aluminum pan when you are cooking a food that has a lot of vinegar in it. Glass and stainless steel are acceptable.

LOW CARB NUTRITION ▶

SOURCES FOR MACRONUTRIENT VALUES

I've had to use several sources to get the carbohydrate, fiber, fat, protein, and alcohol values. Generally, the United States Department of Agriculture web site (www.nal.usda.gov/fnic/cgi-bin/nut_search.pl) is my first choice. This database has over 6,000 items listed. The second source is any book by Corinne Netzer, who is a recognized authority on macronutrient values. The final source is the ingredient list found on the back of most food items. There are a couple of instances where I had to approximate the counts for an item. Generally, everything is consistent and well within any acceptable range of error.

CARB COUNTS

The calculated carb grams in each recipe are not 100 percent accurate. Some are overestimated slightly and some are underestimated slightly. This is due to several factors. Some companies have more carbs in their products than others. For a few items, like capers and key lime juice, I was not able to find the carb values in the USDA database and I had to make a guesstimate. I tended to count spices as 1 gram per teaspoon except for things like dried dill that don't weigh much more than one gram per teaspoon. Despite all this, I can assure you that the calculated values for individual servings are very close to accurate.

HIDDEN CARBS

A surprising number of foods contain hidden carbs. The biggest shock for me was *liver.* Different types of liver have different amounts of carbohydrates, but some weigh in at over 5 percent. *Seafood* can contain a small amount of carbs as well, including *scallops,* which are about 2.4 percent carbs and *shrimp,* which is about 1 percent carbs. Some *soy sauces* have more carbs than others; that made from just soy (tamari) is better than that made from hydrolyzed vegetable protein or the combination of soy and wheat. I buy the soy sauce with the least amount of carbs listed on the label and use those macronutrient values in all of the recipes below. Generally, when you read the list of ingredients for most types of *sausage* (such as brats, Italian, and Polish), there is some type of sugar listed as the first non–meat ingredient. *Balsamic vinegar* can be dangerous to a low carb diet because it typically has a lot of sugar in it. It's just as easy for you to sweeten your own vinegar at the rate of 4 tablespoons of sugar equivalent sweetener to 12 ounces of wine vinegar. Granted, it doesn't have the flavor of balsamic vinegar, but it also doesn't have the carbs. Save the balsamic vinegar for special occasions.

FREEBIES

There are several ingredients in this book that I consider "freebies" but may actually have a very small amount of carbs. These include bouillon cubes, stocks, black pepper, hot peppers, and many herbs and spices if the quantity is less than 1 teaspoon. I've tried to be consistent throughout the book. If you think you need to add a gram or two of carbs per serving because you use a lot of these, go ahead.

FIBER

For those who have an interest in this, the fiber content for a serving can easily be determined by subtracting the available carb grams from the total carb grams.

SUGAR

Needless to say, none of the recipes in this book contain sugar. Sugar is poison and one of the primary reasons that we are on a low carb diet in the first place. However, there are recipes that are sweetened, so I need to establish some kind of standard nomenclature to designate how much of your chosen sweetener you should use, whether it be stevia, saccharin, or, for those outside the United States, cyclamates, which are presently not FDA approved. In order to be consistent so that everyone can prepare these recipes, I have used the designation "sugar equivalent sweetener." So, for instance, when you see, "1 T. sugar equivalent sweetener" you will know that this means to measure out however much of the sweetener you are using that will be as sweet as 1 tablespoon of sugar. All recipes in this book that require sweetener were tested with saccharin. *Please note that the use of aspartame in cooking is not recommended because it tends to break down with heat.*

While we're on the subject of sugar, the following list, according to Dr. Richard Bernstein in his book *Dr. Bernstein's Diabetes Solution,* should be considered sugars and should be avoided because they require insulin: carob, corn syrup, dextrin, dextrose, dulcitol, fructose, glucose, honey, lactose, levulose, maltose, maltodextrin, manitol, mannose, molasses, saccharose, sorbitol, sorghum, treacle, turbinado, xylotol, xylose. Generally, if an ingredient name ends with an "ose," "al," or "ol," you should consider it a sugar.

SWEETENERS

We need to discuss sweeteners for a moment. First, many sugar substitutes, like Equal and Sweet N' Low, actually do have sugar in them. When you read the ingredient list on the package, the first thing you'll see is dextrin or maltodextrin or some other word that end with an "ose," an "al," or an "ol." In order to be conservative, you can count these little packets as a half gram of carbs per packet. Also, look at the ingredient list on the large boxes of sweeteners, such as Splenda. You may find words at the front of the list that resemble one or more of the forbidden sugars listed above.

One final thing needs to be mentioned about sweeteners, and that is their flavor after they have been cooked. I used saccharin to test all of the recipes in which I call for a little sweetener. I used saccharin because it's readily available and it's always sugar-free, unless it's Sweet N' Low. There is always a residual flavor if saccharin is cooked a long time, especially if you use a lot of it. This is one of the tradeoffs we make when we prepare desserts that require a large amount of sweetener. One thing you can do, as I did in the Low Carb Chocolate recipe (see page 256) is to wait until most of the cooking is completed before adding the sweetener. This applies to soups and sauces as well as desserts. For those of you who choose to use a cup of Splenda or the equivalent amount of Equal and Sweet N' Low in your desserts, you should consider adjusting the carb counts. I tend to count them as 12 grams of available carbs per 1 cup sugar equivalent sweetener.

SUGAR-FREE FLAVORED GELATINS

I've found that I'm using more and more sugar-free gelatins for flavorings as time goes on. This will become readily apparent when you look at the dessert section of this book. According to the back of the package, these sugar-free flavored gelatins are a free food exchange for those who follow the American Diabetes Association. When you start looking at the way the calories are presented on the package, they don't add up. According to the nutritional data on the back of the package, the entire box has about 40 calories. There are about four grams of protein in the package which is about 16 calories leaving 24 calories to come from somewhere. According to the ingredients section, there is no fat at all in the package. That leaves 24 calories that probably come from the maltodextrin. At four calories per gram of carbohydrate, this means that there could possibly be an additional, uncounted six grams of carbs in the "sugar free" gelatin or about 1½ grams of carb per serving. For someone like me whose average blood sugar is about 93, this might mean that I eat about 30 grams of carbs per day rather than 25; however, this is not trivial for those diabetics or epileptic children who eat a box of this per day. My solution to the problem is that I use the nutritional values on the package in doing the calculations for the desserts. However, you, as a consumer, should be aware that this could be problematic. If you are an insulin-dependent diabetic or your child is an epileptic, you might consider adjusting the carb counts accordingly. See the section on hidden carbs.

SALT

Salt is included in all of the recipes. Salt enables you to taste the food better. I've heard complaints from low carb dieters that they are tired of eggs for breakfast. Eggs acquire much more flavor with the addition of salt. If you have high blood pressure, you should consult your physician before adding more salt to your diet. However, a low carb diet is diuretic in and of itself and there have been people whose physicians recommended that they add salt to their diet. For those who worry about the potassium/sodium balance, you might want to try using a salt substitute.

VINEGAR

In the process of doing research for this book, I came across conflicting information about vinegar. On the one hand, in the USDA table of food values, cider vinegar is listed as having about 0.9 grams of carbs per tablespoon. On the other hand, in *The Complete Book of Food Counts,* Corinne Netzer lists wine vinegar has having 0 (zero) carbs per tablespoon. In the nutrition information on all of the different brands of vinegar that I looked at, with the exception of the rice wine vinegar, they give the carb count as 0. For our purposes, I count vinegar as a freebie with 0 grams of carbs in these recipes.

SPICES

In these recipes, none of the spices have any carb grams unless they were used in teaspoon quantities.

YOGURT

Yogurt deserves a special mention. Dr. Jack Goldberg claims that in the process of making yogurt, much of the lactose in the milk is converted by the *lactobacillus acidophilus*. This means that a cup of yogurt made with skim milk actually has about 4 grams of carbs instead of having about 12 grams, which means that yogurt actually has less available carbohydrate than cream, about 6 grams of carbs per cup. If you see a place where you can easily substitute non-sweetened yogurt for cream, go ahead and do it and count it as approximately 0.4 grams of carbs per tablespoon.

SOUPS

RUSSIAN CABBAGE SOUP

THE approximate English pronunciation of the name of this Russian cabbage soup is "Lenivye Shchi." Literally translated, it means, "Poor man's soup made the lazy way." I learned to make this soup from my father and have eaten it for the last thirty years. This soup is a staple in my low carb eating and I try to eat it along with a salad (with Italian Dressing—see page 36) several times each month.

QUAN.	INGREDIENT	CARB GRAMS	AVAIL. CARB	FAT	PROTEIN
1 lb.	**HAMBURGER** (77% lean)	0	0	92.4	77.2
2 c.	**GREEN CABBAGE**, chopped	9.6	5.6	0.4	2.6
½ c.	**CARROTS**, grated	5.6	4.0	0	0.5
1 c.	**CELERY**, diced	4.4	2.4	0	0.9
1 c.	**ONION**, sliced thinly	10.0	7.8	0	1.4
2 c.	**STEWED TOMATOES** (one 14½ ounce can will suffice)	17.5	14.0	0	3.5
1 T.	**DRIED PARSLEY**				
1 T.	**GARLIC POWDER**	6.1	6.1	0	1.4
3 t.	**SALT**				
1 t.	**BLACK PEPPER**				
½ t.	**CAYENNE PEPPER** (more or less added to your taste)				
½ c.	**DRY RED WINE** (optional)	2.0	2.0	0	0.4
2 t.	**SUGAR EQUIVALENT SWEETENER**				
	ENOUGH WATER TO MAKE 3 QUARTS				
	TOTALS	55.2	41.9	92.8	87.9
	PER SERVING OF 1 C.	4.6	3.5	7.7	7.3

- Brown the hamburger in a three-quart soup pot. Add all of the remaining ingredients except the sugar substitute. Cover, bring to a boil, reduce heat to medium low, and let simmer 20 minutes, stirring occasionally. Remove from heat, add the sugar substitute, and stir. Let it set, covered, an additional 5 minutes. Stir well before serving. This freezes very well.

- **MAKES ABOUT 3 QUARTS OR ABOUT 12 SERVINGS WITH ABOUT 113 CALORIES PER SERVING.**

BORSCHT

BESIDES having a Russian grandmother, I've been fortunate in my life to work with many native born Russians and I've picked up some of the language. One discussion I've had with several Russians is how to pronounce the name of this soup, that is, whether it should have a "t" sound or a "ch" sound at the end of it. When they began going through various declensions for the word, the native Russians decided that the "ch" sound should go at the end (it should be pronounced "borschch"). We have learned to recognize it with the "t" sound, so that's how I'm putting it in this book.

QUAN.	INGREDIENT	CARB GRAMS	AVAIL. CARB	FAT	PROTEIN
2 lb.	**STEW BEEF** or **CHUCK ROAST** cut into ½ inch cubes	0	0	57.6	174.6
2 T.	**OLIVE OIL**	0	0	26.0	0
½ lb.	**CABBAGE**, shredded	12.3	7.1	0.5	3.2
½ c.	**CARROTS**, grated	5.6	4.0	0	0.5
1 c.	**CELERY**, diced	4.4	2.4	0	0.9
1 c.	**ONION**, sliced thinly	10.0	7.8	0	1.4
2 c.	**BEETS**, sliced (one 15 oz. can is sufficient)	26.3	21.5	0.2	3.2
1 T.	**DRIED PARSLEY**				
1 T.	**GARLIC POWDER**	6.1	6.1	0	1.4
2 T.	**DILL WEED**				
3 t.	**SALT**				
1 t.	**BLACK PEPPER**				
½ t.	**CAYENNE PEPPER** (more or less added to your taste)				
½ c.	**DRY RED WINE** (optional)	2.0	2.0	0	0.4
2 t.	**SUGAR EQUIVALENT SWEETENER**				
	ENOUGH WATER TO MAKE 3 QUARTS				
¾ c	**SOUR CREAM FOR SERVING** (about 1 tablespoon per dollop for 12 dollops)	7.4	7.4	34.3	5.5
	TOTALS	74.1	58.3	118.6	191.1
	PER SERVING OF 1 C.	6.2	4.9	9.9	15.9

- Brown the beef in the oil in a 3 quart soup pot over medium high heat. Add the cabbage and cook until the cabbage begins to wilt. Add half of the dill weed and all of the remaining ingredients except the beets, the sour cream, and the sugar substitute. Cover, bring to a boil, reduce the heat to medium low, and let it simmer 1 hour, stirring occasionally. Add all of the remaining ingredients except the sour cream and bring to a boil. Remove from heat. Let this sit, covered, an additional 5 minutes. Stir well before serving. Serve with a dollop of sour cream on top.

- **MAKES ABOUT 3 QUARTS OR ABOUT 12 SERVINGS WITH ABOUT 172 CALORIES PER SERVING.**

FISH CHOWDER

ONE favorite substitute that we low carbers make is that of cauliflower for potatoes. This variation on New England Clam Chowder is very rich and the cauliflower adds great flavor as well as texture.

QUAN.	INGREDIENT	CARB GRAMS	AVAIL. CARB	FAT	PROTEIN
½ c.	**CARROTS**, grated	5.6	4.0	0	0.5
I c.	**CAULIFLOWER**, chopped coarsely	6.7	1.8	0.3	2.9
½ c.	**ONION**, sliced thinly	5.0	3.9	0	0.7
½ c.	**GREEN ONIONS**, diced	3.7	2.4	0	0.9
½ c.	**CELERY**, diced	2.2	1.2	0	0.5
3 T.	**BUTTER**	0	0	36.3	0
I t.	**SALT**				
¼ t.	**BLACK PEPPER**				
I T.	**DRIED PARSLEY**				
¼ t.	**ROSEMARY**				
¼ t.	**THYME**				
I lb.	**COD**, cut into bite sized pieces	0	0	2.3	80.8
I	**BOTTLE CLAM JUICE** (about 8 ounces)				
½ c.	**DRY WHITE WINE**	0.8	0.8	0	0
I c.	**HEAVY WHIPPING CREAM**	6.6	6.6	83.5	4.9
I c.	**WATER**				
	TOTALS	30.6	20.7	122.4	91.2
	PER SERVING OF I C.	3.8	2.6	15.3	11.4

■ In a 2 quart soup pot, cook the onion, carrots, and cauliflower in the butter over medium high heat until the onions begin to turn clear. In this order add the clam juice, the wine, the cream, and the seasonings. Cover, bring to a boil, reduce the heat to medium low, and let simmer for 15 minutes. Add the remaining ingredients, bring to a boil, reduce heat, and let simmer an additional 5 minutes. Remove from heat and let set 10 minutes before serving.

■ **MAKES ABOUT 8 SERVINGS WITH ABOUT 194 CALORIES PER SERVING.**

NEW ENGLAND CLAM CHOWDER

YOU can't discuss low carb soups without including New England Clam Chowder. This very simple and quick version of the classic has been very well received.

QUAN.	INGREDIENT	CARB GRAMS	AVAIL. CARB	FAT	PROTEIN
4 slices	**BACON**, diced	0	0	82.6	13.2
½ c.	**ONION**, sliced thinly	5.0	3.9	0	0.7
1 c.	**CAULIFLOWER**, chopped coarsely	6.7	1.8	0.3	2.9
7 oz.	**MINCED CLAMS** (about two 3½ ounce cans)	0.2	0.2	0	0.7
1 bottle	**CLAM JUICE** (about 8 ounces)				
½ c.	**HEAVY WHIPPING CREAM**	3.3	3.3	41.8	2.5
2	**CHICKEN BOUILLON CUBES**				
½ t.	**BLACK PEPPER**				
½ t.	**DRIED DILL WEED**				
	ENOUGH WATER TO MAKE 4 CUPS				
	TOTALS	15.2	9.2	124.7	20.0
	PER SERVING OF 1 C.	3.8	2.3	31.2	5.0

- In a 1 quart saucepan, fry the bacon over medium heat until it is crisp. Remove bacon from the fat and set aside, reserving as much fat as possible. To the bacon fat add the onion, cauliflower, clam juice, the juice from canned clams, and the seasoning. Cover and cook at a slow boil until the cauliflower is soft (10–15 minutes). Add the canned clams and remove from the heat. Let it set for 5 minutes, then add the cream and bacon.

- **MAKES ABOUT 4 SERVINGS WITH ABOUT 310 CALORIES PER SERVING.**

MANHATTAN CLAM CHOWDER

MANHATTAN Clam Chowder contains more carbs than its New England counterpart because of the tomatoes. Tomatoes have a lot of natural sugar. However, this recipe is low enough in carbs that we can have it occasionally.

QUAN.	INGREDIENT	CARB GRAMS	AVAIL. CARB	FAT	PROTEIN
4 slices	**BACON**, diced	0	0	82.6	13.2
½ c.	**ONION**, sliced thinly	5.0	3.9	0	0.7
1 T.	**GARLIC POWDER**	6.1	6.1	0	1.4
1 T.	**DRIED PARSLEY**				
1 c.	**CELERY**, diced	4.4	2.4	0	1.0
½ c.	**CARROTS**, grated	5.6	4.0	0	0.5
1 c.	**STEWED TOMATOES**	8.8	7.0	0	1.8
7 oz.	**MINCED CLAMS** (about two 3½ ounce cans)	0.2	0.2	0	0.7
1 bottle	**CLAM JUICE** (about 8 ounces)				
1 t.	**SALT**				
¼ t.	**BLACK PEPPER**				
1 t.	**THYME**				
1	**BAY LEAF**				
½ t.	**SUGAR EQUIVALENT SWEETENER**				
	ENOUGH WATER TO MAKE 4 CUPS				
	TOTALS	30.1	23.6	82.6	19.3
	PER SERVING OF 1 C.	7.5	5.9	20.7	4.8

- In a 1 quart saucepan, fry the bacon over medium heat until well browned. Increase the heat to medium high and fry the carrots and celery for about 2 minutes. Add the onions and cook until they become clear. Drain the clams, reserving the juice. Add everything to the soup pot except the clams (and the sugar substitute if you decide to add it later with the clams). Cover and bring to a boil. Reduce heat to medium low and let it simmer 30 minutes. Stir in the clams and let sit 5 minutes before serving.

- **MAKES ABOUT 4 SERVINGS WITH ABOUT 229 CALORIES PER SERVING.**

CABBAGE AND SEAFOOD SOUP

THE combination of shrimp and cabbage in this recipe produces a different odor than you may be used to, but the flavor is remarkably good. My family really enjoyed it when I made it for them.

QUAN.	INGREDIENT	CARB GRAMS	AVAIL. CARB	FAT	PROTEIN
1 lb.	**COD**, cut into bite sized pieces	0	0	2.3	80.8
1 lb.	**SHRIMP**, shelled	4.1	4.1	5.9	92.2
1 lb.	**CABBAGE**, shredded	24.5	14.1	0.9	6.4
½ c.	**ONION**, sliced thinly	5.0	3.9	0	0.7
½ c.	**DRY WHITE WINE**	0.8	0.8	0	0
1 bottle	**CLAM JUICE** (about 8 ounces)				
½ c.	**HEAVY WHIPPING CREAM**	3.3	3.3	41.8	2.5
3	**CHICKEN BOUILLON CUBES**				
2 c.	**CHICKEN STOCK**				
2 c.	**STEWED TOMATOES** (one 14.5 oz. can is sufficient)	17.5	14.0	0	3.5
1 T.	**GARLIC POWDER**	6.1	6.1	0	1.4
1 T.	**DRIED PARSLEY**				
1 t.	**DRIED BASIL**				
1 t.	**SUGAR EQUIVALENT SWEETENER**				
	TOTALS	61.3	46.3	59.0	187.5
	PER SERVING OF 1 C.	4.1	3.1	3.9	12.5

■ Place the wine, clam juice, 1½ cups of chicken stock, and tomatoes in a 1 gallon soup pot. Bring this to a boil and add the onion, cabbage, bouillon cubes, garlic, parsley, basil, and sugar substitute (unless you decide you want to add it at the end with the shrimp). Cover, reduce the heat to medium low, and let simmer for about 45 minutes. Mix the remaining ½ cup of chicken stock with the cream in a separate bowl. After the vegetables are sufficiently softened, add the stock/cream mixture and the cod to the soup and cook until the fish begins to become flaky. Add the shrimp and bring to a boil again over high heat. Remove from the heat and let it set about 5 minutes before serving.

■ **MAKES ABOUT 15 SERVINGS WITH ABOUT 98 CALORIES PER SERVING.**

BOUILLABAISSE

ANOTHER classic recipe that is remarkably simple and quick (under a half hour to prepare), this is similar to at least one Bouillabaisse that I've had in the past. One of the differences is that this has a lot more protein in it.

QUAN.	INGREDIENT	CARB GRAMS	AVAIL. CARB	FAT	PROTEIN
2 c.	**TOMATOES**, diced coarsely	16.8	12.8	0.8	3.0
2 c.	**WATER**				
1 c.	**CLAM JUICE**				
1 c.	**DRY WHITE WINE**	1.6	1.6	0	0
1 T.	**WORCESTERSHIRE SAUCE**	3.0	3.0	0	0
3	**CHICKEN BOUILLON CUBES**				
½ c.	**ONION**, sliced thinly	5.0	3.9	0	0.7
½ c.	**GREEN ONIONS**, diced	3.7	2.4	0	0.9
1 c.	**CELERY**, diced	4.4	2.4	0	0.9
½ c.	**CARROTS**, diced	5.6	4.0	0	0.5
2 t.	**GARLIC POWDER**	4.0	4.0	0	1.0
2 t.	**DRIED BASIL**				
1 t.	**DRIED DILL WEED**				
1 T.	**DRIED PARSLEY**				
1	**BAY LEAF** (ensure that it is removed before the Bouillabaisse is served)				
1 pinch	**SAFFRON**, if you have it available				
2 T.	**OLIVE OIL**	0	0	26.0	0
½ lb.	**FISH** (cod, haddock, or halibut)	0	0	1.2	40.4
1 c.	**CANNED CRAB MEAT** (about two 6 ounce cans, reserve the liquid for the broth)	5.0	5.0	0	55.0
1 lb.	**SHRIMP**	4.1	4.1	5.9	92.2
12 oz.	**FROZEN LOBSTER MEAT**, thawed (about one 12 ounce can, in bite sized pieces)	1.7	1.7	2.0	63.9
1 t.	**SUGAR EQUIVALENT SWEETENER**				
¼ t.	**ORANGE EXTRACT** (optional)				
½ t.	**FENNEL** (optional)				
	TOTALS	54.9	44.9	35.9	258.5
	PER SERVING OF 1 C.	5.0	4.1	3.3	23.5

- In a 3 quart pot, cook the onions, celery, and carrots in the oil over medium heat until the onions begin to become clear. Add the scallions and cook an additional

2 minutes. Add all the liquids, the tomatoes, the spices, and the bouillon cubes. Bring it to a boil, cover, reduce the heat to medium low, and simmer 15 minutes. Add the fish and cook until it turns opaque and begins to flake, about 5 minutes. Add the shrimp, crab, lobster, and the sugar substitute and bring it to a boil. Turn off heat and let sit 5 minutes before serving.

NOTE: If the shrimp are uncooked before being put into the soup, they should be added at the same time as the fish.

■ MAKES ABOUT 11 SERVINGS WITH ABOUT 140 CALORIES PER SERVING.

SIMPLE TOMATO FISH SOUP

THIS is similar to Manhattan Clam Chowder but it's richer and has more protein. In fact, a large serving of this along with a salad and a glass of red wine will provide a complete meal.

QUAN.	INGREDIENT	CARB GRAMS	AVAIL. CARB	FAT	PROTEIN
½ c.	**ONION,** sliced thinly	5.0	3.9	0	0.7
2 c.	**STEWED TOMATOES** (one 14.5 oz. can is sufficient)	17.5	14.0	0	3.5
2 t.	**GARLIC POWDER**	4.0	4.0	0	1.0
2 T.	**OLIVE OIL**	0	0	26.0	0
1	**BOTTLE CLAM JUICE**				
2 T.	**WHITE VINEGAR**				
½ t.	**LEMON EXTRACT**				
2 T.	**DRIED PARSLEY**				
½ c.	**DRY RED WINE**	2.0	2.0	0	0.4
2 lb.	**FISH,** cut into bite sized pieces	0	0	4.6	161.6
2	**CHICKEN BOUILLON CUBES**				
½ t.	**BLACK PEPPER**				
1 t.	**SUGAR EQUIVALENT SWEETENER**				
1 c.	**WATER**				
	TOTALS	28.5	23.9	30.6	167.2
	PER SERVING OF 1 C.	4.1	3.4	4.4	23.9

- In a 2 quart saucepan, sauté the onions in the oil over medium heat until the onions become clear. Add the liquids and the spices and simmer, covered, for 10 minutes. Add the remaining ingredients and simmer an additional 5 minutes. Remove from the heat and let sit 10 minutes before serving.

- **MAKES ABOUT 7 SERVINGS WITH ABOUT 149 CALORIES PER SERVING.**

SEAFOOD OKRA GUMBO

GUMBO is especially great for low carbers because it provides a lot of protein and it tastes delicious. Thank the Cajuns for creating this for us.

QUAN.	INGREDIENT	CARB GRAMS	AVAIL. CARB	FAT	PROTEIN
10 oz.	**FROZEN OKRA**, thawed	18.9	12.7	0.5	4.8
3 T.	**OLIVE OIL**	0	0	39.0	0
1 c.	**ONION**, sliced thinly	10.0	7.8	0	1.4
1 c.	**CELERY**, diced	4.4	2.4	0	0.9
1 c.	**GREEN PEPPERS**, diced	9.6	6.9	0.2	1.4
½ c.	**CARROTS**, diced	5.6	4.0	0	0.5
2 lb.	**SHRIMP**	8.2	8.2	11.8	184.4
1 lb.	**UNCOOKED CRAB MEAT**	0	0	3.5	78.6
1 T.	**GARLIC POWDER**	6.1	6.1	0	1.4
2 T.	**DRIED PARSLEY**				
2	**BOTTLES CLAM JUICE**, about 8 ounces per bottle				
2 T.	**WORCESTERSHIRE SAUCE**	6.0	6.0	0	0
2 c.	**STEWED TOMATOES** (one 14.5 oz. can will suffice)	17.5	14.0	0	3.5
2	**BAY LEAVES**				
2 t.	**SALT**				
1 t.	**BLACK PEPPER**				
1 t.	**CAYENNE PEPPER** (more or less added to your taste)				
1 t.	**SUGAR EQUIVALENT SWEETENER**				
1 c.	**WATER**				
	TOTALS	86.3	68.1	55.0	276.9
	PER SERVING OF 1 C.	7.2	5.7	4.6	23.1

- In a 3 quart soup pot, sauté the okra over medium heat until it is wilted and real soft to touch, about 5 minutes. Add the onions, celery, bell pepper, and carrots and cook until the onions begin to turn clear. Add liquids and seasoning, cover, bring to a boil, reduce the heat to medium low, and simmer 30 minutes. Remove the bay leaves. Add the remaining ingredients and bring it to a boil again. Remove from the heat and let it set 10 minutes before serving.

- **MAKES ABOUT 12 SERVINGS WITH ABOUT 157 CALORIES PER SERVING.**

CHICKEN AND SMOKED SAUSAGE GUMBO

THIS gumbo is a little more down to earth and a little less costly to prepare than the Seafood Okra Gumbo (page 23). I think chefs Lagasse and Prudhomme would approve.

QUAN.	INGREDIENT	CARB GRAMS	AVAIL. CARB	FAT	PROTEIN
1 pkg.	**FROZEN OKRA** (about 10 ounces), thawed	18.9	12.7	0.5	4.8
1 c.	**ONION**, sliced thinly	10.0	7.8	0	1.4
1 c.	**CELERY**, diced	4.4	2.4	0	0.9
1 c.	**GREEN PEPPERS**, diced	9.6	6.9	0.2	1.4
½ c.	**CARROTS**, diced	5.6	4.0	0	0.5
2 T.	**OLIVE OIL**	0	0	26.0	0
2 c.	**STEWED TOMATOES** (one 14.5 oz. can is sufficient)	17.5	14.0	0	3.5
1 lb.	**BONELESS CHICKEN LEGS**, meat only, uncooked and cut into bite sized pieces	0	0	34.7	86.7
1 T.	**GARLIC POWDER**	6.1	6.1	0	1.4
1 lb.	**SMOKED SAUSAGE**, cut into ½ inch thick slices	12.0	12.0	144.0	66.0
2 T.	**DRIED PARSLEY**				
2	**BAY LEAVES**				
1 t.	**THYME**				
1 t.	**BASIL**				
1 T.	**SALT**				
1 t.	**BLACK PEPPER**				
1 t.	**RED PEPPER FLAKES** (more or less added to your taste)				
1 t.	**SUGAR EQUIVALENT SWEETENER**				
3 c.	**WATER**				
	TOTALS	84.1	65.9	205.4	160.4
	PER SERVING OF 1 C.	7.0	5.5	17.1	13.4

- In a 3 quart soup pot, fry the onions, okra, celery, carrots, and bell pepper over medium high heat until the onions become clear. Add everything else except the smoked sausage, stir well, cover, and bring to a boil. Reduce the heat to medium low and simmer for about 1 hour or until the chicken is tender. Remove the bay leaves. Add the remaining ingredients and let simmer an additional 15 minutes. Remove from heat and let sit 10 minutes before serving.

- **MAKES ABOUT 12 SERVINGS WITH ABOUT 230 CALORIES PER SERVING.**

FRENCH ONION SOUP

I was working in a pub in Darmstadt, Germany, the first time that I tried to make French Onion Soup, and I ruined it beyond repair. Fortunately, the chef forgave me my mistake. The secret is to get the onions real brown, and sometimes (not for low carbers) a little sugar is also added for further caramelization.

QUAN.	INGREDIENT	CARB GRAMS	AVAIL. CARB	FAT	PROTEIN
½ c.	DRY RED WINE	2.0	2.0	0	0.4
1 T.	WORCESTERSHIRE SAUCE	3.0	3.0	0	0
1½ lb.	ONIONS	58.3	46.1	0.8	7.8
4 T.	OLIVE OIL	0	0	52.0	0
2 T.	WATER				
2 t.	SUGAR EQUIVALENT SWEETENER				
1½ quart	EACH OF BEEF AND CHICKEN Enough canned stock to make 3 quarts				
	GRATED PARMESAN CHEESE for serving				
	TOTALS	63.3	51.1	53.0	8.2
	PER SERVING OF 1 C.	5.3	4.3	4.4	0.7

- The first step is to caramelize the onions. In a 3 quart soup pot, fry the 1½ lb. of onions in the olive oil and 2 T. of water over medium heat. This should be covered for the first 5 minutes, just enough time to give the onions a chance to wilt. Remove the lid and continue stirring every 10 minutes. Eventually the water will be evaporated and the onions will start browning. When the onions begin to stick, begin reducing the heat slowly. Eventually, the onions will become very dark and sticky to the touch. They will almost taste burned. At this point, add the wine, sugar substitute (unless you decide to add it at the end), Worcestershire sauce, and the stock, cover, and bring to a boil. Reduce the heat to medium low and let it simmer for 45 minutes, stirring every 10 minutes. Serve with the grated Parmesan cheese (and don't forget to add 0.2 grams of carbs per tablespoon).

- **MAKES ABOUT 3 QUARTS OR ABOUT 12 SERVINGS WITH ABOUT 60 CALORIES PER SERVING.**

GERMAN-STYLE GOULASH

IN German, this variation on goulash is known as *Gulaschsuppe*. I found this recipe on a German recipe site and translated it into this tasty lower carb version.

QUAN.	INGREDIENT	CARB GRAMS	AVAIL. CARB	FAT	PROTEIN
2 lb.	STEW BEEF or CHUCK ROAST cut into ½ inch cubes	0	0	57.6	174.6
½ c.	ONION, diced	6.9	5.5	0	1.0
1 c.	GREEN PEPPERS, diced	9.6	6.9	0.2	1.3
4 T.	OLIVE OIL	0	0	52.0	0
1 c.	TOMATO SAUCE	17.6	14.2	0.4	3.4
1 T.	WHITE VINEGAR				
½ t.	LEMON EXTRACT				
2 t.	GARLIC POWDER	4.0	4.0	0	1.0
½ t.	CAYENNE PEPPER (more or less added to your taste)				
½ t.	CARAWAY SEED				
2	BEEF BOUILLON CUBES				
4 c.	CANNED BEEF STOCK				
1 c.	WATER				
	TOTALS	38.1	30.6	110.2	181.3
	PER SERVING OF 1 C.	3.8	3.1	11.0	18.1

- In a 3 quart soup pot, put 2 T. of oil and fry the beef over medium heat until it is well browned. Remove the meat from the pan, reserving as much oil as possible. Add the remaining oil to the skillet. Fry the onions until they are clear. Add the green peppers, cover, and cook about 10 minutes. Add all other ingredients, cover, bring to a boil, reduce the heat to medium low, and simmer 1 hour (more or less), stirring every 20 minutes.

- **MAKES ABOUT 10 SERVINGS WITH ABOUT 184 CALORIES PER SERVING.**

ITALIAN WEDDING SOUP

I first heard of Italian wedding soup when I was living in the Philadelphia area. The neighborhood restaurant where we would sometimes lunch made it for their patrons. After eating this for the first time, I immediately decided this would be good low carb fare as long as we leave out the rice or small pasta.

QUAN.	INGREDIENT	CARB GRAMS	AVAIL. CARB	FAT	PROTEIN
1 ½ lb.	**CHICKEN BREAST**, uncooked, skinless and boneless, cut into ½ inch cubes	0	0	6.1	157.3
5 c.	**WATER**				
½ c.	**CARROTS**, grated	5.6	4.0	0	0.5
1 c.	**CELERY**, diced	4.4	2.4	0	0.9
1 c.	**GREEN ONIONS**, diced	7.4	4.8	0	1.8
2 t.	**FENNEL** or **ANISE**	1.0	0.2	0.2	0.3
1 T.	**GARLIC POWDER**	6.1	6.1	0	1.4
2 t.	**HERBES DE PROVENCE**	2.0	1.0	0	0
4 c.	**ESCAROLE** (or **ENDIVE**), cut into small pieces	6.7	0.5	0.3	2.5
½ c.	**DRY WHITE WINE**	0.8	0.8	0	0
1 T.	**DRIED PARSLEY**				
1 T.	**SALT**				
2 t.	**SUGAR EQUIVALENT SWEETENER**				
	ENOUGH CHICKEN STOCK TO MAKE 3 QUARTS				
12 T.	**GRATED PARMESAN CHEESE** for serving	2.8	2.8	21.4	31.2
	TOTALS	36.8	23.0	28.0	195.9
	PER SERVING OF 1 C.	3.1	1.9	2.3	16.3

■ Bring all the ingredients except the escarole, chicken stock, and cheese to a boil in a covered 3 quart (or larger) soup pot. Reduce the heat to medium low and let it simmer 30 minutes. Turn the heat to high, add the escarole, and bring the amount to three quarts with however much chicken stock it requires. After it again comes to a boil, reduce the heat to medium low and let it simmer, covered, an additional 15 minutes. Serve with 2 tablespoons of grated Parmesan cheese per bowl.

■ **MAKES THREE QUARTS OR 12 SERVINGS WITH ABOUT 94 CALORIES PER SERVING.**

EGG DROP SOUP— HONG KONG STYLE

QUAN.	INGREDIENT	CARB GRAMS	AVAIL. CARB	FAT	PROTEIN
5 c.	CHICKEN STOCK				
½ c.	DRY WHITE WINE	0.8	0.8	0	0
½ c.	GREEN ONIONS, diced	3.7	2.4	0	0.9
½ t.	DRIED GINGER				
1 t.	WHITE PEPPER (more or less, this is supposed to taste a little warm)				
1 t.	GARLIC POWDER	2.0	2.0	0	0.5
1 t.	ONION POWDER	1.7	1.6	0	0.2
1	BEEF BOUILLON CUBE				
3	EGGS	2.1	2.1	14.4	21.6
¼ lb.	HAM, diced	2.0	2.0	2.0	20.0
1 T.	SESAME OIL	0	0	13.0	0
	SALT to taste				
	TOTALS	11.8	10.9	29.4	43.2
	PER SERVING OF 1 C.	2.0	1.8	4.9	7.2

- In a 2 quart saucepan, bring the chicken stock and wine to a boil. Add the bouillon cube, garlic powder, onion powder, pepper, and the ginger and let it simmer about 5 minutes. Remove from the heat and add the ham and onions. In a separate bowl, scramble the eggs and pour them slowly in a circle into the broth. Finally, add the oil and stir gently.

- **MAKES 6 SERVINGS WITH ABOUT 80 CALORIES PER SERVING.**

SIMPLE PORK STEW

THIS is similar in taste to *caldillo,* a New Mexican green chili stew. This, plus a salad, could be considered an entire meal for two people.

QUAN.	INGREDIENT	CARB GRAMS	AVAIL. CARB	FAT	PROTEIN
I lb.	**PORK ROAST** cut into ½ inch cubes	0	0	32.8	87.9
3 c.	**WATER**				
½ c.	**ONION,** sliced thinly	5.0	3.9	0	0.7
I T.	**PICKLED JALAPEÑOS,** diced (more or less added to your taste)				
2 t.	**GARLIC POWDER**	4.0	4.0	0	1.0
2	**BEEF BOUILLON CUBES**				
½ t.	**SUGAR EQUIVALENT SWEETENER**				
I T.	**PICKLED JALAPEÑOS,** diced (more or less added to your taste for garnish)				
	TOTALS	9.0	7.9	32.8	89.6
	PER SERVING OF I C.	2.3	2.0	8.2	22.4

- In a 2 quart pan with a lid, bring the first 7 ingredients to a boil over high heat. Reduce heat to medium low and continue simmering for an hour, until the meat virtually falls apart when you touch it. Add some small amount of diced pickled jalapeños for garnish just before serving.

- **MAKES 4 SERVINGS WITH ABOUT 171 CALORIES PER SERVING.**

CHICKEN AND ASPARAGUS SOUP

THIS soup was part of the single best meal that I've ever had. Better still, the meal consisted of entirely low carb foods. I was so impressed with it that I sent an e-mail to all of my friends the next day telling them about it.

QUAN.	INGREDIENT	CARB GRAMS	AVAIL. CARB	FAT	PROTEIN
16 oz.	**ASPARAGUS** (one 16 ounce can) sliced into 1 inch pieces. Reserve the liquid for the broth.	9.0	6.0	0	3.0
½ c.	**ONION**, diced	6.9	5.5	0	1.0
½ c.	**GREEN ONIONS**, diced	3.7	2.4	0	0.9
½ lb.	**CHICKEN BREAST**, boneless, skinless, cooked and cut into bite sized pieces	0	0	5.7	65.8
2 T.	**BUTTER**	0	0	26.0	0
2 c.	**CHICKEN STOCK**				
½ c.	**DRY WHITE WINE**	0.8	0.8	0	0
3	**CHICKEN BOUILLON CUBES**				
½ c.	**HEAVY WHIPPING CREAM**	3.3	3.3	41.8	2.5
1 T.	**DRIED TARRAGON**				
2 t.	**DRIED BASIL**				
2 t.	**GARLIC POWDER**	4.0	4.0	0	1.5
	TOTALS	27.7	22.0	73.5	74.7
	PER SERVING OF 1 C.	4.0	3.1	10.5	10.7

- In a 2 quart saucepan, sauté the onions in butter for 5 minutes over medium high heat. Add the stock, wine, asparagus liquid, herbs, and bouillon cubes and simmer 10 minutes. Add the chicken, then the asparagus, and then the remaining ingredients, stirring after each addition. Simmer an additional 10 minutes.

- **MAKES ABOUT 7 SERVINGS WITH ABOUT 150 CALORIES PER SERVING.**

TURKEY AND BROCCOLI SOUP

THIS soup is a real good way to get rid of some of that leftover Thanksgiving turkey and it's very simple to make. If you like, you can substitute some Herbes de Provence for the basil.

QUAN.	INGREDIENT	CARB GRAMS	AVAIL. CARB	FAT	PROTEIN
1 lb.	FROZEN BROCCOLI, thawed and sliced into ½ inch pieces	24.2	10.6	0	14.1
½ c.	ONION, diced	6.9	5.5	0	1.0
½ c.	GREEN ONIONS, diced	3.7	2.4	0	0.9
½ lb.	TURKEY BREAST, boneless, skinless, cooked and diced into bite sized pieces	0	0	5.7	65.8
2 T.	BUTTER	0	0	26.0	0
2 c.	CHICKEN STOCK				
1 c.	DRY WHITE WINE	1.6	1.6	0	0
1 c.	WATER				
3	CHICKEN BOUILLON CUBES				
½ c.	HEAVY WHIPPING CREAM	3.3	3.3	41.8	2.5
2 t.	GARLIC POWDER	4.0	4.0	0	1.5
2 t.	DRIED BASIL				
	TOTALS	43.7	27.4	73.5	84.9
	PER SERVING OF 1 C.	7.3	4.6	12.3	14.2

- In a 2 quart saucepan, sauté the onions in butter for 5 minutes over medium high heat. Add the stock, wine, herbs, and bouillon cubes and simmer 10 minutes. Add the turkey, then the broccoli, and finally the remaining ingredients, stirring after each addition. Simmer an additional 10 minutes.

- **MAKES ABOUT 6 SERVINGS WITH ABOUT 186 CALORIES PER SERVING.**

HUNGARIAN SAUERKRAUT SOUP

QUAN.	INGREDIENT	CARB GRAMS	AVAIL. CARB	FAT	PROTEIN
3 slices	BACON	0	0	61.9	9.9
1 lb.	PORK ROAST cut into ½ inch cubes	0	0	32.8	87.9
2 c.	CANNED SAUERKRAUT (this is about one 16 ounce can), washed (see page 211)	12.2	5.0	0.4	2.6
1 T.	PAPRIKA	3.8	2.4	0.8	1.0
½ c.	ONION, sliced thinly	5.0	3.9	0	0.7
1 T.	GARLIC POWDER	6.1	6.1	0	1.4
½ c.	TOMATO SAUCE	8.8	7.1	0.2	1.7
1 t.	CARAWAY SEED				
3 t.	SUGAR EQUIVALENT SWEETENER				
4 c.	CANNED STOCK				
8 T.	SOUR CREAM for garnish	4.0	4.0	19.0	3.0
2 c.	WATER				
	TOTALS	39.9	28.5	115.1	108.2
	PER SERVING OF 1 C.	5.0	3.6	14.4	13.5

- In a 2 quart saucepan, sauté the bacon over medium high heat until well browned. Add the onion and pork and cook until the pork begins to brown. Add the sauerkraut, garlic powder, tomato sauce, paprika, sugar substitute, and caraway seed and stir. Then add the stock, stir, and bring it to a boil. Reduce the heat and let simmer for 1 hour, covered, stirring every 15 minutes. Serve with a dollop of sour cream.

- **MAKES ABOUT 8 SERVINGS WITH ABOUT 198 CALORIES PER SERVING.**

MEXICAN RED

THIS soup is a variation on *pozole rojo,* a Mexican holiday pork stew that normally has hominy in it. I found it when I was looking for what ultimately became Chickarones Soup (see page 34). Before you begin cooking, please refer to the section concerning *pozole* in the Introduction (see page 6).

QUAN.	INGREDIENT	CARB GRAMS	AVAIL. CARB	FAT	PROTEIN
2 lb.	**PORK ROAST** cut into ½ inch cubes	0	0	65.6	175.8
2 T.	**OLIVE OIL**	0	0	26.0	0
2 c.	**STEWED TOMATOES** (one 15 ounce can is sufficient)	17.5	14.0	0	3.5
4 c.	**BEEF STOCK** (two 15 ounce cans are sufficient)				
1 T.	**GARLIC POWDER**	6.1	6.1	0	1.4
2 t.	**OREGANO**	1.9	0.7	0.3	0.3
1 t.	**GROUND CUMIN**	0.9	0.7	0.4	0.4
1 T.	**PICKLED JALAPEÑOS,** diced finely (more or less added to your taste)				
1 t.	**RED PEPPER FLAKES** (more or less added to your taste)				
½ c.	**ONION,** diced	6.9	5.5	0	1.0
½ c.	**GREEN PEPPERS,** diced	4.8	3.5	0.1	0.7
2 T.	**FRESH CILANTRO,** chopped				
3	**BEEF BOUILLON CUBES**				
½ t.	**BLACK PEPPER**				
1 t.	**SUGAR EQUIVALENT SWEETENER**				
2 T.	**WHITE VINEGAR**				
½ t.	**LEMON EXTRACT**				
1 c.	**WATER**				
	TOTALS	38.1	30.5	92.4	183.1
	PER SERVING OF 1 C.	3.8	3.1	9.2	18.3

- Fry the onions and bell peppers in a 3 quart soup pot over medium high heat until the onions become clear. Increase the heat to high, add the pork, and cook until it begins to brown. Add the remaining ingredients, cover, and bring to a boil. Reduce the heat to medium low and let simmer for an hour, stirring every 15 minutes until the pork is so tender that it falls apart when you touch it.

- **MAKES ABOUT 10 SERVINGS WITH ABOUT 168 CALORIES PER SERVING.**

CHICK-ARONES SOUP

LIKE the preceding recipe, this too is a low carb variation on *pozole*. *Chicarones* are the pork skins that we all enjoy. When I first saw the word "chicarones" in print, I thought immediately of the word "chicken." Before you begin, see the section on *pozole* in the Introduction (see page 6).

QUAN.	INGREDIENT	CARB GRAMS	AVAIL. CARB	FAT	PROTEIN
1 lb.	Boneless, skinless, boneless **CHICKEN BREASTS**, uncooked, cut in half inch cubes	0	0	4.2	104.8
2 T.	**OLIVE OIL**	0	0	26.0	0
1 c.	**TOMATO SAUCE** (one 8 ounce can)	14.0	10.5	0	3.5
4 c.	**CHICKEN STOCK** (two 14½ ounce cans are sufficient)				
½ c.	**DRY RED WINE**	2.0	2.0	0	0.4
½ t.	**LEMON EXTRACT**				
2 T.	**WHITE VINEGAR**				
½ c.	**ONION**, sliced thinly	5.0	3.9	0	0.7
½ c.	**GREEN PEPPERS**, diced	4.8	3.5	0.1	0.7
1 t.	**DRIED OREGANO**				
1 T.	**CHILI POWDER**	4.1	1.5	1.0	0.9
1 T.	**PICKLED JALAPEÑOS** (diced finely, more or less added to your taste)				
1 t.	**SUGAR EQUIVALENT SWEETENER**				
1	**CHICKEN BOUILLON CUBE**				
½ t.	**BLACK PEPPER**				
2 t.	**GARLIC POWDER**	4.0	4.0	0	1.0
1 T.	**FRESH CILANTRO**				
3 oz.	**PLAIN PORK RINDS**, crushed to a powder	0	0	30.0	54.0
1 c.	**WATER**				
	TOTALS	33.9	25.4	61.3	166.0
	PER SERVING OF 1 C.	4.2	3.2	7.7	20.8

- In a 2 quart saucepan, heat the oil to medium high. Add the onion and bell peppers and cook until the onion becomes clear. Add the chicken and cook until the chicken begins to brown. Turn the heat to high, add the remaining ingredients except for the pork rinds, cover, and bring to a boil. Reduce the heat to medium low and let simmer for about 45 minutes, stirring several times. Stir in the pork rinds and continue to simmer for 5 minutes. As an alternative, the pork rinds can be served as a side just like the vegetables mentioned in the Introduction.

- **MAKES ABOUT 8 SERVINGS WITH ABOUT 165 CALORIES PER SERVING.**

SALADS

AND SALAD DRESSINGS

ITALIAN DRESSING

THIS dressing is another staple of my own diet. It makes a salad taste better than anything you could get at a restaurant. There are several variations on this. You can add 2 teaspoons of anise or fennel. My particular favorite is to add ½ cup or 4 tablespoons of grated Parmesan cheese and mix with the dry ingredients. If you like blue cheese dressing, mix the vinegar and dry ingredients in a bowl. Before mixing in the oil, toss in some crumbled blue cheese. For a southwestern variation, add a tablespoon (more or less to your taste) of finely diced pickled jalapeño peppers. The carbs are negligible for this dressing, but still must be counted.

QUAN.	INGREDIENT	CARB GRAMS	AVAIL. CARB	FAT	PROTEIN
1 c.	OLIVE OIL	0	0	206.5	0
½ c.	WINE VINEGAR				
½ c.	WATER				
3–4 t.	SUGAR EQUIVALENT SWEETENER				
1 t.	OREGANO or ITALIAN SEASONING	1.0	0.5	0	0
1 T.	GARLIC POWDER	6.0	6.0	0	1.5
1 t.	ONION POWDER	1.7	1.6	0	0.2
½ t.	DRY MUSTARD	0.6	0.4	0.5	0.4
2 t.	CELERY SALT	1.2	0.8	0.8	0.6
½ t.	BLACK PEPPER				
2 T.	DRIED CHIVES				
½–1 t.	XANTHUM GUM for thickening (optional)				
	TOTALS	10.5	8.8	207.8	2.7
	PER SERVING OF 1 T.	0.3	0.3	6.5	0.1

- Dissolve the sugar substitute completely in the vinegar. Put all ingredients except the oil in a pint jar and shake well. Let this set for 15 minutes or longer. Shake again and add the oil. This does not need to be kept refrigerated. Shake very well before serving.

- **MAKES ONE PINT OR 32 SERVINGS WITH ABOUT 60 CALORIES PER SERVING.**

CREAMY ITALIAN DRESSING

THIS is another variation of the Italian dressing. This one is especially good to take to potluck dinners or barbecues along with a tray of low carb vegetables.

QUAN.	INGREDIENT	CARB GRAMS	AVAIL. CARB	FAT	PROTEIN
1 c.	MAYONNAISE	5.9	5.9	168.5	2.4
½ c.	OLIVE OIL	0	0	103.3	0
⅜ c.	WINE VINEGAR				
2 T.	SUGAR EQUIVALENT SWEETENER				
2 t.	OREGANO or ITALIAN SEASONING	2.0	1.0	0	0
1 T.	GARLIC POWDER	6.0	6.0	0	1.5
2 t.	ONION POWDER	3.4	3.2	0	0.4
2 t.	DRY MUSTARD	2.4	1.4	1.8	1.6
2 t.	CELERY SALT	1.2	0.8	0.8	0.6
1 T.	DRIED CHIVES				
	TOTALS	20.9	18.3	274.4	6.5
	PER SERVING OF 1 T.	0.7	0.6	8.6	0.2

- In a 1 quart bowl, mix the dry ingredients, including the sugar substitute, with the vinegar. Let set for 15 minutes or longer if possible. Add the mayonnaise and mix well. Finally, mix in the olive oil.

- **MAKES ONE PINT OR 32 SERVINGS WITH ABOUT 81 CALORIES PER SERVING.**

FRENCH DRESSING ROUGE

THERE are two major types of standard French dressings: those that are red and use various combinations of tomatoes and paprika and those that resemble some type of vinaigrette. As you can tell from its name, this recipe falls within the first category.

QUAN.	INGREDIENT	CARB GRAMS	AVAIL. CARB	FAT	PROTEIN
1 c.	OLIVE OIL	0	0	206.5	0
½ c.	VINEGAR				
3 T.	TOMATO SAUCE	3.3	2.7	0.1	0.6
½ t.	SALT				
¼ t.	BLACK PEPPER				
2 T.	PAPRIKA	7.6	4.8	1.6	2.0
1 t.	DRY MUSTARD				
2 t.	GARLIC POWDER	4.0	4.0	0	1.0
2 t.	ONION POWDER	3.4	3.2	0	0.4
4 t.	SUGAR EQUIVALENT SWEETENER				
1 t.	RED CAYENNE SAUCE (more or less added to your taste)				
4 T.	WATER				
¼ t.	XANTHUM GUM (optional for thickening)				
	TOTALS	18.3	14.7	208.2	4.0
	PER SERVING OF 1 T.	0.6	0.5	6.5	0.3

■ Dissolve the sugar substitute completely in the water and vinegar. Mix the dry ingredients in a 1 quart bowl. Add all the liquids except for the tomato sauce and oil. Stir well and let the mixture sit for about 15 minutes. Add the tomato sauce, mix again, and let sit another 15 minutes. Finally mix in the oil and pour into a pint jar. Mix well before serving. Keep refrigerated. This will keep several weeks.

■ **MAKES ABOUT 1 PINT OR 2 CUPS OR ABOUT 32 SERVINGS WITH ABOUT 62 CALORIES PER SERVING.**

FRENCH DRESSING BLANC

QUAN.	INGREDIENT	CARB GRAMS	AVAIL. CARB	FAT	PROTEIN
11 T.	OLIVE OIL	0	0	143.0	0
2 T.	VINEGAR				
2 T.	LEMON JUICE	2.6	2.5	0	0.1
½ t.	DRY MUSTARD				
1 T.	WORCESTERSHIRE SAUCE	3.0	3.0	0	0
½ t.	SALT				
¼ t.	BLACK PEPPER				
1 t.	GARLIC POWDER	2.0	2.0	0	0.5
1 t.	ONION POWDER	1.7	1.6	0	0.2
1 t.	SUGAR EQUIVALENT SWEETENER				
	TOTALS	9.3	9.1	143.0	0.8
	PER SERVING OF 1 T.	0.6	0.6	8.9	0.1

■ Dissolve the sugar substitute completely in the vinegar and lemon juice. Place all of the dry ingredients in a pint jar. Add the liquids, except for the oil and shake well. Let this sit about 15 minutes and shake again. Add the oil and shake. Stir well before serving.

■ **MAKES ABOUT 1 CUP OR ABOUT 16 SERVINGS WITH ABOUT 83 CALORIES PER SERVING.**

KRAFT-STYLE CREAMY FRENCH DRESSING

KRAFT'S original recipe calls for the use of skim milk. Our recipe uses real cream. If your kids like the original, they'll love this.

QUAN.	INGREDIENT	CARB GRAMS	AVAIL. CARB	FAT	PROTEIN
4 T.	OLIVE OIL	0	0	52.0	0
4 T.	WATER				
2 T.	HEAVY WHIPPING CREAM	1.2	1.2	10.4	0.6
6 T.	VINEGAR				
4 t.	SUGAR EQUIVALENT SWEETENER				
½ t.	SALT				
2 t.	PAPRIKA	2.5	1.6	0.5	0.7
1 t.	GARLIC POWDER	2.0	2.0	0	0.5
1 t.	ONION POWDER	1.7	1.6	0	0.2
½ t.	XANTHUM GUM (optional)				
	TOTALS	7.4	6.4	62.9	2.0
	PER SERVING OF 1 T.	0.5	0.4	3.9	0.1

- In a microwavable 2 cup bowl, place the water, sugar substitute, and paprika and mix well. Microwave it until it is very warm but not boiling, about 20–30 seconds. Remove from the microwave and add the vinegar, the cream, and then the salt and spices, mixing continuously. If you are going to use the xanthum gum, now is the time to mix it in and let it set for about 15 minutes, stirring every 5 minutes. Let this sit at room temperature at least ½ hour. Refrigerate until used. Mix well before using. This should be used before the cream goes bad.

- **MAKES ABOUT 1 CUP OR ABOUT 16 SERVINGS WITH ABOUT 37 CALORIES PER SERVING.**

RANCH-STYLE DRESSING

QUAN.	INGREDIENT	CARB GRAMS	AVAIL. CARB	FAT	PROTEIN
1 c.	MAYONNAISE	5.9	5.9	168.5	2.4
1 c.	BUTTERMILK	11.7	11.7	2.0	8.1
2 t.	ONION POWDER	3.4	3.2	0	0.4
1 T.	DRIED CHIVES				
2 t.	GARLIC POWDER	4.0	4.0	0	1.0
1 T.	DRIED PARSLEY				
1 t.	PAPRIKA	1.3	0.8	0.3	0.3
¼ t.	CAYENNE PEPPER (more or less added to your taste)				
1 t.	CELERY SALT				
½ t.	BLACK PEPPER				
	TOTALS	26.3	25.6	170.8	12.2
	PER SERVING OF 1 T.	0.8	0.8	5.3	0.4

- Mix the dry ingredients thoroughly with the buttermilk in a 1 quart bowl. Mix in the mayonnaise. Store in a pint jar in the refrigerator.

- **MAKES ABOUT 2 CUPS OR ABOUT 32 SERVINGS WITH ABOUT 53 CALORIES PER SERVING.**

BLUE CHEESE DRESSING

THIS dressing has a special place in my heart because it provided for one of my first compliments when the original edition of this book was published. A professional chef in Atlanta sent me an e-mail saying that she and her husband (also a chef) made the Blue Cheese Dressing for their salads and they had never tasted anything this good.

QUAN.	INGREDIENT	CARB GRAMS	AVAIL. CARB	FAT	PROTEIN
1 c.	**MAYONNAISE**	5.9	5.9	168.5	2.4
2 t.	**ONION POWDER**	3.4	3.2	0	0.4
2 t.	**GARLIC POWDER**	4.0	4.0	0	1.0
2 T.	**DRIED PARSLEY**				
½ c.	**SOUR CREAM**	4.9	4.9	22.9	3.7
2 T.	**LEMON JUICE**	2.6	2.5	0	0.1
2 t.	**SUGAR EQUIVALENT SWEETENER**				
2 oz.	**BLUE CHEESE**, crumbled	1.3	1.3	15.4	12.1
1 t.	**CELERY SALT**				
½ t.	**RED CAYENNE SAUCE** (more or less added to your taste)				
	TOTALS	22.1	21.8	206.8	19.7
	PER SERVING OF 1 T.	0.7	0.7	6.5	0.6

- Dissolve the sugar substitute completely in the lemon juice. Mix everything except the mayonnaise in a 1 quart bowl and then mix in the mayonnaise. Place in a pint jar. Let it set in the refrigerator overnight if possible.

■ **MAKES ABOUT 2 CUPS OR ABOUT 32 SERVINGS WITH ABOUT 64 CALORIES PER SERVING.**

GREEN GODDESS DRESSING

MANY, many years ago, in a galaxy far, far away, one of the better-known salad dressings was called Green Goddess. It was created by a San Francisco chef in the 1920s and was named for a play that was being produced there at the time.

QUAN.	INGREDIENT	CARB GRAMS	AVAIL. CARB	FAT	PROTEIN
1½ c.	MAYONNAISE	8.9	8.9	252.8	3.6
6 T.	TARRAGON VINEGAR				
¼ c.	GREEN ONIONS, diced	1.9	1.2	0	0.5
1 t.	SUGAR EQUIVALENT SWEETENER				
½ oz.	ANCHOVIES WITH THE OIL, mashed well	0	0	0.6	4.1
2 T.	DRIED PARSLEY				
2 T.	DRIED CHIVES				
½ t.	DRIED TARRAGON				
2 t.	GARLIC POWDER	4.0	4.0	0	1.0
2 t.	ONION POWDER	3.4	3.2	0	0.4
	TOTALS	18.2	17.3	253.4	9.6
	PER SERVING OF 1 T.	0.6	0.5	7.9	0.3

- In a 1 quart bowl, dissolve the sugar substitute completely in the vinegar. Mix in the dry ingredients. Mash the anchovies in a separate bowl. Add the green onions and the anchovies to the vinegar mixture and mix well. Finally, mix in the mayonnaise. Put in a pint jar and let set refrigerated at least two hours.

- **MAKES ABOUT 2 CUPS OR ABOUT 32 SERVINGS WITH ABOUT 74 CALORIES PER SERVING.**

THOUSAND ISLAND DRESSING

QUAN.	INGREDIENT	CARB GRAMS	AVAIL. CARB	FAT	PROTEIN
¾ c.	**MAYONNAISE**	4.4	4.4	126.4	1.8
3 T.	**CHILI SAUCE** (see page 235)	3.3	2.5	2.7	0.6
1 T.	**DRIED PARSLEY**				
½ c.	**BELL PEPPER**, diced	4.8	3.5	0.1	0.7
½ t.	**SALT**				
2 t.	**PAPRIKA**	2.5	1.6	0.5	0.7
2 t.	**GARLIC POWDER**	4.0	4.0	0	1.0
¼ t.	**CAYENNE PEPPER** (optional, more or less added to your taste)				
4 T.	**SALAD ONIONS** (see page 84)	3.6	2.8	0	0.4
4 T.	**SWEET RELISH** (see page 85)	2.0	1.2	0.8	0.8
	SALAD ONION JUICE (see page 84), 4 T. (more or less added to your taste)				
2 T.	**WATER**				
1 T.	**VINEGAR**				
2 t.	**SUGAR EQUIVALENT SWEETENER**				
	TOTALS	24.6	20.0	130.5	6.0
	PER SERVING OF 1 T.	0.8	0.6	4.1	0.2

- In a 1 quart saucepan, bring the water, vinegar, salt, and sugar substitute to a boil. Add the bell pepper, stir, and cover. Bring to a boil again, stir, remove from heat, and let cool to room temperature. Empty the pan into a 1 quart bowl and mix in the rest of the ingredients. Add enough of the Salad Onion juice to make a pint. Put it in a pint jar and refrigerate.

- **MAKES 32 SERVINGS WITH ABOUT 40 CALORIES PER SERVING.**

AVOCADO SALAD DRESSING

I specifically made this salad dressing to be used as a variation on guacamole. It has a lot more mayonnaise and it is the perfect accompaniment for your taco salad, without the tortilla, of course.

QUAN.	INGREDIENT	CARB GRAMS	AVAIL. CARB	FAT	PROTEIN
1 c.	**AVOCADO**, mashed or pureed	17.0	5.5	32.2	4.6
2 T.	**LIME JUICE**	2.8	2.7	0	0.1
2 t.	**SUGAR EQUIVALENT SWEETENER**				
2 T.	**TOMATOES**, seeds removed and diced finely	1.1	0.8	0.1	0.2
1 t.	**SALT**				
2 t.	**GARLIC POWDER**	4.0	4.0	0	1.0
½ c.	**MAYONNAISE** (enough to bring the recipe to 2 cups)	3.5	3.5	84.3	1.2
2 T.	**PICKLED GREEN JALAPEÑOS**, diced finely (more or less added to your taste)				
½ t.	**RED CAYENNE SAUCE** (more or less added to your taste)				
2 T.	**SALAD ONIONS** (see page 84)	1.8	1.4	0	0.2
½ t.	**DRIED OREGANO**				
2 T.	**FRESH CILANTRO**, chopped coarsely				
	TOTALS	30.2	17.9	116.6	7.3
	PER SERVING OF 1 T.	0.9	0.6	3.6	0.2

- Dissolve the sugar substitute completely in the lime juice. Mash the avocado and lime juice together in a 1 quart bowl to keep the avocado from darkening. Add the remaining ingredients and mix well. Refrigerate covered until serving. Serve 4 tablespoons of this dressing with 2 loosely packed cups of lettuce.

■ **MAKES ABOUT 2 CUPS OR 32 SERVINGS WITH ABOUT 36 CALORIES PER SERVING.**

PUMPKIN VINAIGRETTE

THIS is a good salad dressing for the fall and the holidays. It also complements any type of pumpkin- or squash-based soup.

QUAN.	INGREDIENT	CARB GRAMS	AVAIL. CARB	FAT	PROTEIN
2 T.	**PUMPKIN PUREE** without sugar	2.25	1.0	0.1	0.5
2 T.	**APPLE CIDER VINEGAR**				
1 t.	**GARLIC POWDER**	2.0	2.0	0	0.5
1 t.	**SUGAR EQUIVALENT SWEETENER** (more or less added to your taste)				
½ t.	**SALT**				
¼ t.	**BLACK PEPPER**				
4 T.	**OLIVE OIL**	0	0	52.0	0
	TOTALS	4.25	3.0	52.1	1.0
	PER SERVING OF ¼ C. OR 4 T.	2.1	1.5	26.1	0.5

- In a 2 cup bowl, dissolve the sugar substitute completely in the vinegar. Add the dry ingredients and mix well. Mix in the pumpkin and finally the oil.

- **MAKES 2 SERVINGS WITH ABOUT 243 CALORIES PER SERVING.**

RASPBERRY POPPY SEED VINAIGRETTE

QUAN.	INGREDIENT	CARB GRAMS	AVAIL. CARB	FAT	PROTEIN
5 T.	OLIVE OIL	0	0	75.0	0
2 T.	RASPBERRY VINEGAR (see page 86)	0.4	0.4	0	0
1 T.	SALAD ONIONS (see page 84)	0.9	0.7	0	0.1
½ t.	DIJON MUSTARD				
2 t.	SUGAR EQUIVALENT SWEETENER				
½ t.	POPPY SEEDS	0.4	0.2	0.6	0.3
1 t.	GARLIC POWDER	2.0	2.0	0	0.5
½ t.	SALT				
2 T.	WALNUTS (optional for garnish)				
	TOTALS	3.7	3.3	75.6	0.9
	PER SERVING OF ¼ C. OR 4 T.	1.9	1.7	37.8	0.5

- In a 2 cup bowl, dissolve the sugar substitute completely in the vinegar. Whisk in the onions, mustard, and dry ingredients. Then slowly whisk in the oil. Serve over salads of spinach, broccoli, or cauliflower with a few chopped walnuts sprinkled on top.

- **MAKES ABOUT ½ CUP OR ABOUT 2 SERVINGS WITH ABOUT 349 CALORIES PER SERVING.**

CRANBERRY VINAIGRETTE

THIS is a good basic vinaigrette recipe. You can just substitute the type of vinegar you want for the cranberry vinegar and—voila!—you have a different vinaigrette. This makes enough dressing for about 4 cups of salad greens.

QUAN.	INGREDIENT	CARB GRAMS	AVAIL. CARB	FAT	PROTEIN
6 T.	OLIVE OIL	0	0	75.0	0
2 T.	CRANBERRY VINEGAR (see page 72)	0.6	0.6	0	0
½ t.	DIJON MUSTARD				
2 t.	SUGAR EQUIVALENT SWEETENER				
1 t.	GARLIC POWDER	2.0	2.0	0	0.5
1 t.	ONION POWDER	1.7	1.6	0	0.2
½ t.	SALT				
	TOTALS	4.3	4.2	75.0	0.7
	PER SERVING OF 1 T.	0.5	0.5	9.4	0.1

- In a 2 cup bowl, dissolve the sugar substitute completely in the vinegar. Whisk in the mustard and dry ingredients. Finally, slowly whisk in the oil.

- **MAKES ABOUT ½ CUP OR ABOUT 8 SERVINGS WITH ABOUT 87 CALORIES PER SERVING.**

LEMON CAPER VINAIGRETTE

CAPERS and lemon juice in a salad dressing? Sounds fancy, doesn't it? It's fortunate for us low carbers that we can use capers rather freely.

QUAN.	INGREDIENT	CARB GRAMS	AVAIL. CARB	FAT	PROTEIN
4 T.	OLIVE OIL	0	0	52.0	0
2 T.	WATER				
2 T.	LEMON JUICE	2.6	2.5	0	0.1
1 T.	CAPERS, drained and chopped	0.4	0.1	0.1	0.2
½ t.	SALT				
½ t.	BLACK PEPPER				
1 t.	OREGANO				
½ t.	GARLIC POWDER	1.0	1.0	0	0
2 t.	SUGAR EQUIVALENT SWEETENER				
	TOTALS	4.0	3.6	52.1	0.3
	PER SERVING OF ¼ C. OR 4 T.	2.0	1.8	26.1	0.2

- In a 2 cup bowl, dissolve the sugar substitute completely in the lemon juice and water. Combine all of the ingredients except the oil in a bowl and whisk well. Slowly add the oil, whisking the whole time.

- **MAKES ABOUT ½ CUP OR ABOUT 2 SERVINGS WITH ABOUT 243 CALORIES PER SERVING.**

TOFU VINAIGRETTE

QUAN.	INGREDIENT	CARB GRAMS	AVAIL. CARB	FAT	PROTEIN
½ c.	OLIVE OIL	0	0	103.3	0
4 oz.	SOFT TOFU, drained and rinsed	2.1	1.8	3.9	7.5
3 T.	DIJON MUSTARD				
2 T.	LEMON JUICE	2.6	2.5	0	0.1
2 T.	WHITE VINEGAR				
2 t.	GARLIC POWDER	4.0	4.0	0	1.0
½ t.	SALT				
4 T.	SALAD ONIONS (see page 84)	3.6	2.8	0	0.4
2 t.	SUGAR EQUIVALENT SWEETENER				
	TOTALS	12.3	11.1	107.2	9.0
	PER SERVING OF 1 T.	0.5	0.5	4.5	0.4

■ In a 2 cup bowl, dissolve the sugar substitute completely in the vinegar and lemon juice. Puree the lemon juice, vinegar, and tofu in blender or food processor until it is smooth. Add the remaining ingredients and continue processing until everything is smooth. Transfer the mixture to a pint jar. Cover and chill. This will keep up to a week or more.

■ **MAKES ABOUT 1½ CUPS OR ABOUT 24 SERVINGS WITH ABOUT 44 CALORIES PER SERVING.**

MOM'S SPECIAL VINAIGRETTE

MY mother could not tolerate acid foods all that well so I created this vinaigrette especially for her. The proteins in the cream neutralize the acid somewhat, making this dressing relatively mild.

QUAN.	INGREDIENT	CARB GRAMS	AVAIL. CARB	FAT	PROTEIN
2 T.	LEMON JUICE (or A VINEGAR OF YOUR CHOICE)	2.6	2.5	0	0.1
2 t.	SUGAR EQUIVALENT SWEETENER				
2 t.	GARLIC POWDER	4.0	4.0	0	1.0
1 t.	PREPARED MUSTARD (any mustard will do)				
1 t.	ONION POWDER	1.7	1.6	0	0.2
¼ t.	SALT				
¼ t.	BLACK PEPPER				
2 T.	HEAVY WHIPPING CREAM	1.2	1.2	10.4	0.6
2 T.	MAYONNAISE	0.8	0.8	21.0	0.4
2 T.	OLIVE OIL	0	0	26.0	0
	RED CAYENNE SAUCE to your taste (a shake or two)				
	TOTALS	10.3	10.1	57.4	2.3
	PER SERVING OF 1 T.	1.3	1.3	7.2	0.3

- In a 2 cup bowl, dissolve the sugar substitute completely in the lemon juice. Stir the dried seasoning into the lemon mixture. Then stir the mustard and cream into the lemon mixture. The mixture will become a little thicker when the cream is added. Mix in the mayonnaise and then the olive oil.

■ **MAKES ABOUT ½ CUP OR ABOUT 8 SERVINGS WITH ABOUT 71 CALORIES PER SERVING.**

GARLIC BLUE CHEESE VINAIGRETTE SALAD

QUAN.	INGREDIENT	CARB GRAMS	AVAIL. CARB	FAT	PROTEIN
3 T.	OLIVE OIL	0	0	39.0	0
1 T.	WINE VINEGAR				
½ t.	COARSE GROUND MUSTARD				
1 t.	SUGAR EQUIVALENT SWEETENER				
½ t.	SALT				
2 t.	GARLIC CLOVES, diced finely	1.9	1.8	0	0.4
½ t.	ONION POWDER	0.9	0.8	0	0.1
1 oz.	BLUE CHEESE, at room temperature, crumbled	0.7	0.7	7.7	6.1
2 c.	HEAD LETTUCE, torn for a salad and packed tightly in the measuring cup	2.2	0.6	0.2	1.2
	TOTALS	5.7	3.9	46.9	7.8
	PER SERVING	5.7	3.9	46.9	7.8

- In a small bowl, dissolve the sugar substitute completely in the vinegar. In a 1 quart bowl, using a fork, mash the garlic with the salt until the garlic is almost a paste. Add the oil and mix thoroughly. Add the mustard, vinegar, and onion powder and mix. Mix in the blue cheese with the fork, again making a paste. Pour over the lettuce, toss, and serve.

- **MAKES 1 SERVING WITH ABOUT 469 CALORIES PER SERVING.**

BROCCOLI SALAD
WITH TARRAGON DRESSING

THIS salad made with broccoli will provide a little respite from the standard lettuce, greens, and cabbage types of salads. It will also be a pleasant surprise for your friends.

QUAN.	INGREDIENT	CARB GRAMS	AVAIL. CARB	FAT	PROTEIN
1 lb.	FROZEN BROCCOLI FLORETS	24.2	10.6	0	14.1
2 t.	GARLIC POWDER	4.0	4.0	0	1.0
1 t.	ONION POWDER	1.7	1.6	0	0.2
2 T.	WHITE WINE VINEGAR or TARRAGON VINEGAR				
2 T.	SWEET RELISH (see page 85)	1.0	0.6	0.4	0.4
2 T.	CHOPPED CHIVES				
2 T.	CHOPPED FRESH TARRAGON (or 1 T. DRIED TARRAGON)				
½ t.	SALT				
¼ t.	BLACK PEPPER				
6 T.	OLIVE OIL	0	0	78.0	0
2 t.	SUGAR EQUIVALENT SWEETENER (more or less added to your taste)				
	TOTALS	30.9	16.8	78.4	15.7
	PER SERVING	7.7	4.2	19.6	3.9

■ Let the broccoli thaw to room temperature. Drain it well before putting it in a 4 cup salad bowl. Mix the remaining ingredients in a separate 2 cup bowl and pour the marinade over the broccoli. Stir well a couple of times. Refrigerate for a couple of hours before serving. This will keep refrigerated several days.

■ **MAKES 4 SERVINGS WITH ABOUT 209 CALORIES PER SERVING.**

MUSHROOM SALAD

QUAN.	INGREDIENT	CARB GRAMS	AVAIL. CARB	FAT	PROTEIN
1 lb.	**BUTTON MUSHROOMS**, well cleaned	21.2	15.7	1.1	9.5
2 t.	**GARLIC POWDER**	4.0	4.0	0	1.0
2 T.	**WINE VINEGAR**				
2 T.	**SALAD ONIONS** (see page 84)	1.8	1.4	0	0.2
2 T.	**CHOPPED CHIVES**				
½ t.	**SALT**				
¼ t.	**BLACK PEPPER**				
6 T.	**OLIVE OIL**	0	0	78.0	0
	TOTALS	27.0	21.1	79.1	10.7
	PER SERVING	4.5	3.5	13.2	1.8

■ Bring 2 quarts of water to a boil in a 3 quart soup pot. Blanch the mushrooms in the boiling water for 1 minute and then cool them in ice water. Drain them well before putting them in an 8 cup salad bowl. Mix the remaining ingredients in a separate 2 cup bowl and pour the marinade over the mushrooms. Stir well a couple of times. Refrigerate for 2 hours before serving, if possible. This will keep refrigerated several days.

■ **MAKES 6 SERVINGS WITH ABOUT 140 CALORIES PER SERVING.**

BROCCOLI, CHEESE, WALNUTS, AND HAM SALAD

QUAN.	INGREDIENT	CARB GRAMS	AVAIL. CARB	FAT	PROTEIN
10 oz.	FROZEN BROCCOLI, diced	15.1	6.6	0	8.8
¼ lb.	HAM, diced	2.0	2.0	2.0	20.0
2 oz.	AMERICAN CHEESE, shredded	1.5	1.5	18.0	12.0
2 T.	SALAD ONIONS (see page 84)	1.8	1.4	0	0
4 T.	WALNUTS, diced	5.5	4.1	17.7	4.3
½ t.	GARLIC POWDER	1.0	1.0	0	0.3
1 t.	SALT (more or less added to your taste)				
6 T.	MAYONNAISE	2.2	2.2	63.2	0.9
2 T.	WHITE VINEGAR				
4 T.	SUGAR EQUIVALENT SWEETENER				
½ t.	DRY MUSTARD	0.6	0.4	0.5	0.4
	TOTALS	29.7	19.2	101.4	46.7
	PER SERVING	7.4	4.8	25.4	11.7

- Thaw and drain the broccoli. Dissolve the sugar substitute completely in the vinegar. Make the dressing by combining the vinegar mixture with the mayonnaise, salt, garlic powder, and mustard in a 1 cup bowl. Pour over the remaining ingredients in your 1 quart salad bowl and mix well. Refrigerate until serving. Stir well before serving.

■ **MAKES 4 SERVINGS WITH ABOUT 295 CALORIES PER SERVING.**

GERMAN-STYLE CUCUMBER ZUCCHINI SALAD

YOU may be familiar with the German-style cucumber salad served in many restaurants. I've added zucchini to the mix for a little variation.

QUAN.	INGREDIENT	CARB GRAMS	AVAIL. CARB	FAT	PROTEIN
½ lb.	CUCUMBERS, peeled and sliced	6.3	4.5	0.2	1.6
½ lb.	ZUCCHINI, sliced	6.5	3.8	0.2	2.6
½ c.	ONION, sliced thinly	5.0	3.9	0	0.7
4 T.	WHITE VINEGAR				
2 T.	SUGAR EQUIVALENT SWEETENER				
½ c.	WATER				
2 t.	SALT				
1 t.	GARLIC POWDER	2.0	2.0	0	0.5
½ t.	BLACK PEPPER				
½ c.	SOUR CREAM	4.9	4.9	22.9	3.7
2 T.	CHOPPED CHIVES, either fresh or dried				
	TOTALS	24.7	19.1	23.3	9.1
	PER SERVING	6.2	4.8	5.8	2.3

- Place the zucchini and cucumbers in a 4 cup salad bowl, add 1 teaspoon of salt, and stir. Let this sit at room temperature for at least 1 hour in order to wilt the vegetables. Pour the water off of the vegetables and gently squeeze out the rest of the liquid. Add the remaining ingredients except the sour cream and chives. Stir and refrigerate for 2 hours. About an hour before serving, stir in the sour cream. For garnish, sprinkle the chives over the salad just before serving. This will stay fresh for several days in your refrigerator.

■ **MAKES 4 SERVINGS WITH ABOUT 81 CALORIES PER SERVING.**

GERMAN GREEN BEAN SALAD

WHEN I visited my niece in Columbia, South Carolina, she took me to dinner at a German restaurant near her apartment on the east side. One of the dishes that we chose was a green bean salad. My niece loved it so much that she asked me to create a recipe for it.

QUAN.	INGREDIENT	CARB GRAMS	AVAIL. CARB	FAT	PROTEIN
2 c.	**GREEN BEANS** (one 15 oz. can is sufficient) drained, reserving the liquid	14.0	7.0	0	3.6
4 T.	**WHITE VINEGAR**				
½ c.	**ONION,** sliced thinly	5.0	3.9	0	0.7
½ t.	**SALT**				
1 t.	**SUGAR EQUIVALENT SWEETENER**				
	TOTALS	19.0	10.9	0	4.3
	PER SERVING	6.3	3.6	0	1.4

- Pour 1 cup of the green bean liquid into a 1 quart saucepan. If there isn't enough green bean liquid, add water to bring it to 1 cup. Add the sliced onions to the saucepan. Then add the remaining ingredients, cover, and bring to a boil over high heat. Remove from the heat and let it cool down to room temperature, stirring occasionally. Refrigerate overnight before serving. The longer it sets, the tastier it gets.

- **MAKES 3 SERVINGS WITH ABOUT 20 CALORIES PER SERVING.**

HOT GARDEN SALAD—
ENGLISH STYLE

IF you really like blue cheese, try this salad. It's a warm salad dressed with a British equivalent called Stilton cheese. If you don't have Stilton cheese, you can substitute Roquefort or Gorgonzola.

QUAN.	INGREDIENT	CARB GRAMS	AVAIL. CARB	FAT	PROTEIN
3 slices	**BACON**, diced	0	0	61.9	9.9
½ c.	**RASPBERRY VINEGAR** (see page 72)				
¼ t.	**CRACKED BLACK PEPPERCORNS**				
4 T.	**OLIVE OIL**	0	0	52.0	0
½ t.	**SALT**				
2 oz.	**STILTON CHEESE**, crumbled	1.3	1.3	15.4	12.1
¼ c.	**RED ONION**, thinly sliced	2.5	2.0	0	0.4
½ c.	**SLICED MUSHROOMS**	1.6	1.2	0.1	0.7
2 t.	**GARLIC**, diced finely	1.9	1.8	0	0.4
1	**HEAD OF CURLY ENDIVE**, roughly chopped	17.2	1.3	0.7	6.4
3 c.	**LETTUCE** or **VARIOUS OTHER SALAD GREENS**	3.3	0.9	0.3	1.8
2 t.	**SUGAR EQUIVALENT SWEETENER**				
	TOTALS	27.8	8.5	130.4	31.7
	PER SERVING	13.9	4.3	65.2	15.9

- Dissolve the sugar substitute in the vinegar. Fry the bacon in the oil in a medium skillet over medium high heat until the bacon is crispy. Add the mushrooms and onions and cook until the onions begin to wilt. Add the garlic and cook about 1 minute. Turn the heat up to high. Stir in the salt and pepper and then add the vinegar/sugar substitute mixture and bring to a boil. Stir in the cheese. When it has melted somewhat, pour over the salad in a 6 cup heat-proof salad bowl, mix well, and serve immediately.

- **MAKES 2 SERVINGS WITH ABOUT 668 CALORIES PER SERVING.**

CAESAR SALADS AND DRESSINGS

AS you probably know, the general ingredients for Caesar salad include oil, egg, an acid, some type of anchovy flavor, garlic, grated Parmesan cheese, romaine lettuce, salt, and pepper. Mayonnaise is a combination of oil and egg and is considered safe from salmonella, so I use it instead of raw egg. The acid is usually either lemon juice or vinegar. Worcestershire sauce is sometimes used in the place of anchovies because most of them are actually made of anchovies. Other ingredients that are sometimes added are mustard and some type of hot peppers. I've included two recipes for Caesar salad dressing for you to make, one very simple and one a little more complex.

CAESAR SALAD

QUAN.	INGREDIENT	CARB GRAMS	AVAIL. CARB	FAT	PROTEIN
2 c.	**HEAD ROMAINE LETTUCE**, bite sized	2.7	0.8	0.2	1.8
4 T.	**FANCY CAESAR SALAD DRESSING** (see page 60)	3.7	3.6	21.9	4.5
1	**COLD HARD BOILED EGG**, diced	0.7	0.7	4.8	7.2
	GRATED PARMESAN or **ROMANO CHEESE** to sprinkle on the finished salad				
	TOTALS	7.1	5.1	26.9	13.5
	PER SERVING	7.1	5.1	26.9	13.5

■ **MAKES 1 SERVING WITH ABOUT 317 CALORIES PER SERVING.**

SIMPLE CAESAR SALAD

QUAN.	INGREDIENT	CARB GRAMS	AVAIL. CARB	FAT	PROTEIN
2 c.	**HEAD ROMAINE LETTUCE**, bite sized	2.7	0.8	0.2	1.8
4 T.	**SIMPLE CAESAR SALAD DRESSING** (see page 61)	6.9	6.5	25.5	6.9
1	**COLD HARD BOILED EGG**, diced	0.7	0.7	4.8	7.2
	GRATED PARMESAN or **ROMANO CHEESE** to sprinkle on the finished salad				
	TOTALS	10.3	8.0	30.5	15.9
	PER SERVING	10.3	8.0	30.5	15.9

■ Wash the lettuce thoroughly. Tear it into bite sized pieces. Pour the dressing over the lettuce in a 1 quart salad bowl and mix well. Dice the eggs and sprinkle them over the top of the salad along with the remaining shredded cheese.

■ **MAKES 1 SERVING WITH ABOUT 370 CALORIES PER SERVING.**

FANCY CAESAR SALAD DRESSING

THIS is the more difficult of the two Caesar salad dressing recipes. It takes a little longer because you have to mash the garlic and the anchovies.

QUAN.	INGREDIENT	CARB GRAMS	AVAIL. CARB	FAT	PROTEIN
8 T.	MAYONNAISE	3.2	3.2	84.0	1.6
4 T.	OLIVE OIL	0	0	52.0	0
6 T.	LEMON JUICE or WHITE VINEGAR (or some combination)	7.8	7.6	0	0.4
2 T.	WORCESTERSHIRE SAUCE	6.0	6.0	0	0
4 T.	GARLIC, diced finely	11.2	10.2	0.2	2.2
6 T.	GRATED PARMESAN CHEESE	1.4	1.4	10.7	15.6
2 t.	SUGAR EQUIVALENT SWEETENER				
1 T.	DIJON MUSTARD (any coarse ground prepared mustard will suffice)				
½ t.	BLACK PEPPER				
1 t.	RED CAYENNE SAUCE (more or less added to your taste)				
2 oz.	ANCHOVY PASTE or MASHED ANCHOVIES (1 can of anchovies, more or less added to your taste)	0	0	2.4	16.4
	TOTALS	29.6	28.4	149.3	36.2
	PER SERVING OF ¼ C. OR 4 T.	3.7	3.6	18.7	4.5

- Put the garlic and sugar substitute in the acid in a 2 cup microwavable container and microwave on high temperature for 15 seconds. Set this aside and let it cool to room temperature. Combine the anchovies and the olive oil in a 2 cup container. Stir the mayonnaise thoroughly into the olive oil mixture and set aside. Combine the remaining ingredients, except the reserved grated Parmesan cheese, with the acid mixture, then stir the mayonnaise mixture thoroughly. Store this in a pint jar.

- **MAKES ABOUT 1 PINT OR 8 SERVINGS WITH ABOUT 201 CALORIES PER SERVING.**

SIMPLE CAESAR SALAD DRESSING

THIS is the quick and easy version of Caesar salad dressing. I've used Thai Fish Sauce to provide the anchovy flavor.

QUAN.	INGREDIENT	CARB GRAMS	AVAIL. CARB	FAT	PROTEIN
½ c.	MAYONNAISE	3.0	3.0	83.4	1.2
½ c.	OLIVE OIL	0	0	103.3	0
6 T.	LEMON JUICE	7.8	7.5	0	0.3
6 T.	THAI FISH SAUCE or WORCESTERSHIRE SAUCE or some combination of the two	18.0	18.0	0	12.0
1 T.	DRY MUSTARD	3.9	2.3	3.0	2.8
3 T.	GARLIC POWDER	18.3	18.3	0	4.2
1 T.	SUGAR EQUIVALENT SWEETENER				
1½ t.	BLACK PEPPER	2.1	1.2	0.2	0.3
½ c.	GRATED PARMESAN CHEESE	1.9	1.9	14.3	20.8
1½ t.	RED CAYENNE SAUCE (more or less added to your taste)				
	TOTALS	55.0	52.2	204.2	55.1
	PER SERVING OF ¼ C. OR 4 T.	6.9	6.5	25.5	6.9

- In a 2 cup bowl, dissolve the sugar substitute completely in the liquids. Mix in the dry ingredients and set them aside. In a separate bowl, mix the mayonnaise and olive oil together and then stir them into the liquid mixture thoroughly.

■ **MAKES 1 PINT OR 8 SERVINGS WITH ABOUT 283 CALORIES PER SERVING.**

CAULIFLOWER SALAD WITH ANCHOVIES

THIS surprising combination that I stumbled upon is absolutely delicious. To top it off, it's a very pretty salad because the dark anchovies and olives contrast with the lighter color of the cauliflower.

QUAN.	INGREDIENT	CARB GRAMS	AVAIL. CARB	FAT	PROTEIN
1 lb.	**FROZEN CAULIFLOWER**, thawed and drained	18.0	12.0	0	12.0
½ oz.	**ANCHOVIES**, mashed well (more or less added to your taste)	0	0	1.5	4.0
8 T.	**ITALIAN DRESSING** (see page 36)	2.4	2.4	52.0	0.8
4 T.	**BLACK OLIVES**, diced coarsely	2.1	1.0	3.4	0.3
	SALT to taste				
	TOTALS	22.5	15.4	56.9	17.1
	PER SERVING	5.6	3.9	14.2	4.3

- Place the cauliflower and olives in a 4 cup salad bowl and set aside. Mash the anchovies well in a 1 cup bowl. Add the Italian Dressing and mix thoroughly. Pour over the cauliflower and olives and mix thoroughly. Refrigerate until serving.

■ **MAKES 4 SERVINGS WITH ABOUT 161 CALORIES PER SERVING.**

COBB SALAD

THIS salad is very close in style to the Cobb salad made famous by the Brown Derby restaurant in Hollywood. For many folks, this is a staple of their low carb eating regimen because it is very high in protein.

QUAN.	INGREDIENT	CARB GRAMS	AVAIL. CARB	FAT	PROTEIN
1 c.	**ICEBERG LETTUCE,** in bite sized pieces	1.1	0.3	0.1	0.6
1 c.	**WATERCRESS,** in bite size pieces	0.4	0	0	0.8
1 c.	**CURLY ENDIVE,** in bite sized pieces	1.7	0.2	0.1	0.6
1 c.	**ROMAINE LETTUCE,** in bite sized pieces	1.3	0.3	0.1	0.9
½ lb.	**COOKED CHICKEN BREAST,** cut into bite sized pieces	0	0	6.8	69.8
6 slices	**BACON,** diced, cooked crisp	0.4	0.4	29.8	19.4
1 cup	**AVOCADO,** peeled and diced in bite sized pieces	11.1	3.6	21.0	3.0
2	**HARD BOILED EGGS,** sliced	1.3	1.3	9.6	14.4
4 T.	**SALAD ONIONS** (see page 84)	3.6	2.8	0	0.4
¾ c.	**FRENCH DRESSING BLANC** (see page 39)	7.0	6.8	107.3	0.6
1 T.	**DRIED CHIVES**				
2 oz.	**CRUMBLED BLUE CHEESE**	1.3	1.3	15.4	12.1
	TOTALS	29.2	17.0	190.2	122.6
	PER SERVING	14.6	8.5	95.1	61.3

- Mix the chives with the French Dressing Blanc in a 1 cup bowl and set aside for at least 15 minutes. In an 8 cup salad bowl, place the greens and the onions and toss with about ½ cup of the dressing. Decorate the top of the salad with the remaining items and drizzle the remaining dressing over them. Serve immediately.

■ **MAKES 2 SERVINGS WITH ABOUT 1,135 CALORIES PER SERVING.**

ZUCCHINI AND MUSHROOM SALAD

THIS marinated salad is very simple to make. The tarragon gives it a unique flavor and it was one of my mother's favorites.

QUAN.	INGREDIENT	CARB GRAMS	AVAIL. CARB	FAT	PROTEIN
½ lb.	**BUTTON MUSHROOMS**, cleaned	7.5	5.7	0.5	4.8
2 c.	**ZUCCHINI**, cut into ¾ inch cubes	7.2	4.2	0.2	2.9
2 T.	**OLIVE OIL**	0	0	51.6	0
4 T.	**WINE VINEGAR**				
4 T.	**DRY WHITE WINE**	0.4	0.4	0	0
1 T.	**WATER**				
1 t.	**SALT**				
½ t.	**BLACK PEPPER**				
2 t.	**SUGAR EQUIVALENT SWEETENER**				
2 t.	**GARLIC POWDER**	4.0	4.0	0	1.5
½ t.	**DRIED TARRAGON**				
1 t.	**ONION POWDER**	1.7	1.6	0	0.2
	TOTALS	23.8	15.9	52.3	9.4
	PER SERVING	7.9	5.3	17.4	3.1

- Place all of the ingredients in a 2 quart saucepan, cover, and bring to a boil over high heat. Reduce the heat to medium low and cook until the zucchini is tender. Remove from the heat and let it cool to room temperature, stirring every 15 minutes. Refrigerate overnight if possible.

- **MAKES 3 SERVINGS WITH ABOUT 190 CALORIES PER SERVING.**

CAULIFLOWER AND BROCCOLI SALAD

QUAN.	INGREDIENT	CARB GRAMS	AVAIL. CARB	FAT	PROTEIN
1 lb.	**FROZEN BROCCOLI AND CAULIFLOWER,** thawed and well drained	20.0	10.0	0	10.0
4 T.	**SALAD ONIONS** (see page 84)	3.6	2.8	0	0.4
½ c.	**GREEN** or **RED BELL PEPPER,** diced	4.8	3.5	0.1	0.7
6 T.	**CREAMY ITALIAN DRESSING** (see page 37)	4.2	3.6	51.6	1.2
½ t.	Salt				
	TOTALS	32.6	19.9	51.7	12.3
	PER SERVING	8.2	5.0	12.9	3.1

■ Mix all ingredients together in a 6 cup salad bowl. Let sit several hours before serving if possible. Mix well before serving.

■ **MAKES 4 SERVINGS WITH ABOUT 149 CALORIES PER SERVING.**

SMOKED TURKEY SALAD
WITH CRANBERRIES

WHEN I was living in Germany, I went to dinner in a town outside of Freiburg and I was served wild pig. I was intrigued that the meal was served with cranberries, and when I asked about it, I was told that cranberries are thought to enhance the flavor of wild meats. This is why cranberries are a part of a traditional Thanksgiving dinner—they're supposed to complement the turkey.

QUAN.	INGREDIENT	CARB GRAMS	AVAIL. CARB	FAT	PROTEIN
1 lb.	**SMOKED TURKEY**, diced in ½ inch pieces	0	0	25.9	133.0
4 c.	**ROMAINE LETTUCE**, torn in bite sized pieces	5.3	1.5	0.3	3.6
4 T.	**RASPBERRY VINEGAR** (see page 72)	0.8	0.8	0	0
½ c.	**CRANBERRIES**	7.0	4.7	0	0.2
4 T.	**SUGAR EQUIVALENT SWEETENER**				
½ c.	**OLIVE OIL**	0	0	103.3	0
1 c.	**CELERY**, diced	4.4	2.4	0	0.9
4 T.	**SALAD ONIONS** (see page 84)	3.6	2.8	0	0.4
1 t.	**GARLIC POWDER**	2.0	2.0	0	0.5
½ t.	**SALT**				
¼ t.	**BLACK PEPPER**				
½ t.	**DRY MUSTARD**				
	EXTRA WINE VINEGAR to taste				
	TOTALS	23.1	14.2	129.5	138.6
	PER SERVING	7.7	4.7	43.2	46.2

- Pour the vinegar in a 2 cup saucepan and bring to a boil. Add the cranberries, sugar substitute, salt, pepper, mustard, and garlic and remove from the heat. Mash the cranberries with the back of a fork so that all of the skins are broken. Add the oil to the pan and let this cool to room temperature. Place the turkey in a 1 quart bowl and pour the marinade over. Mix thoroughly and let it marinate several hours, preferably overnight. When you are ready to serve, toss the lettuce, celery, onions, and marinade mixture in your 8 cup salad bowl.

- **MAKES 3 SERVINGS WITH ABOUT 592 CALORIES PER SERVING.**

NAPA CABBAGE SALAD
WITH BLUE CHEESE

QUAN.	INGREDIENT	CARB GRAMS	AVAIL. CARB	FAT	PROTEIN
2 c.	NAPA CABBAGE, torn to bite-sized pieces and tightly packed	3.0	1.6	0.3	2.1
4 T.	FRENCH DRESSING ROUGE (see page 38)	2.4	2.0	26.0	1.2
2 T.	SALAD ONIONS (see page 84)	1.8	1.4	0	0.2
2 oz.	BLUE CHEESE, crumbled	1.3	1.3	15.4	12.1
	TOTALS	8.5	6.3	41.7	15.6
	PER SERVING	8.5	6.3	41.7	15.6

- Place the cabbage in a 4 cup salad bowl. Stir in the onions and the dressing. Garnish with the blue cheese.

- **MAKES 1 SERVING WITH ABOUT 463 CALORIES PER SERVING.**

CUCUMBER SALAD

THIS is the simplest form of cucumber salad that you can make. To add a little spice, you can use cumin (perhaps ¼ teaspoon, more or less to your taste) or a small dollop of sour cream with each serving.

QUAN.	INGREDIENT	CARB GRAMS	AVAIL. CARB	FAT	PROTEIN
4 c.	**CUCUMBERS**, peeled, seeded, and sliced thinly	13.2	9.6	0.4	3.2
2 T.	**OLIVE OIL**	0	0	26.0	0
4 T.	**SALAD ONIONS** (see page 84)	3.6	2.8	0	0.4
1½ t.	**SALT**				
¼ t.	**BLACK PEPPER**				
1 t.	**GARLIC POWDER**	2.0	2.0	0	0.5
1 t.	**SUGAR EQUIVALENT SWEETENER**				
	WINE VINEGAR to your taste				
	TOTALS	18.8	14.4	26.4	4.1
	PER SERVING	4.7	3.6	6.6	1.0

- Place the cucumbers in a 6 cup salad bowl. Sprinkle 1 t. of the salt over the cucumbers and mix well. Let this sit at room temperature several hours to render the water from the cucumbers. Drain the water off, squeezing the cucumbers slightly to rid them of any excess water. Add the remaining ingredients and mix well. Let it sit at room temperature another hour. Taste to ensure that you have used enough vinegar. Refrigerate overnight if possible.

- **MAKES 4 SERVINGS WITH ABOUT 78 CALORIES PER SERVING.**

ROB'S ITALIAN SPINACH SALAD

ROB is a friend of mine who lived with an Italian family in his youth in the New Jersey area. He recently began a low carb diet on the advice of his physician, and this is one of the recipes that he brought to the table, so to speak. If you're in the mood for something different, you can use mozzarella cheese instead of the Gorgonzola, Genoa salami instead of the bacon, or even try sprinkling grated Parmesan cheese or some onion powder over the salad.

QUAN.	INGREDIENT	CARB GRAMS	AVAIL. CARB	FAT	PROTEIN
4 c.	FRESH SPINACH	4.2	1.0	0.3	3.4
6 T.	OLIVE OIL	0	0	78.0	0
2 T.	BACON BITS	0	0	3.0	6.0
2 oz.	GORGONZOLA CHEESE (you can use any blue cheese if you can't get Gorgonzola)	1.3	1.3	15.4	12.1
½ t.	SALT				
I t.	GARLIC POWDER	2.0	2.0	0	0.5
	BLACK PEPPER to taste				
	TOTALS	7.5	4.3	96.7	22.0
	PER SERVING	3.8	2.2	48.4	11.0

- Ensure that the spinach is well cleaned and dry. In a 6 cup salad bowl, stir the olive oil into the spinach until the spinach is well coated. Add the salt and garlic powder and continue mixing until it is evenly distributed. Serve with the cheese and the bacon bits on top as a garnish.

■ **MAKES 2 SERVINGS WITH ABOUT 488 CALORIES PER SERVING.**

TUNA SALAD BETTE

APPARENTLY, the Divine Miss M is known for eating lots of tuna salad, so much so that she gave out her ingredient list in an interview with a magazine. I think this approximates what she had in mind.

QUAN.	INGREDIENT	CARB GRAMS	AVAIL. CARB	FAT	PROTEIN
6 oz.	**TUNA, PACKED IN OIL** (one 6 ounce can)	0	0	15.0	32.5
2 T.	**DILL PICKLES**, diced	0.7	0.5	0	0.1
2 T.	**SWEET RELISH** (see page 85)	1.0	0.6	0.4	0.4
1	**LARGE EGG, HARD BOILED** and diced coarsely	0.7	0.7	4.8	7.2
½ c.	**CELERY**, diced	2.2	1.2	0	0.5
3 T.	**MAYONNAISE**	1.2	1.2	31.5	0.6
2 T.	**SALAD ONIONS** (see page 84)	1.8	1.4	0	0.2
½ t.	**SALT**				
¼ t.	**BLACK PEPPER**				
½ t.	**PICKLED JALAPEÑOS**, diced (very optional, more or less added to your taste)				
	TOTALS	6.6	4.4	51.7	51.4
	PER SERVING	6.6	4.4	51.7	51.4

- Drain most of the oil off of the tuna. Place all of the ingredients in a 1 quart bowl and mix well.

- **MAKES 1 SERVING WITH ABOUT 689 CALORIES PER SERVING.**

HAM SALAD

YOU can use this as a vegetable dip as well as place it on a salad. I've also made this with chicken and leftover turkey and it's very good.

QUAN.	INGREDIENT	CARB GRAMS	AVAIL. CARB	FAT	PROTEIN
½ lb.	HAM (2% fat)	4.0	4.0	4.0	40.0
2 T.	SWEET RELISH (see page 85)	1.0	0.6	0.4	0.4
2 T.	SALAD ONIONS (see page 84)	1.8	1.4	0	0.2
1 c.	CELERY, diced	4.4	2.4	0	0.9
3 T.	MAYONNAISE	1.2	1.2	31.5	0.6
1 t.	GARLIC POWDER	2.0	2.0	0	0.5
	TOTALS	14.4	11.6	35.9	42.6
	PER SERVING OF 1 T.	0.5	0.4	1.1	1.3

- Place first four ingredients in a food processor and grind until relatively smooth. Pour into a 4 cup bowl and mix in the remaining ingredients.

■ MAKES ABOUT 2 CUPS OR 32 SERVINGS WITH ABOUT 17 CALORIES PER SERVING.

FLAVORED VINEGARS ▶

Flavored vinegars are just another way to add a little excitement to your low carb diet. These vinegars also make great gifts to give your friends and coworkers.

In a covered 1 quart nonreactive pan, bring one cup of vinegar to a boil. Add 1 cup of fruit, stir, and bring to a boil again. Turn off the heat and let it cool to room temperature. Mash the fruit to ensure that as much of its surface area is exposed to the vinegar as possible. (Alternatively, you can use a blender or food processor to process the vinegar mixture.) Place the mixture in a very clean 1 pint container and let it set for a week or more. At the end of the week (or longer), strain the liquid from the solids and discard the solids. Pour the liquid into a pint jar and add white wine vinegar until the jar is full. A pint is equal to thirty-two 1 tablespoon servings. We must assume that all available carbs in the fruit are transferred into the vinegar solution. The carb counts are given below for various fruits. You should use this as you would plain vinegar. If you use any of these in a salad, you shouldn't have to dilute it with water. Another possibility is to add 4 tablespoons of sugar equivalent sweetener (more or less added to your taste) to each 16 ounces bottle of finished flavored vinegar.

STRAWBERRIES—7.2 total grams of available carbs or 0.2 grams carbs per tablespoon

BLACKBERRIES—10.8 total grams of available carbs or 0.3 grams carbs per tablespoon

BLUEBERRIES—16.6 total grams of available carbs or 0.5 grams carbs per tablespoon

CRANBERRIES—9.4 total grams of available carbs or 0.3 grams carbs per tablespoon

RASPBERRIES—5.8 total grams of available carbs or 0.2 grams carbs per tablespoon

SOUR CHERRIES (without pits)—16.4 total grams of available carbs or 0.5 grams carbs per tablespoon

RED OR WHITE CURRANTS (use the raw because the dried are loaded with carbs)—10.7 total grams of available carbs or 0.3 grams carbs per tablespoon

FOR BLUEBERRY–BASIL VINEGAR, thinly slice ¼–½ cup of fresh basil and follow the above procedure. After you strain the residue out, you can add additional basil leaves to the jar for decoration. There shouldn't be any carbs from the basil, so there will be about 16.6 total grams of available carbs or about 0.5 grams carbs per tablespoon.

FOR GINGER–APPLE VINEGAR, use 1 cup of apple cider vinegar instead of white wine vinegar, add 2 teaspoons of sugar substitute and ¼ cup of ginger, peeled and sliced thinly. Mix together in a pint container and let sit for a week or more before using. This must be counted as 0.2 grams of carbs per tablespoon even though it probably isn't that high.

SLAWS

AND SUCH

Several years ago when I was working in Delaware, I would usually take some kind of low carb slaw to work to use for potluck dinners. My boss, whose daughter was a working chef, told me that I made the best slaws that she had ever tasted. The secret is that slaws deserve as much care in their preparation as any other good meal. With all slaws, you should mix your dressing first, unless otherwise specified, and then test it to ensure that it tastes correct. If it isn't sweet enough or salty enough or it's too sour or not sour enough, this is the time to make the adjustment. After it has been mixed and it sets for a while, further adjustments can be made. Many folks have found slaws very convenient because they for provide a lot of variation in their low carb eating plan.

BASIC COLESLAW

IN preparing any slaw, always remember Cole's Law: For any mayonnaise-based salad dressing, it's more efficient to mix all of the water-soluble ingredients first and then add the oils before the dressing is mixed into the vegetables. This well-known cooking principle is named after Cole Robbie, the man who first put it into practice.

QUAN.	INGREDIENT	CARB GRAMS	AVAIL. CARB	FAT	PROTEIN
1 lb.	CABBAGE, shredded	24.5	14.1	0.9	6.4
4 T.	SALAD ONIONS (see page 84)	3.6	2.8	0	0.4
½ c.	GREEN PEPPERS, diced	4.8	3.0	0.1	0.7
2 T.	VINEGAR				
2 T.	SUGAR EQUIVALENT SWEETENER				
1½ t.	SALT				
¾ c.	MAYONNAISE	4.4	4.4	126.4	1.8
1 t.	DRY MUSTARD				
1 t.	GARLIC POWDER	2.0	2.0	0	0.5
	TOTALS	39.3	26.3	127.4	9.8
	PER SERVING	4.9	3.3	15.9	1.2

- Place the vegetables in a 6 cup salad bowl and toss. Mix everything else in a 2 cup bowl, first dissolving the sugar substitute completely in the vinegar, and pour over the vegetables. Toss and let sit at room temperature a for a few hours until the vegetables begin to wilt, stirring occasionally. Refrigerate. This is best if it is made one day prior to serving. It will keep several days in the refrigerator.

- **MAKES ABOUT 8 SERVINGS WITH ABOUT 161 CALORIES PER SERVING.**

EASTERN CAROLINA–STYLE SLAW

WHEN testing, sometimes I foist new recipes off on my family during family dinners. This is convenient for several reasons, but mainly I do it because there are several family members who are really particular about what they eat. Generally, if they are enthused about a recipe, then it is good. This slaw has become a real family favorite.

QUAN.	INGREDIENT	CARB GRAMS	AVAIL. CARB	FAT	PROTEIN
1 lb.	**CABBAGE**, shredded	24.5	14.1	0.9	6.4
½ c.	**GREEN ONIONS**, diced	3.7	2.4	0	0.9
1 c.	**MAYONNAISE**	5.9	5.9	168.5	2.4
2 T.	**VINEGAR**				
2 t.	**CELERY SALT**				
2 T.	**SUGAR EQUIVALENT SWEETENER**				
	TOTALS	34.1	22.4	169.4	9.7
	PER SERVING	4.9	3.2	24.2	1.4

■ Mix the cabbage and onion in a 6 cup salad bowl. In a separate 2 cup bowl, dissolve the sugar substitute completely in the vinegar. Mix in the celery salt and then the mayonnaise. In the 6 cup salad bowl, mix the dressing with the cabbage and onion. Refrigerate until ready to serve. Serve with Eastern Carolina Bar-B-Q (see page 122).

■ **MAKES 7 SERVINGS WITH ABOUT 236 CALORIES PER SERVING.**

CAJUN-STYLE SLAW

QUAN.	INGREDIENT	CARB GRAMS	AVAIL. CARB	FAT	PROTEIN
1 lb.	**CABBAGE, SHREDDED**	24.5	14.1	0.9	6.4
¼ c.	**GREEN PEPPER**, diced	2.4	1.7	0	0.3
4 T.	**SALAD ONIONS** (see page 84)	3.6	2.8	0	0.4
¼ c.	**SCALLIONS**, diced	1.9	1.2	0	0.5
½ c.	**CELERY**, diced	2.2	1.2	0	0.5
4 T.	**SWEET RELISH** (see page 85)	2.0	1.2	0.8	0.8
½ c.	**MAYONNAISE**	3.0	3.0	84.3	1.2
2 T.	**CREOLE MUSTARD** (or any coarse ground mustard)				
2 T.	**OLIVE OIL**	0	0	26.0	0
2 T.	**LEMON JUICE**	2.6	2.5	0	0.1
1 T.	**RED CAYENNE SAUCE** (more or less added to your taste)				
1 t.	**SALT**				
1 T.	**SUGAR EQUIVALENT SWEETENER**				
1 t.	**GARLIC POWDER**	2.0	2.0	0	0.5
1 t.	**PAPRIKA**	1.3	0.8	0.5	0.7
	TOTALS	45.5	30.5	112.5	11.4
	PER SERVING	7.6	5.1	18.8	1.9

- In a 2 cup bowl, mix the mayonnaise, mustard, olive oil, lemon juice, cayenne sauce, salt, pepper, garlic powder, and sugar substitute together for the slaw dressing. Put the remaining ingredients in a 6 cup salad bowl and pour the dressing over them, stirring well. Refrigerate. Stir well before serving.

- **MAKES 6 SERVINGS WITH ABOUT 197 CALORIES PER SERVING.**

SOUTHERN TENNESSEE–STYLE MUSTARD SLAW

THIS slaw is a variant of a dish called Pool Room Slaw in the south-central Tennessee area. Typically it is served with dill pickles on sandwiches, hamburgers, and hot dogs, but we can use it as a side dish. Don't forget the dill pickles.

QUAN.	INGREDIENT	CARB GRAMS	AVAIL. CARB	FAT	PROTEIN
3 c.	GREEN CABBAGE, grated and packed relatively tightly	14.4	8.4	0.6	3.9
5 T.	PREPARED SALAD MUSTARD (use a good mustard and not the "economy" kind)	6.1	2.3	2.4	3.1
2 T.	SUGAR EQUIVALENT SWEETENER				
1 t.	ONION POWDER	1.7	1.6	0	0.2
⅔ c.	DILL PICKLE JUICE				
	- or -				
9 T.	WATER				
3 T.	WHITE VINEGAR				
½ t.	SALT				
	TOTALS	22.2	12.3	3.0	7.2
	PER SERVING OF ¼ C. OR 4 T.	2.8	1.5	0.4	0.9

- Place the dill pickle juice in a 1 quart saucepan. If you don't have dill pickle juice, use the water, salt, and vinegar mixture above in its place. Add the sugar substitute and onion powder to the liquid and bring it to a boil. Add the cabbage and bring to a boil again, stirring every minute or so for 3–4 minutes. The cabbage should wilt. Add the mustard, stir well, and remove from the heat. When it has cooled to room temperature, pour it into a pint jar or freezer container and refrigerate several hours before serving, preferably overnight. It can be frozen and thawed as necessary, but do not freeze it in glass. You can add some cayenne sauce (to taste) if you like. This will keep unfrozen for several weeks.

- **MAKES 8 SERVINGS WITH ABOUT 13 CALORIES PER SERVING.**

KENTUCKY COLONEL–STYLE SLAW

QUAN.	INGREDIENT	CARB GRAMS	AVAIL. CARB	FAT	PROTEIN
1 lb.	**CABBAGE,** shredded	24.5	14.1	0.9	6.4
4 T.	**VINEGAR** (more or less added to your taste)				
3 T.	**WATER**				
8 t.	**SUGAR EQUIVALENT SWEETENER**				
½ c.	**MAYONNAISE**	3.0	3.0	84.3	1.2
2 T.	**HEAVY WHIPPING CREAM**	1.2	1.2	10.4	0.6
2 t.	**ONION POWDER**	3.4	3.2	0	0.4
½ t.	**DRY MUSTARD**	0.6	0.4	0.5	0.4
1 t.	**SALT**				
	TOTALS	32.7	21.9	96.1	9.0
	PER SERVING	6.5	4.4	19.2	1.8

- Place the cabbage in a 6 cup salad bowl and set aside. In a 2 cup bowl, dissolve the sugar substitute completely in the vinegar and water. Add the dry ingredients and mix. Finally, mix in the mayonnaise and cream, pour over the cabbage, and mix well. Refrigerate an hour before serving, if possible.

- **MAKES ABOUT 5 SERVINGS WITH ABOUT 198 CALORIES PER SERVING.**

BAR-B-Q SLAW

THIS type of slaw is traditionally served with barbecue in northern Alabama and southern Tennessee. Chef Emeril Lagasse makes a slaw similar to this, but his is much hotter because he adds a small amount of red or green bell pepper and a tablespoon (more or less added to your taste) of finely diced pickled jalapeño peppers. Feel free to try it yourself.

QUAN.	INGREDIENT	CARB GRAMS	AVAIL. CARB	FAT	PROTEIN
2 c.	**CABBAGE**, shredded	9.6	5.6	0.4	2.6
2 t.	**ONION POWDER**	3.4	3.2	0	0.4
4 T.	**WATER**				
4 T.	**CIDER VINEGAR**				
1 t.	**SALT**				
5 T.	**SUGAR EQUIVALENT SWEETENER**				
	TOTALS	13.0	8.8	0.4	3.0
	PER SERVING OF 2 T.	0.8	0.6	0	0.2

- In a 1 quart saucepan, bring all ingredients except the cabbage to a boil and remove them from heat. Add the cabbage, stir, and let cool. Spoon it into a pint bowl or jar. This will keep for a couple of weeks in the refrigerator. It is ready to serve in a couple of hours and it freezes very well.

- **MAKES ABOUT 16 SERVINGS WITH ABOUT 3 CALORIES PER SERVING.**

GERMAN SLAW

ON a visit to my niece one day, she decided that she wanted to go to a German restaurant for supper. I am always eager to eat German food because I lived in Germany for a while and actually worked in a pub in Darmstadt. We had a slaw very similar to this with our meal that evening. She asked me if I could come up with a recipe for her and this is it.

QUAN.	INGREDIENT	CARB GRAMS	AVAIL. CARB	FAT	PROTEIN
1 lb.	CHOPPED CABBAGE	24.5	14.1	0.9	6.4
1 c.	DICED BELL PEPPER	9.6	6.9	0.2	1.3
½ c.	DICED ONION	6.9	5.5	0	1.0
1 T.	SUGAR EQUIVALENT SWEETENER				
½ c.	OLIVE OIL	0	0	103.3	0
3 T.	WATER				
5 T.	WINE VINEGAR				
1 t.	CELERY SALT				
½ t.	SALT				
½ t.	GROUND MUSTARD SEED				
½ t.	BLACK PEPPER				
2 t.	GARLIC POWDER	4.0	4.0	0	1.0
	TOTALS	45.0	30.5	104.4	9.7
	PER SERVING	7.5	5.1	17.4	1.6

- Mix the cabbage and bell pepper in a heatproof 6 cup salad bowl. In a 1 quart saucepan, mix all of the dry ingredients with the onion, water, and vinegar. Add the oil and bring it to a boil. Pour over the cabbage and stir immediately until it becomes warm. This will only take a minute or two because the temperature of the hot liquid dissipates quickly. Let it cool to room temperature, stirring occasionally. Cover and refrigerate several hours, preferably overnight, before serving.

- **MAKES 6 SERVINGS WITH ABOUT 183 CALORIES PER SERVING.**

HORSERADISH SLAW

IN some of my cooking experiments, I froze fresh cabbage and then thawed it again to make one dish or another. One of the things I discovered is that freezing cabbage produces a slightly bitter flavor that is useful in some recipes. The horseradish in this slaw brings out the natural bitterness of the cabbage.

QUAN.	INGREDIENT	CARB GRAMS	AVAIL. CARB	FAT	PROTEIN
1 lb.	**CHOPPED CABBAGE**	24.5	14.1	0.9	6.4
½ c.	**GREEN PEPPERS**, diced	4.8	3.5	0.1	0.7
½ c.	**SNOW PEAS**, blanched in hot water and then diced coarsely	3.7	2.0	0.1	1.4
4 T.	**SALAD ONIONS** (see page 84)	3.6	2.8	0	0.4
½ c.	**MAYONNAISE**	3.0	3.0	84.3	1.2
4 T.	**SOUR CREAM**	2.0	2.0	9.5	1.5
2 T.	**WHITE VINEGAR**				
1 t.	**DIJON MUSTARD**				
4 t.	**BOTTLED HORSERADISH** (more or less to your taste, added gradually)				
1 T.	**SUGAR EQUIVALENT SWEETENER**				
1 t.	**SALT**				
½ t.	**RED CAYENNE SAUCE** (optional, more or less added to your taste)				
	TOTALS	41.6	27.4	94.9	11.6
	PER SERVING	5.2	3.4	11.9	1.5

- In a 2 cup bowl, dissolve the sugar substitute completely in the vinegar. Add the salt, mustard, onions, cayenne sauce (if used), and horseradish and mix well. Stir in the mayonnaise and then the sour cream. Taste the dressing and adjust the seasoning as needed. Place all of the vegetables in a 6 cup salad bowl and mix. Pour the dressing over the vegetables and toss well. Let this sit at least an hour before serving. Refrigerating overnight is best.

- **MAKES 8 SERVINGS WITH ABOUT 127 CALORIES PER SERVING.**

MORAVIAN-STYLE SLAW

I'VE eaten this kind of slaw for years but didn't know until very recently that it had a real name. This slaw is very colorful and has highly contrasting sweet and sour flavors. Keep in mind that this slaw should ideally be made the day before it is to be eaten because we are, effectively, pickling the vegetables.

QUAN.	INGREDIENT	CARB GRAMS	AVAIL. CARB	FAT	PROTEIN
1 lb.	**CABBAGE**, shredded	24.5	14.1	0.9	6.4
½ c.	**ONION**, diced	6.9	5.5	0	1.0
½ c.	**GREEN PEPPERS**, diced	4.8	3.5	0.1	0.7
2¼ oz.	**CANNED PIMIENTOS**	3.0	3.0	0	1.0
4 T.	**SWEET RELISH** (see page 85)	2.0	1.2	0.8	0.8
½ c.	**WATER**				
½ c.	**WHITE VINEGAR**				
½ c.	**SUGAR EQUIVALENT SWEETENER**				
2 t.	**SALT**				
	TOTALS	41.2	27.3	1.8	9.9
	PER SERVING	5.9	3.9	0.3	1.4

- Mix the cabbage, bell peppers, relish, and pimientos in a heatproof 6 cup salad bowl. Bring the water, salt, and sugar substitute to a boil in a 1 quart saucepan. Add in the vinegar and then the onions. Remove from the heat and pour it over the cabbage mixture. Stir well until the heat dissipates—a couple of minutes. Let this cool to room temperature, stirring occasionally, and refrigerate overnight.

- **MAKES 7 SERVINGS WITH ABOUT 24 CALORIES PER SERVING.**

CHOW CHOW

I first heard Chow Chow mentioned on a TV show many years ago, but didn't know what it was. When I was researching my first cookbook back in 1996, I discovered that it's really just pickled vegetables, so I bought a jar and created this low carb version of it.

QUAN.	INGREDIENT	CARB GRAMS	AVAIL. CARB	FAT	PROTEIN
1 lb.	**CABBAGE**, shredded	24.5	14.1	0.9	6.4
½ c.	**ONION**, sliced thinly	5.0	3.9	0	0.7
½ c.	**GREEN PEPPERS**, diced	4.8	3.5	0.1	0.7
4 T.	**TOMATO SAUCE**	4.4	3.6	0.1	0.9
½ t.	**RED PEPPER FLAKES** (more or less added to your taste)				
½ c.	**WATER**				
¾ c.	**WHITE VINEGAR**				
1 t.	**MUSTARD SEED**				
1 t.	**CELERY SEED**				
1 t.	**GARLIC POWDER**	2.0	2.0	0	0.5
2 t.	**SALT**				
6 T.	**SUGAR EQUIVALENT SWEETENER**				
	TOTALS	40.7	27.1	1.1	9.2
	PER SERVING OF 2 T.	1.3	0.8	0.1	0.3

- Bring all ingredients to a boil in a 2 quart saucepan, stirring occasionally, then remove from heat. Let cool to room temperature and pack in a quart jar. This will keep refrigerated several weeks and will freeze indefinitely.

■ **MAKES ABOUT 1 QUART OR 32 SERVINGS WITH ABOUT 5 CALORIES PER SERVING.**

SALAD ONIONS

THIS is a quick way to make the pickled onions that folks like so much. Salad Onions are one of the basic ingredients you will need in order to make many of the dishes in this book. The pickling process gets rid of a lot of the bitterness in the onions, which makes salads much more enjoyable because the onions become so mild and sweet. I realize that some of you won't make the Salad Onions no matter how easy the task. If you want, you can substitute onion powder for the Salad Onions in the recipes; 2 tablespoons of Salad Onions is about equal to 1 teaspoon of onion powder in terms of the macronutrient values. If you do decide to make this substitution, keep in mind that the food texture will be affected.

QUAN.	INGREDIENT	CARB GRAMS	AVAIL. CARB	FAT	PROTEIN
2 c.	**ONIONS**, diced	27.6	22.4	0.4	3.8
2 t.	**SALT**				
¾ c.	**WATER**				
4 T.	**WHITE VINEGAR**				
1 T.	**SUGAR EQUIVALENT SWEETENER**				
	TOTALS	27.6	22.4	0.4	3.8
	PER SERVING OF 1 T.	0.9	0.7	0	0.1

- Pack the onions tightly in a pint jar. Add the dry ingredients, half the water, all of the vinegar, and then the remaining water. Heat in a microwave on high for about 2 minutes. The jar should be very hot to touch but not boiling. Let it cool to room temperature and cover with a tight lid. Shake well once every hour for a couple of hours. Refrigerate overnight. This is ready to serve the next day.

- **MAKES 32 SERVINGS WITH ABOUT 3 CALORIES PER SERVING.**

SWEET RELISH

THIS is one of the basics that you should make because it is used in several other recipes. This doesn't look like regular sweet relish with sugar, but it makes a good substitute in things like Thousand Island dressing and egg salad.

QUAN.	INGREDIENT	CARB GRAMS	AVAIL. CARB	FAT	PROTEIN
2 c.	**CUCUMBER**, seeded and diced	6.6	4.8	0.2	1.6
1 T.	**MUSTARD SEED**	7.8	4.7	6.0	5.6
2 t.	**SALT**				
⅔ c.	**WATER**				
⅓ c.	**WHITE VINEGAR**				
3 T.	**SUGAR EQUIVALENT SWEETENER**				
	TOTALS	14.4	9.5	6.2	7.2
	PER SERVING OF 1 T.	0.5	0.3	0.2	0.2

- In a 1 quart bowl, mix the cucumbers and dry ingredients together thoroughly. Pack the cucumbers tightly into a pint jar. Add the water and the vinegar. Heat in a microwave on high for about 2 minutes. The jar should be very hot to touch but not boiling. Let it cool to room temperature and then cover with a tight lid. Shake well once every hour for a couple of hours. Refrigerate overnight. This is ready to use the next day. Realistically, you don't get many carbs from the mustard seed, but since there are always some remaining in the jar, we have to count them all.

- **MAKES 32 SERVINGS WITH ABOUT 4 CALORIES PER SERVING.**

BEEF

ENTRÉES

CORNED BEEF AND CABBAGE

THIS dish is traditionally served with potatoes, but we don't need them. I try to make this at least twice each year other than St. Patrick's Day. This can be served as a soup, one cup at a time. Note that we don't get all of the fat calories because we remove some of it from the meat, but it must, nonetheless, be counted.

QUAN.	INGREDIENT	CARB GRAMS	AVAIL. CARB	FAT	PROTEIN
4 lb.	**UNCOOKED CORNED BEEF BRISKET**	2.5	2.5	225.7	266.4
3 lb.	**CABBAGE,** the stem removed from each head and cut into 8ths	73.5	42.3	2.7	19.2
½ c.	**CARROTS,** diced	5.6	4.0	0	0.5
I c.	**CELERY,** diced	4.4	2.4	0	0.9
I c.	**ONION,** diced	13.8	11.2	0.2	1.9
I T.	**DRIED PARSLEY**				
I T.	**GARLIC POWDER**	6.1	6.1	0	1.4
I t.	**BLACK PEPPER**				
2 t.	**SUGAR EQUIVALENT SWEETENER**				
I c.	**DRY WHITE WINE**	1.6	1.6	0	0
	ENOUGH WATER TO MAKE 3 QUARTS				
	TOTALS	107.5	70.1	228.6	290.3
	PER SERVING OF I C.	9.0	5.8	19.1	24.2

- Remove the large layer of fat from the corned beef, but don't throw it away. Place the corned beef and the fat in two quarts of water in a large soup pot, cover, and bring to a boil. Reduce the heat to medium low and let it simmer two hours. Remove the meat and fat from the pot and add everything else to the stock. Again, cover and bring to a boil, then reduce the heat and simmer. Throw the piece of fat away. When the corned beef cools, cut it into bite-sized pieces and return it to the soup. Simmer for at least one more hour.

- **MAKES ABOUT 12 SERVINGS WITH ABOUT 292 CALORIES PER SERVING.**

PHILLY CHEESE STEAK

WHEN I lived in the Philadelphia area, I came to appreciate a good Philly cheese steak sandwich. In some of the better cheese steak places in the Philly area, they use shaved rib eye meat. One of the secrets to a great sandwich is to cook each of the vegetables separately until they are caramelized or browned. This is good alternative to the real thing, given that we can't have the associated bread. A salad with Italian dressing goes well with this.

QUAN.	INGREDIENT	CARB GRAMS	AVAIL. CARB	FAT	PROTEIN
12 oz.	**THINLY SLICED DELI ROAST BEEF**, coarse julienned	0	0	18.2	85.4
½ c.	**ONION**, sliced thinly	5.0	3.9	0	0.7
4 T.	**OLIVE OIL**	0	0	52.0	0
1 t.	**GARLIC POWDER**	2.0	2.0	0	0.5
2 T.	**DRY RED WINE** (you can use water if you don't have any wine available)	0.5	0.5	0	0.1
6 oz.	**PROVOLONE CHEESE**	3.6	3.6	42.9	43.5
1	**BEEF BOUILLON CUBE**				
	BELL PEPPER (optional)				
	MUSHROOMS (optional)				
	HOT PEPPERS (optional)				
	TOTALS	11.1	10.0	113.1	130.2
	PER SERVING	3.7	3.3	37.7	43.4

■ Heat a 10-inch nonstick skillet over medium high heat. Add 2 T. oil and the beef and cook it until the meat is cooking well (in other words, you want to do more than just heat it up). Remove the meat to a plate. In the same skillet over medium heat, add the remaining oil and the onion. You are going to cook the onions until they begin to brown. It is at this point that you add the optional ingredients if you choose and begin to cook them. When they are properly wilted, add the beef back into the skillet along with the wine, the garlic powder, and the bouillon cube. Stir, and bring to a boil. Let simmer covered about 5 minutes. Add the cheese, cover, and let simmer an additional 2 minutes. Stir again, cover, and let simmer still another 2 minutes. If you add any of the optional ingredients, do not forget to account for the increase in carbs.

MAKES 3 SERVINGS WITH ABOUT 526 CALORIES PER SERVING.

ONE-SKILLET *CHILI RELLENOS*

ONE way I decide if I like a Mexican restaurant is by testing their *chili rellenos*. This recipe is patterned after the *chili rellenos* I used to get at one of my favorite Mexican restaurants that unfortunately closed down a few years ago. You can use any kinds of peppers you want so you can provide as much spice to this as you desire.

QUAN.	INGREDIENT	CARB GRAMS	AVAIL. CARB	FAT	PROTEIN
1 lb.	HAMBURGER (77% lean)	0	0	92.4	77.2
½ c.	ONION, sliced thinly	5.0	3.9	0	0.7
2 c.	GREEN PEPPERS, sliced coarsely	19.2	13.8	0.4	2.6
4 T.	WATER				
1	BEEF BOUILLON CUBE				
1 T.	CHILI POWDER	4.1	1.5	1.0	0.9
2 t.	GARLIC POWDER	4.0	4.0	0	1.0
3½ oz.	AMERICAN CHEESE	1.6	1.6	29.6	22.1
3 oz.	MOZZARELLA CHEESE	2.4	2.4	12.8	20.6
	TOTALS	36.3	27.2	136.2	125.1
	PER SERVING	12.1	9.1	45.2	41.7

- In a 10 inch skillet, brown the hamburger and onion over medium high heat. Add the water, the bouillon cube, the chili powder, and the garlic powder, bring to a boil, reduce the heat to medium, and simmer 5 minutes. Stir in the peppers, cover, and simmer again about 5 minutes. Stir, add the cheese, and simmer another 5 minutes. The object is to get the peppers just to the point where they are starting to wilt a little.

- **MAKES 3 SERVINGS WITH ABOUT 610 CALORIES PER SERVING.**

CARNE ASADA

I don't know about you, but Mexican food is one of my favorite cuisines. Here's another dish designed to please your Mexican palate. This can be served with a salad with Guacamole Dressing (see page 224).

QUAN.	INGREDIENT	CARB GRAMS	AVAIL. CARB	FAT	PROTEIN
1 lb.	**CHUCK ROAST** cut into ¼ inch slices	0	0	28.8	87.3
1 t.	**SALT**				
½ t.	**BLACK PEPPER**				
3 T.	**OLIVE OIL**	0	0	39.0	0
¼ c.	**ONION**, diced	3.0	2.8	0	0.5
2 T.	**LIME JUICE**	2.8	2.7	0	0.1
1 t.	**GARLIC POWDER**	2.0	2.0	0	0.5
2 t.	**CHILI POWDER**	2.7	1.0	0.7	0.6
	SALAD ONIONS (see page 84) for serving				
	DICED TOMATOES for serving				
	PICKLED JALAPEÑO PEPPERS for serving				
	GUACAMOLE (see page 244) for serving				
	SALSA (see page 245) for serving				
	TOTALS	10.5	8.5	68.5	89.0
	PER SERVING	5.3	4.3	34.3	44.5

■ Mix everything except the oil in a bowl and let it marinate at least and hour, overnight if possible. To cook, heat the oil in a 10 inch skillet over medium high heat. Coat the skillet well with the oil. Add the marinated beef and extra marinade to the oil and cook to the desired doneness.

■ **MAKES 2 SERVINGS WITH ABOUT 504 CALORIES PER SERVING.**

POLISH-STYLE BEEF

QUAN.	INGREDIENT	CARB GRAMS	AVAIL. CARB	FAT	PROTEIN
2 lb.	**STEW BEEF** or **CHUCK ROAST** cut into ½ inch cubes	0	0	57.6	174.6
½ c.	**ONION,** diced	6.9	5.5	0	1.0
2 T.	**OLIVE OIL**	0	0	26.0	0
½ t.	**BLACK PEPPER**				
1	**BAY LEAF**				
2 c.	**CANNED BEEF STOCK** (1 can of 14.5 ounces is sufficient)				
2	**BEEF BOUILLON CUBES**				
2 t.	**GARLIC POWDER**	4.0	4.0	0	1.0
2 oz.	**DILL PICKLE,** diced				
1 c.	**SOUR CREAM**	9.8	9.8	45.7	7.3
	TOTALS	20.7	19.3	129.3	183.9
	PER SERVING	5.2	4.8	32.3	46.0

- In a 3 quart skillet or soup pot, cook the meat in the oil over medium high heat until it begins to brown. Add the onions and continue cooking until they become clear. Add the remaining ingredients except for the sour cream. Cover and bring to a boil. Reduce the heat to medium low and simmer for about 1 hour, stirring every 15 minutes, until the meat is very tender. Remove from the heat, remove the bay leaf, and stir in the sour cream. Serve with the sauce.

- **MAKES 4 SERVINGS WITH ABOUT 494 CALORIES PER SERVING.**

BARBECUED BEEF SHORT RIBS

SEVERAL years ago in a commentary on National Public Radio, I heard an Atlanta attorney say that for some folks, the notion of "beef barbecue" is an oxymoron while for others, most of whom live west of the Mississippi River, it's a redundancy. No matter where you live, these are the basic beef ribs for your potluck or party.

QUAN.	INGREDIENT	CARB GRAMS	AVAIL. CARB	FAT	PROTEIN
3 slices	BACON, diced	0	0	61.9	9.9
3 lb.	BEEF SHORT RIBS	0	0	455.5	196.0
¼ c.	ONION, diced	3.5	2.8	0	0.5
¼ c.	GREEN PEPPERS, diced	2.4	1.7	0.1	0.3
2 c.	KETCHUP (see page 234)	30.0	24.7	1.3	6.1
1	BEEF BOUILLON CUBE				
2 t.	CELERY SEED				
4 T.	SUGAR EQUIVALENT SWEETENER				
4 T.	WHITE VINEGAR				
½ t.	LEMON EXTRACT				
1 T.	DRY MUSTARD	3.6	2.1	2.7	2.4
2 t.	GARLIC POWDER	4.0	4.0	0	1.0
2 c.	CANNED BEEF STOCK (one 14½ oz. can is sufficient)				
	TOTALS	43.5	35.3	521.5	216.2
	PER SERVING	7.3	5.9	86.9	36.0

■ Cook the bacon over medium heat in a 3 quart (or larger) soup pot until it is well browned and crispy. Remove the bacon pieces and put them aside. Then brown the ribs in the bacon fat. Mix the remaining ingredients together and pour it over the ribs. Cover, bring to a boil, reduce the heat to medium low, and simmer, covered, for 2 hours, stirring every half hour. By this time the meat should be falling off the bone. If the sauce is too thin, continue simmering with the lid off until it thickens to your satisfaction.

■ **MAKES 6 SERVINGS WITH ABOUT 949 CALORIES PER SERVING.**

NOTE that this calorie count is very high but you probably won't consume all of the fat from the ribs.

BOEF À LA STROGANOFF

I consider this is my fancy version of beef stroganoff because I use filet mignon. Simpler versions can also be made with ground beef or deli-sliced precooked beef.

QUAN.	INGREDIENT	CARB GRAMS	AVAIL. CARB	FAT	PROTEIN
2 lb.	**FILET MIGNON**, diced in ½ inch cubes	0	0	170.2	163.6
½ c.	**ONION**, diced	6.9	5.5	0	1.0
4 T.	**OLIVE OIL**	0	0	52.0	0
½ c.	**DRY WHITE WINE**	0.8	0.8	0	0
4 T.	**TOMATO SAUCE**	4.4	3.6	0.2	0.8
2 T.	**DIJON MUSTARD**				
2	**BEEF BOUILLON CUBES**				
2 c.	**BUTTON MUSHROOMS**, diced	6.5	4.8	0.3	2.9
1 c.	**SOUR CREAM**	9.8	9.8	45.7	7.3
½ t.	**FRESH GROUND BLACK PEPPER**				
	TOTALS	28.4	24.5	268.4	175.6
	PER SERVING	7.1	6.1	67.1	43.9

- Heat 2 T. oil over medium high heat in a 3 quart skillet or soup pot. Add the meat and pepper and cook to the desired doneness. Remove the meat to a plate and put aside. Add the remaining oil, onions, and mushrooms to the skillet and cook until the mushrooms are tender. Remove the onions and mushrooms. Over medium high heat, deglaze the pan with the wine, scraping the pan. Return the meat, onions, and mushrooms to the pan. Add the bouillon cubes, mustard, and tomato sauce and simmer, uncovered, about 5 minutes. Add the sour cream, remove from the heat and stir.

- **MAKES 4 SERVINGS WITH ABOUT 804 CALORIES PER SERVING.**

BUL-GO-GEE

A few years before the 1988 Olympic Games in Seoul, I decided that Americans needed a Korean cookbook designed for American tastes. I had been eating Korean food for several years and there were no Korean cookbooks available in English at that time. This is one of the recipes from that unpublished cookbook, modified for low carbers. Bul-Go-Gee is Korean barbecued beef and is one of the staples used in Korean restaurants. Serve this with a little Yaki Mandu Sauce (see page 243) for dipping.

QUAN.	INGREDIENT	CARB GRAMS	AVAIL. CARB	FAT	PROTEIN
1 lb.	CHUCK ROAST cut into ¼ inch thick slices	0	0	28.8	87.3
2 t.	GARLIC POWDER	4.0	4.0	0	1.0
½ c.	GREEN ONIONS, diced	3.7	2.4	0	0.9
2 T.	SUGAR EQUIVALENT SWEETENER				
4 T.	SOY SAUCE	2.0	2.0	0	8.0
1 T.	SESAME SEEDS				
½ t.	BLACK PEPPER				
½ t.	DRIED RED PEPPERS (more or less added to your taste)				
2 T.	SESAME OIL	0	0	52.0	0
1 t.	DRIED GINGER				
	TOTALS	9.7	8.4	80.8	97.2
	PER SERVING	4.9	4.2	40.4	48.6

- Julienne the scallions and then dice them. In a 4 cup bowl, mix all ingredients together, adding the oil in last. Let this sit 1 hour, mixing every 15 minutes. Refrigerate overnight, if possible. You can fry or broil the beef, but it tastes best when cooked on a charcoal grill covered with aluminum foil with holes punched in it. If you decide to fry or broil, do so with a small, sliced onion.

- **MAKES 4 SERVINGS WITH ABOUT 575 CALORIES PER SERVING.**

ITALIAN BEEF

THIS dish is great because it provides us another opportunity for a taste of Italy without the heavy carbs. It goes well with a salad with Italian-style dressing and a little dry red wine.

QUAN.	INGREDIENT	CARB GRAMS	AVAIL. CARB	FAT	PROTEIN
2 lb.	**STEW BEEF** or **CHUCK ROAST** cut into ½ inch cubes	0	0	57.6	174.6
4 T.	**OLIVE OIL**	0	0	52.0	0
½ c.	**DRY RED WINE**	2.0	2.0	0	0.4
4 T.	**TOMATO SAUCE**	4.4	3.6	0.1	0.9
2 c.	**BUTTON MUSHROOMS**, diced	6.5	4.8	0.3	2.9
½ c.	**GREEN PEPPERS**, diced	4.8	3.5	0.1	0.7
½ c.	**ONION**, diced	6.9	5.5	0	1.0
2 T.	**WINE VINEGAR**				
2 t.	**ITALIAN SEASONING**	2.0	1.0	0	0
2	**BEEF BOUILLON CUBES**				
1	**BAY LEAF**				
1 T.	**GARLIC POWDER**	6.1	6.1	0	1.4
2 t.	**SUGAR EQUIVALENT SWEETENER**				
½ c.	**WATER**				
	RED CAYENNE SAUCE (optional to taste)				
	TOTALS	32.7	26.5	110.1	181.9
	PER SERVING	8.2	6.6	27.5	45.5

- In a 3 quart skillet or soup pot, brown the meat in the 2 T. oil over medium high heat. Remove the meat. Add the remaining oil and cook the mushrooms, bell peppers, and onions until the mushrooms are tender. Add all other ingredients. Cover and bring to a boil. Reduce heat to medium low and simmer about an hour. Remove from heat and remove the bay leaf. Serve with the extra sauce from the pot.

- **MAKES 4 SERVINGS WITH ABOUT 456 CALORIES PER SERVING.**

ITALIAN BEEF COVELLI

QUAN.	INGREDIENT	CARB GRAMS	AVAIL. CARB	FAT	PROTEIN
2 lb.	**STEW BEEF** or **CHUCK ROAST** cut into ½ inch cubes	0	0	57.6	174.6
½ c.	**DRY RED WINE**	2.0	2.0	0	0.4
½ c.	**ONION**, diced	6.9	5.5	0	1.0
2 c.	**BEEF STOCK** (one 15 ounce can is sufficient)				
2 t.	**ITALIAN SEASONING**	2.0	1.0	0	0
2	**BEEF BOUILLON CUBES**				
1	**BAY LEAF**				
1 T.	**GARLIC POWDER**	6.1	6.1	0	1.4
1 t.	**SUGAR EQUIVALENT SWEETENER**				
	TOTALS	17.0	14.6	57.6	177.4
	PER SERVING	4.3	3.7	14.4	44.4

- In a 2 quart saucepan, place the beef, onions, seasonings, bouillon cubes, and liquids. Cover the pan and bring it to a boil over high heat. Reduce the heat to medium low and simmer about an hour, stirring every 15 minutes. Remove from the heat and remove the bay leaf. Let it set at least 10 minutes before serving. Serve *au jus*.

- **MAKES 4 SERVINGS WITH ABOUT 322 CALORIES PER SERVING.**

BAR-B-Q BRISKET

BRISKET is the cut of meat that's used in the Kansas City–style barbecue cookoffs. It's used because it has a lot of fat in it and this helps to create smoke. This particular variation is cooked in the oven. Don't forget to serve a lot of Basic Bar-B-Q Sauce for dipping.

QUAN.	INGREDIENT	CARB GRAMS	AVAIL. CARB	FAT	PROTEIN
4 lb.	Beef brisket	0	0	262.2	346.6
1 c.	Onion, diced	13.8	11.0	0	2.0
2 c.	Basic Bar-B-Q Sauce (see page 236)	33.3	29.0	20.0	10.6
2 t.	Garlic powder	4.0	4.0	0	1.0
1 t.	Salt				
½ t.	Black pepper				
½ c.	Water				
	TOTALS	51.1	44.0	282.2	360.2
	PER SERVING	6.4	5.5	35.3	45.0

- Preheat the oven to 400° F. Trim the visible fat off the brisket. Rub the salt, pepper, and garlic onto the brisket. Place the onion in the bottom of a baking pan. Add the water. Place the brisket on top of the onion. Pour the Bar-B-Q Sauce evenly over the brisket. Bake at 400° F for 30 minutes. Reduce heat to 325° F and bake an additional 4 hours.

- **MAKES ABOUT 8 SERVINGS WITH ABOUT 520 CALORIES PER SERVING.**

TEXAS BRISKET

THIS kind of Texas brisket is a little spicier and takes a little more time than regular barbecued brisket. Serve this with some of the cooking sauce and Bar-B-Q Slaw (see page 79).

QUAN.	INGREDIENT	CARB GRAMS	AVAIL. CARB	FAT	PROTEIN
4 lb.	BEEF BRISKET	0	0	262.2	346.6
I c.	CELERY, diced	4.4	2.4	0	0.9
I c.	ONION, diced	13.8	11.0	0	2.0
2 c.	CHILI SAUCE (see page 235)	35.7	26.9	28.3	6.3
I c.	GREEN PEPPERS, diced	9.6	6.9	0.2	1.3
2 T.	SLICED, PICKLED JALAPEÑO PEPPERS (more or less added to your taste)				
2 t.	SALT				
3 T	SUGAR EQUIVALENT SWEETENER				
2 T.	LIQUID SMOKE				
½ t.	ALLSPICE				
½ t.	5 SPICE POWDER				
2 T.	PAPRIKA	7.6	4.8	1.6	2.0
2 T.	GARLIC POWDER	12.2	12.2	0	2.8
4 T.	CIDER VINEGAR				
	TOTALS	83.3	64.2	292.3	361.0
	PER SERVING	10.4	8.0	36.5	45.1

- Trim the visible fat off the brisket. Mix the salt, sugar substitute, liquid smoke, allspice, five spice powder, paprika, garlic powder, and vinegar into a paste. Rub this onto the brisket and let it set for at least two hours.

Put the celery, onion, about one half of the peppers and one cup of Chili Sauce (see page 235) in your roasting pan and stir. Place the brisket in the pan and pour the remaining Chili Sauce and peppers over it. Bake at 350° F for an hour, reduce the heat to 225° F and cook another six to eight hours or until the meat is tender.

- **MAKES ABOUT 8 SERVINGS WITH ABOUT 541 CALORIES PER SERVING.**

POT ROAST

I like to prepare pot roast at least once a month. It's simple and the leftovers can be used in salads or in other places where beef is called for.

QUAN.	INGREDIENT	CARB GRAMS	AVAIL. CARB	FAT	PROTEIN
3 lb.	CHUCK ROAST	0	0	86.4	261.9
2 T.	OLIVE OIL	0	0	52.0	0
½ c.	CARROTS, diced	5.6	4.0	0	0.5
1 c.	CELERY, diced	4.4	2.4	0	0.9
½ c.	ONION, diced	6.9	5.5	0	1.0
2 t.	DRIED PARSLEY				
2 t.	GARLIC POWDER	4.0	4.0	0	1.0
1	BAY LEAF				
2 t.	SALT				
½ t.	BLACK PEPPER				
½ c.	DRY RED WINE	2.0	2.0	0	0.4
½ t.	THYME				
¼ t.	NUTMEG				
2	CLOVES				
2 c.	BEEF STOCK (one 15 ounce can is sufficient)				
	TOTALS	22.9	17.9	138.4	265.7
	PER SERVING	3.8	3.0	23.1	44.3

- Sear the chuck roast in the olive oil in a 3 quart skillet or soup pot over medium high heat. Add the remaining ingredients, cover, and bring to a boil. Reduce the heat to medium low and simmer about 4 hours. Serve *au jus*. Don't forget to remove the bay leaf before serving.

- **MAKES ABOUT 6 SERVINGS WITH ABOUT 397 CALORIES PER SERVING.**

NEW ENGLAND BOILED DINNER

DON'T let the name of this dish fool you; this is pot roast with some cabbage added. A reader of the previous edition just told me that he's been stewing the cabbage separately from the beef and then mixing them when serving. Personally, I like the flavor of the beef cooked in the cabbage.

QUAN.	INGREDIENT	CARB GRAMS	AVAIL. CARB	FAT	PROTEIN
3 lb.	**CHUCK ROAST**	0	0	86.4	261.9
½ c.	**CARROTS**, diced	5.6	4.0	0	0.5
1 c.	**CELERY**, diced	4.4	2.4	0	0.9
½ c.	**ONION**, diced	6.9	5.5	0	1.0
2 lb.	**CABBAGE**, cut into 8ths	49.0	28.2	1.8	12.8
2 t.	**DRIED PARSLEY**				
2 t.	**GARLIC POWDER**	4.0	4.0	0	1.0
2 t.	**SALT**				
½ t.	**BLACK PEPPER**				
2 c.	**BEEF STOCK** (one 15 oz. can is sufficient)				
1 c.	**WATER**				
	TOTALS	69.9	44.1	88.2	278.1
	PER SERVING	10.0	6.3	12.6	39.7

- Place everything in a 3 quart skillet or soup pot. Cover and bring to a boil over high heat. Reduce the heat to medium low and simmer 2–3 hours.

■ **MAKES ABOUT 7 SERVINGS WITH ABOUT 297 CALORIES PER SERVING.**

BEEF BOURGUIGNON

THIS classic beef dish consists of beef and mushrooms served in a red wine sauce. Make a nice salad and save a glass or two of the wine to enjoy with the meal.

QUAN.	INGREDIENT	CARB GRAMS	AVAIL. CARB	FAT	PROTEIN
2 lb.	STEW BEEF or CHUCK ROAST cut into ½ inch cubes	0	0	57.6	174.6
3 slices	BACON	0	0	61.9	9.9
2 T.	OLIVE OIL	0	0	26.0	0
1 c.	DRY RED WINE	4.0	4.0	0	0.8
1 t.	THYME				
½ t.	BLACK PEPPER				
2	BEEF BOUILLON CUBES				
2 t.	GARLIC POWDER	4.0	4.0	0	1.0
½ c.	ONION, diced	6.9	5.5	0	1.0
2 c.	BUTTON MUSHROOMS, sliced	6.5	4.8	0.3	2.9
1 t.	SUGAR EQUIVALENT SWEETENER				
	TOTALS	21.4	18.3	145.8	190.2
	PER SERVING	5.4	4.6	36.5	47.6

- In a bowl, mix the beef, wine, oil, thyme, pepper, and garlic powder and let it set 4 hours at room temperature or overnight in the refrigerator, if possible. In a 3 quart skillet or soup pot, cook the bacon over medium heat until it is well browned and crisp. Add the beef and cook until it begins to brown. Add the onion, cooking until it becomes clear. Add the mushrooms and cook until they begin to wilt. Place the remaining ingredients in the pan, cover, bring to a boil, reduce the heat to medium low, and simmer 1 hour, stirring every 15 minutes.

- **MAKES 4 SERVINGS WITH ABOUT 537 CALORIES PER SERVING.**

STEAK DIANE

TRADITIONALLY, when you have this dish in a restaurant, it is prepared at your table; you are free to do the same at home, especially if you want to impress your guests.

QUAN.	INGREDIENT	CARB GRAMS	AVAIL. CARB	FAT	PROTEIN
2	FILET MIGNON STEAKS, 8 ounces each	0	0	85.1	81.8
2 T.	BUTTER	0	0	26.0	0
2 T.	OLIVE OIL	0	0	26.0	0
1 t.	DIJON MUSTARD				
1 T.	SHALLOTS, diced finely (you can substitute onion if necessary)	1.7	1.7	0	0.3
2 T.	WORCESTERSHIRE SAUCE	6.0	6.0	0	0
2 T.	LEMON JUICE	2.6	2.5	0	0.1
	SALT AND FRESH BLACK PEPPER to taste				
	TOTALS	10.3	10.2	137.1	82.2
	PER SERVING	5.2	5.1	68.6	41.1

■ Pound the steaks with a meat mallet between wax paper until they are ½ inch thickness. Sprinkle both sides with salt and pepper. Heat the 10 inch skillet over medium high heat. Add 1 T. butter and the olive oil. When the butter sizzles, add the steaks and cook on both sides until they are done to your satisfaction. Remove the steaks to a plate and keep them warm. Add the remaining butter and olive oil and sauté the shallots for a minute, add the Worcestershire sauce and lemon juice and reduce the volume to about half. Pour the sauce over the steaks and serve.

■ **MAKES 2 SERVINGS WITH ABOUT 802 CALORIES PER SERVING.**

GRILLED BEEF THAI-STYLE

I'VE made this dish several times and everyone who has had it really likes it. At first glance, it may not be a cooking method that you're all that familiar with, but it works. This is not very hot, despite how it looks.

QUAN.	INGREDIENT	CARB GRAMS	AVAIL. CARB	FAT	PROTEIN
1½ lb.	**FLANK STEAK**, sliced	0	0	62.9	133.0
2	**FRESH GREEN CHILIES**, diced (more or less added to your taste)				
4 T.	**WHITE VINEGAR**				
½ t.	**LEMON EXTRACT**				
½ c.	**RED ONION**, sliced	5.0	3.9	0	0.7
½ c.	**GREEN ONIONS**, diced	3.7	2.4	0	0.9
4 T.	**LIME JUICE**	5.6	5.4	0	0.2
2 T.	**THAI FISH SAUCE**	6.0	6.0	0	4.0
1 T.	**GARLIC POWDER**	6.1	6.1	0	1.4
1 t.	**RED PEPPER FLAKES** (more or less added to your taste)				
1 T.	**FRESH CILANTRO**, chopped (more or less added to your taste)				
1 t.	**DRIED BASIL**				
2 t.	**SUGAR EQUIVALENT SWEETENER**				
	TOTALS	26.4	23.8	62.9	140.2
	PER SERVING	8.8	7.9	21.0	46.7

- Mix the vinegar, lemon extract, and sugar substitute in a small bowl, ensuring that the sugar substitute is dissolved. Marinate the steak in the vinegar mixture, cilantro, chilies, garlic powder, and basil for at least 1 hour. Cook (you can grill, fry, broil, etc.) the beef to desired doneness and place it in a 1 quart bowl. Add the onions and mix well. Add the lime juice, fish sauce, and red pepper flakes, mix well, and serve.

- **MAKES 3 SERVINGS WITH ABOUT 407 CALORIES PER SERVING.**

GOLUBTSI

THIS variation on Russian cabbage rolls is a little more involved than most of the other recipes in this book. There is a simpler method: Make the Bavarian Kraut (see page 108) and add an 8 oz. can of tomato sauce. The simpler variety has the wonderful flavor of cabbage rolls without taking the time and trouble, but this recipe is well worth the work.

QUAN.	INGREDIENT	CARB GRAMS	AVAIL. CARB	FAT	PROTEIN
2 quarts	BOILING SALTED WATER				
12	LARGE CABBAGE LEAVES (about ½ lb., more or less)	12.3	7.1	0.5	3.2
2 lb.	HAMBURGER (77% lean)	0	0	184.8	154.4
2 t.	SALT				
I t.	GARLIC POWDER	2.0	2.0	0	0.5
2	EGGS, beaten slightly	1.4	1.4	9.6	14.4
½ t.	BLACK PEPPER				
½ c.	ONION, diced	6.9	5.5	0	1.0
I c.	BEEF BROTH				
I c.	TOMATO SAUCE	17.6	14.2	0.4	3.4
4 T.	SOUR CREAM	2.0	2.0	9.5	1.5
	TOTALS	42.2	32.2	204.8	178.4
	PER SERVING	10.6	8.1	51.2	44.6

- In a 3 quart soup pot, bring 2 quarts of water and 2 t. of salt to a boil. Place the cabbage leaves in the boiling salted water one at a time until each is wilted. Cool the cabbage leaves in a large bowl of cold water. Mix thoroughly the meats, eggs, seasonings, and onion in a 6 cup bowl. Use one cabbage leaf per roll. Place the leaf on a cutting board and cut the ribs in order to make the leaf lie flat. Fill each leaf with about 3 oz. of the meat mixture (this would be 2–3 heaping tablespoons) in the center. Roll up each leaf, tucking in the ends or using a toothpick to keep them from unrolling. Place the cabbage rolls seam-side down on a plate in preparation for cooking. Bring the beef broth and the tomato sauce to a rolling boil in a 10 inch skillet. Place the cabbage rolls in the liquid one at a time, carefully, in order to maintain them as rolls. Cover and bring to a boil again. Reduce the heat to medium low and simmer 30 minutes. Serve with the sauce from the skillet and a dollop of sour cream.

- **MAKES 4 SERVINGS WITH ABOUT 672 CALORIES PER SERVING.**

HUNGARIAN GOULASH

I'VE been fortunate in the past because I've had access to some very good paprika when making this savory dish. Use as good a paprika as you can find because quality makes a difference.

QUAN.	INGREDIENT	CARB GRAMS	AVAIL. CARB	FAT	PROTEIN
2 lb.	**STEW BEEF** or **CHUCK ROAST** cut into ½ inch cubes	0	0	57.6	174.6
2 T.	**OLIVE OIL**	0	0	52.0	0
3 T.	**PAPRIKA**	11.4	7.2	2.4	3.0
2 t.	**GARLIC POWDER**	4.0	4.0	0	1.0
½ t.	**BLACK PEPPER**				
1	**BAY LEAF**				
½ c.	**ONION**, diced	6.9	5.5	0	1.0
1 c.	**BEEF STOCK**				
1 c.	**SOUR CREAM**	9.8	9.8	45.7	7.3
	TOTALS	32.1	26.5	157.7	186.9
	PER SERVING	8.0	6.6	39.4	46.7

- Fry the beef in the oil in a 3 quart skillet or soup pot over medium high heat until the beef begins to brown. Add the onions and cook until they become clear. Add the remaining ingredients except the sour cream, cover, and bring to a boil. Reduce heat to medium low and simmer 30–45 minutes, stirring every 15 minutes. Serve with the sour cream.

- **MAKES ABOUT 4 SERVINGS WITH ABOUT 568 CALORIES PER SERVING.**

SPANISH MEAT LOAF

QUAN.	INGREDIENT	CARB GRAMS	AVAIL. CARB	FAT	PROTEIN
1½ lb.	HAMBURGER (77% lean)	0	0	138.6	115.8
15	GREEN STUFFED OLIVES, sliced thinly	3.0	3.0	7.5	0
4 T.	TOMATO SAUCE	4.4	3.6	0.1	0.9
1 T.	WHITE VINEGAR				
2 t.	SUGAR EQUIVALENT SWEETENER				
2	EGGS, beaten slightly	1.4	1.4	9.6	14.4
½ c.	ONION, diced	6.9	5.5	0	1.0
1 t.	GARLIC POWDER	2.0	2.0	0	0.5
1 t.	SALT				
	TOTALS	17.7	15.5	155.8	132.6
	PER SERVING	5.9	5.2	51.9	44.2

- Dissolve the sugar substitute completely in the vinegar. Mix all ingredients thoroughly. Bake 1 hour in a bread loaf pan at 350° F.

- **MAKES 3 SERVINGS WITH ABOUT 665 CALORIES PER SERVING.**

BAVARIAN KRAUT

QUAN.	INGREDIENT	CARB GRAMS	AVAIL. CARB	FAT	PROTEIN
1 lb.	**HAMBURGER** (77% lean)	0	0	92.4	77.2
1 lb.	**CABBAGE**, shredded	24.5	14.1	0.9	6.4
½ c.	**ONION**, diced	6.9	5.5	0	1.0
2 t.	**GARLIC POWDER**	4.0	4.0	0	1.0
3	**BEEF BOUILLON CUBES**				
1 t.	**SUGAR EQUIVALENT SWEETENER**				
½ c.	**WATER**				
	TOTALS	35.4	23.6	93.3	85.6
	PER SERVING	11.8	7.9	31.1	28.5

- In a 3 quart skillet or soup pot, brown the hamburger over medium high heat, breaking it up thoroughly while it cooks. Add the onion and cook until it becomes clear. Add the cabbage and cook until it begins to wilt. Add the remaining ingredients and bring to a boil. Cover, reduce the heat to medium low, and let simmer 20 minutes, stirring well every 5 minutes.

- **MAKES 3 SERVINGS WITH ABOUT 426 CALORIES PER SERVING.**

CUBAN-STYLE BEEF

QUAN.	INGREDIENT	CARB GRAMS	AVAIL. CARB	FAT	PROTEIN
1 lb.	**SKIRT STEAK**, sliced thinly	0	0	42.1	89.3
4 T.	**KETCHUP** (see page 234)	3.6	3.2	0	0.8
4 T.	**DRY WHITE WINE**	0.4	0.4	0	0
1	**BEEF BOUILLON CUBE**				
½ c.	**ONION**, sliced thinly	5.0	3.9	0	0.7
1 c.	**GREEN AND RED SWEET BELL PEPPERS**, sliced	9.6	6.6	0.2	1.3
1 t.	**GARLIC POWDER**	2.0	2.0	0	0.5
2 T.	**OLIVE OIL**	0	0	26.0	0
½ t.	**GROUND CUMIN**	0.5	0.4	0.2	0.2
½ t.	**BLACK PEPPER**				
1	**BAY LEAF**				
	TOTALS	21.1	16.5	68.5	92.8
	PER SERVING	10.6	8.3	34.3	46.4

- In a 10 inch skillet, cook the beef in the oil over medium high heat until it is slightly browned. Add the onion and bell peppers and cook until the onions are clear. Add the remaining ingredients, cover, and bring to a boil. Reduce the heat to medium low and let simmer 30 minutes. Remove from the heat and let sit for 10 minutes before serving.

- **MAKES 2 SERVINGS WITH ABOUT 528 CALORIES PER SERVING.**

TWICE-COOKED CUBAN BEEF

THIS is kind of Cuban-style beef, also known as *vaca frita,* is the one used in sand-wiches in many of the Cuban restaurants in Miami.

QUAN.	INGREDIENT	CARB GRAMS	AVAIL. CARB	FAT	PROTEIN
1 lb.	**SKIRT STEAK,** sliced thinly	0	0	42.1	89.3
4 T.	**KETCHUP** (see page 234)	3.6	3.2	0	0.8
½ c.	**WATER**				
1	**BEEF BOUILLON CUBE**				
½ c.	**ONION,** sliced thinly	5.0	3.9	0	0.7
1 t.	**GARLIC POWDER**	2.0	2.0	0	0.5
3 T.	**OLIVE OIL**	0	0	26.0	0
4 T.	**LIME JUICE**	5.6	5.4	0	0.2
1 t.	**SUGAR EQUIVALENT SWEETENER**				
	TOTALS	16.2	14.5	66.1	91.5
	PER SERVING	8.1	7.3	33.1	45.8

- Mix the lime juice and sugar substitute in a small bowl and set aside. Place the steak, ketchup, water, and bouillon cubes in a 10 inch skillet, cover, and bring to a boil over high heat. Reduce the heat to medium low and let it simmer 30 minutes. Remove the meat from the liquid and let it cool to room temperature. (Instead of throwing it away, you can reserve the meat stock for soups.) Let the meat sit at least an hour. Add the garlic powder, sugar substitute, and lime juice mixture to the meat and let it marinate at least a half hour, but preferably overnight, refrigerated. When ready to begin serving, heat the oil in a 10 inch skillet over high heat. Add the meat, reduce the heat to medium high, and cook until the meat begins to crisp. Remove the meat to a platter, leaving as much oil in the skillet as possible. Add the onions to the skillet and cook until slightly browned. Add the onion to the meat and serve.

- **MAKES 2 SERVINGS WITH ABOUT 510 CALORIES PER SERVING.**

CUBAN PALOMILLA-STYLE STEAK

QUAN.	INGREDIENT	CARB GRAMS	AVAIL. CARB	FAT	PROTEIN
1 lb.	**SIRLOIN STEAKS**, cut into ½ inch cubes	0	0	59.1	86.9
2 T.	**OLIVE OIL**	0	0	26.0	0
2 T.	**BUTTER**	0	0	24.2	0
½ c.	**ONION**, sliced thinly	5.0	3.9	0	0.7
1 T.	**GARLIC POWDER**	6.1	6.1	0	1.4
½ t.	**LEMON FLAVORING**				
2 T.	**WHITE VINEGAR**				
½ c.	**WATER**				
1 T.	**LIME JUICE**	1.4	1.4	0	0.1
1 t.	**SUGAR EQUIVALENT SWEETENER**				
2	**BEEF BOUILLON CUBES**				
	FRESH GROUND BLACK PEPPER to taste				
	TOTALS	12.5	11.4	109.3	89.1
	PER SERVING	6.3	5.7	54.7	44.6

- Bring the oil to temperature in a 10 inch skillet over medium high heat. Add the butter and let it begin to sizzle. Add the meat and cook until it begins to brown. Add the onion and cook until it becomes clear. Add the garlic powder, lemon flavoring, vinegar, bouillon cubes, water, and sugar substitute; cover, and bring to a boil. Reduce the heat to medium low and let it simmer one half hour, stirring every 10 minutes. Remove from the heat and drizzle the lime juice over it before serving. Serve with the black pepper.

- **MAKES 2 SERVINGS WITH ABOUT 694 CALORIES PER SERVING.**

CUBAN-STYLE BEEF SKILLET

QUAN.	INGREDIENT	CARB GRAMS	AVAIL. CARB	FAT	PROTEIN
3 slices	BACON, diced	0	0	61.9	9.9
1 lb.	STEW BEEF or CHUCK ROAST cut into ½ inch cubes	0	0	28.8	87.3
½ c.	ONION, diced	6.9	5.5	0	1.0
¼ lb.	SMOKED HAM (2% fat), cut into bite sized pieces	2.0	2.0	2.0	20.0
1 T.	CAPERS	0.4	0.1	0	0.2
2 t.	GARLIC POWDER	4.0	4.0	0	1.0
10	GREEN, STUFFED OLIVES, diced coarsely	2.0	2.0	5.0	0
1 T.	PICKLED JALAPEÑOS, diced finely (more or less added to your taste)				
1 T.	WHITE VINEGAR				
1 c.	WATER				
2	BEEF BOUILLON CUBES				
4 T.	TOMATO SAUCE	4.4	3.6	0.1	0.9
¼ t.	BLACK PEPPER				
1 t.	SUGAR EQUIVALENT SWEETENER				
	TOTALS	19.7	17.2	97.8	120.3
	PER SERVING	6.6	5.7	32.6	40.1

- In a 3 quart pan, fry the bacon over medium high heat until it becomes crisp. Add the beef and cook until the beef begins to brown. Add the onion and cook until it becomes clear. Add the remaining ingredients, cover, and bring to a boil. Reduce the heat to medium low and let simmer for 30–45 minutes, stirring every 15 minutes. Remove from the heat and let set for 10 minutes before serving.

- **MAKES 3 SERVINGS WITH ABOUT 477 CALORIES PER SERVING.**

STEAK FLORENTINE

WHILE I was living in the Charlotte area, a friend of mine returned from a trip to Italy raving about a dish he called Steak Florentine. After several Internet searches, I was able to find and adapt what is otherwise known as *bistecca alla Florentine*. The original recipe calls for New York strip steaks, but I prefer the flavor and texture of rib-eye steaks.

QUAN.	INGREDIENT	CARB GRAMS	AVAIL. CARB	FAT	PROTEIN
1 lb.	RIB-EYE STEAKS (2 steaks about 8 ounces each)	0	0	87.8	79.4
4 T.	LEMON JUICE	5.2	5.0	0	0.2
2 T.	OLIVE OIL	0	0	26.0	0
2	LEMONS SLICES for garnish				
	SALT AND BLACK PEPPER to taste				
	TOTALS	5.2	5.0	113.8	79.6
	PER SERVING	2.6	2.5	56.9	39.8

- Put 2 T. of the lemon juice in a shallow baking dish. Place the steaks in the dish and coat both sides. Place the steaks on a preheated grill at medium heat and cook to your preference, at least 10 minutes for medium. After the steaks are finished cooking, let them sit for a few minutes. Slice across the grain into strips about ½ inch thick and place on the serving dishes. Drizzle with the olive oil and the remaining lemon juice.

- **MAKES 2 SERVINGS WITH ABOUT 681 CALORIES PER SERVING.**

STEAK ITALIANO

THIS is a recipe for rib-eye steak that is marinated in something very close to Italian dressing before being grilled. After the steak has been grilled to the desired doneness, it is then served with more dressing.

QUAN.	INGREDIENT	CARB GRAMS	AVAIL. CARB	FAT	PROTEIN
1 lb.	RIB EYE STEAKS (2 steaks about 8 ounces each)	0	0	87.8	79.4
3 T.	OLIVE OIL	0	0	39.0	0
3 T.	WATER				
2 T.	WHITE VINEGAR				
1 t.	ITALIAN SEASONING				
2 t.	SUGAR EQUIVALENT SWEETENER				
1 T.	SOY SAUCE (tamari)	1.0	1.0	0	1.9
1 t.	GARLIC POWDER	2.0	2.0	0	0.5
1 t.	ONION POWDER	1.7	1.6	0	0.2
	SALT AND BLACK PEPPER to taste				
	TOTALS	3.7	3.6	126.8	82.0
	PER SERVING	1.9	1.8	63.4	41.0

- In a bowl, dissolve the sugar substitute into the liquids. Add the dry ingredients and mix well and then add the oil. Put 4 T. of the marinade into a shallow baking dish. Place the steaks in the dish and coat both sides. Marinate as long as possible. Place the steaks on a preheated grill at medium heat and cook to your preference, at least 10 minutes for medium. After the steaks are finished cooking, let them sit for a few minutes. Slice across the grain into strips about ½ inch thick and place on the serving dishes. Drizzle with the remaining sauce and serve. This marinade is also very good with grilled hamburgers.

- **MAKES 2 SERVINGS WITH ABOUT 742 CALORIES PER SERVING.**

GRILLED HAMBURGERS

WHEN I was in graduate school at the University of Nebraska, some folks from the East Coast moved upstairs from me and they brought their hibachi with them. It seemed like every evening, even when it was snowing and the temperature was near zero, they would have that hibachi cranked up. It was the first time I had ever seen this.

Grilled hamburgers are one of the simpler treats that we low carbers can have. The problem is that we can't have the hamburger bun with them. What we need is a way to embellish them after they are cooked. This is where various sauces and dressings come in.

QUAN.	INGREDIENT	CARB GRAMS	AVAIL. CARB	FAT	PROTEIN
I lb.	**HAMBURGER** (77% lean), divided into 3 patties	0	0	92.4	77.2
	TOTALS	0	0	92.4	77.2
	PER SERVING	0	0	30.8	25.7

- Start with a pound of ground beef and divide this into three patties. Grill each patty to desired doneness. Serve each patty with 2 tablespoons of any of the following:

    With Ketchup (see page 234) add 1.6 grams of carbs
    With Chili Sauce (see page 235) add 1.6 grams of carbs
    With Italian Dressing (see page 36) add 0.6 grams of carbs
    With Creamy Italian Dressing (see page 37) add 1.2 grams of carbs
    With French Dressing Rouge (see page 38) add 1.0 gram of carbs
    With Blue Cheese Dressing (see page 42) add 1.4 grams of carbs
    With Thousand Island Dressing (see page 44) add 1.2 grams of carbs
    With Ranch Dressing (see page 41) add 1.6 grams of carbs
    With Basic Bar-B-Q Sauce (see page 236) add 1.8 grams of carbs
    With South Carolina Mustard Bar-B-Q Sauce (see page 248) add 0.8 grams of carbs
    With Warm Mustard Sauce (see page 249) add 1.8 grams of carbs
    With Yaki Mandu Dipping Sauce (see page 243) add 0.8 grams of carbs
    With Thai Hot Sauce (see page 253) add 2.8 grams of carbs
    With Vietnamese Dipping Sauce (see page 254) add 2.6 grams of carbs
    With Chow Chow (see page 83) add 0.8 grams of carbs
    With Salad Onions (see page 84) add 1.4 grams of carbs
    With Mojo (see page 247) add 1.0 gram of carbs

- **MAKES 3 SERVINGS WITH ABOUT 400 CALORIES PER SERVING.**

PORK

ENTRÉES

PESTO PORK

I first started experimenting with this recipe several years ago because the combination seemed like a natural to me. For those who don't like pork, you can use boneless, skinless chicken thighs.

QUAN.	INGREDIENT	CARB GRAMS	AVAIL. CARB	FAT	PROTEIN
1 lb.	**PORK ROAST** cut into ½ inch cubes	0	0	32.8	87.9
1	**CHICKEN BOUILLON CUBE**				
½ c.	**ONION**, sliced thinly	5.0	3.9	0	0.7
1 T.	**GARLIC POWDER**	6.1	6.1	0	1.4
½ t.	**DRIED BASIL**				
15	**FRESH BASIL LEAVES**, sliced very thinly				
½ t.	**BLACK PEPPER**				
½ c.	**DRY WHITE WINE**	0.8	0.8	0	0
4 T.	**WATER**				
2 T.	**OLIVE OIL**	0	0	25.8	0
6 T.	**GRATED PARMESAN CHEESE**	1.2	1.2	8.4	12.6
	TOTALS	13.1	12.0	67.0	102.6
	PER SERVING	6.6	6.0	33.5	51.3

- Put the olive oil in a 10 inch skillet over medium high heat. Add the pork and brown it well. Add the onion and cook until it is clear. Add the dried basil, garlic powder, pepper, wine, and water, cover, and bring to a boil. Reduce the heat to medium low and let simmer for 30 minutes, stirring every 10 minutes. Add the fresh basil leaves, stir, and let simmer another 3 minutes. Remove from heat and sprinkle the grated Parmesan cheese over the meat, cover, and let sit for 10 minutes.

- **MAKES 2 SERVINGS WITH ABOUT 531 CALORIES PER SERVING.**

OKTOBERFEST RIBS

DURING the cooking process, these ribs provide some of the flavor for the accompanying sauerkraut. You can have your own little Oktoberfest with the addition of some low carb beer and German Green Bean Salad (see page 57).

QUAN.	INGREDIENT	CARB GRAMS	AVAIL. CARB	FAT	PROTEIN
3 lb.	**PORK RIBS**	0	0	230.4	219.4
2 c.	**CANNED SAUERKRAUT** (1 can of about 15 ounces is sufficient)	12.2	5.1	0.3	2.6
½ c.	**ONION,** sliced thinly	5.0	3.9	0	0.7
12 oz.	**LOW CARB BEER** (one 12 ounce can)	3.2	3.2	0	0.9
2 T.	**SUGAR EQUIVALENT SWEETENER**				
1 t.	**CARAWAY SEED**				
1	**BEEF BOUILLON CUBE**				
	TOTALS	20.4	12.2	230.7	223.6
	PER SERVING	4.1	2.4	46.1	44.7

- Rinse the kraut twice (see Sauerkraut Preparation on page 211). Mix the sugar substitute with the beer and make sure it dissolves completely. In the following order, place the kraut, onions, and ribs in a large soup pot. Pour the liquid over the ribs. Sprinkle the caraway seed over the ribs. Cover the pan and bring to a boil. Lower the heat to medium low and simmer very gently for 3 hours.

- **MAKES ABOUT 5 SERVINGS WITH ABOUT 603 CALORIES PER SERVING.**

CAJUN PORK ROAST

QUAN.	INGREDIENT	CARB GRAMS	AVAIL. CARB	FAT	PROTEIN
3 lb.	**PORK ROAST**	0	0	98.4	263.7
1 T.	**PAPRIKA**	3.8	2.4	0.8	1.0
1 t.	**CAYENNE PEPPER** (more or less added to your taste)				
2 t.	**GARLIC POWDER**	4.0	4.0	0	1.0
2 t.	**ONION POWDER**	3.4	3.2	0	0.4
1 t.	**OREGANO**				
1 t.	**THYME**				
2 t.	**SALT**				
½ t.	**WHITE PEPPER**				
1 t.	**BLACK PEPPER**				
1 t.	**CUMIN**				
½ t.	**NUTMEG**				
2 c.	**BEEF STOCK** (one 15 ounce can is sufficient)				
	TOTALS	11.2	9.6	99.2	266.1
	PER SERVING	1.9	1.6	16.5	44.4

- Preheat oven to 450° F. Mix the seasonings and rub them well all over the roast. Pour the stock in the roasting pan, add the roast, cover and cook for 15 minutes. Reduce the heat to 325° F and cook for an additional hour and a half. Let sit 10 minutes before slicing.

■ **MAKES 6 SERVINGS WITH ABOUT 333 CALORIES PER SERVING.**

WISCONSIN PORK STEW

SOUP made with beer? Yup! Except in this case, it's low carb beer. If you serve this with a vinaigrette dressing on your salad, you can use a little bit of the malt vinegar to reinforce the flavor.

QUAN.	INGREDIENT	CARB GRAMS	AVAIL. CARB	FAT	PROTEIN
2 lb.	**PORK ROAST** cut into ½ inch cubes	0	0	65.6	175.8
2 t.	**SALT**				
½ t.	**BLACK PEPPER**				
2 T.	**OLIVE OIL**	0	0	52.0	0
½ c.	**ONION**, diced	6.9	5.5	0	1.0
½ c.	**CARROTS**, diced	5.6	4.0	0	0.5
1 c.	**CELERY**, diced	4.4	2.4	0	0.9
2 t.	**GARLIC POWDER**	4.0	4.0	0	1.0
2 T.	**DRIED PARSLEY**				
1 t.	**CARAWAY SEED**				
1	**BAY LEAF**				
2 c.	**CHICKEN STOCK** (one 15 ounce can is sufficient)				
12 oz.	**LOW CARB BEER** (one 12 ounce can)	3.2	3.2	0	0.9
2 T.	**MALT VINEGAR**				
1 T.	**SUGAR EQUIVALENT SWEETENER**				
	TOTALS	24.1	19.1	117.6	180.1
	PER SERVING	6.0	4.8	29.4	45.0

- In a 3 quart soup pot, brown the meat in the oil over medium high heat. Add the vegetables and cook until the onions become clear. Add remaining ingredients, cover, and bring to a boil. Reduce the heat to medium low and simmer 1 hour, stirring every 15 minutes. Let sit 10 minutes before serving.

- **MAKES 4 SERVINGS WITH ABOUT 464 CALORIES PER SERVING.**

EASTERN NORTH CAROLINA–STYLE BAR-B-Q

THIS regional delicacy requires you to cook the meat twice. First you smoke it until it's about done, then you boil it in a vinegar-based barbecue sauce to complete the cooking. Serve with Bar-B-Q Slaw (see page 79) or Eastern Carolina Slaw (see page 75).

QUAN.	INGREDIENT	CARB GRAMS	AVAIL. CARB	FAT	PROTEIN
6 lb.	**PORK SHOULDER ROAST**	0	0	493.4	454.2
½ qt.	**WATER**				
½ qt.	**CIDER VINEGAR**				
2 T.	**RED PEPPER FLAKES** (more or less added to your taste)				
1 T.	**GARLIC POWDER**	6.1	6.1	0	1.4
1 T.	**ONION POWDER**	5.2	5.1	0	0.7
1 T.	**SALT**				
	TOTALS	11.3	11.2	493.4	456.3
	PER SERVING	1.1	1.1	49.3	45.6

- Smoke the meat according to the instructions that came with your smoker, trying to keep the temperature between 220° and 240° F. Smoking should last 8–10 hours or until the meat comes easily away from the bone. During the last few hours you can gradually increase the temperature to 300° F. Remove the meat to a pan and add the remaining ingredients, bringing to a boil over high heat. Reduce the heat to medium low and let simmer, covered, until the meat is well separated from the bone. If it becomes too late, you can just turn this off and continue it the next day without worrying about refrigeration.

- **MAKES ABOUT 10 SERVINGS WITH ABOUT 631 CALORIES PER SERVING.**

BASIC BAR-B-Q PORK RIBS

QUAN.	INGREDIENT	CARB GRAMS	AVAIL. CARB	FAT	PROTEIN
2½ lb.	COUNTRY-STYLE PORK RIBS	0	0	190.9	192.7
1 c.	BASIC BAR-B-Q SAUCE (see page 236)	16.7	14.5	10.0	5.3
	TOTALS	16.7	14.5	200.9	198.0
	PER SERVING	4.2	3.6	50.2	49.5

- Place ribs in a 3 quart soup pot or skillet. Cover with water, bring to a boil over high heat, reduce heat to medium low, and simmer 30 minutes. Drain the ribs. Place ribs in a roasting pan, then cover them with the Bar-B-Q sauce and bake 30 minutes at 325° F. Stir, making sure to coat ribs, and bake another 30 minutes. Stir a final time and bake a final 30 minutes.

- **MAKES 4 SERVINGS WITH ABOUT 664 CALORIES PER SERVING.**

KANSAS CITY–STYLE
BAR-B-Q PORK RIBS

RECENTLY, I've considered joining the Kansas City Barbecue Society and competing, or at least becoming a judge. Generally, their sauces are tomato-based with the addition of a little acid and a little sweetness. Kind of like this.

QUAN.	INGREDIENT	CARB GRAMS	AVAIL. CARB	FAT	PROTEIN
2½ lb.	COUNTRY-STYLE PORK RIBS	0	0	190.9	192.7
4 T.	SOY SAUCE	2.0	2.0	0	8.0
5 T.	CIDER VINEGAR				
1 t.	GARLIC POWDER	2.0	2.0	0	0.5
½ c.	ONION, diced	6.9	5.5	0	1.0
2 T.	COOKING OIL	0	0	26.0	0
4 T.	SUGAR EQUIVALENT SWEETENER				
1 c.	TOMATO SAUCE	17.6	14.2	0.4	3.4
1 T.	PICKLED JALAPEÑO PEPPERS, diced finely (more or less added to your taste)				
	TOTALS	28.5	23.7	217.3	205.6
	PER SERVING	7.1	5.9	54.3	51.4

- Place the ribs in a 3 quart skillet or soup pot. Cover with water, bring to a boil, reduce heat, and simmer 30 minutes. Drain the ribs. In the meantime, start the sauce by frying the onion in the oil in a 1 quart saucepan over medium heat until the onions become clear. Add the tomato sauce, sugar substitute, soy sauce, vinegar, and peppers. Simmer, stirring occasionally, for 30 minutes. Place the ribs in a low baking dish or roasting pan, then cover them with the sauce and bake at 325° F for 30 minutes. Stir, making sure to coat ribs, and bake another 30 minutes. Stir a final time and bake a final 30 minutes.

- **MAKES 4 SERVINGS WITH ABOUT 718 CALORIES PER SERVING.**

PORK CHOPS DIJON

THE sauce for this recipe has more than a slight mustard flavor. However, it isn't harsh and I encourage you to adjust the sweetness up or down to your taste.

QUAN.	INGREDIENT	CARB GRAMS	AVAIL. CARB	FAT	PROTEIN
1 lb.	**PORK CHOPS**	0	0	20.7	100.0
2 T.	**OLIVE OIL**	0	0	26.0	0
¼ c.	**ONION**, diced	3.5	2.8	0	0.5
3 T.	**DIJON MUSTARD**				
4 T.	**ITALIAN DRESSING** (see page 36)	1.3	1.1	26.0	0.3
1 t.	**SUGAR EQUIVALENT SWEETENER**				
2 T.	**WATER**				
	SALT AND BLACK PEPPER to taste				
	TOTALS	4.8	3.9	72.7	100.8
	PER SERVING	2.4	2.0	36.4	50.4

- Heat the oil in a 10 inch skillet over medium heat. Add the pork chops and sprinkle them with salt and pepper. Brown them on both sides. Remove the chops from the skillet and cook the onions until they become clear. Deglaze the pan with the water. Replace the chops in the pan. Mix all other ingredients into a paste in a 1 cup bowl and pour over the chops. Cover and cook over medium low heat 30–45 minutes until the meat is tender. Let them sit 10 minutes before serving.

- **MAKES 2 SERVINGS WITH ABOUT 537 CALORIES PER SERVING.**

ROSEMARY PORK CHOPS

QUAN.	INGREDIENT	CARB GRAMS	AVAIL. CARB	FAT	PROTEIN
1 lb.	PORK CHOPS	0	0	20.7	100.0
2 T.	BUTTER	0	0	26.0	0
1 T.	OLIVE OIL	0	0	13.0	0
1 t.	ROSEMARY				
1 t.	SAGE				
1 t.	GARLIC POWDER	2.0	2.0	0	0.5
1 t.	ONION POWDER	1.7	1.6	0	0.2
½ t.	SALT				
¼ t.	BLACK PEPPER				
1 c.	DRY WHITE WINE	1.6	1.6	0	0
	TOTALS	5.3	5.2	59.7	100.7
	PER SERVING	2.7	2.6	29.9	50.4

- Make a mixture of the seasonings and mash it onto both sides of each pork chop. Fry the chops in the butter and oil in a 10 inch skillet over medium heat, browning on both sides. Add the wine, cover, and bring to a boil. Reduce the heat to medium low and simmer 30–45 minutes or until the chops are very tender. Remove the chops from the skillet and reduce the sauce to your taste, down to just a few tablespoons, and then pour it over the chops.

- **MAKES 2 SERVINGS WITH ABOUT 481 CALORIES PER SERVING.**

GERMAN BAKED PORK CHOPS

PORK chops in a white wine sauce: a remarkably simple yet elegant recipe to make in your quest for variety.

QUAN.	INGREDIENT	CARB GRAMS	AVAIL. CARB	FAT	PROTEIN
1½ lb.	PORK CHOPS	0	0	31.1	150.0
1 t.	GARLIC POWDER	2.0	2.0	0	0.5
1 t.	ONION POWDER	1.7	1.6	0	0.2
1 t.	CARAWAY SEEDS				
2 t.	PAPRIKA	2.5	1.6	0.5	0.7
½ t.	SALT				
¼ t.	BLACK PEPPER				
1 c.	DRY WHITE WINE	1.6	1.6	0	0
2 T.	WHITE WINE VINEGAR				
1 c.	SOUR CREAM	9.8	9.8	45.7	7.3
1 t.	SUGAR EQUIVALENT SWEETENER				
	TOTALS	17.6	16.6	77.3	158.7
	PER SERVING	5.9	5.5	25.8	52.9

- In a 2 cup bowl, prepare a marinade of everything except the pork chops and the sour cream. Marinate the pork chops for several hours. Place the pork chops in a baking dish and pour the marinade over them. Bake uncovered at 325° F for 1 hour. Check every 15 minutes and add more wine if necessary. When the chops are finished, remove them from the pan. Make sure that you have at least ½ cup of liquid (add more wine if needed) and stir in the sour cream. Pour the sauce over the chops and serve.

- **MAKES 3 SERVINGS WITH ABOUT 466 CALORIES PER SERVING.**

THAI-STYLE PORK SALAD

THIS is a good dish for your summer dinner party, as it can be prepared well ahead of time. The longer you let it cook, the more the flavor is infused in the pork and the more tender the pork becomes. This is best served at room temperature. Make sure that you get enough of the sauce and include a little with every bite.

QUAN.	INGREDIENT	CARB GRAMS	AVAIL. CARB	FAT	PROTEIN
1 lb.	**PORK ROAST** cut into ½ inch cubes	0	0	32.8	87.9
2 T.	**WATER**				
2 T.	**FISH SAUCE**	6.0	6.0	0	4.0
2 T.	**LEMON JUICE**	2.6	2.5	0	0.1
2 t.	**SUGAR EQUIVALENT SWEETENER**				
2 t.	**HOT CHILI PASTE** (from Asian groceries, more or less to your taste. You can use red cayenne sauce in its stead)				
½ c.	**GREEN ONIONS**, diced	3.7	2.4	0	0.9
4 c.	**LETTUCE**, shredded	4.6	1.5	0.3	2.2
½ t.	**DRIED BASIL**				
½ oz.	**FRESH BASIL**, sliced finely				
4 T.	**FRESH CILANTRO**				
2 t.	**GARLIC POWDER**	4.0	4.0	0	1.0
	TOTALS	20.9	16.4	33.1	96.1
	PER SERVING	10.5	8.2	16.6	48.1

- Place the pork, water, fish sauce, dried basil, and garlic in a covered 2 quart saucepan and bring to a boil over high heat. Reduce the heat to medium low and let it simmer for about 45 minutes, stirring every 15 minutes. Remove from the heat, add the onions, and stir very well. Then add the lemon juice, sugar substitute, and chili paste. Stir well and set aside to cool down. Place the lettuce, the cilantro, and the basil in a salad bowl and mix well. Pour the entire meat mixture over the salad mixture. Mix well before serving.

- **MAKES 2 SERVINGS WITH ABOUT 375 CALORIES PER SERVING.**

PORTUGUESE-STYLE PORK WITH CLAMS

WHEN I was surfing the Internet one day looking at pork recipes, I ran across something that incorporated pork and clams in the same recipe. I wrote down the basic ingredients, began testing, and this dish is the result. Try it first without the cloves as the cloves can easily dominate.

QUAN.	INGREDIENT	CARB GRAMS	AVAIL. CARB	FAT	PROTEIN
I lb.	PORK ROAST cut into ½ inch cubes	0	0	32.8	87.9
6 oz.	CLAMS				
½ c.	ONION, diced	6.9	5.5	0	1.0
2 T.	OLIVE OIL	0	0	26.0	0
2 t.	THAI FISH SAUCE	2.0	2.0	0	1.7
½ c.	GREEN PEPPERS, diced	4.8	3.5	0.1	0.7
I	CHICKEN BOUILLON CUBE				
I T.	WHITE VINEGAR				
¼ t.	LEMON EXTRACT				
½ c.	DRY WHITE WINE	0.8	0.8	0	0
2 t.	PAPRIKA	2.5	1.6	0.5	0.7
⅛ t.	GROUND CLOVES (optional)				
2 t.	GARLIC POWDER	4.0	4.0	0	1.0
I t.	DRIED CILANTRO				
I T.	DRIED PARSLEY				
4 T.	TOMATO SAUCE	4.4	3.6	0.1	0.9
I t.	SUGAR EQUIVALENT SWEETENER				
	RED CAYENNE SAUCE (a sprinkle or two to your taste)				
	TOTALS	25.4	21.0	59.5	93.9
	PER SERVING	12.7	10.5	29.8	47.0

■ Separate the clams from the juice in the can, reserving the juice for the stock. In a 10 inch skillet, cook the pork over medium high heat until it begins to brown. Add the onions and peppers and cook until the onions become clear. Increase the heat to high, add the remaining ingredients except for the clams, cover, and bring to a boil. Reduce the heat to medium low and let it simmer for about 45 minutes, stirring every 15 minutes. At this point the pork should fall apart at the touch. Remove from the heat, stir in the clams, and let it set for 10 minutes before serving.

■ **MAKES 2 SERVINGS WITH ABOUT 498 CALORIES PER SERVING.**

CZECH-STYLE PORK AND CABBAGE

THIS is based on a traditional Czech dish. The flavor is supposed to be sweet and sour, so you should have a bottle of wine vinegar available to sprinkle on it just in case it isn't sour enough. You can adjust the amount of cumin a little bit, but the cumin can come to dominate it quickly, so don't play with it too much. At some point, you might want to try this with chicken instead of pork.

QUAN.	INGREDIENT	CARB GRAMS	AVAIL. CARB	FAT	PROTEIN
3 slices	**BACON**, diced	0	0	61.9	9.9
I lb.	**PORK ROAST** cut into ½ inch cubes	0	0	32.8	87.9
½ c.	**ONION**, diced	6.9	5.5	0	1.0
½ lb.	**CABBAGE**, sliced coarsely	12.3	7.1	0.5	3.2
2	**BEEF BOUILLON CUBES**				
I t.	**CUMIN**				
I t.	**CARAWAY SEEDS**				
2 t.	**GARLIC POWDER**	4.0	4.0	0	1.0
2 T.	**WHITE VINEGAR**				
2 t.	**SUGAR EQUIVALENT SWEETENER**				
I c.	**CANNED BEEF STOCK**				
	TOTALS	23.2	16.6	95.2	103.0
	PER SERVING	11.6	8.3	47.6	51.5

- In a 10 inch skillet, fry your bacon over medium high heat until it is well browned. Add the pork and cook until it begins to brown. Remove the meat from the skillet and put it in a separate dish, reserving as much fat in the skillet as possible. Decrease the heat to medium and add the onions to the skillet. Cook the onions, stirring every couple of minutes, until they are well browned. Add the cabbage and cook it until it begins to wilt well. Increase the heat to high, add all of the ingredients to the skillet, cover, and bring to a boil. Reduce the heat to medium low and let it simmer for 45 minutes, stirring every 15 minutes.

- **MAKES 2 SERVINGS WITH ABOUT 668 CALORIES PER SERVING.**

FENNEL PORK AND CABBAGE

QUAN.	INGREDIENT	CARB GRAMS	AVAIL. CARB	FAT	PROTEIN
2 T.	OLIVE OIL	0	0	26.0	0
1 lb.	PORK ROAST cut into ½ inch cubes	0	0	32.8	87.9
½ c.	ONION, diced	6.9	5.5	0	1.0
½ lb.	CABBAGE, sliced coarsely	12.3	7.1	0.5	3.2
2	BEEF BOUILLON CUBES				
½ t.	FENNEL or ANISE				
2 t.	GARLIC POWDER	4.0	4.0	0	1.0
1 t.	SUGAR EQUIVALENT SWEETENER				
1 c.	CANNED BEEF STOCK				
1 T.	WHITE VINEGAR				
½ t.	FRESH GROUND BLACK PEPPER				
	TOTALS	23.2	16.6	59.3	93.1
	PER SERVING	11.6	8.3	29.7	46.6

■ Add the pork to the oil in a 3 quart pan over medium high heat. Cook until the pork begins to brown. Add the onion and cook until the onion becomes clear. Add the cabbage and cook until it begins to wilt. Deglaze the pan with the beef stock and vinegar. Add the remaining ingredients, cover, and bring to a boil. Reduce the heat to medium low and let simmer 45 minutes, stirring every 15 minutes.

■ **MAKES 2 SERVINGS WITH ABOUT 487 CALORIES PER SERVING.**

PORK ANTHONY

WHEN I lived in Charlotte, I used to go to a Chinese restaurant every week owned by a man named Anthony. He had a chicken dish on his buffet every Friday that I loved. I asked him how to make it and this is the result. For those of you who don't like pork, you can use chicken thighs like he did.

QUAN.	INGREDIENT	CARB GRAMS	AVAIL. CARB	FAT	PROTEIN
1 lb.	PORK ROAST cut into ½ inch cubes	0	0	32.8	87.9
2 T.	SESAME OIL	0	0	26.0	0
½ c.	ONION, sliced thinly	5.0	3.9	0	0.7
2 T.	SOY SAUCE	1.0	1.0	0	4.0
2 t.	GARLIC POWDER	4.0	4.0	0	1.0
½ c.	WATER				
	TOTALS	10.0	8.9	58.8	93.6
	PER SERVING	5.0	4.5	29.4	46.8

- Fry the pork in the oil in a 10 inch skillet over medium high heat until it begins to brown. Add the onion and cook it until it begins to brown. Add the remaining ingredients, stir well, cover, and bring to a boil. Reduce the heat to medium low and let simmer 30–45 minutes, stirring every 15 minutes.

- **MAKES 2 SERVINGS WITH ABOUT 470 CALORIES PER SERVING.**

CHICKEN

DISHES

BUFFALO THIGHS

I am a big fan of chicken wings. Several years ago, I decided to try to add a little more flavor to some chicken thighs while keeping with the basic chicken wing notion—vinegar, oil, and some type of pepper sauce.

QUAN.	INGREDIENT	CARB GRAMS	AVAIL. CARB	FAT	PROTEIN
2 lb.	**CHICKEN THIGHS.** Remove the skin and bone and cut into ¾ inch cubes (this should yield about 1 lb. of meat)	0	0	17.6	108.5
2 T.	**OLIVE OIL**	0	0	26.0	0
1 t.	**SALT**				
½ t.	**BLACK PEPPER**				
½ t.	**CAYENNE PEPPER** (more or less added to your taste)				
2 t.	**GARLIC POWDER**	4.0	4.0	0	1.0
2 T.	**WHITE VINEGAR**				
1 T.	**RED CAYENNE SAUCE** (more or less added to your taste)				
½ c.	**ONION,** diced	6.9	5.5	0	1.0
2 t.	**SUGAR EQUIVALENT SWEETENER**				
½ c.	**WATER**				
	TOTALS	10.9	9.5	43.6	110.5
	PER SERVING	5.5	4.6	21.8	55.3

- Fry the chicken, pepper, and salt in the oil in a 3 quart skillet or soup pot over medium high heat until it begins to brown. Add the onions and cook until they become clear. Add the remaining ingredients, cover, and bring to a boil. Reduce the heat to low and simmer for an additional 30 minutes, stirring every 10 minutes. Most of the liquid should have reduced. If it becomes too dry, add a little water. Serve with a slaw of your choice.

- **MAKES 2 SERVINGS WITH ABOUT 436 CALORIES PER SERVING.**

CHICKEN DIABLO

QUAN.	INGREDIENT	CARB GRAMS	AVAIL. CARB	FAT	PROTEIN
2 lb.	**CHICKEN BREAST**, uncooked, boneless, skinless, and cut into ¾ inch cubes (if you use thigh meat instead, you need to add a few fat grams)	0	0	8.3	209.6
2 T.	**OLIVE OIL**	0	0	26.0	0
½ c.	**ONION**, diced	6.9	5.5	0	1.0
1 c.	**GREEN PEPPERS**, diced	9.6	6.9	0.2	1.3
½ c.	**WATER**				
4 T.	**DRY RED WINE**	1.0	1.0	0	0.2
2 t.	**GARLIC POWDER**	4.0	4.0	0	1.0
1 t.	**SALT**				
2 T.	**WHITE VINEGAR**				
½ t.	**BLACK PEPPER**				
2 t.	**CAYENNE PEPPER** (more or less added to your taste)				
4 T.	**TOMATO SAUCE**	4.4	3.6	0.1	0.9
2 t.	**ITALIAN SEASONING**				
	TOTALS	25.9	21.0	34.6	214.0
	PER SERVING	6.5	5.3	8.7	53.5

- Fry the chicken in the oil in a 3 quart skillet or soup pot over medium high heat until it begins to brown. Add the onions and cook until they are clear. Add the remaining ingredients, cover, and bring to a boil. Reduce the heat to medium low and simmer 30 minutes. Remove the lid and reduce the sauce to about ½ cup.

- **MAKES 4 SERVINGS WITH ABOUT 314 CALORIES PER SERVING.**

PEPPERONI CHICKEN

A few years ago, I received an e-mail from a lady who had found this recipe on my cookbook web site and made it for her family for supper to see how they liked it. She said that her teenage son wouldn't let anybody else in the family have any and wanted to know how she could get the cookbook the very next day.

QUAN.	INGREDIENT	CARB GRAMS	AVAIL. CARB	FAT	PROTEIN
2 lb.	**CHICKEN BREAST,** uncooked, boneless, skinless, and cut into ¾ inch cubes (if you use thigh meat instead, you need to add a few fat grams)	0	0	8.3	209.6
2 t.	**OLIVE OIL**	0	0	26.0	0
¼ lb.	**SLICED PEPPERONI**	3.2	3.2	46.8	23.6
½ c.	**ONION,** diced	6.9	5.5	0	1.0
1 c.	**GREEN PEPPERS,** diced	9.6	6.9	0.2	1.3
½ c.	**BLACK OLIVES,** pitted and sliced thinly	4.2	2.0	6.9	0.6
2 t.	**GARLIC POWDER**	4.0	4.0	0	1.0
1 t.	**ANISE** or **FENNEL**				
2	**CHICKEN BOUILLON CUBES**				
½ t.	**BLACK PEPPER**				
½ c.	**DRY WHITE WINE**	0.8	0.8	0	0
¼ lb.	**MOZZARELLA CHEESE,** shredded	3.1	3.1	17.0	27.3
½ c.	**GRATED PARMESAN CHEESE**	1.9	1.9	14.3	20.8
	TOTALS	33.7	27.4	119.5	285.2
	PER SERVING	5.6	4.6	19.9	47.5

- In a large, ovenproof skillet, fry the chicken in the oil over medium high heat until it begins to brown slightly. Add the onions and cook until they begin to clear. Add the remaining ingredients except the pepperoni and cheese, cover, and bring to a boil. Reduce heat and simmer 30 minutes. Turn on the oven broiler. Remove the lid and stir in the pepperoni. Sprinkle the grated Parmesan cheese over the contents of the skillet, then the mozzarella, and put under the broiler until the cheese browns.

- **MAKES 6 SERVINGS WITH ABOUT 388 CALORIES PER SERVING.**

CHICKEN IN RIESLING

CHICKEN and mushrooms in a white wine and cream sauce is a little more involved than just grilling your rib-eye steak, but it does provide a tasty change.

QUAN.	INGREDIENT	CARB GRAMS	AVAIL. CARB	FAT	PROTEIN
2 lb.	**CHICKEN BREAST**, uncooked, boneless, skinless, and cut into ¾ inch cubes (if you use thigh meat instead, you need to add a few fat grams)	0	0	8.3	209.6
4 T.	**BUTTER**	0	0	52.0	0
I	**CHICKEN BOUILLON CUBE**				
½ t.	**BLACK PEPPER**				
½ c.	**ONION**, sliced thinly	5.0	3.9	0	0.7
2 t.	**GARLIC POWDER**	4.0	4.0	0	1.0
2 c.	**BUTTON MUSHROOMS**, cut in half	6.5	4.8	0.3	2.9
I c.	**RIESLING WINE**	1.9	1.9	0	0.2
3 T.	**HEAVY CREAM**	1.2	1.2	15.7	0.9
	TOTALS	18.6	15.8	76.3	215.3
	PER SERVING	4.7	4.0	19.1	53.8

- Fry the chicken in the butter in a 3 quart skillet or soup pot over medium high heat until it begins to brown slightly. Add the onion and cook until it becomes clear. Add the remaining ingredients except the cream, cover, and bring to a boil. Reduce the heat and simmer 30 minutes. Remove the lid, reduce the sauce to ½ cup, and blend in the cream. Serve the chicken with the sauce.

- **MAKES 4 SERVINGS WITH ABOUT 403 CALORIES PER SERVING.**

BURGUNDY CHICKEN

QUAN.	INGREDIENT	CARB GRAMS	AVAIL. CARB	FAT	PROTEIN
2 lb.	**CHICKEN BREAST**, uncooked, boneless, skinless, and cut into ¾ inch cubes (if you use thigh meat instead, you need to add a few fat grams)	0	0	8.3	209.6
2 T.	**OLIVE OIL**	0	0	26.0	0
2 t.	**GARLIC POWDER**	4.0	4.0	0	1.0
½ c.	**ONION**, diced	6.9	5.5	0	1.0
4 c.	**BUTTON MUSHROOMS**, cut in half	13.0	9.6	0.6	5.8
1 c.	**DRY RED WINE**	4.0	4.0	0	0.8
1	**CHICKEN BOUILLON CUBE**				
1 t.	**SUGAR EQUIVALENT SWEETENER**				
	TOTALS	27.9	23.1	34.9	218.2
	PER SERVING	7.0	5.8	8.7	54.6

- Fry the chicken in the oil over medium high heat in a 3 quart skillet or soup pot until it begins to brown slightly. Add the onions and cook until the onions become clear. Add the mushrooms and cook until they begin to wilt slightly. Add the remaining ingredients, cover, and bring to a boil. Reduce the heat to medium low and simmer 30 minutes, stirring every 15 minutes.

- **MAKES 4 SERVINGS WITH ABOUT 320 CALORIES PER SERVING.**

CHICKEN BORDEAUX

THIS is chicken with mushrooms and a little tomato flavor. I suggest serving this with a good salad with French Dressing Blanc (see page 39).

QUAN.	INGREDIENT	CARB GRAMS	AVAIL. CARB	FAT	PROTEIN
2 lb.	**CHICKEN BREAST,** uncooked, boneless, skinless, and cut into ¾ inch cubes (if you use thigh meat instead, you need to add a few fat grams)	0	0	8.3	209.6
2 T.	**OLIVE OIL**	0	0	26.0	0
2 t.	**GARLIC POWDER**	4.0	4.0	0	1.0
½ c.	**ONION,** diced	6.9	5.5	0	1.0
4 c.	**BUTTON MUSHROOMS,** cut in half	13.0	9.6	0.6	5.8
1 c.	**DRY WHITE WINE**	1.6	1.6	0	0
2 t.	**SUGAR EQUIVALENT SWEETENER**				
4 T.	**TOMATO SAUCE**	4.4	3.6	0.1	0.9
1	**CHICKEN BOUILLON CUBE**				
½ t.	**BLACK PEPPER**				
	TOTALS	29.9	24.3	35.0	218.3
	PER SERVING	7.5	6.1	8.8	54.6

■ Fry the chicken in the oil in a 3 quart skillet or soup pot over medium high heat until it begins to brown slightly. Add the onions and cook until the onions become clear. Add the mushrooms and cook until they begin to wilt slightly. Add the remaining ingredients, cover, and bring to a boil. Reduce the heat to medium low and simmer 30 minutes, stirring at least once. Let sit 10 minutes before serving.

■ **MAKES 4 SERVINGS WITH ABOUT 322 CALORIES PER SERVING.**

CHICKEN VINAIGRETTE

QUAN.	INGREDIENT	CARB GRAMS	AVAIL. CARB	FAT	PROTEIN
2 lb.	**CHICKEN BREAST**, uncooked, boneless, skinless, and cut into ¾ inch cubes (if you use thigh meat instead, you need to add a few fat grams)	0	0	8.3	209.6
2 t.	**GARLIC POWDER**	4.0	4.0	0	1.0
1	**CHICKEN BOUILLON CUBE**				
½ t.	**CLOVES**				
½ t.	**CINNAMON**				
1	**BAY LEAF**				
½ t.	**BLACK PEPPER**				
2 T.	**OLIVE OIL**	0	0	26.0	0
½ c.	**ONION**, diced	6.9	5.5	0	1.0
15	**GREEN STUFFED OLIVES**, sliced thinly	3.0	3.0	7.5	0
2 T.	**RED WINE VINEGAR**				
2 T.	**DRY RED WINE**	0.5	0.5	0	0.1
1 T.	**LEMON JUICE**	1.3	1.2	0	0.1
1 T.	**SUGAR EQUIVALENT SWEETENER**				
½ c.	**WATER**				
	TOTALS	15.7	14.2	41.8	211.8
	PER SERVING	3.9	3.6	10.5	53.0

■ Fry the chicken in the oil in a 3 quart skillet or soup pot over medium high heat until it begins to brown. Add the remaining ingredients, cover, and bring to a boil. Reduce heat to medium low and simmer 30 minutes, stirring every 15 minutes. Remove from the heat and remove the bay leaf before serving.

■ **MAKES 4 SERVINGS WITH ABOUT 321 CALORIES PER SERVING.**

CHICKEN DIVAN

WHEN I worked at the MGM Grand in Las Vegas, I spent most of my tenure in the Italian gourmet room. The way that the grated Parmesan cheese is incorporated into the cream in this recipe is almost the exact method we used to make the alfredo sauce at the Grand. Just heat your cream and start stirring in the grated Parmesan.

QUAN.	INGREDIENT	CARB GRAMS	AVAIL. CARB	FAT	PROTEIN
2 lb.	**CHICKEN BREAST**, uncooked, boneless, skinless, and cut into ¾ inch cubes	0	0	8.3	209.6
3 T.	**BUTTER**	0	0	39.0	0
1 c.	**CANNED CHICKEN BROTH**				
1 bag	**FROZEN BROCCOLI**, about 1 pound, thawed	24.2	10.6	0	14.1
½ c.	**ONION**, diced	6.9	5.5	0	1.0
4 T.	**DRY WHITE WINE**	0.4	0.4	0	0
4 T.	**GRATED PARMESAN CHEESE**	0.9	0.9	7.1	10.4
4 T.	**HEAVY CREAM**	3.3	3.3	41.8	2.5
	TOTALS	35.7	20.7	96.2	237.6
	PER SERVING	7.1	4.1	19.2	47.5

- Cook the chicken in the butter in a 3 quart skillet or soup pot over medium high heat until it begins to brown. Add the onion and cook until it is clear. Add the wine and the chicken broth, cover, and bring to a boil. Reduce heat to medium low and simmer 30 minutes. Turn the heat up to medium, add the broccoli, and simmer an additional 15 minutes. Stir in the cream. Add the grated Parmesan cheese slowly, stirring constantly, until the cheese is incorporated into the cream. It will thicken slightly.

- **MAKES 5 SERVINGS WITH ABOUT 379 CALORIES PER SERVING.**

TWENTY CLOVES OF GARLIC CHICKEN

OKAY, it may not be twenty cloves. Surprisingly, as you already know if you've gotten this far, garlic has a lot of sugar in it. According to the USDA, garlic is about one third carbohydrate, most of which is available and is not fiber. However, garlic is considered indispensable by many folks, including me, and this dish is for us.

QUAN.	INGREDIENT	CARB GRAMS	AVAIL. CARB	FAT	PROTEIN
3 lb.	**FRYER** cut into 8 pieces	0	0	14.4	126.4
2 T.	**OLIVE OIL**	0	0	26.0	0
½ c.	**GARLIC CLOVES** peeled	22.5	21.1	0.3	4.3
½ c.	**DRY WHITE WINE**	0.8	0.8	0	0
½ c.	**CANNED CHICKEN STOCK**				
½ c.	**HEAVY WHIPPING CREAM**	3.3	3.3	41.8	2.5
1 t.	**ONION POWDER**	1.7	1.6	0	0.2
	SALT AND BLACK PEPPER to taste				
	TOTALS	28.3	26.8	82.5	133.4
	PER SERVING	9.4	8.9	27.5	44.5

- Preheat oven to 400° F. Spread the garlic cloves in the bottom of a Dutch oven or roasting pan. Pour the wine and oil over the garlic and sprinkle it lightly with salt. Place the chicken on top of the garlic and sprinkle with salt, pepper, and onion powder. Bake 45 minutes or until the dark meat comes off the bone. Return the pan to the top of the stove. Remove the chicken from the pan. Add the chicken stock and the cream and bring to a boil. Let it reduce, uncovered, for 3 minutes or until the sauce meets your taste.

■ **MAKES 3 SERVINGS WITH ABOUT 461 CALORIES PER SERVING.**

CHICKEN BREASTS
WITH MUSHROOMS

THIS is a very simple, quick, yet elegant recipe to prepare for any occasion. Serve it with a little dry white wine and a vinaigrette salad.

QUAN.	INGREDIENT	CARB GRAMS	AVAIL. CARB	FAT	PROTEIN
2 lb.	**CHICKEN BREAST**, uncooked, boneless, skinless, and cut into ¾ inch cubes	0	0	8.3	209.6
2 T.	**OLIVE OIL**	0	0	26.0	0
½ c.	**ONION**, diced	6.9	5.5	0	1.0
½ c.	**GREEN ONIONS**, diced	3.7	2.4	0	0.9
2 c.	**BUTTON MUSHROOMS**, sliced	6.5	4.8	0.3	2.9
2 t.	**GARLIC POWDER**	4.0	4.0	0	0.5
I	**CHICKEN BOUILLON CUBE**				
½ c.	**DRY WHITE WINE**	0.8	0.8	0	0
I t.	**SUGAR EQUIVALENT SWEETENER**				
½ c.	**WATER**				
	TOTALS	21.9	17.5	34.6	214.9
	PER SERVING	5.5	4.4	8.7	53.7

- Fry the chicken in the oil in a 3 quart skillet or soup pot over medium high heat until it begins to brown. Add the onions and cook until the onions become clear. Add the mushrooms and the garlic and cook until the mushrooms begin to wilt. Add the water, wine, sugar substitute, and bouillon cube, cover, and bring to a boil. Reduce the heat to medium low and simmer 30 minutes. Remove the cover and reduce the sauce to your taste.

- **MAKES 4 SERVINGS WITH ABOUT 311 CALORIES PER SERVING.**

RED-COOKED CHICKEN

RED-COOKING sauce is a Chinese master sauce. This means that it is saved between batches and reused, getting richer and richer each time. The carbs in this dish are hard to calculate because all of the carbs are not consumed with each serving. I assume you get one twentieth of the carbs per serving, which is probably an overestimate. This, by the way, makes a very good snack food for those who occasionally get the munchies.

QUAN.	INGREDIENT	CARB GRAMS	AVAIL. CARB	FAT	PROTEIN
10	CHICKEN LEGS	0	0	182.8	303.2
1 c.	SOY SAUCE	8.0	8.0	0	32.0
1 c.	WATER				
1 T.	GARLIC POWDER	6.1	6.1	0	1.4
1 t.	DRIED GINGER				
1 t.	STAR ANISE				
1 t.	SUGAR EQUIVALENT SWEETENER				
½ c.	GREEN ONIONS, diced	3.7	2.4	0	0.9
	TOTALS	17.8	16.6	182.8	337.5
	PER SERVING OF 1 LEG	0.9	0.8	18.3	32.0

- Combine all ingredients except the chicken in a 3 quart soup pot and bring to a boil. Add the chicken and return to boiling. If you don't have enough liquid to cover the chicken, then just add a little more soy sauce and water. Cover the pan and simmer for 30 minutes. Turn off the heat and let stand for 20 minutes. The chicken is ready to serve. It also keeps in the refrigerator for several days. (This dish is good hot or cold.) After cooking, just strain the sauce into a refrigerator container. Allow the fat to remain on top until just before reusing the sauce. To reuse the sauce, remove the fat and boil the sauce for 15 minutes (just a precaution against possible microbe growth) before adding the items to be cooked. Periodically add more seasonings, water, and soy sauce.

■ **MAKES 10 SERVINGS WITH ABOUT 296 CALORIES PER SERVING.**

LIME AND TARRAGON CHICKEN

QUAN.	INGREDIENT	CARB GRAMS	AVAIL. CARB	FAT	PROTEIN
2 lb.	**CHICKEN BREAST**, uncooked, boneless, skinless, and cut into ¾ inch cubes (if you use thigh meat instead, you need to add a few fat grams)	0	0	8.3	209.6
2 T.	**OLIVE OIL**	0	0	26.0	0
2 T.	**LIME JUICE**	2.8	2.7	0	0.1
2 T.	**WHITE VINEGAR**				
½ t.	**LEMON EXTRACT**				
½ c.	**DRY WHITE WINE**	0.8	0.8	0	0
2 t.	**GARLIC POWDER**	4.0	4.0	0	0.5
1 t.	**ONION POWDER**	1.7	1.6	0	0.2
1 t.	**DRIED GINGER**				
½ t.	**DRIED TARRAGON**				
1 c.	**CANNED CHICKEN STOCK**				
4 T.	**TOMATO SAUCE**	4.4	3.6	0.1	0.9
2	**CHICKEN BOUILLON CUBES**				
1 t.	**SUGAR EQUIVALENT SWEETENER**				
	TOTALS	13.7	12.7	34.4	211.3
	PER SERVING	3.4	3.2	8.6	52.8

- Mix the lime juice, vinegar, and lemon extract. Marinate the chicken in the seasonings, the lime juice mixture, and the wine for at least 1 hour if possible. Fry the chicken in the oil in a 3 quart skillet or soup pot over medium high heat for about 10 minutes. Add the remaining ingredients, cover, and bring to a boil. Reduce the heat to medium low and let simmer 30 minutes.

- **MAKES 4 SERVINGS WITH ABOUT 301 CALORIES PER SERVING.**

CHICKEN WITH TARRAGON SAUCE

QUAN.	INGREDIENT	CARB GRAMS	AVAIL. CARB	FAT	PROTEIN
2 lb.	**CHICKEN BREAST**, uncooked, boneless, skinless, and cut into ¾ inch cubes (if you use thigh meat instead, you need to add a few fat grams)	0	0	8.3	209.6
2 T.	**OLIVE OIL**	0	0	26.0	0
1 c.	**DRY WHITE WINE**	1.6	1.6	0	0
1 T.	**DIJON MUSTARD**				
2 t.	**DRIED TARRAGON**				
1	**CHICKEN BOUILLON CUBE**				
4 T.	**HEAVY CREAM**	1.7	1.7	20.9	1.2
½ t.	**FRESH GROUND BLACK PEPPER**				
	TOTALS	3.3	3.3	55.2	210.8
	PER SERVING	0.8	0.8	13.8	52.7

- Fry the chicken in the oil in a 3 quart skillet or soup pot over medium high heat until it begins to brown slightly. Add the wine, pepper, 1 t. of the tarragon, and the bouillon cube, cover, and bring to a boil. Reduce the heat to medium low and let simmer 30 minutes. Stir in the cream and remaining ingredients and let simmer, uncovered, about 10 minutes until the mixture begins to thicken.

- **MAKES 4 SERVINGS WITH ABOUT 338 CALORIES PER SERVING.**

KOREAN BAR-B-Q CHICKEN

MOST of the chicken I've had in Korean restaurants has a sauce made with hot bean paste, which is wonderful but relatively high in carbs. Here's my low carb version of their recipe. You can also cook this under the broiler, but the flavor really comes out when it is grilled.

QUAN.	INGREDIENT	CARB GRAMS	AVAIL. CARB	FAT	PROTEIN
3 lb.	**FRYER** cut into 8 pieces	0	0	14.4	126.4
½ c.	**SOY SAUCE**	4.0	4.0	0	16.0
2 T.	**SESAME OIL**	0	0	26.0	0
1 t.	**SESAME SEEDS**				
3 T.	**SUGAR EQUIVALENT SWEETENER**				
½ c.	**GREEN ONIONS**, diced	3.7	2.4	0	0.9
¼ t.	**BLACK PEPPER**				
½ t.	**CAYENNE PEPPER** (more or less added to your taste)				
1 t.	**DRIED GINGER**				
1 t.	**GARLIC POWDER**	2.0	2.0	0	0.5
	TOTALS	9.7	8.4	40.4	143.8
	PER SERVING	3.2	2.8	13.5	47.9

- Mix all ingredients. Let the chicken marinate 1 hour if possible. Cook slowly over charcoal, basting with the marinade. Discard any marinade that isn't used. Serve with Yaki Mandu Sauce (see page 243) for dipping.

- **MAKES 3 SERVINGS WITH ABOUT 324 CALORIES PER SERVING.**

CHICKEN PAPRIKA

THIS is a variation of the more famous Hungarian Goulash (see page 106). For those who like a little heat, you can add a sprinkle or two of your favorite red cayenne sauce.

QUAN.	INGREDIENT	CARB GRAMS	AVAIL. CARB	FAT	PROTEIN
2 lb.	**CHICKEN BREAST**, uncooked, boneless, skinless, and cut into ¾ inch cubes (if you use thigh meat instead, you need to add a few fat grams)	0	0	8.3	209.6
2 T.	**OLIVE OIL**	0	0	26.0	0
3 T.	**PAPRIKA**	11.4	7.2	2.4	3.0
2 t.	**GARLIC POWDER**	4.0	4.0	0	1.0
½ t.	**BLACK PEPPER**				
½ c.	**ONION**, diced	6.9	5.5	0	1.0
1 c.	**CANNED CHICKEN STOCK**				
1 c.	**SOUR CREAM**	9.8	9.8	45.7	7.3
1	**CHICKEN BOUILLON CUBE**				
1 t.	**SUGAR EQUIVALENT SWEETENER**				
	TOTALS	32.1	26.5	82.4	221.9
	PER SERVING	8.0	6.6	20.6	55.5

- Fry the chicken in the oil in a 3 quart skillet or soup pot over medium high heat until the chicken turns white and begins to brown. Add the onions and cook until they become clear. Add the remaining ingredients except the sour cream, cover, and bring to a boil. Reduce the heat to medium low and simmer 30 minutes. Stir in the sour cream and serve.

- **MAKES 4 SERVINGS WITH ABOUT 434 CALORIES PER SERVING.**

BAKED CHICKEN THIGHS

QUAN.	INGREDIENT	CARB GRAMS	AVAIL. CARB	FAT	PROTEIN
6	**CHICKEN THIGHS** (average size about 4 ounces with the bone in)	0	0	78.6	97.2
	KOSHER SALT				
	TOTALS	0	0	78.6	97.2
	PER SERVING	0	0	39.3	48.6

- Preheat the oven to 500° F. Place the chicken thighs in the baking pan, skin-side up. Sprinkle the chicken skin liberally with kosher salt and rub it in. Place the pan on the top rack in the oven without a lid. Bake for 30–40 minutes. This generates a lot of fat so make sure that the pan will not overflow. Pour the fat off and scrape the bottom of the pan for some very flavorful stuff.

- **MAKES 2 SERVINGS WITH ABOUT 548 CALORIES PER SERVING.**

NOTE that this actually has considerably fewer calories than indicated because most of the fat bakes off the chicken, probably on the order of two ounces or more.

CHICKEN THIGHS IN RASPBERRY VINEGAR SAUCE

YOU can actually use any kind of chicken for this, but I like thighs because they tend to have more flavor. You can serve this with a salad with any berry vinaigrette (see page 48).

QUAN.	INGREDIENT	CARB GRAMS	AVAIL. CARB	FAT	PROTEIN
3 T.	CLARIFIED BUTTER or OLIVE OIL	0	0	39.0	0
4 T.	DRY WHITE WINE	0.4	0.4	0	0
2 T.	RASPBERRY VINEGAR (see page 72)	0.4	0.4	0	0
½ c.	GREEN ONIONS, diced	3.7	2.4	0	0.9
2 t.	GARLIC POWDER	4.0	4.0	0	1.0
1 t.	SUGAR EQUIVALENT SWEETENER				
1 T.	PREPARED MUSTARD, any coarse ground will suffice				
½ c.	WATER				
1	CHICKEN BOUILLON CUBE				
1 t.	PAPRIKA				
¼ t.	CAYENNE PEPPER (more or less added to your taste)				
2 lb.	CHICKEN THIGHS, skin and bone removed, cut into ¾ inch cubes (this should yield about 1 lb. of meat)	0	0	17.6	108.5
	TOTALS	8.5	7.2	56.6	110.4
	PER SERVING	4.3	3.6	28.3	55.2

- Brown the chicken in the butter in a 10 inch skillet over medium high heat. Add the onions and cook for a couple of minutes until the onions begin to become clear. Deglaze the pan with the wine. Add the remaining ingredients, cover, bring to a boil and reduce the heat to medium low. You should turn the chicken at least once to ensure even contact with the sauce. After 30–45 minutes, remove the lid and continue cooking until the sauce is reduced to about half.

- **MAKES 2 SERVINGS WITH ABOUT 489 CALORIES PER SERVING.**

CUBAN-STYLE CHICKEN THIGHS

QUAN.	INGREDIENT	CARB GRAMS	AVAIL. CARB	FAT	PROTEIN
2 lb.	CHICKEN THIGHS, skinned and deboned and cut into ¾ inch cubes (this should yield about 1 lb. of meat)	0	0	17.6	108.5
2 t.	GARLIC POWDER	4.0	4.0	0	1.0
¼ c.	ONION, diced	3.5	2.8	0	0.5
½ c.	DRY WHITE WINE	0.8	0.8	0	0
2 T.	OLIVE OIL	0	0	26.0	0
2 T.	LIME JUICE	2.8	2.7	0	0.1
¼ t.	BLACK PEPPER				
½ t.	SALT				
2 t.	GROUND CUMIN				
1 t.	SUGAR EQUIVALENT SWEETENER				
	TOTALS	11.1	10.3	43.6	110.1
	PER SERVING	5.6	5.2	21.8	55.1

- Brown the chicken in the oil in a 10 inch skillet over medium high heat. Add the onion and cook until it becomes clear. Deglaze the pan with the wine. Add the remaining ingredients, cover, bring to a boil, reduce the heat to medium low, and let it simmer for about 30–45 minutes, stirring every 15 minutes.

- **MAKES 2 SERVINGS WITH ABOUT 437 CALORIES PER SERVING.**

CHICKEN FAJITAS

MANY years ago, I was eating in my favorite local Mexican restaurant when one of the tables close to me received their order of fajitas. It was gorgeous. So I asked the manager how the chef was able to make the fajitas with the just-right browned onions. The secret to the world's best fajitas is . . . drum roll, please . . . soy sauce. The soy sauce is used to provide not only color but also the salt for the food. Serve your fajitas with sides of pickled jalapeños, shredded lettuce, diced tomatoes, various shredded cheeses, Salsa (see page 245), Pico de Gallo (see page 252), or Guacamole (see page 244), and don't forget to count the carbs.

QUAN.	INGREDIENT	CARB GRAMS	AVAIL. CARB	FAT	PROTEIN
2 lb.	**CHICKEN BREAST**, uncooked, boneless, skinless, and cut into ½ inch cubes	0	0	8.3	209.6
1 c.	**ONION**, sliced thinly	10.0	7.8	0	1.4
2 c.	**GREEN PEPPERS**, sliced thinly	19.2	13.8	0.4	2.6
2 t.	**GARLIC POWDER**	4.0	4.0	0	1.0
1 t.	**ONION POWDER**	1.7	1.6	0	0.2
7 T.	**OLIVE OIL**	0	0	91.0	0
6 T	**WHITE VINEGAR**				
½ t.	**LEMON EXTRACT**				
6 T.	**SOY SAUCE**	3.0	3.0	0	12.0
5 t.	**LIME JUICE**	2.2	2.1	0	0.1
4 t.	**SUGAR EQUIVALENT SWEETENER**				
1 t.	**LIQUID SMOKE** (optional)				
1 T.	**DRIED CILANTRO**				
2 t.	**OREGANO**				
4 T.	**WATER**				
	TOTALS	40.1	32.3	99.7	226.9
	PER SERVING	10.0	8.1	24.9	56.7

- First, prepare the marinade for the chicken. In a 1 cup bowl, mix 2 t. of sugar substitute, 4 T. of vinegar, 4 T. of soy sauce, the lemon extract, garlic powder, onion powder, oregano, cilantro, and liquid smoke. Pour this over the chicken in a 2 quart bowl and let it marinate at least 1 hour, the longer the better, stirring occasionally.

- The onions and green peppers are cooked separately and are prepared by the exact same method. To prepare the green peppers, mix 1 T. of vinegar, 1 T. of soy sauce, 1 t. of sugar substitute, 1 t. of lime juice and 2 T. of water in a bowl. Set this aside until you are ready to cook the green peppers. Do the same for the onions.

- Cook the peppers and onions first, before you cook the chicken. In a 3 quart skillet over medium high heat, cook the green peppers in 2 T. of oil until they begin to wilt, stirring occasionally. When they begin to wilt, after about 10 minutes, add the soy sauce mixture and let it reduce a couple of minutes, stirring constantly. Place the peppers in a microwavable bowl and set aside. Repeat this same process for the onions.

- For the chicken, in the same large skillet, cook the chicken in 3 T. of oil over medium high heat until it begins to change color, about 5 minutes. The marinade will begin to boil. When it begins to boil, cover and reduce the heat to medium low. Cook, covered, for about 15–20 minutes. Remove the lid and allow the marinade to reduce to your taste. Heat the peppers and onions in a microwave for a minute just before serving.

■ **MAKES 4 SERVINGS WITH ABOUT 483 CALORIES PER SERVING.**

BEEF FAJITAS

QUAN.	INGREDIENT	CARB GRAMS	AVAIL. CARB	FAT	PROTEIN
	substitute beef for chicken in the Chicken Fajitas recipe				
2 lb.	**STEW BEEF** or **CHUCK ROAST** cut into ½ inch cubes	0	0	57.6	174.6
	TOTALS	40.1	32.3	149.0	191.9
	PER SERVING	10.0	8.1	37.3	48.0

- Beef Fajitas are prepared exactly like the Chicken Fajitas just described except they are cooked longer. After you cover the pan and reduce the heat to medium low, let this cook at least a half hour.

- **MAKES 4 SERVINGS WITH ABOUT 560 CALORIES PER SERVING.**

SHRIMP FAJITAS

QUAN.	INGREDIENT	CARB GRAMS	AVAIL. CARB	FAT	PROTEIN
	substitute shrimp for chicken in the Chicken Fajitas recipe				
2 lb.	**UNCOOKED SHRIMP**, as large as you can afford, peeled and deveined	8.2	8.2	11.8	184.4
	TOTALS	48.3	40.5	103.2	201.7
	PER SERVING	12.1	10.1	25.8	50.4

■ Shrimp Fajitas are prepared exactly like the Chicken Fajitas previously described except they are cooked for a shorter period of time. The cooking time depends on the size of the shrimp, larger shrimp taking longer to cook. Don't cover the pan; reduce the heat to medium low and let this cook until all of the shrimp have turned pink or white, and then cook an additional 5 minutes.

■ **MAKES 4 SERVINGS WITH ABOUT 474 CALORIES PER SERVING.**

THANKSGIVING TURKEY

THANKSGIVING is my favorite meal of the year to cook. Holidays are an especially hard time to maintain your low carb eating, so if I eat mashed potatoes and corn bread dressing only once a year, this will be the day. However, we can minimize the carbs for this day and we can make it an absolutely NO SUGAR day, as all our days should be. You can find recipes for low carb vegetables (see Veggies on the Side page 195) and Pumpkin Pie (see page 257). I have no recipe for low carb mashed potatoes. Sorry.

QUAN.	INGREDIENT	CARB GRAMS	AVAIL. CARB	FAT	PROTEIN
1	TURKEY				
1	MEDIUM ONION, sliced				
1	MEDIUM CARROT, diced				
2	STALKS CELERY, diced				
1 c.	DRY WHITE WINE				
4 c.	WATER				
	SALT AND BLACK PEPPER to taste				
1 T.	GARLIC POWDER				
2 T.	DRIED PARSLEY				
1 T.	PAPRIKA				
1 T.	ONION POWDER				
	TOTALS **PER SERVING OF 4 OUNCES OF WHITE MEAT**	**0**	**0**	**3.3**	**25.0**

- All of this is done on the Wednesday evening before Thanksgiving. Make sure that the turkey is properly thawed if it has been frozen. Remove the neck and the giblets from the turkey. Place it in a baking pan breast-side down. Preheat oven to 400° F. Make sure that you have enough room in the pan to spread the vegetables around the bottom. If you are using a baking bag, this should not be a problem. Spread the vegetables around the bottom of the pan. Pour the wine and the water over the turkey. Sprinkle the salt, pepper, garlic powder, parsley, paprika, and onion powder over the turkey (just dump whatever you have remaining in the liquid). Cover and bake for 30 minutes. Reduce heat to 325° F and plan on cooking about 20 minutes per pound or more. You will know that the turkey is cooked when you can twist the leg bone away from the thigh easily. If you have to work to do it, the bird is not ready. After the turkey is done cooking, turn the heat off and leave it in the oven overnight. It will still be warm the next day. On Thanksgiving day, you can throw away all of the vegetables in the stock, or you can put them in your gravy. The bird will be moist and there will be plenty of stock to serve with it. **If you want to count the carbs in the stock, count it as 1 gram per serving for the spices.**
- This has about 130 calories per serving of 4 ounces of white meat.

CHICKEN
WINGS

As many folks have discovered, chicken wings are the perfect low carb diet food. A lady I know in Florida, a type II diabetic, makes a different kind of chicken wing dish twice a week and a different slaw dish and she never gets bored. As long as she stays on low carb she is able to totally control her diabetes without any medications, so this is a godsend for her. It seems that everyone now has a recipe for chicken wings. They have become a staple in our cuisine. You can get Buffalo wings, Syracuse wings, Montreal wings, Texas wings, Cajun wings, Korean wings—the list is endless. It also seems that everyone has their own way to prepare the "original" recipe for Buffalo wings from the Anchor Bar in Buffalo. One person says you should use only margarine. Another person says that you should use only a certain type of hot sauce. Another person claims that the blue cheese dressing is a dip for the wings and not the celery and yet another says that the proper ratio of hot pepper sauce to oil is 3:1. Whatever the case, wings are especially good for low carb eaters. I've included over a dozen recipes, beginning with my version of the original.

BUFFALO WINGS

QUAN.	INGREDIENT	CARB GRAMS	AVAIL. CARB	FAT	PROTEIN
2 lb.	CHICKEN WINGS, split (this is about 9 wings)	0	0	62.7	80.8
4 T.	BUTTER or MARGARINE	0	0	52.0	0
1 T.	WHITE VINEGAR (optional to dilute the red cayenne sauce)				
1 T.	RED CAYENNE SAUCE (more or less added to your taste)				
1 t.	SALT				
⅛ t.	CELERY SEED (optional)				
¼ t.	CAYENNE PEPPER (optional, more or less to your taste)				
1 t.	GARLIC POWDER (optional)	2.0	2.0	0	0.5
½ t.	BLACK PEPPER (optional)				
½ t.	SUGAR EQUIVALENT SWEETENER (optional)				
	TOTALS	2.0	2.0	114.7	81.3
	PER SERVING	1.0	1.0	57.4	40.7

- Melt the butter in a small saucepan over medium heat. Add the hot sauce, vinegar, the spices, and the salt to the pan. Cook until the sauce thickens slightly and remove the pan from the heat. Fry the wings in 375° F oil until they are brown and crisp. Place the wings in a bowl that can be covered. Add the sauce and shake well insuring that they are evenly coated. After they are coated they can be baked for 10–15 additional minutes at 375° F to "dry up" the sauce. Serve with Blue Cheese Dressing (see page 42) and celery sticks.

- **MAKES 2 SERVINGS WITH ABOUT 683 CALORIES PER SERVING.**

BAKED BUFFALO WINGS

THIS is my favorite kind of Buffalo Wings. I prefer to bake them rather than deep-fry them. This recipe has the added garlic and onion flavor.

QUAN.	INGREDIENT	CARB GRAMS	AVAIL. CARB	FAT	PROTEIN
2 lb.	CHICKEN WINGS, split (this is about 9 wings)	0	0	62.7	80.8
4 T.	BUTTER or MARGARINE	0	0	52.0	0
1 T.	RED CAYENNE SAUCE (more or less added to your taste)				
1 T.	WHITE VINEGAR				
1 t.	SALT				
1 t.	GARLIC POWDER	2.0	2.0	0	0.5
1 t.	ONION POWDER	1.7	1.6	0	0.2
	TOTALS	3.7	3.6	114.7	81.5
	PER SERVING	1.9	1.8	57.4	40.8

- Melt the butter in a small saucepan. Add the hot sauce, vinegar, spices, and the salt to the butter and bring it to a boil. Remove the sauce from the heat. Bake the wings in your baking dish in the oven at 375° F until they are done, about 30–40 minutes. Place the wings in a bowl that can be covered. Add the sauce and shake well, ensuring that they are evenly coated. Serve with Blue Cheese Dressing (see page 42) and celery sticks.

- **MAKES 2 SERVINGS WITH ABOUT 687 CALORIES PER SERVING.**

GARLIC WINGS

QUAN.	INGREDIENT	CARB GRAMS	AVAIL. CARB	FAT	PROTEIN
2 lb.	**CHICKEN WINGS**, split (this is about 9 wings)	0	0	62.7	80.8
4 T.	**OLIVE OIL**	0	0	52.0	0
2 oz.	**CLOVES GARLIC**, whole and peeled	18.9	17.7	0.2	3.7
½ t.	**ROSEMARY**				
½ t.	**THYME**				
1 t.	**ONION POWDER**	1.7	1.6	0	0.2
2 T.	**DRY WHITE WINE**	0.2	0.2	0	0
1 t.	**SALT**				
	TOTALS	20.8	19.5	114.9	84.7
	PER SERVING	10.4	9.8	57.5	42.4

■ Heat your oven to 375° F. Place all ingredients in a casserole, tossing to coat evenly. Cover the casserole and bake 1 hour, stirring a couple of times. Serve with the olive oil as a dip. And don't forget to eat the garlic.

■ **MAKES 2 SERVINGS WITH ABOUT 726 CALORIES PER SERVING.**

MEXICAN WINGS VERDE

I'VE been making these wings for over ten years as a variation on a Mexican dish I got at one of my local restaurants. This is almost like using the wings for soup, so don't forget to consume the broth.

QUAN.	INGREDIENT	CARB GRAMS	AVAIL. CARB	FAT	PROTEIN
2 lb.	**CHICKEN WINGS**, split (this is about 9 wings)	0	0	62.7	80.8
1 c.	**WATER**				
½ c.	**ONION**, diced	6.9	5.5	0	1.0
2	**CHICKEN BOUILLON CUBES**				
1 t.	**GARLIC POWDER**	2.0	2.0	0	0.5
3 T.	**PICKLED JALAPEÑO PEPPERS**, diced (more or less added to your taste)				
	TOTALS	8.9	7.5	62.7	82.3
	PER SERVING	4.5	3.8	31.4	41.2

■ Put all ingredients in a two quart pan, cover and bring to a boil over high heat. Stir, reduce the heat to medium low, and simmer 30–45 minutes, stirring every 10 minutes until the meat falls away from the bones. Serve with some of the stock as a dip.

■ **MAKES 2 SERVINGS WITH ABOUT 463 CALORIES PER SERVING.**

BAR-B-Q WINGS

QUAN.	INGREDIENT	CARB GRAMS	AVAIL. CARB	FAT	PROTEIN
2 lb.	**CHICKEN WINGS**, split (this is about 9 wings)	0	0	62.7	80.8
1 c.	**BASIC BAR-B-Q SAUCE** (see page 236)	16.7	14.5	10.0	5.3
	TOTALS	16.7	14.5	72.7	86.1
	PER SERVING	8.4	7.3	36.4	43.1

- Place all ingredients in a 2 quart saucepan, cover, and bring to a boil. Reduce heat and let simmer about 15 minutes. Remove wings to a baking sheet and bake at 375° F for 30 minutes. Increase heat to 425° F and begin basting with some of the remaining sauce, cooking an additional 15 minutes. Serve with any remaining sauce.

- **MAKES 2 SERVINGS WITH ABOUT 529 CALORIES PER SERVING.**

CAJUN BAR-B-Q WINGS

IT'S been said that Cajun food is one of the true, unique American cuisines. We should give thanks to the likes of chefs Prudhomme and Lagasse for popularizing it. I think they would approve of this recipe.

QUAN.	INGREDIENT	CARB GRAMS	AVAIL. CARB	FAT	PROTEIN
2 lb.	CHICKEN WINGS, split (this is about 9 wings)	0	0	62.7	80.8
3 T.	RED CAYENNE SAUCE (more or less added to your taste)				
3 T.	CAJUN SEASONING	9.0	9.0	0	0
2 T.	COOKING OIL				
1 t.	SALT				
	TOTALS	9.0	9.0	62.7	80.8
	PER SERVING	4.5	4.5	31.4	40.4

- In a 2 cup bowl, mix the red cayenne sauce, Cajun seasoning, and cooking oil. Place the wings in a 2 quart bowl. Pour the seasoning sauce over the wings and mix well. Allow them to marinate as long as possible, at least an hour. Cook these slowly on the grill, basting with any remaining sauce. Serve with red cayenne sauce if desired. Discard any marinade that isn't used.

- **MAKES 2 SERVINGS WITH ABOUT 462 CALORIES PER SERVING.**

KANSAS CITY–STYLE WINGS

QUAN.	INGREDIENT	CARB GRAMS	AVAIL. CARB	FAT	PROTEIN
3 lb.	CHICKEN WINGS, split (this is about 14 wings)	0	0	97.5	125.7
½ c.	DIJON MUSTARD				
2 t.	OLIVE OIL	0	0	26.0	0
2 t.	GARLIC POWDER	4.0	4.0	0	1.0
½ c.	SOY SAUCE	4.0	4.0	0	16.0
½ t.	DRIED GINGER				
1 t.	ONION POWDER	1.7	1.6	0	0.2
1 T.	SUGAR EQUIVALENT SWEETENER				
	TOTALS	9.7	9.6	123.5	142.9
	PER SERVING	3.2	3.2	41.2	47.6

- Dissolve the sugar substitute completely in the soy sauce. Mix all ingredients in a 3 quart bowl and marinate at least an hour. Grill the wings, basting with the sauce. Discard any remaining marinade after the wings are finished cooking.

- **MAKES 3 SERVINGS WITH ABOUT 574 CALORIES PER SERVING.**

CARIBBEAN WINGS

THESE wings are citrus-based, primarily with lime and a little orange flavor. You might want to add some cayenne pepper, perhaps ½ t., to the marinade for a little extra kick.

QUAN.	INGREDIENT	CARB GRAMS	AVAIL. CARB	FAT	PROTEIN
2 lb.	CHICKEN WINGS, split (this is about 9 wings)	0	0	62.7	80.8
4 T.	LIME JUICE	5.6	5.4	0	0.2
¼ t.	ORANGE EXTRACT				
1 t.	GARLIC POWDER	2.0	2.0	0	0.5
1 t.	ONION POWDER	1.7	1.6	0	0.2
1 t.	PAPRIKA	1.3	0.8	0.3	0.3
½ t.	BLACK PEPPER				
1 T.	SOY SAUCE	0.5	0.5	0	2.0
1 t.	SUGAR EQUIVALENT SWEETENER (more or less added to your taste)				
	TOTALS	11.1	9.3	63.0	84.0
	PER SERVING	5.6	4.7	31.5	42.0

- Dissolve the sugar substitute completely in all of the liquids. Combine all ingredients in a 2 quart bowl and marinate for at least an hour. Bake in a covered 10 inch skillet at 350° F for 30–40 minutes. Remove the lid and continue baking until the liquid is reduced to your taste.

■ **MAKES 2 SERVINGS WITH ABOUT 470 CALORIES PER SERVING.**

LEMON WINGS

ACTUALLY, these wings should be named "Lemonade Wings." Intuitively, I really liked the notion of making a sweet lemon-based sauce for wings, and this is it.

QUAN.	INGREDIENT	CARB GRAMS	AVAIL. CARB	FAT	PROTEIN
2 lb.	CHICKEN WINGS, split (this is about 9 wings)	0	0	62.7	80.8
3 T.	SOY SAUCE	1.5	1.5	0	6.0
3 T.	DRY WHITE WINE	0.3	0.3	0	0
3 T.	OLIVE OIL	0	0	39.0	0
½ c.	CANNED CHICKEN BROTH				
2 T.	LEMON JUICE	2.6	2.5	0	0.1
I T.	LEMON ZEST	1.0	0.4	0	0.1
3 T.	SUGAR EQUIVALENT SWEETENER				
I t.	SESAME OIL	0	0	13.0	0
2 t.	DRIED GINGER	2.6	2.2	0.2	0.4
I t.	GARLIC POWDER	2.0	2.0	0	0.5
I t.	ONION POWDER	1.7	1.6	0	0.2
	TOTALS	11.7	10.5	114.9	88.1
	PER SERVING	5.9	5.3	57.5	44.1

- In a 10 inch skillet, fry the wings in the olive oil over medium heat until they begin to brown. Add the remaining ingredients, cover, and bring to a boil. Reduce the heat to medium low and simmer 30–45 minutes. Don't forget to reduce the sauce to your taste before serving.

- **MAKES 2 SERVINGS WITH ABOUT 715 CALORIES PER SERVING.**

PARMESAN WINGS

QUAN.	INGREDIENT	CARB GRAMS	AVAIL. CARB	FAT	PROTEIN
2 lb.	**CHICKEN WINGS**, split (this is about 9 wings)	0	0	62.7	80.8
4 T.	**BUTTER**	0	0	52.0	0
2 T.	**DIJON MUSTARD**				
1 T.	**LEMON JUICE**	1.3	1.3	0	0.1
1 t.	**GARLIC POWDER**	2.0	2.0	0	0.5
1 t.	**ONION POWDER**	1.7	1.6	0	0.2
½ c.	**CANNED CHICKEN STOCK**				
½ t.	**SALT**				
½ t.	**BLACK PEPPER**				
½ t.	**OREGANO**				
½ c.	**GRATED PARMESAN CHEESE**	1.9	1.9	14.3	20.8
	TOTALS	6.9	6.8	129.0	102.4
	PER SERVING	3.5	3.4	64.5	51.2

- In a 10 inch skillet, fry the wings in the butter over medium heat until they begin to brown slightly. Add the remaining ingredients except the grated Parmesan cheese, cover, and bring to a boil. Reduce the heat to medium low and simmer 30–45 minutes. Reduce the sauce to your taste and sprinkle on the grated Parmesan cheese, slowly coating the wings evenly.

- **MAKES 2 SERVINGS WITH ABOUT 799 CALORIES PER SERVING.**

HORSERADISH WINGS

HORSERADISH provides a different kind of "heat" to chicken wings. I know a lot of folks really like horseradish, and these wings will scratch their horseradish itch.

QUAN.	INGREDIENT	CARB GRAMS	AVAIL. CARB	FAT	PROTEIN
2 lb.	CHICKEN WINGS, split (this is about 9 wings)	0	0	62.7	80.8
½ c.	TOMATO SAUCE	8.8	7.1	0.2	1.7
1 T.	WHITE VINEGAR				
4 T.	PREPARED HORSERADISH (more or less added to your taste)				
2 T.	OLIVE OIL	0	0	26.0	0
3 T.	WORCESTERSHIRE SAUCE	9.0	9.0	0	0
1 t.	RED CAYENNE SAUCE (more or less added to your taste)				
½ t.	BLACK PEPPER				
½ t.	SALT				
2 t.	SUGAR EQUIVALENT SWEETENER				
	TOTALS	17.8	16.1	88.9	82.5
	PER SERVING	8.9	8.1	44.5	41.3

- Dissolve the sugar substitute completely in the vinegar and Worcestershire sauce. Put all ingredients in a 2 quart bowl and marinate for at least an hour. Grill until they are cooked, basting with the remaining marinade. Discard any leftover marinade.

- **MAKES 2 SERVINGS WITH ABOUT 598 CALORIES PER SERVING.**

KOREAN-STYLE WINGS

QUAN.	INGREDIENT	CARB GRAMS	AVAIL. CARB	FAT	PROTEIN
2 lb.	CHICKEN WINGS, split (this is about 9 wings)	0	0	62.7	80.8
6 T.	YAKI MANDU SAUCE (see page 243) for marinade	2.3	2.3	0	9.0
	YAKI MANDU SAUCE for dipping				
	TOTALS	2.3	2.3	62.7	89.8
	PER SERVING	1.2	1.2	31.4	44.9

■ Marinate the wings at least 1 hour in a 2 quart bowl. Grill the wings until they are cooked, basting with the marinade. Serve with more Yaki Mandu sauce. Make sure to discard any marinade that isn't used.

■ **MAKES 2 SERVINGS WITH ABOUT 467 CALORIES PER SERVING.**

DRAGON BREATH WINGS

THESE wings give us a little taste of the Orient with a little punch. I've also used this on chicken thighs with very good results. These wings are exceptionally good when they are grilled. Feel free to adjust the sweetness to your taste.

QUAN.	INGREDIENT	CARB GRAMS	AVAIL. CARB	FAT	PROTEIN
2 lb.	CHICKEN WINGS, split (this is about 9 wings)	0	0	62.7	80.8
4 T.	SOY SAUCE	2.0	2.0	0	8.0
1 t.	GARLIC POWDER	2.0	2.0	0	0.5
1 t.	ONION POWDER	1.7	1.6	0	0.2
1 t.	FIVE SPICE POWDER				
4 T.	DRY WHITE WINE	0.4	0.4	0	0
1 T.	SESAME OIL	0	0	13.0	0
2 t.	RED CAYENNE SAUCE (more or less added to your taste)				
2 t.	SUGAR EQUIVALENT SWEETENER				
	TOTALS	6.1	6.0	75.7	89.5
	PER SERVING	3.1	3.0	37.9	44.8

- For the marinade, mix all of the ingredients except the wings in a 2 cup bowl. Place the wings in a 2 quart bowl and pour the marinade over them, coating well. Marinate for at least 1 hour, overnight if possible. Grill until they are done. Baste with remaining sauce. Discard any leftover marinade.

- **MAKES 2 SERVINGS WITH ABOUT 532 CALORIES PER SERVING.**

BAKED WINGS WITH THAI DIPPING SAUCE

I'M not looking to pick a fight here, but I firmly believe that Thai people eat their foods hotter than any other culture in the world. This sauce will give you a taste of Thailand and you can make it as hot or as mild as you like.

QUAN.	INGREDIENT	CARB GRAMS	AVAIL. CARB	FAT	PROTEIN
2 lb.	**CHICKEN WINGS,** split (this is about 9 wings)	0	0	62.7	80.8
I T.	**THAI FISH SAUCE**	3.0	3.0	0	2.0
I T.	**SOY SAUCE**	0.5	0.5	0	2.0
2 T.	**LIME JUICE**	2.8	2.7	0	0.1
2 t.	**SUGAR EQUIVALENT SWEETENER**				
2 t.	**GARLIC POWDER**	4.0	4.0	0	0.5
I t.	**ONION POWDER**	1.7	1.6	0	0.2
½ t.	**DRIED GINGER**				
2 t.	**HOT CHILI PASTE** (from Asian groceries, more or less to your taste. You can use red cayenne sauce in its stead.)				
½ t.	**DRIED BASIL**				
2 t.	**DRIED CILANTRO**				
4 T.	**WATER**				
	TOTALS	12.0	11.8	62.7	85.6
	PER SERVING	6.0	5.9	31.4	42.8

- Prepare the Thai Dipping Sauce by combining the liquids and the spices in a 2 cup bowl. Set the marinade aside. Place the wings in a pan that can be used for baking as well as on top of the stove. Bake at 500° F for 25–30 minutes. Move to the top of the stove and pour off the fat. Turn the heat to medium and deglaze the pan with the Thai Dipping Sauce. Cover and cook an additional 10 minutes. Remove the lid and continue cooking until you've reduced the sauce by half, stirring every couple of minutes. Serve with a small bowl of the sauce for dipping.

- **MAKES 2 SERVINGS WITH ABOUT 477 CALORIES PER SERVING.**

GERMAN-STYLE CHILI WINGS

QUAN.	INGREDIENT	CARB GRAMS	AVAIL. CARB	FAT	PROTEIN
2 lb.	**CHICKEN WINGS**, split (this is about 9 wings)	0	0	62.7	80.8
I T.	**RED CAYENNE SAUCE** (more or less added to your taste)				
I t.	**CHILI POWDER**	1.4	0.5	0.3	0.3
I t.	**ONION POWDER**	1.7	1.6	0	0.2
I t.	**GARLIC POWDER**	2.0	2.0	0	0.5
½ t.	**SALT**				
2 t.	**SUGAR EQUIVALENT SWEETENER**				
2 T.	**TOMATO SAUCE**	2.2	1.8	0.1	0.4
2 t.	**WHITE VINEGAR**				
3 T.	**WATER**				
	TOTALS	7.5	5.9	63.1	82.2
	PER SERVING	3.8	3.0	31.6	41.1

- In a 2 cup bowl, dissolve the sugar substitute completely in the vinegar. Add everything else to make the marinade. In a 2 quart bowl, mix the wings with the marinade. Marinate the wings for at least 1 hour. Bake the wings at 400° F in a covered casserole dish for 40 minutes. Serve with a small bowl of the pan sauce for dipping.

- **MAKES 2 SERVINGS WITH ABOUT 461 CALORIES PER SERVING.**

SEAFOOD
DISHES

One of the most important and surprising discoveries made since I published the first edition of this book in 1996 is that most nonfish seafood, along with liver, contains some amount of carbohydrate. In 1996, everyone assumed that all meat was essentially carb-free. Needless to say, this new information has been taken into account in the recipes below.

SHRIMP with THAI VINAIGRETTE

I first concocted this recipe while living in the Charlotte area. You can always use some fresh basil, finely diced, for a little more flavor and variety.

QUAN.	INGREDIENT	CARB GRAMS	AVAIL. CARB	FAT	PROTEIN
2 t.	**GARLIC POWDER**	4.0	4.0	0	1.0
1 t.	**ONION POWDER**	1.7	1.6	0	0.2
¼ t.	**DRIED GINGER**				
1 T.	**FISH SAUCE** or **SOY SAUCE**	1.0	0.9	0	1.9
3 T.	**LIME JUICE**	4.2	4.0	0	0.2
2 t.	**SUGAR EQUIVALENT SWEETENER**				
1 t.	**DRIED BASIL LEAVES**				
4 T.	**CILANTRO**				
2 T.	**PEANUT OIL**	0	0	26.0	0
1 lb.	**COOKED MEDIUM SIZED SHRIMP**, peeled	5.0	5.0	4.1	94.9
2 t.	**HOT CHILI PASTE** (from Asian groceries, more or less to your taste. You can use red cayenne sauce in its stead.)				
	TOTALS	10.9	10.5	30.1	98.2
	PER SERVING	5.5	5.3	15.1	49.1

- To prepare the vinaigrette, mix the chili paste, garlic, onion powder, ginger, fish sauce, lime juice, sugar substitute, cilantro, and basil in a 2 cup bowl. Let it set for at least 15 minutes and then stir in the oil slowly. Pour the dressing over the shrimp and stir gently. Cover and refrigerate for at least 2 hours, preferably overnight. Stir occasionally to ensure that it stays well mixed.

- **MAKES 2 SERVINGS WITH ABOUT 354 CALORIES PER SERVING.**

SCALLOPS AND CRAB ALFREDO

QUAN.	INGREDIENT	CARB GRAMS	AVAIL. CARB	FAT	PROTEIN
¼ lb.	**CRABMEAT** (uncooked)	0.1	0.1	0.9	20.3
¼ lb.	**SCALLOPS**	2.7	2.7	0.4	18.9
½ c.	**HEAVY CREAM**	3.3	3.3	41.8	2.5
½ c.	**SHREDDED MOZZARELLA CHEESE** (about 3½ ounces)	2.8	2.8	15.1	24.3
3 T.	**GRATED PARMESAN CHEESE**	0.7	0.7	5.3	7.8
2 T.	**BUTTER**	0	0	26.0	0
⅛ t.	**SALT**				
⅛ t.	**DRIED BASIL** (optional)				
	TOTALS	9.6	9.6	89.5	73.8
	PER SERVING	4.8	4.8	44.8	36.9

- In a 10 inch skillet, sauté the crab and scallops (and the basil if you use it) in the butter over medium high heat until mostly cooked. Add the heavy cream and salt and reduce the heat to medium. Add the grated Parmesan cheese gradually, stirring after each addition. Add most of the mozzarella and stir until it thickens. Remove to a casserole dish, add the rest of the mozzarella, and broil in a toaster oven or regular oven until brown and bubbly on top.

- **MAKES 2 SERVINGS WITH ABOUT 570 CALORIES PER SERVING.**

SOUTHWESTERN CRAB "CAKE"

TYPICALLY, crab cakes are made into patties for cooking. Since we don't use a binder such as flour, I decided that it would be easier to make this as a casserole. Keep in mind that, because everything except the egg is cooked before it is mixed, it needs only be cooked long enough to cook the eggs.

QUAN.	INGREDIENT	CARB GRAMS	AVAIL. CARB	FAT	PROTEIN
12 oz.	**CRAB MEAT** (two 6 ounce cans), reserve the liquid and freeze it to be used in a soup at a later point in time	5.0	5.0	0	55.0
2	**EGGS**, scrambled slightly	1.4	1.4	9.6	14.4
2 t.	**GARLIC POWDER**	4.0	4.0	0	1.0
½ c.	**ONION**, sliced thinly	5.0	3.9	0	0.7
2 t.	**DRIED PARSLEY**				
½ c.	**CELERY**, diced	2.2	1.2	0	0.5
½ c.	**GREEN PEPPERS**, diced	4.8	3.5	0.1	0.7
2 T.	**PICKLED JALAPEÑO PEPPERS**, diced finely (more or less added to your taste)				
4 T.	**OLIVE OIL**	0	0	52.0	0
2 t.	**WORCESTERSHIRE SAUCE**	2.0	2.0	0	0
½ t.	**RED CAYENNE SAUCE** (optional, more or less to your taste)				
1 t.	**SALT**				
½ t.	**BLACK PEPPER**				
	TOTALS	24.4	21.0	61.7	72.3
	PER SERVING	12.2	10.5	30.9	36.2

- Preheat your oven to 375° F. In a medium-sized skillet, fry the onion, celery, and bell pepper over medium heat in 2 T. of olive oil until the onions begin to turn clear. Remove from the heat and let cool to room temperature. Blend all ingredients in a quart bowl. Coat a small casserole dish or bread pan with the remaining olive oil. Pour the mixture into the casserole and bake at 350° F about 30 minutes or until a knife inserted into the center comes out clean.

- **MAKES 2 SERVINGS WITH ABOUT 465 CALORIES PER SERVING.**

SALMON LOAF

QUAN.	INGREDIENT	CARB GRAMS	AVAIL. CARB	FAT	PROTEIN
15 oz.	SALMON (one 15 ounce can, reserve and freeze the liquid for use later in a soup)	0	0	35.0	84.0
4 T.	HEAVY CREAM	1.7	1.7	20.9	1.2
2	EGGS, scrambled slightly	1.4	1.4	9.6	14.4
1 t.	SALT				
¼ t.	BLACK PEPPER				
1 t.	PAPRIKA				
2 t.	WORCESTERSHIRE SAUCE	2.0	2.0	0	0
1 c.	CELERY, diced	4.4	2.4	0	0.9
½ c.	ONION, diced	6.9	5.5	0	1.0
2 t.	DRIED PARSLEY				
2 T.	LEMON JUICE	2.6	2.5	0	0.1
	TOTALS	21.0	17.5	65.5	101.6
	PER SERVING	7.0	5.8	21.8	33.9

- Combine all ingredients in a 2 quart bowl and mix thoroughly. Pour into an oiled loaf pan. Bake at 350° F for about 30 minutes or until a knife inserted into the center comes out clean.

■ **MAKES 3 SERVINGS WITH ABOUT 355 CALORIES PER SERVING.**

SHRIMP SZECHWAN

I'VE made this dish perhaps a half dozen times. Most of the recipes for this involve the use of ketchup. We avoid ketchup by incorporating most of the ingredients while we are cooking it. This is a very pretty dish and folks tend to like it. A variation of this is to use diced chicken rather than shrimp, but it must be cooked longer, 20 minutes if the pieces are small, or up to 45 minutes if you cut the chicken in ½ inch cubes.

QUAN.	INGREDIENT	CARB GRAMS	AVAIL. CARB	FAT	PROTEIN
I lb.	UNCOOKED SHRIMP, peeled	4.1	4.1	5.9	92.2
I t.	GARLIC POWDER	2.0	2.0	0	0.5
I t.	DRIED GINGER	1.3	1.1	0.1	0.2
2 t.	DRIED RED PEPPER FLAKES (more or less added to your taste)				
2 T.	SOY SAUCE	1.0	1.0	0	4.0
2 T.	TOMATO SAUCE	2.2	1.8	0.1	0.4
I T.	WHITE VINEGAR				
I c.	GREEN ONIONS, diced	7.4	4.8	0	1.8
I T.	SUGAR EQUIVALENT SWEETENER				
2 T.	PEANUT OIL	0	0	26.0	0
2 t.	SESAME OIL	0	0	8.7	0
2 T.	WATER				
	TOTALS	18.0	14.8	40.8	99.1
	PER SERVING	9.0	7.4	20.4	49.6

- In a 10 inch skillet, heat the peanut oil over high heat. Cook the shrimp over high heat until they turn white. Add the water and soy sauce and bring to a boil. Add the remaining ingredients except the onion and simmer about 5 minutes, stirring to ensure that the shrimp are coated. Add the onion and simmer another 2 minutes.

- **MAKES 2 SERVINGS WITH ABOUT 412 CALORIES PER SERVING.**

SHRIMP RÉMOULADE

QUAN.	INGREDIENT	CARB GRAMS	AVAIL. CARB	FAT	PROTEIN
1 lb.	**COOKED SHRIMP**, peeled	4.2	4.2	6.0	94.1
½ c.	**RÉMOULADE SAUCE** (see page 246)	7.0	6.4	42.2	1.2
	TOTALS	11.2	10.6	48.2	95.3
	PER SERVING	5.6	5.3	24.1	47.7

- Ensure that the shrimp are chilled well. Serve with the Rémoulade Sauce in small bowls for dipping.

- **MAKES 2 SERVINGS WITH ABOUT 429 CALORIES PER SERVING.**

SPICED SHRIMP

WHEN I was a hospital corpsman in the navy and stationed at the Bethesda Naval Hospital in Bethesda, Maryland, I would go to a small pub on Wisconsin Avenue in the District of Columbia and have spiced shrimp. Serve with Cocktail Sauce (see page 250). This is an excellent appetizer and great to take for potlucks or barbecues.

QUAN.	INGREDIENT	CARB GRAMS	AVAIL. CARB	FAT	PROTEIN
1½ lb.	**FRESH SHRIMP,** large and unpeeled with the heads removed	6.2	6.2	8.9	138.3
2 c.	**WATER**				
½ c.	**WHITE VINEGAR**				
4 t.	**LEMON EXTRACT**				
4	**BAY LEAVES**				
1 t.	**CELERY SEEDS**				
3 t.	**PICKLING SPICE**				
4 t.	**ONION POWDER**				
2 t.	**GARLIC POWDER**				
1 T.	**SALT**				
1 t.	**FRESHLY CRACKED BLACK PEPPER**				
2 t.	**CRUSHED RED PEPPER FLAKES** (more or less added to your taste)				
4 T.	**SUGAR EQUIVALENT SWEETENER**				
	TOTALS	6.2	6.2	8.9	138.3
	PER SERVING	1.6	1.6	2.2	34.6

- Place all of the ingredients except the shrimp in a 3 quart pan over high heat. Cover and bring to a boil. Reduce the heat to low and let it simmer 10–15 minutes. Bring to a rolling boil again over high heat and add the shrimp. Let it come to a boil again and cook for 2–3 minutes. Remove from the heat and let it cool to room temperature. Place the shrimp in a quart jar and cover with as much of the cooking liquid as possible. Refrigerate for several days before serving—a week if possible. The longer this stays in your refrigerator, up to a point, the better it is. Count this as about 2 grams of carbs per serving.

- **MAKES 4 SERVINGS WITH ABOUT 165 CALORIES PER SERVING.**

SHRIMP JAMBALAYA

THIS is another dish for which we can thank the Cajuns. This particular version can be made very quickly, on the order of 15–20 minutes.

QUAN.	INGREDIENT	CARB GRAMS	AVAIL. CARB	FAT	PROTEIN
2 lb.	**UNCOOKED SHRIMP**, peeled and deveined	8.2	8.2	11.8	184.4
½ lb.	**BONELESS COOKED CHICKEN**, diced				
½ lb.	**SMOKED POLISH SAUSAGE**, diced	8.0	8.0	68.0	28.0
2 T.	**OLIVE OIL**	0	0	26.0	0
½ c.	**ONION**, sliced thinly	5.0	3.9	0	0.7
1 c.	**GREEN PEPPERS**, diced	9.6	6.9	0.2	1.3
1 c.	**CELERY**, diced	4.4	2.4	0	0.9
1 c.	**GREEN ONIONS**, diced	7.4	4.8	0	1.8
2 t.	**GARLIC POWDER**	4.0	4.0	0	1.0
1 t.	**THYME**				
1 t.	**CAYENNE PEPPER** (more or less added to your taste)				
½ t.	**BLACK PEPPER**				
½ t.	**SALT**				
2 T.	**WORCESTERSHIRE SAUCE**	6.0	6.0	0	0
½ c.	**CANNED CHICKEN STOCK**				
½ c.	**TOMATO SAUCE**	8.8	7.1	0.2	1.7
1 t.	**SUGAR EQUIVALENT SWEETENER**				
	TOTALS	61.4	51.3	106.2	219.8
	PER SERVING	10.2	8.6	17.7	36.6

- In a 3 quart skillet or soup pot, fry the sausage and chicken in the oil over medium high heat until they begin cooking—that is, they aren't just heated up. Add the onions, celery, bell pepper, and scallions and cook until the onions become clear. Add the shrimp and the dry seasonings and cook until the shrimp begin to turn white. Add the remaining ingredients, bring to a boil, and simmer about 5 minutes.

- **MAKES 6 SERVINGS WITH ABOUT 340 CALORIES PER SERVING.**

BAKED FISH

THIS is a quick and easy dish that can be started the night before. The particular version uses Vietnamese Dipping Sauce, but I also like Baked Fish with Thai Dipping Sauce (see page 171), Yaki Mandu Sauce (see page 243), and Mojo (see page 247), among others.

QUAN.	INGREDIENT	CARB GRAMS	AVAIL. CARB	FAT	PROTEIN
I lb.	COD	0	0	2.3	80.8
4 T.	VIETNAMESE DIPPING SAUCE (see page 254)	5.4	5.4	0	2.3
	TOTALS	5.4	5.4	2.3	83.1
	PER SERVING	2.7	2.7	1.2	41.6

- Marinate the fish in 4 T. of the sauce for at least 1 hour, overnight if possible. Bake at 400° F for 15 minutes or until the fish begins to flake. Serve with additional sauce for dipping as needed.

- **MAKES 2 SERVINGS WITH ABOUT 188 CALORIES PER SERVING.**

SHRIMP SCAMPI

THIS is a classic shrimp dish that originated in Italy. When I was working at the MGM Grand in Las Vegas, the sous chef of the Italian kitchen showed me how to make scampi the "real" way, that is, with the addition of a small amount of dried bread crumbs to help thicken the sauce. We don't really need the bread crumbs to enjoy this dish.

QUAN.	INGREDIENT	CARB GRAMS	AVAIL. CARB	FAT	PROTEIN
1 lb.	UNCOOKED SHRIMP, as large as you can afford, cleaned and with the tails remaining	4.1	4.1	5.9	92.2
3 T.	OLIVE OIL	0	0	39.0	0
2 T.	UNSALTED BUTTER	0	0	24.2	0
¼ c.	DRY WHITE WINE	0.4	0.4	0	0
¼ c.	FRESH PARSLEY, chopped finely				
½ c.	GREEN ONIONS, diced	3.7	2.4	0	0.9
2 T.	CAPERS				
2 t.	GARLIC POWDER	4.0	4.0	0	1.0
½ t.	DRIED RED PEPPER FLAKES (optional more or less added to your taste)				
1 pinch	OREGANO (optional)				
2 T.	GRATED PARMESAN CHEESE (optional for garnish)				
	LEMON SLICES (optional for garnish)				
	TOTALS	12.2	10.9	69.1	94.1
	PER SERVING	6.1	5.5	34.6	47.1

- In a 10 inch skillet, fry the shrimp along with the green onions in the olive oil over medium high heat until the shrimp turn pink. Remove the shrimp to the serving plate, reserving as much oil in the skillet as possible. Deglaze the pan with the wine and add the remaining ingredients. Reduce the heat to low and let the butter melt slowly. Pour the sauce over the shrimp.

■ **MAKES 2 SERVINGS WITH ABOUT 522 CALORIES PER SERVING.**

OTHER MAIN COURSES AND APPETIZERS

ONE-PAN PIZZA CASSEROLE

OVER the years, I've received dozens of requests for pizza recipes and there have been debates on various Internet low carb support groups about how to enjoy pizza on a low carb diet. This is my solution to the low carb pizza problem.

QUAN.	INGREDIENT	CARB GRAMS	AVAIL. CARB	FAT	PROTEIN
½ lb.	**ITALIAN SAUSAGE**	6.8	5.0	44.0	39.4
½ lb.	**SLICED PEPPERONI**	6.4	6.4	93.6	47.2
¼ c.	**ONION,** sliced thinly	2.5	2.0	0	0.4
½ c.	**GREEN PEPPERS,** diced	4.8	3.5	0.1	0.7
½ c.	**BUTTON MUSHROOMS,** diced	1.7	1.2	0.1	0.8
4 T.	**DRY RED WINE**	1.0	1.0	0	0.2
1 t.	**ITALIAN SEASONING**				
4 T.	**TOMATO SAUCE**	4.4	3.6	0.1	0.9
½ lb.	**SHREDDED MOZZARELLA CHEESE**	6.2	6.2	34.0	54.6
4 T.	**GRATED PARMESAN CHEESE**	0.9	0.9	7.1	10.4
½ t.	**SUGAR EQUIVALENT SWEETENER**				
	TOTALS	34.7	29.8	179.0	154.6
	PER SERVING	8.7	7.5	44.8	38.7

- In a medium ovenproof skillet, fry the Italian sausage over medium heat until it is cooked thoroughly, breaking it into small pieces. Add the onion and cook until it becomes clear. Add the bell pepper and mushrooms and cook until the mushrooms begin to wilt. Add the seasonings, pepperoni, wine, sugar substitute, and tomato sauce and let it reduce, uncovered, 5 minutes. Turn on the broiler in your oven. Sprinkle the grated Parmesan cheese over the contents of the pan, then the mozzarella. Place under the broiler until the cheese is lightly browned.

- **MAKES 4 SERVINGS WITH ABOUT 588 CALORIES PER SERVING.**

POLISH SAUSAGE AND CABBAGE

THIS dish is a little higher in carbs than our average dish, primarily because of the sugar in the Polish sausage. Otherwise, it's simple and relatively quick to prepare and it's something that a lot of folks like. Have a little mustard on the table for the sausage.

QUAN.	INGREDIENT	CARB GRAMS	AVAIL. CARB	FAT	PROTEIN
4 T.	BUTTER	0	0	52.0	0
½ c.	ONION, sliced thinly	5.0	3.9	0	0.7
1 lb.	CABBAGE cut into 2 inch cubes	24.5	14.1	0.9	6.4
2 lb.	SMOKED POLISH SAUSAGE, sliced in ¼ inch pieces	32.0	32.0	272.0	112.0
2 t.	SUGAR EQUIVALENT SWEETENER				
1	BEEF BOUILLON CUBE				
½ t.	BLACK PEPPER				
1 c.	CANNED BEEF STOCK				
	TOTALS	61.5	50.0	324.9	119.1
	PER SERVING	15.4	12.5	81.2	29.8

- In a 10 inch skillet, cook the onion in the butter over medium high heat until the onion turns clear. Add the cabbage, beef stock, sugar substitute, salt and pepper, and cover and bring to a boil. Reduce the heat to medium low and simmer about 30 minutes, stirring every 10 minutes. Add the sausage and let simmer an additional 10 minutes, stirring a couple of times.

- **MAKES 4 SERVINGS WITH ABOUT 900 CALORIES PER SERVING.**

JAMBALAYA

TRADITIONALLY, this dish is served with rice, but we don't need rice to enjoy it. A good Cajun Style Slaw (see page 76) will go nicely with this.

QUAN.	INGREDIENT	CARB GRAMS	AVAIL. CARB	FAT	PROTEIN
1 lb.	CHICKEN BREAST, uncooked, boneless, skinless, and cut into ¾ inch cubes (chicken dark meat is also good)	0	0	4.2	104.8
½ lb.	HAM (2% fat)	4.0	4.0	4.0	40.0
½ lb.	POLISH KIELBASA, cut in ½ inch cubes	8.0	8.0	68.0	28.0
2 T.	OLIVE OIL	0	0	26.0	0
½ c.	ONION, diced	6.9	5.5	0	1.0
1 c.	GREEN PEPPERS, diced	9.6	6.9	0.2	1.3
1 c.	GREEN ONIONS, diced	7.4	4.8	0	1.8
½ c.	CARROTS, diced	5.6	4.0	0	0.5
1 c.	CELERY, diced	4.4	2.4	0	0.9
2 t.	GARLIC POWDER	4.0	4.0	0	1.0
1 T.	DRIED PARSLEY				
1 t.	SALT				
½ t.	BLACK PEPPER			4.2	104.8
½ t.	CAYENNE PEPPER (more or less added to your taste)				
2 t.	PICKLED JALAPEÑO PEPPERS, diced (more or less added to your taste)				
1 t.	GROUND CUMIN	0.9	0.7	0.4	0.4
2	BAY LEAVES				
½ t.	CLOVES				
¼ t.	THYME				
¼ t.	BASIL				
¼ t.	MACE				
1 c.	WATER				
½ c.	TOMATO SAUCE	8.8	7.1	0.2	1.7
	TOTALS	59.6	47.4	103.0	181.4
	PER SERVING	15.0	11.9	25.8	45.4

- In a 3 quart skillet or soup pot, fry the chicken in the oil over medium high heat until it begins to brown slightly. Add the onion, carrots, and celery and cook until the onion becomes clear. Add all remaining ingredients, cover, and bring to a boil. Reduce the heat to medium low and let simmer 30–45 minutes.

- **MAKES 4 SERVINGS WITH ABOUT 461 CALORIES PER SERVING.**

ITALIAN SAUSAGE AND PEPPERS

THIS has always been one of my favorite meals and I'm very happy that I was able to come up with a low carb variation of it.

QUAN.	INGREDIENT	CARB GRAMS	AVAIL. CARB	FAT	PROTEIN
1 lb.	ITALIAN SAUSAGE (4 links to the pound)	2.9	2.9	134.0	64.4
½ c.	ONION, sliced thinly	5.0	3.9	0	0.7
2 c.	GREEN PEPPERS, diced	19.2	13.8	0.4	2.6
½ c.	DRY WHITE WINE	0.8	0.8	0	0
1	BEEF BOUILLON CUBE				
½ c.	TOMATO SAUCE	8.8	7.1	0.2	1.7
½ t.	ITALIAN SEASONING				
1 t.	SUGAR EQUIVALENT SWEETENER				
4 T.	WATER				
	TOTALS	36.7	28.5	133.6	68.7
	PER SERVING	18.4	14.3	66.8	34.4

- Put the links in the water in a 3 quart pan over medium high heat. Puncture the links with the tip of a knife, one puncture every inch or so. Cover and bring to a boil. After the water has evaporated, the links will begin to fry. Reduce the heat to medium low. Continue frying the links until they are well browned on two sides. Remove the links to a side plate, retaining as much fat in the skillet as possible. Fry the onions and peppers in the oil in the same skillet over medium heat, until the onions begin to clear. Add all ingredients, cover, and bring to a boil. Reduce the heat to medium low and simmer 15–20 minutes, stirring occasionally.

- **MAKES 2 SERVINGS WITH ABOUT 796 CALORIES PER SERVING.**

CREOLE HOT SAUSAGE

THIS is another variation on sausages that taste great when grilled. Take this instead of hamburger to the ball game for your tailgating.

QUAN.	INGREDIENT	CARB GRAMS	AVAIL. CARB	FAT	PROTEIN
2 lb.	GROUND PORK	0	0	173.0	151.9
2 t.	GARLIC POWDER	4.0	4.0	0	1.0
2 t.	SALT				
2 t.	PAPRIKA	2.5	1.6	0.5	0.7
2 t.	ONION POWDER	3.4	3.2	0	0.4
2 t.	ITALIAN SEASONING				
2 t.	CAYENNE PEPPER (more or less added to your taste)				
2 t.	BLACK PEPPER				
4 T.	WATER				
2 t.	SUGAR EQUIVALENT SWEETENER				
	TOTALS	9.9	8.8	173.5	154.0
	PER SERVING OF ONE 4 OZ. PATTY	1.2	1.1	21.7	19.3

- Dissolve the sugar substitute completely in the water. Mix all ingredients thoroughly in a 1 quart bowl. Let this sit refrigerated and covered overnight if possible. Mix again just before using. Shape into patties and grill (or fry) to your taste.

- **MAKES 8 SERVINGS WITH ABOUT 277 CALORIES PER SERVING.**

MEXICAN *CHORIZO*

THE first time I had Mexican *chorizo* I was amazed at the combination of flavors. *Chorizo* is especially good with eggs. Unfortunately, the breakfasts that include *chorizo* also usually include tortillas and *frijoles,* which aren't low carb.

QUAN.	INGREDIENT	CARB GRAMS	AVAIL. CARB	FAT	PROTEIN
2 lb.	GROUND PORK	0	0	173.0	151.9
2 t.	SALT				
4 T.	CHILI POWDER	16.4	6.0	4.0	3.6
1 t.	OREGANO				
2 t.	GARLIC POWDER	4.0	4.0	0	1.0
1 t.	ONION POWDER	1.7	1.6	0	0.2
½ t.	CINNAMON				
4 T.	WHITE VINEGAR				
4 T.	WATER				
1 t.	SUGAR EQUIVALENT SWEETENER				
	TOTALS	22.1	11.6	177.0	156.7
	PER SERVING OF ONE 4 OZ. PATTY	2.8	1.5	22.1	19.6

- Dissolve the sugar substitute completely in the water. Mix all ingredients thoroughly in a 1 quart bowl. Let this sit refrigerated and covered, overnight if possible. Mix again just before using.

■ **MAKES 8 SERVINGS WITH ABOUT 283 CALORIES PER SERVING.**

ITALIAN MEATBALLS

WHEN I lived in Las Vegas, there was an Italian restaurant there that had some of the best food I've ever eaten, and was incredibly inexpensive. As part of their salad bar deal, you got a plate of spaghetti. One of the things they had at the salad bar was leftover cold meatballs in Thousand Island Dressing. It's absolutely delicious. I encourage you to make some Thousand Island Dressing (see page 44) and try it yourself. Otherwise, you would normally serve these with a little tomato sauce and grated Parmesan cheese.

QUAN.	INGREDIENT	CARB GRAMS	AVAIL. CARB	FAT	PROTEIN
2 lb.	HAMBURGER (77% lean)	0	0	184.8	154.4
½ c.	ONION, diced	6.9	5.5	0	1.0
2 t.	GARLIC POWDER	4.0	4.0	0	1.0
2 t.	ONION POWDER	3.4	3.2	0	0.4
1 T.	DRIED PARSLEY				
2	EGGS, beaten slightly	1.4	1.4	9.6	14.4
½ c.	GRATED PARMESAN CHEESE	1.9	1.9	14.3	20.8
4 T.	WATER				
2 T.	OLIVE OIL	0	0	26.0	0
2 t.	SALT				
½ t.	BLACK PEPPER				
½ t.	NUTMEG (optional)				
2 t.	ITALIAN SEASONING				
2 c.	BEEF STOCK (about one 15 ounce can for poaching, you can use water instead, reserve this for a soup after you are finished with it in this recipe)				
	TOTALS	17.6	16.0	363.4	192.0
	PER SERVING	1.1	1.0	22.7	12.0

- Fry the onions in the oil over medium heat until the onions become clear. Let the onions cool. Mix all ingredients, except the stock, thoroughly in a 2 quart bowl. Let this sit for 10 minutes. Form into 2 ounce meatballs (2 ounces is about 2 heaping tablespoons). Bring the stock to a boil in a skillet and immediately reduce the heat to medium. Place the meatballs in the stock, cover, and let simmer 30 minutes, turning after 10 minutes.

■ MAKES 16 SERVINGS WITH ABOUT 256 CALORIES PER SERVING.

CHOPPED CHICKEN LIVER

WHEN I worked in Lincoln, Nebraska, I was asked to develop a menu for a new restaurant. Here is a great low carb dish from that menu that I encourage you to try.

QUAN.	INGREDIENT	CARB GRAMS	AVAIL. CARB	FAT	PROTEIN
1 lb.	CHICKEN LIVERS	15.4	15.4	13.0	80.9
½ c.	ONION, diced	6.9	5.5	0	1.0
2 T.	WATER				
2 T.	OLIVE OIL	0	0	26.0	0
1 t.	SALT				
½ t.	BLACK PEPPER				
2 T.	CHICKEN FAT or MAYONNAISE	0.8	0.8	21.0	0.4
2	EGGS, hard boiled with the shell removed	1.4	1.4	9.6	14.4
	TOTALS	24.5	23.1	69.6	96.7
	PER SERVING OF 1 T.	0.8	0.7	2.2	3.0

- In a 2 quart saucepan, fry the onion in the olive oil over medium high heat until the onions become clear. Add the water, salt, and livers, cover, and bring to a boil. Reduce the heat to medium low and let it simmer 30 minutes. Remove the lid and continue to cook until the liquid evaporates down to only a couple of tablespoons. Remove the pan from the heat and let it cool to room temperature. Refrigerate overnight. The next day, mix the liver and eggs in a food processor and add to the ingredients in the saucepan. The final step is to mix in the chicken fat or mayonnaise.

- MAKES ABOUT 1 LB. OR 32 SERVINGS WITH ABOUT 35 CALORIES PER SERVING.

PIMENTO CHEESE SPREAD

PIMENTO cheese is very popular in the southern United States. The commercial pimento cheese spreads are primarily made of mayonnaise, with only a little cheese and pimentos. This dish has more substance and is a good low carb appetizer, especially when served on celery sticks.

QUAN.	INGREDIENT	CARB GRAMS	AVAIL. CARB	FAT	PROTEIN
12 oz.	DICED or SHREDDED AMERICAN CHEESE	6.0	6.0	108.0	72.0
2¼ oz.	CANNED PIMENTOS, drained	3.0	3.0	0	1.0
2 t.	WORCESTERSHIRE SAUCE	2.0	2.0	0	0
10 T.	MAYONNAISE	3.7	3.7	105.3	1.5
1 t.	SUGAR EQUIVALENT SWEETENER				
1 t.	GARLIC POWDER	2.0	2.0	0	0.5
1 t.	ONION POWDER	1.7	1.6	0	0.2
	DICED PICKLED JALAPEÑOS or DILL PICKLES to taste (optional)				
TOTALS		18.4	18.3	217.7	75.2
PER SERVING OF 1 T.		0.9	0.9	10.9	3.8

- Mix all ingredients in a 4 cup bowl. The flavor improves if you refrigerate it overnight. Try spreading this on grilled hamburgers for a nice change.

■ **MAKES ABOUT 20 SERVINGS WITH ABOUT 117 CALORIES PER SERVING.**

VEGGIES

ON **THE SIDE**

GRANDMA'S GREEN BEANS

SOME southern sage once asked why someone would want to eat green beans that have been cooked only a couple of minutes when they can cook it for a couple of hours and infuse all that flavor into it? My grandmother made the best green beans with a ham bone and onions. The secret to getting all that meat flavor into the beans is to cook them slowly, stir them often, and reduce the liquid to almost nothing. I didn't learn this until I was an undergraduate, after a very long and unsuccessful experiment in cooking beans. These beans provide all of the flavor that my grandmother would appreciate, but they don't require all of the cooking time.

QUAN.	INGREDIENT	CARB GRAMS	AVAIL. CARB	FAT	PROTEIN
2 c.	**GREEN BEANS** (one 15 ounce can is sufficient)	14.0	7.0	0	1.8
1	**CHICKEN BOUILLON CUBE**				
½ c.	**ONION**, sliced thinly	5.0	3.9	0	0.7
2 T.	**BUTTER**	0	0	26.0	0
	TOTALS	19.0	10.9	26.0	2.5
	PER SERVING	6.3	3.6	8.7	0.8

- Place the onion and bouillon cube in the bottom of a 1 quart saucepan. Add the green beans with the liquid and butter, bring to a boil over high heat, reduce heat to medium low, and cook uncovered, stirring every five minutes. You are going to reduce the liquid to about one tablespoon. Turn off the heat and let sit 5 minutes before serving.

■ **MAKES 3 SERVINGS WITH ABOUT 96 CALORIES PER SERVING.**

GERMAN-STYLE HOT CAULIFLOWER SALAD

AS low carbers, there are several dishes that we make where we can use cauliflower to provide the texture of potatoes. This dish is modeled after German potato salad.

QUAN.	INGREDIENT	CARB GRAMS	AVAIL. CARB	FAT	PROTEIN
1 lb.	FROZEN CAULIFLOWER, thawed, drained, and cut into bite sized pieces	18.0	12.0	0	12.0
4 slices	BACON	0	0	82.6	13.2
1 c.	CELERY, diced	4.4	2.4	0	0.9
½ c.	ONION, diced	6.9	5.5	0	1.0
1 t.	SALT				
4 T.	WINE VINEGAR				
¾ c.	WATER				
½ t.	BLACK PEPPER				
1 t.	GARLIC POWDER	2.0	2.0	0	1.0
1 t.	SUGAR EQUIVALENT SWEETENER				
	TOTALS	31.3	21.9	82.6	28.1
	PER SERVING	7.8	5.5	20.7	7.0

- In a 3 quart skillet, cook your bacon over medium heat until it is well browned and the fat is rendered. Add the celery and onion and cook until the onion begins to clear. Deglaze the pan with the liquids, bring to a boil, and add the spices, sugar substitute, and salt. Finally, add the cauliflower. Stir well. Cover and bring to a boil. Stir again and turn the heat off, keeping the lid on. Let this sit for about 5 minutes before serving.

- **MAKES 4 SERVINGS WITH ABOUT 236 CALORIES PER SERVING.**

GERMAN RED CABBAGE

QUAN.	INGREDIENT	CARB GRAMS	AVAIL. CARB	FAT	PROTEIN
1 lb.	**RED CABBAGE**, shredded	27.6	18.6	0.8	6.3
4 slices	**BACON**	0	0	82.6	13.2
½ c.	**ONION**, diced	6.9	5.5	0	1.0
½ c.	**DRY WHITE WINE**	0.8	0.8	0	0
3 T.	**SUGAR EQUIVALENT SWEETENER**				
3 T.	**WINE VINEGAR**				
½ t.	**GROUND CLOVES**				
1 t.	**SALT**				
½ t.	**CARAWAY SEEDS**				
	TOTALS	35.3	24.9	83.4	20.5
	PER SERVING	7.1	5.0	16.7	4.1

- In a 3 quart skillet or soup pot, fry the bacon over medium heat until it is well browned and the fat is rendered. Add the onion and cook until it is clear. Add the remaining ingredients and bring to a boil. Reduce the heat to medium low and simmer slowly, uncovered, for ½ hour to 1 hour. Don't let this dry out.

- **MAKES 5 SERVINGS WITH ABOUT 187 CALORIES PER SERVING.**

ENGLISH RED CABBAGE

GERMANY isn't the only culture that has a national main dish made out of red cabbage. This is the English version and as you will soon see, it's a little more tame.

QUAN.	INGREDIENT	CARB GRAMS	AVAIL. CARB	FAT	PROTEIN
1 lb.	RED CABBAGE, shredded	27.6	18.6	0.8	6.3
½ c.	ONION, diced	6.9	5.5	0	1.0
4 T.	WHITE VINEGAR				
1	BAY LEAF				
4 T.	SUGAR EQUIVALENT SWEETENER				
2 T	BUTTER	0	0	26.0	0
1 t.	SALT				
½ t.	BLACK PEPPER				
4 T.	WATER				
	TOTALS	34.5	24.1	26.8	7.3
	PER SERVING	6.9	4.8	5.4	1.5

- Place everything in a 3 quart pan and cover. Bring to a boil over high heat, reduce the heat to medium low, and simmer at least 1 hour, stirring every 15 minutes. Remove the bay leaf before serving.

- **MAKES 5 SERVINGS WITH ABOUT 74 CALORIES PER SERVING.**

BRUSSELS SPROUTS

THESE might be a little high in carbs, but they are very flavorful. You want to cook them long enough to infuse the meat flavor of the bouillon cubes into the sprouts.

QUAN.	INGREDIENT	CARB GRAMS	AVAIL. CARB	FAT	PROTEIN
10 oz.	**FROZEN BRUSSELS SPROUTS**, thawed, drained, and cut in half if necessary	22.4	11.6	0.9	10.7
2 T.	**BUTTER**	0	0	26.0	0
½ c.	**WATER**				
1	**CHICKEN BOUILLON CUBE**				
½ c.	**ONION**, diced	6.9	5.5	0	1.0
1 t.	**GARLIC POWDER**	2.0	2.0	0	0.5
	TOTALS	31.3	19.1	26.9	12.2
	PER SERVING	10.4	6.4	9.0	4.1

- In a 10 inch skillet, fry the onion in the butter over medium heat until it becomes clear. Add the brussels sprouts and fry for about 5 minutes. Add the remaining ingredients. Bring to a boil, reduce the heat to medium low, and cover. Cook for 15 minutes, stirring every 5 minutes.

- **MAKES 3 SERVINGS WITH ABOUT 123 CALORIES PER SERVING.**

SPINACH AND ARTICHOKE CASSEROLE

QUAN.	INGREDIENT	CARB GRAMS	AVAIL. CARB	FAT	PROTEIN
2 c.	**CANNED ARTICHOKE HEARTS**, drained (one 14 ounce can is sufficient)	37.6	19.5	0.4	11.7
3	**PACKAGES OF FROZEN SPINACH**, thawed with as much liquid as possible squeezed out (about 10 ounces per package)	35.1	15.3	0	20.7
8 oz.	**CREAM CHEESE**, at room temperature	6.1	6.1	75.7	17.3
2 T.	**MAYONNAISE**	0.8	0.8	21.0	0.4
2 T.	**OLIVE OIL**	0	0	26.0	0
4 T.	**HEAVY CREAM**	1.7	1.7	20.9	1.2
¾ c.	**GRATED PARMESAN CHEESE**	2.8	2.8	21.4	31.2
1½ t.	**SALT**				
½ t.	**BLACK PEPPER**				
1	**EGG**, beaten slightly	0.7	0.7	4.8	7.2
	TOTALS	84.8	46.9	170.2	89.7
	PER SERVING	10.6	5.9	21.3	11.2

- Oil the bottom of a 3 quart casserole with olive oil. Layer it with the artichokes. In a separate 2 quart bowl, begin mixing the cream cheese, the mayonnaise, and the heavy cream. When it is thoroughly mixed, stir in the remaining ingredients. When everything is well mixed, pour over the artichokes. Bake at 350° F for 30–40 minutes.

- **MAKES 8 SERVINGS WITH ABOUT 260 CALORIES PER SERVING.**

BAKED ZUCCHINI AND GARLIC

QUAN.	INGREDIENT	CARB GRAMS	AVAIL. CARB	FAT	PROTEIN
1 lb.	**ZUCCHINI**, halved lengthwise	26.1	15.3	0.9	10.4
1 oz.	**WHOLE PEELED GARLIC**	9.3	8.7	0.1	1.8
1 t.	**ONION POWDER**	1.7	1.6	0	0.2
½ t.	**SALT**				
1 t.	**OREGANO** or **ITALIAN SEASONING**				
4 T.	**OLIVE OIL**	0	0	52.0	0
4 T.	**GRATED PARMESAN CHEESE**	0.9	0.9	7.1	10.4
½ c.	**MOZZARELLA CHEESE**	3.1	3.1	17.0	27.3
	TOTALS	41.1	29.6	77.1	50.1
	PER SERVING	10.3	7.4	19.3	12.5

- Mix everything except the cheeses in a 2 quart bowl, making sure the zucchini is evenly coated. Place on a baking sheet and bake at 325° F for 30 minutes. If the garlic isn't quite soft, continue cooking, checking every 5 minutes until it softens. Cover with the grated Parmesan and mozzarella cheeses and brown in the oven.

- **MAKES 4 SERVINGS WITH ABOUT 253 CALORIES PER SERVING.**

WILTED BEAN SPROUTS

IF you've ever eaten at a Korean restaurant, then you know that they bring small dishes of various types of vegetables to eat with your meal. This is a variation on one of those vegetable dishes. These sprouts are delicious with Chinese entrées as well as Korean.

QUAN.	INGREDIENT	CARB GRAMS	AVAIL. CARB	FAT	PROTEIN
2 c.	**BEAN SPROUTS,** from the can, drained well (one 15 ounce can is sufficient)	5.4	3.4	0.1	3.5
½ t.	**SALT**				
I t.	**GARLIC POWDER**	2.0	2.0	0	0.5
I T	**SESAME OIL**	0	0	26.0	0
2 t.	**SESAME SEEDS**	1.4	0.7	4.3	1.6
	TOTALS	8.8	6.1	30.4	5.6
	PER SERVING OF ½ C.	2.2	1.5	7.6	1.4

- Place the sprouts in a 1 quart bowl. Add the salt and garlic and mix. Add the oil, mix well, and refrigerate. Serve cold, about ½ cup per person. This will only keep fresh a few days in your refrigerator.

- **MAKES 4 SERVINGS WITH ABOUT 80 CALORIES PER SERVING.**

WILTED SPINACH

IN my opinion, Koreans really go out of their way to make their vegetables taste good. This recipe is one of the few ways that I will eat spinach, aside from in a salad. This can also be made with zucchini instead of the spinach.

QUAN.	INGREDIENT	CARB GRAMS	AVAIL. CARB	FAT	PROTEIN
½ lb.	FRESH SPINACH	7.9	1.8	0.5	6.4
I t.	SALT				
I t.	GARLIC POWDER	2.0	2.0	0	0.5
2 T.	SESAME OIL	0	0	26.0	0
I T.	SESAME SEEDS	2.1	1.0	4.3	1.6
	TOTALS	12.0	4.8	30.8	8.5
	PER SERVING OF I OZ.	1.5	0.6	3.9	1.1

- Bring 2 quarts of water to a boil in a 3 quart pan. Wash the spinach well. Rinse in the boiling water until the spinach is slightly wilted, then rinse in cold water to stop the cooking. Squeeze out the liquid and put it in a 2 quart bowl. Mix in the dry ingredients, then the oil, and refrigerate. Serve about 1 ounce per person. This will keep, refrigerated, for a couple of days.

- **MAKES 8 SERVINGS WITH ABOUT 42 CALORIES PER SERVING.**

SAUERKRAUT with CRANBERRIES

CRANBERRIES are lower in carbs than most other fruits, so we can use them for flavoring. This variation on sauerkraut is especially good with roast pork.

QUAN.	INGREDIENT	CARB GRAMS	AVAIL. CARB	FAT	PROTEIN
3	**SLICES BACON**, diced	0	0	61.9	9.9
½ c.	**MEDIUM ONION** sliced thinly	5.0	3.9	0	0.7
½ c.	**CRANBERRIES**	7.0	4.7	0	0.2
2 c.	**SAUERKRAUT**, washed thoroughly (see page 211)	12.2	5.0	0.4	2.6
1	**CHICKEN BOUILLON CUBE**				
½ c.	**DRY WHITE WINE**	0.8	0.8	0	0
1 c.	**WATER**				
2 T.	**SUGAR EQUIVALENT SWEETENER**				
1 t.	**CARAWAY SEED** (optional)				
¼ t.	**NUTMEG** (optional)				
½ t.	**CAYENNE PEPPER** (optional, more or less added to your taste)				
	TOTALS	25.0	14.4	62.3	13.4
	PER SERVING	6.3	3.6	15.6	3.4

■ In a 10 inch skillet, fry the bacon over medium heat until it is well browned. Add the onion and cook until it becomes clear. Add the remaining ingredients, cover, and bring to a boil. Reduce the heat to low and stir every 15 minutes until most of the liquid is almost gone—about 1 hour. If it appears that it is getting too dry, add a half-cup of water and continue cooking. Keep in mind that the sauerkraut must cook the full hour in order to absorb all of the flavors; it isn't something that one wants to eat right out of the can or bag.

■ **MAKES 4 SERVINGS WITH ABOUT 168 CALORIES PER SERVING.**

KOREAN-STYLE FRIED GREEN BEANS

QUAN.	INGREDIENT	CARB GRAMS	AVAIL. CARB	FAT	PROTEIN
I lb.	**FRESH GREEN BEANS**, cleaned	32.2	16.8	0.4	8.2
4 T.	**SESAME OIL**	0	0	52.0	0
6	**GARLIC CLOVES**, diced finely	6	6	0	0.4
I t.	**SALT**				
2 T.	**SESAME SEEDS**	4.2	2.0	8.6	3.2
I t.	**SUGAR EQUIVALENT SWEETENER**				
2 T.	**WATER** for steaming				
I qt.	**WATER** for blanching the green beans				
	TOTALS	42.4	24.8	61.0	11.8
	PER SERVING	10.6	6.2	15.3	3.0

■ Snap and wash the green beans if necessary. Bring the quart of water to a boil in a half gallon pan. Place the oil in a 3 quart skillet over medium low heat. Add the beans to the water and let it come to a boil again. Turn off the heat and let the beans sit there for about 5 minutes. Drain the beans. Turn the skillet heat up to about medium. Add the garlic and cook until it begins to brown slightly. Add the beans, the salt, the 2 T. water, and the sugar substitute to the skillet and stir well. Put a lid on the skillet and let it steam for a couple of minutes. Add the sesame seeds, stir again, and let it steam, covered, again for about 5 minutes.

■ **MAKES 4 SERVINGS WITH ABOUT 175 CALORIES PER SERVING.**

SOUTHWESTERN GREEN BEANS

I first ate this dish in a restaurant in Concord, North Carolina, several years ago. It was so good that my friends decided that we needed a low carb version of it and this is what I came up with. These beans go with just about anything, but especially grilled beef.

QUAN.	INGREDIENT	CARB GRAMS	AVAIL. CARB	FAT	PROTEIN
2 c.	**GREEN BEANS** (one 16 oz. can is sufficient)	15.4	8.8	0.3	3.5
½ c.	**ONION,** sliced thinly	5.0	3.9	0	0.7
1	**BEEF BOUILLON CUBE**				
¼ t.	**CAYENNE PEPPER** (more or less added to your taste)				
½ t.	**SUGAR EQUIVALENT SWEETENER**				
	TOTALS	20.4	12.7	0.3	4.2
	PER SERVING	10.2	6.4	0.2	2.1

- Place the onion and bouillon cube in the bottom of a 1 quart saucepan. Add everything else, cover, bring to a boil over high heat, reduce the heat to medium low, and cook 15 minutes, stirring every 5 minutes. Turn off the heat and let sit 5 minutes before serving.

■ **MAKES 2 SERVINGS WITH ABOUT 36 CALORIES PER SERVING.**

TURNIP GREENS

QUAN.	INGREDIENT	CARB GRAMS	AVAIL. CARB	FAT	PROTEIN
1 lb.	**FROZEN TURNIP GREENS**	10.0	4.4	0.4	2.6
2 c.	**BEEF STOCK** (one 15 ounce can is sufficient)				
½ c.	**WATER**				
½ c.	**ONION**, sliced thinly	5.0	3.9	0	0.7
1 T.	**PICKLED JALAPEÑO PEPPERS** (diced, more or less to your taste)				
1 t.	**SUGAR EQUIVALENT SWEETENER** (optional)				
	TOTALS	15.0	8.3	0.4	3.3
	PER SERVING	5.0	2.8	0.1	1.1

- Place all of the ingredients in a 2 quart saucepan. Cover and bring to a boil over high heat. Reduce the heat to medium low and let simmer at least ½ hour. Most of the liquid should be cooked off. If it isn't cooked off, remove the lid and continue cooking until most of the liquid is gone.

- **MAKES 3 SERVINGS WITH ABOUT 17 CALORIES PER SERVING.**

COOKED RADISHES

COOKED radishes are not something we traditionally think of as a vegetable dish. These will provide a pleasant surprise for your guests because they don't resemble raw radishes at all. Their texture is similar to cooked potatoes or beets.

QUAN.	INGREDIENT	CARB GRAMS	AVAIL. CARB	FAT	PROTEIN
2 c.	**RADISHES**, cleaned and quartered	8.3	4.6	0.2	1.4
½ c.	**GREEN ONIONS**, diced	3.7	2.4	0	0.9
2 t.	**SUGAR EQUIVALENT SWEETENER**				
1 c.	**WATER**				
2	**CHICKEN BOUILLON CUBES**				
¼ t.	**BLACK PEPPER**				
	TOTALS	12.0	7.0	0.2	2.3
	PER SERVING OF ½ C.	3.0	1.8	0.1	0.6

- Place everything in a 1 quart saucepan and bring it to a boil over high heat. Cover, reduce the heat to medium, and let it simmer until most of the liquid is evaporated. This will take 15 minutes or more, so it should be stirred several times in the cooking process. Deglaze with an additional 2 T. of water, if necessary, and serve.

- **MAKES 4 SERVINGS WITH ABOUT 11 CALORIES PER SERVING.**

RED CABBAGE
AND CRANBERRIES

QUAN.	INGREDIENT	CARB GRAMS	AVAIL. CARB	FAT	PROTEIN
6 c.	**RED CABBAGE**, shredded	25.8	17.4	0.6	6.0
1 c.	**CRANBERRIES**	14.0	9.4	0	0.4
½ c.	**ONION**, sliced thinly	5.0	3.9	0	0.7
3 T.	**BUTTER** or **OLIVE OIL**	0	0	39.0	0
4 T.	**DRY RED WINE**	1.0	1.0	0	0.2
4 T.	**RED WINE VINEGAR**				
½ c.	**WATER**				
4 T.	**SUGAR EQUIVALENT SWEETENER**				
1 t.	**SALT**				
½ t.	**BLACK PEPPER**				
½ t.	**CINNAMON**	1.8	0.6	0	0.1
	TOTALS	47.6	32.3	39.6	7.4
	PER SERVING	7.9	5.4	6.6	1.2

■ Use a non–aluminum ovenproof pot, 3 quarts if possible. Over medium heat, bring the water and cranberries to a boil. Reduce the heat to low and smash the cranberries with a fork until their skins pop. Increase the heat to high and add the remaining ingredients. Cover and bring to a boil. Reduce the heat to medium low and cook for about 1 hour, stirring well every 10 minutes.

■ **MAKES 6 SERVINGS WITH ABOUT 86 CALORIES PER SERVING.**

SAUERKRAUT

SAUERKRAUT is a very low carb–friendly food because basically, it's pickled cabbage. Many folks don't like sauerkraut and I think that the reason for this is that they have never had it prepared properly. Most folks just open the can and microwave it for 2 minutes. The method of preparation described below provides for a mild but well-flavored sauerkraut and it is the sauerkraut that I use when the ingredient is called for in recipes throughout this book.

QUAN.	INGREDIENT	CARB GRAMS	AVAIL. CARB	FAT	PROTEIN
2 c.	**CANNED SAUERKRAUT** (about 1 can of 15 ounces)	12.2	5.1	0.3	2.6
1	**BOUILLON CUBE**				
½ c.	**ONION**, diced	6.9	5.5	0	1.0
1 T.	**OLIVE OIL**	0	0	13.0	0
¾ c.	**WATER**				
½ t.	**CARAWAY SEED** (optional)				
½ t.	**CAYENNE PEPPER** (optional)				
1 t.	**SUGAR EQUIVALENT SWEETENER** (optional)				
	TOTALS	19.1	10.6	13.3	3.6
	PER SERVING	6.4	3.5	4.4	1.2

- First you need to wash the kraut. Open the sauerkraut can, retaining the lid. Over the sink, using the lid, press the juice out of the sauerkraut. You want to remove as much of the juice as possible. Put the kraut in a 1 quart bowl and cover again with water. Ensure that the water is well mixed in with kraut. Let this sit for as long as possible, at least ½ hour, in order to leach the acid and salt out of the kraut. Squeeze the liquid out of the kraut and it is ready to use.

In a skillet, heat the oil. Add the onion and cook until it becomes clear. Add the sauerkraut, the ¾ cup of water, and the remaining ingredients to the skillet, cover, and bring to a boil. Reduce the heat to medium low and simmer, covered, for about 20 minutes. Remove the lid and reduce the liquid, stirring every 10 minutes. When there is about 4 T. or ¼ cup of the liquid remaining, remove from the heat. Let sit about 5 minutes before serving.

- **MAKES 3 SERVINGS WITH ABOUT 58 CALORIES PER SERVING.**

EGGS
GALORE

BASIC SCRAMBLED EGGS

FOR most folks, scrambled eggs tend to be real plain. I've always liked to add a small amount of various herbs and spices to mine to increase the flavor.

QUAN.	INGREDIENT	CARB GRAMS	AVAIL. CARB	FAT	PROTEIN
3	EGGS, slightly scrambled	2.1	2.1	14.4	21.6
3 T.	HALF AND HALF	1.8	1.8	4.8	1.2
1/8 t.	SALT				
1/2 t.	ONION POWDER	0.9	0.8	0	0.1
1/2 t.	GARLIC POWDER	1.0	1.0	0	0.3
1 pinch	BLACK PEPPER				
2 T.	OLIVE OIL or BUTTER	0	0	26.0	0
	You can add CHEESE, HAM, BACON, SAUSAGE, BELL PEPPER, MUSHROOMS, etc.				
	TOTALS	5.8	5.7	45.2	23.2
	PER SERVING	5.8	5.7	45.2	23.2

■ Place the first 6 ingredients in a 1 quart bowl and mix well with a fork. If you want to add vegetables and/or meat, cook this first in a 10 inch skillet in the olive oil over medium high heat. Add the eggs and continue stirring until they are only slightly runny. Plate the mixture. At this point you can add the cheese and heat in a microwave for about 15 seconds. Try to limit anything that you add to the eggs to under 1/2 cup. In other words, you want more eggs than additions. Make sure you add in any additional macronutrient values for any additional ingredients.

■ MAKES 1 SERVING WITH ABOUT 522 CALORIES PER SERVING.

FRITTATA/ONE-SKILLET QUICHE ▶

Omelets are wonderful for the low carb eater, but they are a little harder to cook than just plain old scrambled eggs because they have to be flipped. The Italian frittata is an omelet that doesn't have to be turned because we steam it instead. Frittata can be converted to a "crustless pie" by pouring into a greased baking dish and baking at 325° F for about 40 minutes for a single helping. A crust can be made of crushed pork rinds if you so desire. Many people prefer to cook their frittata on top of the stove, but it can also be finished in just a short time under the broiler.

QUICHE LORRAINE FRITTATA

TRADITIONALLY, Quiche Lorraine is a pie, crust and all. Once we learn how to make it in the form of a frittata, it becomes much more acceptable for us. This was one of my mother's favorites because she preferred the Gruyère-style cheeses.

QUAN.	INGREDIENT	CARB GRAMS	AVAIL. CARB	FAT	PROTEIN
3	EGGS, slightly scrambled	2.1	2.1	14.4	21.6
3 T.	HALF AND HALF	1.8	1.8	4.8	1.2
1/8 t.	SALT				
1/2 t.	ONION POWDER	0.9	0.8	0	0.1
1/2 t.	GARLIC POWDER	1.0	1.0	0	0.3
1 pinch	BLACK PEPPER				
1/2 t.	NUTMEG				
2 T.	GRATED PARMESAN CHEESE	0.5	0.5	3.6	5.2
2 slices	BACON, diced	0	0	41.3	6.6
1/2 c.	ONION, diced	6.9	5.5	0	1.0
2 oz.	SWISS CHEESE, diced	1.9	1.9	14.8	16.1
	TOTALS	15.1	13.6	78.9	52.1
	PER SERVING	15.2	13.6	78.9	52.1

- Fry the bacon in a 10 inch skillet over medium heat until it is well browned. Add the onion and cook until they become clear. Remove the skillet from the heat and remove the onions and bacon from the skillet, reserving as much oil in the skillet as possible. (You are going to use this oil for cooking the frittata.) After the bacon has cooled, dice it and mix everything except the Swiss cheese in a 1 quart bowl. Again, heat your skillet over medium heat. Stir your egg mixture once more and pour it into the skillet. Add the Swiss cheese and cover. Reduce the heat to low. Cook until the mixture is soft but solid on top. Remove to your plate.

- **MAKES 1 SERVING WITH ABOUT 973 CALORIES PER SERVING.**

CHICKEN AND BROCCOLI FRITTATA

THE combination of chicken, broccoli, and Swiss cheese is always appealing. Here we are combining them with eggs for a low carb dinner for two.

QUAN.	INGREDIENT	CARB GRAMS	AVAIL. CARB	FAT	PROTEIN
6	**EGGS**, slightly scrambled	4.2	4.2	28.8	43.2
6 T.	**HALF AND HALF**	3.6	3.6	9.8	2.4
¼ t.	**SALT**				
1 t.	**ONION POWDER**	1.7	1.6	0	0.2
1 t.	**GARLIC POWDER**	2.0	2.0	0	0.5
1 pinch	**BLACK PEPPER**				
4 T.	**OLIVE OIL** or **BUTTER**	0	0	52.0	0
½ t.	**NUTMEG**				
4 T.	**GRATED PARMESAN CHEESE**	0.9	0.9	7.1	10.4
4 oz.	**COOKED CHICKEN**, diced	0	0	2.9	32.9
¼ c.	**ONION**, diced	3.5	2.8	0	0.5
2 oz.	**SWISS CHEESE**, diced	1.9	1.9	14.8	16.1
1 c.	**FROZEN BROCCOLI**, thawed, drained, and chopped coarsely	9.8	4.3	0.1	5.7
	RED CAYENNE SAUCE to your taste (a shake or two)				
	TOTALS	27.6	21.3	115.5	111.9
	PER SERVING	9.2	7.1	38.5	37.3

- In a 10 inch skillet, fry the onions in 2 T. oil over medium heat until they become clear. Let them cool. Mix everything except the remaining oil and the Swiss cheese in a 1 quart bowl. Heat 2 T. oil in the 10 inch skillet over medium heat. Add the egg mixture to the skillet, sprinkle with the Swiss cheese, cover, and reduce the heat to low. Cook until the mixture firms up.

- **MAKES 3 SERVINGS WITH ABOUT 524 CALORIES PER SERVING.**

SHRIMP QUICHE

QUAN.	INGREDIENT	CARB GRAMS	AVAIL. CARB	FAT	PROTEIN
6	**EGGS**, slightly scrambled	4.2	4.2	28.8	43.2
6 T.	**HALF AND HALF**	3.6	3.6	9.8	2.4
¼ t.	**SALT**				
I t.	**ONION POWDER**	1.7	1.6	0	0.2
I t.	**GARLIC POWDER**	2.0	2.0	0	0.5
I pinch	**BLACK PEPPER**				
2 T.	**OLIVE OIL** or **BUTTER**	0	0	26.0	0
½ c.	**SOUR CREAM**	4.9	4.9	22.9	3.7
I c.	**CANNED SHRIMP** (about 2 cans at 6 ounces per can, reserve and freeze the liquid for a future soup)	1.3	1.3	1.8	29.5
¼ c.	**ONION**, diced	3.5	2.8	0	0.5
½ c.	**CHOPPED GREEN CHILIES** (more or less to your taste, can use finely diced jalapeños instead)				
½ c.	**COLBY CHEESE**, diced	1.7	1.7	20.1	15.7
½ c.	**MONTEREY JACK CHEESE**, diced	0.5	0.5	19.0	16.2
4 T.	**SALSA** for serving (see page 245)	3.6	2.8	0	0.4
	TOTALS	27.0	25.4	128.4	112.3
	PER SERVING	9.0	8.5	42.8	37.4

- Mix the eggs, half and half, spices, sour cream, shrimp, and chilies in a 1 quart bowl. In a 10 inch skillet, cook the onion in the oil over medium high heat until it becomes clear. Slowly pour the egg mixture into the pan, sprinkle the cheese over the egg mixture, cover the pan, and reduce the heat to low. Cook until the mixture is soft but solid on top. Remove to your plate. Spoon the salsa over the top.

- **MAKES 3 SERVINGS WITH ABOUT 569 CALORIES PER SERVING.**

SPINACH QUICHE

I have it on good authority that this is Popeye's favorite quiche. Actually, this is very similar to many other spinach casserole recipes, except this dish is quicker and less of a hassle to prepare.

QUAN.	INGREDIENT	CARB GRAMS	AVAIL. CARB	FAT	PROTEIN
6	EGGS, slightly scrambled	4.2	4.2	28.8	43.2
6 T.	HALF AND HALF	3.6	3.6	9.8	2.4
¼ t.	SALT				
I t.	ONION POWDER	1.7	1.6	0	0.2
I t.	GARLIC POWDER	2.0	2.0	0	0.5
I pinch	BLACK PEPPER				
2 T.	OLIVE OIL or BUTTER	0	0	26.0	0
½ t.	NUTMEG				
½ c.	GRATED PARMESAN CHEESE	1.9	1.9	14.3	20.8
2 T.	LEMON JUICE	1.3	1.3	0	0.1
¼ c.	ONION, diced	3.5	2.8	0	0.5
I box	FROZEN CHOPPED SPINACH, well thawed, with the juice squeezed out (about 10 ounces per box)	11.7	5.1	0	6.9
	TOTALS	29.9	22.5	78.9	74.6
	PER SERVING	15.0	11.3	39.5	37.3

- Mix the spices, grated Parmesan cheese, lemon juice, and spinach with the eggs and half and half in a 1 quart bowl. In a 10 inch skillet, fry the onion in the butter over medium high heat until the onion becomes clear. Pour the egg mixture into the pan, cover, and reduce the heat to low. Cook until the mixture is soft but solid on top. Remove to your plate.

- **MAKES 2 SERVINGS WITH ABOUT 550 CALORIES PER SERVING.**

GERMAN QUICHE

QUAN.	INGREDIENT	CARB GRAMS	AVAIL. CARB	FAT	PROTEIN
6	**EGGS**, slightly scrambled	4.2	4.2	28.8	43.2
6 T.	**HALF AND HALF**	3.6	3.6	9.8	2.4
¼ t.	**SALT**				
1 t.	**ONION POWDER**	1.7	1.6	0	0.2
1 t.	**GARLIC POWDER**	2.0	2.0	0	0.5
1 pinch	**BLACK PEPPER**				
2 T.	**OLIVE OIL** or **BUTTER**	0	0	26.0	0
½ t.	**NUTMEG**				
½ t.	**OREGANO**				
4 T.	**GRATED PARMESAN CHEESE**	0.9	0.9	7.1	10.4
¼ lb.	**HAM** (2% fat)	2.0	2.0	2.0	20.0
¼ c.	**ONION**, diced	3.5	2.8	0	0.5
2 oz.	**SWISS CHEESE**, diced	1.9	1.9	14.8	16.1
1 c.	**FROZEN CAULIFLOWER**, thawed, drained, and chopped coarsely	6.7	1.8	0.3	2.9
½ c.	**SOUR CREAM**	4.9	4.9	22.9	3.7
	TOTALS	31.4	25.7	111.7	99.9
	PER SERVING	10.5	8.6	37.2	33.3

- Mix the eggs, half and half, spices, grated Parmesan cheese, ham, and sour cream in a 2 quart bowl. In a 10 inch skillet, fry the onions and cauliflower in the oil over medium high heat until the onions become clear. Pour the egg mixture into the skillet, sprinkle the mixture with the Swiss cheese, cover the skillet, and reduce the heat to low. Cook until the mixture is soft but solid on top. Remove to your plate.

- **MAKES 3 SERVINGS WITH ABOUT 502 CALORIES PER SERVING.**

SALMON QUICHE

QUAN.	INGREDIENT	CARB GRAMS	AVAIL. CARB	FAT	PROTEIN
6	**EGGS**, slightly scrambled	4.2	4.2	28.8	43.2
6 T.	**HALF AND HALF**	3.6	3.6	9.8	2.4
¼ t.	**SALT**				
1 t.	**ONION POWDER**	1.7	1.6	0	0.2
1 t.	**GARLIC POWDER**	2.0	2.0	0	0.5
1 pinch	**BLACK PEPPER**				
2 T.	**OLIVE OIL** or **BUTTER**	0	0	26.0	0
½ t.	**DILL WEED**				
8 oz.	**CANNED SALMON** (about half of a 15 ounce can will suffice)	0	0	17.5	42.0
¼ c.	**ONION**, diced	3.5	2.8	0	0.5
4 oz.	**SWISS CHEESE**, diced	3.8	3.8	29.6	32.2
½ c.	**SOUR CREAM**	4.9	4.9	22.9	3.7
2 T.	**OLIVE OIL**	0	0	26.0	0
	TOTALS	23.7	22.9	160.6	124.7
	PER SERVING	7.9	7.6	53.5	41.6

■ Mix the eggs, half and half, spices, salmon, sour cream, and Swiss cheese. In a 10 inch skillet, fry the onions in the oil over medium high heat until they become clear. Pour the egg mixture into the skillet, cover, and reduce the heat to low. Cook until the mixture is soft but solid on top. Remove to your plate.

■ **MAKES 3 SERVINGS WITH ABOUT 678 CALORIES PER SERVING.**

CHEDDAR CHILI FRITTATA

QUAN.	INGREDIENT	CARB GRAMS	AVAIL. CARB	FAT	PROTEIN
6	EGGS, scrambled slightly	4.2	4.2	28.8	43.2
6 T.	HALF AND HALF	3.6	3.6	9.8	2.4
1/4 t.	SALT				
1 t.	ONION POWDER	1.7	1.6	0	0.2
1 t.	GARLIC POWDER	2.0	2.0	0	0.5
1 pinch	BLACK PEPPER				
2 T.	OLIVE OIL or BUTTER	0	0	26.0	0
1/2 c.	SHREDDED CHEDDAR CHEESE	0.9	0.9	20.8	16.5
6 oz.	HAM (2% fat)	3.0	3.0	3.0	30.0
1/2 c.	SOUR CREAM	4.9	4.9	22.9	3.7
1/2 c.	ONION, diced	3.5	2.8	0	0.5
2 T.	PICKLED JALAPEÑO PEPPERS, diced (more or less added to your taste)				
	TOTALS	23.8	23.0	111.3	97.0
	PER SERVING	7.9	7.7	37.1	32.3

- Mix the eggs, half and half, cheese, ham, sour cream, and jalapeños. In a 10 inch skillet, fry the onions in the butter over medium high heat until they become clear. Pour the egg mixture into the pan, cover, and reduce the heat to low. Cook until the mixture is soft but solid on top. Remove to your plate.

- **MAKES 3 SERVINGS WITH ABOUT 494 CALORIES PER SERVING.**

GREEN CHILI EGGS

THIS is made in the form a casserole and not a frittata. You can always adapt this to a frittata if you're not making it to feed a crowd.

QUAN.	INGREDIENT	CARB GRAMS	AVAIL. CARB	FAT	PROTEIN
2–3	**FROZEN WHOLE GREEN CHILIES**, seeded and wiped dry (more or less to your taste, can use 2–3 t. of finely diced pickled jalapeños instead)				
I lb.	**GRATED MONTEREY JACK CHEESE**	3.1	3.1	129.2	110.2
12	**EGGS**, well scrambled	8.4	8.4	57.6	86.4
I c.	**SOUR CREAM**	9.8	9.8	45.7	7.3
½ t.	**SALT**				
¼ t.	**BLACK PEPPER**				
I t.	**GARLIC POWDER**	2.0	2.0	0	0.5
I t.	**ONION POWDER**	1.7	1.6	0	0.2
	TOTALS	25.0	24.9	232.5	204.6
	PER SERVING	4.2	4.2	38.8	34.1

- Layer the chilies with the grated cheese in a buttered or greased 13 x 9 x 2 inch baking dish. Combine the eggs and all of the other ingredients in a bowl and pour over the top of the chilies. Bake for 30 minutes at 350° F until it puffs like a soufflé.

- **MAKES 6 SERVINGS WITH ABOUT 502 CALORIES PER SERVING.**

SWABIAN-STYLE BEEF AND EGGS

THIS is a variation on *Katzeng'schrei* (caterwauling), which, according to the source where I found it, was traditional Monday fare in Swabia (modern Baden-Wurttemberg and western Bavaria). Traditionally, leftovers of cooked beef are diced, fried, mixed with lightly beaten eggs, and served with cranberries. You can serve this with a green salad and Cranberry Sauce (see page 251). For variety, you can also add some diced green peppers or some cheese.

QUAN.	INGREDIENT	CARB GRAMS	AVAIL. CARB	FAT	PROTEIN
3	EGGS	2.1	2.1	14.4	21.6
3 T.	HALF AND HALF	1.8	1.8	4.8	1.2
⅛ t.	SALT				
½ t.	ONION POWDER	0.9	0.8	0	0.1
½ t.	GARLIC POWDER	1.0	1.0	0	0.3
I pinch	BLACK PEPPER				
2 T.	OLIVE OIL or BUTTER	0	0	26.0	0
½ lb.	COOKED CHUCK ROAST or DELI ROAST BEEF (or any cooked beef), sliced thinly and cut into small pieces	0	0	26.6	32.1
½ c.	ONION, diced	6.9	5.5	0	1.0
4 T.	WATER				
	TOTALS	12.7	11.2	71.8	56.3
	PER SERVING	6.4	5.6	35.9	28.2

- In a 10 inch skillet, cook the onions in 2 T. of oil until they begin to brown. Add the beef and the water, cover, and cook until it is well heated. Remove the lid and let the liquid evaporate somewhat. Add the eggs and cook until the desired texture is obtained.

- **MAKES 2 SERVINGS WITH ABOUT 458 CALORIES PER SERVING.**

EGG SALAD

EGG salad is typically composed of hard-boiled eggs, mayonnaise, mustard, salt, and pepper. For variation you can include onions, garlic, pickles, peppers, ham, bacon, and various deli meats. This particular recipe is one of my favorite variations. By the way, this makes a wonderful breakfast. Keep in mind that the addition of ½ cup of diced celery adds only about 1.2 grams total available carbs to this or about 0.2 grams available carbs per serving.

QUAN.	INGREDIENT	CARB GRAMS	AVAIL. CARB	FAT	PROTEIN
1 doz.	HARD-BOILED LARGE EGGS	8.4	8.4	57.6	86.4
4 T.	MAYONNAISE	1.5	1.5	42.1	0.6
4 T.	SALAD ONIONS (see page 84)	3.6	2.8	0	0.4
4 T.	SWEET RELISH (see page 85)	2.0	1.2	0.8	0.8
1 t.	SALT				
½ t.	PREPARED SALAD MUSTARD				
1 t.	PREPARED WHITE HORSERADISH (optional, more or less to your taste)				
	TOTALS	15.5	13.9	100.5	88.2
	PER SERVING	2.6	2.3	16.8	14.7

- Boil and peel the eggs as described (see page 231). In a 2 quart bowl, dice the eggs finely with the back of a fork. Mix in the remaining ingredients.

■ **MAKES ABOUT 6 SERVINGS WITH ABOUT 219 CALORIES PER SERVING.**

DEVILLED EGGS

DEVILLED eggs are one of those treats you can find at all of my family get-togethers. This is my sister's recipe and it is everyone's favorite. Suggested additions include: a teaspoon of prepared mustard, a half teaspoon of lemon juice, 2 tablespoons of sour cream, ½ t. hot sauce, garnish with pimientos, ½ t. dry mustard, 1 t. garlic powder, 1 t. Worcestershire Sauce, 2 t. caviar, 2 T. butter, 1 T. diced truffles, 2 T. olives, 1 t. prepared white horseradish, all more or less to your taste.

QUAN.	INGREDIENT	CARB GRAMS	AVAIL. CARB	FAT	PROTEIN
½ doz.	**HARD-BOILED EGGS**	4.2	4.2	28.8	43.2
2 T.	**MAYONNAISE**	0.8	0.8	21.0	0.4
1 t.	**ONION POWDER**	1.7	1.6	0	0
2 T.	**SWEET RELISH** (see page 85)	1.0	0.6	0.4	0.4
½ t.	**SALT**				
	PAPRIKA for garnish				
	TOTALS	7.7	7.2	50.2	44.0
	PER SERVING OF ½ EGG	0.6	0.6	4.2	3.7

- Boil and peel the eggs as described (see page 231). Cut the eggs in half lengthwise. Remove the yolks to a 2 cup bowl. Mash the yolks thoroughly with the back of a fork. Mix the mayonnaise, onion powder, salt, and relish with the yolks. Spoon about 2 teaspoons (more or less) of the yolk mixture back into the egg whites. Garnish with a sprinkle of paprika.

- **MAKES 12 SERVINGS WITH ABOUT 55 CALORIES PER SERVING.**

JUEVOS DEL DIABLO

THIS is a Mexican variation on the Devilled Eggs that we typically eat, but these are spicy hot.

QUAN.	INGREDIENT	CARB GRAMS	AVAIL. CARB	FAT	PROTEIN
½ doz.	HARD-BOILED EGGS	4.2	4.2	28.8	43.2
3 T.	MAYONNAISE	1.2	1.2	31.5	0.6
2 t.	GROUND CUMIN	1.8	1.4	0.8	0.8
1 T.	CAPERS, diced finely	0.4	0.1	0.1	0.2
½ t.	SALT				
1 t.	PREPARED MUSTARD				
1 T.	JALAPEÑO PEPPERS, diced finely (more or less added to your taste)				
	CAYENNE PEPPER for garnish				
	FRESH CHOPPED CILANTRO for garnish				
	TOTALS	7.6	6.9	61.2	44.8
	PER SERVING OF ½ EGG	0.6	0.6	5.1	3.7

- Boil and peel the eggs as described (see page 231). Cut the eggs in half lengthwise. Remove the yolks to a 2 cup bowl. Mash the yolks thoroughly with the back of a fork. Mix the mayonnaise, cumin, capers, peppers, and salt with the yolks. Spoon about 2 teaspoons (more or less) of the yolk mixture back into the egg whites. Garnish with a sprinkle of cayenne and cilantro.

- **MAKES 12 SERVINGS WITH ABOUT 63 CALORIES PER SERVING.**

EGGS À LA RUSSE

QUAN.	INGREDIENT	CARB GRAMS	AVAIL. CARB	FAT	PROTEIN
½ doz.	**HARD-BOILED EGGS**	4.2	4.2	28.8	43.2
3 T.	**MAYONNAISE**	1.2	1.2	31.5	0.6
6	**GREEN STUFFED OLIVES**, diced finely	1.3	1.3	3.2	0
I T.	**CAPERS**, diced finely	0.4	0.1	0.1	0.2
3 T.	**SALAD ONIONS** (see page 84), diced finely	2.7	2.1	0	0.3
2 t.	**DRIED TARRAGON**				
½ c.	**CELERY**, diced finely	2.2	1.2	0	0.5
I t.	**DRIED DILL**				
I T.	**PREPARED HORSERADISH** (more or less added to your taste)				
2 T.	**CAVIAR** for garnish (½ t. per ½ egg, optional)	1.3	1.3	5.2	7.9
	TOTALS	13.3	11.4	68.8	52.7
	PER SERVING OF ½ EGG	1.1	1.0	5.7	4.4

- Boil and peel the eggs as described (see page 231). Cut the eggs in half lengthwise. Remove the yolks to a 2 cup bowl. Mash the yolks thoroughly with the back of a fork. Mix in the mayonnaise, capers, olives, onions, celery, and spices with the yolks. Spoon about 2 teaspoons (more or less) of the yolk mixture back into the egg whites. Garnish with the caviar.

- **MAKES 12 SERVINGS WITH ABOUT 73 CALORIES PER SERVING.**

EGGS STUFFED WITH CRABMEAT

THIS is a unique kind of devilled eggs with some seafood added. You can use salad shrimp instead of crabmeat if you prefer.

QUAN.	INGREDIENT	CARB GRAMS	AVAIL. CARB	FAT	PROTEIN
½ doz.	**HARD-BOILED EGGS**	4.2	4.2	28.8	43.2
6 oz.	**CRABMEAT** (one 6 ounce can, reserve and freeze the liquid for a later soup)	2.5	2.5	0	27.5
½ c.	**CELERY**, diced finely	2.2	1.2	0	0.5
1 t.	**DRY MUSTARD**				
½ t.	**ONION POWDER**	0.9	0.8	0	0.1
½ t.	**GARLIC POWDER**	1.0	1.0	0	0.3
⅛ t.	**SALT**				
1 pinch	**BLACK PEPPER**				
3 T.	**MAYONNAISE**	1.2	1.2	31.5	0.6
	PAPRIKA for garnish				
	TOTALS	12.0	11.9	60.3	72.2
	PER SERVING OF ½ EGG	1.0	1.0	5.0	6.0

- Boil and peel the eggs as described (see page 231). Cut the eggs in half lengthwise. Remove the yolks to a 2 cup bowl. Mash the yolks thoroughly with the back of a fork. Mix everything with the yolks. Spoon 2–3 t. of the yolk mixture into the egg whites, sprinkle with paprika, and refrigerate until needed.

- **MAKES 12 SERVINGS WITH ABOUT 73 CALORIES PER SERVING.**

BASIC PICKLED EGGS

THESE eggs can be found in commercial establishments throughout the South. They will keep at least a month in the refrigerator, and the longer they sit, the better they are. These are supposed to be eaten spicy hot, so they can be served with red cayenne sauce and salt. I like to keep them around not only to gnosh on, but to put on my salads. There are many variations on this recipe, the most common being the inclusion of some type of cayenne pepper in the marinating liquid.

QUAN.	INGREDIENT	CARB GRAMS	AVAIL. CARB	FAT	PROTEIN
11	**HARD-BOILED LARGE EGGS,** cooled and peeled	7.7	7.7	52.8	79.2
½ c.	**WHITE VINEGAR** (plus extra vinegar)				
½ c.	**WATER**				
1 t.	**ONION POWDER**				
1 t.	**GARLIC POWDER**				
4 t.	**SALT**				
2 t.	**CAYENNE PEPPER** (optional—more or less added to your taste)				
	RED CAYENNE SAUCE, a shake or two when serving				
	TOTALS	7.7	7.7	52.8	79.2
	PER SERVING OF 1 EGG	0.8	0.8	4.8	7.2

- Boil and peel the eggs according to the instructions (see page 231). Place the eggs in a quart jar. Bring the other ingredients to a boil and pour over the eggs. If you don't have quite enough liquid to fill the jar, add enough vinegar to cover the eggs. Let the jar cool to room temperature and cover it with a lid. Refrigerate. Shake every couple of days to move the spices around. These are ready to eat within 2–3 days. Because none of the spices are ever consumed, we assume that we are getting minimal carbs from them, so rather than count them entirely, the carb counts from the eggs are just rounded up slightly.

- **MAKES 11 SERVINGS WITH ABOUT 75 CALORIES PER SERVING.**

BOILING AND PEELING EGGS ▶

As low carb eaters, we can eat a lot of boiled eggs. There are better and worse methods to boil and peel eggs. These suggestions come from the American Egg Board in their *Eggcyclopedia*, 3rd edition.

EGG SELECTION

Select eggs that are neither too fresh nor too old—eggs that have been refrigerated a week to ten days. Eggs should be stored small-end up for twenty-four hours before boiling in order to center the yolk.

BOILING

Pierce the shells before cooking. Place the eggs in a single layer at the bottom of a pan. Cover the eggs with cold water an inch above the eggs. Add 2 to 4 tablespoons of salt per gallon of water. Bring the water to a boil quickly, let simmer 5 minutes and remove from heat. Let sit an additional 10 minutes for large eggs (subtract 3 minutes for medium eggs and an additional 3 minutes for small eggs) in the hot water. Cool the eggs as quickly as possible; under cold running water for 5 minutes is suggested.

PEELING

If the eggs aren't going to be used immediately, refrigerate in the shell in the carton for up to a week. Otherwise, crack the shell all over by tapping gently on the counter, then roll the egg around in your palm. Begin peeling with the large end. Holding the egg under water or dipping it in water facilitates the peeling.

SAUCES AND CONDIMENTS

KETCHUP

ONE of the first things that most low carbers complain about is not being able to have ketchup. This recipe has a lot of flavor and is relatively quick to make. Note the subtle combination of sweet and sour flavors.

QUAN.	INGREDIENT	CARB GRAMS	AVAIL. CARB	FAT	PROTEIN
1 c.	TOMATO SAUCE	17.6	14.2	0.4	3.4
¾ c.	WATER				
2 t.	ONION POWDER	3.4	3.2	0	0.4
1 t.	GARLIC POWDER	6.0	6.0	0	1.5
⅜ c.	WHITE VINEGAR				
5 T.	SUGAR EQUIVALENT SWEETENER				
1 t.	SALT				
1 t.	DRY MUSTARD	1.2	0.7	0.9	0.8
1 t.	CINNAMON	1.8	0.6	0	0
	XANTHUM GUM for thickening (optional)				
	TOTALS	30.0	24.7	1.3	6.1
	PER SERVING OF 1 T.	0.9	0.8	0	0.2

- In a heavy, non–aluminum 1 quart saucepan, bring the water, vinegar, and all of the dry ingredients, less the xanthum gum, to a boil over high heat. Reduce the heat to medium low and let simmer for 5 minutes. Add the tomato sauce, bring it to a boil, reduce the heat, and simmer for an additional 10 minutes. Pour into a jar or freezer container and let cool. If it doesn't come to 2 cups, add enough cold water to bring it up to 2 cups. This ketchup should keep in your refrigerator for at least a week. You can also freeze it. If you freeze it, you might want to put it in an ice cube tray or something else which is portioned so that you don't have to thaw and refreeze the whole batch each time you want ketchup. If it is to be used for a noncooking purpose, such as to put on a cheeseburger (without the bun of course), it can be thickened by adding ½ t. of xanthum gum to one cup of the cold ketchup. Sprinkle the xanthum gum over the ketchup and stir well. Stir again every 10 minutes. This should be thoroughly thickened after an hour.

- **MAKES ONE PINT OR 32 SERVINGS WITH ABOUT 4 CALORIES PER SERVING.**

CHILI SAUCE

CHILI Sauce is very similar to ketchup, except it has the added hot flavor along with the sweet and sour combination.

QUAN.	INGREDIENT	CARB GRAMS	AVAIL. CARB	FAT	PROTEIN
1 c.	TOMATO SAUCE	17.6	14.2	0.4	3.4
½ c.	WATER				
2 t.	ONION POWDER	3.4	3.2	0	0.4
½ c.	BELL PEPPER, diced finely	4.8	3.5	0.1	0.7
2 T.	PICKLED JALAPEÑO PEPPERS, diced finely (more or less added to your taste)	0.7	0.4	0.1	0.2
½ c.	CELERY, diced finely	2.2	1.2	0	0.5
1 t.	GARLIC POWDER	2.0	2.0	0	0.5
2 T.	OLIVE OIL	0	0	26	0
4 T.	WHITE VINEGAR				
5 T.	SUGAR EQUIVALENT SWEETENER				
1 t.	SALT				
1 t.	DRY MUSTARD	1.2	0.7	0.9	0.8
1 t.	CINNAMON	1.8	0.6	0	0
½ t.	GRATED NUTMEG	0.6	0.3	0.3	0
½ t.	CLOVE	0.7	0.3	0.5	0
½ t.	ALLSPICE	0.7	0.5	0	0
	XANTHUM GUM for thickening (optional)				
	TOTALS	35.7	26.9	28.3	6.3
	PER SERVING OF 1 T.	1.1	0.8	0.9	0.2

- In a heavy, non-aluminum 1 quart saucepan, add the oil, the onions, the celery, and the peppers and cook over medium high heat until the onions become clear. Add the water, vinegar, sugar substitute, and the dry ingredients, bring to a boil, and simmer 10 minutes. Add the tomato sauce. Reduce the heat to low and cook for about 15 minutes. Pour into a jar or freezer container and let cool. If you freeze it, you might want to put it in an ice cube tray or something else that is portioned so you don't have to thaw and refreeze the whole batch each time you want chili sauce. If it is to be used for a noncooking purpose, such as to use in a salad dressing, and you think it needs to be thicker, it can be thickened by adding ½ t. of xanthum gum to one cup of the chili sauce. Sprinkle the xanthum gum over the chili sauce slowly and stir well. Stir again every 10 minutes. This should be thoroughly thickened after an hour.

- **MAKES ONE PINT OR 32 SERVINGS WITH ABOUT 12 CALORIES PER SERVING.**

BASIC BAR-B-Q SAUCE

QUAN.	INGREDIENT	CARB GRAMS	AVAIL. CARB	FAT	PROTEIN
2½ c.	TOMATO SAUCE	44.0	35.5	1.0	8.5
1 c.	WATER				
2 T.	ONION POWDER	10.4	10.2	0	1.4
2 T.	GARLIC POWDER	12.2	12.2	0	2.8
4 t.	SALT				
2 t.	DRY MUSTARD				
2 t.	BLACK PEPPER				
4 t.	DRIED RED PEPPER FLAKES (more or less added to your taste)				
3 T.	OLIVE OIL	0	0	39.0	0
1 c.	CIDER VINEGAR				
¾ c.	SUGAR EQUIVALENT SWEETENER				
½ t.	LIQUID SMOKE (optional)				
	TOTALS	66.6	57.9	40.0	21.2
	PER SERVING 1 T.	1.0	0.9	0.6	0.3

- In a heavy, non–aluminum 2 quart saucepan, over medium heat, add all of the ingredients and bring it to a boil. Reduce the heat to low and simmer for about 30 minutes. Pour it into a jar or freezer container and let it cool. Refrigerate or freeze the rest until it is needed. Add more or less red pepper to modify hotness. This can be diluted with Ketchup (see page 234) or tomato sauce if your first attempt is too hot.

- **MAKES ABOUT 4 CUPS OR 64 SERVINGS WITH ABOUT 10 CALORIES PER SERVING.**

MEXICAN BAR-B-Q SAUCE

FOR those of us who like Mexican food, this sauce permits us a little taste of Mexico from the grill. Go easy on the peppers when you make this the first time and then adjust the heat to your taste.

QUAN.	INGREDIENT	CARB GRAMS	AVAIL. CARB	FAT	PROTEIN
5–6 T.	**SUGAR EQUIVALENT SWEETENER**				
6 T.	**CHILI POWDER** (more or less added to your taste)	24.6	9.0	6.0	5.4
1 T.	**PICKLED JALAPEÑO PEPPERS,** diced finely (optional for hotness, more or less added to your taste)				
4 T.	**TOMATO SAUCE**	4.4	3.6	0.1	0.9
5 T.	**CIDER VINEGAR**				
2 T.	**OLIVE OIL**	0	0	26.0	0
1 T.	**DRY MUSTARD**				
1 T.	**GARLIC POWDER**	6.1	6.1	0	1.4
½ t.	**SALT**				
1 T.	**RED CAYENNE SAUCE** (optional for hotness, more or less to your taste)				
2 T.	**WATER**				
	TOTALS	35.1	18.7	32.1	7.7
	PER SERVING OF 1 T.	2.9	1.6	2.7	0.6

- In a 1 quart saucepan, bring all ingredients to a boil over high heat. Reduce the heat to medium low and simmer 10 minutes, covered. Taste it and adjust for hotness.

- **MAKES ABOUT ¾ CUP OR ABOUT 12 SERVINGS WITH ABOUT 33 CALORIES PER SERVING.**

TEXAS BAR-B-Q SAUCE

TEXANS like to brag about their barbecue and their barbecue sauce. I bet if you walked into a Texas barbecue in a pair of boots and a cowboy hat with this sauce, they'd never know you weren't a native.

QUAN.	INGREDIENT	CARB GRAMS	AVAIL. CARB	FAT	PROTEIN
1 c.	TOMATO SAUCE	17.6	14.2	0.4	3.4
2 T.	WORCESTERSHIRE SAUCE	6.0	6.0	0	0
½ c.	SUGAR EQUIVALENT SWEETENER				
2 T.	LIME JUICE	2.8	2.7	0	0.1
2 T.	WHITE VINEGAR				
½ t.	LEMON EXTRACT				
2 T.	RED PEPPER FLAKES (more or less added to your taste)				
1 t.	SALT				
2 T.	OLIVE OIL	0	0	26.0	0
½ c.	ONION, diced	6.9	5.5	0	1.0
½ T.	PICKLED JALAPEÑO or CANNED CHIPOTLE PEPPERS, diced (more or less added to your taste)				
1 T.	GARLIC POWDER	6.1	6.1	0	1.4
6 oz.	TOMATO PASTE	32.8	25.8	0.7	6.2
12 oz.	LOW CARB BEER (one 12 ounce can)	3.2	3.2	0	0.9
	TOTALS PER SERVING OF 1 T.	1.6	1.3	0.6	0.3

■ In a 1 quart saucepan, fry the onion in the oil over medium high heat until it becomes clear. Add the remaining ingredients except the tomato paste, cover, and bring to a boil. Reduce the heat to medium low and simmer 20 minutes. Thicken with the tomato paste, and simmer an additional 10 minutes.

■ **MAKES ABOUT 3 CUPS OR 48 SERVINGS WITH ABOUT 12 CALORIES PER SERVING.**

CAJUN-STYLE BAR-B-Q SAUCE

CAJUN cooking is one of the few cuisines native to America and we would be remiss if we didn't provide a Cajun-style barbecue sauce.

QUAN.	INGREDIENT	CARB GRAMS	AVAIL. CARB	FAT	PROTEIN
6 T.	ITALIAN DRESSING (see page 36)	2.0	1.7	39.0	0.5
2 t.	GARLIC POWDER	4.0	4.0	0	1.0
½ c.	ONION, diced	6.9	5.5	0	1.0
1 c.	TOMATO SAUCE	17.6	14.2	0.4	3.4
1 T.	WHITE VINEGAR				
6 T.	SUGAR EQUIVALENT SWEETENER				
2 T.	WORCESTERSHIRE SAUCE	6.0	6.0	0	0
2 t.	CAJUN SEASONING	2.0	2.0	0	0
1 t.	SALT				
½ t.	RED CAYENNE SAUCE (more or less added to your taste)				
	TOTALS	38.5	33.4	39.4	5.9
	PER SERVING 1 T.	1.2	1.0	1.2	0.2

- Combine all ingredients in 1 quart saucepan. Cover and bring to a boil over high heat. Reduce the heat to medium low and simmer for 15 minutes, stirring a couple of times. Let it cool to room temperature. Taste and adjust for heat, acid, and salt before you store in a pint jar in your refrigerator.

- **MAKES 32 SERVINGS WITH ABOUT 16 CALORIES PER SERVING.**

BAR-B-Q SAUCE À L'ORANGE

THIS is a variation on a sauce developed by Chef Emeril Lagasse. This sauce can be used for basting as well as for dipping. You can pulse it in a blender if you want, but I prefer the onion in small pieces. Chef Lagasse uses his sauce on pork, but it works just as well on beef (especially grilled hamburgers), chicken, or baked fish. You can adjust the level of vinegar up or down to control the tartness and adjust the sugar substitute up or down to control the sweetness.

QUAN.	INGREDIENT	CARB GRAMS	AVAIL. CARB	FAT	PROTEIN
1 c.	TOMATO SAUCE	17.6	14.2	0.1	3.4
7 T.	WHITE VINEGAR				
½ t.	LEMON EXTRACT				
½ t.	ORANGE EXTRACT				
3 T.	SUGAR EQUIVALENT SWEETENER				
1 T.	WHOLE GRAIN MUSTARD				
2 t.	GARLIC POWDER	4.0	4.0	0	1.0
½ c.	ONION, diced finely	6.9	5.5	0	1.0
½ t.	RED CAYENNE SAUCE (more or less added to your taste)				
2 t.	WORCESTERSHIRE SAUCE	2.0	2.0	0	0
1	BEEF BOUILLON CUBE				
¼ t.	CAYENNE PEPPER (more or less added to your taste)				
½ t.	DRIED GINGER	0.7	0.6	0.1	0.1
½ t.	BLACK PEPPER				
2 T.	WATER				
	TOTALS	31.2	26.3	0.2	5.5
	PER SERVING OF 1 T.	1.0	0.8	0	0.2

- In a nonreactive 1 quart saucepan, bring the water, vinegar, Worcestershire sauce, lemon extract, orange extract, bouillon cube, onions, and sugar substitute to a boil over high heat. Make sure that the sugar substitute and the bouillon cube are completely dissolved. Remove the pan from the heat and stir in the dry ingredients, then the mustard, and finally the tomato sauce. Store in a pint jar in the refrigerator for a couple of weeks.

- **MAKES ABOUT 1 PINT OR 32 SERVINGS WITH ABOUT 4 CALORIES PER SERVING.**

FRENCH-STYLE BAR-B-Q SAUCE

QUAN.	INGREDIENT	CARB GRAMS	AVAIL. CARB	FAT	PROTEIN
½ c.	SUGAR EQUIVALENT SWEETENER				
½ c.	DRY WHITE WINE	0.8	0.8	0	0
4 T.	WHITE WINE VINEGAR (more or less added to your taste)				
4 T.	OLIVE OIL	0	0	52.0	0
4 T.	DIJON MUSTARD	4.9	1.9	2.0	2.5
I T.	DRIED PARSLEY				
2 t.	GARLIC POWDER	4.0	4.0	0	1.0
¾ t.	SALT				
½ t.	WHITE PEPPER				
½ c.	ONIONS, diced	6.9	5.5	0	1.0
	TOTALS	16.6	12.2	54.0	4.5
	PER SERVING OF I T.	0.7	0.5	2.3	0.2

- In a 1 quart saucepan, sauté your onions in the oil over medium high heat until they become clear. Add the remaining ingredients, cover, and bring to a boil. Reduce the heat to medium low and simmer for about 15 minutes.

- **MAKES ABOUT I ½ CUPS OR 24 SERVINGS WITH ABOUT 24 CALORIES PER SERVING.**

TARTAR SAUCE

IN addition to Cocktail Sauce (see page 250) we always want tartar sauce around when we have seafood. This is especially good on baked or grilled fish. To this you can add at your discretion a few chopped green olives, a few chopped capers, or some chopped fresh parsley.

QUAN.	INGREDIENT	CARB GRAMS	AVAIL. CARB	FAT	PROTEIN
1 c.	**MAYONNAISE**	5.9	5.9	168.5	2.4
4 T.	**SALAD ONIONS** (see page 84)	3.6	2.8	0	0.4
4 T.	**SWEET RELISH** (see page 85)	2.0	1.2	0.8	0.8
2 T.	**LEMON JUICE**	2.6	2.5	0	0.1
2 t.	**SUGAR EQUIVALENT SWEETENER** (optional, more or less to your taste)				
1 t.	**DIJON MUSTARD** (optional)				
¼ c.	**DILL PICKLES**, diced finely (more or less to your taste, optional)				
½ t.	**SALT**				
¼ t.	**BLACK PEPPER**				
	TOTALS	14.1	12.4	169.3	3.7
	PER SERVING OF 1 T.	0.5	0.5	6.5	0.1

- Mix all of the ingredients in a 1 quart bowl and refrigerate in a pint container.

■ **MAKES ABOUT 26 SERVINGS WITH ABOUT 61 CALORIES PER SERVING.**

YAKI MANDU SAUCE

THIS is a Korean sauce that's normally served with Yaki Mandu, a meat dumpling wrapped in noodle dough. We can't have the noodle dough, but we can still enjoy the sauce. As you've probably already seen, I use this sauce in many of the recipes in this book.

QUAN.	INGREDIENT	CARB GRAMS	AVAIL. CARB	FAT	PROTEIN
¾ c.	SOY SAUCE	6.0	6.0	0	24.0
4 T.	WHITE VINEGAR				
½ t.	RED PEPPER FLAKES (more or less added to your taste)				
4 T.	SUGAR EQUIVALENT SWEETENER				
2 t.	CHIVES				
I t.	SESAME SEEDS				
	TOTALS	6.0	6.0	0	24.0
	PER SERVING OF I T.	0.4	0.4	0	1.5

- Heat the first three ingredients in a 2 cup saucepan over high heat. Add the last three ingredients and remove from the heat. Let it cool to room temperature.

- **MAKES ABOUT I CUP OR 16 SERVINGS WITH ABOUT 8 CALORIES PER SERVING.**

GUACAMOLE

WHEN it comes to guacamole, chef Sarah Moulton likes the minimalist approach, meaning nothing too fancy and with as few ingredients as possible. From her perspective, this recipe might be considered to be a little involved. There is a lot of potential for variation in this dish and you can still keep it low carb. You can use sour cream instead of the olive oil, you can add ½ t. oregano, use lime instead of lemon juice, add some fresh cilantro, or even add some horseradish.

QUAN.	INGREDIENT	CARB GRAMS	AVAIL. CARB	FAT	PROTEIN
2 c.	AVOCADOS, diced	22.2	7.2	42.0	5.9
2 T.	OLIVE OIL	0	0	26.0	0
1 t.	GARLIC POWDER	2.0	2.0	0	0.5
½ t.	SALT				
4 T.	PICKLED JALAPEÑOS, diced finely (more or less added to your taste)				
1 T.	LEMON JUICE	1.3	1.3	0	0.1
½ t.	RED CAYENNE SAUCE				
4 T.	SALAD ONIONS (see page 84)	3.6	2.8	0	0.4
4 T.	DICED TOMATO with the seeds removed	2.1	1.6	0.1	0.4
½ t.	SUGAR EQUIVALENT SWEETENER				
	TOTALS	31.2	14.9	68.1	7.3
	PER SERVING OF 1 T.	1.0	0.5	2.1	0.2

- In a 1 quart bowl, mash the avocado and the lemon juice together with either the back of a fork or a potato masher in order to prevent the avocado from turning dark. Add the remaining ingredients and mix well. Refrigerate, covered, until serving.

- **MAKES ABOUT 2 CUPS OR ABOUT 32 SERVINGS WITH ABOUT 22 CALORIES PER SERVING.**

SALSA

MANY years ago, I asked my favorite local Mexican restaurant how they made their salsa because it was remarkably good. This is close to the recipe that I was given. Not only is it good, it's simple and you can adjust the heat to your taste.

QUAN.	INGREDIENT	CARB GRAMS	AVAIL. CARB	FAT	PROTEIN
1 c.	TOMATO SAUCE	17.6	14.2	0.4	3.4
2 t.	WHITE VINEGAR				
½ c.	SALAD ONIONS (see page 84), diced finely	7.2	5.6	0	0.8
4 T.	PICKLED JALAPEÑO PEPPERS, diced finely (more or less added to your taste)				
1 t.	SUGAR EQUIVALENT SWEETENER				
½ t.	SALT				
	TOTALS	24.8	19.8	0.4	4.2
	PER SERVING OF 1 T.	0.9	0.7	0	0.1

- Dissolve the sugar substitute completely in the vinegar and the tomato sauce. Mix all ingredients thoroughly in a 1 quart bowl. This will keep stored in a pint jar in the refrigerator for a couple of weeks.

- **MAKES ABOUT 1¾ CUPS OR 28 SERVINGS WITH ABOUT 3 CALORIES PER SERVING.**

RÉMOULADE SAUCE

IN my travels, I've found that rémoulade sauce has about as many variations as chicken wings. There is a light version and a redder version, probably generated in New Orleans. This is the more classic light version.

QUAN.	INGREDIENT	CARB GRAMS	AVAIL. CARB	FAT	PROTEIN
½ c.	MAYONNAISE	3.0	3.0	84.3	1.2
2 T.	DIJON MUSTARD				
1 t.	GARLIC POWDER	2.0	2.0	0	0.5
4 T.	SALAD ONIONS (see page 84)	3.6	2.8	0	0.4
¼ c.	CELERY, diced finely	1.1	0.6	0	0.2
1 T.	WORCESTERSHIRE SAUCE (more or less to your taste for saltiness)	3.0	3.0	0	0
1 T.	LEMON JUICE	1.3	1.3	0	0.1
1 T.	CAPERS, diced coarsely (optional)				
1 t.	SUGAR EQUIVALENT SWEETENER				
½ t.	SALT				
¼ t.	BLACK PEPPER				
2 t.	DRIED TARRAGON (or you can use 1 T. fresh tarragon)				
2 t.	DRIED PARSLEY (or you can use 1 T. fresh parsley)				
	RED CAYENNE SAUCE, a shake or two optional to your taste				
	TOTALS	14.0	12.7	84.3	2.4
	PER SERVING OF 1 T.	0.9	0.8	5.3	0.2

- Mix the celery, lemon juice, sugar substitute, and salt in a 1 quart bowl and let it sit for 15 minutes. Mix in the remaining ingredients. Refrigerate for at least 30 minutes before serving.

- **MAKES ABOUT 1 CUP OR ABOUT 16 SERVINGS WITH ABOUT 52 CALORIES PER SERVING.**

MOJO

AS someone who works with food for a living, it takes a lot to get me excited about a particular food. This is a low carb version of Mojo, a Cuban barbecue and dipping sauce, and trust me when I say it's really fantastic. I especially like it on grilled pork chops or pork steaks.

QUAN.	INGREDIENT	CARB GRAMS	AVAIL. CARB	FAT	PROTEIN
13 T.	WATER				
3 T.	WHITE VINEGAR				
2 t.	GARLIC POWDER	4.0	4.0	0	1.0
1 t.	ONION POWDER	1.7	1.6	0	0.2
1 t.	GROUND CUMIN	0.9	0.7	0.4	0.4
1 t.	DRIED OREGANO				
1 t.	SALT				
½ t.	BLACK PEPPER				
2 T.	FRESH CILANTRO OR PARSLEY				
½ t.	LEMON FLAVORING				
½ t.	ORANGE FLAVORING				
1 T.	LIME JUICE	1.4	1.4	0	0.1
1 t.	SUGAR EQUIVALENT SWEETENER				
	TOTALS	8.0	7.7	0.4	1.8
	PER SERVING OF 1 T.	0.5	0.5	0	0.1

- Put everything except the cilantro and lime juice in a 2 cup saucepan and bring it to a boil. Remove the pan from the heat and let cool to room temperature. Mix in the cilantro and the lime juice. Store it in the refrigerator for several weeks. Shake well before using. Use this as a marinade for pork and chicken. After the meat is cooked serve a little Mojo as a dipping sauce.

- **MAKES ABOUT 1 CUP OR ABOUT 16 SERVINGS WITH ABOUT 2 CALORIES PER SERVING.**

SOUTH CAROLINA-STYLE MUSTARD BAR-B-Q SAUCE

QUAN.	INGREDIENT	CARB GRAMS	AVAIL. CARB	FAT	PROTEIN
½ c.	CIDER VINEGAR				
⅓ c.	PREPARED MUSTARD	6.5	2.5	2.6	3.3
1 t.	ONION POWDER	1.7	1.6	0	0.2
1 t.	GARLIC POWDER	2.0	2.0	0	0.5
1 t.	RED CAYENNE SAUCE (more or less added to your taste)				
½ t.	SALT				
8 t.	SUGAR EQUIVALENT SWEETENER				
	TOTALS	10.2	6.1	2.6	4.0
	PER SERVING OF 1 T.	0.6	0.4	0.2	0.3

- In a nonreactive 1 quart saucepan, bring the vinegar to a boil over high heat. Add the dry ingredients and mix well. Remove the pan from the heat and mix in the mustard thoroughly. Let it cool to room temperature. Add enough vinegar to bring the volume to 1 cup and mix again.

- **MAKES 1 CUP OR ABOUT 16 SERVINGS WITH ABOUT 5 CALORIES PER SERVING.**

WARM MUSTARD SAUCE

THE "warm" in this recipe refers to temperature and not spiciness. Of course, you can always add a shake or two of red cayenne sauce if you want to warm it up even more. This goes well on hamburgers, hot dogs, or any grilled meat.

QUAN.	INGREDIENT	CARB GRAMS	AVAIL. CARB	FAT	PROTEIN
1 T.	**OLIVE OIL**	0	0	13.0	0
½ c.	**ONION**, diced	6.9	5.5	0	1.0
½ c.	**GREEN PEPPERS**, diced	4.8	3.5	0.1	0.7
1 t.	**GARLIC POWDER**	2.0	2.0	0	0.5
¼ t.	**CELERY SEED**				
½ t.	**SALT**				
½ c.	**PREPARED YELLOW MUSTARD** (any good mustard, such as Dijon, is satisfactory)	9.8	3.8	3.9	5.0
2 t.	**SUGAR EQUIVALENT SWEETENER** (more or less to your taste)				
2 T.	**WATER**				
	TOTALS	23.5	14.8	17.0	7.2
	PER SERVING OF 1 T.	1.5	0.9	1.1	0.5

- In a 2 cup saucepan, cook the onions and bell pepper in the oil over medium high heat until the onions become clear. Reduce the heat to medium, add the water, and then stir in the remaining ingredients. Let it cook for a minute or two, until it is well heated. Remove the pan from the heat and serve immediately.

- **MAKES ABOUT 1 CUP OR ABOUT 16 SERVINGS WITH ABOUT 16 CALORIES PER SERVING.**

COCKTAIL SAUCE

IF you eat seafood, chances are you've been yearning for a low carb version of cocktail sauce. This one provides everything we need in a cocktail sauce without the sugar. If you take a shrimp dish to a potluck, don't forget this. This recipe makes enough for about 2 lbs. of medium-sized shrimp.

QUAN.	INGREDIENT	CARB GRAMS	AVAIL. CARB	FAT	PROTEIN
1 c.	TOMATO SAUCE	17.6	14.2	0.4	3.4
5 T.	WHITE VINEGAR				
5 t.	SUGAR EQUIVALENT SWEETENER				
½ t.	LEMON EXTRACT				
1 T.	PREPARED HORSERADISH (more or less added to your taste)				
1 t.	WORCESTERSHIRE SAUCE (more or less to your taste for saltiness)	1.0	1.0	0	0
½ t.	RED CAYENNE SAUCE (more or less to your taste for heat)				
1 t.	ONION POWDER	1.7	1.6	0	0.2
	TOTALS	20.3	16.8	0.4	3.6
	PER SERVING OF 1 T.	1.0	0.8	0	0.2

- In a nonreactive 1 quart saucepan, bring the vinegar, sugar substitute, and lemon extract to a boil over high heat. Remove the pan from the heat, add to the remaining ingredients, and mix well. Try to let it set for at least a half hour before serving.

- **MAKES ABOUT 21 SERVINGS WITH ABOUT 4 CALORIES PER SERVING.**

CRANBERRY SAUCE

I developed this recipe about four years ago because I needed something to have with my Thanksgiving turkey that didn't contain a lot of sugar. This is a great alternative to the cranberry sauce that everyone else has with their feast.

QUAN.	INGREDIENT	CARB GRAMS	AVAIL. CARB	FAT	PROTEIN
1 c.	**CRANBERRIES**	14.0	9.4	0	0.4
2 c.	**WATER**				
5 T.	**SUGAR EQUIVALENT SWEETENER** (more or less added to your taste)				
1 pkg.	**SUGAR-FREE CRANBERRY FLAVORED GELATIN** (2 c. size; you can substitute raspberry flavored if cranberry isn't available)	0	0	0	4.0
	TOTALS	14.0	9.4	0	4.4
	PER SERVING OF ½ C.	2.8	1.9	0	0.9

- Bring one cup of water and the sugar substitute to a boil in a 1 quart saucepan. Add the cranberries and bring to a boil again. Remove the pan from the heat and mash the cranberries with a fork or potato masher. Dissolve the gelatin in the cranberries, stirring at least 5 minutes. Add the remaining 1 cup of cold water and stir. Pour in your serving bowl and refrigerate several hours.

- **MAKES 5 SERVINGS WITH ABOUT 11 CALORIES PER SERVING.**

PICO DE GALLO

THERE is a Mexican restaurant where I eat occasionally in a little town near where I live. The answer to your question is yes, you can eat lower carb at a Mexican buffet. You can have a taco salad, for instance, without the shell and with lots of guacamole. This restaurant makes a delicious Pico de Gallo and my recipe comes pretty close to it.

QUAN.	INGREDIENT	CARB GRAMS	AVAIL. CARB	FAT	PROTEIN
¾ c.	**ONION**, diced finely	10.4	8.4	0.2	1.4
¾ c.	**TOMATO**, seeds removed and diced finely	6.3	4.8	0.3	1.2
1 t.	**LEMON FLAVORING**				
2 T.	**WHITE VINEGAR**				
1 t.	**SUGAR EQUIVALENT SWEETENER**				
2 t.	**PICKLED JALAPEÑOS**, diced finely (more or less added to your taste)				
1 T.	**LIME JUICE**	1.4	1.4	0	0.1
1 T.	**RAW CILANTRO**, diced finely	0.2	0.1	0	0.1
1 t.	**SALT**				
1 t.	**GARLIC POWDER**	2.0	2.0	0	0.5
	TOTALS	20.3	16.7	0.5	3.2
	PER SERVING OF 1 T.	0.7	0.6	0	0.1

- Bring everything except the lime juice and cilantro to a boil in a 1 quart saucepan. Remove from the heat and add the remaining ingredients. Let this sit for at least an hour, stirring every 15 minutes, before serving. This is better if it is refrigerated overnight.

■ **MAKES ABOUT 28 SERVINGS WITH ABOUT 3 CALORIES PER SERVING.**

THAI HOT SAUCE

YEARS ago when I discovered Thai food, I got this recipe from a Thai family living in my neighborhood. It's especially appropriate now for low carb eating. This sauce is wonderful as a marinade for grilled meats and as a dipping sauce. Thai food is traditionally very hot and the original recipe called for 2 T. of chili paste. You can add different kinds of peppers to vary the flavor of the sauce, but keep in mind that a little goes a long way. Other substitutions include using lemon or lime juice in lieu of the vinegar (and don't forget to add the carbs), adding 1 teaspoon of cilantro, adding up to 2 t. of red pepper flakes, adding up to 1 T. of finely diced dried shrimp, or adding up to 2 t. of sugar substitute.

QUAN.	INGREDIENT	CARB GRAMS	AVAIL. CARB	FAT	PROTEIN
2 T.	FISH SAUCE	6.0	6.0	0	4.0
4 T.	WATER				
2 T.	WHITE VINEGAR				
1 T.	HOT CHILI PASTE (from Asian groceries, more or less to your taste. You can use red cayenne sauce in its stead)				
1 t.	GARLIC POWDER	2.0	2.0	0	0.5
1 t.	DRIED GINGER	1.3	1.1	0.1	0.2
2 t.	ONION POWDER	3.4	3.2	0	0.4
1 t.	DRIED CILANTRO (optional)				
2 t.	DRIED RED PEPPER FLAKES (optional)				
2 T.	DRIED SHRIMP FINELY DICED (optional)				
2 t.	SUGAR EQUIVALENT SWEETENER (optional)				
	TOTALS	12.7	12.3	0.1	5.1
	PER SERVING OF 1 T.	1.4	1.4	0	0.6

- Mix all ingredients in a 2 cup bowl and let it sit for ½ hour, stirring occasionally. If it is too salty or it has too much vinegar, dilute with water, one teaspoon at a time, until it is satisfactory.

- **MAKES ABOUT 9 SERVINGS WITH ABOUT 8 CALORIES PER SERVING.**

VIETNAMESE DIPPING SAUCE

QUAN.	INGREDIENT	CARB GRAMS	AVAIL. CARB	FAT	PROTEIN
½ T.	**PICKLED JALAPEÑOS**, diced very finely (more or less added to your taste)				
I	**FRESH JALAPEÑO** or **CHILI PEPPER**, sliced very thinly (more or less added to your taste)				
I t.	**GARLIC POWDER**	2.0	2.0	0	0.5
3 T.	**WATER**				
2 t.	**SUGAR EQUIVALENT SWEETENER**				
2 T.	**FISH SAUCE**	6.0	6.0	0	4.0
2 T.	**LIME JUICE**	2.8	2.7	0	0.1
	TOTALS	10.8	10.7	0	4.6
	PER SERVING OF I T.	1.4	1.3	0	0.6

- Mix everything in a 2 cup bowl. Store refrigerated for a couple of weeks.

- **MAKES ABOUT ½ CUP OR 8 SERVINGS WITH ABOUT 8 CALORIES PER SERVING.**

DESSERTS

Low carb desserts tend to be very rich on two levels. First, they call for a lot of cream and butter, which makes them very high in calories so we can't eat too much in a single sitting. Second, since we can't use all that trash filler such as flour and corn starch, they tend to be a little more costly than your standard dessert.

LYNNE'S WORLD FAMOUS
LOW CARB CHOCOLATE

THIS was developed by my friend Lynne, known in the low carb world as a Low Carb Muse. She made this dessert part of a low carb diet that helped her lose 170 pounds. Because of the high caloric value per serving, she would eat only one serving per day.

QUAN.	INGREDIENT	CARB GRAMS	AVAIL. CARB	FAT	PROTEIN
1 oz.	UNSWEETENED CHOCOLATE	8.0	3.6	15	2.9
2 T.	UNSALTED BUTTER	0	0	24.2	0
1 T.	HEAVY WHIPPING CREAM	0.6	0.6	5.2	0.3
¼ t.	VANILLA				
16 t.	SUGAR EQUIVALENT SWEETENER (Lynne uses 8 packets of Equal)	4.0	4.0	0	0
2 T.	CRUSHED WALNUTS	2.0	1.0	8.4	3.8
	TOTALS	14.6	9.2	52.8	7.0
	PER SERVING	5.3	4.6	26.4	3.5

- Melt the chocolate and butter carefully in a double boiler. Remove from the heat and stir in the cream, the vanilla, and then the sugar substitute. Fold in the walnuts and pour into a foil-lined pan and chill. Do not use saccharin in this recipe. If you can get cyclamates or other no carb sugar substitutes, you can subtract 2 grams of available carbs from each serving.

- **MAKES 2 SERVINGS WITH ABOUT 270 CALORIES PER SERVING.**

PUMPKIN PIE

AS you may have already gathered, I really like Thanksgiving and one of the main reasons why is pumpkin pie. Although this is still a little high in carbs, it allows us to have the pumpkin pie flavor without the sugar and the crust.

QUAN.	INGREDIENT	CARB GRAMS	AVAIL. CARB	FAT	PROTEIN
2 c.	**CANNED PUMPKIN** (one 15 ounce can is sufficient)	70.0	42.0	0	7.0
2	**EGGS**, slightly scrambled	1.4	1.4	9.6	14.4
3 c.	**SUGAR EQUIVALENT SWEETENER**				
½ t.	**SALT**				
3 T.	**PUMPKIN PIE SPICE**	11.6	9.1	1.4	1.0
1 c.	**HALF AND HALF**	10.4	10.4	26.4	7.2
1 T.	**OLIVE OIL**	0	0	13.0	0
	TOTALS	93.4	62.9	50.4	29.6
	PER SERVING OF ½ C.	15.6	10.5	8.4	4.9

- Preheat the oven to 400° F. Heat the half and half and sugar substitute in a microwave for about 1 minute, giving the sugar substitute a chance to dissolve. Let this cool. Add the oil to the eggs in a 1 quart bowl and blend well. Add the pumpkin, the salt, and the spices and mix thoroughly. Add the half and half and mix well. Oil your baking pan. Bake for 20 minutes. Reduce the heat to 325° F and bake about 50 minutes or until a knife inserted in the center of the pie comes out clean. The top will feel firm to the touch.

- **MAKES 6 SERVINGS WITH ABOUT 137 CALORIES PER SERVING.**

WINE SYLLABUB

QUAN.	INGREDIENT	CARB GRAMS	AVAIL. CARB	FAT	PROTEIN
½ c.	DRY WHITE WINE	0.8	0.8	0	0
½ c	SUGAR EQUIVALENT SWEETENER				
3 T.	LEMON JUICE	3.9	3.8	0	0.2
1 T.	BRANDY (provides about 32 calories)				
1 t.	GRATED LEMON PEEL				
⅛ t.	NUTMEG				
1 c.	WHIPPED CREAM (with, perhaps, a little lemon extract added—see page 263)	2.2	2.2	27.8	1.6
	FRESH BERRIES for serving (optional)				
	TOTALS	6.9	6.8	27.8	1.8
	PER SERVING	1.7	1.7	7.0	0.5

- Combine the wine, sugar substitute, lemon juice, brandy, and lemon peel in a bowl and let it marinate for at least a couple of hours at room temperature or refrigerated overnight. Fold the whipped cream into the marinade gently 2 T. at a time. Spoon into four wine glasses (or bowls, if you prefer) and refrigerate until serving. Garnish with berries if you use them.

- **MAKES 4 SERVINGS WITH ABOUT 80 CALORIES PER SERVING.**

CHOCOLATE PUDDING

FOR those of you who need a chocolate hit every day, here is another solution to your problem. This is one of the basics and it has multiple uses. If you like different flavors mixed with chocolate, you can add ½ t. (more or less added to your taste) of any of the following flavors: banana, amaretto, mint/peppermint, strawberry, coconut, cherry, or lemon. You can also add some peanut butter, cinnamon, almonds and other nuts, instant coffee, or berries. When you serve this as pudding, sprinkle one of those pink or blue packets of sugar substitute over it to make it pretty. If you are going to use this as a pie filling, use the basic Pie Crust (see page 268) and then top it with Whipped Cream (with chocolate flavoring added—see page 263) and sprinkle a little unsweetened powdered chocolate on it.

QUAN.	INGREDIENT	CARB GRAMS	AVAIL. CARB	FAT	PROTEIN
2 c.	HEAVY CREAM	13.2	13.2	167.0	9.8
2–2½ c.	SUGAR EQUIVALENT SWEETENER (more or less added to your taste)				
2	EGG YOLKS	0.6	0.6	8.5	5.6
2 T.	BUTTER (optional)	0	0	24.2	0
½ t.	VANILLA FLAVOR (optional)				
2 t.	XANTHUM GUM				
2 oz.	BAKER'S CHOCOLATE, unsweetened and chopped finely	20.0	8.0	28.0	8.0
1 pinch	SALT				
1 pkg.	UNFLAVORED GELATIN (optional if you are going to use this for a pie filling)	0	0	0	6.0
	TOTALS	33.8	21.8	227.7	29.4
	PER SERVING OF ½ C.	6.8	4.4	45.5	5.9

- Place the cream and the egg yolks in a 2 quart saucepan and mix well. Add the sugar substitute, salt, and the gelatin if it is used. Stir in the chocolate. Over medium low heat, whisking constantly, slowly add the xanthum gum. Ultimately, it will come to a boil. Let it boil 1 minute and remove from the heat. Add the butter and the vanilla, stir well, and let it cool to room temperature. Refrigerate until ready to serve.

■ **MAKES 5 SERVINGS WITH ABOUT 450 CALORIES PER SERVING.**

COCONUT PUDDING

I like to use this pudding as a pie filling. One suggestion is to add a little banana flavoring to it, perhaps ½ t. (more or less added to your taste).

QUAN.	INGREDIENT	CARB GRAMS	AVAIL. CARB	FAT	PROTEIN
2 c.	HEAVY CREAM	13.2	13.2	167.0	9.8
1½–2 c.	SUGAR EQUIVALENT SWEETENER (more or less added to your taste)				
2	EGGS	1.4	1.4	9.6	14.4
2 T.	BUTTER	0	0	24.2	0
2 t.	COCONUT FLAVOR				
½ oz.	COCONUT, shredded, dried, unsweetened (about 4 T. or ½ c.)	3.5	1.2	8.6	1.0
½ t.	VANILLA FLAVOR				
2 t.	XANTHUM GUM				
1 pinch	SALT				
1 pkg.	UNFLAVORED GELATIN (optional if you are going to use this for a pie filling)	0	0	0	6.0
	TOTALS	18.1	15.8	209.4	31.2
	PER SERVING OF ½ C.	3.6	3.2	41.9	6.2

- Place the cream and the eggs in a 1 quart saucepan and mix well. Add the sugar substitute, salt, coconut flavor, and the gelatin (if it is to be used). Stir in the coconut. Over medium low heat, whisking constantly, slowly add the xanthum gum. After a while, it will come to a boil. Let it boil 1 minute and remove from the heat. Add the butter and the vanilla, stir well, and let cool to room temperature. Refrigerate until ready to serve.

■ **MAKES 5 SERVINGS WITH ABOUT 415 CALORIES PER SERVING.**

RICOTTA PUDDING

THIS pudding recipe is modeled on recipes I have for cannoli filling and is meant to be served warm, right out of the oven. Sometimes I add 2 tablespoons of crushed walnuts, which will add 1 gram of available carbs to the entire dish. You might also want to try serving it with a little Chocolate Syrup (see page 264).

QUAN.	INGREDIENT	CARB GRAMS	AVAIL. CARB	FAT	PROTEIN
1 lb.	RICOTTA CHEESE	16.0	16.0	64.0	56.0
3	EGGS, separated	2.1	2.1	14.4	21.6
½ t.	XANTHUM GUM (optional for thickening)				
1½ c.	SUGAR EQUIVALENT SWEETENER				
1 t.	ORANGE EXTRACT				
1 t.	LEMON EXTRACT				
1 t.	VANILLA EXTRACT				
2 T.	BRANDY, COGNAC, WHISKEY, RUM, ETC.				
½ c.	HEAVY WHIPPING CREAM	3.3	3.3	41.8	2.5
1 t.	CINNAMON				
	TOTALS	21.4	21.4	120.2	80.1
	PER SERVING OF ½ C.	3.6	3.6	20.0	13.4

- Preheat the oven to 375° F. Beat the egg whites to a stiff peak with a mixer or whip in a 1 quart bowl. Coat a baking pan with butter or oil. A bread pan is sufficient. In a 2 quart bowl, if you are using the xanthum gum, sprinkle it over the ricotta cheese and mix thoroughly. Mix in the egg yolks, cream, extracts, alcohol, cinnamon, and sugar substitute. Fold in the egg whites and pour into your baking pan. Bake at 375° F for 30 minutes. Turn the heat off and let it sit a few minutes in the oven. Turn it out on your serving dish and sprinkle it with a little extra cinnamon and powdered sugar substitute.

- **MAKES 6 SERVINGS WITH ABOUT 248 CALORIES PER SERVING.**

CHOCOLATE
RICOTTA PUDDING

QUAN.	INGREDIENT	CARB GRAMS	AVAIL. CARB	FAT	PROTEIN
	add cocoa powder to the above recipe				
2 T.	**UNSWEETENED CHOCOLATE POWDER**	6.0	4.0	1.0	2.0
	TOTALS	27.4	25.4	121.2	82.1
	PER SERVING OF ½ C.	4.6	4.2	20.2	13.7

■ The Chocolate Ricotta Pudding is made exactly as described above except that the cocoa powder is added at the same time as the egg yolks.

■ **MAKES 6 SERVINGS WITH ABOUT 253 CALORIES PER SERVING.**

WHIPPED CREAM

THERE are many dishes that require whipped cream, especially desserts. This is a good, general recipe. If it's not to be used for a dessert, you can leave the sugar substitute and the vanilla out.

QUAN.	INGREDIENT	CARB GRAMS	AVAIL. CARB	FAT	PROTEIN
1 c.	HEAVY WHIPPING CREAM	6.6	6.6	83.5	4.9
4 t.	SUGAR EQUIVALENT SWEETENER				
½ t.	VANILLA EXTRACT				
2 T.	UNSWEETENED COCOA POWDER (optional for flavored whipped cream)				
2 T.	RUM, BRANDY, COGNAC, WHISKEY, ETC. (optional for flavored whipped cream)				
1-2 t.	INSTANT COFFEE (optional for flavored whipped cream)				
	TOTALS	6.6	6.6	83.5	4.9
	PER SERVING OF ½ C.	1.1	1.1	13.9	0.8

- The cream should be cold before you begin. Place the cream in a 2 quart mixing bowl along with the sugar substitute and vanilla. Using an electric beater, begin mixing the cream at a low speed until it begins to thicken. Increase the speed of the mixer to medium and continue until you have about 3–4 cups. It will be relatively stiff. If you are using flavorings, now is the time to add them and mix an additional 1–2 minutes. Serve immediately or refrigerate for 2–3 hours.

■ **MAKES MINIMALLY 6 SERVINGS WITH ABOUT 133 CALORIES PER SERVING.**

CHOCOLATE SYRUP

THIS chocolate syrup is real easy to make. You can use it as you would any syrup that contains sugar, which makes it especially good for your children.

QUAN.	INGREDIENT	CARB GRAMS	AVAIL. CARB	FAT	PROTEIN
½ c.	COCOA, unsweetened	23.4	9.1	5.6	8.5
1¾ c.	WATER				
2 c.	SUGAR EQUIVALENT SWEETENER				
⅛ t.	SALT				
½ t.	VANILLA FLAVOR				
¼ t.	XANTHUM GUM				
	TOTALS	23.4	9.1	5.6	8.5
	PER SERVING OF 1 T.	0.7	0.3	0.2	0.3

- Whisk the cocoa and xanthum gum into the water in a 2 quart saucepan. Place it over medium heat and whisk constantly until it comes to a boil. Reduce the heat to low and let it set on the stove for several minutes, stirring occasionally. Remove from the heat and add the sugar substitute, salt, and vanilla. Let it cool to room temperature, stirring occasionally, and pour it into a pint container. This can be stored in the refrigerator for several weeks.

- **MAKES ABOUT 2 CUPS OR ABOUT 32 SERVINGS WITH ABOUT 4 CALORIES PER SERVING.**

COFFEE ICE

THIS is a favorite after-dinner dessert among coffee drinkers. Add a little cinnamon on top of the whipped cream for garnish.

QUAN.	INGREDIENT	CARB GRAMS	AVAIL. CARB	FAT	PROTEIN
4 c.	**COFFEE**, brewed very strongly (you can use instant coffees also—espresso is desired)	3.8	3.8	0	0.9
6 T.	**SUGAR EQUIVALENT SWEETENER** (more or less added to your taste)				
2 c.	**WHIPPED CREAM** (see page 264)	4.4	4.4	55.7	3.3
4 oz.	**LIQUOR** (you can use brandy, cognac, Kahlua, etc. – 80 proof provides 257 calories)				
	TOTALS	8.2	8.2	55.7	4.2
	PER SERVING	2.1	2.1	13.9	1.1

■ Dissolve the sugar substitute completely in the coffee while it is brewing. Let the coffee cool to room temperature and pour it into ice trays. Let it freeze overnight if possible. When you are ready to serve, bring the frozen coffee out of the freezer and crush it as finely as possible. Place the frozen coffee chips in large glasses, one cup in each glass. Add 1 oz. liquor to each glass and top with ½ cup of whipped cream.

■ **MAKES 4 SERVINGS WITH ABOUT 202 CALORIES PER SERVING.**

STRAWBERRY JAM

THIS jam is especially good as an accompaniment for cookies. For those of you who are wine drinkers, you might try using a cup of dry red wine instead of the water, but if you make this substitution be sure to add an additional 1.6 grams of carbs to the total available carbs.

QUAN.	INGREDIENT	CARB GRAMS	AVAIL. CARB	FAT	PROTEIN
2 c.	STRAWBERRIES	21.3	14.3	0.8	1.9
2 T.	LEMON JUICE	2.6	2.5	0	0.1
2 c.	SUGAR EQUIVALENT SWEETENER				
4 t.	LOWER SUGAR SURE-JELL (not the totally sugar-free pectin)				
1 t.	STRAWBERRY EXTRACT				
	ENOUGH WATER TO BRING IT TO 2 C.				
	TOTALS	23.9	16.8	0.8	2.0
	PER SERVING OF 1 T.	0.7	0.5	0	0.1

■ The day before, dice the strawberries coarsely. Mix with the lemon juice and 1 c. of the sugar equivalent sweetener and let it set several hours, overnight if possible. Pour the strawberry mixture into a 1 quart saucepan along with any water needed to bring the volume to 2 c. and the strawberry extract. Stir in the sure-jell until it is dissolved. Turn the heat to medium and bring it to a rolling boil. Reduce the heat to low and let it boil 3–5 minutes. Remove from the heat and stir in the remaining sugar substitute until it is dissolved. Pour into a pint jar or a 2 cup freezer container. This will keep refrigerated several weeks and it can be frozen if you aren't going to use it immediately. Count this as 0.7 grams of carbs per tablespoon, about 0.2 grams of carbs per teaspoon, because of some residual sugar in the sure-jell.

■ **MAKES ABOUT 2 CUPS OR ABOUT 32 SERVINGS WITH ABOUT 3 CALORIES PER SERVING.**

RASPBERRY JAM

QUAN.	INGREDIENT	CARB GRAMS	AVAIL. CARB	FAT	PROTEIN
	substitute raspberries for strawberries in the preceding recipe				
2 c.	**RASPBERRIES**	28.5	11.8	0.9	2.2
	TOTALS	31.1	14.3	0.9	2.3
	PER SERVING OF 1 T.	1.0	0.4	0	0.1

- Follow the directions above for Strawberry Jam. Count this as 0.5 grams of carbs per tablespoon, about 0.2 grams of carbs per teaspoon, because of some residual sugar in the sure-jell.

- **MAKES ABOUT 2 CUPS OR ABOUT 32 SERVINGS WITH ABOUT 2 CALORIES PER SERVING.**

BASIC PIE CRUST

THE Austrians make a dessert called the *Linzer Torte* with a dough made from finely ground nuts, usually hazelnuts or almonds, sugar, flour, and spices. This is the basis for our Basic Pie Crust (see page 270). Lynne, the Low Carb Muse, suggests that if you have any remaining dough after you have made the crust, you should form it into small cookies and cover them with her Low Carb Chocolate (see page 256).

QUAN.	INGREDIENT	CARB GRAMS	AVAIL. CARB	FAT	PROTEIN
8 oz.	**WALNUTS**	44.0	32.8	141.6	34.4
2 T.	**BUTTER**	0	0	24.2	0
3 T.	**SUGAR EQUIVALENT SWEETENER**				
1 T.	**VANILLA EXTRACT**				
2	**EGG WHITES**	0.7	0.7	0	7.0
⅛ t.	**XANTHUM GUM** (optional)				
	TOTALS	44.7	33.5	165.8	41.4
	PER SERVING	5.6	4.2	20.7	5.2

■ Preheat the oven to 350° F. Grease a pie pan. Process the walnuts until they are a powdery paste in your food processor. Mix the walnuts in a 2 quart bowl with the melted butter, sugar substitute, and vanilla extract until the butter is worked all the way through. Use your hands if you really want to hurry the process. Whip the egg whites and the xanthum gum, beginning on a low speed and graduating up to the highest speed, until frothy. Using the electric mixer on the low setting, add the walnut mixture into the egg whites until thoroughly blended. Press the walnut mixture into a pie pan. Bake at 350° F for 15 minutes. Remove from the oven and allow to cool thoroughly.

■ **MAKES 8 SERVINGS WITH ABOUT 224 CALORIES PER SERVING.**

ALMOND CRISPS

THIS is another recipe suggested by someone who has been there since the beginning. For variety, you can coat these with Lynne's Low Carb Chocolate (see page 256), some Strawberry Jam (see page 266), or sprinkle a little powdered sugar substitute on them.

QUAN.	INGREDIENT	CARB GRAMS	AVAIL. CARB	FAT	PROTEIN
¾ c.	**ALMOND SLIVERS**, finely ground	20.2	12.9	54.5	22.2
¾ c.	**SUGAR EQUIVALENT SWEETENER** (more or less to your taste)				
4 T.	**UNSALTED BUTTER**	0	0	48.4	1.0
2 T.	**HEAVY CREAM**	1.2	1.2	10.4	0.6
I T.	**WHITE FLOUR**	6.0	5.8	0.1	0.8
I	**EGG WHITE**	0.3	0.3	0	3.5
½ t.	**ALMOND EXTRACT** (optional)				
	TOTALS	27.7	20.2	113.4	28.1
	PER SERVING OF I COOKIE	1.5	1.1	6.3	1.6

- Melt the butter in a 10 inch skillet over medium heat. Add the flour and stir well until the flour is totally dissolved in the butter. Continue cooking until the flour begins to brown a little. Add the almonds and stir well. Continue cooking, another minute or two, stirring constantly. Remove from the heat. In the meantime, combine the cream, sugar substitute, and egg white (and extract if you use it) in a separate bowl, ensuring that the sugar substitute is dissolved. When the almonds are cooled down to about room temperature add them to the egg white mixture and stir well. Drop by tablespoonfuls onto a well greased cookie sheet. Bake them in a 275°–300° F oven for 15 minutes. Remove the cookies from the cookie sheet and cool on wire racks.

- **MAKES ABOUT 18 SERVINGS WITH ABOUT 68 CALORIES PER SERVING.**

LINZER COOKIES

THESE are as close as we can get to real Austrian Linzer pastry. Serve these with a teaspoon of Raspberry or Strawberry Jam (see page 266) on top, and don't forget to count the carbs. These are also good with a little Chocolate Syrup (see page 264) dripped on them.

QUAN.	INGREDIENT	CARB GRAMS	AVAIL. CARB	FAT	PROTEIN
6 oz.	WALNUTS	31.2	23.1	100.3	24.3
1 t.	CINNAMON	1.8	0.6	0.1	0.1
1 t.	DRIED GINGER	1.3	1.1	0.1	0.2
½ t.	NUTMEG				
⅛ t.	CLOVES				
2	EGG WHITES	0.7	0.7	0	7.0
1 t.	VANILLA				
¾ c.	SUGAR EQUIVALENT SWEETENER				
⅛ t.	XANTHUM GUM				
15 t.	RASPBERRY JAM (see page 267)	4.9	2.2	0.1	0.4
	TOTALS	39.9	27.7	100.6	32.0
	PER SERVING OF 1 COOKIE	2.7	1.8	6.7	2.1

- Mix all of the dry ingredients together. Add the vanilla to the egg whites and whip until they are frothy. Fold the dry ingredients into the egg whites. Spoon the cookies onto a greased cookie sheet, a tablespoon per cookie. Bake them at 350° F for 15 minutes.

- **MAKES ABOUT 15 SERVINGS WITH ABOUT 76 CALORIES PER SERVING.**

COCONUT MACAROONS

THESE are light and very flavorful. For variation, serve some of these with a little Chocolate Syrup (see page 264) and some almond pieces.

QUAN.	INGREDIENT	CARB GRAMS	AVAIL. CARB	FAT	PROTEIN
¾ c.	HEAVY WHIPPING CREAM	5.0	5.0	62.6	3.7
I c.	SUGAR EQUIVALENT SWEETENER				
I t.	VANILLA EXTRACT				
½ t.	XANTHUM GUM				
2	EGG WHITES, whipped with a fork	0.7	0.7	0	7.0
8 oz.	UNSWEETENED COCONUT (about 2½ cups)	55.4	18.4	137.6	15.6
I t.	COCONUT EXTRACT				
	TOTALS	61.1	24.1	200.2	26.3
	PER SERVING OF I COOKIE	2.0	0.8	6.7	0.9

- In a 2 quart bowl, using a whisk or an electric beater on low speed, mix the xanthum gum into the cream until it is thoroughly dissolved. Add the egg whites and continue whisking. Mix in the extracts and the sugar substitute. Finally, using a spoon, mix the coconut into the cream mixture. Drop tablespoons of the mixture onto your greased cookie sheet. Bake at 325° F for about 20 minutes. These should be refrigerated or frozen as soon as they cool to room temperature because the cream will go bad if they are left out.

- **MAKES ABOUT 30 SERVINGS WITH ABOUT 67 CALORIES PER SERVING.**

KEY LIME–STYLE PIE

THIS nice, simple dessert provides the flavor of real Key Lime Pie without the high carb baggage.

QUAN.	INGREDIENT	CARB GRAMS	AVAIL. CARB	FAT	PROTEIN
2 pkgs.	**SUGAR-FREE LIME FLAVORED GELATIN** (2 cup size)	0	0	0	8.0
1¾ c.	**WATER,** boiling				
4 T.	**KEY LIME JUICE** or **REGULAR LIME JUICE** (more or less added to your taste)	5.6	5.4	0	0.2
3 c.	**WHIPPED CREAM** (1 recipe perhaps with a little lemon extract added—see page 263)	6.6	6.6	83.5	4.9
½ c.	**SUGAR EQUIVALENT SWEETENER** (more or less added to your taste)				
	TOTALS	12.2	12.0	83.5	13.1
	PER SERVING	2.0	2.0	13.9	2.2

- Place the boiling water in a 2 quart heat-proof bowl. Stir in the sugar substitute and the gelatin until the gelatin is dissolved. Stir in the key lime juice. Set this in the refrigerator until it begins to thicken slightly, about 30–45 minutes. Then fold in the whipped cream and return it to the refrigerator for at least 1 hour before serving.

- **MAKES 6 SERVINGS WITH ABOUT 134 CALORIES PER SERVING.**

NONALCOHOLIC GRASSHOPPER-STYLE PIE

THIS tastes just like a Grasshopper drink except it has a little extra lime flavor and no alcohol. Try serving this with a little Chocolate Syrup (see page 264).

QUAN.	INGREDIENT	CARB GRAMS	AVAIL. CARB	FAT	PROTEIN
1 pkg.	**SUGAR-FREE LIME FLAVORED GELATIN** (2 cup size)	0	0	0	8.0
1 c.	**WATER**, boiling				
½ t.	**PEPPERMINT EXTRACT** (more or less to your taste)				
3 c.	**WHIPPED CREAM** (1 recipe—see page 263)	6.6	6.6	83.5	4.9
	TOTALS	6.6	6.6	83.5	12.9
	PER SERVING	1.1	1.1	13.9	2.2

■ Place the boiling water in a 2 quart heatproof bowl. Stir in the gelatin and peppermint extract until it is dissolved. Set this in the refrigerator until it begins to thicken slightly, about 30–45 minutes. Then fold in the whipped cream and return it to the refrigerator for at least 1 hour before serving.

■ **MAKES 6 SERVINGS WITH ABOUT 138 CALORIES PER SERVING.**

CHEESECAKE,
ANYONE?

I've compiled several recipes for cheesecakes using various methods of preparation and containing either cream cheese, ricotta cheese, or cottage cheese. Generally, and especially for the noncooked variety of cheesecake, we add some form of gelatin to the mixture to give it body. I encourage you to try each of these recipes with and without the Basic Pie Crust (see page 268). For those of you who don't want to take the time to make a crust, for variety you might try putting a cup of walnut (pecan, almond, etc.) pieces in the bottom of your pan before you pour in the cheesecake mixture.

NO-COOK
CHOCOLATE CHEESECAKE

WE begin our adventure in cheesecakes with a simple Chocolate Cheesecake. Again, for variation, you can add any number of flavorings, depending on your taste.

QUAN.	INGREDIENT	CARB GRAMS	AVAIL. CARB	FAT	PROTEIN
1 c.	**WATER**, boiling				
1 t.	**UNFLAVORED GELATIN** (more or less added for the desired consistency)	0	0	0	2.0
1 t.	**VANILLA EXTRACT**				
16 oz.	**CREAM CHEESE**, at room temperature	16.0	16.0	144.0	32.0
2 oz.	**UNSWEETENED BAKING CHOCOLATE SQUARES**	20.0	8.0	28.0	8.0
2 c.	**SUGAR EQUIVALENT SWEETENER**				
	TOTALS	36.0	24.0	172.0	42.0
	PER SERVING	4.5	3.0	21.5	5.3

- Place the boiling water in a microwavable 2 quart bowl. Dissolve the vanilla and gelatin in the water. Add the chocolate to the bowl and microwave at high temperature for 15 second increments until the chocolate is melted, a total of about a minute. Stir the chocolate well after each repetition in the microwave. After the chocolate is completely melted, stir in the sugar substitute. Cut the cream cheese into small pieces and stir it into the chocolate mixture. Using your electric mixer, make sure that the cream cheese is completely blended into the chocolate. Pour into a buttered pie pan or pie shell and refrigerate several hours until it gels.

■ **MAKES ABOUT 8 SERVINGS WITH ABOUT 227 CALORIES PER SERVING.**

STRAWBERRY-FLAVORED
CHEESE FLUFF

IT'S the whipped cream in this dish that gives it the light texture. It's almost as light as a marshmallow.

QUAN.	INGREDIENT	CARB GRAMS	AVAIL. CARB	FAT	PROTEIN
1 pkg.	**SUGAR-FREE STRAWBERRY FLAVORED GELATIN DESSERT** (2 cup size package)	0	0	0	4.0
1 c.	**BOILING WATER**				
8 oz.	**CREAM CHEESE** at room temperature	8.0	8.0	72.0	16.0
3 c.	**WHIPPED CREAM** (1 recipe with a little strawberry flavor added— see page 263)	6.6	6.6	83.5	4.9
¾ c.	**SUGAR EQUIVALENT SWEETENER** (more or less added to your taste)				
	TOTALS	14.6	14.6	155.5	24.9
	PER SERVING OF ½ C.	1.8	1.8	19.4	3.1

- Place the boiling water in a 2 quart heat-proof bowl. Stir in the sugar substitute and the gelatin until the gelatin is dissolved. Break the cream cheese into small pieces and mix it into the gelatin, stirring after each addition. Use a whisk or an electric mixer to combine them thoroughly. Set this in the refrigerator until it just begins to thicken slightly, about 30–45 minutes. After it has begun to thicken, fold in the whipped cream and return it to the refrigerator for at least an hour before serving.

■ **MAKES 8 SERVINGS WITH ABOUT 194 CALORIES PER SERVING.**

CRANBERRY CHEESECAKE

FOR those of you who prefer a more traditional cheesecake flavor, go ahead and add an additional 8 ounce package of cream cheese and give it a try, but don't forget to adjust the macronutrient values.

QUAN.	INGREDIENT	CARB GRAMS	AVAIL. CARB	FAT	PROTEIN
2 pkg.	**SUGAR-FREE CRANBERRY FLAVORED GELATIN DESSERT** (2 cup size packages)	0	0	0	8.0
1 c.	**WATER**				
8 oz.	**CREAM CHEESE** at room temperature	8.0	8.0	72.0	16.0
3 c.	**WHIPPED CREAM** (see page 263)	6.6	6.6	83.5	4.9
½ c.	**CRANBERRIES**	7.0	4.7	0	0.2
	TOTALS	21.6	19.3	155.5	29.1
	PER SERVING OF ½ C.	2.7	2.4	19.4	3.6

■ Put the water and the cranberries in a blender or food processor and blend until the mixture is relatively smooth. Place the mixture in a 2 cup saucepan and bring it to a boil. If you don't have a blender or food processor then, bring ½ cup water and the cranberries to a boil in a 2 cup saucepan. Mash the cranberries with the back of a fork or a potato masher so that most of them are out of their skin. Add the remaining water and bring it to a boil again. At this point, you have 1 cup of boiling water with the cranberries crushed in it. Place the cranberry mixture in a 2 quart heat-proof bowl. Stir in the gelatin until it is dissolved. Break the cream cheese into small pieces and stir them into the gelatin. Use a whisk or an electric mixer to combine them thoroughly. Set this in the refrigerator until it just begins to thicken, about 30–45 minutes. After it has begun to thicken, fold in the whipped cream and return it to the refrigerator for at least an hour before serving.

■ **MAKES 8 SERVINGS WITH ABOUT 195 CALORIES PER SERVING.**

PUMPKIN CHEESE SOUFFLÉ

THIS dessert soufflé is especially good with walnut pieces added to the bottom of the pan before it is baked. This should be served warm with a dollop of whipped cream.

QUAN.	INGREDIENT	CARB GRAMS	AVAIL. CARB	FAT	PROTEIN
1 c.	UNSWEETENED CANNED PUMPKIN	35.0	21.0	0	3.5
½ c.	HEAVY WHIPPING CREAM	6.6	6.6	83.5	4.9
8 oz.	CREAM CHEESE at room temperature	8.0	8.0	72.0	16.0
½ c.	BOILING WATER				
1 pkg.	UNFLAVORED GELATIN	0	0	0	6.0
1 c.	SUGAR EQUIVALENT SWEETENER				
2	EGGS, separated	1.4	1.4	9.6	14.4
1 t.	VANILLA EXTRACT				
1 t.	CINNAMON	1.8	0.6	0.1	0.1
⅛ t.	CLOVES				
⅛ t.	NUTMEG				
¼ t.	XANTHUM GUM (optional for thickening)				
	TOTALS	52.8	37.6	165.2	44.9
	PER SERVING	8.8	6.3	27.5	7.5

- Preheat the oven to 300° F. Beat the egg whites to a stiff peak. In a 2 quart heat-proof bowl, dissolve the gelatin in the boiling water. Stir in the sugar substitute. Add the cream cheese to the bowl and warm it slightly in the microwave. Make sure that everything is mixed well, using an electric mixer if needed. Add the pumpkin and then the cream, stirring after each addition. Stir in the remaining ingredients except for the egg whites. Fold in the egg whites. Pour the mixture into a buttered dish. Bake on the top shelf of your oven for about 1–1½ hours or until an inserted knife comes out clean. Turn the oven off, crack the oven door, and let the cheesecake sit until it cools to room temperature.

- **MAKES 6 SERVINGS WITH ABOUT 303 CALORIES PER SERVING.**

NEW YORK ITALIAN–STYLE CHEESECAKE

QUAN.	INGREDIENT	CARB GRAMS	AVAIL. CARB	FAT	PROTEIN
3	EGGS	2.1	2.1	14.4	21.6
1 lb.	RICOTTA CHEESE	16.0	16.0	64.0	56.0
8 oz.	SOUR CREAM	9.8	9.8	45.7	7.3
1 c.	SUGAR EQUIVALENT SWEETENER				
1½ t.	ANISE EXTRACT (more or less added to your taste)				
¼ t.	LEMON EXTRACT				
½ t.	XANTHUM GUM (optional for thickening)				
	TOTALS	27.9	27.9	124.1	84.9
	PER SERVING	4.7	4.7	20.7	14.2

■ Preheat the oven to 350° F. Mix everything in a blender or food processor until it is smooth. Pour it into an 8 inch baking pan. You are going to place the baking pan inside another pan and pour 1–2 inches of water into the outer pan, creating a water bath for the cheesecake. Then place both of the pans inside the oven on the top or middle shelf. Bake for 1 hour and then turn the heat off. Crack the oven door and let the cheesecake rest in the oven until it cools to room temperature, about 1 hour.

■ **MAKES 6 SERVINGS WITH ABOUT 262 CALORIES PER SERVING.**

CHOCOLATE RASPBERRY FLAVORED CHEESECAKE

QUAN.	INGREDIENT	CARB GRAMS	AVAIL. CARB	FAT	PROTEIN
1 c.	**WATER**, boiling				
2 pkg.	**SUGAR-FREE RASPBERRY FLAVORED GELATIN** (2 cup size packages)	0	0	0	8.0
8 oz.	**CREAM CHEESE**, at room temperature	8.0	8.0	72.0	16.0
3 T.	**UNSWEETENED COCOA POWDER**	9.0	6.0	1.5	3.0
	TOTALS	17.0	14.0	73.5	27.0
	PER SERVING	4.3	3.5	18.4	6.8

- Place the boiling water in a microwavable 1 quart bowl. Dissolve the cocoa and gelatin in the water. Cut the cream cheese into small pieces and stir it into the chocolate/gelatin mixture. Using an electric mixer, make sure that the cream cheese is totally blended into the mixture. Pour it into a buttered pie pan or pie shell and refrigerate several hours until it gels.

- **MAKES ABOUT 4 SERVINGS WITH ABOUT 207 CALORIES PER SERVING.**

RASPBERRY
COTTAGE CHEESE PUDDING

QUAN.	INGREDIENT	CARB GRAMS	AVAIL. CARB	FAT	PROTEIN
12 oz.	COTTAGE CHEESE	12.0	12.0	15.0	33.0
3 c.	WHIPPED CREAM (see page 263)	6.6	6.6	83.5	4.9
2 pkgs.	SUGAR-FREE RASPBERRY FLAVORED GELATIN (any flavor or combination of flavors will do— 2 cup size packages)	0	0	0	8.0
½ c.	RASPBERRIES for garnish	7.1	3.0	0.2	0.6
1 T.	WATER				
	TOTALS	25.7	21.6	98.7	46.5
	PER SERVING	5.1	4.3	19.7	9.3

- In a 2 quart bowl, stir the gelatin into the cottage cheese and water. Let this sit until the gelatin is thoroughly dissolved, about 15 minutes. After the gelatin is dissolved, prepare the whipped cream. Gently fold the whipped cream into the cottage cheese mixture. Refrigerate it for at least 1 hour before serving.

- **MAKES 5 SERVINGS WITH ABOUT 232 CALORIES PER SERVING.**

NO-BAKE KEY LIME CHEESECAKE

BECAUSE this isn't cooked, you might use twelve packets of Equal in this. You can also try this in a low carb Basic Pie Crust (see page 268).

QUAN.	INGREDIENT	CARB GRAMS	AVAIL. CARB	FAT	PROTEIN
4 T.	KEY LIME JUICE	5.6	5.4	0	0.2
4 T.	WHITE VINEGAR				
2 t.	LEMON EXTRACT				
½ c.	SUGAR EQUIVALENT SWEETENER				
8 oz.	CREAM CHEESE at room temperature	6.1	6.1	75.7	17.3
3 c.	WHIPPED CREAM (see page 263)	6.6	6.6	83.5	4.9
	TOTALS	18.3	18.1	159.2	22.4
	PER SERVING	3.1	3.0	26.5	3.7

- First prepare the whipped cream, adding a little lemon extract. If possible, warm the cream cheese slowly in the microwave in a 2 quart bowl. It should be just warm to touch. Beat the sugar substitute into the cream cheese until the cream cheese is very smooth. Beat in the key lime juice, the vinegar, and the lemon extract. Fold half of the whipped cream into the cream cheese mixture. After panning the cream cheese mixture, cover with the remaining whipped cream.

- **MAKES ABOUT 6 SERVINGS WITH ABOUT 265 CALORIES PER SERVING.**

NUTRITIONAL VALUES
FOR COMMONLY USED INGREDIENTS

QUAN.	INGREDIENT	CARB GRAMS	AVAIL. CARB	FAT	PROTEIN
2 oz.	ALMONDS, slivered finely and chopped	13.0	5.5	27.4	11.6
2 lb.	ALMONDS, toasted and unblanched	208.0	106.3	439.8	185.0
½ oz.	ANCHOVIES WITH THE OIL	0	0	0.6	4.1
2 oz.	ANCHOVIES WITH THE OIL	0	0	6.0	12.0
1 T.	FENNEL or ANISE	3.0	0.7	0.7	0.9
1 c.	FROZEN ARTICHOKES, chopped coarsely	15.4	7.7	0.6	5.2
1 lb.	FRESH ASPARAGUS	20.4	10.9	0.9	10.4
1 lb.	BACON (12 slices)	0	0	247.7	39.5
2 T.	BACON BITS	0	0	3.0	6.0
2 cans	GREEN BEANS (about 15 ounces per can)	28.0	14.0	0	3.5
1 lb.	FRESH GREEN BEANS, cleaned	32.2	16.8	0.4	8.2
2 lb.	STEW BEEF or CHUCK ROAST cut into ½ inch cubes	0	0	57.6	174.6
4 lb.	BEEF BRISKET	0	0	262.2	346.6
10 oz.	FROZEN BROCCOLI, diced	15.1	6.6	0	8.8
1 c.	BROCCOLI, chopped coarsely and wilted	9.8	4.3	0.1	5.7
1 bag	FROZEN BROCCOLI, about 1 pound, thawed and sliced into 1 inch pieces	24.2	10.6	0	14.1
2 T.	UNSALTED BUTTER	0	0	24.2	0
1 lb.	CABBAGE, shredded	24.5	14.1	0.9	6.4
3 c.	RED CABBAGE, shredded	12.9	8.7	0.3	3.0
2 lb.	RED CABBAGE, shredded	55.1	37.1	1.6	12.5
1 c.	GREEN CABBAGE, chopped	4.8	2.8	0.2	1.3
2 c.	NAPA CABBAGE, torn to bite size and tightly packed (bok choi or pak choi)	3.0	1.6	0.3	2.1
8 T.	CAPERS	3.4	1.2	0.4	1.6
½ c.	CARROTS, grated	5.6	4.0	0	0.5
1 c.	CAULIFLOWER, chopped coarsely and wilted	6.7	1.8	0.3	2.9
1 lb.	FROZEN CAULIFLOWER, thawed and drained	18.0	12.0	0	12.0
2 t.	CAYENNE PEPPER	2.0	1.0	0.6	0.4
1 c.	CELERY, diced	4.4	2.4	0	0.9
⅛ lb.	AMERICAN CHEESE, shredded	1.5	1.5	18.0	12.0
2 oz.	BLUE CHEESE, crumbled	1.3	1.3	15.4	12.1
1 c.	CHEDDAR CHEESE	1.7	1.7	41.5	32.9
6 oz.	CREAM CHEESE	4.6	4.6	56.8	13.0

QUAN.	INGREDIENT	CARB GRAMS	AVAIL. CARB	FAT	PROTEIN
1 c.	RICOTTA CHEESE	12.0	12.0	32.0	28.0
1 lb.	RICOTTA CHEESE	16.0	16.0	64.0	56.0
2 lb.	SWISS CHEESE	30.7	30.7	236.3	258.2
1 c.	SWISS CHEESE, diced	4.5	4.5	34.4	37.5
½ lb.	CHICKEN BREAST, boneless, skinless, cooked and diced	0	0	5.7	65.8
2 lb.	CHICKEN BREAST, uncooked, boneless, skinless, and cut into ¾ inch cubes	0	0	8.3	209.6
2 lb.	CHICKEN LEGS	0	0	69.3	173.4
6	CHICKEN THIGHS (average size about 4 ounces with the bone in)	0	0	78.6	97.2
2 lb.	CHICKEN THIGHS. Remove the skin and bone and cut into ¾ inch cubes (this should yield about 1 lb. of meat)	0	0	17.6	108.5
2 lb.	CHICKEN WINGS, split (this is about 9 wings)	0	0	62.7	80.8
32 T.	CHILI SAUCE	35.7	26.9	28.3	6.3
1 T.	CHILI POWDER	4.1	1.5	1.0	0.9
1 oz.	UNSWEETENED CHOCOLATE	8.0	3.6	15	2.9
1 T.	GROUND CINNAMON	5.4	1.7	0.3	0.3
2 cans	MINCED CLAMS (about 3½ ounces per can)	0.2	0.2	0	0.7
1 c.	COCONUT MILK	6.4	6.4	45.3	4.6
1 lb.	COD, cut into bite sized pieces	0	0	2.3	80.8
4 lb.	UNCOOKED CORNED BEEF BRISKET	2.5	2.5	225.7	266.4
16 T.	CORNSTARCH	116.8	115.6	0.1	0.3
1 can	CRAB MEAT (about 6 ounces)	2.5	2.5	0	27.5
2 lb.	CRAB MEAT (uncooked)	0.4	0.4	7.2	162.5
½ c.	CRANBERRIES	7.0	4.7	0	0.2
1 c.	HEAVY WHIPPING CREAM	6.6	6.6	83.5	4.9
1 T.	HEAVY WHIPPING CREAM	0.6	0.6	5.2	0.3
1 c.	SOUR CREAM	9.8	9.8	45.7	7.3
2 C.	CUCUMBER, seeded and diced	6.6	4.8	0.2	1.6
2 lb.	CUCUMBER with peel	25.0	17.8	0.8	6.3
1 t.	GROUND CUMIN	0.9	0.7	0.4	0.4
1 T.	CURRY POWDER	3.7	1.6	0.7	0.8
2	EGGS, scrambled slightly	1.4	1.4	9.6	14.4
½ doz.	HARD-BOILED EGGS	4.2	4.2	28.8	43.2
2 lb.	EGGPLANT	55.1	32.4	1.1	9.3
3	Heads BELGIAN ENDIVE	51.6	3.9	2.1	19.2
1 T.	FENNEL or ANISE	3.0	0.7	0.7	0.9
1 T.	THAI FISH SAUCE	3.0	3.0	0	2.0

QUAN.	INGREDIENT	CARB GRAMS	AVAIL. CARB	FAT	PROTEIN
1 t.	**GARLIC POWDER**	2.0	2.0	0	0.5
2 t.	**GARLIC POWDER**	4.0	4.0	0	1.0
1 T.	**GARLIC POWDER**	6.1	6.1	0	1.4
2 lb.	**GARLIC**, raw	297.6	278.7	3.1	57.2
1 c.	**GARLIC**, crushed	45.0	42.1	0.5	8.6
1 t.	**GARLIC**, crushed	0.9	0.9	0	0.2
2 t.	**GARLIC**, crushed	1.9	1.8	0	0.4
1 T.	**GARLIC**, crushed	2.8	2.6	0	0.5
1 t.	**GINGER**, dried	1.3	1.1	0.1	0.2
3 T.	**GINGER**, grated	2.7	2.3	0.1	0.3
1 lb.	**FRESH GREEN BEANS**, cleaned	32.2	16.8	0.4	8.2
1 c.	**HALF AND HALF**	10.4	10.4	26.4	7.2
¼ lb.	**HAM** (2% fat)	2.0	2.0	2.0	20.0
1 lb.	**HAMBURGER** (77% lean)	0	0	92.4	77.2
4 T.	**S.F. HOISIN SAUCE**	4.4	3.6	7.2	6.8
32 T.	**ITALIAN DRESSING**	10.5	8.8	207.8	2.7
2 lb.	**ITALIAN SAUSAGE**	27.5	19.7	175.9	157.4
2 t.	**ITALIAN SEASONING**	2.0	1.0	0	0
2 T.	**LEMON JUICE**	2.6	2.5	0	0.1
1 T.	**LEMON ZEST**	1.0	0.4	0	0.1
1 c.	**LETTUCE**, shredded or chopped	1.1	0.3	0.1	0.6
2 T.	**LIME JUICE**	2.8	2.7	0	0.1
1 can	**FROZEN LOBSTER MEAT**, thawed, about 12 ounces, in bite sized pieces	1.7	1.7	2.0	63.9
1 c.	**MAYONNAISE**	5.9	5.9	168.5	2.4
1 T.	**MAYONNAISE**	0.4	0.4	10.5	0.2
1 c.	**BUTTERMILK**	11.7	11.7	2.0	8.1
2 lb.	**MOZZARELLA CHEESE**	24.9	24.9	135.9	218.3
2 c.	**BUTTON MUSHROOMS**, diced	6.5	4.8	0.3	2.9
2 lb.	**BUTTON MUSHROOMS**	42.3	31.4	2.1	19.0
1 c.	**CANNED BUTTON MUSHROOMS**, drained	7.7	4.0	0.2	2.9
1 t.	**DRY MUSTARD**	1.2	0.7	0.9	0.8
1 c.	**MUSTARD**, prepared yellow	19.5	7.5	7.8	9.9
1 pkg.	**FROZEN OKRA** (10 ounces)	18.9	12.7	0.5	4.8
1 c.	**BLACK OLIVES**, seeded and sliced thinly	8.4	4.0	13.8	1.2
25	**GREEN STUFFED OLIVES**, sliced thinly	5.0	5.0	12.5	0
½ c.	**ONION**, sliced thinly	5.0	3.9	0	0.7

QUAN.	INGREDIENT	CARB GRAMS	AVAIL. CARB	FAT	PROTEIN
½ c.	ONION, diced	6.9	5.5	0	1.0
2 c.	ONION, diced	27.6	22.4	0.4	3.8
2 lb.	ONIONS	77.7	61.5	1.0	10.4
½ c.	GREEN ONIONS, diced	3.7	2.4	0	0.9
4 T.	SALAD ONIONS	3.6	2.8	0	0.4
2 t.	ONION POWDER	3.4	3.2	0	0.4
1 t.	ONION POWDER	1.7	1.6	0	0.2
1 T.	ONION POWDER	5.2	5.1	0	0.7
2 T.	OLIVE OIL	0	0	25.8	0
1 c.	OLIVE OIL	0	0	206.5	0
1 T.	OREGANO	2.9	1.0	0.4	0.5
2 T.	PAPRIKA	7.6	4.8	1.6	2.0
4 T.	GRATED PARMESAN CHEESE	0.9	0.9	7.1	10.4
1 c.	GRATED PARMESAN CHEESE	3.7	3.7	28.5	41.6
6 T.	GRATED PARMESAN CHEESE	1.2	1.2	8.4	12.6
2 T.	SUGAR FREE PEANUT BUTTER	7.0	5.0	16.0	7.0
1 t.	BLACK PEPPER	1.4	0.8	0	0
2 t.	CAYENNE PEPPER (more or less to taste)	2.0	1.0	0.6	0.4
1 c.	GREEN PEPPERS, diced	9.6	6.9	0.2	1.3
1 c.	JALAPEÑOS, sliced	5.3	2.8	0.4	1.2
1 c.	PICKLED JALAPEÑOS, sliced	6.4	2.9	0.9	1.3
1 c.	RED PEPPERS, diced	9.6	6.6	0.2	1.3
1 c.	YELLOW PEPPERS	11.8	10.1	0	1.9
¼ lb.	SLICED PEPPERONI	3.2	3.2	46.8	23.6
2 lb.	SLICED PEPPERONI	25.6	25.6	374.5	188.7
1 lb.	POLISH SAUSAGE	16.0	16.0	136.0	56.0
4 lb.	PORK RIBS	0	0	307.2	292.5
1 lb.	PORK ROAST cut into ½ inch cubes	0	0	32.8	87.9
6 lb.	PORK SHOULDER ROAST	0	0	493.4	454.2
1 lb.	PORK CHOPS	0	0	20.7	100.0
2 lb.	GROUND PORK	0	0	173.0	151.9
1 c.	RADISHES, sliced thinly and wilted	4.2	0.1	2.3	0.7
2 c.	RASPBERRIES	28.5	11.8	0.9	2.2
2 T.	SWEET RELISH	1.0	0.6	0.4	0.4
2 lb.	SALMON STEAKS, uncooked	0	0	63.7	193.1
2 c.	CANNED SAUERKRAUT (about 1 can of 15 ounces)	12.2	5.1	0.3	2.6
4 T.	SESAME OIL			52.0	

QUAN.	INGREDIENT	CARB GRAMS	AVAIL. CARB	FAT	PROTEIN
2 T.	SESAME SEEDS	4.2	2.0	8.6	3.2
1 lb.	SCALLOPS	10.6	10.6	1.7	75.5
1 lb.	UNCOOKED SHRIMP	4.1	4.1	5.9	92.2
1 lb.	COOKED SHRIMP	4.2	4.2	6.0	94.1
1 c.	CANNED SHRIMP (about 2 cans at 6 ounces per can)	1.3	1.3	1.8	29.5
1 c.	SNOW PEAS, diced	7.4	4.0	0.1	2.7
4 T.	SOUR CREAM	2.0	2.0	9.5	1.5
1 c.	SOUR CREAM	9.8	9.8	45.7	7.3
2 T.	SOY SAUCE (tamari)	2.0	2.0	0	3.8
4 T.	SOY SAUCE	2.0	2.0	0	8.0
1 c.	SUMMER CROOK-NECK SQUASH, sliced thinly and wilted	4.9	0.2	2.8	1.3
2 c.	SWEET SLAW DRESSING	8.9	8.9	252.8	3.6
1 c.	PREPARED SAUERKRAUT	6.1	2.5	0.2	1.3
1 box	FROZEN CHOPPED SPINACH (about 10 ounces per box)	11.7	5.1	0	6.9
2 lb.	SOFT TOFU, drained and washed	16.4	14.6	31.2	59.6
1 c.	TOMATO, diced	8.4	6.4	0.4	1.5
½ c.	TOMATO SAUCE	8.8	7.1	0.2	1.7
1 can	STEWED TOMATOES (14.5 oz)	17.5	14.0	0	3.5
1 can	TUNA, PACKED IN OIL (about 6 ounces)	0	0	15.0	32.5
1 lb.	DELI SMOKED CHICKEN or TURKEY BREAST, sliced and cut into bite sized pieces	0	0	13.3	100.0
¼ c.	WALNUTS, diced	5.5	4.1	17.7	4.3
2 T.	CRUSHED WALNUTS	2.0	1.0	8.4	3.8
2 lb.	WALNUTS	166.6	123.0	534.7	129.7
⅜ c.	WALNUT OIL	0	0	77.8	0
3 c.	WATERCRESS LEAF, cut coarsely	1.2	0	0	2.4
1 T.	HEAVY WHIPPING CREAM	0.6	0.6	5.2	0.3
½ c.	DRY WHITE WINE	0.8	0.8	0	0
1 c.	DRY WHITE WINE	1.6	1.6	0	0
½ c.	DRY RED WINE	2.0	2.0	0	0.4
1 T.	WORCESTERSHIRE SAUCE	3.0	3.0	0	0
2 lb.	ZUCCHINI	26.1	15.3	0.9	10.4

ACKNOWLEDGMENTS

THIS book is the culmination of a journey that began in June 1996. I had just begun my permanent low carb way of eating on May 10th and had joined the low carb list on the Internet. One of the consistent complaints of the list members was that they didn't have any variety in their food choices, so I mentioned that I might be able to write a low carb cookbook. Needless to say they encouraged me. I began work on the book over Fourth of July weekend and spent every spare moment I had on it over the next ten weeks. On September 23rd, I sent out my first mailing of *Everyday Low Carb Cookery,* the first edition of this book. So thanks go to all of the folks on the low carb list who initially encouraged me to write the book.

Two people from that low carb list deserve special mention. The first is Liz Jackson, who has helped me in the past with some recipes and continues to provide input and support. The second is Lynne Axiak, known as the Low Carb Muse to many of us in the low carb world. Lynne is a registered nurse who helped me out with some of the dessert recipes. But best of all, she has always been eager to help educate other folks with her boundless low carb knowledge. Thanks to both of these ladies.

The next person who facilitated my journey is Gretchen Becker. She provided the denouement when she contacted Marlowe & Company on my behalf. Thank you, Gretchen.

Last but certainly not least are the folks at Marlowe & Company. Publisher Matthew Lore had the confidence in me to ask me to update *Everyday Low Carb Cookery,* and thanks to the efforts of editor Sue McCloskey, this revision is significantly more presentable than the original. They both should know that they've made a little boy very happy.